International Directory of
BUSINESS
BIOGRAPHIES

International Directory of
BUSINESS
BIOGRAPHIES

VOLUME 3
M-R

Edited by Neil Schlager
Produced by Schlager Group Inc.

ST. JAMES PRESS
An imprint of Thomson Gale, a part of The Thomson Corporation

THOMSON
⋆
GALE

Detroit • New York • San Francisco • San Diego • New Haven, Conn. • Waterville, Maine • London • Munich

THOMSON

✳

™

GALE

International Directory of Business Biographies
Schlager Group Inc. Staff
Neil Schlager, president
Marcia Merryman Means, managing editor

Project Editor
Margaret Mazurkiewicz

Editorial
Erin Bealmear, Joann Cerrito, Jim Craddock,
Stephen Cusack, Miranda Ferrara, Peter M.
Gareffa, Kristin Hart, Melissa Hill, Carol
Schwartz, Bridget Travers, Michael J. Tyrkus

Editorial Support Services
Luann Brennan

Rights Acquisitions Management
Mari Masalin-Cooper, Shalice Shah-Caldwell

Imaging and Multimedia
Dean Dauphinais, Lezlie Light, Dan Newell,
Christine O'Bryan

Composition
Evi Seoud

Product Design
Jennifer Wahi

Manufacturing
Rhonda Williams

LIBRARY OF CONGRESS CATALOGING-IN-PUBLICATION DATA

International directory of business biographies / Neil Schlager, editor ; Vanessa Torrado-
Caputo, assistant editor; project editor, Margaret Mazurkiewicz ; produced by Schlager
Group.
     p. cm.
         Includes bibliographical references and indexes.
         ISBN 1-55862-554-2 (set hardcover : alk. paper) —
         ISBN 1-55862-555-0 (volume 1) —
         ISBN 1-55862-556-9 (volume 2) —
         ISBN 1-55862-557-7 (volume 3) —
         ISBN 1-55862-558-5 (volume 4)
         1. Businesspeople—Biography. 2. Directors of corporations—Biography.
         3. Executives—Biography. 4. Industrialists—Biography.
         5. Businesspeople—Directories. 6. Directors of corporations—Directories.
         7. Executives—Directories. 8. Industrialists—Directories.
         I. Schlager, Neil, 1966- II. Torrado-Caputo, Vanessa. III. Mazurkiewicz,
         Margaret. IV. Schlager Group.

HC29.I57 2005
338.092'2—dc22
                                         2004011756

British Library Cataloguing in Publication Data.
A Catalogue record of this book is available from the British Library.

Printed in the United States of America
10 9 8 7 6 5 4 3 2

Contents

■■■

PREFACE . . . . PAGE vii–viii

LIST OF ADVISERS ix

LIST OF CONTRIBUTORS xi

LIST OF ENTRANTS . . . . xiii–xxii

ENTRIES

VOLUME 1: A-E 1–466

VOLUME 2: F-L 1–505

VOLUME 3: M-R 1–457

VOLUME 4: S-Z 1–403

NOTES ON CONTRIBUTORS 405–410

NATIONALITY INDEX 411–417

GEOGRAPHIC INDEX 419–425

COMPANY AND INDUSTRY INDEX 427–447

NAME INDEX 449–465

Preface

■■■

Welcome to the *International Directory of Business Biographies (IDBB)*. This four-volume set covers more than 600 prominent business people from around the world and is intended for reference use by management students, librarians, educators, historians, and others who seek information about the people leading the world's biggest and most influential companies. The articles, all of which include bylines, were written by a team of journalists, academics, librarians, and independent scholars. (See **Notes on Contributors**.) Approximately 60 percent of the entrants are American, while 40 percent are from other countries. Articles were compiled from material supplied by companies for whom the entrants work, general and academic periodicals, books, and annual reports. With its up-to-date profiles of important figures from the world of international business, *IDBB* complements the popular St. James Press series *International Directory of Company Histories (IDCH)*, which provides entries on the world's largest and most influential companies. Leaders of many of the companies covered in *IDCH* are profiled in *IDBB*.

INCLUSION CRITERIA

The list of entrants in *IDBB* was developed by the editors in consultation with the academics and librarians serving on *IDBB*'s advisory board. (See **List of Advisers**.) The majority of people profiled here are current or recent chief executives of large, publicly traded companies such as those found on the Fortune 500 and Global 500 lists of companies compiled by *Fortune* magazine. Among this group are familiar names such as H. Lee Scott Jr. of Wal-Mart, Carly Fiorina of Hewlett-Packard, John Browne of BP, and Nobuyuki Idei of Sony. Retired or former executives like GE's Jack Welch and Vivendi Universal's Jean-Marie Messier also make the list, as do a few deceased individuals who were active in the past few years, including Jim Cantalupo of McDonald's and Chung Ju-yung of Hyundai.

In addition, we have included other high-profile individuals whose companies are privately held or are not large enough to make the *Fortune* lists but whose influence makes them valuable candidates for study, such as Kase L. Lawal of CAMAC Holdings, Oprah Winfrey of Harpo Productions, and Terence Conran of Conran Holdings. We also mix in up-and-coming executives who may not currently be chief executives but who are rapidly gaining prominence in the business world; among this group are Indra K. Nooyi of PepsiCo and Lachlan and James Murdoch of News Corporation. For these latter categories, we have attempted to highlight female and minority executives who, even in the early twenty-first century, continue to be underrepresented in the upper echelons of the corporate world.

Readers should note that our aim was to produce balanced, objective profiles of influential executives, and individuals were not disqualified if they or their companies were enmeshed in scandal. Thus, the set includes articles about executives such as Ken Lay of Enron, Dennis Kozlowski of Tyco International, and Martha Stewart of Martha Stewart Living Omnimedia, all of whom were indicted on criminal charges in the early 2000s.

ARRANGEMENT OF SET AND ENTRY FORMAT

The four-volume set is arranged alphabetically by surname. An alphabetical list of subjects is included in the front-matter. Within each entry, readers will find the following sections:

Fact Box: This section provides details about the subject's birth and death dates, birth and death locations, family information, educational background, work history, major awards, and publications. For entrants affiliated with a specific company at the time of publication, the Fact Box also includes the company address and URL address, except in cases where the subject is no longer affiliated with a company.

Main Text: This section provides a narrative overview of the subject's life, career trajectory, and influence. The text includes subheadings to assist the reader in navigating the key periods in the subject's life.

Sources for Further Information: This section lists books, articles, and Web sites containing more information about the subject. Also included here are sources from which quotations are drawn in the main text.

See also: At the end of most articles is a cross-reference to applicable company profiles in the *International Directory of Company Histories*.

INDEXES

IDBB includes four indexes. The **Nationality Index** lists entrants according to their country of birth, country of citizenship (if different from country of birth), and country of long-term residence. The **Geographic Index** lists entrants according to the country of the headquarters of operation or the country where the subject works (if different from country of the headquarters); the index lists entrants according to their employer at the time of publication as well as significant previous companies where they were employed. The **Company and Industry Index** lists entrants according to their current and former companies of employment as well the industries in which those companies operate; in this latter index, industries are listed in small caps, while companies are listed in roman font with upper- and lowercase letters. The **Name Index** lists all entrants as well as other significant individuals discussed in the text.

ACKNOWLEDGMENTS

Numerous individuals deserve gratitude for their assistance with this project. I am indebted to everyone at St. James Press and Thomson Gale who assisted with the production, particularly Margaret Mazurkiewicz, who provided crucial help at all stages of production; I also thank Chris Nasso, Peter Gareffa, and Bridget Travers for their support. At Schlager Group, Marcia Merryman Means elucidated style matters and coordinated the copyediting and fact-checking process, while Jayne Weisblatt and Vanessa Torrado-Caputo provided valuable editorial assistance.

Neil Schlager

SUGGESTIONS WELCOME

Comments and suggestions from users of *IDBB* on any aspect of the product are cordially invited. Suggestions for additional business people to include in future new editions or supplements are also welcomed. Please write:

The Editor
International Directory of Business Biographies
Thomson Gale
27500 Drake Rd.
Farmington Hills, MI 48331-3535

Advisers

Vincenzo Baglieri, PhD
Director, Technology Management Department
Bocconi School of Management
Bocconi University
Milan, Italy

Lyda Bigelow, PhD
Assistant Professor of Organization and Strategy
Olin School of Business
Washington University in St. Louis
St. Louis, Missouri

Diane Davenport, MLS
Reference Manager
Berkeley Public Library
Berkeley, California

Karl Moore, PhD
Associate Professor
Faculty of Management
McGill University
Montreal, Canada

Mohammad K. Najdawi, PhD
Senior Associate Dean and Professor
Department of Decision and Information Technologies
College of Commerce and Finance
Villanova University
Villanova, Pennsylvania

Judith M. Nixon, MLS
Management and Economics Librarian
Purdue University
West Lafayette, Indiana

Contributors

■■■

Elisa Addlesperger

Barry Alfonso

Margaret Alic

Don Amerman

William Arthur Atkins

Kirk H. Beetz

Patricia C. Behnke

Mark Best

Alan Bjerga

Jeanette Bogren

Thomas Borjas

Carol Brennan

Jack J. Cardoso

C. A. Chien

Peter Collins

Stephen Collins

Matthew Cordon

Peggy Daniels

Amanda de la Garza

Ed Dinger

Catherine Donaldson

Jim Fike

Virginia Finsterwald

Tiffeni Fontno

Katrina Ford

Erik Donald France

Lisa Frick

Margaret E. Gillio

Larry Gilman

Meg Greene

Paul Greenland

Barbara Gunvaldsen

Timothy L. Halpern

Lauri Harding

Lucy Heckman

Ashyia N. Henderson

Eve M. B. Hermann

John Herrick

Jeremy W. Hubbell

Dawn Jacob Laney

Michelle Johnson

Jean Kieling

Barbara Koch

Deborah Kondek

Alison Lake

Sandra Larkin

Josh Lauer

Anne Lesser

David Lewis

Jennifer Long

DeAnne Luck

Susan Ludwig

David Marc

William F. Martin

Beth Maser

Doris Morris Maxfield

Ann McCarthy

Patricia McKenna

Lee McQueen

Jill Meister

Carole Sayegh Moussalli

Miriam C. Nagel

Catherine Naghdi

Caryn E. Neumann

John M. Owen

Carol Pech

David Petechuk

Anastasis Petrou

A. Petruso

Luca Prono

Trudy Ring

Nelson Rhodes

Celia Ross

Joseph C. Santora

Lorraine Savage

M. W. Scott

Cathy Seckman

Kenneth R. Shepherd

Stephanie Dionne Sherk

Hartley Spatt

Janet P. Stamatel

Kris Swank

François Therin

Marie L. Thompson

Mary Tradii

Scott Trudell

David Tulloch

Michael Vandyke

Maike van Wijk

Stephanie Watson

Valerie Webster

S. E. Weigant

Kelly Wittmann

Lisa Wolff

Timothy Wowk

Ronald Young

Barry Youngerman

Candy Zulkosky

List of Entrants

■■■

A

F. Duane Ackerman

Josef Ackermann

Shai Agassi

Umberto Agnelli

Ahn Cheol-soo

Naoyuki Akikusa

Raúl Alarcón Jr.

William F. Aldinger III

Vagit Y. Alekperov

César Alierta Izuel

Herbert M. Allison Jr.

John A. Allison IV

Dan Amos

Brad Anderson

Richard H. Anderson

G. Allen Andreas Jr.

Micky Arison

C. Michael Armstrong

Bernard Arnault

Gerard J. Arpey

Ramani Ayer

B

Michael J. Bailey

Sergio Balbinot

Steve Ballmer

Jill Barad

Don H. Barden

Ned Barnholt

Colleen Barrett

Craig R. Barrett

Matthew William Barrett

John M. Barth

Glen A. Barton

Richard Barton

J. T. Battenberg III

Claude Bébéar

Pierre-Olivier Beckers

Jean-Louis Beffa

Alain Belda

Charles Bell

Luciano Benetton

Robert H. Benmosche

Silvio Berlusconi

Betsy Bernard

Daniel Bernard

David W. Bernauer

Wulf H. Bernotat

Gordon M. Bethune

J. Robert Beyster

Jeff Bezos

Pierre Bilger

Alwaleed Bin Talal

Dave Bing

Carole Black

Cathleen Black

Jonathan Bloomer

Alan L. Boeckmann

Daniel Bouton

List of Entrants

Martin Bouygues

Jack O. Bovender Jr.

Peter Brabeck-Letmathe

Richard Branson

Edward D. Breen

Thierry Breton

Ulrich Brixner

John Browne

Wayne Brunetti

John E. Bryson

Warren E. Buffett

Steven A. Burd

H. Peter Burg

Antony Burgmans

James Burke

Ursula Burns

C

Louis C. Camilleri

Lewis B. Campbell

Philippe Camus

Michael R. Cannon

Jim Cantalupo

Thomas E. Capps

Daniel A. Carp

Peter Cartwright

Steve Case

Cássio Casseb Lima

Robert B. Catell

William Cavanaugh III

Charles M. Cawley

Clarence P. Cazalot Jr.

Nicholas D. Chabraja

John T. Chambers

J. Harold Chandler

Morris Chang

Chen Tonghai

Kenneth I. Chenault

Fujio Cho

Chung Ju-yung

Carla Cico

Philippe Citerne

Jim Clark

Vance D. Coffman

Douglas R. Conant

Phil Condit

Terence Conran

John W. Conway

John R. Coomber

Roger Corbett

Alston D. Correll

Alfonso Cortina de Alcocer

David M. Cote

Robert Crandall

Mac Crawford

Carlos Criado-Perez

James R. Crosby

Adam Crozier

Alexander M. Cutler

Márcio A. Cypriano

D

David F. D'Alessandro

Eric Daniels

George David

Richard K. Davidson

Julian C. Day

Henri de Castries

Michael S. Dell

Guerrino De Luca

Hebert Demel

Roger Deromedi

Thierry Desmarest

Michael Diekmann

William Dillard II

Barry Diller

John T. Dillon

Jamie Dimon

Peter R. Dolan

Guy Dollé

Tim M. Donahue

David W. Dorman

Jürgen Dormann

E. Linn Draper Jr.

John G. Drosdick

José Dutra

E

Tony Earley Jr.

Robert A. Eckert

Rolf Eckrodt

Michael Eisner

John Elkann

Larry Ellison

Thomas J. Engibous

Gregg L. Engles

Ted English

Roger Enrico

Charlie Ergen

Michael L. Eskew

Matthew J. Espe

Robert A. Essner

John H. Eyler Jr.

F

Richard D. Fairbank

Thomas J. Falk

David N. Farr

Jim Farrell

Franz Fehrenbach

Pierre Féraud

E. James Ferland

Dominique Ferrero

Trevor Fetter

John Finnegan

Carly Fiorina

Paul Fireman

Jay S. Fishman

Niall FitzGerald

Dennis J. FitzSimons

Olav Fjell

John E. Fletcher

William P. Foley II

Jean-Martin Folz

Scott T. Ford

William Clay Ford Jr.

Gary D. Forsee

Kent B. Foster

Charlie Fote

Jean-René Fourtou

H. Allen Franklin

Tom Freston

Takeo Fukui

Richard S. Fuld Jr.

S. Marce Fuller

Masaaki Furukawa

G

Joseph Galli Jr.

Louis Gallois

Christopher B. Galvin

Roy A. Gardner

Jean-Pierre Garnier

Bill Gates

David Geffen

Jay M. Gellert

Louis V. Gerstner Jr.

John E. Gherty

Carlos Ghosn

Charles K. Gifford

Raymond V. Gilmartin

Larry C. Glasscock

Robert D. Glynn Jr.

Francisco González Rodríguez

David R. Goode

Jim Goodnight

Fred A. Goodwin

Chip W. Goodyear

Andrew Gould

William C. Greehey

Stephen K. Green

Hank Greenberg

Jeffrey W. Greenberg

Robert Greenberg

J. Barry Griswell

Rijkman W. J. Groenink

Andy Grove

Oswald J. Grübel

Jerry A. Grundhofer

Rajiv L. Gupta

Carlos M. Gutierrez

H

Robert Haas

David D. Halbert

Hiroshi Hamada

Toru Hambayashi

Jürgen Hambrecht

John H. Hammergren

H. Edward Hanway

George J. Harad

William B. Harrison Jr.

Richard Harvey

William Haseltine

Andy Haste

Lewis Hay III

William F. Hecht

Bert Heemskerk

Rainer Hertrich

John B. Hess

Laurence E. Hirsch

Betsy Holden

Chad Holliday

Katsuhiko Honda

Van B. Honeycutt

Kazutomo Robert Hori

Janice Bryant Howroyd

Ancle Hsu

Günther Hülse

L. Phillip Humann

Franz Humer

I

Nobuyuki Idei

Robert Iger

Jeffrey R. Immelt

Ray R. Irani

J

Michael J. Jackson

Tony James

Charles H. Jenkins Jr.

David Ji

Jiang Jianqing

Steve Jobs

Jeffrey A. Joerres

Leif Johansson

Abby Johnson

John D. Johnson

John H. Johnson

Robert L. Johnson

William R. Johnson

Lawrence R. Johnston

Jeff Jordan

Michael H. Jordan

Abdallah Jum'ah

Andrea Jung

William G. Jurgensen

K

Eugene S. Kahn

Akinobu Kanasugi

Isao Kaneko

Ryotaro Kaneko

Mel Karmazin

Karen Katen

Jeffrey Katzenberg

Jim Kavanaugh

Robert Keegan

Herb Kelleher

Edmund F. Kelly

Mikhail Khodorkovsky

Naina Lal Kidwai

Kerry K. Killinger

James M. Kilts

Eric Kim

Kim Jung-tae

Ewald Kist

Gerard J. Kleisterlee

Lowry F. Kline

Philip H. Knight

Charles Koch

Richard Jay Kogan

John Koo

Timothy Koogle

Hans-Joachim Körber

Richard M. Kovacevich

Dennis Kozlowski

Sallie Krawcheck

Ronald L. Kuehn Jr.

Ken Kutaragi

L

Alan J. Lacy

A. G. Lafley

Igor Landau

Robert W. Lane

Sherry Lansing

Jean Laurent

Kase L. Lawal

Bob Lawes

Ken Lay

Shelly Lazarus

Terry Leahy

Lee Yong-kyung

David J. Lesar

R. Steve Letbetter

Gerald Levin

Arthur Levinson

Kenneth D. Lewis

Victor Li

Li Ka-shing

Alfred C. Liggins III

Liu Chuanzhi

J. Bruce Llewellyn

Lu Weiding

Iain Lumsden

Terry J. Lundgren

M

Ma Fucai

John J. Mack

Terunobu Maeda

Joseph Magliochetti

Marjorie Magner

Richard Mahoney

Steven J. Malcolm

Richard A. Manoogian

Mohamed Hassan Marican

Reuben Mark

Michael E. Marks

J. Willard Marriott Jr.

R. Brad Martin

Strive Masiyiwa

David Maxwell

L. Lowry Mays

Michael B. McCallister

W. Alan McCollough

Mike McGavick

Eugene R. McGrath

Judy McGrath

William W. McGuire

Tom McKillop

Henry A. McKinnell Jr.

C. Steven McMillan

Scott G. McNealy

W. James McNerney Jr.

Dee Mellor

Jean-Marie Messier

Gérard Mestrallet

Edouard Michelin

Charles Milhaud

Alexei Miller

Stuart A. Miller

Akio Mimura

Vittorio Mincato

Rafael Miranda Robredo

Fujio Mitarai

William E. Mitchell

Hayao Miyazaki

Anders C. Moberg

Larry Montgomery

James P. Mooney

Ann Moore

Patrick J. Moore

Giuseppe Morchio

Tomijiro Morita

Angelo R. Mozilo

Anne M. Mulcahy

Leo F. Mullin

James J. Mulva

Raúl Muñoz Leos

James Murdoch

Lachlan Murdoch

Rupert Murdoch

N. R. Murthy

A. Maurice Myers

N

Kunio Nakamura

Robert L. Nardelli

Jacques Nasser

M. Bruce Nelson

Yoshifumi Nishikawa

Hidetoshi Nishimura

Uichiro Niwa

Gordon M. Nixon

Jeffrey Noddle

Tamotsu Nomakuchi

Indra K. Nooyi

Blake W. Nordstrom

Richard C. Notebaert

David C. Novak

Erle Nye

O

James J. O'Brien Jr.

Mark J. O'Brien

Robert J. O'Connell

Steve Odland

Adebayo Ogunlesi

Minoru Ohnishi

Motoyuki Oka

Tadashi Okamura

Jorma Ollila

Thomas D. O'Malley

E. Stanley O'Neal

David J. O'Reilly

Amancio Ortega

Marcel Ospel

Paul Otellini

Mutsutake Otsuka

Lindsay Owen-Jones

P

Pae Chong-yeul

Samuel J. Palmisano

Helmut Panke

Gregory J. Parseghian

Richard D. Parsons

Corrado Passera

Hank Paulson

Michel Pébereau

Roger S. Penske

A. Jerrold Perenchio

Peter J. Pestillo

Donald K. Peterson

Howard G. Phanstiel

Joseph A. Pichler

William F. Pickard

Harvey R. Pierce

Mark C. Pigott

Bernd Pischetsrieder

Fred Poses

John E. Potter

Myrtle Potter

Paul S. Pressler

Larry L. Prince

Richard B. Priory

Alessandro Profumo

Henri Proglio

David J. Prosser

Philip J. Purcell III

Q

Allen I. Questrom

R

Franklin D. Raines

M. S. Ramachandran

Dieter Rampl

Lee R. Raymond

Steven A. Raymund

Sumner M. Redstone

Dennis H. Reilley

Steven S. Reinemund

Eivind Reiten

Glenn M. Renwick

Linda Johnson Rice

Pierre Richard

Kai-Uwe Ricke

Stephen Riggio

Jim Robbins

List of Entrants

Brian L. Roberts

Harry J. M. Roels

Steven R. Rogel

James E. Rogers

Bruce C. Rohde

James E. Rohr

Matthew K. Rose

Bob Rossiter

Renzo Rosso

John W. Rowe

Allen R. Rowland

Patricia F. Russo

Edward B. Rust Jr.

Arthur F. Ryan

Patrick G. Ryan

Thomas M. Ryan

S

Alfredo Sáenz

Mary F. Sammons

Steve Sanger

Ron Sargent

Arun Sarin

Mikio Sasaki

Paolo Scaroni

George A. Schaefer Jr.

Leonard D. Schaeffer

Hans-Jürgen Schinzler

James J. Schiro

Werner Schmidt

Richard J. Schnieders

Jürgen E. Schrempp

Howard Schultz

Ekkehard D. Schulz

Gerald W. Schwartz

Louis Schweitzer

H. Lee Scott Jr.

Richard M. Scrushy

Ivan G. Seidenberg

Donald S. Shaffer

Kevin W. Sharer

William J. Shea

Donald J. Shepard

Yoichi Shimogaichi

Etsuhiko Shoyama

Thomas Siebel

Henry R. Silverman

Russell Simmons

James D. Sinegal

Carlos Slim

Bruce A. Smith

Fred Smith

O. Bruton Smith

Stacey Snider

Jure Sola

George Soros

William S. Stavropoulos

Sy Sternberg

David L. Steward

Martha Stewart

Patrick T. Stokes

Harry C. Stonecipher

Hans Stråberg

Belinda Stronach

Ronald D. Sugar

Osamu Suzuki

Toshifumi Suzuki

Carl-Henric Svanberg

William H. Swanson

T

Keiji Tachikawa

Noel N. Tata

Sidney Taurel

Gunter Thielen

Ken Thompson

Rex W. Tillerson

Robert L. Tillman

Glenn Tilton

James S. Tisch

Barrett A. Toan

Doreen Toben

Don Tomnitz

Shoichiro Toyoda

Tony Trahar

Marco Tronchetti Provera

Donald Trump

Shiro Tsuda

Kazuo Tsukuda

Joseph M. Tucci

Ted Turner

John H. Tyson

U

Robert J. Ulrich

Thomas J. Usher

Shoei Utsuda

Akio Utsumi

V

Roy A. Vallee

Anton van Rossum

Thomas H. Van Weelden

Daniel Vasella

Ferdinand Verdonck

Ben Verwaayen

Heinrich von Pierer

W

Norio Wada

Rick Wagoner

Ted Waitt

Paul S. Walsh

Robert Walter

Shigeo Watanabe

Fumiaki Watari

Philip B. Watts

Jürgen Weber

Sandy Weill

Serge Weinberg

Alberto Weisser

Jack Welch

William C. Weldon

Werner Wenning

Norman H. Wesley

W. Galen Weston

Leslie H. Wexner

Kenneth Whipple

Edward E. Whitacre Jr.

Miles D. White

Meg Whitman

David R. Whitwam

Hans Wijers

Michael E. Wiley

Bruce A. Williamson

Chuck Williamson

Peter S. Willmott

Oprah Winfrey

Patricia A. Woertz

Y

Shinichi Yokoyama

Dave Yost

Larry D. Yost

Yun Jong-yong

Z

Antoine Zacharias

Edward Zander

John D. Zeglis

Deiter Zetsche

Zhang Enzhao

Zhang Ligui

Zhou Deqiang

Aerin Lauder Zinterhofer

Edward J. Zore

Klaus Zumwinkel

■■■

Ma Fucai
1943–
Chairman, PetroChina

Nationality: Chinese.

Born: 1943, in China.

Education: Beijing Petroleum Institute.

Career: China National Petroleum Corporation, ?–1990, worked in oilfields, various positions; 1990–1996, deputy director, standing deputy director, and director of Shengli Petroleum Administration Bureau; 1996, assistant president; 1996–1998, vice president; 1997–1998, director of Daqing Petroleum Administration Bureau; 1998–2004, president; PetroChina, 1999–, chairman.

Address: PetroChina, World Tower, 16 Andelu, Dongcheng, Beijing 100011, China; http://www.petrochina.com.cn.

Ma Fucai. *Goh Chai Hin/Getty Images.*

■ Until his forced resignation Ma Fucai was in charge of China's largest oil company during the period of rapid economic growth following the Asian financial crisis of 1997 and leading to China's inclusion in the World Trade Organization (WTO). To meet energy needs and promote energy security for China, Ma worked on multiple fronts to improve the efficiency of Chinese oil production, reforming the state-owned oil company China National Petroleum Corporation (CNPC); privatizing a segment of CNPC as the publicly listed PetroChina, the fourth largest of such listed companies; and using CNPC aggressively to increase the output from China's sources of oil.

CNPC led China's oil sector by virtue of its control of 28 separate companies. Though it possessed only 3.7 billion barrels of proven reserves, CNPC increased China's oil supply through additional oil projects in 30 countries. The subsidiary PetroChina owned proven reserves of 10.9 billion barrels of oil and 38.8 trillion cubic feet of natural gas and in China operated eight thousand miles of natural-gas pipeline, 23 refineries, and 13 chemical plants. By 2002 PetroChina employed almost 420,000 people and by 2004 owned over 15,000 gas stations, ranking first among China's oil companies. Under Ma, PetroChina increased oil production through foreign ac-

quisitions and pipeline deals involving countries from Russia to Morocco and in Central America.

BECOMING AN OILMAN

After graduating from the Beijing Petroleum Institute, Ma worked in the oilfields of China—first in Daqing, which opened in 1960, and then in Shengli. Working his way up through China National Petroleum Corporation's administration, he became the head of the Shengli oilfields in 1990. Ma was a consummate oil technocrat who had intimate knowledge of every aspect of the energy industry, from oil drilling and gas exploration to financial management and foreign trade. China's decision to join the Western market economy by pursuing membership in the World Trade Organization in 1986 set all of China's state companies on a path toward Western corporate norms. The economic liberalization eventually triggered a booming economy and a series of high annual growth rates from 1990 onward. Once China became a net importer of oil in 1993, Ma's future as an international oil dealer was set, as he became responsible for securing China's oil supply in order to keep the economic transition going.

Geologically China had little oil wealth (excluding the possibility that offshore explorations would find fields far beyond expectations). After two decades of corporate struggles the optimal combination of private and public oil development yielded CNPC. As a government ministry under Wang Tao, CNPC continued domestic development while investing abroad, in Canada and Peru. China's role as manufacturer of petroleum-based plastic products and as the future home to the largest class of car drivers and consumers (consumption having been encouraged as the solution to the 1997 financial crisis) depended on the securement of oil. China passed Japan as the world's second-leading oil consumer, behind the United States, in 2003. China planned to institute fuel-efficiency and pollution standards more stringent than those of the United States by 2005.

ALL FOR OIL

In 1998 Ma became the number-one oilman in China; due to the political importance of oil, he effectively became a cabinet minister. He immediately implemented a strategy for securing more oil for China that involved the creation of the fourth-largest publicly traded company, improved efficiency in CNPC through management reform, and a pursuit of oil concessions anywhere and with anyone. Ma implemented his strategy using logic based on the ideal technological approach to securing oil for his country, ignoring political, environmental, and cultural considerations.

The restructuring of China's oil ministry into a few large, state-controlled companies in 1993 had not led to the hoped-for efficiency. Ma met with Sinopec, the other large oil company that had been produced by Chinese privatization efforts, in an attempt to streamline both operations by swapping concerns. As a result CNPC gained control of China's northern oil developments, Sinopec the southern. This geographic solution allowed for facility consolidation within both companies—and also made CNPC the larger oil producer. Ma then invested in exploration of western China, an area thought to hold another large oilfield; by 2003 CNPC added five new fields in Western China to its portfolio, which had already comprised China's two largest oilfields, Daqing and Shengli. However, western China failed to yield a third large field, and CNPC resumed its global oil acquisitions with renewed vigor. Exacerbating China's domestic oil situation, Daqing's production had to be lowered that same year in order to conserve oil in light of the poor findings in western China.

After the deal with Sinopec, Ma performed a successful transformation of China's oil ministry by spinning off CNPC's best assets and facilities—excluding China Oil Company, CNPC's profitable Hong Kong company—into PetroChina. Ma then guided PetroChina through its initial public offering (IPO) in 2000. While he succeeded in taking the company to market, he did not succeed in bolstering PetroChina's value to the level of capitalization its reserves and facilities ought to have commanded. Investors in Hong Kong and New York were wary of PetroChina's connections with Sudan, which the U.S. administration had placed on its list of terrorism sponsors. The political ramifications of foreign investment never gave Ma pause, nor did levels of worker satisfaction.

As the head of Daqing production and then as the head of CNPC, Ma bore responsibility for workplace conditions as well as the institution of cost-cutting measures. In the late 1990s CNPC decided to save money by removing a heating subsidy given to workers during the winter in the oilfields. Thousands of workers marched on the main office in protest, but Ma had his way. As a result of the PetroChina spin-off and subsequent reorganization, more than one-half million workers lost their jobs: of the original CNPC employment total of 1.5 million, PetroChina employed less than one-half million as a subsidiary of CNPC; CNPC then reduced its workforce of one million workers to less than one-half million.

THE LOCATION OF OIL MAKES NO DIFFERENCE

Securing a steady oil supply for China was Ma's priority as he cultivated relations in the Middle East and with Russia. The year before Ma took over, CNPC had signed an agreement with Iraq for control of the Al Ahdab oilfield in 1997. As of 2004 China had yet to see any oil from this field, though it nevertheless proved to be a continuing source of tension in Sino-U.S. relations. CNPC also furthered its investment in Sudanese oil despite the problems surrounding PetroChina's IPO. Ma's investment in Syria in 2003 secured for CNPC a major foothold in the Middle East.

After exhaustive lobbying in Russia, in May 2003 Ma succeeded in changing plans for an east-west pipeline that would have gone straight to Japan, but would instead serve China first and Japan second. China regarded the pipeline as intrinsic to development of its northern provinces; Russia saw the pipeline as an inexpensive means of bringing Siberian oil to the world market without incurring extensive shipping costs. The deal seemed to be advantageous to both sides; CNPC's partner, Yukos, surpassed LUKoil as the largest oil company in Russia.

By the fall of 2003, however, the head of Yukos, Mikhail Khodorkovsky, was in jail; he had been the victim of a power play by the Russian president Putin, as he had shirked taxes and challenged Moscow's control of oil pipelines. The pipeline would now serve Japan first, and China would be lucky to receive even a branch line delivering leftovers. The failure of the deal, in addition to lethargy over development elsewhere, meant China would soak up supplies from the world market—instead of from Siberia—helping to drive up the NYSE-listed price of oil to an all-time high of $42 a barrel in May 2004. Once again Ma had neglected politics; this time he turned west toward the Caspian Basin and a deal with Kazakhstan, the next closest neighbor for China's northern oil needs.

While Ma struggled to secure additional oil for China, the profitability of PetroChina continued to improve, setting a record in 2002. During that year's 16th National Congress of the Chinese Communist Party, Ma was elected to the party's Central Committee as part of Jiang Zemin's embrace of capitalism. At the height of his power Ma declared, as reported in *China Chemical Reporter*, "2003 is the year for CNPC to improve performance through management" (May 6, 2004). Ma declared six requirements for the reform of CNPC, revealing his continued commitment to transforming China's oil ministry into a market sector—and also revealing the amount of work yet to be done. Critics of Ma said that his reforms remained tactical but neglectfully apolitical.

"WEN ZE ZHI"

After joining the WTO in 2001, the Chinese government removed legal obstacles to capitalism and began improving its human rights and environmental records. By 2003 *wen ze zhi*, meaning "government accountability system," became a recurring political theme. The system—also known as "take the blame and resign," as noted in *China Daily* (April 30, 2004)—was emblematic of China's new concerns for human safety and environmental health; those in charge of operations involved in causing harm were sacked. Ma, as the number-one oilman and central committee member, would become the poster child of *wen ze zhi*.

In December 2003 a cloud of hydrogen-sulfide gas was released by an explosion at a CNPC-controlled well. The cloud dispersed over 28 towns in Kaixian county and suburban Chongqing. The accident led to the evacuation of 60,000 people from the county; thousands of people suffered side effects and 243 died. Over the next few months the company was shaken, as public outcry demanded accountability. An investigation into the accident blamed the absence of a blowout-prevention device, which had been removed as part of a cost-cutting measure extending the life of the well. Six workers were blamed for following improper procedures at the work site and arrested. Low-level managers were also sacked.

As the person responsible for CNPC's industrial safety, Ma bore the full weight of the accident and tendered his resignation, which the government accepted in April 2004. Undoubt-

edly Ma never would have resigned if not for the principle of *wen ze zhi*; his predecessor had not been pressured to resign when 312 people had died in an oil fire in 1994. Yet China was changing, and the series of sackings in 2003 and 2004 were due not to a sudden epidemic of accidents but the new governmental concern for improving safety through the institution of accountability.

CNPC staff felt Ma's resignation to be unwarranted. As reported by Xu Yihe, one said, "It is just like 'killing chicken to frighten monkeys' which is a Chinese saying to mean punishing someone as a warning to others" (April 21, 2004). After Ma's resignation CNPC facilities sprung a series of chemical leaks leading to the deaths of another 30 people, the hospitalization of 282, and the evacuation of over 150,000. *Wen ze zhi* alone could not improve an energy industry that had developed when the Chinese government had been unconcerned with safety. Sinopec, on the other hand, had in fact invested in safety and consequently suffered very few accidents.

On July 1, 2004, the "Chongqing rule" went into effect. Written by the municipal government of Chongqing, the rule sought to institutionalize *wen ze zhi* such that the accountability, resignations, prosecutions, and firings of workers and managers throughout China after accidents were not simply the normalization of scapegoating. The Chongqing rule declared the rights of the public, news organizations, and governmental representatives to be privy to the accountability system.

Ma's willingness to resign and open acceptance of his responsibility added to his reputation among government officials and industry workers. Resignations normally occurred in ugly, drawn-out manners, but Ma was ready to resign as soon as the government conveyed its desire for him to do so. Such "courage," as referred to by Interfax China Business News, endeared Ma to many (April 15, 2004). His role in the early days of *wen ze zhi* set China on a route toward accountability and the regulation of industry safety. At the very least the removal of oil and chemical facilities from populated areas was sped up as a result of his actions.

See also entry on China National Petroleum Corporation in *International Directory of Company Histories*.

SOURCES FOR FURTHER INFORMATION

"Bad News Off the Agenda for 'Model' State-run Enterprise," *Upstream*, March 19, 2004, http://www.upstream online.com.

"China Industry: President of CNPC Resigns," *Economist Intelligence Unit*, April 27, 2004, p. 28.

Jiang Zhuqing, "Leaders Held Responsible for Accidents," *China Daily*, April 30, 2004.

"Media Praises Ma's 'Courage' Following His Resignation from CNPC," Interfax China Business News, April 15, 2004, http://www.interfax.com/com?item=products&id=5672573.

"Three Companies, Three Focuses," *China Chemical Reporter*, 15, no. 13 (May 6, 2004): 441.

Wonacott, Peter, Jeanne Whalen, and Bhushan Bahree, "China's Growing Thirst for Oil Remakes the World Market," *Wall Street Journal*, December 3, 2003.

Xin Zhiming, "Sewing Up Loopholes in Accountability Process," *China Daily*, May 13, 2004.

Yihe, Xu, "China Energy Watch: CNPC Changes Heads, Problems Ahead," Dow Jones Energy Service, April 21, 2004, http://www.newstoprofitby.com/showpage.cfm?pid=189.

—Jeremy W. Hubbell

■ ■ ■

John J. Mack

1944–

Former president and chief executive officer, Credit Suisse First Boston

Nationality: American.

Born: November 17, 1944, in Mooresville, North Carolina.

Education: Duke University, BA, 1968.

Family: Son of Charlie Machoul (mother's name unknown); married Christy (maiden name unknown); children: three.

Career: Smith Barney, 1968–1970, municipal bond trader and salesman; F. S. Smithers & Company, 1971–1972, bond trader; Morgan Stanley, 1972–1976, bond salesman, fixed income department; 1976–1977, vice president; 1977–1979, principal; 1979–1984, managing director; 1985–1992, head, worldwide taxable fixed income division; 1992–1993, chief operating officer; 1993–1997, president; Morgan Stanley Dean Witter & Company, 1997–2001, president, chief operating officer, and director; Credit Suisse First Boston, 2001–2004, chief executive officer; Crédit Suisse Group, 2003–2004, co–chief executive officer.

John J. Mack. *AP/Wide World Photos.*

EARLY YEARS

■ With 2002 revenue of $5.7 billion Credit Suisse First Boston (CSFB), once known as the venerable Donaldson, Lufkin & Jenrette, was a unit of Crédit Suisse Group. Despite its European roots the company was a top U.S. investment firm, combining the investment banking prowess of its predecessor and of its parent. CSFB operations included investment and merchant banking, securities underwriting and management, research, securities trading, and top-ranked fixed income product services. John J. Mack was named CEO of the firm in 2001 and immediately began transforming the then beleaguered company into a lean, client-focused organization. His knack for cost cutting along with a refusal to coddle investment bankers was a reality check to an organization that was spending money faster than it was earning it.

The son of a Lebanese immigrant, Mack learned from his parents the value of hard work. His father worked as a door-to-door salesman selling needles and thread and eventually opened a small store. Mack's mother cooked for sick people in the community. For a first-generation immigrant, life in a small southern town was not easy. A gifted athlete, Mack attended Duke University on a football scholarship and ran a late-night snack shop out of his dormitory room. His first job on Wall Street was at Smith Barney, where he started as a municipal bond trader and salesman. The next major firm he worked at was Morgan Stanley, where under his watch the bond-trading operation was consistently profitable. Mack's reward was a quick ascent on the corporate ladder. In 1993 Mack replaced the investment banker Robert Greenhill as president of Morgan Stanley, earning a reputation as a charismatic leader, brilliant dealmaker, and diligent cost cutter. The last trait won him the nickname "Mack the Knife."

INCONSPICUOUS EXECUTIVE WITH A COMPETITIVE STREAK

His 1994 compensation package totaled $2.5 million, but Mack avoided the lavish lifestyle common to many Wall Street executives. The main decoration in his office was a large painting of a woman swimming underwater. Mack's fiercely competitive streak, however, was a perfect fit for Wall Street. *Fiasco*, the 1997 book by Frank Partnoy, a former Morgan employee, featured Mack's testosterone-induced management style. According to Partnoy, Mack routinely paced the company's trading room, screaming, "There is blood in the water. Let's go kill."

In 1997 Mack brokered the merger of his firm and Dean Witter Discover & Company, adding Dean Witter's strength as a retail brokerage to Morgan Stanley's investment banking might. Mack ceded the CEO position to Philip Purcell, his Dean Witter counterpart, expecting to ascend to the top spot again. He resigned in January 2001 when Purcell refused to outline a succession plan. Three months later Crédit Suisse named Mack CEO.

TURNING AROUND A CULTURE

Crédit Suisse was the biggest challenge of Mack's career. The company was in dire need of disciplined management. CSFB was under investigation for breaching regulatory practices in the United States, the United Kingdom, Sweden, Japan, and India. The U.S. government was investigating CSFB's initial public offering (IPO) allocation. The West Coast technology banker at CSFB, Frank Quattrone, turned the firm into a technology-IPO powerhouse. In the post-Internet boom, however, these deals left the firm vulnerable.

Mack restored order. He shifted employees' focus from increasing the value of their bonus checks to delivering value for clients. Mack set about breaking down the silos in the firm, whereby units and executives in the company had been working in isolation. Mack sold the philosophy that teamwork, not big egos, would seal the company's success. Mack, who believed he could transform the culture in three years, told Patrick McGeehan of the *New York Times*, "It never came to my mind that I couldn't get people to change" (January 27, 2002).

Not everyone was on board. A dismayed employee told Michelle Celarier, of *Investment Dealers Digest*, "Mack is saying we're one firm. But these are people who enjoyed being left alone" (March 24, 2003). Others criticized Mack's management style. A former CSFB banker told Celarier, "Everyone repeats whatever he says; it's a mantra. If you go against him, he flips out."

LESS PAY, MORE LOYALTY

Mack's most impressive feat was reining in CSFB's out-of-control spending. He cut 10,000 jobs and eliminated more than $3 billion in costs. When Mack joined the company, an astonishing 60 percent of CSFB's bonus pool was guaranteed. He persuaded the firm's bankers to give back $421 million in cash pay, meeting with employees one on one. According to Patricia Sellers, of *Fortune*, Mack told the employees, "Look, we're not making money. We have a lot of young people here who aren't going to get bonuses unless you give up some money. It's about fairness and building a great firm. Trust me. I'll remember what you did."

At the same time Mack built loyalty. After one employee agreed to cut his pay package, Mack showed his gratitude. Knowing that the employee was an ardent fan of the Duke University basketball team, Mack had the Duke coach Mike Krzyzewski call the employee. According to Sellers, Krzyzewski, who spoke to the employee for approximately an hour, said, "I said to this guy: I'm best friends with John Mack. He's a cold S.O.B. I just want you to know that what you did today warmed his heart. That's what leadership is all about."

THE LURE OF A CHALLENGE

During the first quarter of 2004 CSFB's parent company, Crédit Suisse Group, reported that first-quarter profit was more than six times the earnings in the quarter a year earlier. Net profit soared more than sixfold to $1.4 billion, compared with a gain of $279 million previously, as business conditions improved. Mack told Fiona Fleck of the *New York Times*, "2003 was a critical turning point for C.S.F.B. We set out to be consistently profitable, and we were. I am confident that C.S.F.B. is now well positioned to build on its progress and achieve growth in 2004 as global markets rebound" (February 13, 2004). Turning CSFB into a profitable firm was Mack's obsession. He told Sellers, "This has been the biggest challenge, the most interesting challenge. 'Fun' is not the right word. Do you have fun when you work out? No. You do it because it makes you feel good afterward. It gets your blood pumping." In June 2004 Mack announced that when his contract expired on July 12, 2004, he would step down as co-CEO of Crédit Suisse Group and as CEO of Credit Suisse First Boston.

See also entry on Crédit Suisse Group in *International Directory of Company Histories*.

SOURCES FOR FURTHER INFORMATION

Celarier, Michelle, "Fixer-Upper: John Mack Faces the Challenge of His Life at CSFB," *Investment Dealers Digest*, March 24, 2003.

Fleck, Fiona, "Crédit Suisse Rebounds To a Profit," *New York Times*, February 13, 2004, Section W, Column 6, Business/Financial Desk, p. 1.

McGeehan, Patrick, "His Rallying Cry at First Boston: Smaller, Cleaner, Fairer," *New York Times*, January 27, 2002.

Partnoy, Frank, *Fiasco*, New York: W. W. Norton & Company, 1997.

Sellers, Patricia, "The Trials of John Mack," *Fortune*, September 1, 2003, p. 98.

—Tim Halpern

■■■
Terunobu Maeda
1945–
President and chief executive officer, Mizuho Holdings

Nationality: Japanese.

Born: January 2, 1945, in Japan.

Education: University of Tokyo, LLB, 1967.

Career: Fuji Bank, 1968–2000, director and general manager of Credit Planning Division, director and general manager of Corporate Planning Division, managing director of Public and Financial Institution Group, chief financial officer, and deputy president; 2000–2001, vice president; Mizuho Holdings Corporation, 2001, president and CEO.

Address: Mizuho Financial Group, 1-5-5 Otemachi, Chiyoda-ku, Tokyo, Japan; http://www.mizuho-fg.co.jp.

■ Terunobu Maeda was president and CEO of Japan's Mizuho Holdings, the first bank with $1 trillion in assets and the largest financial services company (by assets) in the world. A victim of the bursting of Japan's economic bubble and declining stocks, Mizuho suffered from persistent mountains of bad debt and apathetic management. After a steady stream of financial losses and a massive computer glitch that affected 2.5 million transactions, Maeda was seen as a weak leader shirking responsibility.

NAMED PRESIDENT OF THE WORLD'S LARGEST BANK

Terunobu Maeda joined Fuji Bank in 1968 after graduating from the University of Tokyo with a bachelor of laws degree. Through the years he served in a variety of capacities, as director and general manager of the Credit Planning Division, director and general manager of the Corporate Planning Division, managing director of the Public and Financial Institution Group, chief financial officer, deputy president, and vice president.

Fuji Bank, along with Dai-Ichi Kangyo Bank and the Industrial Bank of Japan (IBJ), merged in September 2000 to

Terunobu Maeda. © *Reuters NewMedia/Corbis.*

form Mizuho Holdings. Mizuho Holdings thus became the largest bank in the world in terms of assets, surpassing even Citigroup. Japan's regulatory Financial Services Agency (FSA), saw the integration as the ultimate example of consolidation of Japanese banks as they tried to cope with massive loan defaults.

In November 2001, six months into the fiscal year, Mizuho Holdings reported a loss of ¥265 billion ($2.1 billion). The company then stated a net loss of ¥600 billion ($4.9 billion) for the fiscal year ended March 31, 2002. To assume responsibility for the bank's huge losses, Mizuho Holdings' president, Katsuyuki Sugita; Fuji Bank's president, Yoshiro Yamamoto; and IBJ's president, Masao Nishimura, resigned. The resignations were designed to rejuvenate management. One move toward that end was the appointment of Terunobu Maeda, a vice president of Fuji Bank, to replace Sugita as president and

CEO of Mizuho Holdings. Yamamoto was first considered but was later rejected in favor of the younger Maeda. At a time when the bank wrote off ¥2 trillion ($16.2 billion) in bad loans, up from a projected ¥1.03 trillion ($8.3 billion), some critics suggested that a clean sweep of all management was a necessary approach.

CLAIMED NO DAMAGE AFTER COMPUTER CHAOS

On April 1, 2002, when the three merged banks officially went online as one megabank, a malfunction in the network software crippled the computer system. Money transfers were delayed or not delivered at all, customers were billed for transfers that did not go through, and customers were double-billed for transactions performed on automatic teller machines (ATMs). All told, seven thousand ATMs were shut down, 60,000 accounts were debited twice for the same transaction, and customers incurred a total of ¥1 billion ($7.7 million) in damages. In the first five days of operation, 800,000 utility and credit card transfers and withdrawals were inaccurate, affecting customers of such companies as Tokyo Electric Power, Tokyo Gas, Nippon Telegraph & Telephone, and Credit Saison Company. The glitches affected about 2.5 million ATM transactions.

Maeda immediately assembled an emergency team to analyze the problem. Days later, in an unusual move, Japan's parliament, the Diet, summoned Maeda to explain the fiasco. The Diet rarely required top bank executives to explain operational mistakes. Maeda at first apologized and asked for more time to fix the problems. But he stunned the public when he shamelessly told the Diet that the malfunction had not caused damage to users.

Politicians were angry and feared that the computer debacle and the ongoing debt problems of Japan's banks would erode people's faith in the Japanese financial system and that they would pull their money out in droves. They complained that Mizuho had embarrassed Japan internationally. In the *Economist*, Shintaro Ishihara, governor of Tokyo, which was Mizuho's largest depositor, said of the bank, "Maybe it wouldn't be so bad if it was forced out of business" (April 27, 2002).

FSA's chief, Hakuo Yanigisawa, even considered punishing Mizuho. Maeda responded that his bank would contend with those responsible. Maeda noted in the *Japan Times*, "Once operations resume and we know how and why the troubles occurred, we will clarify responsibility, including my own, and take appropriate action" (April 17, 2002).

Tokyo Electric had considered filing a lawsuit. After two weeks the power company giant was still waiting for ¥5.2 billion ($40 million), encompassing 547,000 delinquent or missing automatic transfers. In response, Maeda announced that Mizuho would compensate its corporate customers for financial damages and would pay the penalties that customers were charged for delays in paying loans and credit card bills. Mizuho paid roughly ¥9.8 billion ($74.7 million) to Tokyo Electric.

RECEIVED PAY CUT IN DISCIPLINARY ACTION

The computer debacle was only a symptom of greater problems indicative of Mizuho's management climate. Although they had had years to prepare, management of the three banks engaged in power struggles and infighting over who would oversee the network integration of the banks' computer systems. Complacency, lack of preparation, poor communication, and management's neglect of the computer system's progress plagued the company. Management even dismissed requests by utility companies to test the debit system and requests by FSA inspectors for progress reports before the system went online.

Investigations by the FSA and Mizuho traced the computer fiasco to a chief information officer originally from Dai-Ichi Kangyo Bank who had failed to notify top management about a possible large-scale system failure for fear of delaying the April 1 launch. Maeda said in *Japan Times*, "The officer in charge of computer systems did not think the glitches that appeared during the tests could not be overcome, and no information to the contrary was passed on" (June 20, 2002).

The FSA announced disciplinary action against Mizuho. Short of stepping down, Maeda, along with Mizuho Bank's president, Tadashi Kudo, and Mizuho Corporate Bank's president, Hiroshi Saito, agreed to a 50 percent reduction in salary for six months. Mizuho Holdings itself punished 114 executives and employees responsible for computer malfunctions with 15–30 percent pay cuts. This disciplinary action was the largest for any Japanese banking firm in response to a scandal. The FSA also issued a business-improvement order to Mizuho to strengthen its internal control and submit progress reports on methods to prevent another recurrence of computer failures. Another operations mess would require Mizuho's top management to go. Despite the reprimands and preventive measures, analysts were doubtful that Mizuho's intensions to improve were sincere.

In the midst of the computer scandal, Mizuho Holdings announced its performance for fiscal 2001, ended March 31, 2002. Mizuho reported a group net loss of ¥976 billion ($7.7 billion). For fiscal 2001 the bank was able to dispose of ¥2.38 trillion ($18.8 billion) in debt, a 218 percent increase from fiscal 2000. Maeda praised the achievement, saying that Mizuho's bad-debt write-offs had accelerated in the past year. This was in line with the Japanese government's demands that the nation's banks shed their bad debt over three years or face government intervention.

APOLOGIZED TO SHAREHOLDERS

At a June 2002 meeting, Maeda apologized to about 1,800 shareholders for the computer meltdown. In *Mainichi Shimbun*, he said, "Problems with the settlement system, which is a social infrastructure, adversely affected our customers and shareholders. I apologize for that. We are firmly determined to create a new business model" (June 25, 2002). Maeda also expressed regret for the bank's bad performance. Some shareholders criticized the board members' lack of crisis management and encouraged those at the top to change their ways or resign.

In a climate of plunging stocks and critical health for Japan's top banks, FSA's new bank minister, Heizo Takenaka, pronounced no Japanese bank "too big to fail" and threatened stricter regulatory policies. In October 2002 Maeda was literally unable to show his face. Addressing an invitation-only banking conference hosted by Merrill Lynch in Tokyo, he read from a prepared statement, nose down, with only the top of his head toward the audience. Commenting in *Newsweek*, one attendee observed, "It was the worst presentation in the world, not a single number or target in it. [Maeda] didn't give the impression that he was chairman of the world's largest bank" (October 21, 2002).

PRESENTED NEW STRATEGY

Takenaka put his foot down to the banks, which were plagued by write-offs, low interest rates, and falling land and stock prices. He urged them to dispose of nonperforming loans and force no-hope borrowers into liquidation. With bank stocks trading at record lows, Takenaka threatened that the government would nationalize the weakest lenders. Maeda disagreed, quoted in the *New York Times* as saying, "Nationalization is not the best way for managing our business. It is more efficient to handle this privately, and we can do it" (November 26, 2002). Maeda also added his voice to the top seven Japanese banks, which carried a combined ¥26.8 trillion ($216 billion) in bad loans, in objecting to the government's plan to bail out the struggling banks.

At the end of 2002, after seeing Mizuho's share price drop below ¥100,000 ($793.65), Maeda unveiled a new restructuring strategy. He planned to reduce the pay of top executives and board members by 30 percent, cut 6,300 jobs (or 21 percent) of the workforce, lower salaries by 10 percent, close 120 branches worldwide, and sell preferred shares to raise capital. In all, the efforts were expected to reduce costs by $1.3 billion, or 20 percent, by March 2005.

Analysts believed that Mizuho's changes would not be enough without government intervention. Some thought that the bank would fail in 2003. Even investors pushed down the company's shares to nearly half their value in September 2002.

But Mizuho stayed afloat by selling its safest assets, government bonds; raising funds from other financial institutions and business corporations; and cutting lending to Japanese corporations in an attempt to stave off possible bad debts.

LOSING CUSTOMERS' TRUST

Mizuho's financing methods were being criticized by the media, and Mizuho's management team was being humiliated. Economists who had hoped Mizuho (whose name means "fresh harvest of rice") would be an example of recovery now viewed the company as a symbol of the failure of the Japanese economy. Financial advisers said that the bank needed to regain the trust of customers, investors, and business partners. The Japanese government raised fears that the country's banking system was headed for a meltdown. Maeda himself was being criticized for not taking responsibility for the bank's deteriorating performance and for not being a strong leader.

Maeda countered with a declaration to "resolve all fear for the future of the bank" and to remain in office to oversee his bank's turnaround. Nevertheless, at a February 2003 shareholders' meeting, attendees rejected a confidence motion against Maeda, who had failed to control the bank's bad debts. For the 2002 fiscal year ending March 31, 2003, Maeda once again found himself apologizing for a group net loss of ¥1.95 trillion ($16.4 billion), but he was at least able to praise the achievement of successfully raising ¥1 trillion ($8.4 billion).

DISAPPOINTING IMAGE OF MANAGEMENT

In a commentary on the rapid decline of Mizuho's management structure, the *Weekly Post* described the company's near empty executive suite. Half of the 12 executives remained. The empty office reflected the forlorn image of Maeda, CEO of the world's largest bank. The thin man with a plain view of life spoke to others softly and often cast his eyes down. He was said to arrive at work at 7:00 a.m. and have lunch precisely at 12:00 p.m. Some people described him as a rationalist and a mystery man, while others said that he looked like a mayor's assistant in a small town. A former executive of Mizuho said that part of Mizuho's problems stemmed from appointing Maeda as its president.

In March 2004 Japan's House of Representatives Committee on Financial Affairs held a panel with the presidents of four major banking groups. Maeda reported that Mizuho Financial was conducting tests for an integrated computer system in an effort to avoid a repeat of the company's computer debacle of the previous year.

See also entries on Fuji Bank, Ltd. and Mizuho Financial Group Inc. in *International Directory of Company Histories*.

SOURCES FOR FURTHER INFORMATION

Belson, Ken, "Pressure Is Building on Banks in Japan," *New York Times*, November 26, 2002.

Bremmer, Brian, "Japan's Cracked Banking Colossus," *BusinessWeek*, December 23, 2002.

"Crisis Facing Mizuho Financial Group Symbolizes Ailing Japanese Economy," *Weekly Post*, May 19–25, 2003.

"Financial Giant Announces Punishment for Its Top Staff," *Japan Times*, June 20, 2002.

"Heads Begin to Roll over Mizuho Fiasco," *Japan Times*, April 17, 2002.

"In a Hole, Digging Deeper," *Economist*, December 14, 2002, pp. 66–67.

Merrell, Caroline, "Investors Support Mizuho's $37bn Share Issue," *Times*, February 6, 2003.

"Mizuho Financial Group's Executives Get 17 Million Yen Remuneration on Average," *Kyodo News International*, June 25, 2002.

"Mizuho Head Apologizes over Huge ATM Blunder," *Mainichi Shimbun*, June 25, 2002.

"Three Top Mizuho Execs Get Pay Cuts for ATM Botchery," *Mainichi Shimbun*, June 9, 2002.

"Undispensable," *Economist*, April 27, 2002, pp. 72–73.

Wehrfritz, George, "Flat on Its Back," *Newsweek*, October 21, 2002, pp. 52–53.

—Lorraine Savage

■ ■ ■

Joseph Magliochetti
1942–2003
Former president and chief executive officer, Dana Corporation

Nationality: American.

Born: 1942, in River Forest, Illinois.

Died: September 22, 2003.

Education: Hillsdale College, 1969; Harvard University, 1985.

Family: Married Kathleen (maiden name unknown); children: three.

Career: Victor Manufacturing, 1966–1967, management trainee; Dana Corporation, 1967–1975, management trainee in a number of sales, engineering, and manufacturing positions; Dana's Churubusco Distribution Center, 1975–1978, plant manager—service-parts group; Dana-Spicer Clutch Division, 1978–1979, general manager; 1979–1980, vice president and general manager; Dana Engineering (part of Dana Europe), 1980, director of drive-train components; Dana Europe, 1980–1985, president; Dana North American Operations, 1985–1990, group vice president; 1990–1992, president—automotive; 1992–1996, president; Dana Corporation, 1996–1997, president; 1997–1999, chief operating officer; 1999–2003, president and chief executive officer; 2000–2003, chairman of the board of directors.

Awards: Triangle Award and Automotive Hall of Fame Distinguished Service Citation, Motor & Equipment Manufacturers Association, 2002.

■ The automotive executive Joseph Magliochetti served the Dana Corporation for 37 years, from 1966 to 2003, and was ultimately named CEO and chairman. During his career with Dana, Magliochetti held a number of domestic and international positions. He gained a wealth of experience in the global economy, both with domestic and international projects. He also developed Dana's e-commerce initiatives and repositioned the company to focus on long-term technology.

Dana Corporation is one of the world's largest independent designers and manufacturers of components, modules, and complete systems that automobile, commercial, off-highway, and industrial vehicle manufacturers use to assemble new vehicles. It also supplies replacement parts for automobile companies in the aftermarket sector. Dana's core products include axles, brakes, and drive shafts, along with engine, filtration, fluid-system, sealing, and structural products. Customers include original equipment manufacturers, such as Ford, General Motors, Toyota, DaimlerChrysler, and BMW. Dana employs approximately 60,000 people worldwide and operates hundreds of technology, manufacturing, assembly, distribution, and customer-service facilities in more than 30 countries.

DANA CAREER

Magliochetti began his automotive career as a management trainee with Victor Manufacturing in Chicago, Illinois, in 1966. He had declined an employment offer with Dana before taking the job with Victor and rejected another job offer from Dana just before the company acquired Victor in 1967. After Dana management finally got Magliochetti on its team, he served in a variety of sales, engineering, and manufacturing positions at several Dana divisions. In 1975 he moved to the service-parts group as plant manager of the Churubusco Distribution Center. He was promoted to general manager of the Spicer Clutch Division (Toledo, Ohio) in 1978 and was named that division's vice president and general manager the following year.

In 1980 Magliochetti was named director of drive-train components for Dana Engineering (London, England), a part of Dana Europe. Later that year he was appointed president of Dana Europe with responsibility for all operations in Europe and the Middle East. In 1985 Magliochetti returned to the United States as group vice president of North American Operations. In 1990 he became president of the automotive division of North American Operations. He was promoted to president of North American Operations in 1992 and was appointed to the Dana Policy Committee.

Magliochetti was promoted to president of Dana Corporation in 1996 and was elected to the company's board of directors later that year. In 1997 he was appointed chairman of Dana's World Operating committee. In that same year he was elected COO and remained at that post until 1999. He was named CEO in February 1999, after Southwood "Woody"

Morcott resigned from the position. Magliochetti became chairman of the board of directors in April 2000.

MAGLIOCHETTI IN CHARGE

Owing to the economic slowdown that began in 2000, Dana Corporation was struggling as a direct result of diminishing automobile production and slow U.S. vehicle sales. Automobile manufacturers began to cut back production to reduce inventories, and heavy truck manufacturing companies were already in the process of contracting their businesses. All of Dana's customers began to pressure the company to cut costs.

Although Magliochetti had headed the company for only 18 months, he began a restructuring plan in 2000 that cut 10,000 jobs and closed 11 facilities. This strategy included implementing online warehouse distribution, selling some non-core facilities, and reducing capital-spending plans by $150 million, to less than $400 million. Looking to increase Dana's return on investment, Magliochetti moved its North American axle production out of existing plants and consolidated all such production into nine facilities run by its Spicer Driveshaft Division. Dana's 2000 profits dropped about 44 percent—on a sales decline of 6 percent—to $12.3 billion. Its share price sank from $30 to $15. By the end of 2001 Magliochetti continued to see his company struggle. However, he was unchanged in his defense of his company's fundamental strength. By the end of 2002 Magliochetti had closed a total of 39 plants, consolidated others, and cut 20 percent of its pre-2000 workforce of 70,000 employees. In the first six months of 2003 Magliochetti saw Dana turn around—earning $93 million, compared with a $177 million loss during the first half of 2002.

TECHNOLOGY DRIVEN

Despite the pressure from the declining stock market and the contracting manufacturing industry, Magliochetti directed the company's affairs with technology in mind. Knowing that technology would drive Dana's growth, Magliochetti spent $287 million on research and development in 2000 with the goal of developing proprietary (private) technologies and products that would give the company an edge over its formidable competitors, such as Delphi and Visteon—large suppliers spun off from the automobile makers General Motors and Ford, respectively. Rather than expand through acquisitions, Magliochetti felt that in order to protect Dana's long-term margins, the company had to grow with innovations.

One of the concepts that Magliochetti used to advance this technological growth was "megatronics"—the science of incorporating emerging technologies into traditional products. For instance, the cylinder-head gasket—a traditional low-technology product—was modified to include state-of-the-art sensors, which were able to monitor engine temperatures.

Magliochetti also made Dana a leader in manufacturing modular parts, which helped decrease the number of parts used to assemble an automobile from 10,000 to 6,000. For instance, one module might call for a comprehensive driveline complete with clutch, transmission, driveshaft, and axle. Magliochetti focused on offering module products either directly or through strategic partnerships. Dana continued to focus on joint ventures to prepare for increased modularity use.

Magliochetti saw great potential with long-term employees who had experienced the volatile cyclical market in which Dana operated. He stated that his top-level management team averaged 27 years of service. With such experience, Magliochetti's team looked forward to growing the company by offering new products and becoming a supplier to the new modular manufacturing sector.

BATTLING A HOSTILE TAKEOVER ATTEMPT

During 2002 and into 2003 Magliochetti was leading the company in a tremendous battle to protect itself from a hostile takeover attempt by Larry D. Yost, CEO of rival ArvinMeritor. The company, based in Troy, Michigan, was a supplier of shocks, struts, suspensions, and exhaust systems and made a $15-per-share, $2.2 billion hostile takeover bid in July 2003. Magliochetti rejected the offer, saying that the antitrust concerns and divestitures that would result from a merger would make the deal pointless. Dana became a takeover target after suffering net losses of $182 million in 2002 and $298 million in 2001 and a 33 percent drop in its share price from the end of 2001 until July 8, 2003, the day ArvinMeritor made its offer. At Magliochetti's last public appearance at the University of Michigan, he described the takeover attempt as totally inadequate with regard to the best interests of Dana's shareholders.

PASSING AWAY

Dana announced on September 23, 2003, that Magliochetti had passed away on the previous evening. After a two-week hospitalization for removal of his gallbladder, he died from complications of pancreatitis. Dana announced that Glen Hiner would serve as acting chairman of the board of directors. Hiner, one of Dana's longest-serving directors, said in a news release that Magliochetti "was a wonderful man, not only respected but also beloved by his friends and colleagues. . . . [who] served with great distinction for more than three decades and was an outstanding leader. He built a culture of integrity and a strong organizational structure" (Dana press release, September 23, 2003).

No one knew whether Magliochetti's death would make Dana a more vulnerable target for takeover. Scott Upham, an analyst with J. D. Power and Associates, said in the *Detroit News*, "His absence is going to bring a lot of things into question during the next couple of weeks. The company is 100 years old and has very solid management from the top down" (September 24, 2003). By November 2003 ArvinMeritor had abandoned its hostile takeover bid for Dana. As a result, Dana stock increased about 45 percent from the end of November 2003 to February 2004. For the first time in more than 50 years, the board of directors at Dana looked outside its own management members for a new CEO. Michael J. Burns, a lifelong General Motors executive, was named CEO, president, and a director of the board of directors in the early part of February 2004, taking the helm on March 1.

CIVIC ACTIVITIES AND AWARDS

Magliochetti led many business and civic initiatives, both locally and nationally. He served on the board of directors of BellSouth (beginning in March 2000) and CIGNA Corporation and was a member of the U.S. Business Roundtable and its policy committee and a member and former chairman of the Motor and Equipment Manufacturers Association (MEMA) board of directors. He also was a member of the Automotive Original Equipment Manufacturers Association and the Automotive Service Industry Association. Magliochetti served on the board of the National Association of Manufacturers and was a member of the U.S.-Japan Business Council and the MEMA/JAMA (Japan Automotive Manufacturers Association) Liaison Committee to cultivate automotive trade relations with Japan. He also served on the U.S. Department of Commerce Auto Parts Advisory Committee and on the inde-pendent nominating committee to recommend directors for the New York Stock Exchange.

Locally, Magliochetti was actively involved in many community organizations, including the United Way of Greater Toledo, for which he served as the 2002 Toledo-area campaign chairman. He also was chairman of the Toledo Symphony board and a member of the board of directors of the Toledo Museum of Art and the Center of Science and Industry.

An avid sportsman, Magliochetti often invited industry analysts to join him on hunting and fishing trips. He was ranked number 197 among the country's best chief executive golfers in a survey by *Golf Digest* magazine. In 2002 Magliochetti was awarded the Automotive Hall of Fame Distinguished Service Citation in honor of his contributions to the motor vehicle industry as well as the MEMA Triangle Award, which recognized his leadership and advocacy on behalf of the automotive industry.

See also entry on Dana Corporation in *International Directory of Company Histories.*

SOURCES FOR FURTHER INFORMATION

"Dana Chairman & CEO Joe Magliochetti Passes Away; Board Names Acting Chairman, Acting President," Dana press release, September 23, 2003, http://www.dana.com/news/pressreleases/prpage.asp?page=1318.

Garsten, Ed, "Dana Chief's Death May Upset Takeover Bid: Magliochetti Led Opposition to $2.2 Billion ArvinMeritor Offer," *Detroit News*, September 24, 2003.

—William Arthur Atkins

Marjorie Magner

1949–

Chairman and chief executive officer, Global Consumer Group, Citigroup

Nationality: American.

Born: 1949, in Brooklyn, New York.

Education: Brooklyn College, BS, 1969; Krannert School of Management, Purdue University, MSIA (master of science in industrial administration), 1974.

Family: Children: one.

Career: Chemical Bank, 1974–1987, various positions including managing director of the chemical-technologies division at the time of her resignation; Citigroup (including predecessor company Commercial Credit, later known as CitiFinancial), 1987–2003, various positions; 2003–, chairman and CEO of Global Consumer Group.

Awards: Helen Keller Achievement Award, American Foundation for the Blind, 2001; named one of *Fortune* magazine's 50 Most Powerful Women, 2000–2003; named one of *US Banker* magazine's 25 Most Powerful Women in Banking, 2003; awarded honorary doctor of management degree, Purdue University, 2004.

Address: Citigroup, 399 Park Avenue, New York, New York 10043; http://www.citigroup.com/citigroup/homepage.

■ Marjorie Magner was promoted to chairman and chief executive officer (CEO) of Citigroup's highly profitable Global Consumer Group in August 2003 after almost two decades with Citigroup, the New York financial-services giant that emerged from the merger of the Travelers Group and Citicorp in 1998. She served as the Global Consumer Group's chief operating officer (COO) from April 2002 until her promotion. Under her leadership the organization, including retail banking, credit cards, and consumer finance, generated more than half of Citigroup's revenue during the first two quarters of 2003. Including her employment at Commercial Credit, a predecessor company, Magner had been with Citigroup since 1987. Associates depicted her as a personable leader whose drive, enthusiasm, and passion were tempered by a low-key personality.

EARLY CAREER

Following her graduation from the Krannert School of Management at Purdue University in 1974, Magner joined the Chemical Bank operations division, where her business-focused master's degree made her unique in a work environment dominated by men. Even though her gender was notable, and sometimes an issue, she forged ahead. When she was excluded from meetings held by male coworkers, she showed up without an invitation. "It was very brazen and I wasn't a particularly brazen person in those days. But I would show up and say, 'I know you forgot to tell me about this meeting, but it's okay. I'm here now, let's start.' They didn't do it much after that," she was quoted as saying (*US Banker*, October 2003). By the time she left Chemical she was managing director of the chemical-technologies division.

MOVES TO CITIGROUP

Magner started her Citigroup career at Commercial Credit, a forerunner of Citigroup, in 1987. Her move followed that of her Chemical Bank mentor, Robert Willumstad, who was a vice president when she started at Chemical. In addition to their common work experience, the two shared Brooklyn roots. Magner told the *New York Daily News* that "People from Brooklyn are a little scrappy. It's a hard working community with high expectations" (August 7, 2003). Her responsibilities steadily increased; she served as president, CEO, and then chairman of CitiFinancial, the successor company to Commercial Credit. In 2000 she became head of Citigroup's Primerica Financial Services and Citibanking North America, and by 2002 she had been named COO of the Global Consumer Group.

SIGNIFICANT PROMOTION

In August 2003 Magner was promoted to chairman and CEO of the Global Consumer Group, reporting to Bob Willumstad. She had earned the respect of Citigroup Chairman and CEO Sandy Weill, who praised her for her skills in acquisitions and consolidations, a key Citigroup business strategy, and for her integrity. The appointment was part of Citigroup's succession plan for Weill, then in his early 70s. At the time of her promotion, Magner's responsibilities included North

American Retail Banking, the Global Retail Banking product, CitiFinancial North America, CitiCapital, and Women and Company, which offered professional women financial services tailored to their needs. Analysts praised her as a high-caliber leader with extensive Citigroup experience that equipped her well for the job. Analyst Ken Worthington of CIBC World Markets said that "She is one of the best operators this company has. She has a tremendous track record" (*New York Daily News*, August 7, 2003).

MANAGEMENT STYLE

Magner, as described by associates and analysts at the time of her 2003 promotion, was a calm and steady executive who motivated her employees through high expectations and confidence in their abilities. Although Magner told *US Banker* that her management style was almost "boring" because it was so consistent (September 2003), one analyst commented that she was a "quality executive who knows the businesses very well" (*American Banker*, August 7, 2003).

Magner served on the board of trustees for Brooklyn College, and she was a member of the dean's advisory council of the Krannert School of Management at Purdue. She also sup-

ported Krannert by returning as a guest lecturer in the 2003 Purdue Old Masters program. She had previously been on the boards of directors for the Welfare to Work Partnership, Dress for Success Worldwide, Port Discovery Children's Museum (Maryland), and the Maryland Business Roundtable for Education.

See also entry on Citigroup Inc. in *International Directory of Company Histories.*

SOURCES FOR FURTHER INFORMATION

De Paula, Matthew, "#2 Marjorie Magner," *US Banker*, October 2003, p. 28.

Dunaief, Daniel, "Citi Shatters Glass Ceiling," *New York Daily News*, August 7, 2003.

"Hits and Has-Beens," *US Banker*, September 2003, p. 12.

Julavits, Robert, "Citi Veteran Takes Helm of Global Consumer Unit," *American Banker*, August 7, 2003, p. 2.

—S. E. Weigant

■■■
Richard Mahoney
1934–
Retired chief executive officer and chairman, Monsanto

Nationality: American.

Born: January 30, 1934, in Springfield, Massachusetts.

Education: University of Massachusetts, BS, 1955; LLD, 1983.

Family: Married Barbara Marsden Barnett, 1956; children: three.

Career: Monsanto, 1962–1965(?), product development specialist; 1965–1967, marketing manager for new products; 1967–1971, marketing manager for bonding products and divisional sales director; 1971–1974, sales director for agricultural division; 1974–1975, international operations director for agricultural division; 1975, general manager of the overseas division of the agricultural division; 1975–1976, corporate vice president and managing director of Monsanto Agricultural Products; Monsanto Plastics and Resins, 1976–1977, group vice president and managing director; 1977–1980, executive vice president; 1980–1981, president; 1981–1983, chief operating officer; Monsanto Company, 1983–1986, president and chief executive officer; 1986–1995, chief executive officer and chairman.

Awards: Frederick S. Troy Alumni Achievement Award, University of Massachusetts, 1981; Honorary Fellowship, Exeter College, Oxford, 1986.

■ As chief executive officer and chairman of Monsanto, Richard John Mahoney oversaw the transformation of a conservative and financially troubled chemical company into an innovative leader in biotechnology and pharmaceuticals. His goal was to make Monsanto recession resistant by reducing its exposure to business-cycle fluctuations and oil prices. He was known for his aggressive and demanding management style, maintaining high pressure on his subordinates, and keeping the company under his tight control.

Richard Mahoney. *Rob Kinmouth/Getty Images.*

TRANSFORMING MONSANTO

Mahoney began his career at Monsanto in 1962, working his way up in new-product development and sales. He made a name for himself in agricultural chemicals, Monsanto's most successful division. In 1976 he moved to Monsanto Plastics and Resins, becoming president in 1980 and chief operating officer in 1981.

By the late 1970s big oil companies were taking over the petrochemical industry. The cost of raw materials soared, and Monsanto had serious financial control problems. CEO Jack Hanley began to move the company into biotechnology. Hanley picked Mahoney to succeed him as CEO in September 1983 and as chairman in 1986.

In his first year as CEO, Mahoney drastically cut costs and businesses. He sold off Monsanto's petrochemical-based commodity chemical, paper, and polystyrene divisions that accounted for about $4 billion in annual sales. Although many analysts thought he had undersold them, they had no place in Mahoney's long-term strategy. Between 1986 and 1990, Mahoney sold off 18 Monsanto units, merged one, and closed another, while acquiring three new higher-margin businesses. He concentrated Monsanto's resources on specialty chemicals, agricultural products, pharmaceuticals, and biotechnology. During that period sales increased 31 percent to $9 billion, and earnings rose 26 percent to $546 million.

BUYING G. D. SEARLE AND COMPANY

In 1985 Mahoney bought Searle pharmaceuticals for $2.8 billion. Analysts thought that he grossly overpaid. He told *Forbes* in February 1986, "Our objective is to be one of the four or five major pharmaceutical companies." Mahoney doubled Searle's research budget to $200 million annually. Calan SR, Searle's drug for angina treatment, was remade into a popular medication for high blood pressure, with sales of $240 million in 1988. However, sales fell as generic versions were introduced. In addition, Searle faced hundreds of lawsuits over its Copper-7 intrauterine contraceptive device. Nevertheless, between 1985 and 1991, Searle's sales rose from $600 million to $1.5 billion.

As patents on Calan SR and Searle's NutraSweet, the best-selling artificial sweetener, approached expiration, Mahoney kept prices low, hoping for customer loyalty. He told *Forbes* in January 1992, "You dare not violate the customer's confidence." Instead, by lowering manufacturing and other costs, Monsanto challenged other companies entering the market because it was already a low-cost provider. When competition in the diet-soft-drink market threatened NutraSweet, Mahoney oversaw the introduction of several new products, including a low-fat ice cream.

PROTECTIVE STRATEGIES

Chemicals still accounted for about 60 percent of Monsanto's assets, and Mahoney continued to invest research and capital in those units as well as in agriculture and animal nutrition. As much as possible, Mahoney protected Monsanto's profitable businesses while its new divisions matured. Chemical products, including shatterproof windows, detergents, and stain-resistant carpets, still accounted for half of Monsanto sales in 1989.

In 1987 Monsanto's patent on Lasso—the most widely used herbicide in the United States for corn and soybean crops—expired. Mahoney threatened to discount Lasso for private-label distributors, discouraging competitors. New application methods and sales efforts for Lasso and Roundup—an all-purpose, globally best-selling herbicide and the most

successful new chemical in years—boosted company earnings. When Roundup's patent expired in 1991, Mahoney slashed its price.

In 1992 Mahoney again restructured Monsanto's chemical operations, laying off 2,500 employees and closing several smaller plants. He was quoted in *Forbes* as saying, "Efficiency isn't doing less. Efficiency is doing smarter. Picking the right things to do and then doing them well" (January 6, 1992).

EARLY ENTRY INTO BIOTECHNOLOGY

According to a 1983 story in *Forbes*, Monsanto's young genetic engineers presented Mahoney with a diploma "For Mastering the Arcane Art of Molecular Biology" shortly after he became CEO. Mahoney told the magazine, "I think biotechnology will be at least as important to the chemical industry in the nineties as petrochemicals were in the thirties and forties" (October 24, 1983). He spent an unthinkable 10 percent of Monsanto's research and development money on biotechnology—$1 billion, which during the 1980s was an unthinkable amount. By 1984 he had spent $150 million to build a life sciences research center. Mahoney put venture capital into rising biotechnology companies, such as Genentech and Amgen, and linked Monsanto with university research.

Monsanto's first biotech product—bovine somatotropin—was a growth hormone for cows that increased milk production. Soon after developing the product, Monsanto introduced porcine somatotropin to grow leaner pigs. In addition to being one of the world's first biotechnology companies, Monsanto was considered by many analysts to be the best.

MANAGEMENT STYLE

Like his idol Winston Churchill, Mahoney concentrated on long-term strategy. However, he believed that a company as large as Monsanto required a 20 percent annual return on equity to become a great corporation. He was extremely tough. To reach this goals, Mahoney was extremely tough on his employees, raising the stakes as soon as he projected that a target would be met.

Mahoney was given to lecturing employees and making overstated pronouncements. A Monsanto executive told *Fortune* in February 1989, "I made a mistake on a trip once and he tore into me on the plane home. For the entire flight he told me that I wasn't living up to my potential." According to that article, subordinates viewed Mahoney as a man with a huge ego that constantly needed stroking. He listened but did not understand what others said and had little empathy for his employees. He did not believe that he could be wrong about anything. Some saw him as a great employee motivator. When asked to describe his style, Mahoney told *Fortune*, "I am demanding, not mean. Forgiveness is out of style, shoulder shrugs are out of fashion. Hit the targets on time without excuses" (February 27, 1989).

Monsanto had a reputation as a polluter, and growing environmental concerns lowered the reputation and credibility of the entire industry. In 1990, faced with having to report a 1987 release of 20 million pounds of toxic emissions, Mahoney decided to go on the offensive. He announced that within four years Monsanto would voluntarily reduce toxic air emissions to 10 percent of its 1987 levels. He went on the lecture circuit, touting Monsanto's environmental stewardship and arguing that the industry had to make environmental quality a top priority if it was to prevent the imposition of tough government regulations. Mahoney told *Financial World*, "Our overall goal is zero effect on public perceptions" (January 23, 1990).

Mahoney retired as Monsanto's CEO and chairman in March 1995, remaining a director and chairman of the executive committee for another year. He later became a board member and head of the governance committee for Union Pacific, the world's largest railroad.

See also entry on Monsanto Company in *International Directory of Company Histories.*

SOURCES FOR FURTHER INFORMATION

Chakravarty, Subrata N., "Taking Risks Is What They Pay You For," *Forbes*, pp. 44–45.

Lane, Randall, "Do the Right Thing," *Forbes*, January 6, 1992, p. 109.

McGough, Robert, "A Matter of Perception," *Financial World*, January 23, 1990, pp. 43–44.

Nulty, Peter, and Karen Nickel, "America's Toughest Bosses," *Fortune*, February 27, 1989, pp. 40–46.

Smith, Geoffrey, "Culture Shift," *Forbes*, October 24, 1983, pp. 68–70.

—Margaret Alic

■■■
Steven J. Malcolm
1948–
Chairman, president, and chief executive officer, Williams Companies

Nationality: American.

Born: September 1948, in St. Louis, Missouri.

Education: University of Missouri, Rolla, BA, 1970.

Family: Married Gwen (maiden name unknown); children: one.

Career: Cities Gas Company, ?–1984, refining, marketing, and transportation services; Williams Companies, 1984–1986, director of business development, Williams Natural Gas Company; 1986–1989, director of gas management, Williams Natural Gas Company; 1989–1993, vice president of gas management and supply; 1993–1994, senior vice president and general manager of the midcontinent region, Williams Field Services; 1994–1996, senior vice president and general manager of gathering and processing, Williams Field Services; 1996–1998, senior vice president and general manager, Midstream Gas and Liquids; 1998–2001, president and chief executive officer, Williams Energy Services; 2001–2002, president and chief operating officer; 2002–, chairman, president, and chief executive officer.

Address: The Williams Companies, One Williams Center, Tulsa, Oklahoma 74172; http://www.williams.com.

■ As the chief executive officer of the Williams Companies, Steven J. Malcolm sought to give the company a new profile, as an integrated natural gas company that was streamlined and simplified. He envisioned a smaller, more profitable company with fewer lines of business. Although he was pleased with his company's progress, he said at the 2004 annual meeting: "We're proud of where we are today, but getting here has not been easy." He noted further that he had been compelled to make some difficult decisions to restore the financial standing that had long been associated with Williams. "We are working to expand on the progress we've made over the last two years in reducing our cost structure and the size of our organization to reflect Williams' smaller, less complex base of businesses," he added (press release, May 20, 2004).

Malcolm joined Williams in 1984 as director of business development for Williams Natural Gas Company after working at Cities Gas Company in refining, marketing, and transportation services. He served as the company's vice president of gas management and supply and had been director of gas management services. He then served as senior vice president and general manager of the midcontinent region for Williams Field Services. In 1996 Malcolm was named senior vice president and general manager of Midstream Gas and Liquids for Williams Energy Services, and in 1998 he became president and CEO of Williams Energy Services. Continuing to move up the corporate ladder in a difficult and volatile business, Malcolm was named chairman of Williams in May 2002, having been appointed CEO the previous January.

Throughout his career with Williams, Malcolm saw the advantages of streamlining the company to concentrate on its core natural gas business as the main source for profitability and generating cash flow. The Oklahoma-based Williams Companies moves, manages, and markets a variety of energy products, including natural gas, liquid hydrocarbons, petroleum, and electricity. Financial results, say stock-market analysts, can fluctuate, reflecting lower sales of natural gas and crude and refined oil. Malcolm emphasized that the company was being managed differently to fit a different business environment. His strategy was to build liquidity and cut costs, to generate cash by selling assets that did not fit into his new and sharply defined business focus.

In the 2004 annual meeting Malcolm said that Williams was in a much stronger financial position than it had been a year earlier: "2003 was a year in which we focused almost exclusively on executing our multi-year plan, designed to rebuild our financial strength and take advantage of our best common capabilities." The company, he noted, has sold more than $6.5 billion in assets, and refocused "our operations around a core of world-class natural gas assets" (Williams). More importantly, he added, the company had reduced total long-term debt by $2.7 billion.

This progress, added Malcolm, had not gone unnoticed, as the company's stock and bond prices had moved significantly higher. "Some have suggested that we are the turnaround story of our sector," he said, adding that the higher stock price reflected "the market's acceptance and confidence in, both our restructuring and our plans for the future" (Williams).

Malcolm was particularly optimistic about Williams's exploration and production (E&P) business. Even among the company's peers, he said, Williams's E&P business was unique, thanks to its extraordinary reserves and production expertise. The company's production continued to grow, and it had a 10-year window of opportunity as well as about 9 to 10 years of potential natural gas finds in the Powder River Basin area. Malcolm said the company would continue to allocate the lion's share of its capital expenditures to developing production of natural gas within this area, which he said would generate an attractive return on capital. That focus, however, did not indicate a shortage of growth possibilities in other business areas of the company, he added.

Malcolm said that he was excited about the performance of Williams's midstream business, which had recently completed and put into service a major platform in the eastern Gulf of Mexico. Midstream business includes the gathering of natural gas and its transportation and storage—in other words, every step in the process leading to actual delivery of the final product. The Gulf of Mexico was providing the greatest growth potential, perhaps surpassing the projected volumes of all other projects. Besides the growth in offshore operations, Malcolm predicted that Williams would maintain a strong position in onshore projects. In Wyoming, for example, he noted that Williams produced 50 percent of the natural gas derived from the state.

In reviewing the company's financial picture, Malcolm saw a continued improvement in its debt status as being tremen-dously important to the company's restructuring. He felt strongly that despite some tough times, Williams was "a company that's back on track" (Williams). In addition to his duties with Williams, Malcolm served on the boards of the Tulsa Area United Way, Tulsa Community Foundation, YMCA, and St. John Medical Center, and the University of Tulsa board of trustees.

See also entry on Williams Companies, Inc. in *International Directory of Company Histories.*

SOURCES FOR FURTHER INFORMATION

"CEO Says Williams Energy Services Is One of the Top 25 Independent E&P Companies Today," *Wall Street Transcript,* March 1, 2001.

"Chairman Reviews Williams' Financial Progress at Annual Meeting," press release, May 20, 2004, http://www.williams.com/newsmedia/2004/20040520_595.htm.

Inc. Staff Icon Group International, *Williams Companies, Inc. (The): International Competitive Benchmarks and Financial Gap Analysis,* San Diego, Calif.: Icon Group International, October 2000.

"Williams Companies, Inc.," http://premium.hoovers.com/subscribe/co/people/bio.xhtml?COID=11638&&PID=12879043.

—Stephen H. Collins

■ ■ ■

Richard A. Manoogian
1936–
Chairman and chief executive officer, Masco Corporation

Nationality: American.

Born: 1936, in Detroit, Michigan.

Education: Yale University, BA, 1960.

Family: Son of Alex Manoogian (founder, Masco Corporation); married; children: three.

Career: Masco Corporation, 1968–1985, president and chief operating officer; 1985–, chairman and chief executive officer.

Address: Masco Corporation, 21001 Van Born Road, Taylor, Michigan 48180; http://www.masco.com.

■ Richard Manoogian joined Masco Corporation in 1958. He was elected chairman and chief executive director in 1964 and took over leadership of the company in 1968 when he was named president and chief executive officer. He became chairman in 1985. Originally known as the Masco Screw Products Company, Masco had been founded by Richard's father, Alex Manoogian, eight days before the U.S. stock market crash of 1929. The primary business was manufacturing machined automotive parts. The company later expanded operations into the building and home improvement industries. In the 1950s Masco revolutionized the faucet industry by perfecting the design of the single-lever hot and cold faucet. The Delta faucet was one of the first one-handled faucets on the market and quickly became the best-selling faucet brand in the United States. The success was due in part to Masco's innovation in marketing and product distribution. The company was the first to market faucets directly to mass market consumers via television advertisements. The result was a shift in distribution from plumbing wholesalers to retail outlets.

Masco manufactured a variety of consumer products that included Merillat cabinetry, Delta and Peerless faucets, Behr paints and stains, Weiser locks, Thermador appliances, and Baldwin brass. The company's manufacturing facilities were located throughout the United States and Europe. The international operations were located primarily in Belgium, Denmark, Germany, Holland, Italy, Spain, and the United Kingdom. The company's common stock was offered for public trade in 1936.

MANAGING EXPANSION

The first 10 years of Manoogian's tenure with Masco were spent working with his father to increase the company's value from $55 million to $8 billion. This goal was met primarily through mergers and acquisitions. Masco acquired more than one hundred companies in the 1960s through 1980s. The strategy was to reinvest surplus earnings and create opportunities for new growth into different, but related, market sectors.

Masco's strength was automation of the manufacturing process. Manoogian wanted to apply experience and success to new industries, such as furniture and other home furnishings. This effort produced mixed results. The acquired cabinetry business developed into a core product line that greatly increased Masco's income. However, acquisition of several furniture makers proved ill-advised.

PROFIT LOSSES AND SHAREHOLDER CRITICISM

There were several issues with the furniture manufacturing acquisitions. First, the furniture industry did not lend itself easily to automated manufacturing. The process of making furniture required too much handwork, and product lines were vastly diverse, so few opportunities existed for mass production of furniture components. In addition, Manoogian acquired several companies that had been fierce competitors and had no real intention of working together effectively once they shared the same parent company. Finally, the furniture and home furnishings market was struggling in a down economy, and sales were sagging. As a result, the questionable investment decisions caused Manoogian great difficulty with Masco's shareholders.

In addition to the furniture fiasco, there was trouble in the industrial division of the company. In the 1980s Manoogian had spun off the industrial parts manufacturing operation to create Masco Tech, which did not perform well and incurred further losses. Because Masco was a 50 percent owner of

Masco Tech, investors were extremely displeased with Manoogian's performance. He promised to sever ownership of Masco Tech but was unable to find a buyer for the struggling company.

Major criticisms were that Manoogian was running Masco as a private family business although stock was publicly held. Shareholders were angry about diversification attempts and Manoogian's investment in noncore competencies such as home furnishings. Although revenue climbed an average of 10.3 percent annually throughout the 1990s, Masco wrote off $841 billion owing to poor business decisions, and there was approximately $1.2 billion of debt on the books.

By the mid-1990s the damage done by the floundering furniture business was readily apparent. With a flat economy, consumer confidence was down and a dramatic decrease in the number of home remodels and major improvements being done translated into decreasing demand for Masco's products. Masco Tech's poor performance contributed to the mounting losses. Masco's stock performance rating slipped, and shareholders became even more displeased about the diversification attempts. When Standard & Poor's downgraded Masco's credit risk rating, Manoogian was finally forced to recognize that the furniture division was dragging down the performance of the entire company. Manoogian sold the business in a leveraged buyout by management, and the company took a $650 million dollar write-off. The sale of Masco Tech was completed in 2000.

RECOVERING PROFITABILITY

Admitting that the shareholders' criticism was fair, Manoogian turned his attention to debt reduction, share buyback, and a different acquisition strategy. To recover losses and resume growth, Masco needed a new growth income generator. Manoogian separated the building products division from the industrial businesses in an attempt to reduce the bottom-line impact of economic cycles in the automotive and housing mar-

kets. In 1996 Manoogian effected a culture change at Masco. He initiated severe cost-cutting measures and reduced his own salary from $1.4 million to $1 annually. These combined efforts were successful in stabilizing the company's bottom line and restoring profitability.

Associates described Manoogian as straightforward and talkative, the kind of person who would not stop working long enough to eat lunch. He served on the boards of directors for Ford Motor Company, Bank One Corporation, and Metaldyne Corporation. Manoogian was one of the foremost collectors of 19th-century American paintings. His collection of more than one thousand paintings was valued at more than $250 million, making it one of the most complete in the United States. Under Manoogian's leadership, Masco was a substantial contributor to educational, civil, and cultural organizations, primarily through the Masco Corporation Foundation.

See also entry on Masco Corporation in *International Directory of Company Histories.*

SOURCES FOR FURTHER INFORMATION

"Manufacturers," *Forbes*, October 11, 1999, p. 338.

Reingold, Jennifer, "The Masco Fiasco," *Financial World*, October 24, 1995, pp. 32–34.

Romero, Gina, "Art Imitates Masco," *Forbes*, October 24, 1988, p. 398.

Rossant, Juliette, "Throwing in the Towel," *Forbes*, February 26, 1996, p. 14.

Salomon, R. S., Jr., "Can an Old Boss Learn New Tricks?" *Forbes*, July 29, 1996, p. 102.

Tatge, Mark, "A Leaky Affair," http://www.forbes.com/global/2002/1209/028.html.

—Peggy K. Daniels

Mohamed Hassan Marican

1952–

President and chief executive officer, Petroliam Nasional Berhad (Petronas)

Nationality: Malaysian.

Born: October 18, 1952, in Sungai Petani, Malyasia.

Education: Malay College Kuala Kangsar, 1971.

Family: Married Puan Sri Noraini Mohamed Yusoff.

Career: Touche Ross & Company, 1972–1980; Hanafiah Raslan and Mohamed, 1980–1989, partner; Petronas, 1989–1995, senior vice president (finance); Petronas Gas Berhad, 1991–, chairman; Petronas, 1995–, president and chief executive officer; Petronas Dagan Berhad, 1995–, chairman; Malaysia International Shipping Corporation Berhad, 1997–, chairman; Perusahaan Otomobil Nasional Berhad (Proton), 2000–2003, director and chairman.

Awards: Dato' Setia Sultan Mahmud Terengganu, with the title of Dato', 1992; Seri Paduka Mahkota Terengganu, with the title of Dato', 1996; Panglima Setia Mahkota, with the title Tan Sri, 1997; Commandeur de la Légion d'honneur, France, 2000; Friendship Medal, Vietnam, 2001; Panglima Negara Bintang Sarawak, with the title of Datuk Seri, 2003.

Address: Petroliam Nasional Berhad, Level 31-33, Tower 1, Petronas Twin Towers, Kuala Lumpur City Centre, 50088 Kuala Lumpur, Malaysia; http://www.petronas.com.my.

Mohamed Hassan Marican. *Ernest Goh/Getty Images.*

■ Mohamed (Mohd) Hassan Marican has been a key part of the management team responsible for turning Petronas, Malaysia's state-owned oil company, into a truly multinational corporation with a record of consistently steady profits. Trained as an accountant, Marican was described by analysts as forthright and a strong advocate for strict fiscal discipline. Marican stressed the importance of teamwork, and he insisted that Petronas employees meet high standards of integrity and professionalism. As head of a state-owned firm, he worked closely with and earned the trust of Malaysia's prime minister. He effectively balanced the identity of Petronas as a national firm with its commercial goals through a largely successful strategy of expansion and integration.

ARRIVING AT PETRONAS AND EXPANDING ITS GLOBAL REACH

After graduating from college in Malaysia, Marican moved to London and trained as an accountant. Upon his return to Malaysia, he worked in a high-paying position as a partner in an accounting firm before joining Petronas in 1989 as senior vice president of finance. The company was founded in 1974 as a state-owned company, and its national mission focused on managing Malaysia's oil-and-gas resources as well as continuing to develop the country's petroleum industry. Petronas was at the forefront of industrial and technological development in Malaysia, and its agenda has been closely tied to the government's nation-building goals. Until the late 1980s Petronas focused primarily on regulating Malaysia's domestic resources, and it was only with the arrival of Marican, along with Chairman Azizan Abidin, that the company pursued a more aggressive global strategy.

Consistent with Malaysian Prime Minister Mahathir Mohamed's stance that his government served as an advocate for underdeveloped countries, Petronas sought partnerships in countries that other petroleum companies avoided or were restricted from investing in. In 1997 Petronas teamed with Chinese partners to turn Sudan into an oil exporter, which occurred in less than two years. Despite a U.S. embargo, Petronas partnered with a French company and launched a successful operation in Iran. Petronas was one of the first companies to invest in post-apartheid South Africa, purchasing a 30 percent stake in Engen, its largest oil-refining company. For Marican, Petronas's partnership strategy worked well, because the company sought associations with those who shared the Petronas philosophy and work ethic and in which Petronas was treated as an equal. Similarly, partnering countries were increasingly attracted to Petronas because of its nation-building experience, both in Malaysia and elsewhere. To ensure that its partnership strategy remained balanced, Petronas invested in all areas of the petroleum business, from shipping to refining.

After more than a decade of expansion, Petronas had a presence in 35 countries, with almost 80 percent of its revenues coming from global partnerships and exports. By 2003 Petronas reported over $21 billion in revenue, with a net profit of almost $4 billion. Marican refused to take credit for the company's success and insisted that its accomplishments were "based on solid teamwork" (*New Straits Times*, May 9, 2003). Marican further explained that Petronas insisted on "commitment, professionalism, integrity and honesty" from its workers, which ensured "that things are done in a proper and professional way." To effectively manage Petronas's global concerns, Marican spent half of each year visiting the company's sites around the world.

LEADING A STATE-OWNED COMPANY

One of the biggest challenges Marican faced was in leading a company owned by the state and hence vulnerable to political pressure. Malaysia's other state-owned and politically connected companies were well known for mismanagement and corruption. Other state-owned petroleum companies, such as Indonesia's Pertamina, also did not fare well and often became hotbeds for handing out patronage. Although the path Petronas took under Marican set it apart from other state companies, the company became involved in politically sensitive situations. In the wake of the Asian financial crisis of the mid-1990s, Petronas was called on to bail out a shipping operation controlled by the prime minister's son. Petronas also bought control of the Malaysian automaker, Proton, and the possibility was raised of the company's buying Malaysia Airlines. With

its considerable cash reserves, Petronas was asked by the government to serve as a property developer, taking over ownership, for example, of the Petronas Towers in Kuala Lumpur.

Analysts raised concerns about the fact that Petronas was asked to serve as a kind of treasury for the Malaysian government that might be called upon to rescue state-owned or politically sensitive corporations whenever necessary. Observers worried that the more involved Petronas became in activities not related to its core petroleum business, the more its resources would be stretched and the more uncertain the company's long-term outlook would become. Since Petronas reported directly to the prime minister's office, its full financial reports were not made public, thus depriving the company of the total fiscal transparency of which Marican was an advocate. Yet Marican defended Petronas's involvement in these non-core activities, stating that national necessity required the company to act. He also argued that Petronas would recoup at least some of its investment and whatever resources it had committed to auxiliary ventures aiding national development. For example, the Petronas Twin Towers would raise property values in Kuala Lumpur. Experts stated that it was a testimony to Marican and the Petronas management team that the company fared as well as it did when dealing with outside demands.

A GLOBAL PHILOSOPHY

Marican's interests in multinational cooperation went beyond his duties for Petronas. In 2003 he presented a proposal to the World Conference of Islamic Scholars for the formation of what he called an Islamic Development Bank (IDB). Funded by a small percentage of the value of oil produced by its member countries, IDB would be run as a public corporation, with its governing board consisting of representatives with business experience from each country. Marican projected that even with the small initial investment the bank could be worth almost $3 billion. He argued that the proposed IDB not only would provide its member countries with economic benefits but also would alleviate some of the burdens associated with borrowing from external sources. By fostering fiscal independence, Marican suggested that the IDB would help governments focus on such issues as health care and education and would encourage cooperation among IDB countries.

Apart from the IDB proposal, Marican continued to be a strong advocate for the kind of sustainable development that he and Petronas proved could be successful. Marican noted (at the Sixth SPE International Conference on Health, Safety, and Environment in Oil and Gas Exploration and Production, March 20, 2002) the great difficulty in creating sustainable development, which he thought must meet four goals: "social progress that recognizes the needs of everyone, effective protection of the environment, prudent use of natural resources," and maintenance of high levels of economic growth. In keeping with the partnership strategy he had spearheaded for Petronas, Marican argued for increased cooperation among petroleum companies, governments, aid agencies, and nongovernmental organizations to reach the goals he outlined. Marican's development philosophy was shaped by his commitment to the Petronas mission. In his view, Petronas was formed to serve its home country and thus had an obligation to return what it could to the community. As part of Petronas's business culture, this domestic mission extended to the company's global partnerships. Marican remained committed to serving the global communities of which Petronas was a part.

See also entry on Petronas in *International Directory of Company Histories.*

SOURCES FOR FURTHER INFORMATION

Jayasankaran, S., "Global Reach," *Far Eastern Economic Review*, August 12, 1999, p. 10.

———, "Saviour Complex," *Far Eastern Economic Review*, August 12, 1999, p. 14.

Lopez, Leslie, "A Well-Oiled Money Machine," *Far Eastern Economic Review*, March 13, 2003, p. 40.

Marican, Mohamed Hassan, "Partnerships for a Sustainable Future," Sixth SPE International Conference on Health, Safety, and Environment in Oil and Gas Exploration and Production, March 20, 2002.

"Petronas Builds on Its Competitive Strengths," *Euromoney*, September 2003, pp. 16–17.

"Professionalism, Integrity the Keys," *New Straits Times*, May 9, 2003.

"Visions of Success," *New Straits Times*, May 9, 2003.

—Carol Pech

■ ■ ■
Reuben Mark
1939–

Chairman and chief executive officer, Colgate-Palmolive Company

Nationality: American.

Born: January 21, 1939, in Jersey City, New Jersey.

Education: Middlebury College, BA, 1960; Harvard Business School, MBA, 1963.

Family: Son of Edward Mark and Libbie Berman; married Arlene Slobzian (music therapist); children: three.

Career: U.S. Army, 1961, infantry officer; Colgate-Palmolive Company, 1963–1972, advertising trainee, then various marketing and management positions; 1972–1973, president and general manager in Venezuela; 1973–1974, president and general manager in Canada; 1974–1975, vice president and general manager of Far East division; 1975–1979, vice president and general manager of household-products division; 1979–1981, group vice president of domestic operations; 1981–1983, executive vice president; 1983–1984, COO; 1983–1984, president; 1984–1986, CEO; 1986–, chairman and CEO.

Address: Colgate-Palmolive Company, 300 Park Avenue, New York, New York 10022; http://www.colgate.com.

■ In the transitory business climate of the 21st century, Reuben Mark was a throwback to an earlier era: he was a true "company man," working only for Colgate-Palmolive Company for more than 40 years. It would be practically impossible to overstate his contribution; in his two decades as chief executive of the $9.1 billion consumer-products giant, Colgate-Palmolive's stock bested that of GE throughout the GE CEO Jack Welch's tenure. Rather than making the talk-show circuit to tout his success, Mark could be found committing himself to extensive educational philanthropy and the improvement of corporate governance. While he set a universally positive example for his CEO peers, Mark would have been the last person to say anything about it.

A FATEFUL BEGINNING

Born in Jersey City, the industrial town that then housed Colgate's headquarters and its largest domestic plant, Mark's family moved to Long Island before his first birthday. His education took him first to Middlebury College in Vermont, where he studied economics, and later to Harvard Business School, where he earned his MBA in 1963. In 1961 he spent six months as an army officer.

Upon leaving Harvard, Mark joined Colgate-Palmolive as a trainee in its advertising department. He had other offers, including one from archrival P&G; he contended that his decision was influenced by geography—he didn't want to move to Cincinnati—but an unidentified friend offered another reason in *Fortune* magazine: "I think he felt he could probably move faster and higher at Colgate. It just wasn't as competitive internally as P&G" (May 11, 1987).

INTERNATIONAL WORK PREPARES HIM TO LEAD A MULTINATIONAL

Indeed, Mark rose steadily through the ranks, holding various marketing and management positions around the world until he took over control of the company's Venezuelan subsidiary in 1972. Since Colgate traditionally earned the lion's share of its profits in international markets, overseas operations, which spanned 70 countries, were the best place for Mark to gain visibility as an executive.

Historically press-shy, Mark agreed with the media's assessment that he was just as comfortable with Colgate's factory workers as he was with Wall Street analysts. During a 1991 trip to the company's facilities in Mexico City he disarmed nervous employees by joking in fluent Spanish. In one of his rare public interviews, published in *Fortune*, Mark reflected upon the importance of such rapport: "I remember as a young boy walking with my father, who was treasurer of a food company, through one of their plants. A worker who was stirring something in a huge vat yelled down with a big grin, 'Hi, Mr. Mark,' and my father called back, 'How you doing, George?' It meant a lot to me that my father, a management guy, had a good relationship with people in the plant" (May 11, 1987).

Mark's command of Spanish and his early focus on Latino markets served Colgate well. By the early 2000s Latinos were the fastest-growing ethnic group in the country: America's Latino population grew 61 percent, from 21.9 million to over 35 million, from 1990 to 2001. This demographic group was forecast to wield $900 billion in spending power by 2007.

CHARMING ANALYSTS AND EMPLOYEES

Mark became CEO in 1984 and, additionally, chairman in 1986. Unlike his predecessors, Mark met often with analysts and institutional investors to herald Colgate. Historically the results were bullish and the analysts enthusiastic. Emma Hill, an analyst with Wertheim Schroder & Company, noted in *Fortune*, "He spoke at a seminar I arranged, and by the time he got done talking, everybody wanted to run right out and buy Colgate stock. I've never seen anything like it. More than any other chairman I have seen, Reuben has Wall Street eating out of his hands" (May 11, 1987). His buoyant enthusiasm extended to his other corporate commitments. When Mark, a director on the AOL Time Warner board since 2001, purchased shares of the company, a fund manager reversed his negative position on AOL stock.

Under Mark's tenure, Colgate experienced seven straight years of double-digit earnings-per-share growth. Colgate stock outperformed GE stock from 1984, when Mark became CEO, through 2001, when the head of GE Jack Welch retired.

LONG-TERM RESULTS TRUMP SHORT-TERM GAIN

In the mid-1990s, when stocks had nowhere to go but up, Mark was one of the only major American CEOs to emphasize the effect corporate culture had on sound governance. Around the same time Enron's Ken Lay, for example, was pushing his board and top managers to devise elaborate schemes in order to defraud investors. In 2003 Colgate's board earned a top score from GovernanceMetrics International for its governance practices—an honor achieved by a mere 17 of 1,600 companies tracked. CBS MarketWatch reported that Ric Marshall, the CEO of The Corporate Library, the independent research firm, said, "After almost three years of stories of powerful leaders violating standards of ethics, Mark is an example of a CEO doing a good job" (September 18, 2003).

EDUCATION MATTERS MOST

Mark's staunch business beliefs extended to activities outside his company. While charitable commitments were part and parcel of the modern CEO's job description, Mark's investment in education went far beyond the boardroom and had deep, personal meaning for him. His wife was a music therapist, school psychologist, and full-time teacher for elementary and high-school students.

Under Mark's leadership and coordination, Colgate adopted a once-beautiful New York City school that had lost its lus-

ter. The school was a virtual war zone and in total chaos. Colgate sponsored the school's rehabilitation, dismissing the principal and senior managers and restructuring the unit into three middle schools and one high school. Colgate employees sat on the school's advisory board, offering management, budget, and technical expertise. Mark described Colgate's activities at this school extensively in the May 1994 issue of *Chief Executive* magazine: "We were confronted with the inadequacies of the New York City school system. I was stunned to see how kids were being treated—they were essentially warehoused until they turned 16 or dropped out. What's worse, they didn't have educational advocates. Education truly is the most crucial problem that we as a country face and everyone, every single individual, every single organization, can do something about it. The most important thing Colgate contributed was not money, but people—people who helped develop curriculum and systems, people who helped in governance, people who acted as mentors. We provided physical space for meetings and educational materials. It was not a classic adopt-a-school project in which we write a check and the school spends it. But if I as CEO had not been involved at the beginning, my people would not have felt free to spend their time or energy on the project or been allowed to take time off from work to get involved. That's why the key is getting the most senior people interested. They can rally to the cause people throughout the organization."

RESULTS, NOT RECOGNITION, COUNT

By the early 2000s Colgate-Palmolive faced increased competition from P&G. In 2001 P&G beat Colgate to the tooth-whitener market with the launch of Crest White Strips. Colgate countered with Simply White, but sales lagged, and retailers complained of excess inventory. While Mark himself was a proven winner, the company's long-term prospects were by no means certain.

Mark was up to the challenge. With retirement planned for sometime between 2006 and 2008, he remained interested only in results and continued to shun the spotlight—he even declined an interview with a publication honoring him as a finalist for CEO of the year. He believed it offensive for one person to take credit for the efforts of an entire organization. Said The Corporate Library's Marshall, "Mark stands out precisely because he does not stand out. That's what a CEO is supposed to do: quietly build value for shareholders without ostentatious show. Those are the people that keep the market going" (September 18, 2003).

See also entry on Colgate-Palmolive Company in *International Directory of Company Histories.*

SOURCES FOR FURTHER INFORMATION

"Colgate's Mark: Teaching Corporate Citizenship," CBS MarkctWatch, September 18, 2003.

"Finding What Really Works in Education," *Chief Executive*, May 1994, p. 48.

Steinbreder, John H., "The Man Brushing Up Colgate's Image," *Fortune*, May 11, 1987, p. 106.

—Tim Halpern

■ ■ ■

Michael E. Marks

1950–

Chief executive officer, Flextronics International

Nationality: American.

Born: December 31, 1950.

Education: Oberlin College, BA, MA, 1973; Harvard University, MBA, ca. 1976.

Family: Married Carole (maiden name unknown); children: two.

Career: Flextronics, 1989–1990, plant manager; Metcal, ca. 1990–ca. 1993, president and chief executive officer; Flextronics International, 1993–1994, chairman; 1994–2003, chairman and chief executive officer; 2003–, chief executive officer.

Awards: Named one of the Heroes of U.S. Manufacturing, *Fortune*, 2000; CEO of the Year, *Electronic Business*, 2003.

Address: Flextronics International, 2090 Fortune Drive, San Jose, California 95131; http://www.flextronics. com.

Michael E. Marks. © *Ed Quinn/Corbis SABA.*

■ Michael E. Marks became chief executive officer of Flextronics International, an electronics-manufacturing-services company, in 1994. With Marks at the helm, a nearly bankrupt Flextronics that was ranked 22nd in the industry grew over 10 years to become an industry leader with over $14 billion in revenues a year. Marks was highly regarded by his colleagues, employees, and customers, who described him as an enthusiastic visionary who had successfully navigated the company through challenging times in the industry.

EARLY YEARS

Marks was raised in St. Louis and had an early introduction to business leadership: his father owned and ran an air-conditioner distributorship. Working alongside his father and brothers, Marks was taught to appreciate customer relationships and to value innovation. He told *Electronic Business*, "My father was a very ethical man, very sensitive to his employees" (December 1, 2003). Marks went on to earn both bachelor's and master's degrees in psychology from Oberlin College in Ohio. He spent a year with the Cleveland police department formulating an entrance exam before heading to Harvard Business School to earn a master's in business administration. At the time, Marks's interests differed from those of most of his classmates; his intent was to run a small business rather than a large corporation.

After graduation Marks began working for a coal company that would later fold. The experience helped to shape his attitude toward corporate structure: "It was the most dysfunctional place I ever worked, with lots of channels and fiefdoms" (*Electronic Business*, December 1, 2003). Marks returned to St. Louis in the early 1980s to be near his father, who was gravely ill, and to run a $10-million-a-year computer company. His father died in 1981, but his interest in the industry was piqued. The computer job was "a humbling experience" in Marks's words, and he aspired to learn more (*Electronic Buyers' News*, December 20, 1999). With his wife and two children in tow, Marks relocated to the geographical center of the U.S. electronics sector, Silicon Valley in California.

STARTING OUT AT FLEXTRONICS

Marks began working for Flextronics in the late 1980s, first as a consultant and then as manager of a California plant. He later admitted that he was not entirely prepared for the position: "I didn't really know much about world-class manufacturing." At least one customer agreed, suggesting that Marks read Richard Schonberger's 1986 book *World Class Manufacturing: The Lessons of Simplicity Applied*. The book was "a real eye-opener" for Marks, who had barely passed the one manufacturing class he had taken while a student at Harvard (*Institutional Investor*, March 15, 2004). He was drawn in particular to Schonberger's description of how to streamline manufacturing processes and the importance of focusing on the customer.

In 1990 Marks left Flextronics and became president and chief executive officer of Metcal, a maker of precision systems for electronics manufacturing. Flextronics was in the midst of a financial upheaval: its Asian plants were sold off in 1990 and its U.S. operations had collapsed. Marks had left a favorable impression on the executives of the Asian spin-off, Flextronics International, and was asked to join the board of directors in 1991. Despite the challenges facing the company, Marks saw potential in the company and in the burgeoning outsourcing trend. He left his job at Metcal and convinced several venture-capital firms to fund a takeover of the company to the tune of $15 million. Marks became chairman of the Flextronics board in 1993 and was appointed chief executive officer in January 1994.

TAKING THE LEAD

Marks had his work cut out for him. The company was rated only 28th among contract-manufacturing (CM) companies and made less than $100 million a year in revenue. Marks had an idea for making the company more efficient and cost-effective: vertical integration, or controlling multiple stages of the manufacturing process, from production to warehousing to shipping. Vertical integration had been used prominently by the automotive manufacturer Henry Ford in the 1920s, but at the time no other contract manufacturer was applying the concept. Marks's plan for Flextronics was to open plants in low-cost locations such as Asia and Eastern Europe and to create industrial parks that would bring suppliers to where the products were being manufactured. Marks also felt that a strategy called demand-flow manufacturing, in which products are made only as orders come in to avoid a backlog of inventory, would allow for even greater cost and efficiency savings.

Marks's strategies paid off. Louis Miscioscia, an analyst for Lehman Brothers, said that Flextronics was "the first and so far only CM to move to these megacampuses, a low-cost strategy that no one else has replicated. . . . [Marks] is considered by many in the supply chain industry to be more visionary than the other guys" (*Electronic Business*, December 1, 2003). Within Marks's first year at the helm of Flextronics, the company was listed on NASDAQ, the venture-capital firms were paid off, and two acquisitions were completed to add to the company's capabilities.

Over the next six years Flextronics underwent a period of rapid growth, coinciding with a boom in the electronics-manufacturing industry. While other electronics-manufacturing-services (EMS) companies were growing at an average rate of 20 percent per year, Flextronics was growing at 60 percent. By 2000 sales had reached $10.5 billion, and the company's customers included Cisco, Nokia, Hewlett-Packard, Motorola, and Ericsson. Marks had taken Flextronics from the 22nd- to the 4th-rated EMS provider worldwide, with the goal of taking over the number-one spot by 2001. In 2000 Marks was named by *Fortune* magazine as one of six "Heroes of U.S. Manufacturing."

WEATHERING THE STORM

In the early 2000s the technology sector suffered a downturn, and the electronics-manufacturing market crashed. Flextronics, however, went on to claim the title of industry leader in December 2001, surpassing Solectron Corporation. Revenues for fiscal year 2004 were posted at $14.5 billion. Marks reacted quickly in the face of declining trends by employing broad cost-cutting measures, including closing 40 plants and laying off thousands of employees. As of 2004 the company still employed nearly 100,000 employees at approximately one hundred plants. Vertical integration through Flextronics's global industrial parks also helped to offset losses.

Colleagues and analysts credited Marks's vision and innovation for helping the company weather the storm. Bob McNamara, managing director at Broadview International, an investment bank, said of Marks: "To call him a visionary is not an overstatement. He's always been one step ahead of the trends in the industry" (*Electronic Business*, December 1, 2003). Analyst Chris Whitemore agreed: "Marks is usually two or three years ahead of everyone else in the field" (*Chief Executive*, July 2004).

MANAGEMENT STYLE

Marks's disdain for bureaucracy and red tape helped create a nonconventional corporate structure at Flextronics's headquarters. He avoided meetings whenever possible and purposely kept the layers of management to a minimum. By his own admission he was not a micromanager and gave his executives financial and creative latitude to make major decisions. "I've surrounded myself with people who are bright and enthusiastic and don't want a lot of direction. We grew at 60 percent a year for six or seven years. If you don't have this kind of organization, you can't grow like that. . . . I set expectations and judge people by results. By definition, if you give people a lot of rope, some will hang themselves. So I occasionally fire people" (*Electronic Business*, December 1, 2003).

His leadership style garnered much respect from his employees. Flextronics's chief operating officer, Mike McNamara, told *Electronic Business*, "Marks lets you run your own business as long as you produce results. He doesn't believe in complex structures, reports or endless reviews. He allows us to innovate." Humphrey Porter, president of Flextronics Europe, added, "Marks is one of these guys who is enormously collaborative. He's completely at home with the janitor or the CEO. He makes whoever he is working with a part of the team" (December 1, 2003).

Colleagues and customers described Marks as enthusiastic, energetic, curious, and observant. Analyst Miscioscia said, "He's charismatic, and he's always bullish on something. But he's usually on the money." Ursula Burns, a senior vice president with Xerox, one of Flextronics's customers, called Marks "funny and personable. He talks fast, moves a lot and is hyper. He doesn't know it, but we call him the Energizer bunny" (*Electronics Business*, December 1, 2003).

LOOKING AHEAD

In 2003 Marks stepped down as chairman of the Flextronics board, recommending that another board member, Richard Sharp, take the lead role. He maintained that the transition was in the best interests of shareholders and was not foreshadowing imminent retirement. A 53-year-old Marks told *Chief Executive* in July 2004: "The transition will be when I'm in my sixties." He looked forward to spending his free time with his family and indulging in his hobbies, which included basketball, skiing, bicycling, and playing piano.

See also entry on Flextronics International Ltd. in *International Directory of Company Histories.*

SOURCES FOR FURTHER INFORMATION

Bylinksy, Gene, "Heroes of U.S. Manufacturing: Michael Marks," *Fortune*, March 20, 2000, p. 192.

Doebele, Justin, "Flex Forward: Flextronics' Michael Marks Says that Outsourcing Can Only Get Much, Much Bigger," *Chief Executive*, July 2004.

"Michael Marks of Flextronics International," *Institutional Investor International Edition*, March 15, 2004, pp. 12–14.

Roberts, Bill, "Michael Gets High Marks," *Electronic Business*, December 1, 2003.

Sheerin, Matthew, "Michael E. Marks, Flextronics: Transformed Struggling Company into a Top-tier Global Contractor," *Electronic Buyers' News*, December 20, 1999, p. 64.

———, "One on One: Why Flextronics' CEO Sleeps Well at Night," *Electronic Buyers' News*, August 30, 1999, p. 1.

—Stephanie Dionne Sherk

■■■
J. Willard Marriott Jr.
1932–
Chairman and chief executive officer, Marriott International

Nationality: American.

Born: March 25, 1932, in Washington, D.C.

Education: University of Utah, BS, 1954.

Family: Son of John Willard (the founder of Hot Shoppes and its successor, Marriott Corporation) and Alice Sheets (a civic leader); married Donna Garff, 1955; children: four.

Career: Hot Shoppes, Inc., 1959–1964, vice president of hotel operations; 1964, executive vice president; Marriott–Hot Shoppes, Inc., 1964–1967, president; Marriott Corporation, 1967–1972, president; 1972–1985, CEO and president; Marriott International, 1985–1997, chairman, CEO, and president; 1997–, chairman and CEO.

Awards: Business Leader of the Year, Georgetown University, School of Business Administration, 1984; Service Above Self Award, Rotary Club at JFK International Airport, 1985; American Manager of the Year, National Management Association, 1985; Golden Chain Award, *Nation's Restaurant News*, 1985; Inductee, Hall of Fame, *Consumer Digest*, 1986; Citizen of the Year, Boy Scouts of America, 1986; Restaurant Business Leadership Award, *Restaurant Business*, 1986; Gold Plate, American Academy of Achievement, 1986; Inductee, Hall of Fame, Hotel and Motel Association, 1986; Inductee, Hall of Fame, Culinary Institute of America, 1987; Hospitality Executive of the Year, Pennsylvania State University, 1987; Silver Plate, *Lodging Hospitality*, 1988; Executive Officer of the Year, *Chief Executive Officer*, 1988; Signature Award, California Chapter, National Multiple Sclerosis, 1988; Good Scout Award, Boy Scouts of America Greater New York Council, 1990; Commitment to Excellence Award, Suburban Hospital, 1993; Silver Plate, International Foodservice Manufacturers Association, 1993; Inductee, Hall of Honor, Hospitality Industry, 1998.

Publications: *The Spirit to Serve: Marriott's Way* (with Kathi Ann Brown), 1997.

Address: Marriott International, Corporate Headquarters,

J. Willard Marriott Jr. *AP/Wide World Photos.*

Marriott Drive, Washington, D.C. 20058-0001; http://www.marriott.com.

■ J. Willard Marriott Jr. was born into, raised by, and worked his way up through the ranks of the Marriott family business. By 2004 Marriott International, which originated with a small A&W Root Beer stand in Washington, D.C., opened in 1927 by John Willard and Alice Sheets Marriott, had become a globally leading hospitality management and service company. Under the younger Marriott's direction, Marriott International grew into a billion-dollar hotel and resort empire comprising over 140,000 employees at more than 2,600 lodging properties located in the United States and 63 other countries and territories.

Marriott Jr. was widely recognized in the hospitality industry for his visionary expansion of the company's lodging division. The company was consistently ranked as one of the industry's most admired and one of the best places to work, as reported by *Fortune* magazine. In addition to being at the forefront of the business of providing hospitality, Marriott Jr. has shown himself to be a devoted educational philanthropist. Under his leadership, Marriott aimed to aggressively increase its brand exposure and the overall success of its businesses. The company committed itself to offering outstanding customer service, ample opportunities for executive advancement, and noteworthy returns for both shareholders and owners.

GROWING UP MARRIOTT

Newlyweds J. Willard Marriott Sr. and Alice Sheets Marriott moved to Washington, D.C., from Marriott Settlement, Utah, in 1922. Together in 1927 they launched a small, nine-seat root-beer stand using $6,000 in loans. Later that year they added hot Mexican-style food to their menu and adopted the name Hot Shoppe. The one restaurant soon expanded into the Hot Shoppes chain, which eventually evolved into the Marriott hotel and resort empire. The tiny enterprise flourished in spite of the Great Depression, and the Marriotts—who were hard-working and dedicated Mormons—soon diversified into airline catering, cafeterias, and institutional food service. J. Willard Marriott Jr. was born during the early years of the development of the family business.

SHOE INSPECTION

Before working at the family business, Marriott Jr. polished his father's shoes so that they would be ready for church on Sundays. One Saturday he had to rigorously scrub the shoes to remove a gummy substance that his father had picked up during work from the previous week. It took the boy hours to properly clean the shoes—so that he might pass his father's grueling inspection. In *Spirit to Serve: Marriott's Way*, Marriott Jr. wrote about his father, "Perfection was one notch below the desired result" (1997). The younger Marriott learned a valuable lesson from that early experience: to stick with any job until it was done right.

FIRST MARRIOTT JOB

In 1941, at the age of 14, Marriott Jr. was old enough to learn about the family business from the ground floor; he took his first company job stapling invoices together for the accounting department. He quickly learned that his father used a hands-on management approach and that both parents were very conservative and never took anything for granted, especially success. Marriott Jr. was fond of quoting his father (who

was quoting Winston Churchill) as saying, "Success is never final" (1997). That conservative work ethic would remain with Marriott Jr. throughout his life.

Marriott Jr. continued working at his parents' Hot Shoppes while attending the prestigious St. Albans Prep School in Washington, D.C. He cooked hamburgers, washed dishes, and mopped floors; through this work and through exposure to his parents' work he learned some of the skills that he would need later in his career with the company. Marriott Jr. recalled on the company Web site, "When I was a kid, we used to sit around the table at home and all we would talk about was the business." While attending the University of Utah, Marriott Jr. worked at the fountain and in the dish room, cleaning counters and floors, serving customers, and cooking, at a Hot Shoppe restaurant in Salt Lake City.

FULL-TIME LODGING EXECUTIVE

After receiving his bachelor's degree in banking and finance in 1954, Marriott Jr. became a lieutenant with the U.S. Naval Reserves, spending two years as a ship's service supply officer aboard the U.S.S. *Randolph*. In 1956 he returned full-time to his parents' company. By that time, the Marriotts' food-service customers included hospitals, schools, and highway rest stops, in addition to the expanding divisions of Hot Shoppes and In-Flite, an airline catering service.

Upon Marriott Jr.'s return to the family business, an exciting and promising new development was taking place: the building of the company's first motel, Twin Bridges Motor Hotel, in Arlington, Virginia. As the company's first venture into the lodging industry the hotel would become very important to Marriott Jr.

Eager to manage his own piece of the family enterprise, Marriott Jr. asked his father to place him in charge of the small hotel division. The senior Marriott agreed, even though his son had been back in the business for only eight months. Marriott Jr. immediately faced the challenges and hurdles of running a new business: he was responsible for everything from hiring architects and securing general contractors to preparing last-minute details for the grand opening of the new hotel. He applied the lessons he had earlier learned from his father; part of his ethic was to understand every facet of the business by using a hands-on approach to management.

Marriott Jr. enjoyed every aspect of his work, completely immersing himself in the job—amassing ideas, ultimately successful or not, and slowly building the newly formed hotels as well as the systems needed to run them from the ground up. He was instituting the Marriott "badge of quality" from a solid foundation of hard work, dedication, and old-fashioned common sense.

RENAMING THE COMPANY

In 1964 John Willard Marriott Sr. appointed his son, at the age of 32, president and a member of the board of directors of Marriott–Hot Shoppes. At this time Marriott Jr. convinced his father that to achieve growth within the company they needed to take on debt from the equity they had built up. He told his father that to bring about fundamental internal change—that is, to complete the evolution from a handful of local businesses into a global enterprise—they would need the three Ds: development, deals, and debt.

During the next three years, Marriott Jr. turned Marriott–Hot Shoppes into an international company by purchasing an airline-catering kitchen in Venezuela and expanding its restaurant operations to include the Big Boy and Roy Rogers restaurant chains. In its 40th-anniversary year, the company changed its name from Marriott–Hot Shoppes to Marriott Corporation.

THE BASIC PHILOSOPHY

In 1972 Marriott Jr. assumed the role of CEO, replacing his father but maintaining the latter's conservative business practices. Marriott Jr. had learned that the hotel business depended on balancing excellent customer service and clean, comfortable accommodations with controlled costs. As quoted by Logan Rochelle in her book of business biographies, Marriott continued operating under his father's basic philosophy: "to make sure our associates are very happy and that they enjoy their work, so they go the extra mile—take care of customers and have fun doing it. A lot of companies go through the motions, but they don't go the extra mile" (2002).

Marriott Jr. began to implement his dream for the business: expanding the lodging division through acquisitions and development of new brands. Under his direction, the company quickly established complex financing techniques and built an effective in-house construction operation. By the early 1980s Marriott Jr. had transformed the company into one of the world's largest real-estate developers, building more than $1 billion in hotel properties annually.

As the number of the company's full-service hotels increased, Marriott Jr. continued his aggressive plans to develop a series of lodging brands. Beginning in 1983 with Courtyard by Marriott, the company introduced new hotel lines ranging from economy to luxury accommodations; these innovations in the hospitality industry were often far ahead of what the competition was doing—or even planning. In 1984 Marriot entered the vacation time-share business.

CHAIRMAN AND CEO UPON FATHER'S DEATH

Marriott stepped into the role of chairman following his father's death in 1985. He immediately took charge of the entire company's operations, traveling globally to manage what had become the world's largest hotel chain—by that time, an average of two Marriott hotels opened each week. Marriott Jr. narrowed Marriott's focus on lodging, senior accommodations, and contract services by divesting the company of its fast-food and family restaurants.

By 1986 the company's publicly traded stock split 5 for 1. Respect within the hospitality industry was growing for the very successful company; in 1988 *Chief Executive* magazine named Bill Marriott "CEO of the Year" and *Fortune* magazine included him on its list of the "25 Most Fascinating Business Leaders." One of the reasons given by experts as to why the Marriott family ran such an impressive business was their attention to detail. For example, over the years the Marriotts collected information on how to properly clean a room in a consistent and high-quality manner, eventually developing an instruction guide that laid out 66 separate steps such that each hotel room would be cleaned in less than 30 minutes. Every aspect of the business was based on such natural and logical methods of performing tasks and services.

MARRIOTT INTERNATIONAL IS BORN

In 1993 Marriott Jr. helped to split the former company into two separate companies: Marriott International, a lodging and services management company, and Host Marriott Corporation, focusing on real-estate and airport concessions. The acquisition of the Ritz-Carlton Hotel Company helped to continue Marriott International's growth.

THE SPIRIT TO SERVE

In 1997 Marriott named William J. Shaw, a 22-year company veteran, to the posts of president and chief operating officer. Also that year Marriott Jr. coauthored a book with Kathi Ann Brown about his business philosophy, entitled, *The Spirit to Serve: Marriott's Way*. Therein, Marriott Jr. talked openly about all of the many facets of his business life, including the mistakes he had made. He realized that failures were just as important as successes in learning over a lifetime how to develop a successful business. Marriott Jr. remarked frequently on the virtues of taking care of employees, listening well, and not wasting time on regret. He attributed the company's rapid expansion in part to early standard operating procedures and internal training programs; noting that if they had had to create a new hotel each and every time without the use of standard procedures, they would not have been so successful.

Marriott Jr. cited competitors' lack of reliability and uneven standards, as compared with Marriott, in referring to the company's developing and maintaining superior quality across the spectrum of its businesses. He was proud to point out that the original hands-on, personal-inspection management approach—which had been first used more than 75 years prior in a small root-beer stand—was still a part of Marriott's philosophy and culture.

A FACE WITH THE NAME

As of the early 2000s Marriott Jr. continued to travel an average of 150,000 miles each year in visiting Marriott sites. In *Spirit to Serve* he said, "If you're in the service business and your name is above the door, it's important for people to be able to link a face to a name. I want our associates to know that there really *is* a guy named Marriott who cares about them, even if he can only drop by every so often to personally tell them so" (1997). Marriott Jr.'s oldest son, Steve, said of his father, "He loves to go through a hotel, greeting people. He told me once that he'd rather be doing that than anything else" (1997). Marriott Jr. himself admitted at the end of the 20th century, "The truth is, I'm still having fun after 40 years" (1997).

CHARITY AND FAMILY

In spite of his busy travel schedule, Marriott Jr. served on several boards, including the National Geographic Society, the Naval Academy Endowment Trust, and the National Urban League. He also volunteered each week with The Church of Jesus Christ of Latter-Day Saints and supported a number of community organizations.

Bill Marriott Jr. and his wife, Donna, who were married in 1955, had three sons and one daughter: Steven, John, David, and Deborah. The Marriotts' four offspring gave them 12 grandchildren. Following in their father's footsteps, the Marriott children all worked in various positions within the family company; the three sons all worked full-time for Marriott International.

See also entry on Marriott International, Inc. in *International Directory of Company Histories.*

SOURCES FOR FURTHER INFORMATION

Marriott, J. Willard Jr., and Kathi Ann Brown, *The Spirit to Serve: Marriott's Way*, New York City, N.Y.: HarperBusiness, 1997.

Marriott, Richard E., "Building a Family Legacy: The Marriott Story," http://marriottschool.byu.edu/story/MarriottStory.pdf.

Marriott Web site, http://www.marriott.com.

Rochelle, Logan, and Julie Halverstadt, *100 Most Popular Business Leaders for Young Adults: Biographical Sketches and Professional Paths,"* Greenwood Village, Colo.: Libraries Unlimited, 2002.

—William Arthur Atkins

R. Brad Martin

1951–

Chairman and chief executive officer, Saks Incorporated

Nationality: American.

Born: 1951.

Education: University of Memphis, BA, 1976; Owen Graduate School of Management, Vanderbilt University, MBA, 1980.

Career: Proffitt's (later became Saks), 1989–, chairman, president, and general-merchandise manager; chief executive officer.

Address: Saks Incorporated, 750 Lakeshore Parkway, Birmingham, Alabama 35211; http://www.saksincorporated.com.

■ R. Brad Martin was best known for his leadership of Saks Fifth Avenue, the beleaguered luxury retailer. The chairman and chief executive officer of Saks Incorporated, he struggled to keep Saks Fifth Avenue afloat amid low sales, industry criticism, and uncertain chain identity.

The parent company's 383 midmarket regional stores operated under the names Proffitt's, McRae's, Younkers, Parisian, Herberger's, Carson Pirie Scott, Boston Store, Bergner's, and Saks Off 5th, along with a mail-order business, Folio, and the luxury chain Saks Fifth Avenue. Saks Incorporated was listed on the New York Stock Exchange with a market value over $4 billion. In 2004 the company had 55,000 employees, $5.9 billion in revenues, and the number of department stores had decreased to 240.

FROM SOUTHERN LEGISLATOR TO DEPARTMENT STORE MAGNATE

Martin spent the 1970s and 1980s as a Tennessee state representative, and he also made a fortune in real estate. He then decided to try his hand in the retail sector. Martin was the principal investor in the group that acquired Proffitt's in 1984. At that time the company operated five department stores in metropolitan Knoxville, Tennessee, with annual revenues of approximately $40 million. When Martin joined the company's management in 1989, Proffitt's was a $75-million company.

Martin applied his political wheeling and dealing skills to the boardroom. *BusinessWeek* called him a "savvy dealmaker with a thirst for acquisitions" (July 3, 2000). He first made his mark in regional midmarket stores and purchased Carson Pirie Scott, Herberger's, and Parisian. In 1998 he acquired the troubled Saks Fifth Avenue chain for $2.1 billion, adding around 360 stores in 39 states to his corporation. At the time, Saks was the fourth-largest department store in the United States, with annual revenues over $6 billion. The purchase moved him into the ranks of luxury retailers. *Forbes* called Martin "a numbers guy with a knack for consolidation and cost-cutting [and] just-folks southern manners" (January 21, 2002).

THE FUR COAT'S NOT-SO-SILVER LINING

Martin's success in the midmarket department stores did not transfer to Saks Fifth Avenue, his supposed cash cow. Neiman Marcus and Kohl's were formidable rivals to Saks Fifth Avenue, and the new chain struggled for a couple years while sales continued to fall. To boost sales Martin introduced new clothing lines and promoted in-house expert Christina Johnson to chief executive of the chain. He also consolidated operations such as credit-card processing, legal services, and logistics. To motivate company buyers, he created a new compensation and bonus plan tied to performance. Construction costs for new stores were also cut.

Martin tried to create a cozier feel in the revamped stores with coffee shops and more colorful decor and by adding a less-pricey clothing line. His take on luxury was unique: "Luxury does not need to be exclusive or aloof, or, could we say, snooty" (*BusinessWeek*, September 9, 2002). To appeal to more customers, Martin invested $30 million in an e-commerce site to increase traffic to the store and provide more products to current customers. He spent tens of millions of dollars on the Web site, which generated at most $25 million a year in income. Martin pushed forward despite negative results, firing many Saks veterans in the process. In 2003 he began to add youthful, more stylish shoes and jeans to attract teens and younger women. In January 2002 *Forbes* accused

Martin of "mixing mass with class" and "suffering from an identity crisis" because of its mix of teen styles with pricey adult items (January 21, 2002).

By 2002 Martin's luxury purchase was still afflicted by recession, increased competition, and $1.3 billion in debt. Though this caused him to sharply scale back on planned expansion, between 1998 and 2002 Martin opened 14 new Saks Fifth Avenue stores, expanded 12 more, and closed four. In July 2002 he was forced to sell the Saks credit-card operation to Household International. Saks Fifth Avenue was hard-hit by the drop in tourism to New York City following the terrorist attacks on the World Trade Center in 2001.

Martin told *Business Week* that "It's taken longer to get to where I wanted, but I'm pleased with our progress" (July 3, 2000). But analysts commented that the company had spread itself too thinly with its new acquisition, and that marketing and the Saks image needed work. The company appealed mainly to older, wealthy shoppers and failed to incorporate differences in regional tastes. Martin tried opening stores in second-tier markets and adding moderately priced store brands. To assist him, Johnson accounted for the chain's problems when she trained her buyers and looked at contemporary clothing lines for the new stores.

Saks Incorporated made a small profit in 2002 and then lost $45.8 million in the first half of 2003. Wall Street pressured Martin to sell off the sickly Saks Fifth Avenue, to which he responded, "Ain't gonna happen" (*Business Week*, September 9, 2002). In 2003 he brought in a former Bristol-Myers Squibb president to streamline the organization, create management teams, and increase communication among groups within the corporation. Only two new stores were planned through 2005.

See also entry on Saks Inc. in *International Directory of Company Histories*.

SOURCES FOR FURTHER INFORMATION

Grow, Brian, "Saks Fights Off the Ravages of Age," *Business Week*, September 9, 2002, http://www.keepmedia.com/pubs/BusinessWeek/2002/09/09/25871?from=search.

Pascual, Aixa M., "Still Seeking Synergy at Saks," *Business Week*, July 3, 2000, http://www.keepmedia.com/pubs/BusinessWeek/2000/07/03/23711?from=search.

Wells, Melanie, "He Stoops to Conquer," *Forbes*, January 21, 2002, http://www.keepmedia.com/pubs/Forbes/2002/01/21/198111?from=search.

—Alison Lake

Strive Masiyiwa

1961–

Founder and chief executive officer, Econet Wireless Holdings

Nationality: Zimbabwean.

Born: 1961, in Zimbabwe.

Education: University of Wales, BS, 1983.

Family: Married Tsitsi (maiden name unknown; director, Econet charitable trust); children: four.

Career: Zimbabwe Posts and Telecommunications Corporation, 1984–1988, senior engineer, then principal engineer; Retrofit Engineering, 1988–1994, founder and CEO; Econet Wireless Holdings, 1994–, founder and CEO; Associated Newspapers of Zimbabwe, 2000–, chairman.

Awards: Businessman of the Year, Republic of Zimbabwe, 1990; Manager and Entrepreneur of the Year, Republic of Zimbabwe, 1998; Ten Most Outstanding Young Persons of the World, Junior Chamber International (JCI), 1999; Global Influentials, *Time*, 2002.

Address: Econet Wireless International, 107 Johan Avenue, P.O. Box 785743, Sandton 2146 South Africa; http://www.econetwireless.com.

Strive Masiyiwa. *AP/Wide World Photos.*

■ Strive Masiyiwa was the maverick founder, chairman, and CEO of Econet Wireless Holdings, a diversified international telecommunications group based in South Africa with operations on three continents. A devout Christian noted for his determination and social conscience, Masiyiwa was called a hero for helping millions of Africans gain access to the modern world through affordable cellular telephones.

EDUCATION AND EARLY CAREER

Strive Masiyiwa was born in 1961 in Zimbabwe, which was then called Rhodesia. When he was seven, his family fled the country as Ian Smith's embattled government began to crumble. The family settled in Kitwe, a city in north central Zambia known for its copper mines. Masiyiwa's mother was an entre-

preneur with interests in retail sales, small-scale farming, and transportation. His father worked at first in one of the nearby mines but later joined the family business. By the time Masiyiwa was 12 years old, his parents could afford to provide him with a coveted European education. They sent him to private school in Edinburgh, Scotland. When he graduated in 1978, he traveled back to Zimbabwe, intending to join the anti-government guerilla forces there. "One of the senior officers told me 'Look, we're about to win anyway, and what we really need is people like you to help rebuild the country'" (*Time*, December 2, 2002). Masiyiwa took the man's advice and returned to school in Britain, earning a degree in electrical and electronic engineering from the University of Wales in 1983. He worked briefly in the computer industry in Cambridge, England, but soon returned to Zimbabwe in 1984, hoping to aid the country's recovery after the war of independence it had won in 1980.

Masiyiwa joined the Zimbabwe Posts and Telecommunications Corporation (ZPTC), the state-owned telephone company, as a senior engineer. ZPTC quickly promoted him to the position of principal engineer. Masiyiwa became frustrated with the government bureaucracy, however, and left ZPTC in 1988 to start an electrical contracting firm named Retrofit Engineering. He was chosen as Zimbabwe's youngest-ever Businessman of the Year in 1990.

THE START OF ECONET

Masiyiwa recognized the great potential for wireless telephones in sub-Saharan Africa because the region had only two fixed-line telephones for every hundred people in the 1990s. He saw that wireless networks would be quicker and less expensive to build than land-based networks that required stringing miles of telephone lines across rough terrain. Wireless telephone service would also be less vulnerable than traditional landlines to the theft of copper wire for resale. Masiyiwa first approached ZPTC about forming a mobile telephone network in Zimbabwe. The company wasn't interested, however, saying that cell phones had no future in the country.

Masiyiwa then decided to create a cell phone network on his own. He sold Retrofit Engineering in 1994 and started to finance Econet Wireless through his family company, TS Masiyiwa Holdings (TSMH). He met with fierce opposition, first from ZPTC, which told him it held a monopoly in telecommunications, and second from the Zimbabwean government, which swamped him with red tape and demands for bribes. As a devout Christian, Masiyiwa was opposed to paying bribes and kickbacks to government officials. He decided to pursue his case through the courts. After a landmark four-year legal battle that went all the way to the nation's Supreme Court, Econet finally won a license to provide cell phone service in Zimbabwe. The court declared that the government monopoly on telecommunications had violated the constitution's guarantee of free speech. Econet's first cell phone subscriber was connected to the new network in 1998.

While Masiyiwa waited to gain the government's approval for operations in Zimbabwe, he was able to start a cell phone network in neighboring Botswana. Econet Wireless Holdings then established a presence in over 15 countries, including other African nations, New Zealand, and the United Kingdom. The company also diversified into satellite communications, fixed-line telephone services, and Internet service.

Masiyiwa decided to relocate his family and the Econet headquarters to the Republic of South Africa in 2000. Some observers suggested that he was going into exile from his homeland once again. Masiyiwa himself said simply that South Africa was the best place from which to launch a multinational corporation because it had the continent's most vibrant economy.

ONGOING STRUGGLES

Masiyiwa further antagonized the Zimbabwe government when TSMH bailed out the financially strapped opposition newspaper, the *Daily News*. Masiyiwa eventually became a major shareholder in the newspaper's parent company, Associated Newspapers of Zimbabwe, as well as the company's chairman. The government responded by shutting down the newspaper in the fall of 2003. The paper continued to publish sporadically, though, through early 2004, and maintained an online version from South Africa. Masiyiwa sued for permission to restart the presses in Zimbabwe. The Zimbabwean government countered by starting criminal proceedings against four *Daily News* directors in June 2004 on charges of illegally publishing the paper without a license. Government officials also threatened to revoke Econet's license to operate in Zimbabwe at that time.

The board of directors of Econet Wireless Nigeria (EWN), a company in which Masiyiwa held a stake, ousted him in 2003 when he failed to acquire necessary financing. A critic told South Africa's *Financial Mail* that Masiyiwa "'talks up a storm' but often falls short on his promises to raise capital" (December 5, 2003). The board turned instead to Vodacom, a large South African telecommunications firm, which agreed to provide capital in return for management rights. According to the *New York Times*, however, Masiyiwa vowed to regain control of EWN. He said, "We've taken on Goliaths before" (January 15, 2004).

"Strive is driven by focus, determination and passion," Norman Nyazema told the *Financial Mail*. "Failure is not an option, no matter how many obstacles are thrown in his way" (December 5, 2003). Nyazema, who was a professor of pharmacology at South Africa's University of the North and chairman of Econet Wireless Zimbabwe (EWZ), had gone to school with Masiyiwa.

In the early months of 2004 Econet signed a 50/50 joint-venture agreement with Allied Technology (Altech), a South African information technology company. With Altech's capital and Econet's experience in telecommunications, the new company—dubbed Newco—announced its intention to pursue an aggressive expansion strategy in the developing countries of Africa and Asia.

Masiyiwa became a role model for other young African entrepreneurs through his vision and persistence. He won numerous national and international honors, including a place on *Time* magazine's list of the world's most promising young executives in 2002. Masiyiwa attributed his success in part to the ethical integrity he developed through the devotional practice of reading the Bible for an hour every morning. He served on the boards of such international development agencies as the Southern African Enterprise Development Fund and the Rockefeller Foundation. He and his wife Tsitsi also founded and funded a charitable trust that had provided scholarships for more than five thousand AIDS orphans as of 2003.

See also entry on Newco, Inc. in *International Directory of Company Histories.*

SOURCES FOR FURTHER INFORMATION

Bidoli, Marina, "A Tough Nut," *Financial Mail* (South Africa), December 5, 2003, p. 22.

Itano, Nicole, "The Maverick Behind a Telecom Deal," *New York Times*, January 15, 2004.

"Judgment Day," *The Economist* (U.S.), October 10, 1998, p. 76.

Katzenellenbogen, Jonathan, "Slapping Lions from Mugabe to Vodacom," *Business Day* (South Africa), November 17, 2003, http://www.bday.co.za/bday/content/direct/1,3523,1484436-6099-0,00.html.

Njanji, Susan, "Zimbabwean Media Bosses in Court Once More," *Independent Online* (South Africa), http://www.iol.co.za/index.php?click_id=84_id=qw1086799501847Z511_id=1, June 9, 2004.

Robinson, Simon, "Strive Masiyiwa: Founder of Econet Wireless," *Time*, December 2, 2002, p. 69.

—Kris Swank

■ ■ ■
David Maxwell

1930–

Retired chairman and chief executive officer, Federal National Mortgage Association (Fannie Mae)

Nationality: American.

Born: May 16, 1930, in Philadelphia, Pennsylvania.

Education: Yale University, BA, 1952; Harvard Law School, JD, 1955.

Family: Son of David Farrow and Emily Ogden Nelson; married Joan Clark Paddock, 1968.

Career: U.S. Navy, 1955–1959, naval officer; Obermayer, Rebmann, Maxwell, and Hippel, 1959–1967, associate, partner; State of Pennsylvania, 1967–1968, insurance commissioner; 1968–1969, secretary of administration; 1969–1970, budget secretary; U.S. Department of Housing and Urban Development, 1970–1973, general counsel; Ticor Mortgage Insurance Company, 1973–1981, president and chief executive officer; National Housing Task Force, 1978–1988, vice chairman; Federal National Mortgage Association (Fannie Mae), 1981–1991, chairman and chief executive officer; Centre Partners, director of business and nonprofit organizations.

Awards: Named one of the 10 Greatest CEOs of All Time by *Fortune* magazine, 2003; 1993 Housing Person of the Year award, National Housing Conference; the Maxwell Awards of Excellence are given annually in honor of David Maxwell by the Fannie Mae Foundation.

■ David Maxwell transformed the Federal National Mortgage Association (Fannie Mae), the largest investor in residential mortgages in the United States, from a financially unstable, floundering company into a stable, profitable company that helped low- to middle-income families obtain mortgages. He was described as an innovative and skillful leader whose vision helped motivate employees and management.

THE ORIGINS OF AN IDEA

Maxwell began his career as an attorney in Philadelphia after serving one tour of duty in the U.S. Navy. In 1960 his desire to implement innovative ideas led him to run for the U.S. Congress. Although his candidacy was unsuccessful, he found a new outlet for his ideas in 1967 as he moved into state and national government positions. From 1970 to 1973 he served as general counsel for the U.S. Department of Housing and Urban Development (HUD). During that time he learned more about the desire for low-income housing and mortgage loans for higher risk, lower-income families.

RECOGNITION OF A NEED

After leaving his position at HUD, Maxwell took the position of chairman and chief executive officer at Ticor, a provider of mortgage-guaranty insurance. From this unique vantage point, he could see who obtained mortgages and whether they were able to keep paying on them, which led to his observation that the "division between the housing haves and have-nots in this country [is] getting worse" (*Wall Street Journal*, May 19, 1989). In fact, from 1978 to 1985 the number of poor households increased 19 percent and the federal sponsorship of low-income housing decreased. Maxwell saw that there was a large pool of individuals—immigrants, single-parent families, and minorities—who wanted homes but would have to pay 50 to 80 percent of their salaries toward a mortgage. Most companies were unable to supply reasonable mortgages and mortgage-guaranty insurance to this high-risk population.

APPLICATION OF A VISION

When the immense and financially troubled Fannie Mae, which was losing $1 million a day, approached Maxwell in 1981, he was poised and ready for the challenge of turning around the congressionally chartered company. Maxwell first focused on standard financial changes, such as selling $10 billion worth of unprofitable mortgages and increasing Fannie Mae's financial flexibility by separating its stock prices from their close ties to volatile interest rates. Next, he created an overarching goal to revitalize Fannie Mae and dedicate it to helping others. Maxwell's vision was to frame the restructuring of Fannie Mae "around a mission: strengthening America's social fabric by democratizing home ownership" (*Fortune*, July 21, 2003).

WORKING FOR CHANGE

After the initial hard work of turning Fannie Mae into a stable, profitable company, Maxwell further democratized home ownership by serving on the National Housing Task Force in 1987-1988. As part of the task force, he called attention to the trend in which American incomes were not keeping pace with the costs of housing, and he recommended several strategies to refocus federal-housing policy to help low-income individuals afford housing. In 1998 the Fannie Mae Foundation recognized Maxwell's hard work by developing the Maxwell Awards of Excellence program to encourage, recognize, and give financial awards to community-based nonprofit groups that succeed in creating housing to meet the needs of low-income families and individuals.

A TUMULTUOUS RETIREMENT

When Maxwell retired as chairman in 1991, Fannie Mae was earning $4 million a day and had a $1.36 billion annual profit. The company was profitable enough that Maxwell considered separating it from its congressional charter, which provided some tax breaks and exemption from certain securities rules, but he was convinced by other executives at the company to keep the charter. Despite Maxwell's amazing turnaround of the company, controversy in Congress arose over his initial $27-million retirement package because many felt a government-sponsored agency should not pay such a large amount. Maxwell, concerned about the impact of his retirement payment on Fannie Mae, chose to forgo his second $5.5-million payment and requested that it be used to finance low-income

housing. Despite this offer, Congress passed legislation in 1992 requiring closer oversight of Fannie Mae. The legislation did not reduce Fannie Mae's profitability, and the company expanded its programs for low-income families and provided $1 trillion in financing for a program to buy loans on apartments for low-income families.

Since his retirement from Fannie Mae, Maxwell has served on the boards of Financial Security Assurance Holdings Limited, the Potomac Electric Power Company, and SunAmerica. He has continued his commitment to public policy problem-solving through his positions as chairman of the board of the Urban Institute and as trustee of the Brookings Institution and several other civic organizations.

See also entry on Federal National Mortgage Association in *International Directory of Company Histories.*

SOURCES FOR FURTHER INFORMATION

Barrett, Amy, "Fannie Mae Has Been Wearing Her Thinking Cap," *BusinessWeek*, June 6, 1994, p. 104.

Collins, Jim, "The 10 Greatest CEOs of All Time: What These Extraordinary Leaders Can Teach Today's Troubled Executives," *Fortune*, July 21, 2003, p. 58.

Zipser, Andy, "Gimme Shelter (A Special Report): Extremes—Broken Promises: Low-Cost Housing Stock Shrinks Even as the Need for It Grows," *Wall Street Journal*, May 19, 1989.

—Dawn Jacob Laney

■■■

L. Lowry Mays

1935–

Chief executive officer and chairman of the board, Clear Channel Communications

Nationality: American.

Born: July 24, 1935, in Houston, Texas.

Education: Texas A&M University, BS, 1959; Harvard University, MBA, 1962.

Family: Son of Lester T. and Virginia (Lowry) Mays; married Peggy Pitman, July 29, 1959; children: four.

Career: Russ & Company, c. 1962–c. 1970, investment banker; Mays – Company, c. 1970–1974, investment banker; Clear Channel Communications, 1975–, president, chief executive officer, chairman of the board.

Address: Clear Channel Communications, 200 E. Basse Road, San Antonio, Texas 78209; http://www.clearchannel.com.

■ As founder, chief executive officer, and chairman of Clear Channel Communications, one of the largest broadcast and outdoor advertising companies in the world, L. Lowry Mays built his empire from one radio station purchased in 1974 as an investment. Mays used his many radio and television holdings—and later billboard advertising after he entered that business in the late 1990s—to sell cross-platform packages to advertisers. He was concerned with satisfying his advertising customers and offering them value for their dollar. Another focus of Mays's corporate energy, especially late in his career, was the negotiation of deals to acquire more properties for Clear Channel.

A native of University Park, Texas, Mays graduated from Highland Park High School in 1953. He earned money for college by working as a roughneck on an oil rig. Mays then entered Texas A&M University, where he was a member of the Air Force ROTC. He was granted a BS degree in petroleum engineering in 1959. After working briefly in that industry, Mays was called into active duty by the U.S. Air Force and

went to China. Upon his return, he decided to continue his education by entering Harvard Business School. By the time he had earned his MBA in 1962, he was interested in finance and the stock market.

BOUGHT FIRST RADIO STATION

Mays returned to Texas and spent the next decade working as an investment banker in San Antonio. In the early 1970s Mays was helping some investors arrange a deal to purchase a local radio station; two individuals dropped out, and Mays bought it himself with Red McCombs, a local car dealer. The purchase marked the beginning of their broadcast empire. (McCombs remained a passive investor in Clear Channel for a number of years.) The co-owners of KEEZ-FM (later known as KAJA-FM) changed the station's format to country, increased its promotional budget, and hired more sales staff. The increase in advertising sales soon made the station profitable.

As the first radio station became a success, Mays became a very active station manager, leaving investment banking behind. He learned about the radio business and began lobbying for deregulation of the broadcast industry. Within two years Mays and McCombs had bought three more radio stations, and in 1975 they founded a company, Clear Channel Communications. Mays served as president and chief executive officer. The pair continued to invest in radio, using some of the techniques that had worked at KEEZ, including investing in promotion, increasing sales staff numbers to increase ad sales, and making favorable deals with advertisers. Initially Mays sought out stations in midsized markets that were not doing well and often bought from sellers who were not particularly savvy entrepreneurs. His method expanded the audience for many of his radio stations and led to increased revenue.

BOUGHT FIRST TELEVISION STATION

Because of Mays's success in radio, Clear Channel was able to go public in 1984, with Mays holding a majority of stock. Mays then looked toward a new broadcast market to conquer: television. Clear Channel bought its first television station in 1988, an independent station in Mobile, Alabama. In the late 1980s Clear Channel bought other television stations in Tucson, Arizona; Wichita, Kansas; and Memphis, Tennessee. As he did in radio, Mays emphasized unique promotions. Several of his stations were Fox affiliates, and he developed the first Fox Kid's Club around afternoon cartoons, offering membership cards and fun deals for kids. By 1990 Clear Channel owned 18 radio stations and six television stations.

While many media companies at this time were losing money, Clear Channel remained profitable. Mays was able to expand his company rapidly in the mid-1990s because of federal deregulation, which allowed companies to own more stations in one market, while containing costs and increasing revenues at his stations. Clear Channel was worth over $3 billion in 1996. By 1997 the company owned 178 radio stations, 11 radio networks, and 18 television stations. In the late 1990s Mays began expanding Clear Channel internationally, first by purchasing 24 radio stations in Australia and later by adding other holdings in the United Kingdom and China, among other markets. By this time Mays was focusing much of his attention on acquisitions for Clear Channel while managers handled the day-to-day operations of the company.

INVESTED IN BILLBOARDS

One of Clear Channel's most profitable new markets in the late 1990s was outdoor advertising, primarily billboards. By 1998 Mays's company owned 88,000 billboards. As time went on, billboards became an important source of revenue for the company and another cross-platform selling tool for his sales staff. All three arms of Clear Channel greatly benefited from further deregulation of the broadcast industry at the end of the 1990s. In 1999 Mays bought out AMFM, the largest broadcasting company in the United States, to add even more radio stations, television stations, and billboards. With this merger, Clear Channel became the largest radio station owner and outdoor advertising company in the world.

Mays made another big deal in 2000, when Clear Channel merged with SFX Entertainment. SFX promoted and produced live entertainment, primarily concerts, and operated related venues as well as a sports marketing and management firm. Mays believed that this deal would allow Clear Channel a new angle for offering advertising and marketing while diversifying the company. Although there was no doubt that Clear Channel remained successful (in 1999 alone, the company had annual revenues of $3 billion and a market capitalization of $40 million), this move was somewhat controversial as it was seen as a conflict of interest. Tom Hicks, the previous owner of AMFM and now a major shareholder of Clear Channel, owned two major sports franchises (the Texas Rangers and the Dallas Stars) while McCombs owned one (the Minnesota Vikings). Mays was also criticized for sometimes owning every station in a market and controlling concert tours; both of these perceived monopolies were believed to stifle competition. Mays had to address such issues by appearing before a legislative committee on Capitol Hill in the early 2000s.

HAD BRAIN SURGERY

Such controversy did not stop Mays and Clear Channel, nor did a failing economy in the early 2000s. By 2003 Mays was worth $1.2 billion, and his company had holdings in 66 countries. Clear Channel owned 1225 radio stations in the United States alone, as well as 36 television stations and 800,000 billboards. Though Mays was near retirement age, he continued to work hard while grooming his two sons, Mark and Randall, to replace him. Mark Mays was forced to serve as interim CEO in the spring of 2004 after Mays underwent brain surgery because of a blood clot and brain swelling. Mays temporarily left his position as CEO to recover.

See also entry on Clear Channel Communications, Inc. in *International Directory of Company Histories.*

SOURCES FOR FURTHER INFORMATION

Anderson Forest, Stephanie, "The Biggest Media Mogul You Never Heard Of," *BusinessWeek*, October 18, 1999, p. 56.

Bryce, Robert, "What? A Quiet Texas Billionaire?" *New York Times*, March 19, 2000.

Chen, Christine Y., "The Bad Boys of Radio," *Fortune*, March 3, 2003, p. 118.

"L. Lowry Mays," *Broadcasting & Cable*, November 10, 1997, p. HF28.

Lorek, L. A., "Lowry Mays; The Quiet Empire Builder," *San Antonio Express-News*, October 12, 2003.

Poole, Claire, "The Accidental Broadcaster," *Forbes*, June 8, 1992, p. 58.

—A. Petruso

■ ■ ■

Michael B. McCallister

1952–

President and chief executive officer, Humana Incorporated

Nationality: American.

Born: May 27, 1952, in Shreveport, Louisiana.

Education: Louisiana Tech University, BA, 1974; Pepperdine University, MBA, 1983.

Family: Married Charlene Gray; children: two.

Career: Humana Incorporated, 1974–1975, finance specialist; Community Hospital, Humana Incorporated, 1975–1978, executive director for finance; Humana Hospitals in Huntington and West Anaheim, California, 1978–1985, executive director; Humana Hospitals in West Hills and Canoga Park, California, 1985–1988, executive director; Humana Hospital, Phoenix, Arizona, 1988–1989, president; Human Health Care Plans, Phoenix, Arizona, 1989–1992, vice president; Humana Health Care Plans, San Antonio, Texas, 1992–1996, vice president; Humana Incorporated, 1996–1997, division president for Texas, Florida, and Puerto Rico; 1997–1999, senior vice president, health systems management; 1999–2000, senior vice president and office chairman; 2000–, president and chief executive officer.

Awards: Tower Medallion Award, Louisiana Tech University, 2003.

Address: Humana Incorporated, Humana Building, 500 West Main Street, Suite 300, Louisville, Kentucky 40202-4268; http://www.humana.com.

■ Michael B. McCallister climbed the ladder at Humana Incorporated for 26 years before being named its president and chief executive officer in 2000. As the company grew into one of the largest hospital and health-care companies in the United States, McCallister held a series of executive positions at different hospitals in California, Texas, and Arizona. He rose to upper-level management positions during the 1990s, making his mark as a senior vice president during a time when the company faced large financial losses. After McCallister became president and CEO of the company in 2000, he led the com-

pany's turnaround through such innovative ideas as paperless health care management products and consumer-driven health-care plans.

EDUCATION AND EARLY CAREER

McCallister was born in Shreveport, Louisiana, in 1952. He remained in his home state to attend college at Louisiana Tech University in Ruston, graduating in 1974. At the time McCallister completed his degree, Humana was less than 15 years old. The company, originally called Extendicare, was formed in 1961 by two young lawyers and other investors who developed, owned, and operated a nursing home business. For the remainder of the 1960s the company acquired more nursing homes and expanded its business to include hospitals. By 1974 Extendicare had purchased about 10 hospitals and changed its name to Humana.

McCallister joined Humana in 1974 as a finance specialist, working in the company's headquarters in Louisville, Kentucky. After a year he returned to Louisiana to serve as executive director of finances for Community Hospital in Springhill, which was a branch of Humana. In 1978 McCallister moved again, accepting a position as executive director for Humana hospitals in Huntington and West Anaheim in California. He remained there from 1978 through 1985, during which time he earned an MBA degree from Pepperdine University in Malibu, California.

Humana grew rapidly throughout the 1970s. By the early 1980s it was the world's largest hospital company, owning more than 80 hospitals. McCallister saw the company's growth at first hand, which later helped him deal with change inside the corporation after he moved into upper-level management positions. In 1985 he moved to Humana Hospitals in Canoga Park, California, and served as executive director there until 1988.

MOVING INTO UPPER MANAGEMENT

McCallister became the president of Humana Hospital in Phoenix, Arizona, in 1988. During the following year, he was elected to serve as Humana's vice president for Humana Health Care Plans in Phoenix, where his job required him to integrate health care and hospital plans. McCallister was transferred to San Antonio, Texas, in 1992 to serve in the same capacity. Humana then spun off its hospital business in 1993 to form a new company known as Galen Health Care, Incorporated. After Humana left the hospital business, McCallister's position in San Antonio was concerned only with health care.

McCallister remained in San Antonio until 1996, when he was named president of the company's Division I, which included its operations in Texas, Florida, and Puerto Rico. In 1997 he became senior vice president for health systems management at the company's headquarters in Louisville. He held that position through 1999, when he was appointed Humana's senior vice president and office chairman, reporting directly to company chairman David A. Jones.

McCallister distinguished himself in the late 1990s. He oversaw Humana's large-group commercial, Medicare, Medicaid, workers' compensation, and military health care businesses. He worked closely with David A. Jones, the company's chairman and interim chief executive officer, to develop a plan to improve the company's performance. Humana faced huge losses in 1999, and McCallister was largely responsible for putting its turnaround plan into action. Although the company expected to post overall losses, it also experienced significant gains in gross revenue. "Mike's role in producing these results was absolutely essential," Jones said of McCallister (February 3, 2000).

PRESIDENT AND CEO

Humana named McCallister as president and chief executive officer in 2000. "I look forward to working with my colleagues to continue building on the momentum we have established in the last several months [in 1999]," McCallister said when he took the helm (February 3, 2000). McCallister indicated that the company would focus on its core health insurance businesses and sell off its peripheral assets. McCallister's role as president and CEO began on a sour note, however, when he announced that the company had lost $382 million in 1999. Although the results were not unexpected, McCallister felt compelled to pledge that the company would return to profitability.

McCallister promoted several innovations that gained the attention of the healthcare community. In 2001 he introduced an all-digital health plan computer product called Emphesys, which was designed to transfer all medical provider transac-

tions to the Internet and eliminate the use of paper. "We have a track record of being able to transform our company in a very large-scale way," McCallister said in 2001. "New technologies are providing us not just with information, but with actionable information. That's something this industry hasn't had in the past and it sets the stage for us to transform ourselves yet again" (*Managed Healthcare Executive*, November 1, 2001).

During the following year, McCallister unveiled a revolutionary consumer-driven healthcare plan. He recognized that managed care no longer provided cost savings; Humana's healthcare costs for its own employees had increased 19.2 percent in 2002 alone. The new consumer-driven plans allowed employees to make their own decisions about their healthcare plans, with employers contributing to each employee's tax-free personal account or allowance.

McCallister's strategies paid off for Humana, which experienced a 60-percent increase in profits in 2003. By 2004 Humana was ranked by *Business Week* as one of the top-performing companies in the United States.

See also entry on Humana Inc. in *International Directory of Company Histories.*

SOURCES FOR FURTHER INFORMATION

Benko, Laura B., "Uphill Fight for Humana's New Chief," *Modern Healthcare*, February 14, 2000, p. 8.

Groeller, Greg, "New CEO Hopes To Heal Humana," *Orlando Sentinel*, February 4, 2000, p.B1.

Hansen, Fay, "Driving Savings with Consumer-Driven Health Care," *Workforce Management*, February 1, 2003, pp. 36–40.

"Humana Names Michael B. McCallister President and Chief Executive Officer," press release, February 3, 2000, http://humana.softshoe.com/employment_ops/our_culture/vision_ceo.html.

McCue, Michael T., "The Paperless Evolution," *Managed Healthcare Executive*, November 1, 2003, pp. 22–28.

"Online Extra: A Sharp Eye on Humana's Health," *Business Week Online*, April 5, 2004, http://www.businessweek.com/magazine/content/04_14/b3877648_mz073.htm.

—Matthew C. Cordon

■■■
W. Alan McCollough
1950–
Chairman, president, and chief executive officer, Circuit City Stores

Nationality: American.

Born: 1950.

Education: Missouri Valley College, BS, 1971; Southern Illinois University, MBA, 1974.

Career: U.S. Navy, minesweeper operations officer; Milliken and Company, cost accountant, director of quality, manufacturing plant manager, director of marketing; Circuit City Stores, 1987–1989, general manager of corporate operations; 1989–1991, assistant vice president; 1991–1994, president of central operating division and corporate vice president; 1994–1997, senior vice president of merchandising; 1997–2000, president and COO; 2000–2002, president and CEO; 2002–, chairman, president, and CEO.

Address: Circuit City Stores, 9950 Mayland Drive, Richmond, Virginia 23233; http://www.circuitcity.com.

W. Alan McCollough. *Chris Kelly/Getty Images.*

■ The electronics retail executive W. Alan McCollough was chairman, president, and chief executive officer of the national technology-services and retail company Circuit City Stores, headquartered in Richmond, Virginia, as of 2004. McCollough took over the leadership of the company in June 2000—succeeding Richard L. Sharp, who remained chairman of the company—after 13 years of extensive experience in merchandising and store management, two of the retailer's primary operating areas.

SECOND-LEADING U.S. ELECTRONICS RETAILER

The primary business unit of Circuit City Stores was the Circuit City Group, which was the second-largest U.S. electronics retailer as of 2004 (behind Best Buy Company, which had fewer stores in fewer markets but higher sales). Circuit City owned stores in over six hundred U.S. locations, with most designated as superstores—that is, as very large stores with broad selection and competitive prices selling a wide variety of products, including consumer electronics (such as audio and video equipment), personal computers, movies, music, games, and entertainment software. The Circuit City Web site provided shoppers with extensive product information, direct shipment of purchases, real-time inventory status of products in stores, and Express Pick-up, enabling customers to order goods online and obtain them at specified stores.

The company previously ran over 30 shopping-mall-based Circuit City Express outlets. The company also established the used-car seller CarMax in 2002. At the time of McCollough's ascendancy to the helm of Circuit City, CarMax was the nation's leading specialty retailer of used cars and a rapidly growing new-car retailer. By 2004 there were 40 CarMax locations across the United States.

CIRCUIT OF LEADERSHIP

McCollough began his professional career with the textile manufacturer Milliken and Company. Over his 12 years at Milliken, McCollough held various positions, including cost accountant, director of quality, manufacturing plant manager, and director of marketing. McCollough joined Circuit City in 1987 as general manager of corporate operations. Within two years he was named assistant vice president, directing the development of a large number of store operating procedures designed to promote quality and uniform service across the company's large and rapidly expanding store base. Along with these responsibilities McCollough led the implementation of the company's distributed point-of-sales system, which was used throughout the organization.

From 1991 to 1994 McCollough was vice president of Circuit City and president of the company's central operating division, which comprised more than one-third of the company's stores. In 1994 he became senior vice president in charge of merchandising, a post that involved responsibilities for all merchandise selection, purchasing, and inventory management. During the next three years McCollough developed sturdy working relationships with the vendor community that extended over the entertainment-software, consumer-electronics, major-appliance, and personal-computer industries. McCollough became president and chief operating officer in 1997, which made him responsible for activities involving human relations and resources, management information systems, merchandising, store operations, and planning.

McCollough became chief executive officer of Circuit City in June 2000. A few months before this time, the outgoing CEO Sharp said of McCollough, "Alan's extensive experience in the critical areas of our business, his commitment to our high-quality consumer offers, and his outstanding leadership talents make him the ideal person to guide our company into the next decade" (January 3, 2000). As CEO, McCollough directed the continuing growth and development of both the Circuit City and CarMax automobile superstore businesses. In June 2002 McCollough was elected chairman of the board of directors.

LAGGING BEHIND BEST BUY IN 2000

Upon becoming Circuit City's chief executive officer, McCollough found the company lagging behind Best Buy in such financial data as sales, sales per square foot, and return on investment. Although both stores saw slower sales in the first half of 2000, Best Buy doubled its stock value in the same period that Circuit City saw its value remain flat.

McCollough began implementing a detailed plan involving a new store format, tests of a stand-alone appliance-only concept (in which a small store would sell only appliances), the

rolling out of new merchandising displays, and continuation of the expanding digital-product cycle in consumer electronics. Circuit City would stock more products on store shelves and place registers near entrances, allowing consumers to more easily help themselves to products and to navigate the store in a more efficient manner—what McCollough called a "grab-and-go" climate. A combination of commissioned sales counselors and hourly employees were put in rotation at each store. This new employment policy contrasted the historically exclusive use of commissioned personnel; the switch helped reduce operating expenses.

McCollough also expanded the number of high-technology products offered by Circuit City outlets, including digital cameras, 35-millimeter cameras, software titles, and video games. New merchandising displays were created in order to better highlight the products and services available through the various alliances the company maintained with companies such as AOL and Sony. By shifting Circuit City's product lines and introducing higher-margin, new-technology products, McCollough hoped to rely less on sales from computers and other home-office products, whose profit margins continued to erode.

ELIMINATING APPLIANCES

McCollough initiated a plan to eliminate major appliances from the main Circuit City locations in order to provide more space on the selling floor and in the warehouse for the expanded product categories. While the company's gross margins for appliances were in line with other products, the storage and delivery costs of the oversized items were much greater than for smaller products. McCollough also added that the appliance category did not have the same growth potential as consumer electronics, as the selling of appliances was a cyclical business tied to housing starts and other economic factors. McCollough remarked that 70 percent of customers bought appliances as replacements for older models.

In the end McCollough found that the company needed an extra 20,000 square feet of additional floor space per store in order to accommodate all of the high-growth products it wanted to sell. With Lowe's, Home Depot, Sears, and other companies all involved in the appliance market, McCollough decided it would not be in the company's best interest to pursue further appliance sales.

In 2000 McCollough opened 25 new stores and remodeled 30 to 35 existing stores, each with a new open, warehouse-style format—hardwood floors and bright signs replaced the former red, black, and chrome design scheme, and wider aisles, higher ceilings, and "great sight lines" were introduced. McCollough wanted the bold new atmosphere of Circuit City to impress customers from the moment they walked into stores. Test markets for the consumer electronic-only format included

Richmond, Virginia, and Miami, West Palm Beach, Tampa, Fort Meyers, and Orlando, Florida. Along with these actions, McCollough tested an appliance-only format in six stand-alone locations in Florida. McCollough also led Circuit City to implement an Internet-based training program for store-level associates.

YEAR-END RESULTS

By the beginning of the last quarter of 2000 Circuit City continued to lag behind Best Buy despite McCollough's initiatives. However, McCollough continued to believe that the new product cycle, format changes, and merchandising improvements would help Circuit City better compete with Best Buy. By the end of 2000 McCollough saw improvement in sales at existing stores that had undergone remodeling to replace the defunct appliance business. McCollough slowed the pace of total-store overhauls, hoping to strengthen the company's brand identity and returns on investment with a less expensive future remodel (that of $1.5 million per store rather than $2.5 million).

SEEING IMPROVEMENT

In 2001 McCollough began a new marketing program designed to better communicate Circuit City's new look and product offerings to consumers. He hired Fiona Dias as senior vice president of marketing in order to run marketing as a separate division rather than as part of another division as had been done in the past. In the first part of 2001 sales lost through the removal of appliances were balanced by overall sales increases resulting from overhauled store layouts and operations. Later in the year McCollough announced the company's new advertising slogan: "Circuit City—We're With You." McCollough sought to improve customer service through an overhaul of internal operations—using Six Sigma, an accepted business philosophy fostering customer satisfaction, as its guideline.

STILL UNDECIDED WITH STORE FORMATS IN 2002

McCollough spun off CarMax in the first quarter of 2002, after CarMax's business matured as customers bought used cars rather than new ones during the economic downturn of the early 2000s. McCollough hoped that separating the two businesses (Circuit City and CarMax) would permit the management of each to better focus on financial and operational objectives. With respect to Circuit City, after a year and a half of testing several formats and programs, the company had yet to determine a clear-cut remodeling plan for its aging store base.

McCollough announced that Circuit City would redesign three hundred of its stores to house new video departments, complete with seating areas for the full home-theater experience, to better merchandise the high-growth television category; the company had already been doing this in all newly built stores. McCollough later announced that two other formats would also be tested, one in Chicago, Illinois, and another in the Baltimore–Washington, D.C., area. This announcement caused some disruption on Wall Street, as Circuit City had difficulty communicating with the analyst community. Such issues continued to have adverse affects on the company's stock price and analyst reports.

2003 AND BEYOND

At the beginning of 2003 McCollough continued to focus on updating Circuit City's store base, streamlining operations, and polishing its consumer image. After two full years in a state of transition, the chain store seemed unable to move forward. McCollough contended that the company had made much progress over those two years, although he admitted that the company still had a long way to go before accomplishing its goals. After successfully spinning off CarMax, McCollough abandoned the smaller, mall-based Circuit City Express stores and the stand-alone appliance concept, which had never truly materialized.

McCollough's largest focus was on remodeling and redecorating Circuit City's existing stores. He expanded the home-office category, complete with personal computers, software, and accessories, and the entertainment software section, to help boost foot traffic and bring in younger consumers. However, Wall Street analysts were still unsure about the future of Circuit City, as they waited for the company to finish remodeling its store base and to announce a growth plan. Analysts felt both projects were long overdue, especially considering the opposition of Best Buy, which was far ahead in terms of the executing of a growth plan, brand positioning, and building of vendor relationships. While Circuit City had advanced several positive store prototypes, other stores remained outdated and poorly suited to the evolving consumer-electronics market.

Over the nine months ending November 30, 2003, Circuit City revenues fell 4 percent to $6.5 billion, paralleling the weak retail-sales environment caused by the general economic slowdown. Net losses from continuing operations rose 52 percent to $83.3 million, reflecting declining gross-profit margins and increased remodeling and relocation expenses. McCollough planned to move Circuit City to the next phase of its remodeling program in two hundred stores in 2004. However, the company had been on the remodeling path for some time and had yet to see improvements in returns.

See also entry on Circuit City Stores, Inc. in *International Directory of Company Histories.*

SOURCES FOR FURTHER INFORMATION

Heller, Laura, "Circuit City Future Shift: McCollough to Step Up," *Discount Store News*, January 3, 2000.

—William Arthur Atkins

■■■
Mike McGavick
1958–
Chairman, president, and chief executive officer, Safeco Corporation

Nationality: American.

Born: 1958, in Seattle, Washington.

Education: University of Washington, BA, 1983.

Career: The Rockey Company, 1983–1986, vice president; Washington Round Table, 1986–1988, vice president; U.S. Senator Slade Gorton, 1989–1991, chief of staff and campaign manager; The Gallatin Group, 1991–1992, partner; American Insurance Association, 1992–1995, director of Superfund Improvement Project; CNA, 1995–1996, vice president of New Ventures; 1996–1997, senior financial officer of Commercial Lines Group; 1997–2001, president and COO of Financial Corporation; Safeco Corporation, 2001–2003, president and CEO; 2003–, chairman, president, and CEO.

Address: Safeco Corporation, Safeco Plaza, 4333 Brooklyn Avenue Northeast, Seattle, Washington 98185; http://www.safeco.com.

■ In 2004 the insurance and financial-services company executive Michael S. (Mike) McGavick was president, chief executive officer, and chairman of the board of directors of the Seattle, Washington–based Safeco Corporation—the second-largest commercial insurance operation in the United States. When McGavick was selected as Safeco's new leader, the company was sinking rapidly due to severe operational and management problems. Safeco was in need of major retrenching—as phrased by technical analysts—and McGavick said of the company and its employees on the Safeco Web site, "I'm going to reach out to people throughout the company. Our employees' creative ideas and innovative thinking will unlock the full potential of Safeco, providing shareholders with the returns they deserve" (January 30, 2001). McGavick proved able to do just what he said he would do—but not without making many tough decisions, many of which were not well received. However, those decisions ultimately helped to bring Safeco back to its traditionally successful role as a major multiline insurance company in the United States.

INSURANCE THE SAFECO WAY

Safeco, a Fortune 500 company with annual revenues of about $7.36 billion as of 2003, sold a comprehensive array of insurance and financial investment products and services through a U.S. network of over 17,000 independent agents, brokers, and financial advisors. Its family of companies provided products that included auto, business, casualty, home, life, and property insurance; investments such as life-insurance annuities, mutual funds, and stock purchase plans; group excess-loss medical and retirement plans and services for businesses; and asset management, surety bonds, and trust services.

PUBLIC AFFAIRS STARTS CAREER

McGavick became vice president of The Rockey Company, the Seattle, Washington–based public-affairs firm in 1983. Through his early professional career, McGavick held a number of public-affairs positions, including, from 1986 to 1988, vice president of the Seattle-based Washington Round Table, a nonpartisan policy-research group composed of the top executives (including chief executive officers) of Washington's largest corporations; campaign manager for U.S. Senator Slade Gorton's successful reelection campaign in 1988; chief of staff for Gorton from 1989 to 1991; and partner with The Gallatin Group, the Seattle-based public affairs firm, from 1991 to 1992.

INSURING HIS PROFESSION

McGavick began his insurance career in 1992, spending three years as director of the Superfund Improvement Project for the American Insurance Association in Washington, D.C. In that position he worked as a prime negotiator for the insurance industry with the U.S. Congress, federal agencies, and groups concerned about reforming the country's superfund environmental laws.

Before joining Safeco, McGavick held a number of executive positions at the Chicago, Illinois–based CNA Financial Corporation starting in 1995. During this time he was responsible for managing and improving CNA's relationship with its independent-agent distribution system and engineering CNA's e-commerce strategy. McGavick served from 1995 to 1996 as vice president of New Ventures; from 1996 to late

1997 as senior financial officer of Commercial Lines Group; and from 1997 to 2001 as president and chief operating officer of Financial Corporation. As president and chief operating officer of CNA Financial, the company's largest operating unit, McGavick was responsible for the majority of the company's commercial insurance business. He began a successful turnaround of CNA's commercial operation when he reformulated the workforce distribution and implemented a completely new underwriting technique.

BEFORE MCGAVICK CAME ON BOARD

Unable to deal with the results of Safeco's traditional-business acquisitions, stock analysts, shareholders, and independent agents criticized company management, especially beginning in 1999 and throughout 2000. In particular, after Safeco announced in January 2001 that earnings were below expectations for the fifth consecutive quarter, Standard & Poor's removed the ratings of Safeco and its related entities from CreditWatch (S&P's service highlighting the potential direction of a rating). It lowered Safeco's credit rating and senior unsecured-debt rating from "A-" to "BBB+"; financial security was downgraded from "strong" to "good"; and the company was judged as having become much more likely to be negatively affected by adverse business conditions.

TAKING OVER AT A CRITICAL JUNCTION

The global management-search firm Russell Reynolds Associates, based in New York City, performed an extensive hiring process with Safeco in which the members of the board of directors reviewed over one hundred candidates for the position of chief executive officer; McGavick eventually won out. He took over the position of president and chief executive officer in January 2001 from William G. Reed Jr., who assumed the chairmanship of the board of directors. As found on the company Web site, Reed said of McGavick upon his appointment, "Mike understands the prestige Safeco has always enjoyed, and he has demonstrated the capacity to build and lead a strong team of executives" (January 30, 2001); Reed went on to say, "Mike's ideas, energy, and leadership ability clearly stood out among this field of proven business leaders."

McGavick joined Safeco at a difficult time in the company's history. In 1997 Safeco made a major acquisition when it bought the large property-casualty insurer American States. Instead of helping Safeco to become a more diversified, well-rounded financial-services leader, the acquisition nearly bankrupted the company, as the purchase was made for too much money and at the top of the underwriting cycle (such that Safeco had to reduce rates in order to maintain market share in an already unprofitable business climate). Operating earnings dropped throughout the next year, and by the end of 1999

Safeco's combined expense ratio of 108.4 percent was for the first time in its history worse than the industry average of 106.9 percent.

MANAGEMENT TEAM FORMED

McGavick assembled an outstanding management team in order to counter Safeco's problems and turn the company around for the benefit of shareholders, customers, and distribution partners alike. One of the most important members of his management team was Michael LaRocco, who was formerly GEICO's vice president. LaRocco was hired by McGavick to become the president and chief operating officer of Safeco's personal-lines business. LaRocco ultimately performed critical actions to help McGavick reverse Safeco's plummeting position.

RETURNING TO EXCELLENCE

From the start McGavick assured Safeco's independent agents that the company's primary distribution focus—that of an independent-agency brand—would remain as it had in the past; on the other hand, he implied that the company might eliminate its homeowners market due to tremendous losses.

McGavick immediately launched a series of initiatives to return Safeco to its long tradition of excellence. His first action was to reduce the company's stock dividend by about half in order to redirect the money toward the company's growth. His second move was to write off $1.2 billion ($911 million after taxes) in goodwill obtained from the American States acquisition. The huge one-time charge succeeded in clearing the balance sheet of negativity. Thirdly, McGavick sold the profitable Safeco Credit Company to GE Capital in order to reduce debt.

With short-term debt cut by 50 percent, McGavick began a series of layoffs and consolidations in order to reduce corporate expenses. He downsized Safeco's workforce by about 10 percent, or around 1,200 jobs. McGavick's next concern was the homeowners business, which was losing enormous amounts of money. McGavick told his troops that he did not intend to exit the market entirely but would if he were forced to do so. With McGavick guiding analysis and research, management members eventually decided to raise prices for all homeowner accounts. Another problem spot seen by McGavick was the property-casualty business unit. He assigned LaRocco to reorganize Safeco's direct-marketing strategy; LaRocco modeled the new strategy after GEICO's operations, resulting in lower business-model costs particularly with respect to distribution expenses.

McGavick also invested in technology during Safeco's turnaround. He directed Safeco management to install a common technology platform to handle homeowners, automobile, and small commercial businesses. McGavick rationalized this additional expense by assuming that once the company had recovered from its downturn it would be able to significantly reduce expenses associated with the new investment.

POSITIVE RESULTS WITHIN 11 MONTHS

Under McGavick's leadership, management at Safeco took strong actions to improve the performance of core business lines, strengthen the balance sheet with a noticeable turnaround in market capitalization, and reduce core distribution expenses, meanwhile investing in training and new technologies that were aimed at improving customer service and product distribution, respectively. McGavick accomplished this feat with five core directives in mind: to focus on the qualities that made an organization unique in its industry; to do whatever might be necessary, even if it involved performing "radical surgery," as phrased by McGavick; to "take the pain" earlier

rather than later; to invest in new systems and infrastructures; and to communicate so that actions backed up words.

Safeco turned its financial performance around in 2002, generating net income of more than $300 million, the company's best results in four years.

See also entry on SAFECO Corporation in *International Directory of Company Histories.*

SOURCES FOR FURTHER INFORMATION

Mitchell, Jim, "SAFECO Names CNA Executive Mike McGavick New President and CEO: Gary Reed Elected Chairman," Safeco press release, January 30, 2001, http://www.safeco.com/safeco/news/archive/2001_0130.asp.

—William Arthur Atkins

■■■
Eugene R. McGrath

1942–

Chairman, chief executive officer, and president, Consolidated Edison Company of New York

Nationality: American.

Born: 1942, in Yonkers, New York.

Education: Manhattan College, BS, 1963; Iona College, MBA, 1980; Harvard University, Advanced Diploma, 1989.

Career: Consolidated Edison Company of New York, 1963–1978, engineer and management trainee; 1978–1981, vice president; 1981–1982, senior vice president; 1982–1989, executive vice president; 1989–1990, president and COO; 1990–, chairman, CEO, and president.

Awards: Leaders in Management Award, Pace University, 1997; Honorary Doctorate of Commercial Science, Pace University, 1997.

Address: Consolidated Edison Company of New York, 4 Irving Place, New York, New York 10003; http://www.coned.com.

Eugene R. McGrath. © *Ron Sachs/Corbis*.

■ Eugene McGrath was the chairman and chief executive officer of Consolidated Edison Company of New York, the largest utility in one of the largest urban metropolitan areas in the world, New York City. A native New Yorker, McGrath spent his entire professional career with Con Edison. He joined the company in 1963 immediately after receiving his bachelor's degree in mechanical engineering from Manhattan College. McGrath started his career with Con Edison as an engineer and management trainee in the operating and customer-service divisions. Moving into management, McGrath became responsible for running fossil-fuel and nuclear power plants. He moved progressively into more responsible positions, earning a promotion to vice president in 1978; in 1981 he was made senior vice president, in 1982 executive vice president. McGrath was named president and chief operating officer in 1989 and accepted the position of chairman and chief executive officer in 1990.

The umbrella company Consolidated Edison supplied electric, natural gas, and steam-power services to New York City and neighboring areas of Westchester County. Energy was delivered to more than four million customers through several distribution companies, including Consolidated Edison Company of New York and Orange and Rockland Utilities. Con Edison sold its energy-generating plants in the late 1990s in the course of the restructuring of New York's electric industry; the company then became primarily focused on transmitting and distributing energy resources generated by other companies. Con Edison continued to own and operate one of the largest steam-distribution systems in the world, serving the densely populated New York City borough of Manhattan.

McGrath believed that the decision to divest Con Edison of its power-generating facilities and focus on distribution was critical to the ongoing success of the company as well as to the continued stability of New York City's energy supply. His belief was based on the understanding that the city had developed a vertical infrastructure in which stable provision of adequate electrical power was critical for public safety and welfare. The majority of the city's structures were high-rises, housing a dense population that was entirely reliant on electricity to move other utility services such as water and natural gas. The underground subway system was also wholly dependent on a steady supply of electrical power.

By more concertedly focusing Con Edison on the delivery of energy resources, McGrath laid the foundation for what was called one of the most stable and reliable electricity systems in the world. Although the sales of the generating plants were at first controversial, they were ultimately lauded as intelligent business moves that positioned Con Edison to effectively handle two major challenges that appeared in the following years.

MANAGEMENT UNDER CRISIS

On September 11, 2001, two hijacked airplanes were crashed into the World Trade Center towers in New York City. The true extent of the damage caused by this catastrophic attack was incalculable; thousands of lives were lost, parts of Manhattan were destroyed, and daily operations were completely shut down.

The public responses from Con Edison and from McGrath in particular were widely praised. Within weeks electricity was restored to the devastated area surrounding the World Trade Center. Rebuilding efforts moved efficiently, with destroyed substations being quickly replaced. McGrath became personally involved in the response to the crisis by contacting other corporate leaders to ask for their assistance in attempting to restore normalcy to New York. Perhaps the most important factor behind the rapid replacement of downed substations was McGrath's phone call to the head of General Electric requesting a special rush order on the needed equipment; thus, the speed of the repairs was generally attributed to McGrath's decisive leadership and personal intervention, though he pointed to overlaps in the electrical system and the training of Con Edison staff as more critical factors. He remarked upon the dedication, commitment, and bravery shown by his company's employees, publicly praising their efforts during the emergency.

Con Edison's emergency responsiveness was tested once again on August 14, 2003, when a significant portion of the eastern United States and Canada experienced a sudden and complete loss of electrical power. The cause of the blackout was unclear; it quickly spread westward as far as Michigan, Ohio, and Ontario, Canada, taking power-generating plants and distribution centers offline within minutes. Such a complete and rapid shutdown required careful and thoughtful restoration of service, and McGrath was again praised for his quick leadership in safely restoring power to all of New York City within 29 hours of the initial outage. McGrath again redirected this praise to the customer-service mindset of Con Edison employees, who activated emergency backup plans and followed established policies to restore service with no reported injuries to consumers or Con Edison staff or damage to major equipment.

MANAGEMENT STYLE AND PHILOSOPHY

McGrath's management style stressed factors such as emergency preparedness, security, identification and mitigation of potential risks, and open communication with public-safety and law-enforcement agencies. Described as a dedicated leader and a giant in the energy industry, McGrath bore a direct and straightforward demeanor incorporating civic responsibility and responsiveness. Associates saw him as a hands-on chairman who was able to motivate and challenge Con Edison's workforce. McGrath was credited with spurring the evolution of Con Edison's corporate culture from stuffy and stolid to consumer- and service-oriented. He implemented revolutionary programs such as negotiable energy rates for businesses—a practice largely unheard of at the time of its institution. In 1999 McGrath established the pioneering Power Your Way program, which allowed consumers to choose their preferred suppliers for electricity and natural gas.

In the somewhat turbulent 1990s era of deregulation and restructuring of the electrical and utility industries, McGrath was committed to helping Con Edison and its workforce smoothly complete the transition. He strongly supported workforce education and development initiatives to help Con Edison employees gain the familiarity and experience necessary to work with new technologies. He created an educational facility to train and retrain workers in the skills required by the changing industry; the investment resulted in a dedicated and loyal workforce with a strong shared commitment to the corporate goals of efficiency, cost savings, civic responsibility, and service. Under McGrath, Con Edison maintained steady growth even as utility companies in other parts of the United States struggled. His management strategy was credited with facilitating the achievement of approximately $2.6 billion in rate reductions and cost savings, much of which was passed on to consumers.

Over the course of his 40-plus years at the helm of Con Edison, McGrath repeatedly demonstrated his commitment to his industry and to serving the residents of New York City. Under his guidance Con Edison developed programs and information services such as the Energy Education Campaign. This public-service advertisement program distributed information to citizens with regard to energy conservation as well as infrastructure issues within the energy industry. Believing that an informed public would be able to make better decisions regarding utilities and energy consumption, McGrath worked to involve businesses and individuals in planning for the future of New York City's energy supply. Con Edison's Citizen Participation Plan was developed to build consensus and involve consumers in the process of future siting and development of much-needed gas plants. Of his own view on the responsibilities of his position, McGrath told *Crain's New York Business*, "When I fly into New York at night and I see the lights lit up, I still feel pretty good about that. I feel how important this is" (April 9, 2001).

CIVIC INVOLVEMENT

McGrath was involved in numerous industry, civic, educational, and service organizations. He was the chairman of the Committee of the Energy Association of New York State and of the Union Square Partnership. He served on the boards of directors for the Edison Electric Institute, AEGIS Insurance Services, the American Woman's Economic Development Corporation, Atlantic Mutual Insurance Company, Barnard College, the Business Council of New York State, the Fresh Air Fund, the Hudson River Foundation for Science and Environmental Research, Manhattan College, the Partnership for New York City, Schering-Plough Corporation, and the Wildlife Conservation Society. McGrath was a member of the Committee to Encourage Corporate Philanthropy, the Council on Foreign Relations, the Economic Club of New York, the Development Advisory Council for the Lower Manhattan Development Corporation, the National Academy of Engineering, and the New York City Public/Private Initiatives. He was also a member of the Energy Committee of the New York Building Congress.

See also entry on Consolidated Edison Company of New York, Inc. in *International Directory of Company Histories*.

SOURCES FOR FURTHER INFORMATION

Fredrickson, Tom, "In Charge of the Light Brigade," *Crain's New York Business*, June 17, 2002, p. 48.

Lentz, Philip, "Con Ed Fighting to Keep Savings in Big Merger," *Crain's New York Business*, October 18, 1999, p. 1.

———, "Leading the Charge into Deregulation," *Crain's New York Business*, April 9, 2001, p. 29.

McGrath, Eugene R., "Testimony before the House Committee on Energy and Commerce," September 4, 2003, http://www.coned.com/PublicIssues/pi_testimony_McGrath-09-2003.html.

Misonzhnik, Elaine, "Con Ed Chairman Promises We Will Survive the Summer," *Real Estate Weekly*, June 13, 2001, p. 22.

Norman, James R., "A Beleaguered Tax Collector," *Forbes*, December 20, 1993, pp. 47–48.

Stavros, Richard, "The Best of the Best: Five Electric Utility Chiefs Are Showing True Leaderships for Their Companies and for an Entire Industry," *Public Utilities Fortnightly*, May 15, 2003, p. 28.

—Peggy K. Daniels

■■■
Judy McGrath
1954–
President, MTV Networks Group

Nationality: American.

Born: July 2, 1954, in Scranton, Pennsylvania.

Education: Cedar Crest College, BA, 1974.

Family: Married; children: one.

Career: National Advertising, copywriter; *Mademoiselle*, senior writer; *Glamour*, copy chief; Warner Amex Satellite Entertainment Company/MTV Networks Group, 1981–1987, copywriter, on-air promotions; 1987–1991, editorial director; 1991–1993, creative director; 1993–1994, copresident and creative director; 1994–2000, president, MTV and MTV2; 2000–2003, chairman, interactive music; 2000–, president.

Awards: Community Achievement Award, Do Something Foundation, 2000; Founder's Award, Rock the Vote, 2001; Matrix Award, New York Women in Communications, 2001; Humanitarian Award, Martell Foundation, 2003; Television Century Award, PROMAX&BDA, 2004.

Address: MTV Networks, 1515 Broadway, New York, New York 10036; http://www.mtv.com.

■ Judy McGrath was president of MTV Networks Group, one of the world's top brands. Originally started as a cable channel devoted to showing music videos, MTV grew to encompass news, talk shows, and reality programming and made forays into online entertainment and news. McGrath was with the company from its beginning in 1981, rising from copywriter to creative director and eventually occupying the top management position. Although she officially outgrew MTV's core demographic of 18- to 34-year-olds sometime in the late 1980s, McGrath continued to exude interest in and excitement about the tastes of MTV viewers. She remained aware of youth trends with extensive surveys of the target audience and listened closely to the opinions of the college interns who cycled through MTV's corporate offices.

Judy McGrath. *Matthew Peyton/Getty Images.*

AN EYE ON THE BIG APPLE

McGrath grew up in Scranton, Pennsylvania, but knew early on that she wanted to find a career in New York. She was a voracious reader of *Rolling Stone* and the *New York Times* arts and leisure section. McGrath became convinced that the people she read about were the kind of people she wanted to know. She attended Cedar Crest College and earned a bachelor's degree in English. Her writing ability combined with a passion for music that was instilled in her by her father led McGrath to formulate a goal of working for *Rolling Stone.*

McGrath made it to New York not long after graduating and took a job working for the Condé Nast publishing house. She was a copywriter for *Mademoiselle* and a senior writer for *Glamour.* McGrath still had her sights set on *Rolling Stone* when a friend told her that a new cable start-up called MTV was hiring writers. Drawn to the musical content, McGrath made what would become a characteristic leap into the void.

BUILDING THE MTV BRAND

In the early years at MTV, McGrath and others were working with very small budgets, creating advertising and promotions and formulating ideas in-house. Even after becoming successful, MTV continued to work this way. Within two years of going on the air, MTV was turning a profit. In 1984 McGrath helped launch the first-ever MTV Video Music Awards. In 1990 McGrath, acting as editorial director, was responsible for the creation of television's first reality show, called *The Real World*.

Throughout the 1990s McGrath took on extra projects, working hard to climb MTV's corporate ladder. In 1991 she became creative director and worked to bring another side to the teen-focused network. In 1992 she helped launch the Choose or Lose voter registration campaign to spark interest in the presidential election. The following year she produced MTV's inaugural ball for President Bill Clinton. She also developed the Fight for Your Rights campaign—the first of which addressed issues of violence.

McGrath was responsible for the launch of *Beavis and Butt-Head* in 1993. This animated series inspired outrage among critics because of its gross humor but was one of MTV's most successful programs. *Beavis and Butt-Head* created more impact than any previous cable program. Under McGrath's leadership MTV continued to draw audiences and ratings throughout the 1990s. With an increasing focus on original programming, MTV Networks Group in 1996 launched MTV2, which followed the mostly video format that MTV had pioneered.

MANAGEMENT STYLE

McGrath's willingness to take bold steps was evident. When she was offered the job at MTV, the company was an unknown cable start-up. It was not her dream job of writing for *Rolling Stone*, but McGrath had seen it as an opportunity to move up. In the new and undefined territory of cable television and especially in the freewheeling world of MTV, McGrath successfully took on leadership positions. Her philosophy for keeping MTV lively and timely was to keep constant tabs on the interests of the youthful audience.

One of the most influential elements of the MTV programming strategy was abandoning the strategy every three to four years. Under McGrath's supervision MTV constantly reinvented itself to meet the demands of its demographic. The result was that in 20 years MTV penetration went from fewer than one million to more than 333 million households worldwide. In 1999 an Interbrand survey ranked MTV the world's most valuable media brand, valued at $6.4 billion.

McGrath's management style included an open-door policy that allowed anyone to pitch ideas for new content. McGrath was responsive to ideas from interns and especially from members of MTV's target demographic. McGrath always considered MTV to be revolutionary and maintained that goal through constantly challenging the prevailing programming. When choosing employees McGrath looked for people she could trust and let them do what they wanted.

McGrath's policies and beliefs worked. In 2004 MTV played a significant role in Viacom's (MTV's parent company) 12 percent increase in income to $6.8 billion in the first quarter. Ratings for MTV and Comedy Central had increased. The two networks had more gross ratings points in their target demographic of 18- to 34 year-olds than any other television outlet. MTV itself had six of the top 10 programs on cable television.

As MTV Networks Group president, McGrath was responsible for MTV, MTV2, VH1, CMT (Country Music Television), and Comedy Central. Tom Freston, the CEO of MTV, commented in a company press release on McGrath's abilities, "[She] is a remarkably talented creative executive who has brilliantly led MTV from one success to another, growing the business dramatically along the way."

SOURCES FOR FURTHER INFORMATION

Gunther, Marc, "This Gang Controls Your Kids' Brains," *Fortune*, October 27, 1997, pp. 172–177.

Morris, Chris, "MTV Reaches Out to Audience Via Research," *Billboard*, September 26, 1998.

Richardson, Lynda, "She Wants Her MTV: Actually, She's Got Her MTV," *New York Times*, June 11. 2003.

Russel, Deborah, "Presidency of MTV to Be Solo Performance for Judy McGrath," *Billboard*, July 23, 1994, pp. 5–6.

—Eve M. B. Hermann

William W. McGuire

1948–

Chairman and chief executive officer, UnitedHealth Group

Nationality: American.

Born: 1948, in Troy, New York.

Education: University of Texas at Austin, BA, 1970; University of Texas Medical Branch at Galveston, MD, 1974.

Family: Married Nadine M.; children: two.

Career: University of Texas Health Science Center, 1974–1978, internal medicine resident, chief resident, and pulmonary fellow; Scripps Clinic and Research Foundation, 1978–1980, researcher; Colorado Springs, Colorado, cardiopulmonary medicine, 1980–1985, practicing physician; Peak Health Plan, 1985–1988, president and COO; United HealthCare Corporation, 1988–1989, executive vice president; 1989–1991, president and COO; 1991–1998, chairman and CEO; UnitedHealth Group, 1998–, chairman and CEO.

Awards: 50 Best CEOs in America, *Worth*, 2001.

Address: UnitedHealth Group, 9900 Bren Road East, Minnetonka, Minnesota 55343; http://www.united healthgroup.com.

William W. McGuire. © *Layne Kennedy/Corbis.*

■ In 2004 former pulmonologist Dr. William W. McGuire was the chief executive officer and chairman of the board of directors of the Minnetonka, Minnesota–based UnitedHealth Group, a company with more than 18 million medical members.

and Medicaid options (members of the American Association of Retired Persons were served through the Ovations unit); Uniprise, which handled health plans for large companies; Specialized Care Services, which offered vision care, dental care, and transplant services; and Ingenix, which provided health-information consulting and publishing as well as drug-development and marketing services.

CARING FOR HEALTH

McGuire expanded UnitedHealth Group to the point where it offered a variety of health-care plans and services through four business segments. Those four units included Health Care Services, which managed HMO (health maintenance organization), PPO (preferred-provider organization), and POS (point-of-service) plans as well as various Medicare

EARLY LEADERSHIP QUALITIES LEAD TO MEDICINE

McGuire showed early leadership qualities as a teenager when he led his Clear Creek High School basketball team to a successful 28-3 season; as the six-foot-five-inch center, he was considered the brains behind the team. McGuire went on to become a Doctor of Medicine, graduating summa cum laude from the University of Texas Medical Branch at Galveston.

Upon graduation McGuire worked from 1974 to 1978 as an internal medicine resident, chief resident, and pulmonary fellow at the University of Texas Health Science Center in San Antonio. Between 1978 and 1980 McGuire conducted basic research in immunopathology of the lung at Scripps Clinic and Research Foundation in La Jolla, California.

From 1980 through 1985 McGuire was a practicing physician in Colorado Springs, Colorado, specializing in cardiopulmonary medicine. During this time he served as chairman of the Colorado Foundation for Medical Care, Region 111 (1984–1985), as well as of its Professional Review Committee (1982–1984). McGuire held board certification in internal medicine and pulmonary medicine and was a member of the National Institutes of Health National Cancer Policy Board.

McGuire was then employed at Peak Health Plan in Colorado, where he served as vice president of Health Systems from 1985 to 1986; as medical director of Coastguard, Peak's insurance subsidiary, from 1985 to 1986; and as president and chief operating officer from 1985 to 1988. He joined United HealthCare Corporation when the company acquired Peak, thus beginning his flight up to the company's top corporate position.

TRANSITION TO UNITEDHEALTH GROUP

McGuire joined United HealthCare Corporation, which later became known as UnitedHealth Group, in November 1988, becoming its executive vice president. McGuire was appointed a member of the board of directors and chief operating officer in May 1989. He became president of the company in November 1989, a position he held until May 1991. In February 1991 McGuire became chief executive officer and three months later, in May, added the position of chairman of the board of directors to his official responsibilities. McGuire retained these positions when the company was renamed UnitedHealth Group in 1998.

ADDING FEATURES/PLUGGING GAPS

When McGuire took over the helm at UnitedHealth Group, the company was a regional health maintenance organization (HMO). At this time McGuire was concerned that the company did not offer sufficient options to its customers and decided to identify niches that could be entered to both plug up those gaps and bring more profit to the company. McGuire immediately began to direct company managers toward pricing services and products in accordance with anticipated costs while carefully managing the cost structure of those services and products. McGuire wholeheartedly believed that the results of these commitments in all of its business segments would become evident as the company continued to reorganize and streamline.

CUSTOMER DRIVEN

From the start McGuire felt that the most successful health-care companies were those that offered precisely the products and services that consumers wanted. During his first few years as leader of UnitedHealth, McGuire strived to provide flexibility in the choice of doctors and hospitals, broader access to services, and a wider range of services and products. At the same time he aimed to create a powerful growth strategy that would allow UnitedHealth to compete effectively in an increasingly crowded marketplace. That company would possess the size, level, and operating efficiencies necessary to consistently increase profits for shareholders.

ACQUIRING AND EXPANDING

To fulfill his vision McGuire negotiated the acquisition and expansion of about 30 or so businesses during his first 14 years as company leader. One of his largest deals was completed in 1998, when he brokered a merger with Humana. With the merger McGuire intended for UnitedHealth to become the most profitable health-care company in the United States by providing customers with accessible, high-quality, and affordable health-care services. McGuire predicted that the larger company would realize tremendous economies of scale, superior administrative efficiency, and an industry-leading service platform. He went on to say that the new company would be able to provide more affordable products to a larger number of people and in a more efficient manner.

STRONG FINANCIAL POSITION RESULTS

Following the merger UnitedHealth operated in 48 states, Puerto Rico, and internationally, including in Hong Kong, Singapore, and South Africa. Its workforce numbered 50,000 and the company had a strong financial position with more than $13 billion in total assets and more than $6 billion in shareholder equity.

UnitedHealth went on to become one of the most diversified health-services companies in the United States. In 2003 McGuire saw the company gain about 35 percent in net-income growth, to about $1.8 billion, and 15 percent in sales growth, to about $28.6 billion. By 2004 the company claimed about one in seven U.S. citizens as customers—38 million people in all. The original $605-million-a-year regional HMO company had transformed into a diversified conglomerate that had given shareholders a roughly 35-fold return on investments since the time McGuire became its leader.

Although McGuire was unsure that results in 2004 would better those of 2003, he was confident that UnitedHealth remained well positioned. One of McGuire's key accomplishments as chief executive officer was the formation of a diverse portfolio of health plans, which helped to increase the customer base by almost 10 percent to 50 million. McGuire saw UnitedHealth grow into the country's largest health-services company. A second key accomplishment was the creation of a program that tracked the performance of cardiology centers so that patients could find the best locations for treatment.

STRESSFUL BUT STRONG OUTLOOK

It was expected that the climate around McGuire would continue to be stressful in the future, as increasing competition and diminished consolidation opportunities would hamper the company's growth rate. Health-care costs continued to rise at double-digit rates, which put further stress on profits. McGuire received much publicity as well as criticism for his hefty 2002 pay package of $58 million in cash and exercised stock options. He admitted that his salary was large but countered by noting that he had given his shareholders enormous gains since he came to lead the company.

CHALLENGING THE HEALTH-CARE COMMUNITY

Many people within the health-care industry considered McGuire a blunt person, especially outspoken with regard to the existing health-care system. During the 2003 keynote address at the annual institute of the American Association of Health Plans, McGuire challenged the health-plan community to "step above the micro, incremental issues of the day and help drive discussion to a higher level"; he went on to say, "Between the health-care system that exists today and the health-care system we imagine, there lies significant opportunity to make health-care services more accessible for all Americans, to improve the quality of care, and to help individuals take a more active role in their own health and well-being" (May/June 2003).

THE PERSON BEHIND THE LEADER

McGuire was considered a maverick among executives in the health-care industry. Almost all other heath-care companies stayed away from serving Medicaid recipients; in 2002 McGuire bought AmeriChoice Corporation, a company that served Medicaid recipients, believing that the federal government would eventually add to its funding of the program. Whether or not the government would see fit to do this, McGuire still believed UnitedHealth could make a profit producing high-quality service for a segment of the population he described as "vulnerable."

BUTTERFLIES

McGuire had a long interest in butterflies, formally known as the order of Lepidoptera. He made several discoveries in the field, was considered a well-regarded expert, and had several butterflies named after him—one of them a brown central-Texas insect now called *Euphyes mcguirei*. As his career took him higher in the professional health-care field, he never lost sight of his early interest in Lepidoptera. Particularly intriguing to McGuire was the group of small butterflies known as skippers in the families Hesperiidae and Megathymidae. While he and his family lived in the southwestern United States—Texas, Southern California, and Colorado—McGuire studied, collected, and made many notable discoveries, specifically with respect to his special butterflies. During this time and after moving to his present home in Wayzata, Minnesota, McGuire published a number of professional papers describing the biology and ecology of skippers, particularly the Holarctic genus *Hesperia*.

EXTRACURRICULAR ACTIVITIES

McGuire was a member of the board of directors of Healtheon Corporation in Santa Clara, California, and the Minnesota Business Partnership. McGuire also served as an advisor to the American Board of Internal Medicine in Philadelphia, Pennsylvania. He was elected to the Institute of Medicine in 1997 and served on the Health Care Services Board of the Institute of Medicine in Washington, D.C. He was a board member of the Minnesota Orchestral Association and a trustee of the Minneapolis Institute of Arts.

McGuire and his wife, Nadine, established the William W. McGuire and Nadine M. McGuire Family Foundation. One of their donations was a $3 million gift in 2002 to create the McGuire Institute for Biodiversity and the Environment at the University of Florida, for the study of the diversity of animals and plants as well as the environment. McGuire also donated his personal 30,000-insect collection to the university. Another donation was a gift of $4.2 million in 2000 to establish the McGuire Center for Lepidoptera and Environmental Research, which would house one of the world's largest collections of butterflies and moths. McGuire's foundation provided free copies of *Clinical Evidence*, a text of proven current medical practices, twice yearly to every doctor and many nurses in the United States.

SOURCES FOR FURTHER INFORMATION

Bethall, Tom, "Leading by Example: Health-Plan CEOs Helping to Reshape the Health-Care Policy Debate," *Healthplan*, May/June 2003, http://www.aahp.org/Content/NavigationMenu/Inside_AAHP/Healthplan_Magazine/May_June_2003__COVER_STORY__Leading_by_Example.htm.

—William Arthur Atkins

■■■
Tom McKillop
1943–
Chief executive officer, AstraZeneca

Nationality: British.

Born: March 19, 1943, in Ayrshire, Scotland.

Education: University of Glasgow, BS, 1965; PhD, 1968.

Family: Son of Hugh McKillop and Annie Wilson; married Elizabeth Kettle; children: three.

Career: ICI Corporation, 1969–1975, research scientist; 1975–1978, head of Natural Products Research in ICI Phamaceuticals (ICIP); 1978–1980, director of research in France for ICIP; 1980–1984, chemical manager for ICIP; 1984–1985, general manager of research for ICIP; 1985–1989, general manager of development for ICIP; 1989–1994, technical director of ICIP; Zeneca Group, 1994–1996, CEO of Zeneca Pharmaceuticals; 1996–1999, CEO; AstraZeneca, 1999–, CEO.

Awards: Honorary LLD, Manchester, 1999; Honorary DSc, Glasgow, 2000; Honorary DSc, Leicester, 2000; Honorary DSc, Huddersfield, 2000; Honorary Doctor of Laws, University of Dundee, 2003; 25 Managers to Watch, *BusinessWeek*, 2001; Knighthood, from Queen Elizabeth II, 2002.

Address: AstraZeneca, 15 Stanhope Gate, London, W1Y 6LN, United Kingdom; http://www.astrazeneca.com.

■ Sir Thomas (Tom) McKillop presided over the 1999 merger of Zeneca Group—formerly ICI Pharmaceuticals—with Astra of Sweden, forming the new London-based company AstraZeneca, at the time the fifth-largest drug manufacturer in the world. McKillop began his career as a research scientist but eventually rose through the ranks to management positions. Although the names changed and the businesses he worked for went through considerable development, McKillop was one of those rare individuals in the modern corporate world who stayed with the same company for more than 30 years.

EARLY CAREER

McKillop, a miner's son from Ayrshire, Scotland, never imagined for himself a career in business; his early ambitions

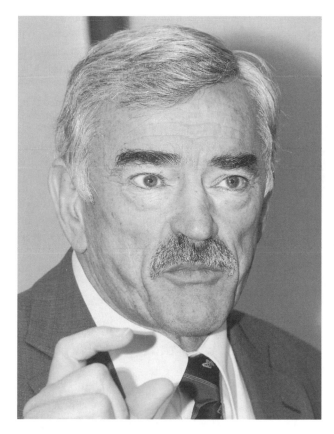

Tom McKillop. *Indranil Mukherjee/Getty Images.*

were in the field of chemistry. He obtained both a bachelor's degree with honors and then a doctorate through his study of carbonium ion rearrangements at Glasgow University. He then went on to do postdoctoral research in Paris.

In 1969 McKillop joined ICI Corporation as a research scientist and began slowly rising through the ranks. He was initially employed in ICI's corporate research laboratory but in 1975 moved over to the Pharmaceuticals division. He held a number of research positions in that division, including director of research at the company's France-based facility from 1978 to 1980 and chemical manager from 1980 to 1984. Further promotions saw McKillop gradually leave his scientific-research roots behind and enter the world of buiness management; he became ICI Pharmaceuticals' general manager of research in 1984, then general manager of development in 1985, then technical director in 1989. In the last position McKillop was in charge of international research, development, and production.

ICI BECOMES ZENECA

Imperial Chemical Industries (later ICI) had begun business in the United Kingdom in 1926. Before World War II the company that had been primarily an explosives and dye-stuffs manufacturer became involved in drug making at the behest of the British government, developing an antimalarial drug for British troops. After the war ICI's senior management concluded that pharmaceuticals would be important in the future and put together a team of scientists that became ICI Pharmaceuticals as of 1957. At first the division incurred consistent losses, but the company's long-term investment paid dividends 20 years later when ICI scientists discovered beta-blockers, the first drugs to be found effective in the treatment of hypertension.

Zeneca Group was created by a demerger from ICI in January 1993, wherein chemical activities were effectively separated from the biosciences side of the business. Zeneca was built on three former business units of ICI: the pharmaceutical, agricultural-chemical, and specialty-chemical units. McKillop was appointed chief executive officer of Zeneca Phamaceuticals in 1994, and two years later became executive director of Zeneca Group.

ZENECA MERGES WITH ASTRA

In December 1998 the announcement was made that Zeneca would merge with Astra, the Swedish pharmaceutical company. Astra was founded in 1913 and was active in pharmaceutical research, development, manufacture, and marketing in four main areas: gastrointestinal, cardiovascular, respiratory, and pain control. At the time of the merger Astra's key products included Losec (omeprazole), a gastrointestinal drug that was the world's best-selling pharmaceutical; Xylocaine, the world's best-selling local anesthetic; and a number of respiratory drugs. At that time Zeneca's key products included Dirpivan (propofol), the world's best-selling injectable general anesthetic, and a range of oncology drugs such as Zoladex (goserelin acetate), Casodex (bicalutamide), Nolvadex (tamoxifen citrate), and Arimidex (anastrozole). Zeneca was also the producer of a number of agrochemicals, such as Gramoxone, Fusilade, Touchdown, and Surpass, all herbicides; Karate, an insecticide; and Amistar, a fungicide. Astra and Zeneca were two companies with similar product areas as well as similar science-based cultures.

McKillop was chosen to be the CEO of the newly formed company, which would be called AstraZeneca. In many ways McKillop was an unexpected choice, as he had never run such a large corporation and bore a background in research rather than in business. However, he did have a 30-year history with Zeneca and had witnessed and taken lessons from all of the changes the company underwent through that period of time. McKillop's reputation for working long hours—which was made possible by his ability to function normally on only fours hours of sleep a night—enabled him to oversee the completion of the merger that created AstraZeneca in only 80 days. In February 1999 the Zeneca shareholders approved the merger, which was then approved by both the European Commission and the U.S. Federal Trade Commission. AstraZeneca officially came into being on April 6, 1999.

Business analysts would point to the merger as a prime example of how successful such unions could be. The new company soon realized operational and research savings and also found itself with a greater ability to spur long-term growth and offer more strategic financial options. In a speech to shareholders McKillop referred to the unification as a "merger of equals" (May 19, 1999); he credited its success to the broad acceptance employees and shareholders had for the new company. Considered by others to be a plain-spoken, no-nonsense manager, McKillop's honest and forthright approach to the merger sidestepped the uncertainty often experienced in such deals. At the time the merger was the largest ever in Europe and created the world's fifth-largest pharmaceuticals company. McKillop remarked during the new company's first shareholders meeting, "From being two medium-sized companies, we are now one at the very top" (May 19, 1999).

Far from resting on his laurels, McKillop continued to innovate and expand, beginning with a spin-off merging of AstraZeneca's agricultural-chemical business with Novartis's crop-protection and seed business. The move was unexpected, as the two companies were seen as rivals, but both benefited. The deal was completed in 2000, creating Syngenta, the world's largest agrochemical company, with a market share at inception of almost 23 percent.

MANAGEMENT STYLE

McKillop was said to maintain a hands-on approach at AstroZeneca, which he was particularly capable of doing thanks to his years working throughout the many levels of the company, giving him broad insight into all aspects of operations. In 2001 *Business Week* named McKillop one of its top "25 Managers to Watch."

The pharmaceutical industry was always shaped by the successes or failures of long-term research projects; yet while a long-term approach was vital, McKillop recognized that with the expiration of patents and the widespread manufacture of generic equivalent drugs the industry was always in flux. He told *Business Week*, "You have to reinvent the business every decade" (January 8, 2001).

McKillop and AstraZeneca took matters of corporate social responsibility very seriously. McKillop told Euractiv.com, a

European Union News and Policy organization, "We believe wherever we operate we should be a contributory part of that community" (March 17, 2004). AstraZeneca's commitment to tuberculosis research—for which a research laboratory was opened in Bangalore, India—was an example of how the company viewed its wider role in the world. McKillop suggested that such philanthropy should be seen as a good business practice for a drug-making company, as a positive public image could make a firm the preferred choice of conscientious customers. In a competitive marketplace and in an industry often beset with public-relations problems, his approach won widespread praise.

PUBLIC LIFE

McKillop strongly supported higher education and research in his roles as prochancellor of the University of Leicester, a member of the Society for Drug Research, and a trustee of the Darwin Trust of Edinburgh. He also served as chairman of the British Pharma Group and of the NorthWest Science Council. In June 2002 he was appointed president of the European Federation of Pharmaceutical Industries and Associations (EFPIA) at its General Assembly in Bruges for a two-year term, having previously served as the federation's vice president. He served as a nonexecutive director with Lloyds TSB Group, Amersham International, and several other companies.

McKillop listed his interests as sports, reading, music, and—emblematic of his hands-on approach to both life and business—carpentry. He received knighthood in the 2002 Queen's Birthday Honours list for services to the pharmaceuticals industry. In recognition of his work and commitments to education and the wider community, he was the recipient of a number of honorary degrees, from Manchester in 1999 and from Glasgow, Leicester, and Huddersfield in 2000.

See also entries on AstraZeneca PLC and Zeneca Group PLC in *International Directory of Company Histories.*

SOURCES FOR FURTHER INFORMATION

"AstraZeneca: A Look at a Key Feature of AstraZeneca Business," Biz/ed, http://www.bized.ac.uk/compfact/astrazen/az9.htm.

Capel, Kerry, "AstraZeneca: A Drug Merger That's Working," *BusinessWeek*, November 15, 1999, p. 36.

McKillop, Thomas, "Full Interview with Tom McKillop, CEO AstraZeneca, President EFPIA," March 17, 2004, http://www.euractiv.com/cgi-bin/cgint.exe/1912988-752?204&OIDN=2250104&-home=search.

Speech by Tom McKillop at AstraZeneca Information Meeting in Stockholm, May 19, 1999, AstraZeneca press release, http://www.astrazeneca.com/pressrelease/269.aspx.

"The Top 25 Managers—Managers to Watch: Thomas McKillop, StarZeneca," *BusinessWeekOnline*, January 8, 2001, http://www.businessweek.com/2001/01_02/b3714031.htm.

—David Tulloch

■■■

Henry A. McKinnell Jr.
1943–
Chairman and chief executive officer, Pfizer

Nationality: Canadian.

Born: February 23, 1943, in Vancouver, British Columbia, Canada.

Education: University of British Columbia, BA, 1965; Stanford University Graduate School of Business, MBA, 1967; PhD, 1969.

Family: Son of Henry A. McKinnell Sr. (owner and operator of cargo vessels) and wife (name unknown); married (divorced); children: four.

Career: American Standard, 1969–1971; Pfizer, 1971–1979, various international posts; 1979–1985, president of Pfizer Asia; 1992–1995, executive vice president; 1995–97, executive vice president and CFO; 1997–1999, executive vice president and president of Global Pharmaceuticals Group; 1999–2001, president of Global Pharmaceuticals Group, president, and COO; 2001–, chairman and CEO.

Awards: Top CEO in the Pharmaceutical Industry, *Institutional Investor*, 2003; Global Leadership Award, United Nations Association of the United States of America, 2003; Corporate Service Award, Woodrow Wilson Institute for International Scholars, 2003; Cleveland E. Dodge Medal for Distinguished Service to Education, Columbia University Teachers College, 2003.

Address: Pfizer, 235 East 42nd Street, New York, New York 10017; http://www.pfizer.com.

■ Dr. Henry A. McKinnell Jr. became chief executive officer of Pfizer in January 2001 and chairman of the board in April 2001 after holding a series of senior executive positions spanning more than 32 years with the company. During his time at Pfizer, McKinnell helped turn the company from a leader in the pharmaceutical industry into a "transforming force" with the acquisitions of Warner-Lambert in 2000 and Pharmacia in 2003 and the subsequent successful integration of both firms, forming a behemoth that earned $45 billion in

2003. Observers described McKinnell as polished, stately, and avuncular, yet also exacting, passionate, and sometimes impatient. A deeply moral man, McKinnell expanded Pfizer's philanthropic activities both in the United States and in the developing world.

PERSONAL BACKGROUND

McKinnell was a third-generation Canadian brought up in Vancouver, British Columbia. He went to a Christian Brothers school through the eighth grade, an experience that imbued him with a strong moral code. His father owned and operated cargo vessels; during his teen years and through college he spent school vacations working on his father's ships as a deckhand and first mate. He gained a penchant for racing Austin Healey sports cars in events sponsored by the Sports Car Club of America and spent two summers racing many West Coast tracks, from Vancouver to Los Angeles.

He enrolled at the University of British Columbia intending to major in chemical engineering and eventually become a college professor. He described himself as an average student with a greater focus on extracurricular activities than academics during the first half of his five-year stint at the university. He then married and decided to "get serious," switching his major to business administration and finishing second in his class.

Based on his achievement McKinnell received a $10,000-a-year fellowship to the Stanford Business School, a tidy sum at that time—it was in fact more money than most full-time jobs offered. He accepted and earned a doctorate within three and a half years. Although he received several offers to join business-school faculties as an assistant professor, McKinnell instead elected to gain practical experience in the business world. He accepted his first job at American Standard, turning down an offer from Pfizer. After working in Brussels for two years, he accepted a position with Pfizer in Tokyo for what he thought would be another two-year period, after which he would return to academia.

An early riser, McKinnell woke up between four and five in the morning and put in 11- to 12-hour days at the office. He lived in Manhattan and on the weekends went to a retreat home in Greenwich, Connecticut, where he enjoyed swimming, fishing, skiing, and bike-riding. An avid sportsman, he ran a full marathon while living in Japan and competed in four mini-triathlons in Greenwich.

EARLY CAREER AT PFIZER: A GLOBAL FOCUS, AN UPWARD PATH

When McKinnell joined Pfizer in 1971 in Tokyo, he requested sales training, a request that was initially puzzling to his new employer given his possession of a doctorate. But McKinnell brushed past the perceived diminutive nature of sales positions, knowing that understanding how sales worked would be essential to understanding a business as a whole. His request was granted, and he developed an appreciation for pharmaceutical sales, medical marketing, product development, and product commercialization. This knowledge, coupled with early exposure to international business, laid the foundation for a career at Pfizer that spiraled inexorably upward until McKinnell was named chief executive officer in 2001.

After three years in Tokyo, Pfizer gave McKinnell an opportunity that was rare for a 30-year-old who still thought he would get back to teaching: the chance to run Pfizer's operations in Iran and Afghanistan, which comprised a fully self-contained pharmaceutical business. The opportunity allowed McKinnell to learn about all aspects of the business—sales, marketing, manufacturing, operations, and product development.

Subsequently, McKinnell was named president of Pfizer's Asia Division, based in Hong Kong, until 1984. His first post in the United States came afterward in corporate strategic planning, where he was instrumental in convincing Pfizer's board of directors to alter the company's capital structure in order to implement a share repurchase program. This move was significant in that up to that time Pfizer had been debt-free; the new program would require that the company borrow in order to buy back its own shares. McKinnell effectively argued that the company's long-term growth prospects would more than offset the interest that would accrue in paying back the loan. His assessment proved right and successive chief financial officers continued the program.

McKinnell continued to move quickly up the corporate ranks. He was named chief financial officer, his first finance job, and president of Pfizer's U.S. Pharmaceutical Division in 1994. By 1997 he was again promoted: as president of Pfizer's Global Pharmaceuticals Group, the company's principal operating division, he was responsible for worldwide pharmaceutical operations. He was executive vice president from 1992 to 1999 and then president and chief operating officer from May 1999 to May 2001. In January 2001 he took over the reins as chief executive officer from William C. Steere Jr., with whom McKinnell had worked closely for over a decade. By May 2001 he added the position of chairman of the board.

Steere had ended his decade-long tenure as CEO having achieved his goal of making Pfizer the number one company in the world, which had come with the 2000 merger of Pfizer and Warner-Lambert. With the company having achieved the industry leadership position just as he entered the role of chief executive, McKinnell wanted to articulate a new vision that would push Pfizer to ever greater heights. He faced some daunting challenges: an industry under attack due to pricing issues, patent expirations for several blockbuster drugs (with sales of at least $1 billion), and growing calls to expand the availability of prescription drugs to the needy and those without insurance. McKinnell would have to apply his considerable executive, political, and leadership skills to address these issues.

AT THE HELM OF PFIZER: NEW VISION, GREATER ACHIEVEMENTS

One of McKinnell's first actions as CEO was to gather a group of the 25 most senior managers to define a new vision and mission for Pfizer. McKinnell posed a simple yet compelling question: "How do we move beyond number one?" With McKinnell leading, the group decided that Pfizer's new vision would be to hold a position as "the world's most valued company to patients, to customers, to business partners, to colleagues, and to communities where we work and live" (Becker, March 2002). In order to achieve this transformation, the group defined six areas that needed change, most of which had been addressed by early 2004.

FOCUS ON CORE BUSINESS: HUMAN PHARMACEUTICALS

As CEO, McKinnell continued to implement a key strategy he had been espousing since arriving at Pfizer's New York headquarters: to focus Pfizer on human pharmaceuticals by selling off noncore businesses. Indeed, in early 2004 human pharmaceuticals was the largest business segment, making up 92 percent of Pfizer revenues. At that time Pfizer announced plans to review some 60 noncore consumer products for possible sale. In 2002 and 2003 Pfizer divested itself of several of these noncore business units.

IMPLEMENTING THE VISION THROUGH STRATEGIC MERGERS AND ACQUISITIONS

What set Pfizer apart from the hundreds of other large corporations who had attempted large-scale mergers in the hopes of achieving operational efficiencies and increased competitiveness was that under McKinnell's leadership the company successfully completed not one but two mergers of big pharmaceutical companies. In 2000 Pfizer acquired Warner-Lambert, which had been marketing Lipitor, one of the world's most prescribed drugs of those used for lowering levels of low-density lipoprotein (LDL), or "bad" cholesterol. The acquisition saved the combined company some $2.5 billion; the new market share exceeded the two companies' previous market shares combined, increasing from 7.8 percent to 8.2 percent.

In April 2003 Pfizer completed the acquisition of Pharmacia Corporation, another major drug manufacturer, for $56 billion. Market share increased to 11 percent among world pharmaceuticals. Pfizer now had 10 drugs generating annual sales of $1 billion each and one drug with sales of over $8 billion. By 2004 Pfizer marketed eight of the world's 25 best-selling medicines and 14 products considered leaders in their therapeutic categories. The company had over 130,000 employees worldwide and a pipeline of over two hundred projects in research and development.

McKinnell sought to fill out the R&D pipeline with strategic acquisitions of biotechnology companies. In December 2003 Pfizer announced the acquisition of Esperion Therapeutics, the biopharmaceutical company that developed therapies targeting high-density lipoprotein (HDL) to treat cardiovascular disease. Other acquisitions were expected in 2004.

DELIVERING THE NUMBERS: PFIZER'S FINANCIAL PERFORMANCE

McKinnell consistently delivered numbers that kept Wall Street analysts humming. In 2001 Pfizer earned revenues of $29 billion and a net income of $7.8 billion, up 11 percent and 109 percent over 2000, respectively. These numbers reflected the acquisition of Warner-Lambert. In 2002 Pfizer earned revenues of $32.4 billion and a net income of $9.1 billion, up 12 percent and 17 percent over 2001, respectively.

Pfizer posted 2003 revenues of $45.2 billion, up 40 percent over 2002—but a net income of only $3.9 billion, down 57 percent from 2002. These numbers were reported under GAAP ("generally accepted accounting practices") and reflected the charges incurred as a result of the acquisition of Pharmacia. In financial reports Pfizer reconciled these GAAP numbers to numbers that took into account purchase-accounting rules, which required inclusion of noncash charges. In the adjusted numbers net income became $12.7 billion, up 28 percent over 2002.

CORPORATE CITIZENSHIP

Pfizer had always had a long tradition of good corporate citizenship; under McKinnell's leadership the tradition expanded. In 2002 Pfizer donated $2 million each working day through various channels. Rather than as an obligation, McKinnell viewed corporate philanthropy more synergistically, noting that "when we help patients in need, we enhance our

standing with physicians, win respect in local communities, and create better working relationships with regulatory authorities. When we keep our people out of hospitals and enable them to function as productive members of society, we bolster economies and become the allies of governments" (Flynn, September 2003). This philosophy positioned Pfizer favorably; but McKinnell forthrightly acknowledged that Pfizer's approach was as good for profits and shareholders as for patients and communities.

In March 2002 McKinnell was appointed by President George W. Bush to the Presidential Advisory Council on HIV/AIDS, which was established to formulate recommendations on how best to ensure the highest quality research, prevention, and treatment for the disease. McKinnell traveled to African nations that had been hit particularly hard by HIV/AIDS, meeting with government leaders, nongovernment organizations (NGOs), and health-care providers in order to formulate a strategy to combat the disease.

Launched in December 2000, the Diflucan Partnership Program was initiated with the Government of South Africa in a public-private venture. At no charge health-care workers distributed Pfizer's Diflucan, a drug that fought two opportunistic fungal infections that together struck over half of African patients with full-blown AIDS. Pfizer later expanded the program to 12 other African countries. At the end of 2002 the program had distributed almost three million doses worth over $100 million and trained approximately 11,000 health-care professionals in the latest AIDS-care practices.

Pfizer was the first U.S. pharmaceutical company and the largest U.S. company overall to sign the United Nations Global Compact, created by the U.N. Secretary General Kofi Anan to distribute the benefits of globalization across all nations.

Back home McKinnell took a proactive step to control Medicaid costs in Florida. He contacted Governor Jeb Bush and suggested that, as prescription drug costs accounted for only 10 percent or $70 million of the state's overall Medicaid bill, some of the money could be used for patient education and counseling that would in turn create better health awareness. Pfizer carefully monitored the results of the program, hoping that McKinnell's unorthodox approach would create favorable outcomes and be duplicated in other states. On another thorny domestic health-care issue, McKinnell expanded the availability of prescription drugs to low-income seniors on Medicare. The Pfizer for Living Share Card provided needed medications for a flat $15 fee to qualified seniors.

After the terrorist attacks on New York and Washington, D.C., on September 11, 2001, Pfizer donated medicines, health-care products, and supply services to those in need. Pfizer and the Pfizer Foundation pledged $10 million to the relief effort and the company also matched approximately $430,000 in employee contributions. Yet another humanitarian effort was referred to as "Hank's Peace Corps" within Pfizer. Approximately 20 to 25 medically and technically trained people spent six months to a year working in developing countries, helping health-care providers, faith-based workers, and members of NGOs improve countries' health-care delivery services.

BLENDING EAST AND WEST: AN "AGGRESSIVE CONSENSUS-SEEKING" MANAGEMENT STYLE

Two factors characterized McKinnell's management style: consensus seeking and cross-functional teamwork—both practices originating from his early exposure to Japanese-style management techniques.

Associates at Pfizer described McKinnell as "an aggressive consensus seeker" at a time when many American corporations were run under a military-style command-and-control structure. McKinnell was a leader who encouraged open discussion of issues but knew how to bring closure to them. Deftly finding that zone of agreement where all minds involved could back a final decision, McKinnell effectively imported consensus-seeking to Pfizer.

While most American companies struggled to improve internal operations by breaking down the barriers to communication inherent in silo-like functionally oriented organizations, Pfizer instead adopted a Japanese-style cross-functional team structure. Teams were composed of members of different functional areas who met together regularly over long periods—sometimes years—to see a product through all the processes of development, regulatory approval, and consumer marketing.

The would-be scholar and college professor was able to cultivate a culture of agreement and collaboration at a time when corporate chieftains typically operated with a hierarchical mindset and expected subordinates to follow the chains of command that they had successfully climbed. That Hank McKinnell was able to develop this leadership style while climbing to the same top job as his contemporaries suggests that what worked for him also worked for Pfizer.

Industry analysts gave positive assessments to McKinnell's performance at Pfizer through 2004. As he continued to promise double-digit returns, the company remained a Wall Street favorite. Referring to the two successful megamergers, one industry observer noted that Pfizer was in a "league of its own" (Becker, March 2002). Another analyst noted that Pfizer was at the "peak of its game."

Media observers covering Pfizer attempted to present McKinnell even-handedly. Lee Clifford of *Fortune* magazine described McKinnell as "polished, tall, stately, and stiff with a barely perceptible Canadian accent" (October 30, 2000). John Simons, also of *Fortune*, characterized him thus: "warm and

avuncular one minute, exacting and impatient the next, McKinnell is an odd cross between Mr. Rogers and the cranky Dr. 'Bones' McCoy from Star Trek. In a single conversation, he can deliver a stirring monologue about curing the world's ills, then launch into a stern rant against consumer activists who think drug companies charge too much for their wares" (Boersig, October 2003).

Robert L. Joss, the Dean of the Stanford Graduate School of Business, was proud of one of his most successful alumni: "When we see in one of our alumni a person of integrity, an effective manager at the highest levels, and a business leader who understands that business is a social institution which must keep the public trust, we—as a school of management— want to recognize those achievements. Hank McKinnell has demonstrated in every way that he is a leader—as the head of the largest pharmaceutical company in the world, as the overseer of the firm's tremendous research efforts aimed at improving the human condition, and as a corporate citizen" (Lee, February 18, 2001).

THE FIRST AMONG EQUALS: MCKINNELL'S REPUTATION IN THE INDUSTRY AND COMMUNITY

The clearest indication of McKinnell's reputation among his peers was his election in 2001 as chairman emeritus of the industry's leading trade organization, the Pharmaceutical Research and Manufacturers of America (PhRMA), a group composed of the CEOs of leading research-based pharmaceutical and biotechnology companies. In his first address McKinnell laid out a blueprint for a reformed health-care system in the 21st century. McKinnell was also chairman of PhRMA's Business–Higher Education Forum.

After ascending to the chief executive's role, McKinnell garnered a series of accolades. In 2003 *Institutional Investor* magazine named McKinnell the top CEO in the pharmaceutical industry. He was also named chair of Pfizer's Executive Committee, was a member of the Pfizer Leadership Team, and was a director of Pfizer since June 1997. He was a member of the influential Business Roundtable (BRT), an organization of business leaders; vice chairman of the BRT's Corporate Governance Task Force; and chairman of its SEC subcommittee. McKinnell sat on the boards of several companies, including ExxonMobil Corporation, Moody's Corporation, and John Wiley & Sons. He was chairman of the Stanford University Graduate School of Business Advisory Council and a Fellow of the New York Academy of Medicine and the Massachusetts Institute of Technology Corporation. McKinnell also sat on the boards of trustees of several organizations in New York City.

Under McKinnell's leadership Pfizer's reputation rose as well. In February 2003 *Fortune* magazine ranked Pfizer 14th on the list of the World's Most Admired Companies. In October 2003 *Med Ad News*, a leading industry publication, named Pfizer the Most Admired Pharmaceutical Company in the industry. In March 2003 *Investor Relations Magazine* awarded Pfizer the Best Corporate Governance award. In 2002 the *Journal of Philanthropy* named Pfizer the world's most generous company. In 2001 *Fortune* named Pfizer the second smartest company in America, after General Electric.

See also entry on Pfizer Inc. in *International Directory of Company Histories.*

SOURCES FOR FURTHER INFORMATION

Becker, Don C., "Prescription for Success," *Greenwich*, March 2002, pp. 94–102.

Boersig, Charles, "Pfizer, Amgen, Allergan Top the List," *MedAdNews*, October 2003, p. 1.

Clifford, Lee, "Tyrannosaurus Rex," *Fortune*, February 18, 2001.

Colvin, Geoffrey, "How to Avoid an M and A Hangover," *Fortune*, August 21, 2001.

Flynn, Don, "McKinnell's Heart Beats for World's Faith-Based Groups," *Spiritual Herald*, September 2003.

Simons, John, "King of the Pill," *Fortune*, March 30, 2003.

Warren, Chris, "Merge, Grow, Repeat," *Continental*, December 2003, pp. 35–37.

—Carole S. Moussalli

■ ■ ■

C. Steven McMillan

ca. 1946–

Chairman, chief executive officer, and president, Sara Lee Corporation

Nationality: American.

Born: ca. 1946.

Education: Auburn University, BS; Harvard Business School, MBA.

Career: McKinsey & Company, 1973–1976, management consultant; Sara Lee Corporation, 1976–1979, president and CEO of Aqualux water-processing division; 1979–1982, president and CEO of Electrolux-Canada affiliate; 1982–1986, president and CEO of Electrolux; 1986–1990, senior vice president for strategy development; 1990–1993, head of packaged-meats, bakery, and food-service businesses; 1993–1997, head of packaged-meats, bakery, food-service, coffee, groceries, and household and body-care businesses; 1997–2001, chairman, president, and COO; 2001–, chairman, CEO, and president.

Address: Sara Lee Corporation, Three First National Plaza, Chicago, Illinois 60602-4250; http://www.saralee.com.

■ C. Steven McMillan became the chief executive officer of Sara Lee in 2001, capping a career with the corporation that stretched back over a quarter of a century. He came to head the company at a time of crisis, when John H. Bryan, the previous head of the corporation and one of the longest-serving executives of any Fortune 500 company, retired after 25 years at the helm and corporate stock had dropped precipitously after a failed restructuring attempt. McMillan made part of his mission as president and CEO to eliminate redundancies among the company's diverse manufacturing structures, spin off businesses that did not relate to Sara Lee's core interests—food, underwear, and household products—and spur the company's growth, centralizing oversight and concentrating on marketing rather than manufacturing.

McMillan responded to the crisis he inherited by emphasizing speed and profitability, eliminating the jobs of about 5 percent of the corporation's workforce, and restructuring food

holdings. In order to raise money he sold off stock in some of the company's most profitable holdings and disposed of the least profitable subdivisions altogether; Coach leather goods, Champion athletic wear, and PYA/Monarch food service were among the labels that McMillan sold either altogether or in part. He then authorized the purchase of companies that, though geographically more diverse, produced goods that were closer to Sara Lee's redefined core interests. The company acquired Uniao, the Brazilian coffee manufacturer and distributor; Sol y Oro, the Argentine underwear firm; Earthgrains, the bakery and frozen-dough company based in St. Louis, Missouri; and a stake in the Johnsonville Sausage Company, also located in the United States.

LONGTIME MANAGER

By the time he stepped into the head office at Sara Lee, McMillan had logged a great deal of experience in management. He worked for McKinsey & Company, the Chicago, Illinois–based management-consulting company, between 1973 and 1976. He then left consulting to join Sara Lee Corporation as the president and chief executive officer of the Aqualux water-processing division. He stayed with Aqualux for three years before being promoted to president and CEO of Sara Lee's Electrolux-Canada affiliate; in 1982 he became president and CEO of Electrolux. In 1986 he was promoted to senior vice president for strategy development of the entire corporation. Four years later he became the head of the packaged meats, bakery, and food-service businesses, and three years after that he added responsibility for coffee, groceries, and household and body-care businesses. That same year he was named to the corporate board of directors, and in 1997 he was promoted to chairman, president, and chief operating officer; his further promotion to chief executive officer occurred in 2001.

FROM A LOVING PARENT

The modern Sara Lee Corporation originated in the late 1930s, when the Canadian businessman Nathan Cummings created a business called Consolidated Foods. In 1956 Cummings's company merged with the Kitchens of Sara Lee, a firm created by Charles Lubin, who had given his daughter's name to his company. After 10 years Consolidated branched out into apparel and household goods, and in 1985 the company officially changed its name to Sara Lee Corporation, "to identify itself with its best-known brand," according to writer Gene Epstein of *Barron's* (June 26, 2000). By the end of the century Sara Lee boasted almost 140,000 employees in over 40 different countries and marketed such well-known brands as Ball Park, Brylcreem, Chock Full o'Nuts, Earthgrains, Hanes, Hillshire Farms, Jimmy Dean, Playtex, Ty-D-Bol, and Wonderbra.

STUMBLING FORWARD

Even before McMillan took over as CEO in 2001, Sara Lee had undergone several severe crises in management and public relations. In 1998 the Bil Mar Foods division of the corporation unknowingly distributed hot dogs and lunch meat infected with the bacterium *lysteria* from one of its Michigan plants. The bacteria were responsible for a minimum of 15 deaths and six miscarriages due to food poisoning; about 80 other serious cases of illness were linked to the infestation. Sara Lee ended up paying $200,000 in fines and an additional $3 million to help fund research of food-borne diseases. The company also settled a class-action lawsuit filed on behalf of the families of those who died or were made seriously ill by the bacteria; the settlement totaled around $5 million.

Sara Lee's stock prices took a hit when the public became aware of the company's responsibility for the minor outbreak. Shares had been trading at over $30 in 1998; by the spring of 2000 share value had dropped by more than half, bottoming out at $14 in March. As chairman and president McMillan announced a sound strategic plan in July 2000 that helped bring stock values up to about $19 a share by that autumn. In 2001, thanks to McMillan's cost-cutting measures, the corporation posted earnings of $2.3 billion despite an absence of an increase in revenues. In 2002 revenues actually shrank, to about $1 billion by midyear. Sales in early 2003 dropped another 2 percent, even though overall profits increased by nearly 5 percent.

In the spring of 2003 another public-relations disaster struck, as Sara Lee found itself under investigation by the federal government for potential misreporting of rebates issued to grocers in the Netherlands by the company's Dutch arm. Pallavi Gogoi declared in *BusinessWeek*, "There is no evidence so far that Sara Lee made any improper payments" (May 26, 2003). Meanwhile McMillan blamed members of his sales staff for overreporting rebate information to the executives of U.S. Foodservice—Sara Lee's Dutch food-management company—and to the auditing firm Deloitte & Touche. Although he continued to insist that the corporation's records were accurate, stockholders received the news with cynicism. By May 2003 stock prices had fallen once more, by almost a quarter.

Still another factor in Sara Lee's struggle to redefine itself was the fluctuating European currency market and the weak-

ening U.S. economy. The declining euro, which was introduced in the European Union while Sara Lee was undergoing corporate restructuring and reorganization, made earnings from European businesses worth less than had been anticipated. In addition investors felt that McMillan had failed to develop and promote new products that would help turn the company's finances around and capture market shares from rivals like Kraft; Sara Lee's crop of businesses were simply not performing up to expectations. Long-established brands like L'eggs and Chock Full o'Nuts lost sales to competing products. McMillan's acquisition of Earthgrains was challenged by investors; by paying $2.8 billion for the company—which was the second-largest bakery in the United States—McMillan had effectively almost doubled Sara Lee's debt. The gains he had expected to materialize from the Earthgrains acquisition had yet to appear, and investors began to believe that the CEO had paid more than the St. Louis–based company was worth. The $300 million in anticipated growth had failed to materialize.

CROSSED FINGERS

Yet McMillan had made the purchase of Earthgrains not just for its product line but also for its distribution system, wherein almost five thousand routes were used to put products directly into stores nationwide. Ownership of that system meant that Sara Lee would no longer be dependent on outside distributors to place its products in stores. Through the addition of the Earthgrains distribution system Sara Lee products would be made directly available to over 60 percent of the U.S. population. McMillan explained in a corporate media release, "The new business will be more competitive and certainly more profitable than our separate, existing operations" (July 2, 2001). That increased competitiveness, he believed, would translate into profits for shareholders.

See also entry on Sara Lee Corporation in *International Directory of Company Histories*.

SOURCES FOR FURTHER INFORMATION

Barboza, David, "Fast Cars, Harleys, and Cheesecake," *New York Times*, July 15, 2001.

Epstein, Gene, "Just Desserts," *Barron's*, June 26, 2000, p. 28.

Forster, Julie, "Sara Lee: Changing the Recipe—Again; McMillan Expects Results in '03, but Will Investors Wait?" *BusinessWeek*, September 10, 2001, p. 125.

Gogoi, Pallavi, "Sara Lee: No Piece of Cake; CEO McMillan Has Cut Costs, but Investors Want Growth," *BusinessWeek*, May 26, 2003, p. 66.

"Sara Lee Corporation Taps Veteran Leader as Next CEO," *Sara Lee Corporation*, January 27, 2000, http://www.saralee.com/newsroom/news_release_popup.aspx?id=31.

"Sara Lee Corporation to Acquire Earthgrains for $2.8 Billion: Becomes Number-Two Player in Fresh Bread Category," *Sara Lee Corporation*, July 2, 2001, http://www.saralee.com/newsroom/news_release_popup.aspx?id=57.

"Sara Lee Pleads Guilty, Will Pay $4.4 Million over Tainted Meat," *Wall Street Journal*, June 25, 2001.

Weber, Joseph, "No Cakewalk at Sara Lee: The Incoming CEO Has a New Plan—but Will It Suffice?" *BusinessWeek*, June 12, 2000, p. 56.

—Kenneth R. Shepherd

Scott G. McNealy

■ ■ ■

1954–

Cofounder, chairman, and chief executive officer, Sun Microsystems

Nationality: American.

Born: November 13, 1954, in Columbus, Indiana.

Education: Harvard University, BA, 1976; Stanford University, MBA, 1980.

Family: Son of Raymond William McNealy (business executive) and Marmaline (maiden name unknown; homemaker); married Susan Ingemanson, 1994; children: four.

Career: Sun Microsystems, 1982–1984, vice president, manufacturing and operations; 1984–1999, chairman, president, and chief executive officer; 1999–2002, chairman and chief executive officer; 2002–2004, chairman, president, and chief executive officer; 2004–, chairman and chief executive officer.

Address: Sun Microsystems, 4150 Network Circle, Santa Clara, California 95054; http://www.sun.com.

Scott G. McNealy. *AP/Wide World Photos.*

■ With three other young entrepreneurs, Scott G. McNealy founded Sun Microsystems in 1982. Despite having no technical background, McNealy's leadership helped to develop Sun into one of the world's leading computer companies. The success of the business rested upon McNealy's determination, business acumen, and ability to motivate those who worked around him. Many analysts commented on McNealy's willingness to take risks and reinvent the company in order to adjust to changing industry conditions. In particular, McNealy's dedication to the company vision, "the network is the computer," meant that Sun was ideally placed to take advantage of the rise of the Internet in the mid-1990s.

McNealy gained a reputation as a brash and aggressive CEO, notorious for his outspoken comments about his business rivals. McNealy was Microsoft's harshest and most vocal critic throughout the 1990s, and he was called on to testify during congressional hearings into competition in the software industry. His willingness to poke fun at himself and his rivals

resulted in memorable wisecracks and some colorful publicity stunts, making him one of the more unconventional CEOs in corporate America. However, despite the loud public persona, those who worked closely with McNealy emphasized his business insight, his appreciation of his coworkers, and his ability to relate to many different types of people. While McNealy could not be regarded as a typical CEO, the company he built in many ways typified the phenomenal growth and technological achievement that was associated with Silicon Valley during the last two decades of the twentieth century.

EARLY EXPERIENCE

Growing up, McNealy gained exposure to the business world through his interest in his father's job as a manager at American Motors. His father eventually became vice chairman of the company, and the experience of watching American Motors decline was important in shaping the younger McNealy's understanding of business. Sports were also important in McNealy's early life. He developed early passions for hockey and golf, which continued into adulthood; McNealy was named the top CEO golfer by *Golf Digest* in 2002, and he continued to play hockey into his 40s. When the McNealy family settled in Bloomfield Hills, Michigan, McNealy attended the elite Cranbrook prep school. He valued the atmosphere at the school, especially the experience of being around bright people and being treated as an adult, which he said better prepared him for life at college. Although he was not a dedicated student, McNealy was able to gain entrance to Harvard. He enrolled as a premedical student, intending to become a doctor, but switched to economics. This was due mainly to the influence of an economics teacher, Bill Raduchel, who was later to join him as chief information officer at Sun. Despite listing his main interests at college as beer and golf, McNealy managed to graduate from Harvard in 1976.

While trying to gain entrance to Stanford Business School, McNealy spent two years working as a plant foreman at Rockwell International, in a factory that made body panels for tractors. This practical experience in a manufacturing environment proved to be extremely valuable. McNealy later said that this was better preparation for running a company than anything he learned at Harvard or Stanford. Eventually accepted into Stanford, on his third attempt, McNealy was one of the few MBA students to concentrate on manufacturing, rather than finance. Upon graduation in 1980 McNealy went to work for FMC Corporation, building Bradley tanks for the U.S. Army. In 1981 he took a job as manufacturing manager with Onyx, a small company manufacturing computers. While he had no technical knowledge of the computer industry, McNealy's manufacturing experience and people skills impressed the CEO at Onyx, Doug Broyles: "We brought him on as director of operations, and put manufacturing and purchasing under him. Within a couple of weeks, Scott had the 50-year-old manufacturing guy's respect and they were working as a team. Scott went out on the line and talked to people" (*High Noon*). Throughout his career, and despite his privileged background, McNealy cultivated an image as a down-to-earth, blue-collar workingman, which appealed to many people.

STANFORD UNIVERSITY NETWORK

McNealy's manufacturing experience did not make him an obvious candidate for founding a Silicon Valley start-up company. However, in 1982 a college friend from Stanford made McNealy an exciting offer. Vinod Khosla was a passionate and driven entrepreneur, with an exciting vision for the future of computing. He met Andy Bechtolsheim, a PhD student who was working on a project called the Stanford University Network, or SUN. Khosla recognized that Bechtolsheim's work

could provide the solution to his idea of a powerful workstation to replace the minicomputers that software engineers were using. This workstation would operate while plugged into a computer network, allowing for electronic collaboration. Khosla invited McNealy to join the project because of his valuable business and manufacturing experience. A fourth member of the team, Bill Joy, was brought in for his programming genius to develop a Unix operating system for the prototype workstation.

The four men, all in their 20s, had very little business experience between them, but they had passion and ambition to make Sun Microsystems a success. The first Sun-2 workstations hit the market in late 1982. Few people in the industry took the upstarts seriously. At the time, Apollo Computers dominated the workstation market, and its staff joked about the "kids" at Stanford. But after Sun beat out Apollo for a crucial deal to supply workstations to Computervision, it was apparent that they had to be taken seriously. Sun's aggressive campaign for the contract, even after Computervision had originally decided to go with Apollo, became a hallmark of Sun and of McNealy's business style.

Initially, McNealy's position within the company was as vice president of manufacturing. Khosla, as the visionary force behind the new company, was CEO. But it soon became apparent that it was McNealy, not Khosla, who was providing leadership to the company's expanding workforce. Of the four founders, only McNealy had the personal skills and experience to deal with the varied demands of running a company. As McNealy described his role in these early days, "I couldn't program anything. I still can't program anything. I wasn't the technical guru. I wasn't the visionary. I was kind of the glue that kept everybody together and helped enunciate what our goals were, how we're going to get there, and kind of cleaned up after the engineers and made sure the customers got what we promised them" ("Scott McNealy Oral History"). This ability to crystallize and implement the vision of others became one of McNealy's strengths throughout his career.

Increasing dissatisfaction among staff and board members over Khosla's performance as CEO led to his leaving Sun in 1984. As the only obvious successor, McNealy was named interim CEO, but the board was concerned that this brash young man, who often lacked tact or discretion, did not have the business acumen required to run the company. A search outside the company failed to produce a suitable alternative, however, and the board decided to stick with McNealy. This was a big gamble, as McNealy was inexperienced, had little technical knowledge of the industry, and had a reputation for cockiness and arrogance. However, his confidence, energy, and total commitment to making the company succeed helped convince the board that he could do the job. Their faith proved well founded. As Sun Microsystems developed from a brash renegade into an industry powerhouse, so too did its CEO.

CHALLENGES

McNealy faced many challenges over the next two decades. His abilities were questioned at times and his response to these challenges highlighted some of his main attributes as a leader. One of the first major trials McNealy faced as CEO came in 1989, when, after several years of rapid growth, Sun posted its first quarterly loss. The company had grown at a phenomenal rate, surpassing its main competitor in 1987 and reaching $1 billion in revenue in 1988, but such rapid growth caused difficulties. Under McNealy's leadership, Sun had placed heavy emphasis on gaining market share, often at the expense of profit margins. Problems with internal systems meant that it was unable to manage production and keep up with demand for its products. At the same time, several key executives left the company, raising questions about McNealy's management style. Some business analysts suggested that the company had outgrown McNealy's abilities as CEO.

In response, McNealy instituted changes in the company's strategy that showed his maturity as a business leader. He put new focus on the importance of costs as well as growth and developed new internal accounting processes that controlled spending. He also made the crucial decision to consolidate Sun's products, basing everything around the new microprocessor developed by Sun's own engineers, the SPARC chip. Other products based on the Intel chip or Motorola technologies were discarded. This was risky, as market acceptance of Sun's new technology was not yet established.

McNealy also initiated an important restructuring of the company during the early 1990s. He reorganized the company into seven planets, each of which represented sales and marketing focused around a specific product line. The new decentralized structure had positive and negative outcomes, which highlighted McNealy's strengths and weaknesses as a leader. While most people agreed that transformation was necessary, in practice executives bickered with each other over their own agendas. Rather than provide his team with practical guidance on how each planet was supposed to interact with the others, McNealy preferred to move on and focus on the next challenge, the next big sale. He often gave more attention to the newer technologies, while neglecting the older, more established parts of the business. This resulted in jealousy and tension between different areas. Nevertheless, the new structure did allow the various businesses within Sun to focus on establishing their own markets, without interference from the others. Many believe that the reorganization enabled the company as a whole to foster innovation in a way that would not have been possible in a more centralized business.

"THE NETWORK IS THE COMPUTER"

At the same time, Sun repositioned itself and carved out a new market away from workstations. Since the company's inception, McNealy had been a strong proponent of the slogan "the network is the computer." This meant that the true value of the computer did not come from the machine you could see on your desk, but instead from the power it derived from being connected to other computers. Sun's commitment to this model meant their machines had always been built with network capabilities, and they were much more powerful than PCs. As businesses began to understand the benefits of data networking in the early 1990s, Sun's workstations were ideally positioned to evolve into network-server computers. With the rise of the Internet, Sun's network slogan finally became clear to most people, and Sun's servers were at the center of the Web revolution. As the Merrill Lynch analyst Steven M. Milunovich claimed in a 1999 *BusinessWeek* article, "If you want to know where the computer industry is going, ask Sun" (January 18, 1999). McNealy's long-term dedication to the network vision had finally paid off.

The launch of Java also identified Sun as a leader of Internet-based technology. Java was a programming language developed by Sun's software engineers in the early 1990s. It was unique because it was not tied to a particular computer operating system. This meant it could be run on almost any computer at any time, provided that the computer had a Java interpreter. Therefore, it was ideal for the Internet environment, where millions of computer users needed to be able to talk to each other in one universal computer language. McNealy saw Java as the basis of a completely new platform for the computing world, one that could challenge the dominance of Microsoft. Inevitably, this would bring him into direct conflict with Microsoft.

THE BATTLE WITH MICROSOFT

When McNealy helped to found Sun, Microsoft had little presence in the industry. Before long, however, the industry would have to grapple with the growing dominance of Microsoft's Windows operating system combined with the Intel computer chip, an alliance that became known as Wintel. McNealy was quick to recognize that Wintel technology would eventually threaten Sun's key markets. As he saw it, Microsoft's CEO, Bill Gates, had a flawed vision for computing that dominated the industry due to Microsoft's unfair business practices. Never one to shy away from directly criticizing his competitors, McNealy's rhetoric reached new heights in the battle against Microsoft.

McNealy's attacks on the company certainly won Sun publicity, but not all were convinced that this was necessarily positive attention. Some people felt that McNealy's anti-Microsoft zeal crossed the line into obsession. For instance, banning all Sun employees from using software such as Microsoft PowerPoint was not popular, as staff needed to be able to operate with Microsoft products when dealing with customers. Many customers were also worried by McNealy's attacks on Microsoft and his apparent inflexibility over the issue of Wintel technology. What they wanted was to be able to run both kinds of technology, not to have to choose between them. McNealy's stubborn insistence that Sun would stand apart from Microsoft was in some senses ignoring the real world in which people needed to be able to operate with both.

The case of Java indicated how difficult cooperation between the two companies was. In 1996 Sun and Microsoft worked out a deal that licensed Microsoft to include Java in its Windows operating system. As the vast majority of desktop computers were running Windows, Sun needed Microsoft to incorporate Java if it was to become a truly universal computer language. At the same time, Microsoft had to use Java because it had been slow to reposition itself in the new world of Internet computing. The deal quickly collapsed, however, with Sun alleging that Microsoft violated the contract by making changes to Java that were incompatible with Sun's own systems. Inevitably, Sun sued Microsoft for breach of contract in 1997.

THE NEW MILLENNIUM

The 1990s had proved to be a great decade for Sun and McNealy. The company had been transformed into an innovative leader in the information-technology industry, and in Java it had one of the most exciting new technologies of the era. McNealy's vision for the Information Age and his crusade against Microsoft's monopoly gained him an appreciative audience. He became one of the most high-profile high-tech CEOs, winning over audiences with his willingness to poke fun at himself as well as his competitors. In a 1996 *BusinessWeek* article, Sun's former treasurer, Thomas J. Meredith, saw this as one of McNealy's key strengths: "His humor and ability to raise a crowd to its feet is in many respects exactly what you need in CEOs and leaders of today's industry" (January 22, 1996).

However, the year 2000 heralded the beginning of Scott McNealy's most difficult period as CEO. With the crash of the dot.com and telecommunications industries and an economic recession exacerbated by the September 11, 2001, terrorist attacks, technology spending plummeted. Sun faced increased competition in its server market from companies producing cheaper alternatives. Sales of Sun products were also badly affected by the Linux operating system, an open-source software that was free to anyone who could download it off the Internet. By 2004 Sun faced 12-consecutive quarters of shrinking

revenues, and it had been posting losses since 2002. The credit-rating agency Standard & Poor's dropped Sun's rating again in 2004, and substantial staff layoffs were announced. McNealy faced criticism for his apparent inability to return the company to profitability. Some analysts predicted the eventual demise of the company.

These factors were behind the shocking announcement in April 2004 that Sun and Microsoft were calling a truce. Microsoft would pay Sun $2 billion to resolve lawsuits, and the two companies agreed to work toward making their technologies more compatible. Many in the industry read the deal as a capitulation by McNealy. It also sparked speculation that he was approaching the end of his time as Sun CEO. Analysts questioned whether McNealy could work closely with Microsoft, when so much of his earlier motivation had come from trying to prevent Microsoft from gaining total control of the industry. There was little doubt that Sun needed to be taken in a new direction if it was to survive, and some people were unsure if McNealy was the right person to do this. McNealy's name was also mentioned as a possible successor at Oracle Corporation if Larry Ellison were to step down as CEO. But McNealy continued to lead the company that he helped to found, relying on continued innovation and new products to return his company to profitability.

See also entry on Sun Microsystems, Inc. in *International Directory of Company Histories.*

SOURCES FOR FURTHER INFORMATION

"Face Value—Desperate Embrace," *Economist*, April 10, 2004, p. 54.

Hof, Robert D., "Scott McNealy's Rising Sun," *BusinessWeek*, January 22, 1996, pp. 66–72.

Hof, Robert D., Steve Hamm, and Ira Sager, "Sun Power," *BusinessWeek*, January 18, 1999, pp. 64–70.

Schlender, Brent, "The Adventures of Scott McNealy— Javaman," *Fortune*, October 13, 1997, pp. 70–76.

"Scott McNealy Oral History," http://www.cwheroes.org/ oral_history_archive/mcnealy/2003.pdf.

Southwick, Karen, *High Noon: The Inside Story of Scott McNealy and the Rise of Sun Microsystems*, New York: John Wiley & Sons, 1999.

—Katrina Ford

■■■
W. James McNerney Jr.

1949–

Chairman and chief executive officer, 3M

Nationality: American.

Born: August 22, 1949, in Providence, Rhode Island.

Education: Yale University, BA, 1971; Harvard University, MBA, 1975.

Family: Son of Walter James McNerney (professor of public health); married (first wife's name unknown; divorced); married Haity; children: three (first marriage), two (second marriage).

Career: Procter & Gamble, 1975–1978, brand manager; McKinsey & Company, 1978–1982, senior manager; GE Mobile Communications, 1982–1988, general manager; GE Information Services, 1988–1989, president; GE Financial Services and GE Capital, 1989–1991, executive vice president; GE Electrical Distribution and Control, 1991–1992, president and chief executive officer; GE Asia-Pacific, 1993–1995, president; GE Lighting, 1995–1997, president; GE Aircraft Engines, 1997–2000, president and chief executive officer; 3M, 2000–, chairman and chief executive officer.

Awards: Vision for America Award, Keep America Beautiful, 2002; one of the Best Managers of 2003, *BusinessWeek*, 2003; CEO of the Year, *Industry Week*, 2003.

Address: 3M Corporate Headquarters, 3M Center, Saint Paul, Minnesota 55144-1000; http://www.3m.com.

W. James McNerney Jr. *AP/Wide World Photos.*

■ W. James McNerney was the first outsider to head 3M in the conglomerate's 100-year history. His success in this role cemented McNerney's reputation as one of America's most respected business leaders. An executive at General Electric since 1982 McNerney was one of CEO Jack Welch's leading protégés, a star of the highly vaunted GE leadership development system. McNerney's public profile soared in 2000, when he became one of the three contenders in the race to become CEO when Welch retired. When the position went to Jeffrey R. Immelt, McNerney accepted the offer to move to 3M.

Some observers predicted that McNerney's desire to import GE methods into 3M would clash with the culture of innovation and independence that was 3M's hallmark. However, McNerney's managerial qualities enabled him to instigate profound changes in the company while largely maintaining the trust of employees. McNerney was widely praised by staff and analysts as a dynamic and effective leader.

EARLY CAREER

McNerney attended Yale University, where he was on the baseball team with George W. Bush, and then Harvard Business School. After graduation, McNerney's first position was with Procter & Gamble, a company famous for its consumer products such as Pampers disposable diapers and Tide laundry detergent. At Procter & Gamble, McNerney worked in brand management for Ivory soap. He then moved to the management consultancy firm McKinsey & Company for four years.

GE TRAINING GROUND

In 1982 McNerney joined GE as general manager of GE Mobile Communications. Over the next 18 years he held seven positions at GE. Such movement was typical of the GE leadership development model, whereby promising managers moved from job to job every two or three years. The aim was to provide managers with diverse experience and exposure. By the time McNerney was named president and CEO of GE Aircraft Engines in September 1997, it had become obvious to observers that he was being groomed as a possible successor to Welch. McNerney developed a reputation as a skilled team builder and proved his ability to grow the businesses with which he was involved at GE. In particular, during McNerney's time as CEO at GE Aircraft Engines, revenue increased from $6.3 billion, the 1996 figure, to $10.6 billion in 1999. Profits increased from $1.2 billion to $2.1 billion. With McNerney at the helm, GE Aircraft Engines became the second largest profit-making division in GE, behind GE Capital. A major success during this time was restoration of the relationship between GE and Boeing, which led to a deal whereby GE90 engines were supplied to Boeing 777 jets. Boeing executives cited McNerney's sincerity, focus, and decisive, hands-on style as key factors in his success. Although he likely received many lucrative offers from outside GE, McNerney was committed to staying in the race for the top job.

OUTSIDER AT 3M

When Immelt was named Welch's successor in November 2000, McNerney and the third candidate, Robert J. Nardelli, became the most hotly recruited executives in corporate America. As a star of the GE system, McNerney faced extreme expectations of success. The day McNerney was named 3M's next CEO, replacing the retiring Livio D. DeSimone, the price of 3M shares jumped 11 percent. Some observers were skeptical about whether the GE "hotshots" could perform outside the confines of GE, and there were doubts about whether a company as insular as 3M would accept an outsider.

3M, established in 1902 as the Minnesota Mining and Manufacturing Company, had a long tradition of achieving innovation by allowing its researchers the independence to pursue their projects without interference from management. This approach had produced thousands of successful products, including household names such as Scotch tape, Scotchguard fabric protector, and Post-It notes. 3M leaders had always been chosen from within the company and were therefore largely committed to protecting the existing company culture. In the late 1990s, however, economic conditions changed. Although

still a sound performer, 3M had been affected by weakening overseas markets, which had a negative effect on revenue. In particular, the 1997–1998 downturn in the Asian economies hurt 3M, as did the high value of the U.S. dollar in 1996–2000. The company's share price also slipped as the U.S. stock market came to the end of a 10-year growth period. In addition, analysts believed that the 3M leadership lacked dynamism and that the venerable company was underperforming.

3M OR "3E"?

McNerney's mandate when he arrived at 3M was to reinvigorate the company. In particular, he aimed to reestablish the company as a growth venture with double-digit growth figures, whereas 3M had been achieving approximately 5 percent. McNerney focused his strategy on initiatives in five key areas: sourcing, indirect costs, e-productivity, 3M Acceleration, and Six Sigma. McNerney faced the difficult task of increasing efficiency and discipline in business while not stifling the innovation for which 3M was famous. One of McNerney's first moves as CEO was to order a global restructuring that cost approximately six thousand jobs, approximately 7 percent of the total workforce. Because this approach seemed to mirror that of Welch, infamous for his job cuts at GE, there were fears that McNerney was trying to turn 3M into "3E." Another profound change that raised fears of a GE takeover was McNerney's drive to implement Six Sigma into 3M. Six Sigma was the management method developed at Motorola in the early 1980s to eliminate inefficiencies and errors. The process was adopted by Welch and expanded to all parts of GE. McNerney also imported the GE system of grading employees to identify and reward performance, a program quite alien to the 3M culture. In addition, McNerney embarked on a major program of acquisitions as part of the aim of increasing sales growth at 3M. GE had been adept at integrating new business, but analysts questioned 3M's lack of experience in this area.

A crucial part of McNerney's strategy was his 3M Acceleration initiative, which targeted the research and development culture at 3M. In a company that prided itself on its independent and unconventional research culture, this program struck at the heart of the company's values. Before McNerney's arrival, research and development was spread equally across the various business divisions. This style was based on the premise that all divisions should be encouraged to innovate and grow and that great things could arise from the most unprepossessing beginnings. The purpose of the acceleration program was to focus resources on projects that looked promising and to cull projects that did not. Some observers and employees feared that in modifying 3M's eclectic approach to fostering innovation, McNerney risked destroying the very elements that had made 3M great.

MANAGING CULTURAL CHANGE

From the outset of his tenure as CEO at 3M, McNerney was careful to emphasize he was trying to improve the existing 3M culture, not replace it with the GE culture. In an article in *Fortune*, McNerney was quoted as saying, "I'm not showing up at 3M with a cultural tool kit that I'm going to transplant" (January 8, 2001). Several factors in McNerney's management approach allayed fears of a GE takeover. He did not arrive at 3M with a band of GE executives in tow and instead emphasized the quality of the people already at 3M. As a result, 3M staff accepted the concept that they were the ones driving change. Many 3M managers noted that McNerney, instead of dictating changes, encouraged the managers to recognize 3M's assets and identify opportunities. Some of the staff welcomed the accompanying sense of rejuvenation. As one senior employee said in an interview in *Fortune*, "He's delivered a very consistent message. There's a sense of speed and a sense of urgency" (August 12, 2002). The ability to clearly communicate his vision for the company and empower his employees was McNerney's main asset during the initial period of transition at 3M. Many observers cited McNerney's low-key style and lack of arrogance as important factors in his success. In the age of the celebrity CEO, McNerney preferred to avoid the spotlight and instead concentrated on building relationships with those around him at 3M.

By the beginning of 2004 McNerney had moved out of the shadow of Welch and GE. Financial indicators ensured general optimism about the success of McNerney's strategy at 3M. Revenue increased 11.6 percent, to $18.2 billion in 2003, and net income increased 21.7 percent to $2.4 billion. The value of 3M stock increased 38 percent over 2003. In late 2003 rumors that McNerney would head Boeing were proved wrong when he announced he would be staying with 3M. Business analysts agreed that McNerney's work at 3M was not over, and most observers remained uncommitted about whether Six Sigma and 3M Acceleration had improved or detracted from 3M's traditional strengths. Nevertheless, the initial success of McNerney's tenure at 3M resulted in his being held up as an example of the benefits of injecting new blood into long-established companies. McNerney's challenge in 2004 was to prove that his business strategy had improved 3M's organic growth rate—the growth in sales revenue from products developed within 3M as opposed to those acquired from outside businesses. The outcome would indicate whether McNerney's drive for efficiency and discipline was compatible with the 3M culture of innovation. In 2004 McNerney was on the boards of directors of Boeing, Procter & Gamble, and the Greater Twin Cities United Way.

See also entries on 3M Company, General Electric Company, and Procter & Gamble Company in *International Directory of Company Histories.*

SOURCES FOR FURTHER INFORMATION

Arndt, Michael, "3M: A Lab for Growth?" *BusinessWeek*, January 21, 2001, pp. 50–51.

"The Best and Worst Managers of 2003—The Best Managers: James McNerney," *BusinessWeek*, January 12, 2004, p. 61.

Brady, Diane, "The Corporation: Succession—The Jet Powered Candidate," *BusinessWeek*, October 2, 2000, p. 132.

"I'm Not Taking a Cultural Tool Kit to 3M," *Fortune*, January 8, 2001, p. 86.

McClenahan, John S., "New World Leader: 3M Co.'s James McNerney, CEO of The Year, Is Committed to Operating Excellence and Organic Growth through Innovation, International Strength, Leadership Development, and Six Sigma," *IndustryWeek*, January 2004, pp. 36–39.

Miller, William H., "New Leader, New Era," *IndustryWeek*, November 2001, pp. 48–49.

—Katrina Ford

Dee Mellor

1957–

Vice president and general manager, GE Healthcare

Nationality: American.

Born: June 7, 1957.

Education: University of Massachusetts, BS, 1978.

Family: Married Gary (last name unknown); children: two.

Career: General Electric, 1978, manufacturing management program; 1979–1995, positions in GE Aircraft Engine's supply-chain division, manufacturing, quality control, and materials and logistics; GE Engine Services, 1995–1998, various positions; 1998–2000, product-support manager; 2000–2002, general manager of U.S. and Asian service operations; GE Medical Systems (now GE Healthcare), 2002–, vice president and general manager of global-supply chain.

Awards: Named one of the Global Inflentials, *Time*, 2002; named College of Engineering Alumna of the Year, University of Massachusetts, 2003.

Address: GE Healthcare, 300 North Grandview Boulevard, Waukesha, Wisconsin 53188; http://www.gehealth care.com.

■ Diane (Dee) Mellor spent her career at General Electric (GE) in a variety of engineering roles, but she was best known in her position as vice president and head of global supply-chain operations for GE Healthcare. Mellor's primary talent was her ability to lead her employees and officers through frequent changes in technology, products, and training. Her substantial problem-solving skills, quick mind, and ability to set and meet long-term goals led to an increase of component production by 20 percent in her first 18 months as head of global supply-chain operations. Coworkers and employees described Mellor as an intelligent and energetic leader who motivated employees to complete difficult tasks in a productive and efficient manner.

STARTING ON THE ENGINEERING PATH

Mellor's early push toward becoming an engineer was supported by her academic environment, her family, and her own aptitude and intelligence. Engineering was an unusual goal for a woman at a time when men dominated the field. Mellor's parents fully supported her in her career choice. Her mother, Pat, told her that she could do anything she wanted "even if it wasn't fashionable for a woman at the time" (*Landmark*, November 2002). Through their natural competitiveness her brothers unwittingly helped her develop the toughness and ability to stand her ground that she needed to break into the male-dominated field. Mellor's aptitude in the sciences allowed her to combine her senior year of high school and her freshman year of college in 1974 at Quinsigamond Community College. In 1975 she enrolled at the University of Massachusetts, and in 1978 she was one of only three women to graduate with a degree in industrial engineering and operations research.

MORE PUZZLES TO SOLVE

Mellor began a management-training program at GE in 1978. Following completion of the program she began to work as an engineer in the manufacturing of jet engines. She flourished in the pressure-cooker atmosphere of the GE aircraft-engine division, whose tough managers were no match for her quick intellect and ability to solve problems. Mellor began as a process engineer and over the next 10 years met every challenge placed in front of her. At 35 years of age, she earned the opportunity to run a GE aircraft-engine-parts plant in Wilmington, North Carolina. She was the first woman ever to run an engine line. Five years later, in 1992, she spearheaded GE's $1.6-billion acquisition-integration of Greenwich Aviation Services. In 1995 Mellor became head of GE's worldwide aircraft-engines product-support operation. She continued to thrive in the intense environment of GE engineering. As she learned new things and solved additional problems, GE was large enough to provide new challenges.

ON-TIME AND ON-BUDGET

In 2000 the chief financial officer of GE Medical Systems (now GE Healthcare) recognized Mellor's hard work, global experience, and ability to pull projects and personnel together and invited her to head GE Medical Logistics. The position provided Mellor a new challenge, and she proved to be a success. At GE, she said, "there isn't a job I've had that I haven't loved, because you are always being challenged and being put in places where you can learn and grow" (*Landmark*, November 2002). Mellor increased productivity in the components department to levels that had not been achieved before. She found efficient ways to keep plants thriving in the United States and get products where and when they needed to go. She also used her decision-making skills to determine a project's short- and long-term profitability. For example, in 2001 she had to make the tough decision on where to relocate the plant that manufactured a crucial part of a CT scanner. She could move the plant to India, where it would show short-term growth but no market expansion, or to China, where the manufacturing market had room to expand. Although India had a proven team and facility, she chose China because it had growth potential and an experienced pool of material scientists.

In addition to her global perspective and creation of production plants overseas, Mellor had success in keeping U.S.-based plants profitable and hiring. She had a decisive, efficient, and intelligent management style and utilized her skills to keep specialized employees and managers trained and up to date on new products and their production methods. Also, she made sure that the company continually evaluated production-line procedures in search of improvement.

MENTORING

Mellor recognized that she developed critical skills on surviving in the corporate environment through her family life, high-school career, and experience breaking into the male-dominated world of engineering. To pass on her experiences to other women seeking to advance in the corporate world, Mellor was instrumental in beginning a women's network at GE in 1997 focused on "enabling and empowering women" early in their careers (*Landmark*, November 2002). As an executive on the team, she helped focus the group on the practical issues of professional development such as finding mentors, writing resumes, giving presentations, pushing back when pushed, and creating local networks. Through projects such as the GE women's network, Mellor found herself being joined by a growing number of female executive and engineers.

See also entry on General Electric Company in *International Directory of Company Histories*.

SOURCES FOR FURTHER INFORMATION

Megnin, Ria, "Holden Native Engineers a TIME-worthy Career," *Landmark*, November 2002.

Thottam, Jyoti, "2002 Global Influentials," *Time*, November 22, 2002.

—Dawn Jacob Laney

■■■
Jean-Marie Messier
1956–
Former chairman and chief executive officer, Vivendi Universal

Nationality: French.

Born: December 13, 1956, in Grenoble, France.

Education: École Polytechnique, BS, 1976; attended École Nationale d'Administration, 1980–1982.

Family: Married Antoinette (maiden name unknown); children: five.

Career: French Ministry of Economy and Finance, 1982–1986, auditor of state-owned companies; 1986–1988, advisor to the minister of economy, finance, and privatization; Lazard Frères et Compagnie, 1988–1994, general partner; Compagnie Générale des Eaux (CGE), 1994–1996, chief executive officer; 1996–1998, chief executive officer and chairman; Vivendi Universal, 1998–2002, chief executive officer and chairman.

Awards: Person of the Year, French-American Chamber of Commerce, 2000; Chevalier de la Légion d'Honneur, government of France, 2001.

Publications: *J6M.com. Faut-il avoir peur de la nouvelle économie?*, 2000.

Jean-Marie Messier. *AP/Wide World Photos.*

■ Jean-Marie Messier put himself and France on the map as a global business presence during his tenure as the chairman and CEO of Vivendi Universal, a media conglomerate that at one time was second only to AOL Time Warner in size and income. A graduate of two of France's most prestigious educational institutions, Messier nonetheless found himself behind bars in the summer of 2004 on criminal charges related to possible insider trading and other breaches of French securities law.

EDUCATION AND EARLY CAREER

Jean-Marie Messier was born in 1956 in Grenoble, a city in the Alps of southeastern France. The son of an accountant,

he was a serious and hardworking student in his high school years. Although he failed on his first attempt to gain entry to the École Polytechnique, the training ground of France's business elite, he retook the entrance examinations the following year and was admitted. He did well in his studies, graduating from the school with high marks in 1976. Messier then attended the École Nationale d'Administration, or ENA, the traditional educational route to a high position in the French government. After completing his course of study at ENA in 1982, he worked for four years in the French ministry of finance as an auditor of state-owned corporations. He became the chief of staff of the French finance ministry in 1986, several months before his thirtieth birthday.

Instead of climbing higher up the political ladder, however, Messier surprised observers by leaving government service in 1988 for a position with Lazard Frères et Compagnie, a major

French investment bank. Messier quickly became the youngest partner in the bank's history. During his years at Lazard, Messier gave advice to French companies about expanding their businesses in the United States. A French journalist said of him at the time, "He was someone who was having an exceptional career. He was growing in power very quickly. He got the reputation of someone who was a very quick thinker" (*BBC News*, July 19, 2002).

THE MAKEOVER OF CGE

Messier's next step in his career was to join the Compagnie Générale des Eaux, or CGE, in 1994 as its chief executive. CGE was an old-fashioned French water company, founded by Emperor Napoleon III in 1853. Its chief businesses in the early 1990s were garbage collection and sewage plant operation. Messier lost little time, however, in remaking CGE after he moved up to the chairman's position in 1996. He began to sell off divisions of the company that he considered outdated and to turn CGE into a media and telecommunications firm. In 1998 the company's name was changed to Vivendi Universal to fit Messier's new image of it.

Messier's first major move after the name change was to purchase a larger stake in Canal Plus, a French television company that produced programs associated with high culture. This purchase was followed by a wave of acquisitions of media and high-technology companies; at one point in 1999, Messier was completing an average of a deal per month. He became the most famous businessman in France. One analyst compared Messier's compulsive deal-making to substance addiction: "When you control media it's like when you control the world. That's what Messier wanted to do" (*BBC News*, July 19, 2002).

Far from shrinking from the attention of the press, Messier appeared to enjoy the limelight. In 2000 he published his autobiography, *J6M.com*, whose title was certainly revealing. The six Ms stood for "(Jean)-Marie Messier, moi-même, maître du monde," which can be translated as "Jean-Marie Messier, me myself, master of the world."

TAKING ON THE UNITED STATES

In 2000 Messier made his most ambitious acquisition—one that attempted to break the American hold on the worldwide media industry. He announced a $34-billion merger with Seagram, a liquor company based in Canada that had gradually turned itself into a media giant. He also completed Vivendi's buyout of Canal Plus. The French public approved of Messier's merger with Seagram at the time because it appeared to be a successful challenge to what they considered American domination of global media. The president of France personally congratulated Messier, and the French-American Chamber

of Commerce honored him as their Person of the Year for 2000. At the presentation of the Chamber's award, the French Ambassador to the United States praised Messier as "the prototype of a new breed of French executives that dispels the traditional clichés about France" (October 18, 2000).

Messier's buying spree was not over, however. In May 2001 Vivendi Universal acquired Houghton Mifflin, an American book publisher with a fine reputation for its lines of textbooks and reference works. This purchase was significant because it followed the collapse of the so-called dot-com bubble, when most corporate executives began to pull back on mergers and acquisitions.

Messier then turned French public opinion against him when he purchased a home in New York. According to a report in the *Daily Telegraph*, Messier used $17.5 million of Vivendi Universal's funds to buy a penthouse on Park Avenue in Manhattan. This purchase symbolized the beginning of Jean-Marie Messier's rise on the social ladder in New York City, but it also represented betrayal to the French. After Messier moved his family to the new apartment, the French began to regard his business deals in the United States as threats to the purity of French culture. Messier further insulted his compatriots when he made a remark in late 2001 to the effect that "the French cultural exception is dead." This remark was widely regarded as hostile criticism of the French government's subsidies of art and culture. The *Daily Telegraph* reported that "... President Jacques Chirac and Prime Minister Lionel Jospin weighed in, warning [Messier] against trampling all over French culture. Protestors have thrown rotten eggs at his office windows and the French media have reared up in indignation" (April 20, 2002).

DOWNFALL

The collapse of Messier's ambitions was almost as sudden as his rise. Part of the problem was financial. Vivendi had grown almost entirely through buyouts. As the dot-com bubble faded, it appeared that Messier had paid too much for some of his acquisitions. In addition, he had been paying for these acquisitions with stock shares rather than cash. His acquisitions strategy worked as long as Vivendi's share prices remained high, but when prices began to fall toward the end of 2001, the company found itself in serious trouble. At the close of 2001 Vivendi recorded the largest single loss—$14 billion—in the history of French business.

Another factor in Messier's downfall was his management style. According to the authors of *The Man Who Tried to Buy the World*, Messier had two very different faces. "In public, Messier played the role of a modern, approachable chief executive who believed in collegial management. Inside the company, he could appear authoritarian, sometimes cutting" (Johnson and Orange). One notable instance of Messier's inability to foresee the results of his authoritarian behavior was his firing of Pierre Lescure, the head of Canal Plus, in April 2002. The employees of the television company were furious; they flooded into the company's studios, stopped program transmission, and broadcast their protests live from the studios.

In addition to being high-handed, Messier also relied on his charismatic personality to sway the emotions of board members rather than using reason and logic to convince them of the wisdom of his business deals. Messier displayed an uncanny ability to play down the downside and pump up the upside of almost any situation. In essence, his superior communication abilities enabled him to persuade his fellow executives and even Vivendi's board to bypass rational decision-making processes in favor of being mesmerized by his ability to sell his vision. The predictable result of these emotionally charged meetings was a series of poor decisions and financial misadventures.

A week after the staff protests at Canal Plus, Messier had to answer to Vivendi's board at the company's annual general meeting. He defended himself, but was pressured to step down by the American as well as the French members of the board. Finally Jacques Chirac, the President of France, sent some of his allies in the French business community to increase the pressure on Messier. Messier finally resigned from Vivendi on July 1, 2002.

FURTHER DISGRACE

After being ousted by Vivendi, Jean-Marie Messier sat on the sidelines and watched his successor, Jean-René Fourtou, take over as chairman and CEO. Fourtou, the former chairman of Rhône-Poulenc, promptly sold an 80-percent stake of Vivendi's entertainment line to NBC, a General Electric company. Fourtou also reversed Messier's acquisitions strategy by breaking up Vivendi into smaller units and selling some of its assets. He was credited with rescuing the company from bankruptcy.

Meanwhile, Jean-Marie Messier made yet another deal that was characteristic of his flamboyant style—he negotiated an unheard-of severance package of EUR 20.5 million. This arrangement went sour as soon as the U.S. Securities and Exchange Commission (SEC) charged Messier with securities fraud. He settled with the SEC by using his severance package as part of the deal. Vivendi agreed in 2003 to pay the SEC $50 million to settle the action but without admitting liability, while Messier was barred from holding directorships in American firms for 10 years.

Worse was yet to come. Less than two years after resigning his position at Vivendi, Messier was arrested by the French police in June 2004 on charges of illegal share dealings. According to the *Wall Street Journal*, the charges were related to four issues: "Vivendi's massive stock buybacks after the Sept. 11, 2001, terrorist attacks; possible insider trading by Vivendi officers in December 2001; the accuracy of Vivendi's financial disclosures; and whether Vivendi should have consolidated three partly owned telecommunications subsidiaries in its accounts" (June 22, 2004). Critics of Vivendi's buyback maintained that it was an attempt to support the price of Vivendi's shares before the crucial results of the merger with Seagram were published.

Prior to Messier's resignation from Vivendi, he served on the boards of Alcatel, BNP-Paribas, Cegetel, Compagnie de Saint-Gobain, and LVMH-Moët Hennessy Louis Vuitton. He was also a member of the New York Stock Exchange.

See also entries on Canal Plus and Vivendi Universal S.A. in *International Directory of Company Histories*.

SOURCES FOR FURTHER INFORMATION

Broughton, Philip Delves, "Another Fine Messier," *Daily Telegraph*, April 20, 2002.

Bujon de l'Estang, François, Remarks at the Presentation of the Person of the Year Award 2000 to Jean-Marie Messier, October 18, 2000, http://www.info-france-usa.org/news/statmnts/2000/vivendi.asp.

Carreyou, John, "Vivendi Ex-CEO Held, Questioned in Probe of Firm," *Wall Street Journal*, June 22, 2004.

Henley, Jon, and Mark Milner, "Messier Arrested in Shares Inquiry," *The Guardian*, June 22, 2004, http://money.guardian.co.uk/businessnews/article/0,11507,1244601,00.html.

Johnson, Jo, and Martine Orange, *The Man Who Tried To Buy The World: Jean-Marie Messier and Vivendi Universal*, New York: Portfolio, 2003.

"The Rise and Fall of Jean-Marie Messier," *BBC News*, July 19, 2002, http://news.bbc.co.uk/2/hi/business/2138445.stm.

Smith, Alex, and Katherine Griffiths, "Fat Cat Moi? I Have Let Down My Shareholders, So I Have Decided to Give Back My Pounds 3m Payoff," *The Independent*, August 19, 2003.

—William F. Martin

■■■

Gérard Mestrallet

1949–

Chairman and chief executive officer, Compagnie de Suez

Nationality: French.

Born: April 1, 1949, in Paris, France.

Education: École Polytech, 1968; École Aviation Civile, 1971; Institute for Study of Politics; National School of Administration, 1978.

Family: Son of Georges Julien Marie and Paule Andrée Augustine (Besnard); married Joëlle Emillienne Renée Arcens, 1974; children: three.

Career: Compagnie de Suez, 1984–1986, vice president of special projects; 1986–1991, executive vice president; 1991–1995, executive director and chairman of the management committee of Société Générale de Belgique; 1995–1997, chairman and chief executive officer; Suez Lyonnaise des Eaux, 1997–2001, chairman of executive board; Suez, 2001–, chairman and chief executive officer.

Address: Compagnie de Suez, 16 rue de la ville l'Eveque, 75008, Paris, France; http://www.suez.com.

Gérard Mestrallet. *AP/Wide World Photos.*

■ Gérard Mestrallet became the chairman and chief executive officer of Compagnie de Suez in 1995. He made a bold choice to change the company's focus shortly after taking over, beginning Suez's transformation from a marginal financial company into a profitable water, gas, and electric provider. Mestrallet was known as a steady and reliable manager who persevered in globally expanding his company. As a result of his successes he was able to focus not just on maximizing profits but also on creating safer water supplies on a global scale. He was described as neither harsh nor difficult but as hardworking with great expectations for his employees and his company. Once Suez had attained sizable profits and expanded globally, Mestrallet knew that his transformation had been successful.

EDUCATION AND EARLY CAREER

Mestrallet graduated from the French engineering school Polytechnique in 1968 and then went on to study at the well-

known National School of Administration, earning a degree in 1978. In 1984 he was hired by Compagnie de Suez to serve as vice president of special projects. He worked his way up through the ranks at Suez, serving as executive vice president, then as executive director and chairman of the management committee, and finally as chairman and chief executive officer. Over the years Mestrallet proved his worth to the company; he would be entrusted with many important decisions.

SUEZ BEGINS A TRANSFORMATION

When Mestrallet took over as chairman and CEO in 1995, he spent some time questioning whether or not Suez could become a truly profitable financial company. After studying options for nearly six months, he decided that Suez should change its focus; he gambled that the company could become a global provider of energy services. He believed that a great need for global growth existed in the utilities industry, and that in meeting those needs Suez could earn substantial amounts of money. Mestrallet sold the subsidiary Indosuez to Crédit Agricole, and Suez made the jump into utilities.

"Mestrallet wants to be a world leader in supplying water, gas, and electricity to municipalities, states, and countries. He's already a large part of the way there: Suez Lyonnaise des Eaux now gets more than 65 percent of its revenues from those core businesses" (*Institutional Investor*, July 1998). Mestrallet envisioned Suez being able to provide water, gas, electricity, and waste collection as well, at which point the company would be unique worldwide in its offering of that combination of services. To achieve his grand vision, Mestrallet would have to overcome various obstacles, especially through operations in the developing world. Frequently endeavors did not work out as planned; Suez had to wait for better times. Yet patience often paid off; for example Suez came to modernize and manage water, electricity, and wastewater treatment services in all of Casablanca, Morocco, a city of five million people.

PURCHASES NALCO

In 1999 Mestrallet and Suez purchased Nalco Chemical Company, the water treatment group based in Naperville, Illinois. As Nalco had possessed the world's largest water treatment facility, the acquisition was important for Suez, as it could then provide services to over 50,000 customers in 120 countries. Mestrallet was happy with the transaction, noting in an article distributed by the Associated Press, "The acquisition of Nalco Chemical Company fits perfectly into our strategic plan, which emphasizes international expansion and the integration of our core businesses" (June 29, 1999). Mestrallet thought it especially important to own businesses in the United States, knowing that if Suez wished to be a worldwide company, it would need to forge partnerships with U.S. firms.

Mestrallet believed that with the Nalco purchase Suez would be able to offer more services and products—especially in water, energy, and waste—and to better integrate those services. At the end of 1999 Mestrallet's goals for the company were being realized; Suez was an industry leader in providing water to 77 million people and wastewater services to 52 million people worldwide.

SERVES AS ADVISOR

Mestrallet not only ran Suez successfully but also served as an advisor to many groups and individuals around the world. He worked with important leaders to help make their cities more desirable places to live and more efficient centers for business growth. He conferred with Lee Myung Bak, the mayor of Seoul, South Korea, on the Seoul International Busi-

ness Advisory Council; together they hoped to make Seoul the center of economic development in northeastern Asia. Mestrallet also advised to Tung Chee Hwa, the chairman of the special administrative zone of Hong Kong. The two worked to develop a positive image for the city so that businesses would want to establish themselves there. Mestrallet also worked with Chen Liong Yu, the mayor of Shanghai, to create a better image for the Chinese commercial center.

COMMITS TO SUSTAINABLE DEVELOPMENT

Mestrallet believed it essential not only to provide services such as water, gas, and electricity but also to do so with minimal impact on the environment. In terms of sustainable development he aimed to develop ways to run his business in a financially successful manner without having a negative effect on resources in the process. While admitting that his first and foremost responsibility was to earn profits for his company, he remarked in *OECD Observer*, "Economic responsibility means always understanding the risks associated with one's business better in order to anticipate, control, and hedge them; their cost to the community, not just the company can be unbearable" (May 2002).

Suez was a global leader in providing people with essential services on a daily basis. Mestrallet continually worked toward improving his company, trying to minimize the use of raw materials and ensure that little waste was produced. He thought these considerations were common sense; when managing a resource, one would not want to let any of it go to waste. As he described in *OECD Observer*, he maintained such a conservative approach through hard work and dedication: "The key is to articulate a strong vision and share it as widely as possible, so that it is translated concretely into management and decision making" (May 2002). Over the course of three years he created a standard of performance for all of his employees to follow; in the end all followed a unifying principle, so that each division could do its part in working toward a common goal.

A DIFFICULT YEAR

Mestrallet felt confident about his vision and goals for the future when speaking in 2001; however, Suez did not perform well in 2002. Company shares lost two-thirds of their value due to rising debt levels and low electricity prices. Mestrallet was disappointed; he created a new plan for Suez. Thanks to the high debt levels he was forced to halt expansion efforts across the Atlantic. In *Utility Week* he put forth "five clear objectives: a streamlined organization; a cost-cutting purge; much lower net debt; reduced exposure to emerging country risk; and the establishment of self-financed business lines" (March 28, 2003). Mestrallet sold riskier investments and continually reevaluated his business plan, making key decisions that would ideally have positive effects in the future.

MANAGEMENT STYLE

Gérard Mestrallet was a calm leader who made educated and careful decisions when it came to expanding his company. He took control of Suez at a time when it was necessary to make big changes; he successfully turned the financial services company into a global leader in the provision of gas, electricity, and water to many countries around the world. He sold unnecessary assets and bought into markets that were viable for Suez. He led by example and was always willing to give his time and energy. Mestrallet was relentlessly focused on turning his company into a global leader, and Suez met this goal by 2002. Even in difficult times Mestrallet did not get discouraged but simply altered his business plans accordingly.

SOURCES FOR FURTHER INFORMATION

"Creating a Gusher in Power and Energy: Unlike Some of His Peers, Mestrallet Has Largely Avoided Overpaying for Assets," *BusinessWeek*, June 17, 2002, p. 42.

"Making Money from Water," *Institutional Investor International Edition*, July 1998, v23, i7, 21.

Mestrallet, Gérard, "Q&A with Suez's Gérard Mestrallet," *BusinessWeek Online*, June 17, 2002, http://www.businessweek.com/@@JIV**oYQoHj91xYA/magazine/content/02_24/b3787605.htm.

_____, "The Suez Commitment: An Interview with Gérard Mestrallet," *OECD Observer*, May 2002, p. 21.

Ockenden, Karma, "The Suez Corral," *Utility Week*, March 28, 2003, p. 26.

Philips, Ian, "French Firm Pours It On," Associated Press, June 29, 1999.

—Deborah Kondek

■■■
Edouard Michelin
1963–
President and chief executive officer, Groupe Michelin

Nationality: French.

Born: August 13, 1963, in Clermont-Ferrand, France.

Education: École centrale de Paris, BS, 1985.

Family: Son of François Michelin (company president) and Bernadette Montagne; married; children: five.

Career: French navy, 1987–1989; service on nuclear submarine; Groupe Michelin, 1989–1991, worker and plant manager; Michelin North America, 1991–1993, president and chief operating officer; Groupe Michelin, 1999–, president and chief executive officer.

Publications: Forward for *Challenge Bibendum: Oui aux voitures propres,* Expédition, 2001.

Address: Compagnie Général des Établissements Michelin, 4 rue de Terrail, 63040 Clermont-Ferrand Cedex, France; http://www.michelin.com.

■ Edouard Michelin was groomed by his father to take over the Groupe Michelin, a tire maker founded in the late nineteenth century by André Michelin. Edouard ran Michelin's U.S. operation in the early 1990s before becoming president and chief executive officer in 1999. Edouard inherited a truly global company and led it to overtake its rival Bridgestone/Firestone. Michelin changed his company's tradition of secrecy and took leadership in the promotion of a sustainable global automobile culture.

LE DAUPHIN

Edouard Michelin was born in Clermont-Ferrand, in the heart of the French Auvergne, on August 13, 1963. He was the youngest son of François and Bernadette Michelin. From the beginning Edouard was seen as the dauphin, or designated successor of his family's very hereditary company. His eldest brother, Etienne, had chosen the priesthood, while the next in line, Damien and Benôit, were not regarded by their father as management material.

Edouard Michelin. *AP/Wide World Photos.*

Edouard seemed to have the business acumen of his father and his grandfather and the desire to succeed them. The youngest Michelin followed in the footsteps of his great-great uncle André, the company founder, by studying engineering at the École centrale in Paris. Upon Edouard's graduation in 1985, François started him at the bottom, making tires on the assembly line at Carmes. Edouard used a false identity at work, but everyone knew who he was. Edouard learned purchasing, research, and all aspects of the company, and he was then posted as an apprentice to Michelin's research center in Greenville, South Carolina. Shortly after he began working there, he was drafted into the French navy, where he demonstrated his leadership skills by serving as an officer on a nuclear submarine.

Michelin returned to the family firm in 1989. He was first placed in charge of a factory in France, and then became president and chief operations officer of Michelin North America in 1991. He returned to France in 1993, where he became a full partner alongside his father and René Zingraff. His father had begun preparing him for the succession. Michelin's structure was unique for a company of its size and reputation. It remained an old-fashioned joint-stock company with what Herbert Lottmann described in his book *The Michelin Men* as a "nineteenth-century management structure," in which the partners were mutually liable. François owned few company assets but all potential liabilities. This structure nonetheless allowed himself, Zingraff, and Edouard to make rapid decisions in the name of Michelin.

During the 1990s there were rumors that Michelin was in trouble. The company's stock remained sluggish, and its shareholders were often left in the dark as to what was happening. Secrecy was a trait of the Michelin culture. In March 1990, François laid off 16,000 workers, one-eighth of the company payroll.

In 1995 Edouard was given the task of explaining Michelin's new European strategy, in which every plant would specialize rather than having all plants making the same thing. Michelin would no longer be organized by country, but by product category. This move cut costs and doubled profits. The following year two new factories were opened in France. The company was evolving from a French to a truly global firm. Of its 114,000 employees, only 15,000 now worked in Clermont-Ferrand and only 15,000 in the rest of France. Only about 15 percent of Michelin tires were now made in France. Over a quarter were made in the rest of Europe, a fifth in the United States, and the remaining 40 percent elsewhere around the world.

In spite of the company's growth, it continued to lose ground in the late 1990s to Bridgestone, the Japanese tire firm that had acquired Ford's supplier, Firestone. Such was the situation when François Michelin felt ready to retire and make way for his talented but perhaps unpredictable son. For François, Edouard was the perfect choice to run the company. He had worked his way up through the ranks and observed how Michelin was run for a decade. On June 12, 1999, François retired after appointing Edouard president.

"L'AMERICAIN"

Edouard Michelin took over the tire company's reins at a tough period in its long history. Faced with competition from Bridgestone/Firestone, he announced in September 1999 a plan, agreed upon with his father, to eliminate 7,500 jobs in Europe over three years. Some 2,000 job reductions were planned for North America as well. Notice of these reductions at a time when company earnings were rising upset the Socialist government of Lionel Jospin. Edouard, for his part, did not denounce the government's policy of a 35-hour workweek, which many French managers saw as unrealistic and detrimen-

tal to productivity. In spite of this, France's powerful and militant unions protested.

Edouard, now nicknamed "L'americain" due to his overseas experience, responded to the criticism by striving to change Michelin's secretive image. He began to hold press conferences and even let reporters into his factories. Edouard defended the layoffs as necessary in cutting overhead costs and improving competitive efficiency against Bridgestone, but saw them as a justification for a more open stance in communicating with the media and the shareholders.

Edouard used different marketing strategies in different parts of the world. In France, Michelin could still be presented as quintessentially French, as defining what France was all about. In the rest of the European Union, Edouard marketed Michelin as a European company, and in Asia and Latin America as a global one. In the United States, given the growing anti-French sentiment, Michelin presented itself chiefly as an American tire company.

Tires were not the only major product for which Michelin was noted. For decades Michelin had been renowned in both France and Europe for its famous maps and tour guides. The guides originally presented lists of upscale restaurants and hotels that would appeal to the French bourgeoisie. As France became more prosperous, the guides now included restaurants and hotels that appealed to those with modest income. The guides became available in English, Dutch, German, Spanish, Italian, Portuguese, and Japanese and sold up to 100,000 copies annually, accounting for 2 percent of company revenue. Edouard marketed Michelin maps and guides in the United States as well, but they were considerably less popular there, as Americans preferred to buy American-made guides.

EDOUARD MICHELIN'S MANAGEMENT STYLE

Michelin sought to adapt the family firm to a new generation and new global conditions, but slowly and with respect for the company's French traditions. As he explained to Paul Betts of the *Financial Times*, the transition from father to son was gradual and evolutionary. The partnership structure in which Edouard and René Zingraff risked unlimited liability was retained. Edouard defended it as "an added long term commitment to the business, to transparency, honesty, communication and performance." He made clear to Betts his rejection of the American shareholder and corporate-raider philosophy: "I get quite frustrated by the way financial markets consider enterprises as a mere commodity, a stock pick." Global capital markets were to him easily turned into "weapons of mass destruction." Michelin, on the other hand, would follow a long-term strategy that allowed it to ride out global booms and recessions.

Edouard considered his personal style to be more managerial and less entrepreneurial than his father's: "His philosophy was not to have too much organisation," he told Betts, but "as we managed the transition step by step," even François recognized the need and told his son that the company "clearly needed to introduce more organisation." By 2001 Michelin was enjoying steady growth. When Firestone's sales plummeted as the result of a number of accidents involving SUVs, Michelin became the leading tire company in the world.

MICHELIN'S CRUSADE FOR SUSTAINABLE VEHICLES

In addition to maintaining Michelin's brand identity and its new leadership in automotive tires, Edouard Michelin was very concerned about the future of the vehicles that used his tires. The automobile was here to stay and selling in growing numbers throughout the world. How could the earth's ecosystem possibly support all these new vehicles? Edouard was an early champion of the development of clean, fuel-efficient vehicles, which he did by sponsoring the Challenge Bibendum.

The first Challenge Bibendum was held in 1998. Edouard invited the world's automakers to compete in producing the most economical and environmentally friendly cars and trucks. "We do it because we believe it is the right thing to do," he told the Malaysian *Berhad Straits Times* (October 12, 2003). "It is Michelin's belief that the automotive industry needed an unbiased forum to demonstrate its commitment to cleaner, greener technologies." In 2002 natural gas and electric cars competed. In 2003 Edouard chose Sonoma, California, as the site of the contest because of California's tough emission laws. Hydrogen cars, trucks, and buses joined the competition. Ameri-can, Japanese, European, and other vehicles competed not in laboratories but in actual driving conditions. Michelin evaluated them on style, speed, quietness, impact safety, emissions, and fuel efficiency. Edouard Michelin realized that he did not have easy answers for making the cars less environmentally harmful. As he prepared to hold the 2004 Challenge Bibendum in China, he could at least feel comfortable that he provided a yearly forum for automakers and others to seek those answers.

See also entry on Compagnie Général des Établissements Michelin in *International Directory of Company Histories.*

SOURCES FOR FURTHER INFORMATION

Albakry, Salehuddin, "Michelin's Green Drive Fuels Change," *Berhad New Straits Times* (Malaysia), October, 12, 2003.

Betts, Paul, "The New Michelin Man Gets Rolling: Interview Edouard Michelin: Strong," *Financial Times*, April 25, 2003.

Crumley, Bruce, "Radial Changes," *Time Europe*, May 20, 2002, p. 107.

Harp, Stephen L., *Marketing Michelin: Advertising and Cultural Identity in Twentieth-Century France*, Baltimore: Johns Hopkins University Press, 2001.

Lottman, Herbert R., *The Michelin Men, Driving an Empire*, London: I.B. Taurus, 2003.

—David Charles Lewis

■■■
Charles Milhaud

1943–

President of the directory of the Caisse Nationale des Caisses d'Épargne

Nationality: French.

Born: February 20, 1943, in Sète, France.

Education: Attended University of Montpellier.

Family: Son of Georges (savings-bank manager) and Fernande (maiden name unknown; homemaker). Married, 1964 (divorced, 1967); married Gisèle (maiden name unknown), 1969; children: two.

Career: Caisse Nationale des Caisses d'Épargne, 1964–, various positions including president.

Awards: Légion d'honneur, 1996; decorated with L'ordre national du Mérite, Laurent Fabius, 2002.

Address: Caisse Nationale des Caisses d'Épargne, 5, rue Masseran, 75007 Paris, France.

Charles Milhaud. © *AFP/Corbis*.

■ "I prefer consensus to the use of force," Charles Milhaud claimed in 2003 (*Le Figaro*, January 13, 2003). Through a combination of political astuteness and sheer doggedness, Milhaud rose to the top position of the Caisse d'Épargne Group and eventually ruled over it as his personal fiefdom. He transformed the loosely organized network of franchises into France's top savings bank, and through an aggressive policy of mergers and acquisitions he created the third largest French banking group. Under his direction, a narrowly focused collective became a major banking enterprise.

Under Milhaud the Caisse d'Épargne Group was a cooperative bank composed of a network hub, La Caisse Nationale des Caisses d'Épargne (CNCE), the Federation Nationale des Caisses d'Épargne, 34 regional Caisses d'Épargne, the Crédit Foncier de France and its subsidiary companies, and specialized national and regional subsidiary companies, 4,700 agencies, 26 million clients, and over 50,000 employees. It disposed of over 18 billion euros in assets under his term at the helm. In 2003 Milhaud moved to consolidate his control over the organization by purchasing the stake in its partner bank,

the Caisse des Depots et Consignations (CDC), held in their joint holding company Eulia and its investment bank CDC IXIS. After his reelection to the head of the group in 2003 he detailed his vision of a global French banking dynasty.

FROM THE BOTTOM UP: A FAMILY HISTORY

Charles Milhaud was one of the more colorful and formidable figures in French banking and business, which is all the more extraordinary for his relatively ordinary origins in a country traditionally skeptical of self-initiating achievers. Milhaud was born into a family that had been former French colonial settlers in Algeria. His grandfather was a self-made man and worked hard to secure for his family a modest existence. He eventually became a skilled laborer and journeyman. Milhaud's father was obliged to leave school in order to work, and he oversaw a vineyard in Algeria. His mother sold bread locally from a car.

The family returned to France shortly before resistance to French colonial rule began. They landed in the fabled Italian fishing town of Sète on France's Côte d'Azure, beloved for its summer festival that includes drunken longboat jousting matches and frequent bleacher brawls. There, the father found work in a local savings bank and eventually rose to become manager.

In Sète they lived in a crowded, working-class neighborhood but enjoyed a middle-class life. Milhaud's parents attentively oversaw the education of their six children and emphasized the traditional values of hard work, persistence, and family loyalty. Both parents were scrupulously involved in the children's schoolwork and mindful of academic achievement.

Though a diligent student at the École Victor-Hugo and the Lycée Paul-Valéry, a heart condition prevented Milhaud from participating in the school's recreational activities. Following the lycée Milhaud studied physics with minors in math and chemistry at the University of Montpellier. He married young, and without financial recourse abandoned his studies to begin work in his father's business. He soon came to the attention of Léopold Suquet, a noted Sétois figure and president of the local Caisse d'Épargne.

GRABBING THE REINS: NETWORKING AND NEGOTIATING

Suquet was a locally influential member of the French Socialist party and at one time worked with the French Socialist interior minister, Jules Moche. Under Suquet's mentorship Milhaud made an early mark on the local Caisse by updating accounting methods and overseeing the installation of a computer banking system.

He also joined the Syndicat Unifié (SU), whose directors comanaged the different Caisses. An opportunity for advancement occurred when the SU decided against appointing one of its directors to represent the Caisses within the national trade union, the CGC. By the end of the 1970s Milhaud, having won the appointment, was SU's president at the CGC. Ambitious, enterprising, and militant, Milhaud assiduously cultivated his connections as a Freemason during this period.

In 1980 Milhaud was appointed assistant general manager of the Caisse d'Épargne des Bouches-du-Rhône et de la Corse, the second largest concern in the Caisse d'Épargne network. The head of the SU in Marseille, Ange Piazza, set Milhaud on his unwavering path to the top when he convinced the SU president, Claude Pelat, of Milhaud's skills as a union negotiator. Pelat was a close colleague of Valery Giscard d'Estaing, who was then running a tight campaign against François Mitterrand for president of France.

His association with Pelat during the election was the turning point in Milhaud's career. His image as a leftist and tough union negotiator at war with, or at least defiant of, France's centralized authority, made him a symbol of the tensions between provincial France and Paris. Through judicious maneuvering he allied himself with the rising stars of the SU and the Caisse d'Épargne, and in 1983, after heading a reform committee, he became director general of the Caisse d'Épargne and member of the Centre National des Caisses d'Épargne et de Prévoyance (CENCEP). Two years later he took over as president of the Caisse d'Épargne des Bouches-du-Rhône et de la Corse and was appointed to a seat on the board of trustees of CENCEP.

In 1999 Milhaud seized power over CENCEP in what has been described as a "putsch." The opportunity arrived when the Jospin government decided to reform the group, soon to become the CNCE, and its obsolescent statutes. Due to his avid support of reforms, Milhaud had been the ministry of finance's favorite to succeed René Barberye when Barberye's mandate as president of the directory expired later that year. The decision was made, however, to appoint the banker Christian Giacomotto as president. Milhaud was appointed to head the board of trustees of the CNCE.

Relying undoubtedly on his skills as a negotiator, his political image, and his network of friends, Milhaud nevertheless managed to secure the presidency of the directory from the government in exchange for acquiring the problematic Crédit Foncier de France, which the government was more than glad to be rid of and which he, at the helm of CNCE, was to successfully turn around.

LE BOSS: BIGGER IS BETTER

Milhaud was described both by his admirers and his detractors as an "atypical" French banker if only for having stood in stark contrast to the elitist and highly exclusive banking establishment made up of the tax inspectors. "He is a complete opportunist, unscrupulous and unprincipled. Duplicity and betrayal are his only rules of conduct. . . . He has no talent except for scheming . . . ," railed an establishment insider (*L'Express*, November 27, 2003). His admirers, however, hailed him as an antiestablishment visionary and a committed regionalist from the south of France who delighted in his local accent, a radical socialist who is able to compromise, a patriot of France, and an inveterate football fan.

His business strategy was simple: "Some of the lower level managers say to me at times, 'We need a breather. We are working like dogs.' But I can't stop." Milhaud added, "I don't like to manage. I like to build." An establishment insider put it differently: "He wants it all. He would buy out everything down to the corner computer store if it flattered his ego" (*Le Point*, October 17, 2003). Milhaud was seriously doubted when he first ascended the ranks of French finance, and many dismissed him as simply not up to the task. The idea of a provincial savings bank pretending to play with bigger banking entities struck them as preposterous. Though atypical in a culture that scorns the atypical, Milhaud was to prove them sorely wrong.

His main successes between 1999 and 2003 involved substantial changes in the Caisse d'Épargne system. As a manager, he doubled its capacity, achieving a solid 11.9 percent return on assets. He modernized computer and commercial systems, and he quelled labor unrest, though relations with the unions remained tense. As a strategist, he strengthened the position of Crédit Foncier de France by acquiring 60 percent of Banque SanPaolo and the insurance company AGF's stake in Entenial, thus turning Crédit Foncier into an asset and engine of growth. Most significantly, he merged with a close rival, Daniel Lebegue's CDC, and gained control of CDC IXIS, creating the financial holding company Eulia. These gains permitted him to expand a once purely domestic operation into a European and global enterprise. Summarizing his accomplishments, Milhaud said, "The Caisses had no back bone. We needed to give them one. That's what we did" (*Le Point*, October 17, 2003).

The key to understanding this baffling success in such a hostile environment may be provided by the following anecdote: During the social unrest of 1968 Milhaud would go to the Bank of France packing a pistol in his belt in order to guarantee that his clients got their money (*Le Figaro*, January 13, 2003). It is difficult to imagine any of his adversaries, products of the privileged institutions of the grandes écoles (which have long educated France's governing and management elite), taking such initiative on behalf of lower-income clients.

THE MACHINE MARCHES ON: ALL THE WAY TO WALL STREET

Milhaud's candidacy for a second term as leader of the Caisses was, not surprisingly, met with a vociferous campaign to block his reappointment. He was, nonetheless, the sole candidate for the post, making it difficult for his opponents to unseat him. The efforts against him appeared at best to be thinly veiled attempts to discredit him as either incompetent or corrupt. The Inspection des finances, for example, released reports dated July 1985, May 1988, and February 1997 detailing irregularities and inconsistencies in his management practices, notably his misapplication of fiscal rules and regulations and the elevated costs of unnecessary studies and external consultations. He was, however, neither convicted nor sanctioned for any of these charges.

Milhaud saw his own legacy as being his lasting imprint on the Caisse d'Épargne, a large, universal bank that would remain long after he was gone. Others saw his legacy differently. The little round man with the air of a friar, who once contemplated joining the church not to be a priest but to be a bishop, had set an example of a new and largely belligerent business culture that traditionalists in France vigorously resisted. That, however, is a legacy Milhaud himself would no doubt relish. If his critics complained that he succeeded by not playing according to the establishment's rules, he in fact succeeded precisely because he played by their rules while not playing their game.

Considered by his critics to be unscrupulous, cunning and duplicitous, Milhaud has been characterized as a man who would stand in no one's shadow, who honored promises and agreements only if they honored his ambitions, who kept tight control over his employees by playing musical chairs with their careers and who enforced a company consensus by keeping loyal cadres in comfortable and rewarding managerial positions. When asked if he had any designs on the American market, he replied enthusiastically: "Yes, that interests the Groupe Caisse d'Epargne . . . we have to be there . . . we are a real bank . . . and everybody better get used to it" (*Les Echos*, October 3, 2003).

SOURCES FOR FURTHER INFORMATION

Bruno, Abescat, "Finances; Milhaud le placement maison," *L'Express*, November 27, 2003.

"Charles Milhaud; L'Ecureuil, c'est lui," *Le Point*, October 17, 2003.

Guerin, Jean-Yves, "Charles Milhaud: 'je préfère le consensus aux coups de force,'" *Le Figaro*, January 13, 2003.

Mayer, Francis, and Charles Milhaud, "Une bonne gouvernance génère l'efficacité, sans conflit paralysant," *Les Echos*, October 3, 2003.

Morris, Jennifer, "Daniel Lebegue and Charles Milhaud," *Euromoney*, March 8, 2002.

—John Herrick

■■■
Alexei Miller
1962–
Chairman of the Management Committee, Gazprom

Nationality: Russian.

Born: January 31, 1962, in Leningrad, Soviet Union.

Education: Leningrad Institute for Finance and Economics, BA, 1984; PhD, 1989.

Career: Leningrad Research Institute of Civil Construction, 1984–1986, engineer-economist; Leningrad Finance and Economic Institute, 1990, researcher; St. Petersburg Mayor's Office, Foreign Economic Relations directorate, 1991–1996, head of markets monitoring department; St. Petersburg Seaport, 1996–1999, director; Baltic Pipeline System Company, 1999–2000, general director; Russian Federation, 2000, Deputy Energy Minister; Gazprom, 2001–, chairman of the management committee.

Awards: Merits before Fatherland Award of II degree, Russia; Award of Sergiy Radonezhskiy of II degree of the Russian Orthodox Church; Patriarch Honorable Award, Russia.

Address: Gazprom, 16 Ul. Nametkina, Moscow 117884, Russia; http://www.gazprom.ru/eng.

Alexei Miller. *AP/Wide World Photos.*

■ Alexei Miller became the chairman of the Gazprom management committee in 2001 after the board of directors removed Rem Vyakhirev. Under Vyakhirev Gazprom was mismanaged, turning into a gas giant that was struggling both financially and internally; Miller was chosen to transform Gazprom back into a successful company again. Bearing a doctorate in economics, he took a more technical view of company finances and made difficult and controversial desicions. His significant changes in Gazprom's management brought profits and company unity in only three years.

EDUCATION AND EARLY CAREER

Miller was born on January 31, 1962, in Leningrad. He graduated from high school in 1979 and attended the Lenin-grad Finance and Economics Institute, where he studied economics. He earned his degree in 1984 and went on to work as an engineer-economist in the general planning division of the Leningrad Research Institute of Civil Construction. He went back to school at the Finance and Economics Institute in 1986, earning his PhD in economics in 1989. He worked for a variety of organizations before President Vladimir Putin appointed him as chairman of Gazprom with responsibility for turning the company around. He had been the director of development and investments at the St. Petersburg Seaport, the largest seaport in northwestern Russia, and later the general director of the Baltic Pipeline System Company. In 2001 he became Gazprom's management committee chairman. Miller's appointment was surrounded by much controversy, as he had many opponents, but he met with substantial success through hard work and determination.

GAZPROM

After taking over as chairman of Gazprom, Miller achieved early victories in gaining firm control of the Russian gas giant. Many interest groups, old Gazprom managers, and other oil companies had been especially displeased with Miller's appointment; they did not want to see a strong leader at the helm because they wished to take advantage of the company, which had been in chaos. Allegations surfaced that managers had been stealing from the company and that many of Gazprom's business deals had not been in its own favor. Miller made rapid progress in asserting his authority when he forced the board to buy back Purgaz, the gas-producing subsidiary of which Gazprom had lost control in 1999. Miller's goal was simple: to recover Gazprom's lost assets.

While his goals were straightforward and clearly good for the company, many still did not want Miller to succeed. In fact rumors about him were spread around, including allegations that he had been fired after only five months on the job. Other oil companies especially wanted Gazprom to remain in disarray so that they could attain cheap assets. Sabrina Tavernise wrote in the *New York Times*, "Miller took the helm at Gazprom after years of mismanagement and lack of investment had driven the company into decline" (December 19, 2001). Miller needed to create a coherent plan for turning Gazprom back into the gas giant it had been in the past.

FOCUSES ON IMMEDIATE PROBLEMS, NOT RESTRUCTURING

Miller decided that the company's problems would be solved in focusing on three areas in particular: he would reacquire gas assets lost in previous years, reversing Gazprom's declining gas output; he would ensure that no employees were stealing from the company; and he would "concentrate on consolidating government control over Gazprom by replacing people associated with ex-CEO Rem Vyakhirev with executives loyal to Putin" (January 31, 2002). Miller did not immediately conceive a precise reorganization plan for the company, however, because he did not feel it to be necessary.

In June 2002 Miller attended Gazprom's annual shareholders' meeting as one of six state representatives, at which meeting he related some of his successes. He had been able to rein in theft by top managers and had recovered production assets that had been sold to controversial gas traders.

CONTINUES TO RESHAPE GAZPROM

Miller thought it necessary to reachieve financial stability at Gazprom before increasing capitalization. The deputy chairman and financial chief Vitaly Savelyev left the company in 2002 because he had been unable to reduce short-term debt. Miller replaced him with Boris Yurlov, who he believed would

introduce a more conservative plan for financial recovery. Miller took criticism for the appointment; an *FSU Energy* article suggested, "Former Gazprom chairman and Russian prime minister Viktor Chernomyrdin—deemed by many to be the godfather of the asset-stripping schemes at Gazprom before Miller's arrival—is trying to persuade the presidential administration that Miller should be removed" (May 31, 2002). Miller worked through such rumors, reshaping the company's board by replacing members who bore allegiance to the former chairman.

By 2003 Miller had made sizable progress at Gazprom, having devised a long-term strategy that would be implemented over a period of 25 years. He centered his plan around the development of five core production areas. As stated in an article in *Gas Connections*, he moved toward "improving tax and pricing policies, setting up a favorable investment climate, and creating a competitive domestic market" (June 12, 2003). His plan relied on the European market, which he stated would continue to be a priority for Gazprom. Miller also wanted to expand into the Asia Pacific region when the company had gained sufficient strength.

Gazprom had bought back many of its lost assets, and the company was slowly moving toward financial stability. Yet not everyone appreciated Miller's hard work and difficult decisions, arguing that he was paying excessive prices to buy back assets that had been lost under the previous management.

GAZPROM BEGINS TO GROW

Under Miller's guidance Gazprom reached financial stability in only three years. The company met its gas production goals for 2003 and moved from a state of restabilization to one of growth. Net profits were expected to exceed RUR 200 billion in 2003. Miller worked concertedly during his tenure to bring together a team of like-minded professionals who would work their hardest to pull Gazprom out of debt and chaos. He established a new corporate spirit, wherein employees persevered and cooperated in order to achieve common goals. Miller chose his employees with care and treated them with respect. In bringing Gazprom out of its crisis, he gave much of the credit to his dedicated employees.

LOOKED TOWARD EXPANSION

While he stated that Europe would be Gazprom's major export market, Miller looked for additional channels through which to spur the company's growth. He hoped to expand into Asia Pacific and studied the markets in China, Japan, and Korea, where Gazprom might increase both production and profits. The company planned to diversify its services to include offerings of electricity and liquefied natural gas; Miller even hoped to gain access to the liquefied gas market in the

United States, for which Gazprom was still in the preinvestment study phase by mid-2004. Miller also looked to raise gas prices in Russia as part of his long-term growth strategy. He did not plan on breaking Gazprom apart into smaller companies, nor did he agree with the idea of privatization. Gazprom had been created as a large, public company and would stay that way under Miller's leadership.

MANAGEMENT STYLE

Miller had an assertive management style and was able to overcome many obstacles when he became Gazprom's chairman. He nurtured a new office climate, in which employees were loyal to both him and the company. He fired top employees who lacked such loyalty, sending a message throughout the company's ranks. Gazprom's staff became comprehensively supportive and filled with professionals who all wished to better their company.

During his leadership at Gazprom, Miller dealt with criticism from many individuals; his tactics proved successful in the end. He bought back many of the assets Gazprom had lost during its years of mismanagement, increasing gas production.

After three years Gazprom had reached the point where it was making a profit and looking toward new ways to expand.

See also entry on OAO Gazprom in *International Directory of Company Histories.*

SOURCES FOR FURTHER INFORMATION

"Gazprom Finance Chief Resigns," *FSU Energy*, May 31, 2002, p. 11.

"Gazprom Replaces CEO, Improves Prospects for Eurobond," *Euroweek*, June 1, 2001, p. 14.

"Miller Bullish on Russian Gas," *Gas Connections*, June 12, 2003, p. 9.

"Miller Rules Out Gazprom Reform," *NEFTE Compass*, January 31, 2002, p. 3.

Tavernise, Sabrina, "Did Russia's Gas Giant Just Glimpse the Future?" *New York Times*, December 19, 2001.

—Deborah Kondek

■ ■ ■
Stuart A. Miller
1957–
President and chief executive officer, Lennar Corporation

Nationality: American.

Born: 1957.

Education: Harvard University, BS, 1979; University of Miami, JD, 1982.

Family: Son of Leonard (founder, Lennar Corporation) and Susan Miller; married Vicki; children: four.

Career: Lennar Corporation, 1982–1992, officer; 1992–1997, vice president; 1997–, president and chief executive officer; LNR Property Corporation, 1997–, chairman of the board.

Awards: America's Most Powerful People, *Forbes*, 2000.

Address: Lennar Corporation, 700 Northwest 107th Avenue, Miami, Florida 33172; http://lennar.com.

■ Stuart Miller served as president, CEO, and director of Lennar Corporation, a homebuilder and provider of financial services. In 1997 under Miller's leadership Lennar spun off the commercial real estate and management operations into LNR Property Corporation, where Miller served as chairman of the board. During his tenure at Lennar Corporation, Miller led the company through a series of acquisitions that resulted in rapid growth and profitability. As of 2004 Lennar had built more than 500,000 houses, and annual revenues exceeded $6 billion. Coworkers and analysts described Miller as an innovative and driven leader who also was known for his imaginative and unconventional motivational style.

LEARNING FROM HIS FATHER'S EXAMPLE

Lennar Corporation had always been part of Stuart Miller's life. As the son of Lennar's cofounder, Leonard Miller, the younger Miller grew up in 1960s Miami watching his father's business grow. Miller did not take his position as the boss's son lightly. He had inherited his father's hard-working and entre-

preneurial nature and desired to make his own way and earn his own money as soon as he was able. At the age of 11 Miller began mowing the lawns of Lennar's model houses. By his teens Miller was working odd jobs around Lennar's construction sites to save money for a car.

Miller left Florida for Harvard University. After receiving his undergraduate degree, Miller attended the University of Miami Law School, being graduated in 1982. Having achieved his educational goals, Miller returned to the company he had grown up with. He was intent on demonstrating his leadership skills, helping grow the family business, and continuing his educational development in the realm of business.

A CAREER AS A HOMEBUILDER

Miller helped grow Lennar into one of the largest house builders in the United States. A key to the company's success was its ability to branch out into all aspects of construction services. The company's operations included house construction and sales, land development, mortgage financing, title insurance, closing services, insurance agency services, high-speed Internet access, cable television, and alarm installation and monitoring services. Miller understood that by diversifying Lennar's operations, he could tap into all the needs of house buyers and provide them with a complete service platform.

Miller understood that intelligent and well-researched land acquisitions were essential to the company's success. By closely following the markets across the country, Lennar was able to acquire prime property in depressed markets poised for a comeback. For example, in the late 1990s the San Francisco Bay area housing market crashed. In response Lennar bought property in the area at a reduced price, believing that the market would eventually come back. It did, and Lennar prospered. "We respond to opportunities," Miller said in an interview with Marilyn Alva of *Investor's Business Daily*. "We recognize that market trends do change" (June 18, 2003).

Under Miller's leadership Lennar developed a dual-faceted marketing program, which allowed buyers to choose between custom and standard options packages. The custom packages, called the "Design Studio," worked much as did other custom builder programs by allowing customers to choose finish options at one of Lennar's design studios. With its standard options package, the "Everything's Included" program, Lennar was able to keep its costs and prices below those of competitors by building relatively simple houses and including all the options buyers wanted in the base price. For the program to be successful, Miller realized that Lennar had to do its homework. The company performed extensive consumer research and conducted customer surveys to identify the upgrades buyers wanted most. "Because we simplify our processes and keep our overhead low, we're able to keep our costs lower—and use that reduction as the mechanism to provide some of the desired upgrades in the base price," Miller said in an interview with Bill Lurz of *Professional Builder*.

In another move that demonstrated Miller's foresight to adapt to the changing face and needs of American house buyers, Lennar began building multifamily dwellings in urban areas. Although primarily a purveyor of single-family houses, management saw shrinking land supplies in areas such as metropolitan Miami and responded to the changing needs of the aging baby boomer generation. In certain areas where baby boomers were relocating, Miller guided Lennar to shift away from subdivisions to build more condominiums, thus satisfying an important demographic group while responding to land shortages. Many experts agreed that the versatility and adaptability Miller commanded allowed Lennar to ride the waves of volatility in the housing market. "Lennar's broad swath across all the housing market opportunities gives them an ability to manage through all cycles," one business analyst told Alva (June 18, 2003).

MILLER FOCUSES ON ACQUISITIONS AND GROWTH FOR LENNAR

Under Miller's leadership Lennar earned a reputation for rapidly acquiring small house-building companies and successfully turning those acquisitions into viable branches of Lennar. This string of acquisitions enabled Lennar to expand rapidly in the 1990s and 2000s. Lennar acquired two homebuilders in Texas in 1995 and two in California in 1996. In 1998 Lennar acquired the North American Title Company, a purveyor of title and escrow services in Arizona, California, and Colorado. In 2000 Lennar gained significant growth nationally with the acquisition of U.S. Home Corporation. With this merger Lennar doubled in size. In 2001 Lennar acquired nine homebuilders.

While business acquisitions were not uncommon among large companies, the ability to carry out so many acquisitions successfully took forethought and insight. Miller said that his process of determining whether an acquisition would work was to analyze whether the acquisition would make Lennar a better company. Miller conducted extensive financial, cultural, and marketing research.

MANAGEMENT STYLE

Throughout his tenure managing Lennar Corporation, Miller focused on making every employee feel accountable and responsible for the growth and success of the corporation. At the same time he made extensive efforts to foster an atmosphere of creativity and fun in and around the office. Miller believed that empowered and happy employees were vital to the success of the company.

Early in his career with Lennar, Miller attended a seminar at the Disney Institute, a management training program run by Walt Disney Company. He returned to Lennar impressed by Disney's philosophy that motivated employees to be friendly regardless of their positions within the company. As a reflection of this philosophy Lennar began a tradition of wearing name tags that bore only first names and no job titles. In a company that was growing so rapidly that many employees did not know all of their coworkers by name, these name tags fostered an intimate and relaxed environment.

For many employees Miller's management style gave everyday business an unexpected twist at Lennar's Miami headquarters. On Fridays, before regularly scheduled meetings, Miller played music and danced with employees. He did not assign parking for executives and had no reserved space himself. Miller also instituted the production of lighthearted holiday videos that were distributed and shown to all Lennar employees to laud their accomplishments and encourage further success in the upcoming year. Miller mixed this creativity with a disciplined approach to management. All employees played a part in Lennar's commitment to maximizing return on net assets. Each of Lennar's 50 divisions sent Miller a monthly, one-page report showing whether it was meeting its financial goals.

Of the many influences in his life, Miller found the writings of children's author Dr. Seuss especially relevant and applicable to his business philosophy. Miller was known to use Seuss's writings during business meetings and training sessions to boost the confidence of employees or illustrate an important lesson. For example, to break tension in a meeting with U.S. Home Corporation managers during the 2000 acquisition, Miller sat on the conference room floor and gave a reading from Dr. Seuss's classic book, *Oh, the Places You'll Go!*. According to an article by Evan Perez in the *Wall Street Journal*, Miller and other executives wrote their own nursery rhymes in the style of Dr. Seuss. "Where's the Wow?" taught that to stand out from a crowd requires ambition that comes only from within. "Where's the How?" told of using research, practice, and simplicity to succeed. The books were illustrated by the company's advertising firm and published in hardcover for internal use.

Miller was responsible for starting the Lennar tradition of using a children's fable to demonstrate the company's values. Each new employee received a card imprinted with "Scratchings from the Little Red Hen," a story adapted from a popular children's tale. Lennar's version told of a little red hen digging for worms during a drought while an arrogant rooster waited in vain for worms to come to him. The hen was able to eat and prosper because of her work ethic, whereas the rooster's lack of initiative left him weak and hungry. "It's a very simple story," Miller told Perez. "It speaks about challenges and how you deal with them" (July 27, 2001). The little red hen story became a rite of passage of sorts for Lennar employees. New employees were encouraged to recite and memorize this tale of an underdog. The fable also illustrated the creativity and drive Miller brought to Lennar in his own tale of challenges and success at the helm of one of the largest house building corporations in the United States.

See also entry on Lennar Corporation in *International Directory of Company Histories.*

SOURCES FOR FURTHER INFORMATION

Alva, Marilyn, "Builder's Opportunism Hits Nail on the Head," *Investor's Business Daily*, June 18, 2003.

Cook, Lynn, "Lennar Corp: Raise the High Roof Beam," *Forbes*, January 8, 2001, pp. 122–123.

Fields, Gregg, "Changing with Times Keeps Lennar a Leader," *Miami Herald*, June 9, 2003.

Lurz, Bill, "One on One: Lennar's Team," *Professional Builder*, July 1999, pp. 77–78.

Perez, Evan, "Happy Homemaker: Lennar Corp. Thrives as Residential Builder," *Wall Street Journal*, July 27, 2001.

—Jennifer Long

■ ■ ■
Akio Mimura
1940–
President, Nippon Steel Corporation

Nationality: Japanese.

Born: November 2, 1940, in Japan.

Education: Tokyo University, BS, 1963.

Career: Fuji Iron & Steel, 1963–1970; Nippon Steel Corporation, 1970–2000; 2000–2003, vice president; 2003–, president.

Address: Nippon Steel Corporation, 6-3 Otemachi 2-chome, Chiyoda-ku, Tokyo 100-8071, Japan; http://www.nsc.co.jp/shinnihon_english.

■ Akio Mimura joined Fuji Iron & Steel after graduating from Tokyo University in 1963 and remained with the company following its 1970 merger with Yawata Steel, which resulted in the formation of Nippon Steel Corporation. Mimura had been involved in marketing prior to being named president in early 2003. His appointment continued a company practice of rotating the top spot between executives from Nippon's two predecessor firms; Akira Chihaya, who served as president from 1998 to 2003, had begun his career at Yawata. The change in management came after Nippon's agreement to form an alliance with Sumitomo Metal Industries and Kobe Steel; the change also followed Mimura's successful guidance of the company through negotiations with the auto industry on steel-price increases.

As president Mimura was responsible for implementing a three-year plan to improve profitability, which had been threatened by increases in the costs of materials and by protectionist tariffs imposed by other countries, including the United States. In the summer of 2003 Mimura went to New York City, becoming the company's first chief executive to visit overseas investors. His career followed a traditional Japanese path: he offered lifelong service to a single corporation and bore a public persona that was strictly limited to his corporate role—except for the disclosure of an enthusiasm for golf, which was also typical of Japanese executives.

In June 2003 Akio Mimura was named chairman of the Japan Iron & Steel Federation, the powerful industry organiza-

tion representing 136 member companies and trade associations. This post was traditionally held by the president of the country's largest steel producer, which at the time was Nippon Steel; by January 2004, however, Nippon's market capitalization had dropped to second place behind JFE Holdings. JFE was created in 2003 through a merger between Kawasaki Steel Corporation and NKK Corporation. Nippon's stock price was further depressed in September 2003 by a gas explosion at its Nagoya plant.

Steel, while playing a central role, had not been Nippon's sole focus for over 20 years. In order to reduce its dependence on a single industry, the company diversified in the 1980s, forming a New Materials unit in 1984, to make silicon wafers, and an Electronics division in 1986. At that time Nippon also entered joint ventures with IBM Japan, Hitachi, and C. Itch, forging its way into the electronics and telecommunications markets. A semiconductor division was added in 1993 but was sold in 1999. As of 2004 Nippon Steel's peripheral operations included engineering, construction, chemicals, nonferrous metals, ceramics, electronics, information and communications, and urban development.

Nippon's first joint venture in China—Guangzhou Pacific Tinplate—was launched in 1997. In July 2003 Nippon Steel signed an agreement with China's largest steelmaker, Shanghai Baoshan Iron and Steel Company, to manufacture steel sheeting for automobiles. Further, a new factory was scheduled to open in Shanghai in 2005. The expanding Chinese economy provided a rapidly growing market for Japanese steel, and by late 2003 more than 20 percent of Japanese steel exports went directly to China. In fiscal 2004 Nippon Steel had its first profitable year since 2001, which was largely attributed to demand from China; however, steep increases in the costs of raw materials made continued growth in profits unlikely.

See also entry on Nippon Steel Corporation in *International Directory of Company Histories.*

SOURCES FOR FURTHER INFORMATION

"Mimura to Succeed Chihaya as Nippon Steel President," *Southeast Asia Iron & Steel Institute Newsletter*, January 22, 2003, http://www.seaisi.org/news_detail.asp?ID=1141&y=Year&m=Month.

"Nippon Steel Recasts Strategies," *Nikkei Weekly*, January 12, 2004.

"Nippon Steel to Name Vice Pres. Mimura as New President," Nikkei Report, January 22, 2003.

—Sandra M. Larkin

■■■
Vittorio Mincato
1936–
Chief executive officer, Eni

Nationality: Italian.

Born: 1936, in Torrebelvicino, Italy.

Career: Eni, 1957–1977, various positions, eventually became director of administration and finance for Lanerossi; 1977–1984, director of administration; 1984–1988, assistant to the chairman; 1989–1990, director of human resources; 1990–1993, chairman and CEO of Savio and chairman of Enichem Agricoltura; 1993–1995, deputy chairman and CEO of Enichem; 1996–1998, chairman of Enichem; 1998–, CEO.

Address: Eni, Piazzale Enrico Mattei 1, 00144 Rome, Italy; http://www.eni.it.

■ An accountant by training, Vittorio Mincato spent his entire professional career at the Italian oil and gas company Eni. After 40 years of rising through Eni's ranks he had given up any hope of ever reaching the top spot; then in 1998 he was finally selected to be the CEO. Mincato succeeded without the support of the political establishment, a rarity in Italian business.

Vittorio Mincato. *AP/Wide World Photos.*

EARLY CAREER

Mincato was born in 1936 in Torrebelvicino, Italy. In 1957 he began his long career with the oil and gas firm Eni. Until 1977 Mincato worked for Lanerossi, Eni's textile division, eventually rising to the position of director of administration and finance. He returned to the parent company in 1977 to serve as director of administration; from 1984 until 1988 he served as assistant to the chairman. Mincato moved to the post of director of human resources in 1989, then from 1990 to 1993 served as the chairman and CEO of Eni's textile-machinery company Savio; at the same time he served as the chairman of Enichem Agricoltura, Eni's fertilizer subsidiary. Mincato helped to privatize both Savio and Enichem Agricoltura. From 1993 to 1995 he held the position of deputy chairman and CEO of Enichem, Eni's petrochemical subsidiary. Then from 1996 to 1998 Minato was chairman of Enichem, where he focused on restructuring and privatization.

BECOMES CEO AT ENI

In November 1998, when the former chief executive Franco Bernabe left the company to become the CEO at Telecom Italia, Mincato became CEO at Eni. Some believed that the company should have brought in an outsider to fill the vacancy, but fears of provoking internal strife by doing so led to the selection of the longtime Eni employee Mincato. He took over at a particularly difficult time for the company: international oil prices were low, and the looming liberalization of the Italian gas market further threatened profits.

After taking over as CEO, Mincato made clear that he would strictly apply the company's statutes giving all executive power to the chief executive, which attitude was occasionally the source of tension. Soon after Mincato became CEO, a power struggle developed between him and the Eni chairman Renato Ruggiero. As the former director-general of the World

Trade Organization, Ruggiero wanted to take on a more active role in running the company and threatened to step down if he was not given broader authority. Yet Mincato was not willing to cede any of his CEO powers, which were outlined in the company statutes. The board of directors stepped in with a compromise in which the CEO would retain overall management powers but the chairman would be given a role in the company's international activities; Ruggiero proved unwilling to accept the compromise for long, resigning in September 1999. Mincato explained the situation to the *Financial Times*: "I did not launch a war to defend my position. At the end of the day the statutes clearly established there was only one CEO" (October 12, 1999). He added that the conflict never became personal.

Mincato's struggles continued into 2000, when the Italian government, which had been trying to assert greater influence over the country's leading companies, attempted to force Mincato to resign. The government still owned 35 percent of Eni and thus wielded a certain degree of leverage within the firm; authorities hoped to give more powers to the new chairman Gianmaria Gros-Pietro. In fact, as Mincato had resisted state interference with Eni's operations the government was seeking to replace him entirely with someone less independent. State officials eventually went as far as to attempt to change the company's statutes in April 2000 in order to give more management powers to the chairman. Mincato indicated that if the government altered the statutes, he would resign; Eni's board of directors rejected the proposed changes, however, and Mincato remained on as CEO.

Upon becoming CEO, Mincato had fully outlined his plan for the company. First, he resolved to refocus Eni on its core oil and gas activities while divesting the company of certain other activities. Second, he wanted the company to focus on growth, especially through alliances and joint ventures. Third, Mincato promised to deal with the liberalization of the domestic gas market. The company had once held a near monopoly over the Italian gas market, but government deregulation had ended that situation; Mincato hoped to make up for lost profits by selling gas abroad to countries such as Croatia and Greece. Finally, he planned to expand into the electricity market. Mincato informed the *Financial Times*, "Our interest is based on the possibility of a gas company becoming integrated downstream into power generation to stabilize or increase sales and revenues in the short term" (October 12, 1999).

EXPANSION PLANS

In spite of his initial plans Mincato came to acquire a reputation for not being interested in international expansion. He informed the *Financial Times* that he was, in fact, keen on such expansion, but observed that he was nevertheless "often depicted as a domestic animal, a defender of national borders" (Oc-

tober 12, 1999). He went on to say that such portrayals were simply not true, pointing to a chemical alliance he had helped forge with Union Carbide in 1995. Mincato also claimed that he began talks with the French company Elf Aquitaine, though a merger never occurred. Mincato did admit to the *Financial Times* that he believed Eni needed to grow before it could successfully expand beyond Italy's borders. He stated, "Our weakness is our size and our priority is to grow. The fastest way is through acquisition and we have ample financial means to do so" (October 12, 1999).

In 2000 Mincato thought he had found a suitable acquisition: Eni attempted to buy the midsized British oil company Enterprise, at first outbidding Amerada Hess. Mincato commented in the *Financial Times*, "Eni has never before undertaken an operation of this size" (December 22, 2000). Minato worked for months on a friendly merger offer in an attempt to convince shareholders to accept the bid. The purchase of Enterprise would have given Eni a presence in both the North Sea and North Africa; the company also would have acquired reserves in Indonesia and Venezuela. However, by 2002 the merger attempt had failed. Another major defeat for Mincato came when the Saudi company Sabic called off talks to buy Eni's petrochemicals division. The Saudis had been concerned about the large investments that would have been required in order to fully comply with environmental laws.

The Italian government criticized Mincato for being too cautious. With his mandate set to expire in May 2002, some state officials wanted to seize the opportunity to remove him from the CEO position. Rumors surfaced that Mincato would be transferred to the chairman's position, thus absolving him of most of his power. One analyst informed the *Financial Times*, "Eni was prudent not to overpay for Enterprise and the Sabic deal was not easy to bring off, but the combination reinforces the view that Mr. Mincato might be made chairman in order to bring in new management" (April 18, 2002).

Officials wanted Eni to be involved in the deals being made by the world's biggest oil companies. Also the government was displeased that the proposed deal with the French company Elf Aquitaine never materialized. Nevertheless Minato felt that an immediate megamerger was not in Eni's best interests. He told the *Financial Times*, "Megamergers were above all guided by a defensive logic. They have been looked upon essentially as a means of further reducing costs while gaining economies of scale. But they also incur costs which are often high. First and foremost is the cost of eventual cultural clashes, which are the main reason for such ventures to fail" (May 28, 2001).

To sidestep such clashes of corporate culture, Mincato looked throughout Europe, avoiding the United States; Eni proceeded to purchase the relatively small British Borneo and Lasmo companies. Of those acquisitions Mincato told the *Financial Times*, "We had never before bought foreign companies and the result has already helped internationalize our own culture" (May 28, 2001). A concrete example of that internationalization was the hiring of the Irishman Hugh O'Donnel as the head of Saipem, Eni's oil-services subsidiary, marking the first time a non-Italian had held such a high-ranking post in the company. To further the company's global interests Mincato bought reserves around the world, including in Iran and Russia.

MUSIC, NOT POLITICS

As was witnessed in a few of his struggles, Mincato preferred not to combine politics with business. He remarked in the *Financial Times*, "Politics and industry do not mix well" (May 28, 2001). Although Eni's headquarters were located in Rome, Mincato spent much of his time in Milan in order to stay clear of the political wrangling in the capital city. Mincato also spent a significant amount of time in Milan because he was a music lover and enjoyed frequenting the city's famous La Scala opera house. He enjoyed reading musical scores, and his favorite composer was Wagner.

See also entry on ENI S.p.A. in *International Directory of Company Histories*.

SOURCES FOR FURTHER INFORMATION

Betts, Paul, "Eni Faces More Top Management Turmoil," *Financial Times*, April 12, 2000.

———, "Eni Resolves Power Struggle between Chiefs," *Financial Times*, September 23, 1999.

———, "Italy Hopes New Brooms Will Calm Its Corporate Giants," *Financial Times*, November 19, 1998.

———, "A Quiet Baritone on Italy's Oil and Gas Stage," *Financial Times*, May 28, 2001.

———, "Wagner Fan Sets Record Straight on Alliances," *Financial Times*, October 12, 1999.

Buchan, David, and Andrea Felsted, "Lasmo Falls into the Arms of Its Latin Lover," *Financial Times*, December 22, 2000.

Kapner, Fred, "Aggressive Eni Plans Rise in Oil and Gas Output," *Financial Times*, January 15, 2002.

———, "Blow for Eni Chief as Sabic Ends Talks," *Financial Times*, April 18, 2002.

—Ronald Young

Rafael Miranda Robredo

1949–

Chief executive officer, Endesa

Nationality: Spanish.

Born: 1949, in Burgos, Spain.

Education: Comillas University, BS, 1973; E.O.I., MS.

Career: Tudor, 1973–1984, group technical director; Campofrio, 1984–1987, vice chief executive officer; Endesa, 1987–1997, managing director; 1997–, chief executive officer.

Address: Endesa, Ribera de Loira 60, 28042 Madrid, Spain; http://www.endesa.es.

■ In 1997 Rafael Miranda Robredo became CEO of Spain's state-owned Empresa Nacional de Electricidad (Endesa), the country's largest electric company. An industrial engineer by training, Miranda joined Endesa in 1987 as managing director after stints with several other Spanish companies. After a decade as managing director, Miranda became CEO, leading Endesa through a period of government deregulation of the electricity sector in Spain. He implemented sweeping changes at the company and greatly increased its presence internationally.

EARLY CAREER

Miranda was born in Burgos, Spain. He graduated with a degree in industrial engineering from Comillas University in 1973. He later earned a master's degree in management science from the industrial organization institute E.O.I. Miranda's first job was with Tudor, a manufacturer of electrical batteries. At Tudor, Miranda served as group technical director. After more than a decade at Tudor, in 1984 he moved on to work at Campofrio, where he was responsible for the industrial division. In 1987 Miranda joined Endesa as managing director, a post he held until becoming CEO in 1997.

PRIVATIZATION AND LIBERALIZATION

With the deregulation of the electricity sector in Spain in 1998, Miranda had to make Endesa fit for competition. He told the *Financial Times* that "with liberalization, the business will change dramatically" (September 23, 1997). Before liberalization the government heavily regulated the electric industry in Spain and guaranteed large profits for companies such as Endesa. Top management rarely worried about marketing or customer satisfaction. Layoffs of workers were exceedingly rare.

With the 1998 deregulation, Endesa would have to face real competition for markets and customers for the first time. The government also planned to privatize the state-owned electric company. Furthermore, the government no longer guaranteed a minimum profit, and customers were free to select their electricity provider. To make matters worse for Miranda, the government reduced electricity rates between 1997 and 1999. Facing such circumstances, Miranda told the *Wall Street Journal* that "nothing will ever be the same. We are faced with the task of remaking Endesa in a competitive environment" (October 6, 1997).

In response to the government's liberalization of the electricity market in Spain, Miranda announced to the *Financial Times* that "corporate efficiency and shareholder value are now our twin priorities" (May 12, 1998). Miranda implemented a three-pronged strategy to deal with deregulation. First he sought diversification by moving beyond the electric industry. For example, Endesa purchased the Spanish telephone company Retevisón. Miranda also moved Endesa into other areas, such as water management, that held the promise of high growth. Second he planned international expansion, particularly into Latin America. Third he looked for ways to cut costs by eliminating jobs and reducing operational and maintenance costs. Thus between February and October 1997 Miranda cut some eight hundred jobs at Endesa, mostly through early retirements. In May 1998 he announced that he planned to cut the company's labor force of about 25,000 by 36 percent over the next four years in anticipation of privatization. In another cost-saving move, in 1998 Miranda streamlined Endesa's seven electricity generation distribution units into a single organization in order to eliminate duplicated costs.

Business analysts largely approved of Miranda's changes at Endesa, and most issued "buy" recommendations for the company's stock. Nicolás Fernández of Ibersecurities told the *Wall Street Journal* that "after 2000, diversification and cost-cutting should kick in to boost profits" (November 12, 1998). Merrill

106

Lynch informed the same newspaper that "management actions to accelerate cost-cutting and share buybacks more than offset worries about Latin American devaluations and any retail-share overhang" (November 12, 1998). At the same time, some government officials worried that Miranda's moves would actually strengthen Endesa's dominance of the electricity market rather than open it up to competition as they had hoped.

LATIN AMERICAN EXPANSION

Like many Spanish firms during the 1990s, Endesa sought to expand its presence in Latin America. Miranda argued that Spanish companies had an advantage in Latin America, telling the *Financial Times*, "Latin Americans are different from the Spanish, but we come from the same roots. We understand the idiosyncrasies of the countries there" (September 23, 1997). Such an attitude was a reflection of Miranda's overall belief that foreign investment was a key component to maintaining Endesa's leadership in the Spanish electricity sector. Because the government planned to privatize the company, profitable foreign expansion was a major selling point to investors, and Latin America seemed a logical place for Miranda to start. While electricity demand in Spain was growing by about 2 percent every year, in Latin America demand was increasing by 8 percent annually. In late 1997 Endesa announced that it would even transfer its international division to Latin America. Miranda told the *Financial Times*, "That's where the assets are. The executives can be close to the problems and the opportunities" (September 23, 1997).

Endesa's most significant Latin American acquisition came in August 1997, when Miranda negotiated the purchase of 26 percent of Enersis, a Chilean electric company and the largest utility in Latin America. Endesa also led a consortium that acquired the two main electric companies in Colombia in September 1997. In addition, the company had a presence in Brazil, Argentina, and Peru.

However, economic problems in Latin America hurt Endesa's expansion into the region. Miranda largely downplayed the economic crises in Latin America, pointing to the fact that the region accounted for only 6 or 7 percent of Endesa's total profits. In addition, he argued that Latin American electric companies were largely unaffected by the economic woes. Despite such claims, Endesa was hurt by Enersis's large debt. This situation had a negative effect on Endesa's credit rating, led to a one-third drop in the company's share value, and forced a reduction of Miranda's investment plan.

Miranda faced another sort of problem in Chile. Spain attempted to extradite the former Chilean dictator Augusto Pinochet for human rights violations against Spanish citizens residing in Chile. However, many Chilean business leaders opposed Spanish interference in Chilean politics. Endesa and Mi-

randa became scapegoats for the actions of Spain. Some former shareholders of Enersis even brought a criminal suit against Miranda. The Endesa CEO, however, brushed the suit aside as having no legal basis.

FAILED MERGER

In 2000 Miranda attempted to forge a merger between Endesa and Iberdrola, Spain's other leading electric company. Miranda argued that the merger of the two electric giants would create a strong Spanish power firm capable of competing with companies from the rest of Europe and the United States. He told the *Financial Times* that "the merger will allow us to be a global player" (October 20, 2000).

However, for the deal to succeed, Miranda would have to overcome Spain's antitrust laws. He claimed that the merger would aid rather than hinder competition in the Spanish power sector. He informed the *Financial Times* that "what we seek is a balance, or trade off between forging a stronger, more efficient Endesa as a result of the takeover, and injecting more competition into the domestic electricity market" (October 20, 2000). While the new company would initially control some 80 percent of the electricity market in Spain, it would eventually divest itself of some assets, allowing new players to compete. To this end Miranda proposed that thermal and hydroelectric plants be sold off in the form of three new companies by 2003. He believed that only this sort of sale would lead to approval of the merger by the government competition commission. He went so far as to admit that Endesa would even have to rid itself of some valuable assets, telling the *Financial Times*, "We won't be able to get rid of unwanted assets and keep the best because we simply won't be allowed to do so" (October 20, 2000). Furthermore, he hoped to divest through asset swaps with other European companies in order to gain access into such countries as France, Italy, and Germany.

In early 2001 Spain's competition commission delivered a confidential, nonbinding report on the merger. Then, citing the conditions imposed by the government on Endesa's takeover of Iberdrola, Miranda called off the merger. He argued that these conditions would have made it virtually impossible to create shareholder value for the new company. While he would have preferred the merger, Miranda announced a new strategy for Endesa that included continued cost-cutting, asset sales, and geographic expansion. He said that he planned to cut Endesa's costs by 35 percent. In addition, the company would sell assets in order to raise additional capital. This capital could then be used to expand Endesa's presence in Europe. Such European expansion marked a shift in focus for the company. In the late 1990s Endesa had largely focused on Latin America. However, deregulation and liberalization of electricity markets in European countries made expansion attractive. Miranda reported to the *Wall Street Journal* that "it's the moment to make the jump to Europe" (March 15, 2001). By expanding, Miranda hoped to follow the German and French models of creating large and powerful electric companies that were capable of growing and diversifying.

Several obstacles blocked Miranda's new plan. First a power crisis in California made European governments more cautious about opening up their energy markets. Second, at the European Union Summit in Stockholm, Sweden, in March 2001, France refused to agree to a concrete timetable for the full liberalization of its energy sector. Endesa was able to acquire 30 percent of SNET, a small French power group. However, Miranda met stiff resistance to his attempts to buy stakes in Dutch utility companies.

Slow European expansion and problems in Latin American markets led to economic problems for Miranda and Endesa. The company suffered double-digit declines in 2002 and in the first quarter of 2003. However, by the second quarter of 2003 Endesa was once again turning a profit. The turnaround was largely a result of the resolution of debt issues at Enersis in Chile. Miranda negotiated for months with banks before he finally succeeded in extending the maturity of Enersis's debt, which in turn restored investors' confidence in Endesa.

See also entries on Campofrio Alimentacion S.A. and ENDESA S.A. in *International Directory of Company Histories.*

SOURCES FOR FURTHER INFORMATION

Burns, Tom, "Endesa to Cut Labour Force by 36 Percent over Four Years," *Financial Times*, May 12, 1998.

———, "Endesa Looks for European Benefits," *Financial Times*, January 12, 2001.

Burns, Tom, and Leslie Crawford, "Power Merger Chiefs on the Defense," *Financial Times*, October 20, 2000.

"Endesa Builds Latin America Presence," *Financial Times*, September 23, 1997.

Schafer, Thilo, "Expansion Plans Facing New Obstacles," *Financial Times*, April 20, 2001.

Vitzhum, Carlta, "After Scrapping Merger, Endesa Charts a New Course for Growth," *Wall Street Journal*, March 15, 2001.

———, "Endesa Hangs Its Hopes on Restructuring: Spanish Utility Grapples with Latin Woes, Sliding Electric Rates," *Wall Street Journal*, November 12, 1998.

———, "Spain's Endesa Pitches $7 Billion Offering: Electric Utility, Facing Deregulation, Expands Overseas," *Wall Street Journal*, October 6, 1997.

—Ronald Young

■■■
Fujio Mitarai
1935–
President and chief executive officer, Canon

Nationality: Japanese.

Born: September 23, 1935, in Kamae, Oita (Kyushu), Japan.

Education: Chuo University, BA, 1961.

Family: Married Chizuko (deceased 2002); children: at least two.

Career: Canon Inc., 1961–1979?, accountant; 1979–1989, president and chief executive officer of Canon USA; 1989–1995, managing director; 1995–, president; 1997–, chief executive officer.

Awards: Named Person of the Year by PhotoImaging Manufacturers & Distributors Association, 1998; named one of the world's top 25 managers by *BusinessWeek*, 2001.

Address: Canon, 30-2, Shimomaruko 3-chome, Ohta-ku, Tokyo 146-8501, Japan; http://www.canon.com.

Fujio Mitarai. *AP/Wide World Photos.*

■ As chief executive officer of Canon, the Japanese camera and office technology manufacturer, Fujio Mitarai introduced his unique blend of Western and Japanese management styles. When the company was struggling to remain profitable, he overhauled the corporate structure, cutting costs, streamlining production, and improving profits substantially. Mitarai's inimitable management style inspired the phrase "the Mitarai way."

ENTERING THE FAMILY BUSINESS

Growing up, Mitarai watched his three brothers follow in their father's footsteps and embark on careers in medicine, but he had different dreams. Though he could speak only Japanese, Mitarai yearned to travel overseas. In 1961 he joined Canon, the company cofounded by his uncle Takeshi Mitarai. Five years later Mitarai's uncle transferred him to the United States. The move was an attempt to compete with Nikon and

Pentax, which then dominated the U.S. camera market. Mitarai was one of just seven employees working in the Canon headquarters in Manhattan.

The company's first earnings report, which Mitarai put together, suggested that Canon had made a mere $6,000 on $3 million in sales. The IRS became suspicious and visited the Canon office. After a close inspection, the auditors suggested that Canon close its unprofitable U.S. headquarters and put the money in the bank, where it would at least earn interest. For Mitarai the advice was a wake-up call. He knew his uncle's company could be profitable if it cut costs and improved sales. A few years later he was promoted to the head of North American camera sales. He traveled around the country promoting Canon's cameras, staying in cheap hotels to save money.

Mitarai spent 23 years in the United States, eventually becoming president of Canon USA. Under his leadership Canon successfully launched several new products. For example, the Canon AE-1, introduced in 1976, was the first affordable 35 mm camera with automatic exposure. The AE-1 made it easy for amateur photographers to take professional-looking pictures, and it helped propel Canon to the head of the single-lens-reflex camera market. In 1987 Canon released its EOS (Electronic Operating System) automatic-focusing camera. With a focusing motor inside its lens, the EOS focused faster and with less light than did other cameras.

Mitarai also expanded Canon's printer and copier businesses, introducing cheaper, faster, smaller machines. In 1984 Canon joined forces with Hewlett-Packard, with Canon designing the laser printer and Hewlett-Packard supplying the software, packaging, and marketing. By 2001 the collaborative effort had secured 70 percent of its market. In 2000 Canon released a line of faster and more reliable digital copiers. Canon effectively ran Xerox out of the low-cost copier market and increased its share of the high-end corporate copier market to become the leading producer of copy machines in the world.

While in America, Mitarai often sought advice from top CEOs, including Jack Welch of General Electric, with whom he regularly played golf. Mitarai carried their advice with him when he returned to Japan in 1989.

LEADERSHIP AT CANON JAPAN

What Mitarai found on his return home alarmed him. In the late 1980s Canon comprised a dozen individually run divisions, many operating in the red. As senior managing director, Mitarai tried to push American-style cost-cutting measures, but Canon executives were not paying attention. In 1995 Mitarai's cousin Hajime Mitarai, then the president of Canon, suddenly died. The company's board passed over six other executives to place Mitarai in the position.

Finally able to put his ideas into action, Mitarai overhauled Canon's financial structure. Instead of focusing on sales (as Japanese executives typically do), he focused on profits. To reduce debt, he eliminated divisions selling unsuccessful products, such as PCs, electric typewriters, and liquid crystal displays. He merged the remaining divisions into four: copiers, printers, cameras, and optical equipment. To increase coordination among the divisions, he directed Canon's managers to adopt consolidated balance sheets, enabling them to see instantly which divisions were successful and which were struggling. He also started having daily lunch meetings with senior managers and monthly meetings with middle managers, in which he personally explained his vision and outlined what needed to be done. He relentlessly pushed his staff to cut costs and increase profits. "I changed the mindset at Canon by getting people to realize that profits come first," he told *Business Week International* (February 11, 2002). In 1997 Mitarai was named the company's CEO.

Within five years of taking over, Matarai had tripled both the company's net profits and its stock value, even as Japan floundered in a recession and the world financial outlook remained shaky. He introduced new budget-planning methods and reduced inventory to improve cash flow management. Moreover, unlike most companies, Canon used its own funds for capital investment rather than borrowing money.

MANAGEMENT STYLE

Some of his colleagues dubbed Mitarai's unyielding obsession with the bottom line the "Mitarai way." His way blends the Western focus on profit with traditional Japanese values. Like American corporations, Canon offers monetary incentives to boost sales and encourage ingenuity. Workers undergo a series of "tests" beginning at age 25; those who do well can make as much as 80 percent more money than their peers. However, the company also promises lifetime employment—a common practice in Japan. Mitarai's blended approach made for loyal, yet driven, employees.

Mitarai long held the belief that Canon's employees are more important than its investors, but some analysts complained that his investor relations left much to be desired. The company's financial reports were often confusing, offering stockholders little insight into Canon's products and strategies. In fact, the Japan Financial Analysts Association placed Canon at the bottom of its rating of 20 companies in terms of openness, information, and overall performance.

In a country where most CEOs are merely figureheads, Mitarai stood out. "He's active in leading the company. He's pretty driven," Steve Appleton, head of semiconductor maker Micron Technology, told *Fortune* (October 14, 2002). Despite being firmly in charge, however, Mitarai relied heavily on input from his executives before making any move. For example, when he wanted to introduce a new production technique, he first spent weeks trying to convince senior executives. He finally won them over. The new system, called cell production, turned out to be one of the best cost-cutting measures in the company's history. Mitarai replaced expensive assembly lines with more efficient groups, or cells, of people who work on one product to completion. The cell production system enables a dozen workers to match the output of 30 workers on the old assembly lines. Streamlining allowed the company to save an estimated $300 million, increase productivity by 30 percent, and to save thousands of feet in factory space. "Many company managers now look up to Mitarai as a role model," Yoshio Nakamura, senior managing director of the Japanese business organization Keidanren told *Business Week* (September 16, 2002).

LOOKING TO THE FUTURE

By the early 2000s Mitarai was focusing on Canon's future. He announced in 2001 that he was investing $810 million in research and development over the next three years. Instead of simply building stand-alone copiers and printers, he wanted to design machines that could communicate with one another and integrate into an office network. In 2004 he announced that Canon was preparing to roll out a new technology called the surface-conduction electron-emitter display, which would be used in large-screen televisions and other devices. Mitarai also expanded his business into the consulting arena, helping corporations plan their business equipment needs.

As part of his continuing effort to cut costs, Mitarai began to move some of the company's operations overseas. In 2002 Canon opened a laser-printing plant and three copier factories in China to take over the production of low- and mid-range copiers that were previously produced in Japan. Canon was expected to have moved 40 percent of its production out of Japan by 2005. Mitarai was also looking at potential acquisitions in the United States and Europe, specifically in the biotechnology and information technology sectors.

Unlike many corporate CEOs, Mitarai was less concerned with his salary than with the success of his company. "I'm mo-tivated by my ambition of turning Canon into a truly excellent company," he told *BusinessWeek Online* (September 13, 2002). His goal was to make Canon number one in cameras, ink-jet printers, and semiconductor manufacturing equipment over the next few years.

See also entry on Canon Inc. in *International Directory of Company Histories*.

SOURCES FOR FURTHER INFORMATION

Holstein, William J., "Canon Takes Aim at Xerox," *Fortune*, October 14, 2002, p. 215.

Kunii, Irene M., "How East Meets West at Canon," *BusinessWeek Online*, September 13, 2002, http://www.businessweek.com/bwdaily/dnflash/sep2002/nf20020913_4948.htm.

———, "International Business: Japan: He Put the Flash Back in Canon," *BusinessWeek*, September 16, 2002, p. 40.

———, "The Pain, the Pain: Canon's Cutting Edge," *BusinessWeek International*, February 11, 2002, p. 16.

—Stephanie Watson

■■■
William E. Mitchell
1944–
President and chief executive officer, Arrow Electronics

Nationality: American.

Born: March 13, 1944, in Los Angeles, California.

Education: Princeton University, BS, 1966; University of Michigan, MS, 1967.

Family: Son of John Stewart Mitchell and Helen Fine; married Jan Marie Scheyer; children: three.

Career: Exxon Corporation, 1969–1972, analyst; 1972–1973, department manager; Raychem Corporation, 1973–1976, operations manager; Raychem International, 1977–1985, regional manager; 1985–1988, vice president and general manager; Raychem Corporation, 1988–1991, senior vice president, industrial group; 1991–1993, senior vice president, electronics group; Nashua Corporation, 1993–1994, president and chief operating officer; 1994–1995, president and chief executive officer; Sequel, 1995–1999, chairman, president, and chief executive officer; Solectron Corporation, 1999–2002, executive vice president, president of the Solectron Global Services division; Arrow Electronics, 2003–, president and chief executive officer.

Address: Arrow Electronics, 50 Marcus Drive, Melville, New York 11747; http://www.arrow.com.

■ William E. Mitchell was elected president and chief executive officer for Arrow Electronics in 2003 after spending 30 years in the electronics industry. After graduating from Princeton University and the University of Michigan, Mitchell worked for Exxon Corporation for four years. He joined Raychem Corporation in 1973 and worked in a variety of capacities in finance, manufacturing, international sales, and marketing. From 1993 to 2002 he served as president and chief executive officer of Nashua Corporation; chairman, president, and chief executive officer at Sequel; and executive vice president for Solectron Corporation. He also served as president of Solectron Global Services, which he built into a $1.2 billion business. His reputation in managing electronic services led to his appointment with Arrow.

EARLY CAREER

Mitchell was born in Los Angeles. As a talented student, he enrolled at Princeton University, where he studied engineering and graduated in 1966 with a bachelor of science degree. He then enrolled in graduate school at the University of Michigan, where he was named as a National Science Foundation Fellow and earned a master of science degree in engineering in 1967. Mitchell began his professional career in 1969 as an analyst at Exxon Corporation's office in New York City. In 1972 he accepted a position as department manager for Exxon in Baton Rouge, Louisiana.

JOINS RAYCHEM

Raychem Corporation was one of the first pioneers in Silicon Valley in California. The company was formed in 1957 when its founder, Paul M. Cook, then an engineer at the Stanford Research Institute, began conducting experiments in his garage. He tested the effects of radiation chemistry on plastics (the name Raychem is a shortened form of "radiation chemistry") and discovered a method for heat-shrinking plastic. This process is used to heat-shrink plastic in packages for meat products and for enclosing coaxial telephone cable.

Raychem had grown into a major force in the technology sector by 1973. Mitchell returned to his native California that year to join Raychem at its headquarters in Menlo Park as an operations manager for the company's energy division. He served in manufacturing operations until his promotion to the position of regional manager for Raychem International in 1977. As regional manager for the international group of the company from 1977 to 1985, his position focused on North and South America.

Raychem grew at an average of 25 percent per year during its first 25 years in business, but growth began to slow in the 1980s. After the company invested more money into its research and development section, profits began to decline. In 1985 the company was forced to lay off more than five hundred employees. Nevertheless, Mitchell earned a promotion during that year based on his work with the international group; he became vice president and general manager of Raychem International.

In 1988 Mitchell was promoted to senior vice president in charge of the industrial group, and during a series of organizational changes by Raychem in 1991, he was named senior vice president in charge of the electronics group. "Bill Mitchell . . . has done an excellent job of restoring growth and profitability to our industrial divisions," said Raychem Chief Executive Officer Robert Saldich in 1991. "His experience in bringing Raychem products to a diverse group of industrial customers will enable us to take a fresh look at our electronics sector as it continues to shift from primarily defense business to a more commercial business" (Business Wire, March 26, 1991).

BECOMES PRESIDENT OF NASHUA CORPORATION

Mitchell remained at Raychem as senior vice president until August 1993, when he was appointed president and chief operating officer of Nashua Corporation, based in Nashua, New Hampshire. Mitchell was also named a director of the company. Nashua offered a wide array of products and services, including coated-paper products, computer products, office supplies, and photofinishing services. The company praised Mitchell's experience when he joined the company. "Bill's leadership abilities will enable Nashua to build on its past successes and aggressively pursue the opportunities offered through our technologies and capabilities," the company's chief executive officer, Charles E. Clough, said of Mitchell (Union Leader, August 13, 1993).

Nashua gained some notoriety during Mitchell's time with the company. Nashua sponsored a private school at a local plant in Albany, New York, which was designed to connect education with industry by maintaining a heavy focus on industry within its curriculum. "I think it's an exciting concept," Mitchell said when he visited the school in 1994 (Times Union, July 12, 1994). The school was known as the Learning Space and was open to children ages 5 through 13. Nashua also received a Certificate of Environmental Achievement from the Environmental Protection Agency in 1994 for participating in a pollution-prevention initiative known as the 33/50 Program, which was designed to reduce certain high-priority toxic chemicals by 33 percent in 1992 and by 50 percent in 1995. "This award demonstrates Nashua's commitment to reducing pollution and preserving our environment," Mitchell said when he received the award on behalf of the company. "Nashua continues to recognize the important role that corporations can play in environmental protection" (Business Wire, August 22, 1994).

Mitchell replaced Clough as the company's chief executive officer in 1994. Under Mitchell's leadership prior to his appointment as CEO, Nashua sold its computer-products division, known as Nashua Precision Technologies, and established a commercial-products group, which was designed to streamline the organization. "We have laid a foundation that will guide Nashua's profitable growth in the future as a cus-

tomer-oriented, market-driven, innovative company with outstanding marketing, service, technical and manufacturing capabilities," Mitchell said in 1994. "Today, Nashua is better positioned to capitalize on its global market opportunities" (Business Wire, July 25, 1994).

Mitchell's plan failed. Nashua Precision Technologies became known as Cerion and saw its sales double between 1994 and 1995. During the same time period, Nashua Corporation saw its market value and stock price plummet, and many blamed Mitchell for the company's problems. According to an article in the Boston Globe, Mitchell "croaked sales by trying to force a plethora of niche products through a single sales force," referring to the company's new commercial-products group (May 8, 1996). Mitchell left the company in 1995 under pressure from Nashua's board of directors.

A NEW START

Mitchell was recruited in 1995 to become chairman, president, and chief executive officer of Sequel, a privately held company based in California. At the time, Sequel focused its primary business on repair and maintenance of computer disk drives. He was responsible for the company's international operations, including those in the United Kingdom, Malaysia, and Penang. In his four years with the company, he converted its focus to computer-services outsourcing.

Mitchell's experience with computer outsourcing proved to be valuable when he was hired in 1999 as executive vice president of Solectron Corporation, which provided customized electronics-manufacturing solutions to original-equipment manufacturers. The company created a new division, Solectron Global Services, and made Mitchell its president. Solectron Global Services offered a full range of services for the product lines of Solectron's client manufacturers, which allowed the manufacturers to focus their attention on the development of new products.

Solectron grew significantly between 1999 and 2002, acquiring a number of companies as it increased its business. Under Mitchell's direction, Solectron Global Services became a $1.2 billion business, and Mitchell was responsible for the division's management, strategic development, and new-business-development opportunities. He was involved in 11 of Solectron's acquisitions during his time with the company.

ELECTED PRESIDENT AND CEO AT ARROW ELECTRONICS

Mitchell's success at Solectron gained the attention of Arrow Electronics, one of Solectron's competitors. Arrow wanted to improve its relationship with electronics-manufacturing-services (EMS) providers, and Mitchell's experience led Arrow to elect him as its president and chief executive officer in January 2003. Analysts said that the move was strategic on the part of Arrow. "I've watched Mitchell grow the services business at Solectron," said an analyst with Merrill Lynch. "It has become the fastest growth unit for the last couple of years. With Arrow's push into the services business to raise gross profit margins, Mitchell's appointment is a strategic move" (*Electronic Buyer's News*, January 20, 2003).

When he was hired, Mitchell said that the pace of the position at Arrow attracted him. One of his first challenges was to work toward improving the relationship between EMS providers and distributors, which were often tense due to a high level of competition. Regarding EMS providers and distributors, Mitchell said, "I think they have complementary skill sets and operate in different parts of the supply chain. We will continue to build the relationship" (*Electronic Buyer's News*, January 20, 2003). Mitchell spent much of his first year with the company working to make it operate more efficiently. He also focused the company's attention on Asia, where he spent a considerable amount of time while he was employed at Solectron. Mitchell also served on the board of directors for Rogers, a manufacturer and marketer of specialty polymer and electronics materials.

See also entries on Arrow Electronics, Inc., Exxon Corporation, Nashua Corporation, Raychem Corporation, and Solectron Corporation in *International Directory of Company Histories*.

SOURCES FOR FURTHER INFORMATION

Bailey, Steve, and Steven Syre, "A Battle for Survival," *Boston Globe*, May 8, 1996.

Dalton, Richard J., Jr., and Mark Harrington, "Hoping to Take Arrow's Business Up," *Newsday*, January 18, 2003.

"Mitchell Is Appointed Nashua Corp. President," *Union Leader*, August 13, 1993.

"Nashua Appoints William E. Mitchell as Chief Executive Officer," Business Wire, July 25, 1994.

"Nashua Corporation Receives EPA Award," Business Wire, August 22, 1994.

Nelis, Karen, "On-Site School Gives Students Industrial-Strength Edge," *Times Union*, July 12, 1994.

"Raychem Announces Organizational Changes," Business Wire, March 26, 1991.

Schrage, Michael, "Raychem Finds Hi-Tech Niche," *Washington Post*, October 6, 1985.

Sullivan, Laurie, "Arrow Electronics Lands One-Two Punch," *Electronic Buyer's News*, January 20, 2003, p. 1.

—Matthew C. Cordon

Hayao Miyazaki
1941–
Chief executive officer, Studio Ghibli

Nationality: Japanese.

Born: January 5, 1941, in Tokyo, Japan.

Education: Gakushuin University, BA, 1963.

Family: Son of Katsuji Miyazaki (aircraft-parts manufacturer); married Akemi Ota (animator); children: two.

Career: Toei Animation, 1963–1971, animator; A Pro, 1971–1973, animator and director; Zuiyo Pictures, 1973–1978, animator and director; Tokyo Movie Shinsha, 1979–1982, director; Tokuma, 1982–1998, director; Studio Ghibli, 1985–1998, director and producer; 1999–, CEO.

Address: Studio Ghibli, 1-4-25, Kajino-cho, Koganei-shi, 184, Japan; http://www.ntv.co.jp/ghibli.

■ The director, producer, animator, and storyteller Hayao Miyazaki was the leader of one of the most successful animated motion picture studios in the world, Studio Ghibli. The studio arose out of his success with the motion picture *Nausicaä of the Valley of the Wind*, and its continued success was wholly dependent on the motion pictures that he wrote and directed. In the 1990s he created the most successful films in the history of Japan, setting numerous box-office records. While his films were already popular among anime enthusiasts worldwide, a distribution deal with Disney Studios in 1996 brought several of Miyazaki's works to broader audiences; he had established himself as an innovator and artist at least equal in stature to Walt Disney himself. As a leader Miyazaki attracted to his productions some of Japan's finest writers, artists, directors, and producers, as well as the outstanding composer Joe Hisaishi, whose scores for Miyazaki's films became classics themselves.

EARLY LIFE

Miyazaki was born on January 5, 1941, in Tokyo. He was one of four sons of Katsuji Miyazaki, who worked in the family business Miyazaki Airplanes, which manufactured parts for warplanes. Miyazaki indicated later in life that he felt guilty that his family had profited from Japan's efforts in World War II. His dislike of militarism would be reflected in such films as *Nausicaä of the Valley of the Wind* and *Porco Rosso*. Partly to escape the American bombing of Tokyo and partly to be closer to the Miyazaki Airplanes factory in Kanuma City, Katsuji Miyazaki moved his family to Utsunomiya City, where they lived from 1944 to 1946. During this period the young Hayao may have become familiar with the forest that would figure prominently in *My Neighbor Totoro*. His mother was sick with spinal tuberculosis from 1947 to 1955, staying in a hospital for three of those years; this state of affairs prefigured the family situation presented in *My Neighbor Totoro*.

In 1958 Miyazaki became interested in animated movies, his imagination having been stirred by *Hakujaden* (Legend of the White Snake), a motion picture that was produced by Toei Animation and was Japan's first color feature-length anime. At that time, however, Miyazaki wanted to be not an animator but a comic-book artist. He majored in economics and political science at Gakushuin University, graduating in 1963, but his heart was in the arts, especially as they appealed to children; he pursued his interest in comic books as a member of the university's children's literature club.

In April 1963 Miyazaki became an animator for Toei Animation, which produced both theatrical motion pictures and television series. He was taught the basics of animation and began at the bottom of the artistic hierarchy, laboriously filling in the cel-by-cel movements of characters and objects; he found the work enjoyable and therein probably learned to accurately draw characters. He impressed many of his coworkers with his fertile imagination and proposed numerous story ideas to the studio; he quickly became a leader in the animators' union. In 1964 he met the animator Akemi Ota, who would become his wife in 1968. That year the first motion picture in which he played a major role was released: *Prince of the Sun*, a collaboration with the chief animator Yasuo Otsuka and the director Isao Takahata. Takahata would later serve as the producer for some of Miyazaki's own movies.

GROWING INDEPENDENCE

In 1971 Miyazaki joined Takahata at A Pro, where he became involved in a failed effort to make an animated feature of *Pippi Longstockings*. In June 1973 he moved to Zuiyo Pictures, where he designed the scenes for *Heidi: Girl of the Alps*. By then he had established himself as an outstanding background-scene artist for both motion pictures and television animation. During the 1970s in addition to motion pictures he worked on *manga*, or graphic novels. The year 1979 saw the release of the first important picture directed by Miyazaki, *Lupin III: The Castle of Cagliostro*. In the early 1980s he began one of his most popular *manga* series, based on the character Nausicaä, a princess living in a future where humanity is in peril of extinction.

In 1982 the Tokuma production company asked Miyazaki, who was by then an instructor for beginning animators and a very experienced director of television cartoons, to make the Nausicaä stories into an animated feature. Miyazaki brought in Takahata to produce the film, while he wrote the screenplay, created the story board, and painted the scenes and the characters that would be used by his animation team. Work began in 1983; *Nausicaä of the Valley of the Wind* was released in 1984. The film was not a smash hit, but it proved profitable at the box office, and out of its success Tokuma created Studio Ghibli—which Miyazaki pronounced "jee-blee," after the Italian word for a dry Saharan wind as well as the name for a World War I aircraft. *Nausicaä* later proved to be a landmark achievement, as it had set a precedent for much of the Japanese anime that would follow, introducing realistically drawn characters and grim themes.

STUDIO GHIBLI

While Studio Ghibli produced motion pictures by people other than Miyazaki, for the most part the studio's reputation rested on what he accomplished. He directed *Laputa: Castle in the Sky*, which was released in 1986. (When later released by Disney, the word *Laputa* was dropped because of offensive connotations for Spanish speakers.) The film exhibited Miyazaki's love of all things flying—featuring an airborne castle—and included two of his recurring preoccupations: an interest in caring for nature and a mistrust of military organizations. The year 1988 saw the release of one of the greatest children's motion pictures ever made, *My Neighbor Totoro*, which ironically almost brought about the death of Studio Ghibli. The picture was released as a cofeature with Takahata's *Grave of the Fireflies*, a story of misery, hopelessness, and prolonged, agonizing deaths. The pairing was a terrible mismatch, and Japanese audiences stayed away from both films. Miyazaki saved *My Neighbor Totoro* with a canny marketing campaign for stuffed toys based on figures in the movie; the figures caught on and were popular well into the 2000s. With its depiction of the real forest near where Miyazaki had lived while a boy, the film inspired an environmentalist movement in Japan. Characters from the movie became part of Studio Ghibli's logo as well as symbols of the studio's motion pictures.

Next came 1989's *Witch's Delivery Service* (renamed *Kiki's Delivery Service* in America), which gained an international following. Miyazaki remarked that he set the picture in a world where World War II never happened; the seaside city where Kiki settles down appears to be French, but it is populated by a variety of ethnic groups. The motion picture was a box-office hit, setting records in Japan. In 1992 *Porco Rosso* (sometimes called *The Crimson Pig*) was released, wherein Miyazaki indulged his passion for aircraft by depicting strange and wonderful airplanes based on actual planes from the 1920s. In his drawings Miyazaki sometimes depicted himself as a large pig; *Porco Rosso* featured a World War I ace who was turned into a pig. *Whispers of the Heart* of 1995 was a charmer that appealed more to teenage girls than to boys; the film introduced the Baron, a cat that would reappear in 2002.

Miyazaki then wrote the screenplay, drew the complete story board (as he usually did), and directed *Princess Mononoke*. He was criticized in the Japanese press for undertaking something that presumably no animated motion picture could accomplish: the telling of a grand epic on a massive scale. When released in Japan in 1997, *Princess Mononoke* was a smash hit, surpassing the success of *E.T.* and setting a record in grossing over $150 million. The film was a major achievement by an artist and leader at the height of his powers—but in the making of the film Miyazaki may have already been losing his eyesight; he used computer animation extensively in the movie's production, even though he very much preferred each cel to be hand-drawn. *Princess Mononoke* was the first of Miyazaki's movies to attract a large American audience. In 2001 Miyazaki topped that film with *Spirited Away*, perhaps the greatest animated motion picture ever made and widely deemed one of the best motion pictures of any kind. Therein Miyazaki united brilliant painted backgrounds with cogent characterization, all while making a fantasy world seem more real than the real world. The movie featured Miyazaki's love for children as well as his environmentalist concerns but above all his wonderful storytelling. *Spirited Away* broke all Japanese box-office records and was a popular success around the globe.

THE DISNEY DEAL

In the mid-1990s, Studio Ghibli's parent company, Tokuma, hit hard times. Fortunately the big box-office success in Japan of *Kiki's Delivery Service* had attracted the attention of Disney; Disney offered a deal that would relieve Tokuma of its financial burdens in exchange for the distribution rights worldwide—save in Southeast Asia—for motion pictures produced by Studio Ghibli. Miyazaki's approval was required to complete the deal; he gave it, explaining that he already had more money than he could possibly spend in one lifetime and that Tokuma had helped him out when he had needed it. The deal was formalized in 1996 and underwent revisions thereafter, such as the later addition of DVD distribution rights for Disney.

The motion pictures distributed by Disney would be released under the Buena Vista and Miramax labels. Although Disney had declared that it wanted to bring Miyazaki's genius to the world without tampering with the movies, it did not keep its promise. The ending of *Spirited Away* was slightly altered, and *Kiki's Delivery Service* dropped a background appearance of Miyazaki himself while adding dialogue not in the Japanese original. Meanwhile for some reason the Disney Store refused to sell Studio Ghibli movies in its shops.

A RENEWAL

On January 14, 1998, Miyazaki had announced that he would be leaving Studio Ghibli. His eyesight was failing, and he believed that he could not guarantee as high a quality of art in his motion pictures as he wished. He intended to make small films for the Studio Ghibli Museum—insisting that the museum should be full of children being noisy—and to train young animators. Yet on January 16, 1999, he returned as the *shocho*, or leader, of Studio Ghibli, taking a strong role in asserting organizational discipline and focusing employees on their tasks. Using computer animation to help maintain artistic control of his creations, he directed the fine *The Cat Returns* (2002), which featured the Baron from *Whispers of the Heart*, and *Lord Howl's Castle* (2004), based on the novel by Diana Wynne Jones.

SOURCES FOR FURTHER INFORMATION

Feldman, Steven, "Hayao Miyazaki Biography, Revision 2," Nausicaa.net, June 6, 1994, http://www.nausicaa.net/miyazaki/miyazaki/miyazaki_biography.txt.

Momoe, Mizukubo, "It's Child's Play for Studio Ghibli," *Look Japan*, June 2002, pp. 34–36.

—Kirk H. Beetz

■■■
Anders C. Moberg
1950–
Chief executive officer, Royal Ahold

Nationality: Swedish.

Born: 1950, in Smaland, Sweden.

Family: Married (wife's name unknown); children: three.

Career: IKEA Group, 1970–1986, various positions; 1986–1999 president and chief executive officer; Home Depot, 1999–2002, president, international division; Royal Ahold, 2003–, chief executive officer.

Awards: International Award, National Retail Federation, 1992.

Address: Albert Heijnweg 1, 1507 EH Zaandam, The Netherlands; http://www.ahold.com.

■ As president of IKEA Group from 1986 to 1999 Swedish-born Anders C. Moberg played a key role in the company's global expansion. After nearly 30 years of working under IKEA's autocratic founder, Ingvar Kamprad, Moberg left the furniture retailer to become president of the international division of Home Depot but less than three years later resigned when Home Depot cut back on its plans for overseas expansion. In 2003 Moberg resurfaced with Royal Ahold, having been named CEO of the Dutch supermarket conglomerate, which had expanded too quickly and taken on an excessive level of debt, a situation exacerbated by an accounting scandal that cost Moberg's predecessor his job. For Moberg the challenges at Ahold were formidable. At stake were not only the company's future but also Moberg's hard-won reputation. Moberg was certainly well suited for the task of running a global business. A true internationalist, the gregarious Moberg, married to a woman who was half German and half Norwegian, was fluent in Danish, English, French, and German in addition to his native tongue of Swedish. Moberg was considered hardworking, efficient, and innovative—traits put to the test as he attempted to bring order to Ahold's far-flung operations, return the company to profitability, and establish a sound base for sustainable growth.

Anders C. Moberg. *AP/Wide World Photos.*

SMALAND VALUES INFLUENCE BOTH IKEA AND MOBERG

Moberg was born in 1950 in Smaland, a small, rock-strewn town in Sweden approximately 400 kilometers south of Stockholm. He was the son of a farmer and a teacher. Growing up on a farm, Moberg naturally learned the importance of hard work, simplicity, and thriftiness—all values reinforced by his community. At the age of only 14 Moberg took a job at a local sawmill, going to work at 6 o'clock in the morning. He recalled that every morning he saw Ingvar Kamprad driving to work. Moberg likely did not suspect he would spend almost three decades of his life working closely with Kamprad, IKEA's founder.

When Moberg began working at the sawmill, Kamprad had recently opened his first IKEA store outside of Sweden. Like Moberg, Kamprad had grown up on a farm. Kamprad displayed an early penchant for business, at the age of five buying matches in bulk and reselling them individually at a profit. Later in childhood he peddled Christmas cards, pens, watches, and other cheap trinkets. Kamprad was only 17 when he started a mail-order business, registering it as a company in 1943. Kamprad named the company IKEA, an acronym formed from his initials and the first letters of Elmtaryd, the family farm, and Agunnaryd, the Smaland parish where he was born. IKEA did not start selling furniture by mail order until 1952. Kamprad applied to furniture the Smaland values that proved influential in both his and Moberg's business careers: striving for affordable, good-looking, and functional furniture to serve a modest and decent life. The virtues of thriftiness, efficiency, and innovation found full expression in 1955 when an IKEA employee decided to ship a table with the legs packed under the tabletop. The result was the birth of furniture consumers could assemble themselves and an idea that transformed IKEA into an international concern. The first retail outlet was opened in 1958 in Almhult, Sweden. Stores were opened in Norway in 1963 and Denmark in 1969.

JOINS IKEA IN 1970

In 1970, at the age of 19, Moberg dropped out of college and went to work for IKEA in the mail-order department in what he intended to be a temporary position. He was quickly taken by the spirit of the company, became an enthusiastic employee, and caught the eye of Kamprad, who took on the young man as his protégé. Moberg was shuffled among departments to gain a fuller understanding of how IKEA worked. In 1974, in his first trip outside of Sweden, Moberg was dispatched to Zurich, Switzerland, to open an IKEA store, the first outside of Scandinavia. In a June 5, 1997, profile in *The European*, Moberg recalled, "It was a good thing I knew something about construction because a lot of the decisions about store building fell on me." Over the next five years Moberg opened stores in Germany and Austria. In 1979 he was groomed on the operational side, serving six months as a vice president of the German store, the highest-grossing store in the IKEA chain. Moberg was subsequently named the president of the Switzerland/Austria operation, a position he held until 1982, when he became the head of the French unit.

Moberg displayed a creative side to his personality by playing a key role in the shaping of the IKEA brand in the early 1980s. The company was in danger of becoming pigeonholed as a cheap furniture outlet when Moberg began to pursue the marketing angle that economy was a virtue, a belief that had been instilled in both Moberg and Kamprad while growing up in Smaland—as evidenced by IKEA's policy that executives travel economy class and stay in two- and three-star hotels. Smaland natives were so legendary for their parsimonious ways that "Smalander" jokes were a staple of Swedish folk humor. Moberg-inspired advertising compared IKEA furniture to more expensive, upscale furniture, employing tag lines such as "IKEA is not for the rich but for the wise." Once the idea of equating IKEA with a smart, practical decision was well established in the mind of the consumer, the advertisements took another leap forward: IKEA furniture was lushly photographed in palatial settings with no text at all.

NAMED IKEA'S PRESIDENT AT AGE 35

Although a number of executives in the organization were more experienced than Moberg, Kamprad in September 1986 selected the young-looking 35-year-old Moberg to become the president of IKEA's worldwide organization. Moberg told Hale Richards in an interview for the *European* that he was as surprised as anyone by the decision: "I was stunned. I had literally never dreamed of such a thing happening to me" (June 5, 1997). Although he had spent 16 years at IKEA, Moberg was not fully ready to run the company and for a few years appeared somewhat uncomfortable in the role of chief executive. Kamprad, only in his early sixties, was still on board as chairman and was still very much involved in running the company. He provided Moberg with adequate time to gain confidence in the job. The pair spent considerable time traveling together, often pausing to take the pulse of ordinary consumers in the belief that such work was too important to be delegated to others. Moberg often recalled a seven-hour train trip through France—in a second class coach—during which Kamprad conducted impromptu market research with "what seemed like 5,000 French people. I couldn't get him to stop" (June 5, 1997). But Moberg proved no different from his mentor, having absorbed IKEA's culture and rivaling Kamprad as its embodiment. Talking about the self-reliance of IKEA employees, Moberg explained to the *European*, "We like to give our coworkers a lot of responsibility and a chance to fulfill individual potential. Personalities and talents flower within our group" (June 5, 1997). He could have easily been talking about himself, a college dropout who rose through the ranks to a position of prominence just short of that held by the company's founder.

When Moberg was more comfortable in his capacity as IKEA's president, Kamprad began to step back and allow his protégé to truly carry out his job, although by his own admission Kamprad could not resist meddling on occasion. Moberg spent approximately one-half of his time out of the office, visiting stores and meeting with local managers as well as being actively involved in product development. Once an active participant in sports, playing soccer and handball, Moberg came to prefer spending his limited free time with his wife, son, and two daughters.

Moberg faced a number of challenges at IKEA. Soon before Moberg was named president the company entered the U.S. market and proceeded to expand confidently. IKEA faced stiff competition in the United States from big-box rivals such as Wal-Mart and Target and from Ethan Allen Interiors and Pier 1 Imports. In 1990, immediately before the U.S. economy lapsed into recession, IKEA became overly ambitious, acquiring five California stores owned by STOR Furnishings International. The stores proved unprofitable, an experience that sobered Moberg and the rest of IKEA's management. Not only in America but also in Europe, IKEA found business becoming increasingly competitive. Moreover, IKEA failed to successfully adapt its furnishings to conform to American tastes. The situation grew bad enough that in 1995 Moberg warned that IKEA was in a state of crisis. Under his leadership the company rebounded. Over the next two years IKEA closed two of its 21 North American stores and cut office staff. It also placed a greater emphasis on designing products more suited to the U.S. market. For example, deeper kitchen cabinets suited the size of larger American appliances, and sofas were softer. As a result of these changes the U.S. business showed considerable improvement.

LEAVING IKEA AFTER 29 YEARS

As the end of the 1990s approached it appeared that Kamprad would not be retiring any time soon. He also did not appear inclined to turn over Moberg's job to any of his three sons, all of whom worked as IKEA managers. Kamprad was so adamant that his sons not be tempted to one day fight over control of the business that in 1984 he made an irrevocable gift of all of his equity in IKEA to a Dutch charitable foundation, thus preventing his children from inheriting the company. Although his position at IKEA appeared secure, Moberg accepted the post when Home Depot approached him in 1999 about heading its international division. The reason the 49-year-old Moberg offered was simple enough: "I wanted to do something else after 29 years at IKEA" (*Wall Street Journal*, March 23, 1999). In the press observers speculated that Moberg left because he concluded it was unlikely he would ascend to the chairmanship of the company.

Moberg joined Home Depot as president of the international division in September 1999, as the retailer was about to enter Argentina and Chile as part of a major international expansion. Moberg also opened Home Depot outlets in Mexico and Canada and was charged with assessing the possibilities of expansion into Europe and Asia, but his tenure at the company proved short-lived, and he left no lasting mark. As Home Depot's U.S. sales growth began to slow, the company quickly retreated, opting instead to focus its attention on rebuilding its core domestic business. In October 2001 Home Depot sold off its South American operations, and in January 2002 Moberg decided it was time to resign and pursue other opportunities.

ROYAL AHOLD BECKONS

Moberg sat out more than a year before deciding on his next career move. He found it in the Dutch supermarket conglomerate Royal Ahold, which in 2003 was mired in an accounting scandal that rivaled those of Enron and WorldCom. Moberg was hired in May 2003 to replace the CEO Cees van der Hoeven, who in the previous decade had spent $19 billion on acquisitions to grow Ahold into a global business earning $65 billion a year. Early in 2003 the company announced that it had overstated its profit by at least $500 million over the previous two years. This news resulted in van der Hoven's ouster. At the center of the controversy was the distributor U.S. Foodservice, a 2000 acquisition. Two of this company's managers were accused of taking advantage of the subsidiary's poor tracking system to inflate the amount of promotional rebates received from suppliers. In addition, the rebates were booked prematurely, creating a false impression of profitability for both U.S Foodservice and its corporate parent.

Although Moberg lacked a background in food retailing, his appointment to the top post at Ahold was generally well received. Moberg was very much a global executive, had held positions of authority at two well-respected retailers, and was not a Dutch insider, giving him the opportunity to see the company with fresh eyes and the freedom to clean house. Soon after Moberg accepted the job, the accounting irregularities deepened. The amount of overstated earnings was recalculated to $1.1 billion and stretched back to 2000. Moberg's challenges, however, extended well beyond steering the company past the accounting scandal. In its rapid rise, Ahold had taken on far too much debt and was in many ways a disjointed collection of assets.

Taking over as acting CEO until the appointment was formally approved at the annual general meeting of shareholders later in the year, Moberg quickly exhibited the strengths he had cultivated since the start of his business career. As he and Kamprad had done many times at IKEA, Moberg took to the road. He paid visits to numerous Ahold supermarkets in Europe and the United States, getting to know the business as well as talking with employees and customers. On the other end of the spectrum, Moberg met with members of the financial community to help buoy investor confidence. In a speech delivered to shareholders on September 4, 2003, Moberg was able to offer a general vision for the company. His view of Ahold and a broad-brush approach to solving its problems were very much a reflection of his character. Moberg espoused simplicity and efficiency, pointing out that Ahold had lost its focus, attempting "to be everything to everybody. That's expensive! For example: we are in hypermarkets, compact hypers, supermarkets, convenience stores and even in discount. In addition, we run production facilities and own specialty stores and pharmacies." Moberg also considered the corporate structure too complex, with "too many overlapping initiatives at different levels and unclear responsibilities." As a result the company had difficulty providing efficient controls. Moberg also espoused practicality, maintaining that many underperforming assets had to be sacrificed. He emphasized that Ahold needed to change its mindset, revealing his belief in the importance of creating a sound corporate culture and esprit de corps. Most important, Moberg wanted to make customers the company's top priority, a philosophy in keeping with the values he had learned during his 30 years at IKEA.

Even before he presented his thoughts to shareholders, Moberg had started the process of divesting noncore assets, exiting from South America and Asia. To the surprise of many Moberg announced that he did not believe it was in the company's best interest to sell U.S. Foodservice. The foodservice market in the United States was estimated to be worth in excess of $160 billion. The largest national player, SYSCO, controlled only 15 percent of the market. In second place, U.S. Foodservice had an 11 percent share, or more than $18 billion. Because there was so much room for growth Moberg decided it was worth devoting the time and resources necessary for getting the business on track and growing.

SALARY CONTROVERSY

Moberg discovered that heading a public company posed a different set of problems than he faced at privately-held IKEA. He found himself caught up in a minor scandal of his own involving the amount of his pay. Many shareholders were infuriated and grilled him about his salary at the September 2003 meeting. Moberg's two-year contract was worth $6.8 million, high by Dutch standards, and seemed especially lavish in light of the company's recent accounting irregularities. Moreover, Moberg had a severance package of $11.35 million collectable even if he were to resign immediately as well as 125,000 shares of stock he could cash in as well. Some shareholders requested that the pay package be renegotiated and that the vote on Moberg's post be postponed until the next shareholders' meeting. Henny de Ruiter, the chairman of the board, refused; the vote took place; and Moberg was appointed. The controversy over his pay did not abate, however.

Moberg's negotiation of a lucrative contract was less a reflection of greed than of his practical nature. Moberg maintained that when he agreed to take the job he had little information about the true state of Ahold's affairs on which to base his decision. The amount of his pay, in his opinion, was simply a function of the risk he was assuming. If his ability to serve as an effective CEO were to be derailed by unknown circumstances that had occurred before he took over, his reputation would be damaged and his career prospects diminished through no fault of his own. By October 2003 Moberg and the Ahold board had agreed to a restructuring of his contract whereby much of his salary was tied to his meeting seven

criteria. In what was likely part truth and part face-saving, Moberg said that he was comfortable with the new arrangement because after spending several months analyzing Ahold, he was reassured about the risk he was taking and no longer needed the guarantees of the original contract.

Moberg formalized the ideas he presented to the shareholders and launched a new financial plan and strategy called "Road to Recovery," which was intended to put Ahold on course to return to an investment-grade portfolio by the end of 2005. U.S. Foodservice also was implementing a three-step plan to turn around its business. Moberg estimated that because of the need to calm shareholders, assuage creditors, and take care of corporate governance matters, he was able to devote only approximately 20 percent of his time to actually running the business. As he explained to the *Wall Street Journal,* "Instant information these days means you can't hide in the executive suite. . . . Sometimes you ask yourself if it is possible to fulfill all the demands on you and whether you have the right balance" (November 24, 2003). Although daunting, it was a challenge Moberg appeared well prepared to take on.

See also entries on The Home Depot, Inc., IKEA Group, and Koninklijke Ahold N.V. in *International Directory of Company Histories.*

SOURCES FOR FURTHER INFORMATION

Bilefsky, Dan, "CEOs in Europe Try to Regain Trust," *Wall Street Journal,* November 24, 2003.

Colangelo, Michael, "IKEA's World: A Unique Structure and Philosophy Speeds This Swedish Furniture Giant Ahead," *HFD: The Weekly Home Furnishings Newspaper,* May 25, 1987.

Crouch, Gregory, "Dutch Grocer Tries to Calm Furor Over Pay," *New York Times,* September 18, 2003./ bibcit.composed>

Hagerty, James R., and Almar Latour, "Home Depot Adds Moberg of IKEA for Foreign Push," *Wall Street Journal,* March 23, 1999.

Moberg, Anders, address to shareholders, September 4, 2003, http://www.ahold.com/investorrelations/events/ 030904_Final_presentation_GM.pdf.

Reilly, David, and Kelly Greene, "Ahold's Choice for Chief Executive Cheers Investors," *Wall Street Journal,* May 5, 2003.

Richards, Hale, "Preacher Spreads IKEA's Gospel," *European,* June 5, 1997.

Timmons, Heather, "Ex-Chief of Ikea Is Named Top Executive at Royal Ahold," *New York Times,* May 3, 2003.

—Ed Dinger

■ ■ ■

Larry Montgomery

1949–

Chief executive officer and chairman of the board of directors, Kohl's Corporation

Nationality: American.

Born: 1949.

Career: Block's, 1985–1987, executive management positions culminating in chief executive officer; L. S. Ayres, 1987–1988, executive management positions including senior vice president and director of stores, general merchandise manager, Softlines; Kohl's Corporation, 1988–1993, senior vice president, director of stores, 1993–1996, executive vice president of stores, 1996–2000, vice chairman of board of directors, 1999–, chief executive officer, 2003–, chairman of the board.

Address: Kohl's Corporation, N56 W17000 Ridgewood Drive, Menomonee Falls, Wisconsin 53051; http://www.kohls.com.

■ Department store chain executive R. Lawrence "Larry" Montgomery—a thirty-year-plus veteran of the retailing industry—was the CEO and chairman of Fortune 500 company Kohl's Corporation. Montgomery ran the company according to its three basic customer-oriented concepts of value, brands, and convenience. Through a long-established philosophy of being a family-focused, specialty discount department store, Kohl's offered customers a mix of national-brand and private-brand casual clothing and home furnishings at discount prices in stores that are convenient to drive to and have inside environments that are organized in an orderly and friendly manner.

Kohl's Corporation operated almost 600 stores in 37 states as of the beginning of 2004, with about half of these stores located in midwestern states. Kohl's competes with discount stores such as Wal-Mart, Target, and Kmart and with middle-level department stores such as Sears, Penney's, Mervyn's, and Macy's. During his time as CEO, Montgomery continued to grow Kohl's within the company's core midwestern region while steadily expanding into other U.S. markets—hoping eventually to mold Kohl's into a national chain.

RETAILING CAREER

Montgomery began his retail career in 1972 and over the next dozen years gained experience in a variety of jobs in the industry. From 1985 to 1987 he held executive management positions of increasing responsibility at Block's, a division of Allied Stores Corporation. He eventually became the CEO at Block's. In 1987-1988 he was employed in various executive management positions including senior vice president and director of stores, and general merchandise manager of Softlines at L. S. Ayres, a division of May Department Stores.

Montgomery joined Kohl's Corporation in 1988 as its senior vice president, director of stores. He was promoted to executive vice president of stores in February 1993 and joined the board of directors in 1994. He became vice chairman of Kohl's board of directors in 1996. In February 1999 he advanced to CEO after William Kellogg stepped down from the position (while retaining the position of chairman) in order to concentrate on Kohl's extensive expansion efforts. Montgomery assumed the chairmanship of the board in February 2003.

HOW MONTGOMERY MADE KOHL'S UNIQUE

Montgomery directed his management team to concentrate on middle-income customers who shop for their families and homes at Kohl's. Montgomery stocked the company's stores with (on average) about 80 percent national brands and about 20 percent Kohl's own private store brands. By maintaining strong merchandising relationships with top national brands of products, Montgomery was able to carry such easily recognized brands as Champion, Dockers, Haggar, Jockey, Lee, Levi's, Krups, Nike, OshKosh B'Gosh, Pfaltzgraff, Reebok, Vanity Fair, and others that are not typically available at discount stores. Montgomery felt that offering so many national brands—unlike Target, for example, which handled very little national-brand apparel—enabled customers to go to any Kohl's in the country and know exactly what products they will find there, thus saving them time and effort.

Montgomery also emphasized the best prices for its products. By controlling internal costs, Kohl's was able to sell its merchandise at prices that were generally lower than those found in department stores. As important a consideration as price was availability: Montgomery ensured that Kohl's products were in stock, historically with an in-stock position that averages about 90 percent, higher than the industry average.

Knowing that service and prices were not the only features considered by shoppers, Montgomery made sure that Kohl's stores were convenient and attractive to customers. He avoided placing stores in shopping malls, preferring instead locations that offered easy access in and out of the store. He emphasized the importance of keeping the stores clean inside and out, with well-lit parking lots.

RACETRACK DESIGN

Part of the design used by Montgomery in all Kohl's stores was a layout modeled after a racetrack. This simple design, as Montgomery explained, allowed shoppers to move past all of a store's merchandise in an easy and flowing manner. Montgomery hoped that such a design would continue to distinguish his stores from other retail stores, whose complicated layouts are often confusing to customers. Montgomery did not want people to feel as if they were walking around a warehouse with no idea where anything was located.

Working against the conventional retail philosophy that stores should keep people shopping as long as possible, Montgomery continued a basic concept of making sure that his customers could shop quickly while still spending more money. Montgomery believed that customers could spend less time in his stores but still buy more items when products were arranged in a simple and logical manner in an environment that was attractive to the eye.

OPENING-DAY FANFARE

Montgomery made sure that when the company entered new markets, it was done with much public fanfare. He planned grand openings in a grand way. For instance, at various points from 2001 through 2003, Kohl's opened 15 stores in Atlanta with one opening-day celebration and did the same with 13 stores in the Northeast (including Long Island, Connecticut, and New Jersey) and 12 stores in Houston. Montgomery prepared for these major events with "blitz teams," as they were called, of Kohl's employees from other stores who helped prepare the new stores for their openings.

In advance of such openings, Montgomery coordinated media advertising (such as television commercials, radio commercials during heavy drive times, and newspaper inserts, especially on Sundays) to announce the new store or stores. Generally, a series of a half-dozen commercials on various media outlets emphasized Kohl's ample and convenient parking, discount prices, wide assortment of brand names, and useful shopping/stroller carts (especially helpful for parents with children). Stores were first prepared with a "soft opening," which provided employees the chance to familiarize themselves with the Kohl's system before actual customers entered the store.

With regard to management aspects of supervision, logistics, and distribution, Montgomery believed that the more stores that were grouped together in a major market, the greater the efficiencies that resulted. In fact, many of Kohl's competitors used similar strategies for entering new markets, but according to industry analysts, Montgomery's management team at Kohl's always did a much better job in overall effectiveness when compared with these companies.

LEADING UP TO CHANGE

Over a 10-year period before Montgomery became leader of Kohl's, the company had increased sales at about 23 percent annually. This consistent success record was achieved by adhering to a strict strategy that gave Kohl's a reputation for being both a retail discounter and a department store. Management was able to persuade department store customers to shop at Kohl's by offering department store-like products at better prices. In addition, the management team was able to persuade discount store customers to shop at Kohl's because it provided the same variety of goods at a fraction of the square footage of other discounters because of its unique store design and centralized checkouts. At an average of 86,000 square feet, Kohl's stores were about half the size of most department stores. Shoppers liked the easy-to-walk-around stores.

During these 10 years, however, the competition saw what was happening with Kohl's successful policy and gradually copied it. In addition, during 2003 Kohl's expanded into California with the opening of 28 stores in the greater Los Angeles area, which distracted Montgomery and his management team from other stores due to the stiff competition—especially that of Mervyn's and Macy's—already located in the area. Montgomery soon saw complaints from Kohl's customers about a climate that was less organized and checkout lines that were regularly longer than normal. At the same time, Kohl's was adding numerous new lines to its stores, along with expanding many of its regular lines, forcing stores into a crowded environment. As a result, same-store sales declined 1.6 percent in 2003, a drastic departure from the 6 to 8 percent annual increase for most of the previous ten years. With less merchandise being sold, inventories increased, which forced markdowns to be taken. As a result, net income in 2003 dropped 8.1 percent to $591.2 million from the previous year's $643.4 million. Montgomery realized that a new strategy had to be implemented.

REFOCUSING ON CORE STRENGTH

With Kohl's in the midst of major problems, Montgomery decided to refocus the company on its traditional core strength: providing easy and convenient shopping in its stores. Thus, Montgomery cut store inventories by an average of 17 percent and removed all but necessary styles and sizes for its products. By December 2003 (during fiscal year 2004) Montgomery added new brands such as a new fashion line by fashion model/television personality Daisy Fuentes; a new line (that expanded the brand) of Gloria Vanderbilt Home towels, sheets, comforters, and bath mats; Estée Lauder cosmetics; and Laura Ashley Lifestyles bathroom and bedding accessories.

With this new strategy in place, Montgomery predicted that 2004 earnings per share would grow 25 percent to $2.15, as compared with $1.72 in 2003. Relying on expansion that often involved buying bankrupt retailers or building new stores on old department store locations, Montgomery planned to have stores in every region and every major metropolitan market (and many smaller ones) by 2006.

The company opened 85 new stores in fiscal 2003 (for a total of 542 stores) and planned to open about 95 more in fiscal 2004 and another 95 in fiscal 2005. With sales productivity levels at near the top of the industry—Kohl's sells $258 per square foot compared with $190 at Federated or May Department Stores—Montgomery was pleased with the progress his company made in 2003. He felt that his management staff had done what most competitors had been unable to do—a great job at marketing their stores. In fact, Montgomery succeeded in making Kohl's a popular place for young people to shop (both with and without their parents)—an accomplishment not seen at such retailers as Kmart, Sears, and Wal-Mart. With net sales in 2003 crossing the $10 billion milestone, Kohl's was positioned for success well into the twenty-first century.

HELPFUL COMMUNITY CITIZEN

Montgomery worked hard to make Kohl's a dedicated citizen within its communities. Through its program Kohl's Cares for Kids(r), the company—to name just three activities—raised money for Children's Hospital (most recently with the help of *Clifford the Big Red Dog*, from the popular children's television show), recognized youngsters who volunteered (even commissioning a scientific study managed by Vanderbilt University to find ways by which adults could stimulate youth volunteerism), and offered gift cards as fundraisers for schools and youth groups. Kohl's also developed Kohl's Kids Who Care, which recognized humanitarian efforts among America's youth.

See also entry on Kohl's Corporation in *International Directory of Company Histories.*

SOURCE FOR FURTHER INFORMATION

"Kohl's Recognizes America's Young Humanitarians," http://www.kohlscorporation.com/2003PressReleases/News0811Release.htm.

—William Arthur Atkins

■ ■ ■

James P. Mooney

1947–

Chairman and chief executive officer, OM Group

Nationality: American.

Born: December 19, 1947, in Berea, Ohio.

Education: Quincy University, BA, 1970.

Family: Son of James B. Mooney (founder of Mooney Chemicals).

Career: Mooney Chemicals, 1971–1975, various positions; 1975–1991, CEO and president; OM Group, 1991–1994, CEO and president; 1993–1994, chairman, CEO, and president; 1994–, chairman and CEO.

Awards: George S. Dively Entrepreneurship Award, Harvard Business School Club of Northeastern Ohio, 2000.

Address: OM Group, 50 Public Square, 3500 Terminal Tower, Cleveland, Ohio 44113-2204; http://www.omgi.com.

■ The chemical and materials manufacturing executive James P. Mooney was the CEO and chairman of OM Group, an international company that produced metal-based specialty products and related materials. Mooney was dedicated to maintaining the high quality that had historically characterized the company's products; although OM Group's components were a small expense in other companies' total manufacturing and processing costs, Mooney was well aware that the components were exceptionally critical in ensuring well-made finished products. Mooney consciously built up the company's reputation for being a reliable provider of innovative products with superior technical quality around the world.

MAJOR METAL MAKER

Through its operating subsidiaries, the Cleveland, Ohio–based OM Group was a leading vertically integrated global manufacturer and marketer of metal-based (especially cobalt, nickel, and copper) specialty organics (compounds based on carbon) and inorganics (compounds not based on carbon), chemicals, powders, alloys, and related materials. Such OM materials were used in about 30 major industries, including aerospace, appliance, automotive, ceramics, computer, construction, catalysts, electronics, hard-metal tools, magnetic media, paints and inks, petrochemicals, rechargeable-battery chemicals, rubber, and stainless steel. As of 2004, in 50 countries worldwide OM Group employed about 1,400 people, all of whom were involved in the various processes required to make and market about 625 products to about 1,700 corporate customers.

Mooney maintained OM Group manufacturing facilities and administrative offices in North America, Europe, Africa, Asia, and Australia. Under Mooney these facilities evolved to the extent where OM Group became the world's leading consumer, refiner, and producer of cobalt-based specialty chemicals (operating the largest cobalt smelter and refinery); a leading global producer of nickel inorganics, electroless nickel, and nickel powders; and the world's third-largest processor of platinum-group metals into final materials. OM Group also produced specialty chemicals and materials derived from barium, calcium, iron, manganese, potassium, rare earth metals, stainless steel, zinc, and zirconium. In all Mooney led OM Group to become one of the three largest specialty-chemical companies in the United States.

FAMILY-BASED BUSINESS

Founded in 1946 as Mooney Chemicals by James B. Mooney—James P. Mooney's father—the family company experienced success for nearly six decades, primarily in the area of metal carboxylates (any salt or ester of any organic acid that contains the carboxyl group). The younger Mooney joined the company in 1971, taking various positions that eventually led to his taking over for his father as president and CEO in 1975. At this time he made a series of key acquisitions in order to expand the company's role in the manufacturing and marketing of raw materials and metal-based chemicals.

GROWING WITH MERGER

In 1991 Mooney guided the company through a merger with the two European chemical companies Outokumpu

Chemicals of Finland and Vasset of France (both of which were units of Outokumpu Metals & Resources of Helsinki, Finland). The merger occurred when Outokumpu decided to sell its cobalt chemical business in order to focus on mining. After negotiations with Mooney, Outokumpu acquired all of the Mooney family's stock in Mooney Chemicals except for about 4 percent, which was retained by Mooney's father; OM Group was formed, with Mooney remaining as CEO and president, holding the latter position until 1994.

In 1993 Mooney took the company public, becoming chairman of the board of directors. OM Group was first listed on NASDAQ and later moved to the New York Stock Exchange in December 1996. With OM Group's merger and consequent conversion into a public company, Mooney intended to quickly bring operations to an international level and expand the company's line of metal chemicals into three new industrial sectors: batteries, magnets, and steel.

ENLARGING WITH ACQUISITIONS

Mooney acquired companies with the goal of building on OM Group's core business in raw materials and metal-based chemicals. One of Mooney's major accomplishments after orchestrating the merger was the 1996 acquisition of the North Carolina–based SCM Metal Products for $122 million. SCM was the world's largest producer of copper powders, and Mooney saw the company as a good strategic fit within OM Group. Another important acquisition was that of the Newark, New Jersey–based Fidelity Chemical for $80 million in 1997. The addition of Fidelity allowed Mooney to expand his company into the high-technology electronics industry—specifically into markets for memory disks for printed circuit boards, information storage, and metal finishing. Also in 1997 Mooney purchased the privately held Auric Corporation, a producer of electroplating chemicals and metal concentrates.

OM Group more than doubled in size in 2001 when Mooney acquired the precious-metals and metals-management unit of the Germany-based Degussa Metals Catalyst Cerdec. This purchase gave Mooney the ability to operate within the areas of automotive catalysts, electroplating, emission-control devices, fuel cells, jewelry, metals trading, and technical materials.

COMPETITIVE ADVANTAGES

With this last merger and several subsequent acquisitions, Mooney had developed OM into a company with many competitive advantages, one of the largest and most unique of which was its vast capability for metal separation. The company could separate many metals then refine and process them for application in various industries on a global basis. For instance, OM could extract and process a nearly pure percentage of both cobalt and copper from the same project. Thanks to this ability Mooney was able to increase business opportunities in the marketplaces of North America, South America, and Asia.

AWARDS AND ACCOLADES

Early in 2002 Mooney's company became an outstanding player in the specialty-chemical industry, with a management team that was developing many new, unique products. The Cleveland newspaper *Plain Dealer* added OM Group to its list of Top Ten Companies in 2001, mostly because the company had posted 24 consecutive quarters of earnings and earnings-per-share improvement and had grown an average of 18.5 percent annually since it had been taken public in 1993.

FIRST REAL DIFFICULTY

Moody started to have problems when in November 2002 the company's share price fell from $30 to about $6.50. At that time it became public knowledge that the company had been forced to reduce the value of its $108 million inventory as a result of lower cobalt prices. Earlier in the year, while both prices and demand had been low, Moody had raised the amount of cobalt OM Group had held in storage after predicting, inaccurately, that prices would rise; he had also anticipated additional sales to the Department of Defense's Defense Logistics Agency. Conditions within OM Group deteriorated further when the company reported disappointing earnings for its third quarter in 2002 and expectations of continued weakness in future earnings; OM also announced the necessity to institute a large restructuring plan in order to come into compliance with credit agreements. Faced with a mandatory payment on a huge margin call, Mooney was forced to sell over 710,000 shares of his stock in the company, which were worth more than $22 million—reportedly 90 percent of his net worth.

RESTRUCTURING PLAN

In December 2002 Mooney began a restructuring program that involved, in part, a realignment of OM Group's corporate and management structure. The company was divided into three business units—Nickel, Cobalt, and Precious Metals—which would be run by global vice presidents who would report directly to Mooney. The three new units, along with existing research-and-development and metals-management operations, allowed Mooney to institute better performance efficiencies within the company. The executive committee was reduced from four to two members: the chief executive officer, Mooney, and the chief financial officer, Tom Miklich. Miklich oversaw the communications, human-resources, information-technology, and legal departments of the company.

Knowing that he needed help, Mooney hired Credit Suisse First Boston as a financial consultant for the aggressive restructuring program he was implementing in order to strengthen the balance sheet and improve cash flow. Mooney announced in April 2003 that the company would have a $327.9 million net loss for 2002, mostly due to the one-time restructuring charge of $329.7 million that would be taken in the fourth quarter; still, he hoped to quickly return the company's performance to the level it had previously enjoyed.

At about this time Mooney announced that in order to reduce debt he would be discontinuing the production of tungsten fine powders, closing the company's tungsten-carbide fine-powders reclamation and cobalt-recycling facility at St. George, Utah, and selling the company's precious-metals unit along with other smaller units. Such efforts allowed Mooney to shift OM's focus back to the base-metals business surrounding cobalt and nickel-based products.

ANALYSIS AND FUTURE OUTLOOK

Analysts who followed OM Group felt that part of Mooney's problem laid with his huge expansion activities early on, which included the 2001 purchase of Degussa's catalyst business. After years of dealing with Mooney and his management team—who had gained a reputation for negotiating ruthlessly in every deal they made—traders of OM's metals did not prove especially sympathetic with the company's deteriorating condition.

As of the first quarter of 2004 Mooney announced that the company would delay its 2003 fourth-quarter and full-year results. This was due, according to Mooney, to complications with the U.S. Securities and Exchange Commission relating to previous filings made by the company. With high metal prices and increasing demand in many of its markets, Mooney was confident that the company could deliver higher sales, improved margins, and increased operating profits in the first quarter of 2004.

Mooney's plans for future growth included additional geographic expansion in Central and South America as well as a particular focus on the Asia Pacific region. Mooney wished to guide OM Group to the forefront of several emerging industries, including electronic chemicals and rechargeable-battery chemicals. He targeted the growth of OM products that were being used with increasing frequency in such high-demand items as memory disks, printed circuit-board assemblies, battery chemicals, and solder plating.

Mooney expanded OM Group through the development and marketing of technologically advanced product innovations—functions for which the company had been historically reputed. Worldwide, Mooney directed the company to provide the highest-quality products through an efficient and secure raw-material resourcing and manufacturing/supply chain. OM's unique vertical integration—which extended from base metals and concentrates to finished metal products and included extensive operations with metal powders, alloys, and specialty chemicals—gave its customers essential products at competitive prices. Mooney also developed a worldwide network of Technical Centers of Excellence, which shared the knowledge and technologies that OM Group had developed over the years with other companies in order to provide solutions for a vast array of technical situations.

OTHER ACTIVITIES

Mooney was a member of the board of trustees of The Cleveland Clinic Foundation. He led OM to become involved as an active corporate participant in the Responsible Care Program, an alliance formed within the chemical industry to promote working relationships with public-interest organizations, citizen groups, and state and local governments. Mooney was associated with the National Paint and Coatings Association; the National Federation of Paint, Technology, and Chemicals Management Council, as a past officer and chairman; and the Chemical Manufacturers' Association. He was also a member and director of the Cobalt Development Institute.

See also entry on OM Group, Inc. in *International Directory of Company Histories.*

SOURCES FOR FURTHER INFORMATION

"About Us," OM Group, http://www.omgi.com/aboutus/default.htm.

"Board of Directors," OM Group, http://www.omgi.com/aboutus/boardofdirectors.htm.

"Our History," OM Group, http://www.omgi.com/aboutus/ourhistory.htm.

—William Arthur Atkins

■■■
Ann Moore

1950–

Chairwoman and chief executive officer, Time

Nationality: American.

Born: 1950, in Biloxi, Mississippi.

Education: Vanderbilt University, BS, 1971; Harvard Business School, MBA, 1978.

Family: Daughter of Monty Sommovigo and Bea (maiden name unknown); married Donovan Moore (private wealth manager for Bessemer Trust); children: one.

Career: Time, 1978–1979, financial analyst; 1979–1981, media manager of *Sports Illustrated*; 1981–1984, assistant circulation director of *Fortune*, then circulation director of *Money* and then of *Discover*; 1984–1988, general manager of *Sports Illustrated*; 1988–1989, associate publisher of *Sports Illustrated*; 1989–1991, founding publisher of *Sports Illustrated for Kids*; 1991–1993, publisher of *People*; 1993–1998, president of *People*; 1998–2001, president of *People* group; 2001–2002, executive vice president; 2002–, chairwoman and CEO.

Awards: Matrix Award, Women in Communications, 1994; 50 Most Powerful Women in American Business, *Fortune*, 1998–2003; Civic Leadership Award, AOL Time Warner, 2003.

Address: Time, Rockefeller Plaza, New York, New York 10019; http://www.aoltimewarner.com.

Ann Moore. © *Najlah Feanny/Corbis.*

■ Ann Moore was appointed CEO and chairwoman of Time, the magazine-publishing arm of the media and publishing company Time Warner, in July 2002. As president and publisher of the very popular *People* magazine in the 1990s, Moore expanded the weekly's circulation base and advertising revenue. She also successfully launched a group of new magazines, such as *In Style*, based on the premise of the flagship title. Colleagues and media commentators remarked on Moore's passion for magazine publishing, describing her managerial style as both personable and direct.

EARLY DECISION TO WORK FOR TIME

In 1971 Moore graduated with a degree in mathematics from Vanderbilt University in Nashville and then worked in bookselling in Boston. In 1978 she graduated with an MBA from Harvard Business School, where as one of only a handful of female MBA graduates she received 13 job offers. Moore was an avid magazine reader, and her ambition was to work in magazine publishing; she consequently accepted the lowest-paid job she had been offered, that of financial analyst at Time.

In her early years at Time, Moore gained experience in circulation and marketing. An avid sports fan, her first executive role was as media manager of *Sports Illustrated* in 1979. Two years later she was appointed assistant circulation director of *Fortune* before moving on to become the circulation director of *Money* and then of *Discover*. Moore returned to *Sports Illus-*

trated as general manager in 1984, becoming the magazine's associate publisher four years later.

Moore's ability to take a Time title to new readers was first demonstrated in 1989 when she was appointed founding publisher of *Sports Illustrated for Kids*. Drawing upon her existing client network, Moore paved the way for the new title by pre-selling advertising pages. She also established an unusually close working relationship between the magazine's editorial section and its marketing and circulation divisions. The founding editor of *Sports Illustrated for Kids* John Papanek later praised Moore's business model in which the metaphorical "church" and "state" were integrated in a highly effective manner.

EXPANDS AND DIVERSIFIES THE *PEOPLE* GROUP

In 1991 Moore became the publisher of *People*, a title appealing primarily to women, and two years later became the magazine's president. Moore believed that the very successful publication could grow larger still if marketed more specifically to readers interested in women's fashion and popular journalism. In an interview with *Advertising Age* in 2001 Moore referred to Time's "inability to understand you could make money marketing to women" (June 4, 2001). Until the 1990s Time published mainly financial and sporting magazines and marketed its titles almost entirely to an educated male readership.

Moore added beauty and fashion sections to *People* and changed its format from black-and-white to color. She also increased the proportion of advertising pages and changed the magazine's issue day from Monday to Friday so as to coincide with weekend shopping trips. Although the new direction in which Moore was taking the magazine met with a cautious response from Time senior management, her innovations proved successful. From 1991 *People* surpassed Time's traditional leader, *Time* magazine, in advertising revenue; by 2001 the gap had become considerable, with *People* earning $723.7 million to *Time*'s $666 million. In 2002 *People* earned one-third of Time's total revenues.

As president of *People* Moore established a pattern of successful magazine launches that further showed her all-around strengths in both the marketing and editorial aspects of magazine publishing. Along with spin-offs such as the Australian version of *People*, entitled *WHO*, Moore created four highly successful magazines at biyearly intervals between 1994 and 2000: *In Style, People en Español, Teen People*, and *Real Simple*.

In Style, launched in 1994, was the first magazine of its kind to include fashion, celebrity lifestyles, and shelter (interior design, architecture, and gardening) content. *In Style* reflected Moore's belief, expressed in a *Brandweek* interview in 1999, that "runway fashion didn't work and it was celebrities who were the trend spotters in America" (March 8, 1999). The new title drew cautious responses from both Moore's higher-ups at Time and sponsors but, as with the revamped *People*, was immediately successful with readers. By 2000 *In Style* was Time's 15th-biggest-selling title, with a circulation of 1.4 million.

Research into the cultural and demographic trends in the Latino and teenage communities preceded Moore's next new titles, *People en Español* and *Teen People*, launched in 1996 and 1998 respectively. The latter was simultaneously launched in print and online, reflecting the high Internet-literacy rates among teenagers. By 1999 *People en Español* was the most popular Spanish-language title in the country, and *Teen People*—then only a year old—ran second only to rival magazine *Seventeen* in advertising pages and circulation.

Moore's success in extending the *People* concept to new readers stemmed from her awareness of the importance of appointing the best and most suitably qualified executive teams to manage the new titles. This awareness was especially important at a company with little tradition in marketing magazines to female readers. Moore worked closely with her subordinate managers, such as *People*'s Nora McAniff, *In Style*'s Ann W. Jackson and *People en Español*'s Lisa Quiroz.

As a publisher Moore possessed what McAniff, in an interview with *Brandweek*, called "this homespun quality—that ability to just home in on what the average person on the street cares about" (March 8, 1999). This trait of Moore's was evident in her commitment to "cause marketing"—that is, the support of charities significant to one's clients. One such charity backed by Moore was Gilda's Club, a cancer support group named in honor of the comedienne Gilda Radner. Such corporate support affirmed the community-oriented values Moore believed to be prominent among her readers—and which she herself also held—while also increasing the profile of her magazines.

APPOINTMENT TO CEO/CHAIRWOMAN

In 1998 Moore was appointed president of the *People* group; in March 2001 she acquired responsibility for Time's *Parenting* group. Three months later she was appointed vice president to Time while still overseeing both the *People* and *Parenting* groups. Moore was appointed to the role of CEO and chairwoman of Time in July 2002, soon after the merger between Time Warner and AOL.

A "PEOPLE" PERSON

Moore's colleagues describe her as an extroverted and vibrant executive. McAniff, who described Moore as embodying the spirit of *People*, stated in *Brandweek*, "She loves the razzle dazzle, she loves the celebrities, she loves the glitz, and she's probably the first person who really has embraced that in a major way and helped bring the franchise to life for our constituencies, whether they're advertisers or consumers" (March 8, 1999). Critics, on the other hand, faulted Moore as brash, especially in contrast to the low-key style of the previous CEO and chairman Don Logan. Moore herself described her managerial style as collaborative, and she was known for treating her staff well.

PREPARES TIME FOR CHANGE AND NEW MARKETS

As the CEO and chairwoman of Time, Moore appointed two new vice presidents, McAniff and John Squires, previously the president of *Entertainment Weekly*. She emphasized Time's long-term financial objectives over quarter-to-quarter performance and promised both acquisitions and launches of new titles. In late 2002 she announced the closure of *Sports Illustrated Women* and *Mutual Funds*. In April 2004 Moore announced the establishment of a new low-price monthly women's title, *All You*, to be launched in September 2004. Moore served on the boards of directors of Avon Products and the Wallace Foundation.

SOURCES FOR FURTHER INFORMATION

Carr, David, "Inheriting the Burden of Success at Time Inc.," *New York Times*, July 22, 2002.

Cotts, Cynthia, "Poor Ann Moore," *Village Voice*, November 27, 2001, p. 32.

Fine, Jon, "Teaching Boys' Club How to Reach Women," *Advertising Age*, June 4, 2001, p. S2.

Granatstein, Lisa, "People Person," *Brandweek*, March 8, 1999, p. S50.

Seglin, Jeffrey L., "Her Hopes, Her Dreams," *Folio*, October 2002, pp. 24–32.

—Ann McCarthy

■ ■ ■

Patrick J. Moore
1954–

Chairman of the board, president, and chief executive officer, Smurfit-Stone Container Corporation

Nationality: American.

Born: September 7, 1954, in Chicago, Illinois.

Education: DePaul University, BS, 1981.

Family: Married Beth (maiden name unknown); children: three.

Career: Continental Bank, 1986–1987, assistant vice president; Jefferson Smurfit Corporation, 1987–1990, assistant treasurer; 1990–1993, treasurer; 1993–1998, vice president; 1994–1996, general manager, industrial packaging division; 1996–1998, chief financial officer; Smurfit-Stone Container Corporation, 1998–2002, vice president and chief financial officer; 2002–, president and chief executive officer; 2003–, chairman of the board.

Address: Smurfit-Stone Container Corporation, 150 North Michigan Avenue, Chicago, Illinois 60601-7568; http://www.smurfit-stone.com.

■ Patrick J. Moore served as chairman of the board, president, and chief executive officer of Smurfit-Stone Container Corporation, a major seller and producer of commodity paper and packaging products. Moore emerged in leadership positions after beginning at Jefferson Smurfit, a predecessor to Smurfit-Stone, as an assistant treasurer in 1987. He was named vice president and chief financial officer at Jefferson Smurfit in 1996 and held the same position at Smurfit-Stone from 1998 through 2002. In 2002 Moore was named president and chief executive officer. The following year he was named chairman of the board. Known for his focus on the organization Moore directed Smurfit-Stone through financial times that were difficult owing to poor economic conditions.

DEVELOPING INTEREST IN MONEY AND FINANCE

Moore attributed his interest in money and finance to his roots in a neighborhood on the south side of Chicago, Illinois.

In an interview with Pam Droog of *St. Louis Commerce Magazine*, Moore said of his early years, "Everyone lived in a little two- or three-bedroom, post-war bungalow, with tons of kids. So I guess since I grew up not having a heck of a lot, I always dreamed of having more" (July 2002). To finance his tuition at DePaul University, Moore worked at Continental Bank, which offered a tuition reimbursement program. He was graduated in 1981 with a bachelor of science degree in business administration and later took some graduate accounting and finance classes. By the time he was 32 Moore had been named assistant vice president of Continental Bank.

JOINS JEFFERSON SMURFIT

In 1987 Moore accepted a position as treasurer at one of Continental's customers, Jefferson Smurfit Corporation, which was based in Saint Louis, Missouri. Jefferson Smurfit, a packaging company, originated in Ireland and made its first move into the United States in 1974. Through a series of acquisitions the company had grown dramatically. Between 1985 and 1987, the year Moore joined the company, Jefferson Smurfit revenues had risen from $630.4 million to $1.1 billion. Moore told Droog he found Smurfit to be "a very interesting company," noting, "It has always been very growth-oriented, entrepreneurial in nature, and it rewards people who perform well" (July 2002). Moore climbed the ranks rapidly, becoming treasurer in 1990, vice president and treasurer in 1993, and vice president and general manager of the company's industrial packaging division in 1994.

Moore continued his ascension within Jefferson Smurfit in 1996, when he was appointed vice president and chief financial officer. By the following year, Jefferson Smurfit had grown to having sales of more than $4 billion per year. Jefferson Smurfit's primary source of revenue came from its container and containerboard section. Other revenue came from production of folding cartons and boxboard, reclamation of wood and newsprint, and industrial and consumer packaging.

NAMED VICE PRESIDENT AND CHIEF FINANCIAL OFFICE OF SMURFIT-STONE

In May 1998 Jefferson Smurfit announced that it would purchase Stone Container Corporation, which was based in Chicago. Stone Container had become a major figure in the cardboard products industry in the 1980s through a series of buyouts. By 1989 Stone was generating $6 billion in revenue, but it also had accumulated approximately $3 billion in debt. The debt load during the 1990s caused Stone to sell several of its assets and eventually to agree to merge with Jefferson Smurfit. The companies merged under the name of Smurfit-Stone Container Corporation. Just months after the merger was announced, Moore was named vice president and chief financial officer of Smurfit-Stone. Moore assumed the position with the difficult task of overseeing major divestment of the assets of the merged company. Through the late 1990s and early 2000s Smurfit Stone made continued efforts to reduce debt and downsize by closing plants.

ASSUMES ROLE OF PRESIDENT, CHIEF EXECUTIVE OFFICER, AND CHAIRMAN OF THE BOARD

Amid the difficult financial climate Moore's leadership abilities stood out. When Raymond M. Curran, who had served as president and chief executive officer of Smurfit-Stone since 1999, announced his retirement in January 2002, the company's board elected Moore to the positions. Moore's ability to handle company finances as well as a large operating division within the company led to his appointment. A year after his appointment as president and chief executive officer, Moore replaced Michael W. J. Smurfit as chairman of the board. Working in what Moore correctly predicted to be a difficult operating environment, Smurfit-Stone in 2002 and 2003 continued to tighten its operating focus, to reduce debt, and to lower production costs. Nevertheless, the company continued to struggle in a weak economy. Throughout much of 2003 and 2004 Moore worked to scale down the company's business to meet regional needs.

MANAGEMENT STYLE

Moore's performance as chief financial officer and vice president at Jefferson Smurfit and Smurfit-Stone earned him accolades from the company. Michael Smurfit, then chairman of Smurfit-Stone's board of directors, commented in 2002, "In recent years, [Moore] has demonstrated outstanding financial stewardship in guiding our leveraged company through complex transactions and challenging business conditions. [He] has earned respect and admiration among Smurfit-Stone employees at all levels" (January 4, 2002). Moore likewise had earned the respect of those outside the company. According to New York analyst Mark Wilde in an article by James B. Arndorfer, while Curran was known as a "deal guy," Moore was "more focused on the organization" (February 11, 2002).

In addition to developing relationships with customers, Moore devoted a considerable amount of time to communicating with employees through meetings, conference calls, newsletters, video tapes, and visits to facilities. He told Droog "people development" was a very important role to him. "I spend a lot of time making sure we have the right people in place for succession planning, training and development" (July 2002).

TIES TO SAINT LOUIS AND CHICAGO

Although Smurfit-Stone's headquarters was in Moore's hometown of Chicago, Moore remained in Saint Louis, where he had moved in 1987 to join Jefferson Smurfit. In an interview with the *St. Louis Post-Dispatch*, Moore said he was committed to Saint Louis. He was highly active in his community, serving on the Regional Chamber and Growth Association. Moore served on the Saint Louis metropolitan board of the YMCA and was active in such charities as Boys Hope Girls Hope, Big Shoulders, and the Commercial Club of Chicago. He also served as a director of Archer Daniels Midland Company.

See also entries on Continental Bank Corporation and Smurfit-Stone Container Corporation in *International Directory of Company Histories*.

SOURCES FOR FURTHER INFORMATION

Arndorfer, James B., "Smurfit-Stone's CEO Seeking Way Out of Tight Economic Box," *Crain's Chicago Business*, February 11, 2002.

Droog, Pam, "Local Impact, Global Perspective," *St. Louis Commerce Magazine*, July 2002, http://www.stlcommercemagazine.com/archives/july2002/profile.html.

"Is Smurfit-Stone All Boxed In?" *BusinessWeek*, February 2, 2004, pp. 2–3.

"Smurfit-Stone Container Corporation Elects Patrick J. Moore President and CEO, Succeeding Ray M. Curran," Smurfit-Stone Container Corporation press release, January 4, 2002, http://www.smurfit-stone.com/content/news/news_112.asp.

Tucci, Linda, "Smurfit-Stone Chief Likes Calling St. Louis Home," *St. Louis Post-Dispatch*, March 14, 2003.

—Matthew C. Cordon

■■■
Giuseppe Morchio
1947–
Former chief executive officer, Fiat Group

Nationality: Italian.

Born: November 20, 1947, in Rapallo, Genoa, Italy.

Education: Politecnico di Genova (Genoa Polytechnic University), BS, 1974.

Family: Married; children: two.

Career: Manuli Group, 1974–1980, cable engineer; Pirelli Group, 1980–1986, director of logistics; Pirelli Coordinamento Pneumatici, 1986–1989, vice president of operations for the tire sector; Pirelli Neumaticos, Spain, 1989–1992, chief executive officer and chairman of the board; Pirelli Tyre North America, 1992–1993, chief executive officer and chairman of the board; Pirelli Cavi S.p.A., 1993–1995, chief executive officer; Pirelli Cavi e Sistemi S.p.A., 1995–2001, chief executive officer and chairman of the board; Fiat Group, 2003–2004, chief executive officer.

Giuseppe Morchio. *AP/Wide World Photos.*

■ Giuseppe Morchio made the tough decisions wherever he worked and was an intimidating figure among his employees. He persistently searched for data that would tell him whether a particular business operation was making money or losing money and whether to sell or cut an operation or invest more money in it to enhance profits. He enjoyed traveling and reading and was avowedly passionate about cars, although his favorite hobby was sailing. Bookish, round-faced with a heavy jaw, and wearing round eyeglasses, he was physically unimposing, but he made his presence felt in any job he held.

RUBBER

Morchio attended the Genoa Polytechnic University, where he earned a degree in mechanical engineering. In 1974 he was hired by the Manuli Group, also known as Manuli Rubber, where he worked as a cable engineer. For the next twenty years the focus of his work would be cables for trans-

mitting power or information. The Manuli Group was a small company compared with other cable manufacturers, and the industrial giant Pirelli Group offered more room for advancement.

Pirelli had been manufacturing tires for about a hundred years when Morchio joined it in 1980, and it was famous for its Formula One racing tires. Morchio became the director of logistics for tires. In 1986 he was promoted to vice president of operations for Pirelli's tire division, the Pirelli Coordinamento Pneumatici, where he proved to be an able and demanding manager. His work gave him experience in the requirements of manufacturing and in coordinating an international operation, because Pirelli tires were sold throughout much of the world.

In 1989 Morchio was made the chief executive officer (CEO) and chairman of the board of Pirelli Neumaticos in Spain, a promotion in the importance of his title but actually somewhat of a comedown because Pirelli's operations in Spain were not as important to the company as was directing its tire operations. Perhaps his employers wanted to give him international experience by sending him abroad, or perhaps he himself wanted a position where he was the boss of all day-to-day activities. In 1992 he moved on to Pirelli Tyre North America, becoming its CEO and chairman of the board. While in the United States he probably became familiar with the technologies and American companies that would be important in his building Pirelli into one of the world's foremost cable companies.

CABLES

In 1993 Morchio was called back to Italy and appointed CEO of Pirelli Cavi. Pirelli was losing money and Morchio set to work focusing the company's management on improving the bottom line and emphasizing new technology. Morchio worked his managers hard, calling underlings in the middle of the night and on weekends to talk business. By 1995 Pirelli had returned to profitability and Morchio was appointed CEO and chairman of the board of the holding company Pirelli Cavi e Sistemi. He was now in an ideal position to exercise his skills because he controlled not only the manufacture of tires and cables but Pirelli's diverse holdings in energy-transmission and telecommunications systems.

Morchio's promotion of research and development made Pirelli a world leader in the technology demanded by expanding communications systems such as the Internet. In December 1996 Pirelli sued the American company CIENA Corporation for patent infringement. CIENA countersued, and Pirelli counter-countersued. This resulted in a messy two-year ordeal, but on June 11, 1998, Pirelli resolved its lawsuits against CIENA, with Pirelli dropping its lawsuits in exchange for a $30 million payment and regularly paid royalties on CIENA's continuing use of Pirelli patents. The agreement was reached during direct talks between Morchio and Patrick H. Nettles, president and CEO of CIENA. It was an example of Morchio's willingness to become personally involved in resolving a corporate conflict.

On June 25, 1998, Pirelli Cables and Systems introduced the TeraMux Hyper-Dense WDM system, with 128 channels and a 1.28 terabit transmission. Data had a tendency to break down when transmitted over cables, but the TeraMux system cut expenses by reducing the need for reassembling data. On October 1, 1998, Morchio directed a gift of 4.5 million shares of Pirelli common stock to Pirelli employees worldwide. The minimum number of shares received by an employee was 591. Morchio said the gift was to celebrate Pirelli's 125th anniversa-ry, but he hoped the gift would foster a sense of community among employees and a commitment to the growth and prosperity of Pirelli by giving its employees at all levels an interest in the company's success.

By 1999 Pirelli had 65 factories and 20,000 employees. Morchio sold some of the company's fiber-optics- and component-manufacturing facilities to Cisco Systems for $2.1 billion. Much of the money was reinvested. For instance, on December 15, 1999, Pirelli provided $13.8 million to American Superconductor Corporation for development of high-temperature superconducting wires for energy transmission. Pirelli and American Superconductor had been collaborating on research, and the investment was intended to help bring the superconducting wires to a level that could be tested on a large scale. Superconducting was a young technology, mostly because superconductors had in the past required temperatures near absolute zero in order to work. A high-temperature superconducting wire could save power companies million of dollars because, in theory, no force would be required to transmit electricity over unlimited distances.

By 2000 Morchio had turned Pirelli into the world's foremost manufacturer of power cables. On February 11, 2000, Pirelli purchased the cable business of the United Kingdom's BICCGeneral for $216 million. Morchio hoped this would enhance Pirelli as an energy provider. On May 25, 2000, Pirelli introduced new optical-cable components that could handle higher bandwidths for the Internet than were currently available. In addition, Pirelli offered new fiber cables FreeLight and DeepLight, which had applications in the high-speed transmission of data. By investing in research and filing for and defending patents for new technology, Pirelli's cable business had become not only valuable but huge. The Pirelli Group cashed in on some of the value it had created by selling to Corning its 90 percent ownership of Optical Technologies, a cable and fiber-optics company based in Delaware, for $3.9 billion. Corning agreed to buy another $100 million in other Pirelli properties in the United States. This meant that Pirelli realized $6 billion in 1999 and 2000 from business created after Morchio took Pirelli's helm. Morchio planned to invest the money from the sales in research, Pirelli's fiber-optics business at home, and the company's tire, underwater-systems, and energy businesses.

On December 28, 2000, Pirelli split its energy and telecommunication division into two divisions, one devoted to energy cables and the other to telecommunication cables, each with its own CEO. That month Morchio cashed in $150 million in stock options, and in January 2001 he retired. He planned to travel, especially around the Mediterranean, and to live a life of leisure, but Morchio was driven to achieve, and his leisurely life did not last long.

THE WOES OF FIAT

The Fiat Group had once been a powerhouse in Europe. In Italy in the 1980s, 60 percent of automobiles sold were manufactured by the subsidiary Fiat Auto; by 2000 this had fallen to 30 percent and was continuing to drop. In a plan to revitalize its automobile business, Fiat Group sold 20 percent of Fiat Auto to General Motors for $2.5 billion, with an option to sell the remaining shares to General Motors in early 2004. In 2000 Fiat Auto lost $1.2 billion, while Fiat Group as a whole lost $4.5 billion. Fiat Group was 30 percent owned by the Agnelli family, descendants of Fiat's founder and part of Italy's social elite. Family leader Giovanni Agnelli was determined to hold on to Fiat Auto.

By the end of 2002 Fiat was $7.5 billion in debt, and General Motors saw its huge investment dwindle to a little over $200 million in value. In early 2003 Giovanni Agnelli died of prostate cancer and his brother Umberto was elected chairman of the board of the Fiat Group. Fiat Group was losing millions of dollars per day, and Umberto Agnelli was under pressure to fix Fiat Group's problems quickly. On February 28, 2003, Umberto hired Morchio as the new CEO of Fiat Group. Morchio would be given a free hand in Fiat Group's day-to-day operations, an unusual agreement because the Agnellis had traditionally controlled corporate affairs. Umberto Agnelli and Morchio proved to be a good team; Agnelli kept his end of the agreement, leaving Morchio free to restructure Fiat Group, but he proved to be an astute businessman whose insights in Fiat Group's businesses helped Morchio. Morchio relished the challenge, asserting in April 2003, "When Mr. Umberto Agnelli called me, I had no hesitation. This is the biggest industrial company in the country, with so many problems but also with huge turnaround potential" (*Forbes.com*, June 25, 2003).

Morchio quickly declared his intention to retain Fiat Auto as part of Fiat Group, which was an enormous company with 190,000 employees scattered through numerous divisions around the world. Fiat Auto was the foundation of the group, but Fiat Group had diversified so much during the 1980s and 1990s that Fiat Auto was no longer vital to the group's success. Fiat Group owned energy companies, telecommunications companies, industrial-equipment manufacturers, farm-equipment manufacturers, insurance companies, and more.

Even so, Fiat Auto was the biggest division, the seventh-largest manufacturer by volume of automobiles and trucks in the world, selling about 2.5 million vehicles per year. It accounted for 7.4 percent of the European automobile market, down from 14 percent in the early 1990s. Fiat Group as a whole accounted for 4.8 percent of Italy's gross national product. Morchio and Agnelli decided that Fiat Auto and related industrial businesses offered the greatest potential for growth in Fiat Group and would form the heart of Fiat Group's recovery. Morchio quickly determined that the infusion of money

from General Motors and bank loans in 2002 was not enough to restart Fiat Auto. In May 2003 he approached General Motors for an investment of another $1 billion, but General Motors, noting the steep increase in Fiat Auto's losses, declined.

FOUNDATIONS FOR RECOVERY

On March 22, 2003, Morchio began selling some of Fiat Group's assets to raise some of the money that modernizing and retooling Fiat Auto's factories required. He sold the profitable insurance company Toro Assicurazioni for $2.5 billion. On April 7, 2003, he sold Fiat's aerospace division, Fiat Avio, to the Carlyle Group for $1.7 billion. This still left him $800 million short of the $5 billion he believed would be necessary to revive Fiat Auto. He then recapitalized Fiat Auto by issuing new stock in the company, thus raising over $1 billion. This large stock offering diluted General Motors's share of the company from 20 to 10 percent, and General Motors threatened to sue for breach of contract, saying that the issuing of new shares invalidated its contract with Fiat Group. Morchio felt he could avert this threatened action: In a separate agreement, General Motors and Fiat Group were collaborating on making drivetrains for automobiles, and the demand for the products of this joint venture was already outstripping supply. Morchio hoped that the potential profits from this venture might dissuade General Motors from taking hostile action against Fiat Group. Meanwhile, Morchio was looking elsewhere for partners to help share the costs of developing new vehicles, and he found a new partner in Japan's Suzuki; Fiat and Suzuki agreed to jointly manufacture a sport-utility vehicle in Budapest, Hungary, with Fiat providing its diesel engine. The companies hoped to begin manufacturing the vehicle in 2005, with each company selling the vehicle under its own brand name.

In June 2003 Morchio revealed his long-term plans for revitalizing Fiat Group. He said that one objective was for the corporation to break even in 2004; another was to turn a profit in 2006. These would be daunting tasks, but Morchio was a whirlwind of activity, flowing through offices and factories, a large notebook full of figures under one arm, restlessly searching for ways to cut costs and for investment opportunities. His plan had five steps. The first was to cut costs by $1.1 billion. To do this Fiat Group would close the factories of Iveco, its truck-manufacturing company, and of CNH, which made farm and industrial equipment. This was part of his plan to close 12 factories during 2003 and 2004, mostly outside of Italy. The closings would result in laying off 12,300 employees, 2,800 of them in Italy. Morchio planned to hire 5,400 people in marketing and research as part of the second step, which was to increase spending on research from an annual $100 million to $1.2 billion. The third step was to have Fiat Group retrench its automobile manufacturing by reducing its European output to 1.6 million vehicles per year. Following this retrenchment the fourth step was to have Fiat Auto introduce several new, more stylish models of automobiles, with the objective of increasing Fiat Auto's share of the European automobile market by 9% by 2006. Fiat Group owned the Ferrari, Maserati, and Alpha Romeo brands, each of which had a reputation for poor after-sales service. Thus, the fifth step was to make service more available by investing $450 million dollars over three years to expand the number of Fiat dealers.

By 2003 business credit-rating companies such as Standard & Poor's rated Fiat Group's stock as junk grade; one of Morchio's ambitions was to have the stock rated investment grade by the middle of 2004. Part of his plan to achieve this was to introduce a series of new automobiles that were well suited to the modern European market. In the past, Fiat had dominated with small cars that fit well in the narrow streets of old European cities, but a decline in the quality of Fiat's automobiles and the introduction of better-made Japanese cars had hurt its sales. Prior to Morchio's arrival on the scene, Fiat Group had tried to return to profitability by manufacturing big automobiles to compete with those of BMW; large automobiles had high profit margins, whereas small cars such as Fiat's Punto had very slim profit margins. Morchio pointed Fiat Group back in the direction of small economy cars, investing in research and development for over a dozen new models from all automobile divisions to be introduced by 2006, while updating current models. The new Idea and Panda models were released in November 2003. It was a happy day for Fiat when European automobile journalists voted the Panda the European Car of the Year for 2004.

AN UNEXPECTED ENDING

It was perhaps a sign of just how bad times had been for Fiat Group when Morchio was praised in the press for reducing losses for the first quarter of 2004 to a mere $242 million, down from $800 million the year before. Banks renewed their interest in investing in Fiat Group, and Morchio persuaded them to extend deadlines for payments on outstanding loans. Automobile sales were picking up, and Fiat Group was making inroads in his old specialty, the development of energy and telecommunications cables. In February 2004 Morchio had Edison and Fiat Engineering sell stock to raise capital for improvements. It seemed as though Fiat Group would actually meet Morchio's goal of breaking even in 2004.

In April 2004 there was an eight-day-long strike at one of Fiat Group's most modern factories, in Melfi. The Melfi factory made components that were used in almost every other Fiat Group factory, and the strike slowed or halted production throughout much of Fiat's European manufacturing centers, cutting automobile production in half. To the surprise of many, including union leaders, Morchio personally met with union leaders to negotiate a settlement to end the strike. The

CEO of Fiat was traditionally treated like royalty and was expected to delegate negotiations with unions to a lower level executive. During a marathon session with the representatives of three striking unions, Morchio and union leaders worked out an agreement.

On May 10, 2004, the factory in Melfi resumed full production after three weeks of below-normal activity. Morchio said that the agreement he reached with the unions was burdensome for Fiat but necessary for its recovery. The strike settlement included a monthly pay increase of $126. Morchio believed that, although second-quarter 2004 income was hurt, Fiat would recover its losses over the rest of the year, putting its recovery back on track.

Morchio continued his efforts to revitalize Fiat Group by hiring outsiders for important executive positions. As CEO of Fiat Auto he hired the Austrian Herbert Demel, then president and CEO of Magna Steyr, an automobile-parts manufacturer. On May 5, 2004, Morchio hired the former head of Ford Motor Company's European operations, Martin Leach, to be CEO of Maserati. Bringing in such experienced outsiders was part of Morchio's long-term plan to revitalize Fiat Group's corporate culture.

On May 27, 2004, Umberto Agnelli died from stomach cancer. Morchio wanted to replace Agnelli as chairman of the board, which would allow him to continue remaking Fiat Group in his own way. On May 30, 2004, the board of directors for Fiat Group met, and the Agnelli family reasserted its control of the company by adding two family members to the board of directors. The CEO of Ferrari, Luca Cordero di Montezemolo, was named chairman of the board. For the Agnelli family di Montezemolo was a logical choice; he was a loyalist who had been with Fiat for 30 years. He had also been Morchio's subordinate for the previous 15 months. Morchio reportedly regarded the election of di Montezemolo as a breach of his agreement with Fiat Group and the Agnellis that he would be given a free hand in revitalizing the corporation. He resigned almost immediately after the snub. Although di Montezemolo said that Fiat Group would continue to follow Morchio's plans to the letter, Morchio quickly became a nonperson at Fiat Group, with references to him disappearing from company records.

See also entries on Fiat SpA and Pirelli S.p.A. in *International Directory of Company Histories.*

SOURCES FOR FURTHER INFORMATION

Bremner, Richard, "A Tale of Two Dynasties," *Management Today*, January 7, 2004, pp. 44–48.

Ciferri, Luca, "Microcar Fascinates Fiat CEO," *Automotive News Europe*, December 1, 2003, p. 17.

Levine, Gregory, "Faces in the News," *Forbes.com*, http://
www.forbes.com/2003/06/25/cx_gl_0625facesam.html.

Wildt, Mathias, "Fiat's Morchio Narrows Losses With New
Models, Asset Sales," *Bloomberg.com*, http://
quote.bloomberg.com/apps/
news?pid=10000085&sid=aev0jdT309dM&refer=europe.

—Kirk H. Beetz

Tomijiro Morita

1941–

President, Dai-ichi Mutual Life Insurance Company

Nationality: Japanese.

Born: 1941.

Education: University of Tokyo, 1964.

Family: Married (spouse's name unknown).

Career: Dai-ichi Mutual Life Insurance Company, 1964–1996, various positions; 1996–1997, vice president; 1997–, president.

Address: Dai-ichi Mutual Life Insurance Company, 1-13-1 Yuraku-cho, Chiyodku, Tokyo, 100-8411, Japan; http://www.dai-ichi-life.co.jp.

Tomijiro Morita. *Kazuhiro Nogi/Getty Images.*

■ Tomijiro Morita spent his career with Dai-ichi Mutual Life Insurance Company, becoming its president in 1997. Morita joined the firm in 1964 after graduating from the University of Tokyo, and he developed a reputation as one of the toughest salespeople in the insurance industry in Japan. He revitalized Dai-ichi's sales division and proved to be a strong negotiator for insurers with the Japanese Ministry of Finance during difficult financial times in the early 1990s. As Dai-ichi's president he steered the company through insurance deregulation, forming a series of strategic alliances and partnerships with other companies to maintain and improve his company's financial position.

BEGINNINGS AT DAI-ICHI MUTUAL INSURANCE COMPANY

Morita studied karate at the University of Tokyo, where he graduated in 1964. He joined Dai-ichi Mutual Life Insurance Company after graduation. During his second year with the company, he was appointed to the company labor union's executive committee. The chairman of the union at the time was Takahide Sakurai, who later became president of the company. Sakurai served as a mentor to Morita as Morita continued his career at Dai-ichi.

For a number of years, beginning primarily in 1970s, Japan enjoyed phenomenal economic success. By the late 1980s Japan was maintaining what was commonly referred to as a "bubble economy," with the country experiencing optimum growth over a period of several years. During this period Morita stood out among his peers as a fierce sales competitor. In 1990, however, Japan's bubble economy burst, leading to a major economic downturn. Morita once again distinguished himself in the sales and marketing aspects of Dai-ichi's business when the company focused, in part, on realignment of asset portfolios.

JOINING DAI-ICHI'S BOARD AND RISING IN MANAGEMENT

Based largely on his performance in the sales sector, Morita earned a seat on Dai-ichi's board in 1991. The board placed him in charge of fund management for the company. He assumed the position as the lead negotiator for the insurance industry with officials from the Ministry of Finance in a major dispute involving Japanese housing lenders, known as *jusen*. By the mid-1990s, seven of the eight leading mortgage companies had neared insolvency, with the lenders suffering from debt of approximately ¥65 trillion. While the insurance industry was only one of several interested parties involved as the Ministry of Finance sought to find an acceptable bailout plan, Morita's service in this capacity earned him respect within the insurance industry.

Morita and Sakurai maintained a strong partnership throughout Morita's career with Dai-ichi. Like Morita, Sakurai had joined Dai-ichi following his graduation from the University of Tokyo in 1955. Sakurai rose through the ranks to become president of Dai-ichi in 1987. The partnership between Morita and Sakurai was one "which rival firms came to fear as the driving force behind Dai-ichi's aggressive marketing strategy" (March 7, 1997).

Morita was groomed for a leadership position in Dai-ichi when he was promoted in 1996 to the position of vice president. In 1997 the company announced that Sakurai would become chairman of Dai-ichi, replacing Shinichi Nishio. Sakurai said he chose to move aside as president with the hope that new management could steer the company through expected and forthcoming financial changes in Japan. The company then selected Morita as its new president.

TAKING OVER AS PRESIDENT OF DAI-ICHI

Dai-ichi had long been Japan's second-largest insurance company, behind Nippon Life Insurance Company. Reflecting what newspaper accounts referred to as a "rather pugnacious business personality," Morita immediately challenged Nippon, saying that one of Dai-ichi's goals was to overtake Nippon for the top position in the industry (March 7, 1997). Dai-ichi's selection of Morita, with his background in sales and marketing, was consistent with a trend among Japanese insurance companies. Like Dai-ichi, Nippon and Mitsui Mutual Life Insurance Company in 1997 selected presidents known for their marketing skills.

The expected radical reforms in Japan's financial markets began to take place a year after Morita assumed the role of president at Dai-ichi. The Japanese legislature enacted the Financial System Reform Act of 1998, which deregulated the insurance, banking, and securities industries. Insurance companies were permitted to set their own prices on policies, a situation that was unprecedented. Similar reforms allowed foreign competitors to enter Japanese business, thus increasing competition among firms. Known as Japan's financial "Big Bang," the new reforms were intended to encourage greater private investment in Japan.

At the press conference where he was introduced as Dai-ichi's new president in 1997, Morita maintained that the company would focus its business on insurance sales and assets investments, expressing caution about the company's entering new businesses. Following deregulation, however, Morita directed Dai-ichi to form a series of strategic alliances with other insurance companies and businesses. The first of these alliances took place in 1998, when Morita announced that Dai-ichi had agreed to a partnership with the Industrial Bank of Japan. The two companies agreed to increase their investments in each other in an effort to strengthen each company's finances. Morita conceded that reform had progressed more quickly than he had expected. Referring to the company's initial caution regarding the effect of deregulation, Morita said, "We had been considering a new strategy at our own pace, but we realized we would miss a partner if we stuck to our own schedule" (*Asahi Shimbun*, October 3, 1998).

CONTINUING AGGRESSIVE BUSINESS STRATEGIES

Morita introduced a number of momentous changes at Dai-ichi in order to steer the company through deregulation. Part of the company's new approach, Morita said in 1999, was to overhaul its marketing strategy. The company had previously centered its focus on indemnity against death. Under the new vision, however, the strategy focused on a plan for the insured's life, including planning for old age. In an interview with the *Yomiuri Shimbun* (May 4, 1999), Morita observed, "As people grow older, the issue of life during their old age becomes more important to them, even if they took out insurance policies in their 20s and 30s. Therefore, it has become all the more necessary for us to present our clients with a clear image of what life in their senior years will be like financially."

Alliances and partnerships remained an important part of Dai-ichi's strategy as well. In 2000 the company announced the formation of alliances with two major insurance companies. Dai-ichi and Yasuda Fire and Marine Insurance Company agreed to join their sales focuses and mutually develop their products. Shortly thereafter, Dai-ichi announced an alliance with American Family Life Assurance Company of Columbus, Ohio, whereby the companies agreed to market and develop their products jointly. While analysts considered many of these moves to be defensive measures, the company in 2004 remained the second-largest life insurance company in Japan.

LEADER WITHIN THE INSURANCE INDUSTRY

Morita's respect within his industry was represented in 1999, when he was appointed chairman of the Life Insurance Association of Japan. During his term as chairman, he was vocal about pertinent issues affecting the insurance industry, maintaining that life insurance played an enhanced social role in Japan with support from both the private sector and the public sector. He was also critical of certain governmental actions, such as the development of state-sponsored term and whole life insurance policies.

SOURCES FOR FURTHER INFORMATION

"Analysis: Dai-ichi Mutual Buckles Down Revenues Through Tie-Ups," *Nikkei Report*, January 7, 2004.

"IBJ, Dai-ichi Mutual Life Form Strategic Alliance," *Asahi Shimbun*, October 3, 1998.

"Japan Life Insur Chief: Insur Companies Still Under Pressure," *Dow Jones Interactive News*, March 17, 2000.

Kurokawa, Shigeki, "Dai-ichi Mutual Life Insurance Faces Big Bang," *Yomiuri Shimbun*, May 4, 1999.

"Morita to Take Charge of Japan's Dai-ichi Mutual Life," *Asia Pulse*, March 7, 1997.

—Matthew C. Cordon

■■■
Angelo R. Mozilo
1939–
Cofounder, chairman, and chief executive officer, Countrywide Financial Corporation

Nationality: American.

Born: 1939, in New York, New York.

Education: Fordham University, BS, 1960.

Family: Married Phyllis (maiden name unknown); children: five.

Career: United Mortgagee Servicing Corporation, 1953–1968; Countrywide Financial Corporation (formerly Countrywide Credit Industries), 1969–, cofounder, chairman, and chief executive officer.

Awards: Named to the Hall of Fame, National Association of Home Builders, 1995; Ellis Island Medal of Honor, 1999, National Ethnic Coalition of Organizations; National Housing Person of the Year, 2004, National Housing Conference; Horatio Alger Award, 2004, Horatio Alger Association; James E. West Fellowship Award, Boy Scouts of America; Albert Schweitzer Award, Alexander von Humboldt Foundation; Special Achievement Award for Humanitarian Service, National Italian American Foundation; Pepperdine University, honorary LLD.

Address: Countrywide Financial, 4500 Park Granada, Calabasas, California 91302-1613; http://www.countrywide.com.

■ Angelo Mozilo cofounded Countrywide Financial Corporation, a diversified financial-services company, in 1969. Under the leadership of Mozilo and his colleague David Loeb, Countrywide was transformed from a two-man office into a mortgage-banking powerhouse with approximately five hundred U.S. branches and over $400 billion in new loans in 2003. With over 50 years of experience in the mortgage business, Mozilo was described as a hands-on manager who was not afraid to take risks and who had high expectations for his employees and a fierce determination to be the best.

LEARNING THE ROPES

Mozilo's parents were first-generation Italian Americans who had little formal schooling, and they impressed on him early the importance of hard work and a good education. He began working in his father's butcher shop at the age of 12 and as a messenger for a Manhattan mortgage lender at 14. While attending Fordham University, Mozilo continued to work for the mortgage company. After graduating in 1960 with a degree in marketing and philosophy, he decided against the family business and began working full-time for the firm.

Soon after, the company merged with a competitor, Lomas Realty Securities, founded by industry pioneer David Loeb. The 21-year-old Mozilo became Loeb's protégé, and when their company was bought out in the late 1960s, the two decided to start their own mortgage bank. They named it Countrywide Credit Industries, although at the time the company consisted of a single office for the two entrepreneurs, with Mozilo as the sole salesperson.

COUNTRYWIDE'S EVOLUTION

For five years Mozilo and Loeb ran the company like the traditional mortgage lender, offering limited types of loans and relying on salespeople to sell them. Then, in 1974, Mozilo and Loeb took a novel approach: they created a branch office and relied on advertisements, not salespeople, to generate business, with the idea that the money no longer being used for sales commissions could be directed at taking the company nationwide. The single California branch office led to the opening of five more offices in the state by the late 1970s, and a total of 40 offices in nine states by 1980. Mozilo's vision of a "countrywide" mortgage lender was becoming a reality.

Despite volatile interest rates in the 1980s, Mozilo led the continued rapid growth of Countrywide by expanding the types of loans it offered, utilizing innovative technologies to streamline business, taking the company public in 1985, and diversifying the company's financial services to include wholesale-loan origination, correspondent lending, and servicing departments. When interest rates began to fall in 1991 and homeowners rushed to refinance, Countrywide emerged as a mortgage-lending powerhouse; its diversification plan helped to offset the ups and downs of interest rates in the 1990s. The company changed its name to Countrywide Financial Corporation in 2002 to reflect its diversified services.

Mozilo remained true to his vision of organic growth, bucking the growing industry trend of consolidation. By doing so, Countrywide was able to capture market share and gain new sales talent during the merger upheaval. During the 1990s, Mozilo also began to recognize that affordable and available housing was a national concern. Through an initiative called We House America, Countrywide committed to offering affordable lending to minorities and lower-income borrowers. In a 2003 lecture at the National Housing Center in Washington, DC, Mozilo stated that "the American dream of homeownership is always our steadfast mission and we must never allow it to become a cliché" (*Mortgage Banking*, February 2003). In 2004 Mozilo was honored with the National Housing Conference's Housing Person of the Year award for his commitment to reducing the barriers to homeownership. He also served as the president of the Mortgage Bankers Association of America in 1991-1992.

MANAGEMENT STYLE

Mozilo's leadership style was key to Countrywide's successes. By his own admission, he had a reputation for being demanding—"I'm perceived as a tough guy, a son of a bitch" (*Forbes*, November 27, 2000)—and he expected the same kind of dedication from his employees. "For me it's corporate culture. They must be quick to adapt. If not, they're jettisoned" (*Mortgage Wire*, November 5, 2003). Despite his high expectations, he instilled in his workers great pride in the company; as of 2004 his top 15 employees had averaged 21 years with Countrywide. His intrepid and competitive nature extended to his personal life, where he relished adventurous vacations such as helicopter skiing and fishing in Central America.

EXIT PLAN

In 2001 Mozilo signed a 10-year contract with Countrywide that called for him to continue as CEO for five years, and then serve as a consultant for another five. Harley W. Snyder, a member of Countrywide's board of directors, said of the deal: "Angelo Mozilo is one of the most important and influential figures in the history of mortgage banking. This agreement ensures that Countrywide will have the opportunity to benefit from his vision, leadership and unmatched expertise over the next decade" (*American Banker*, June 5, 2001).

See also entry on Countrywide Credit Industries, Inc. in *International Directory of Company Histories*.

SOURCES FOR FURTHER INFORMATION

Condon, Bernard, "Last Man Standing," *Forbes*, November 27, 2000, p. 108.

"Countrywide Aims for #1," *Mortgage Wire*, November 5, 2003, p. 1.

Mozilo, Angelo R. "Barriers and Obstacles: Closing the Homeownership Gap," *Mortgage Banking*, February 2003, p. 15.

"Mozilo Signs 10-Year Pact with Countrywide," *American Banker*, June 5, 2001, p. 19.

"Straight Shooter," *Mortgage Banking*, October 1991, pp. 46–52.

—Stephanie Dionne Sherk

■■■
Anne M. Mulcahy
1952–
Chairman and chief executive officer, Xerox Corporation

Nationality: American.

Born: October 21, 1952, in Rockville Centre, New York.

Education: Marymount College, BA, 1974.

Family: Married Joe Mulcahy (sales manager); children: two.

Career: Xerox, 1976–1991, field sales representative; 1992–1995, vice president, human resources; 1996–1997, vice president and staff officer, customer operations worldwide; 1998, senior vice president and chief staff officer; 1999–2000, president, general markets operations; 2000–2001, president and chief operating officer; 2001–2002, president and chief executive officer; 2002–, chairman and chief executive officer.

Address: Xerox Corporation, 800 Long Ridge Road, Box 1600, Stamford, Connecticut 06904; http://www.xerox.com.

Anne M. Mulcahy. *Photo by Frank Veronsky; courtesy of Xerox Corporation.*

■ Anne M. Mulcahy became the first woman CEO in Xerox's history in August 2001 and its first female chairman in January 2002 thanks largely to her skill in turning around the deeply troubled copying and printing giant. She ordered a restructuring that cut annual expenses by $1.7 billion, slashed 25,000 jobs, and sold $2.3 billion worth of noncore assets to reduce Xerox's long-term debt. Mulcahy also paid a $10 million fine and restated five years of Xerox's revenues to quiet an embarrassing accounting scandal; the Securities and Exchange Commission had accused the company of bending its numbers to meet Wall Street's expectations. Colleagues praised her for achieving a minor miracle through honesty, communication, and a willingness to tackle tough tasks.

AN UNUSUAL BACKGROUND FOR A CEO

The only daughter in a family with four boys, Mulcahy was encouraged by her parents to compete equally with her broth-ers. This upbringing taught her not only to handle criticism but to listen to it as well—an ability that has helped her to make difficult decisions. After completing her primary education at a Catholic school, she earned a degree in English and journalism at Marymount College. She then spent 16 years working as a sales representative for Xerox and thought for years about quitting to spend more time with her sons. In May 2000 the Xerox board picked Mulcahy to be president and CEO-in-waiting. "I never expected to be CEO of Xerox. I was never groomed to be CEO of Xerox. It was a total surprise to everyone, including myself," she later said (*Fortune*, June 9, 2003).

But Mulcahy had qualities that Xerox badly needed. She was straightforward, hardworking, and disciplined, and she was fiercely loyal to Xerox—the company, the brand, and the people. Her coworkers described her as both compassionate and tough. "Part of her DNA is to tell you the good, the bad, and the ugly," said one colleague (*Fortune*, June 9, 2003). Mulcahy's willingness to work side by side with subordinates gave her unusual credibility and permitted her to galvanize dispirited Xerox workers.

LEADING BY LISTENING

In the early days of her reign as president, Mulcahy logged 100,000 miles in visits to far-flung Xerox locations. She held town-style meetings to address matters such as Xerox's possible bankruptcy and closure. The meetings were quite contentious, but Mulcahy answered as honestly as possible. She managed to boost morale by giving workers a reason to be hopeful and committed to the company. As she later elaborated, "If you schmooze and spin your communications, it comes back to bite you in your ability to establish credibility with people" (*Fortune*, June 9, 2003). Mulcahy saw communication as the most important tool for a leader. "I believe strongly that my success as a leader is driven by my commitment to understanding and meeting customer's requirements as well as developing and nurturing a motivated and proud workforce" (Kharif, *Business Week Online*).

Xerox had stopped listening to its customers, and Mulcahy's background in sales undoubtedly gave her a perspective that saved the life of the technology giant. The company had lost focus on the market. It neglected to change its cost model, maintaining its strategy despite obvious signs from customers that it no longer worked. Mulcahy, known for being an ex-

tremely focused and decisive woman, placed the company's emphasis back on sales and refused to tolerate subordinates who performed poorly.

While Xerox bounced back, by 2004 it had not experienced the kind of growth it knew during its heyday. Mulcahy sought to reinvigorate the company by dedicating $1 billion annually to research and development. She planned to expand into consulting services by helping companies better manage their document flows and by setting up computer networks. Analysts expressed doubts that Xerox could change its image and learn new areas, but the firm's stock continued to rise under Mulcahy's leadership.

See also entry on Xerox Corporation in *International Directory of Company Histories.*

SOURCES FOR FURTHER INFORMATION

Kharif, Olga, "Anne Mulcahy Has Xerox by the Horns," *BusinessWeek online*, http://www.businessweek.com/technology/content/may2003/tc20030529_1642_tc111.htm.

Morris, Betsy, "The Accidental CEO," *Fortune*, June 9, 2003, pp. 42–47.

Mulcahy, Anne, "Lead Your Employees Through Hell and Back," *Business 2.0*, December 2002, p. 91.

Pryme, Kristy, "Mulcahy's Rise to Power," *Computer Dealer News*, September 12, 2003, p. 46.

—Caryn E. Neumann

■ ■ ■
Leo F. Mullin

1943–
Chairman, Delta Airlines

Nationality: American.

Born: January 26, 1943, in Maynard, Massachusetts.

Education: Harvard University, AB, 1964; MS, 1965; MBA, 1967.

Family: Son of Leo (high school principal) and Alice (schoolteacher); married Leah Malmberg; children: two.

Career: McKinsey & Company, 1967–1973, associate; 1973–1976, principal; Consolidated Rail Corporation, 1976–1981, senior vice president, strategic planning; First Chicago Corporation, 1981–1984, senior vice president; 1984–1991, executive vice president; American National Bank and Trust Company, 1991–1993, chairman; First Chicago Corporation, 1993–1995, chief operating officer; Unicom/Commonwealth Edison, 1995–1997, vice chairman; Delta Airlines, 1997–1999, chief executive officer; 1999–2004, chairman of the board and chief executive officer; 2004–, chairman of the board.

Address: Delta Airlines, 760 Doug Davis Drive, Atlanta, Georgia 30354; http://www.delta.com.

Leo F. Mullin. *AP/Wide World Photos.*

■ Leo F. Mullin spent nearly 30 years rising through leadership positions within several different fields, including banking and transportation, before becoming the chief executive officer of Delta Airlines in 1997. He turned the company's finances around during his first three years as CEO; however, Delta had to struggle along with the rest of the airline industry following the terrorist attacks on the United States in September 2001. Mullin, who held three degrees from Harvard University, became embroiled in controversy when company documents revealed that he and other executives had been paid large sums of money in the form of cash bonuses and payments to pension plans during a time in which the company was asking its employees to accept wage cuts. Mullin stepped down as CEO of Delta at the end of 2003.

EDUCATION AND EARLY CAREER

Leo Mullin grew up in a sound educational environment in Maynard, a small town in eastern Massachusetts. He was one of eight children born to a high school principal and a schoolteacher. Mullin remained in his home state to attend Harvard University, where he studied engineering as an undergraduate. He completed his bachelor's degree in 1964, followed by a master's degree in applied physics and applied mathematics in 1965. Mullin remained at Harvard, receiving a master's degree in business administration from the Harvard Business School in 1967.

Mullin was hired as an associate at McKinsey & Company, a financial consulting service in Washington, D.C., in 1967 and remained with the company for nine years. He was promoted to principal or partner of the firm in 1973 and continued working for McKinsey until 1976. Mullin had his first experience in the transportation industry when he became senior vice president for strategic planning at the Consolidated Rail Corporation (Conrail) in Philadelphia in 1976.

Mullin continued his rise into the ranks of upper management in 1981 when he was hired as the senior vice president of the First Chicago Corporation, the tenth largest bank in the United States. He was later promoted to executive vice president in 1984 and remained in that position until 1991. Between 1991 and 1993, Mullin served as the chairman of the American National Bank and Trust Company in Chicago, a subdivision of First Chicago. His rise through the company culminated in his appointment as the bank's president and chief operating officer in 1993. In 1995 Mullin transferred to Unicom and its subsidiary, Commonwealth Edison, as the Chicago company's vice chairman. Mullin joined Unicom at a time when the utility company had had to adjust to industry deregulation.

AN OUTSIDER CEO

Mullin's next position represented a surprising change for the company that hired him. Until 1997 Delta Airlines had never hired a chief executive officer who had not risen through the company's own ranks. Delta had, however, experienced several crises in the course of the 1990s. During the early part of the decade, the company struggled with a series of financial problems caused by expensive expansion projects. The problems in turn forced the CEO at that time, Ron Allen, to make deep cutbacks. Although Delta had made some financial gains under Allen's direction, its internal morale and customer service had suffered. After several clashes with the company's board, Allen was forced out as CEO.

Delta looked outside its own management when it hired Mullin after a three-month search. Although Mullin had had no experience in managing airlines when he took over as CEO in August 1997, he did not regard his inexperience as a disadvantage. He referred to himself at the time as a "student of companies" (*Atlanta Journal-Constitution*, August 16, 1997). Mullin promised to restore a balance between improving Delta's financial situation and dealing with other important factors, including customer service and relations with employees.

Mullin gained the respect of observers in his first few months with Delta as a result of his open and earnest leadership style. Delta's stock prices climbed during its first year under Mullin's direction. Delta announced its first billion-dollar profit in 1998, and the company's stock price rose to an all-time high of $143 per share. Customer service also improved during Mullin's first year as CEO.

Mullin added the title of chairman of the board to his resume in 1999, but some long-standing problems resurfaced. The company began negotiations with its pilots' union in September 1999. During a meeting in October, the pilots raised a number of concerns regarding the company's dealings with its personnel. Although Delta's pilots were paid the highest salaries in the industry, they felt considerable animosity toward the company's management as a result of deep cutbacks experienced during the early 1990s.

A LEADER IN CRISIS

Delta's profitable run under Mullin ended in 2000 and 2001, as labor costs and fuel prices both escalated. Delta reached an agreement with the pilots' union in June 2001 that provided for a 24–39-percent increase in the pilots' pay. The contract was expected to cost the company $2.5 billion. Delta's profits continued to slide.

The next crisis occurred less than three months later, when the terrorist attacks on the United States on September 11, 2001 crippled the airline industry. All civilian airplanes were grounded for several days after the attack. The interruption in service cost the industry an estimated $120 million per day. Although none of the planes that were hijacked by the terrorists belonged to Delta, the disaster affected all the major airlines.

Within weeks of the terrorist attacks, however, Mullin emerged as an industry spokesperson. He addressed congressional committees on several occasions, requesting federal aid for the airlines and asking Congress to approve mergers between airlines. Thanks to Mullin—who was considered the appropriate industry executive to speak because he "has the ability to communicate that some others don't"—Congress agreed to rescue the ailing airlines (*Los Angeles Times*, September 21, 2001).

CONTROVERSY OVER SALARY

Delta shared the ongoing financial problems that affected all the major carriers following the September 11 attacks. The company sought concessions from the pilots' union, asking the pilots to accept significant pay cuts. The pilots stood firm. As many as 16,000 Delta employees were laid off between the early part of 2001 and the end of 2003, resulting in a sharp drop in employee morale. The first wave of staff reductions were the result of voluntary retirements and buyouts that took place after the company announced potential layoffs. Flight attendants were the group most heavily affected in 2002 and early 2003, although the cuts affected just about every job category in the company.

Although Mullin retained his position as an industry leader through 2002, his reputation was tarnished when reports revealed that Delta had paid as much as $43 million to its executives in the form of cash bonuses and payments to executive pension funds. These pension funds could not be touched in the event that the airline was forced to declare bankruptcy.

Delta's performance rating declined in 2003 along with employee morale and customer satisfaction. Mullin was unable to win concessions from the pilots' union even though Delta tried to cut the pilots' compensation by as much as 31 percent. Amid the turmoil, Mullin abruptly announced his retirement as CEO of Delta in November 2003. He remained as the company's chairman for part of 2004. Although Mullin claimed that the timing of his retirement came at a "perfect break point," analysts assumed that the move was necessary because the pilots were unlikely to agree to wage cuts as long as Mullin remained at the head of the company (*Washington Post*, November 25, 2003).

Apart from Mullin's duties at Delta, he was widely known for his involvement with civic and business organizations, including the Museum of Natural History in Chicago, the Chicago Chamber of Commerce, and the Chicago Urban League.

See also entries on Commonwealth Edison, Consolidated Rail Corporation, Delta Air Lines, Inc., and First Chicago Corporation in *International Directory of Company Histories*.

SOURCES FOR FURTHER INFORMATION

Adams, Marilyn, "Delta CEO Mullin Navigates a Complex, Turbulent Course," *USA Today*, August 27, 2003.

Alexander, Keith L., "Delta Chairman, CEO Announces Plans to Retire," *Washington Post*, November 25, 2003.

Fonti, Nancy, "Delta's Chief Braces for Stressful Period," *Atlanta Journal-Constitution*, September 15, 2001.

Grantham, Russell, "Mullin Leaves Checkered Record as CEO," *Atlanta Journal-Constitution*, January 2, 2004.

Peltz, James F., "Delta's CEO Emerges as Industry Voice," *Los Angeles Times*, September 21, 2001.

Saporta, Maria, "Delta CEO Emerges as Industry Leader," *Atlanta Journal-Constitution*, May 30, 2002.

Thurston, Scott, "A New Delta Team, Inside and Out," *Atlanta Journal-Constitution*, August 16, 1997.

—Matthew C. Cordon

■■■
James J. Mulva

1946–

President and chief executive officer, ConocoPhillips

Nationality: American.

Born: June 19, 1946, in Oshkosh, Wisconsin.

Education: University of Texas, BBA, 1968; MBA, 1969.

Family: Married Miriam (maiden name unknown), 1969; children: two.

Career: Phillips Petroleum Company, 1973–1974, management trainee and treasurer; 1974–1976, assistant treasurer; 1976–1980, manager of foreign exchange and investment; 1980–1984, vice president and treasurer of Europe/Africa; 1984–1985, manager of corporate planning; 1985–1986, assistant treasurer; 1986–1988, treasurer; 1988–1990, vice president and treasurer; 1990–1999, chief financial officer; 1994–1999, president and chief operating officer; 1999, vice chairman; 1999–2002, chairman, president, and chief executive officer; ConocoPhillips, 2002–, president and chief executive officer.

Awards: Named Petroleum Executive of the Year by a representative group of senior oil executives at the 23rd annual Oil and Money Conference, 2002.

Address: ConocoPhillips, 600 North Dairy Ashford, P.O. Box 2197, Houston, Texas 77252-2197; http://www.conocophillips.com.

James J. Mulva. *AP/Wide World Photos.*

■ James Mulva served as president and chief executive officer of Phillips Petroleum Company. During his tenure at Phillips, Mulva guided the company into profitable markets in Europe and Russia and headed the successful merger of Phillips with Conoco to form ConocoPhillips. Coworkers and industry peers described Mulva as a capable leader who was able to implement new technology, learn from other companies' mistakes, and direct financial decisions to meet and exceed corporate goals.

AN INTRODUCTION TO THE IMPORTANCE OF OIL

After graduating from the University of Texas with a BBA in finance and an MBA in business administration, Mulva im-

mediately began a tour of duty in the U.S. Navy. During his first two years in the Navy, he was stationed on Bahrain Island. At that time, Bahrain and Saudi Arabia were producing enormous amounts of oil and natural gas, and Mulva was able to learn about the size and importance of the energy industry. After exposure to the production side of the sector, Mulva became intrigued by the complexity and geopolitical impact of the financial aspects of the energy industry.

USING FINANCIAL SKILLS IN A CORPORATE SETTING

In 1973 Mulva completed his tour of duty in the Navy and decided to enter the energy industry in the financial end of the business. During his job search, Mulva found a position in the treasury department at Phillips Petroleum Company that was a good entry-level fit. This job provided Mulva with the challenge he was looking for as well as practical financial knowledge and an introduction to the petroleum industry. Although Mulva had begun at Phillips without a plan to become a high-level executive, he was promoted based on his hard work and his ability to analyze a situation and determine a solution that resulted in profit to the company.

GOING GLOBAL

Mulva worked carefully through successive positions at Phillips to build the company's long-term security and assets. This work called for an understanding of the global market and culture before many U.S. companies in the sector had ventured outside the United States. As vice president and treasurer of the Europe/Africa division of Phillips from 1980 to 1984, Mulva had to make critical oil-related decisions about where to focus assets. During a time when many oil companies were drilling in the Middle East, Mulva avoided Middle Eastern oil purchases and concentrated instead on new finds in other world locations. For example, in 1994 Phillips began focusing on the first offshore oil field in China to begin oil production. After becoming CEO of Phillips in 1999, Mulva continued this trend to keep assets focused in the North Sea, Venezuela, Asia, North America, Kazakhstan, and Russia. By concentrating on new markets in Europe, South America, and Asia, Mulva made a stable long-term investment that avoided acquisition of assets in volatile Middle East reserves.

Mulva did not completely avoid volatile markets. In June 2004, when Russia began to privatize its oil industry, Mulva strongly pursued a 25 percent share of the Russian oil company Lukoil. He believed that he would have the ability to make the companies more efficient and profitable and increase assets while stabilizing the Russian economy. Although Mulva felt that his plan would enhance the business and social climate in Russia, the long-term success of Mulva's Russian proposal was still unknown in the early 2000s.

Beyond purchasing assets in foreign markets, Mulva tried to pass on to his counterparts in foreign oil companies some of the knowledge he gained by entering the global market early in its development. Mulva focused on executives in foreign oil companies in such countries as Russia and China by helping them train their management personnel, handle new technology, and cooperate with transnational companies.

NOT JUST GAS

Although Phillips Petroleum Corporation was not immediately associated with plastics production, a large portion of the global industry Mulva was working with in Asia included production of polyethylene plastics made from natural gas liquids. In 1996 Mulva assisted Phillips in creating a joint venture agreement to produce polyethylene plastic in China. By the time Mulva became CEO in 1999, Phillips was also involved in the manufacture of polyolefin plastics and other chemicals.

NEW TECHNOLOGY

Mulva's career in the petroleum industry spanned several technological changes in the way the industry obtained oil. The land-based oil derricks in Oklahoma discovered by the Phillips brothers had been replaced by offshore drilling and creation of pipelines. New refinery processes meant application of new technology and, with it, new regulations. In the face of these changes, Mulva advocated creation of a federal system of regulations that refiners should accept "because that is what their customers, stakeholders, and constituents are demanding" (*Oil Daily*, March 25, 2003).

In 2004 Mulva led ConocoPhillips to join a U.S. Department of Energy pilot project experimenting with the use of hydrogen-based transportation. As part of the project, ConocoPhillips planned to equip several fueling stations with the ability to dispense liquid and gaseous hydrogen made from both fossil fuels and renewable energy sources. Although the hydrogen-based technology was in its infancy, the project allowed ConocoPhillips and the other members of the project team to evaluate hydrogen's potential as a new transportation technology. Mulva recognized that to ensure long-term growth for the company, ConocoPhillips had to become a leader in the pursuit and implementation of cleaner energy sources. Mulva underlined his commitment to new sources of fuel by actively seeking out such projects as the U.S. Department of Energy pilot project on hydrogen-based technology.

In addition to leading the industry in the examination of new technology, Mulva looked toward increased benefits for customers. Mulva and his team developed the ConocoPhillips "fleet card," a credit card that can be used at Conoco gas stations, Phillips 66 gas stations, and 76 gas stations. Unlike other gas company cards, it is accepted at many local maintenance facilities as well. To assist clients with tracking and paying their bills, online account management is available.

MANAGEMENT STYLE

Mulva's financial background allowed him to analyze new ideas and proposals carefully, to examine the bottom line, and effectively to predict the ideas' long-term financial impact on the firm. This methodical approach helped him create a strategic plan to meet and exceed corporate goals and decide which new technologies would be profitable. Mulva also maintained a level of transparency in his actions that emphasized his honesty in business. As he frequently said, "If you don't have your health and your integrity, you don't have much to offer" (*Con-*

ocoPhillips Newsroom, May 16, 2003). This transparency increased in importance in 2001, when it was learned that energy executives at Enron, an interstate and intrastate natural gas pipeline company also involved in trade of commodities, had manipulated financial statements to create an illusion of success. The discovery of the deception resulted in a financial crash that lost investors' money and bankrupted the company. After the Enron scandal, regulators took a close look at other energy companies and their executives. Mulva's policy of transparency and honesty protected Phillips from suspicions of financial mismanagement. In 2002 Mulva's peers acknowledged his leadership and ability in an increasingly difficult business environment by presenting to him the Petroleum Executive of the Year award.

COMMUNITY OUTREACH

Given Phillips's global presence, Mulva felt that it was important to try to bring something other than jobs and oil to its operation locations. Primary among these goals was Mulva's desire to ensure that the company's operations did not have an adverse impact on community health and safety. This meant that proper safety measures had to be put in place to avoid increases in air, water, and land pollution as well as to protect the community from product spills. Also important to Mulva was the concept of contributing to the communities in which Phillips's employees worked. Phillips, and later ConocoPhillips, supported business internship programs, continued scholarship programs (such as the Phillips 66er's Scholarship Program), and established the Phillips Petroleum Endowed Professorships and Exchange Fellowships.

ENVIRONMENTAL CONCERNS

In 2000 Mulva faced a tragic situation when a K-resin chemical tank exploded at a Phillips Petroleum Company chemical plant in Pasadena. The explosion killed one worker, seriously burned four workers, and injured 65 other employees. The resulting fire also produced toxic fumes that spread over the surrounding neighborhoods. The blast was especially worrisome because it was the third time in 11 years that an explosion had occurred at that plant. In the wake of the disaster, Mulva had to answer accusations that Phillips's attempts to cut costs had endangered their employees, created an unsafe work environment, and resulted in the large explosions. To salvage Phillips's reputation for safety and its concern for its workers, Mulva and Phillips paid a large Occupational Safety and Health Administration (OSHA) fine for safety violations, concentrated on improving plant safety, and cooperated with investigators to help establish accountability for the explosions.

Following the 1989 Exxon *Valdez* incident, in which approximately 11 million gallons of oil were spilled out of a dam-

aged oil tanker off the coast of Alaska, worldwide public attention was focused on petroleum companies and their environmental records. Although Mulva's time as CEO did not begin until five years after the spill, the *Valdez*'s legacy and legislation were a constant concern that shaped the operations of the petroleum company. As Phillips's CEO, Mulva focused on the environmental impact of petroleum operations. He was determined to learn how to increase Phillips's holdings of oil through exploration and production without damaging the environment. Given the ability of most of Phillips's products to cause environmental destruction if spilled, Mulva directed frequent safety inspections of production operations, trained employees in safe practices, and instituted more safety measures to ensure that an incident like the *Valdez* accident would not occur.

CAREFUL ACQUISITIONS AND MERGERS LEAD TO PROFIT

As CEO of Phillips, Mulva created a five-year strategic plan that used several mergers and acquisitions to make the company more competitive and increase oil exploration and production. Through increasing oil exploration and production, Phillips hoped to avoid being taken over by the huge companies resulting from the mergers of medium-sized businesses, such as Exxon and Mobil and Chevron and Texaco.

In February 2000 Phillips joined its chemical and plastic operations with Chevron to create the Chevron Phillips Chemical Company. For Phillips, the plastics and chemical portion of the company began to decline in strategic importance as an asset as Phillips focused on a new strategic plan for the oil-and-gas sector of the business and a series of explosions at Phillips plants in 1999 and 2000 created public image problems. Through the spin-off and joint venture, Mulva helped create a global chemical production company with an excellent financial position, more assets, and enhanced growth prospects.

In April 2000 Mulva led Phillips in the acquisition of the Alaskan oil-and-gas production assets of the Atlantic Richfield Company in an attempt to boost its upstream exploration and production. The Alaskan assets were sold to satisfy the terms of a legal settlement that resulted from the large BP Amoco/ Arco merger. The assets augmented Phillips's holdings in a nonvolatile location and increased the company's barrels of oil equivalence to 2.2 billion reserve barrels of oil and 340 thousand new barrels per day of production.

The 2001 merger with the Tosco Corporation, a refining, marketing, and transmission business, helped Phillips grow its refining business to become the second largest in the United States and the third-largest seller of motor gasoline in the United States. Phillips also added Tosco's large convenience store market and 6,400 gas stations to its lists of assets. Next came Phillips's merger with Conoco to become ConocoPhillips. Nationally, this merger moved the combined company to a position as the largest refiner in the United States and the third-largest energy company. Internationally, the merger put ConocoPhillips into position as the sixth-largest energy company in the world. At the time Mulva became CEO in 1999, the company's assets were about $15 billion; after the merger was completed in 2002, the company's assets exceeded $75 billion. Mulva had learned more about large oil company mergers by watching carefully the successes and failures of the merger of Mobil and Exxon in 1998 and Chevron and Texaco in 2001. He chose a financial strategy that focused more on saving money and cutting capital spending than on growth in the first years. The strategy produced enhanced financial returns and less debt for ConocoPhillips. By the end of the first quarter of 2004, the company had an income of $1.9 billion and had come very close to paring its debt down to 32 percent of its capital.

See also entry on Phillips Petroleum Company in *International Directory of Company Histories.*

SOURCES FOR FURTHER INFORMATION

Merolli, Paul, "ConocoPhillips CEO Optimistic about Refiners' Future Despite Challenges," *Oil Daily*, March 25, 2003, p. 1.

Mulva, Jim, "Change the World: Commencement Remarks to UT MBA Graduates," May 16, 2003, *ConocoPhillips Newsroom*, http://www.conocophillips.com/news/speeches/051603_utbiz.asp.

O'Hanlon, John, "James J. Mulva, Chairman and Chief Executive Officer, Phillips Petroleum Company-Interview," *Wall Street Corporate Reporter*, December 14, 2000.

—Dawn Jacob Laney

Raúl Muñoz Leos

1940–

General director, Pemex

Nationality: Mexican.

Born: 1940.

Education: Attended Universidad Nacional Autonoma de Mexico.

Career: Du Pont México, ?–2000, various positions, eventually became president and general director; Petroleos Mexicanos (Pemex), 2000–, general director.

Address: Avenida Marina Nacional 329, Colonia Huasteca, 11311 Mexico D.F., Mexico; http://www.pemex.com.

■ Beginning in 2000 Raúl Muñoz Leos served as general director of Petroleos Mexicanos (Pemex), the state-owned Mexican oil company that had a monopoly over the country's petroleum reserves. President Vicente Fox appointed Muñoz Leos to the Pemex post to improve the efficiency and profitability of a company marred by inefficiency and corruption. Before going to Pemex, Muñoz Leos spent most of his career at DuPont Mexico, where he served as both president and general director. Muñoz Leos planned to bring this private-sector experience to Pemex.

DUPONT MEXICO

When Muñoz Leos took over at DuPont Mexico, the company mainly produced for local consumption. With the implementation of the North American Free Trade Agreement (NAFTA) in the early 1990s, Muñoz Leos was forced to revise his business strategy. NAFTA created both opportunities for exports and competition from imports. Muñoz Leos told Mary Suter of *Business Mexico* that "since NAFTA, our focus has been different in that all of our manufacturing operations must be internationally competitive and we design them for their optimum capacity." DuPont Mexico was no longer producing mainly for the Mexican market but also began to expand its exports to all of the Western Hemisphere as well as to Asia and Europe. In 1994 exports accounted for 31 percent of sales. By

1995 that figure had increased to 44 percent. Muñoz Leos looked more to the export sector because free trade resulted in increasing competition in DuPont's many enterprises, including fibers, paints, and pesticides. Muñoz Leos told Suter that "whatever we do, we have to consider all the global competitors that are with us in different fields. We have a lot of competitors because of our wide variety of products, but the common denominator is that all competitors are international, if not global. We are all competing on cost and to provide the best quality and the best service" (December 1, 1997).

Muñoz Leos believed that textiles would be the key to DuPont Mexico's export strategy. His company had the advantage of producing well-known fibers such as nylon, Dacron polyester, and Lycra spandex. He claimed that DuPont Mexico was developing a world-class quality concept in apparel manufacturing, which would lead export-led growth for his firm. On the other hand, products destined for local consumption were hurt the most, especially during hard economic times. Paint, for example, was too bulky for export. When the domestic market shrank, Muñoz Leos was forced to look for ways to reduce production costs and improve distribution.

While at DuPont, Muñoz Leos emphasized environmental management. During his time at DuPont, the company reduced atmospheric emissions in general and eliminated emissions of chlorofluorocarbons. Muñoz Leos also led the cleanup of heavily polluting operations. For example, Muñoz Leos spent $22 million to clean up DuPont's plant at Coatzacoalcos. He also reduced waste at the company's facility in the port city of Altamira, the base for the global manufacture of titanium dioxide. In Altamira the company invested $50 million to convert a sand by-product into a water-purifying chemical. Furthermore, under Muñoz Leos's leadership, DuPont Mexico organized product stewardship programs with customers, such as recycling drums used to transport chemicals. Of the environmental programs, Muñoz Leos told Suter, "this involves a lot of training and communication so that we ensure through our distributors and customers that products are used correctly and disposed of properly. From raw material to the end user, we take ownership of the correct applications of all products—for use, transportation, storage, and disposal" (December 1, 1997).

In the December 2000 issue of *Business Mexico*, Muñoz Leos shared many of his ideas about management at DuPont with the magazine's editors. He emphasized that productivity and training of personnel were key components of his management style. In regard to productivity, Muñoz Leos stated that "we look at productivity as another important element in competitiveness and we compare ourselves with international competitors so as to have the most aggressive benchmarks." He indicated that by setting high standards, DuPont would find better ways to increase the company's productivity.

Muñoz Leos emphasized the importance of the training and development of personnel, saying the company allocated significant resources to this area. He told *Business Mexico* that "we continuously provide courses, seminars, and special training sessions to help our employees strive for higher-responsibility jobs." At DuPont, Muñoz Leos implemented a program in leadership skills, first for the top managerial levels then for the entire population of the company. He believed that such a program helped to get employees to work together on the company's long-term objectives.

PEMEX

In 2000 Vicente Fox of the opposition Partido Acción Nacional (PAN; National Action Party) won the presidential election in Mexico, wresting power from the Partido Revolucionario Institucional (PRI; Institutional Revolutionary Party), which had won every Mexican presidential election since the Revolution early in the 20th century. During the election campaign Fox suggested that he might privatize Pemex. When he took office, Fox named Muñoz Leos director general of Pemex, citing his successful corporate background at DuPont. Like Fox, Muñoz Leos was an advocate of opening state-run industries to the private sector. After winning the election, Fox said that he would not privatize Pemex. However, he indicated that the oil firm needed to adopt a "business outlook" and become more cost-effective. Fox charged Muñoz Leos with transforming Pemex into the world's best oil company.

In 1938 the Mexican government nationalized the country's oil industry. Until that time, foreign oil companies from the United States and Great Britain had dominated Mexican petroleum production. In response to this foreign domination, the Mexican president Lazaro Cardenas had appropriated the foreign oil holdings in Mexico. The result was a state-owned monopoly known as Petroleos Mexicanos (Pemex). The government prohibited foreign ownership in the industry, and Pemex came to represent Mexican economic independence from powerful international corporations. Thus more than just a company, Pemex became a symbol of Mexican sovereignty. Expropriation Day continued to be celebrated in Mexico.

Pemex developed into Mexico's largest company and possessed some of the world's richest oil reserves. By the time Muñoz Leos became the company's director general in 2000,

Pemex employed approximately 130,000 workers and had $40 billion in sales. The company consistently ranked among the world's top five oil producers. It was a major exporter of oil to the United States. Every gas station in Mexico was supplied by Pemex.

For much of its history Pemex had functioned as an arm of the PRI, Mexico's dominant political party. The PRI had used Pemex as a cash cow. Most of the company's profits had gone directly to the government, sometimes accounting for as much as one-third of the Mexican government's revenues. This diversion of Pemex's profits often led to lack of investment, because the company had to obtain government approval to fund new projects. Such constraints created a company that lacked incentives to expand, which in turn led to limited oil exploration and lower production levels. For example, despite great potential reserves in the Gulf of Mexico, Pemex did not develop the technology for deepwater exploration and extraction. This situation stood in stark contrast to the case of the Brazilian state-owned oil company Petrobras, which became a world leader in deepwater technology.

Pemex suffered throughout its history from large-scale corruption, sometimes amounting to more than $1 billion annually. Corruption not only siphoned off money but also inhibited new projects. Officials knew that any new, large-scale project would only invite corruption, leading to delays and spiraling budgets.

The Pemex executive Othon Canales Treviño, who was in charge of competitiveness and innovation, complained of the corruption and inefficiency at Pemex. He was quoted as follows by *Alexander's Oil and Gas Connections*: "We want to act like a company. Pemex isn't a company. It isn't Pemex, Inc. We're not a government ministry either. We are something weird. Our behavior changes depending on whom we are dealing with. To the Finance Ministry, we're their biggest taxpayer. To Congress, we're something else. To our customers, sometimes we're an opportunity and sometimes we're a threat" (February 20, 2003).

TRANSFORMATION OF PEMEX

Within months of taking over at Pemex, Muñoz Leos emphasized that he would restructure the company. He sought a cultural transformation at Pemex by ending the "spend your budget approach" and implementing an attitude of productivity, cost reduction, and competitiveness. He hoped to free Pemex from the government budget, end the public sector culture, and operate the company as if it were a private company. He wanted the company to be concerned with the quality of its operations, not just the quantity. He told Simon Webb of *Business Mexico* that "we are engaged in an ambitious program to improve operations and efficiency." Muñoz Leos indicated that his goal was to achieve such a change within five years.

Among his initial steps was improving Pemex's refining operations and its storage and distribution practices.

There was initial concern about Muñoz Leos's appointment. Critics cited his lack of decisiveness and oil industry experience. Roger Diwan of the Petroleum Finance Company told Jennifer Galloway of *Latin Finance*, "I don't think he can change the culture. You need someone very strong at the helm. He wants to change the culture of Pemex over 10 years. Unless he wants to come and cut the heads off of a lot of people, I say to him 'good luck.'"

Muñoz Leos and Fox witnessed the difficulties in changing Pemex when one of Fox's first steps was to make four new appointments to the company's board of directors. The board had been filled with government and union leaders. Fox, however, appointed four prominent private businessmen to the board, an act that received much criticism. Some critics demanded that Fox remove these newly appointed board members, but the president initially refused. Strong opposition in the Mexican Congress led the president to remove his controversial appointees.

Muñoz Leos began to carry out Fox's orders by negotiating a short-term financing solution to lighten Pemex's tax burden. He claimed that the development of strategic projects was limited by a lack of money. To a large degree, this lack was due to the fact that since an oil crash in the early 1980s, the Mexican government had heavily taxed the company. The result was annual losses of more than $1 billion. In March 2001 Muñoz Leos told *Business Mexico* that "Pemex hasn't grown in the last 15 or 18 years and we have to reverse this tendency of stagnation toward vigorous growth that will allow us to have more resources to contribute as taxes." However, the new Pemex boss was quick to point out that such growth required more money and that the government would have to channel more funds into new projects or else Pemex would have to cut back on production. Furthermore, Muñoz Leos argued that a lack of investment also led to problems of safety and pollution because the company could not afford to properly deal with these issues. For example, major explosions in 1984 and 1992 killed more than eight hundred persons in Mexico City and Guadalajara.

While many Mexicans saw Pemex as a symbol of their country's economic independence from foreign capital, Muñoz Leos claimed that Mexicans themselves had to accept part of the blame for the company's woes. He told Tim Weiner of the *New York Times* that "it is us, the Mexicans, who have stunted the growth of Mexico's oil industry" (February 1, 2003). Muñoz Leos also sought to reestablish links with foreign oil companies by forging alliances with the private sector in areas such as petrochemicals and oil refining. While Mexican law prohibited private ownership rights, private domestic and foreign firms were able to sign service contracts with Pemex to provide services such as drilling wells. Muñoz

Leos argued that without foreign investment, production levels would decrease, and the decrease would hurt the Mexican economy.

Another problem that Muñoz Leos faced was that Pemex employed too many people. Many of the company's employees had little real purpose. Pemex had approximately 130,000 workers when Muñoz Leos took over, twice the number actually needed. For example, Pemex employed approximately two times the number of workers as the state-owned oil company in Venezuela, which produced roughly the same amount of oil. The government had often used Pemex jobs as a tool of political patronage, rewarding loyal followers with jobs in the Mexican oil industry. These jobs were much sought after, because the government provided many attractive and costly benefits, such as free hospitals and schools for employees. Such a system can be dangerous, because unqualified workers sometimes get jobs. Such inexperienced employees, usually family and friends of existing workers, often caused accidents at Pemex facilities. In addition, Pemex was notorious for "no-show jobs," in which people who no longer worked for the company continued to collect a paycheck by providing a percentage to union bosses. Muñoz Leos asked Galloway, "How do you tell a significant portion of your staff that they don't have a job anymore? That takes some doing." In particular, Muñoz Leos faced a difficult task in cutting jobs because the Pemex labor union was very strong and resisted any attempts to reduce the company's workforce.

In addition to reducing the size of Pemex's workforce, Muñoz Leos hoped to improve the quality of the company's management. He emphasized that he would hire qualified and driven managers to run Pemex. He told Galloway, "We will be making personnel changes as required, starting with strengthening our corporate staff so that we can provide stronger leadership and exercise more discipline and control in operations and projects."

In addition to dealing with the issue of excess employees, one of Muñoz Leos's priorities on taking over at Pemex was to make the company's four operating groups work together more efficiently. In 2001 Muñoz Leos told Webb, "What we wanted to do is establish solid guidelines and proper controls to create greater coordination between the units. Pemex has not grown for 18 years and our strategic plan is to strengthen each of the separate units to create a whole that is more than just a sum of its parts."

By 2003 Muñoz Leos had admitted that change had come slowly but surely. He told Weiner, "You turn the battleship's wheel many times to turn the ship one degree. We are working on a culture change. The focus of our change is to help Pemex be able to compete with the world leaders in the oil business" (February 1, 2003). Despite the slowness of change, Muñoz Leos did achieve a certain degree of success over his first several years at Pemex. For example, in 2003 he obtained $4 billion from the Mexican government to expand production. In that year Pemex output reached an all-time high, its reserves were growing, and some private-sector participation had begun.

Even with the influx of money, Pemex did not have enough capital to produce enough oil for the Mexican market. Despite its vast petroleum deposits, the country continued to import gasoline. Because the company's refineries were running at full capacity, in 2003 Mexico imported one-fourth of its gasoline from the United States. Many experts believed the changes were too little and too late. David Shields, an energy expert based in Mexico City, told Brendan Case of the *Dallas Morning News*, "The changes needed to solve this problem are taking place too slowly to correct the trend and eliminate the risk of collapse" (September 20, 2003).

The independent oil analyst George Baker summed up the challenge facing Muñoz Leos. He explained to Weiner, "Here's a man who comes in from the private sector, from DuPont, which meets international standards as a business, and he faces political problems that would never apply in a business context" (February 1, 2003). Baker later elaborated to Case that "industrial logic points in one direction for Pemex. Tradition, vested interests and populism point in another" (September 20, 2003).

See also entry on Petroleos Mexianos in *International Directory of Company Histories.*

SOURCES FOR FURTHER INFORMATION

Case, Brendan, "Pemex Must Change or Die, Observers Say," *Dallas Morning News*, September 20, 2003.

Galloway, Jennifer, "Mexico's Capital Connection," *Latin Finance*, May 2001.

"New Business: Pemex Rebirth," *Business Mexico*, March 1, 2001.

"Strategy: Productivity," *Business Mexico*, December 1, 2000.

"Strategy: Training," *Business Mexico*, December 1, 2000.

Suter, Mary, "Advanced Chemistry: Exports and Local Sales Add Up to Potent Formula for DuPont Mexico," *Business Mexico*, December 1, 1997.

"To Change Mexico, Fox Must First Change Pemex," *Alexander's Oil and Gas Connections* 8, no. 4, February 20, 2003, http://www.gasandoil.com/goc/company/cnl30873.htm.

Webb, Simon, "Pemex Shake-up," *Business Mexico*, April 1, 2001.

Weiner, Tim, "As National Oil Giant Struggles, Mexico Agonizes over Opening It to Foreign Ventures," *New York Times*, February 17, 2002.

———, "Mexican Energy Giant Lumbers into Hazy Future," *New York Times*, February 1, 2003.

—Ronald Young

■■■
James Murdoch
1972–
Chief executive officer, British Sky Broadcasting Group

Nationality: British.

Born: December 13, 1972, in London, United Kingdom.

Education: Attended Harvard University.

Family: Son of Rupert (businessman) and Anna Maria Torv Murdoch; married Kathryn Hufschmid (marketing executive); children: one.

Career: Rawkus Entertainment, 1995–1998, executive; News Corporation, 1998–2000, executive and manager of Web operations; Star TV, 2000, chairman and chief executive officer; British Sky Broadcasting Group, 2003–, chief executive officer.

Address: British Sky Broadcasting, Grant Way, Isleworth, United Kingdom TW7 5QD; http://www.sky.com.

■ At the age of 30, James Murdoch was much younger than most of his counterparts when he became chief executive officer of British Sky Broadcasting Group (BSkyB) in 2003. Never before had someone so young run a FTSE 100 company. The move was not without controversy. Shareholders of BSkyB, Britain's dominant television service, questioned Murdoch's qualifications and complained that he received the position only because his father was chairman of the company. Executives who worked with Murdoch, however, called him an instinctive leader—just like his father.

Murdoch was the son of Rupert Murdoch, chief executive of News Corporation, a $14 billion media empire that included both newspaper and television companies across North America, Europe, and Asia, including the *Times* of London. Other News Corporation companies included Fox Network, *TV Guide*, HarperCollins book publishers, and 20th Century Fox.

SHADOW OF FATHER'S MEDIA CORPORATION

Murdoch was born on December 13, 1972, in London, the oldest of three children of Rupert and Anna Torv Murdoch.

James Murdoch. *AP/Wide World Photos.*

He was reared mostly in New York City, where his father had offices as owner of the *New York Post*. From the beginning, the family business was woven into the fabric of James Murdoch's life. As Murdoch grew, so did his father's media empire. Business talk dominated dinner table conversations, and the elder Murdoch's competitiveness shined through, even when he played games with his children.

At the age of 15, Murdoch landed an internship at the *Sydney Mirror*, the once-struggling paper his father had bought and turned around. Murdoch gained notoriety at the paper by falling asleep covering a press conference. A photographer from the rival *Sydney Morning Herald* snapped some pictures, and Murdoch found himself splashed across its pages. In the mid-1990s, after graduating from the New York City prep school Horace Mann, Murdoch headed to Harvard University to study film and history. At Harvard, Murdoch made his mark as a cartoonist for the *Harvard Lampoon*.

RAWKUS ENTERTAINMENT

Unlike his siblings, who graduated from college and went to work for the family business, Murdoch was determined to prove his own worth in his own way. In 1995 he dropped out of college to form an independent record label with two high-school friends. The Manhattan-based label, called Rawkus Entertainment, signed such bands as the hip-hop Rose Family and the glam-metal band Motor Baby. Further shunning his father's straitlaced corporate world, Murdoch got tattoos, died his scraggly hair blond, and pierced his eyebrow. Rawkus Entertainment was moderately successful, and it proved a good training ground for Murdoch. "I don't want to be cocky, but we're fast learners," Murdoch remarked to the *New Yorker*. "You learn pretty quickly when you're spending money and not getting results" (September 16, 1996).

By 1998 Rawkus was turning a $2.5 million annual profit and was bought by Rupert Murdoch and absorbed into News Corporation. James Murdoch had become part of the family business and was overseeing News Corporation's tiny music division. He then was put in charge of News Corporation's Web operations. He persuaded his father to invest in a number of Internet ventures, which eventually suffered heavy losses. At one point, News Corporation took a $300 million write-off for dot-com investments made at James Murdoch's request.

STAR TV

Although Murdoch had lost money for his father, Rupert Murdoch had faith in his son and in 2000 named Murdoch chairman and chief executive officer of Star TV, News Corporation's Asian division. When James Murdoch arrived in Hong Kong to take over operations, he had to work hard to earn the respect of his colleagues. Trying to fit in with his coworkers, Murdoch wore simple slacks and long-sleeved shirts to work, forgoing a tie.

Star TV, the world's largest satellite network, had become a part of News Corporation in 1995. When James Murdoch took over, its programming was being broadcast in 53 Asian countries in seven languages. In China and India alone, Star TV produced 16,000 hours of original programming. But it had yet to turn a profit, losing approximately £100 million a year. Murdoch changed that. He streamlined operations and focused on producing local programming for local markets, concentrating his efforts on India and China, Asia's largest markets. Star TV's Hindi version of *Who Wants to Be a Millionaire* became so popular advertisers could no longer ignore the broadcaster's impact. In 2002 Star TV drew its first profit.

BRITISH SKY BROADCASTING

Although Murdoch was successful with Star TV, investors grumbled in 2003 when he was appointed chief executive of the British-based digital television network BSkyB, which operated more than 400 channels of sports, movies, entertainment, and news. His salary stood at $2.4 million a year for three years. Murdoch was ready for the job and prepared to approach the new challenge just as he had the past one. His first task was to win over his colleagues. As Murdoch told *AdAgeGlobal*, "first and foremost, if you're in a new organization, you have to earn people's respect and loyalty. . . . If they have hang-ups about who you are, that's really not my concern. I'm more concerned with getting the team together and driving it forward."

Murdoch succeeded in his career by taking a less top-down approach than other executives. He leaned on his capable team of managers, letting them do their work without trying to manage every detail. He also relied on his father, speaking to him nearly every day. "This is a very smart executive," Murdoch's former colleague Matt Jacobson told Valerie Block of *Crain's New York Business*. "Even if his last name didn't start with an M, I'd have a lot of respect for him" (August 10, 1998). When Murdoch took over BSkyB in 2003, all eyes were watching. Before Murdoch took such a high-profile job in the family business, analysts believed his older brother, Lachlan, would succeed their father at the helm of News Corporation. Opinions changed after James Murdoch took over BSkyB.

See also entry on British Sky Broadcasting Group plc in *International Directory of Company Histories*.

SOURCES FOR FURTHER INFORMATION

Block, Valerie, "The Dutiful Son: Spare Murdoch Heir, a High-Tech Kid, Waits Patiently to Rotate into New Post," *Crain's New York Business*, August 10, 1998.

Fabrikant, Geraldine, and Mark Landler, "Just Which Murdoch Will Become the Next Rupert?" *New York Times*, October 8, 2000.

Gibson, Owen, "Ivy League to Isleworth: 'My Relationship with the Chairman Will Be Like That of Any Chief Executive,'" *Guardian*, November 10, 2003.

"A Grass-Roots Murdoch," *New Yorker*, September 16, 1996, p. 44.

"Like Father, Like Son," *Economist*, November 8, 2003, p. 64.

Normandy, Madden, "James Murdoch," *Advertising Age*, January 26, 2004.

"Young Murdoch's Asian Adventure," *AdAgeGlobal*, May 2001, p. 30.

—Lisa Frick

Lachlan Murdoch

1971–

Deputy chief operating officer, News Corporation Limited

Nationality: British, but considers himself Australian.

Born: September 8, 1971, in London, United Kingdom.

Education: Princeton University, BA, 1994.

Family: Son of Rupert Murdoch (chairman and chief executive of News Corporation) and Anna (Torv) Murdoch-Mann (author); married Sarah O'Hare (model).

Career: Queensland Newspapers, 1994–1995, general manager; News Limited, 1995–1997, deputy chief executive; 1997–1999, chairman and chief executive officer; News Corporation, 1999–2000, senior vice president; 2000–, deputy chief operating officer.

Address: News Corporation, 1211 Avenue of Americas, 8th Floor, New York, New York 10036; 2 Holt Street, Sydney, Australia, NS 2010; http://www.newscorp.com.

■ As 2004 began, Lachlan Murdoch continued to generate speculation about whether he would one day become heir of News Corporation Limited, the multinational company ruled by his father, CEO Rupert Murdoch—comprising newspapers, books, magazines, movies, music, and television. With the elder Murdoch showing no signs of retiring, Lachlan Murdoch rose to deputy COO and made his mark on the *New York Post* along with Fox Broadcasting. The scrutiny that comes with a famous surname, along with justified speculation from analysts about whether he was capable of leading News Corporation, made Murdoch an easy target for criticism among industry insiders and analysts. The stakes were nothing less than control of one of the most influential media empires in the world.

LEARNING THE ROPES

News Corporation is among the largest media corporations, though with 2003 revenues of about $20 billion, it lags far behind Time Warner and Walt Disney. The company's 82 percent owned Fox Entertainment Group includes a spate of operations, such as Fox Broadcasting (consisting of the Fox TV network's 200 U.S. affiliates), Twentieth Century Fox (which produces movies and TV programs and maintains a large programming library), and a 34 percent stake in the DI-RECTV parent Hughes Electronics. News Corporation also owns 35 U.S. television stations as well as cable and satellite operations in Asia, Australia, Europe, and Latin America.

Rupert Murdoch's vast empire created for Lachlan Murdoch the opportunity to learn the business one asset at a time. Lachlan Murdoch began working in the business as a printing press cleaner on weekends when he was in high school in the United States. Fresh from Princeton University, where he earned a bachelor of arts in philosophy, he moved to Australia in 1994 to begin his training in the family-owned Queensland Newspapers.

At first glance he seemed an unlikely corporate type, let alone a corporate successor. A rock climber with a lizard tattoo, he traveled around Sydney on a pricey motorcycle. Ever aware of rumors and speculation that his role in his father's company was more a result of bloodline than business savvy, he ultimately chose to tone down his image. In his own words, "I think because of my father—or my relationship with him—the thing I have to do is be extra cautious and to prove myself. I have to prove I'm serious" (*Independent*, May 7, 1995). Opportunity to do just that arrived in 1997, when he was promoted to chief executive of News Limited.

But his time in Australia was not without controversy. Still green, Murdoch found himself in the midst of the Super League debacle—a wayward attempt by News Limited to create the rugby Super League, which nearly killed the sport's popularity and cost the company an estimated $200 million.

HEIR APPARENT

The most formative promotion of Murdoch's career occurred in 1999, when he arrived in the United States to take over the company's print operations, including the *New York Post* and the Harper Collins Publishing Group. This ambitious step placed an even bigger spotlight on Murdoch, who had previously enjoyed relative obscurity in Australia. The new position also earned Murdoch admission into the company's inner circle, the office of the chairman, placing him in direct contact with the company's top six executives.

Around that time, his father told an interviewer that it was the consensus of "the kids" that Lachlan—the middle child—would one day take over the company. Rupert Murdoch has long expressed a preference for Lachlan to succeed him in the top spot at News Corporation. In October 2000 Lachlan Murdoch took another step toward achieving that goal when he was named News Corporation's deputy chief operating officer.

As Lachlan Murdoch's clout increased, so did the comparisons to his father. Mitch Stern, chairman of Fox Television Stations and Twentieth Television, said that Murdoch was "a lot like [Rupert]. . . . He's engaging and curious. Intelligent. And, I'd say—and this is where they stand out from the rest of the industry—a gentleman with a high sense of integrity. Pretty good drinker; good taste in wine. The kind of person you welcome into a meeting. He comes in with his sleeves rolled up. And you're into it" (*New York Observer*, November 24, 2003).

In February 2002 Murdoch was elected to the Fox board of directors, and in May 2002 he was named publisher of the *New York Post*. By then he had implemented important changes, including cutting the paper's single-copy price from 50 cents to 25 cents in 2000. He also led the construction of a $250 million production plant in the Bronx, New York, that allowed quality color printing.

In November 2003 Murdoch's brother, James, was named the chief executive of British Sky Broadcasting, a firm with more than $5 billion a year in revenues (News Corporation owned more than 35 percent of Sky News in 2002). This move caused some to speculate that James Murdoch had usurped his brother's place as Rupert Murdoch's presumed heir. Furthermore, it prompted increased concerns from analysts, who wondered whether either child should be the chosen one. Said Uri D. Landesman, a portfolio manager for Federated Investors, a major investor in News Corporation, "Look, the easiest way for a company to handle family is just say 'no family.' That way you don't have to make decisions about whether the kid is ready or not. But that is obviously not going to happen here" (*New York Times*, December 28, 2003).

ADDED RESPONSIBILITIES

In early 2004 Murdoch added another project to his growing responsibilities: filling the void left by the sudden exit of Fox TV network's chairman, Sandy Grushow. The shake-up placed Murdoch at the helm of the network, which made an estimated $400 million profit in 2003, thanks to such stalwart shows as *American Idol* and *The Simpsons*. It was a crucial test: Fox began 2004 in a ratings slump. The second edition of *Joe Millionaire* garnered awful ratings while an *American Idol* spin-off was killed before it ever debuted.

Murdoch seemed determined to live up to the biblical edict that the original John D. Rockefeller was fond of quoting: "To him who much is given, much is required" (Luke 12:48, Oxford Study Edition: "The New English Bible," Oxford University Press, 1976, chpt. 4). He appeared neither to have shied away from major responsibility nor to have become distracted by the illusions of show business or the uncertainties of the future. In 2003 Rupert Murdoch had this to say: "I look after my health pretty well, and I intend to be the active driver of the company for a long time yet, probably to the frustration of all my relatives" (*New York Times*, December 28, 2003).

See also entry on News Corporation Limited in *International Directory of Company Histories*.

SOURCES FOR FURTHER INFORMATION

Kirkpatrick, David, "Murdoch Gets a Jewel. Who'll Get His Crown?" *New York Times*, December 28, 2003.

Milliken, Robert, "Lachlan Murdoch; Heir to the Sun and Sky," *Independent* (London), May 7, 1995.

Pappu, Sridhar, "Lachlan Murdoch, Spiky Punk Heir Right for Post?" *New York Observer*, November 24, 2003.

Salamon, Julie, "Television: An American Story; A Family That Tried to Be Both Rich and Good" *New York Times*, October 1, 2000.

—Tim Halpern

Rupert Murdoch

1931–

Chairman and chief executive officer, News Corporation

Nationality: American.

Born: March 11, 1931, in Melbourne, Australia.

Education: Worcester College, MA, 1953.

Family: Son of Keith Arthur Lay (journalist) and Elisabeth Joy Greene (philanthropist); married Patricia Brooker (airline stewardess; divorced); children: one; married Anna Torv (journalist and novelist; divorced); children: three; married Wendi Deng (secretary); children: two.

Career: *Daily Express* (London), 1953–1954, subeditor; *Adelaide News*, 1954–, publisher; Southern TV (Adelaide, Channel 9), 1959–, owner; Sydney *Daily* and *Sunday Mirror*, 1960–, publisher; *Australian*, 1964–, founder and publisher; London *News of the World*, 1969–, publisher; London *Sun*, 1969–, publisher; News International, 1969–1987, chairman of the board; 1969–1981, chief executive officer; News Corporation, 1979–, CEO; Times Newspapers Holdings, 1982–1990, chairman of the board; News Corporation, 1991–, chairman of the board; Twentieth Century Fox, 1992–, CEO and chairman of the board; Fox Inc., 1992–, CEO and chairman of the board; News International, 1994–1995, chairman of the board; Times Newspapers Holdings, 1994, chairman of the board; Fox Entertainment Group, 1995–, CEO; British Sky Broadcasting, 1999–, chairman of the board; Shine Ltd., 2001–, CEO and chairman of the board.

Awards: Humanitarian of the Year, United Jewish Appeal, 1997.

Address: News Corporation, 3rd Floor, 1211 Avenue of the Americas, New York, New York 10036-8701; http://www.newscorp.com.

■ Keith Rupert Murdoch was small, pudgy, short tempered, and blunt spoken; he was also charismatic, charming even to his enemies, and patient when criticized. A very complex man whom even his wives had trouble understanding, Murdoch created a media empire that was like his personality—contradictory, large, and dominating. He liked to describe

Rupert Murdoch. *AP/Wide World Photos.*

himself as colorless and boring, but numerous accounts by those who worked with him attested to his having been a stirring leader who could galvanize his employees to achievements that had seemed impossible.

THE EDUCATION OF RUPERT MURDOCH

Murdoch's father was Sir Keith Murdoch, who had been knighted for services to the crown and was a national hero in Australia. He was also one of the 20th century's most celebrated journalists: he was credited with revealing the truth about Britain's invasion of Gallipoli during World War I and with changing the British government's policy as a result, with troops being withdrawn from Turkey. Murdoch grew up in a spacious home near Melbourne and spent much of his time on a sheep ranch owned by his family.

The elder Murdoch was already severely ill with heart trouble when he sent his son to college in Oxford, England. The younger Murdoch developed an unsavory reputation for partying rather than studying, but his father's friend Lord Beaverbrook, publisher of the *Daily Express* (London), gave him work at the newspaper, where he quickly picked up Beaverbrook's flair for sensational headlines and snappy, short-sentenced prose. At the time Murdoch was a socialist who celebrated Lenin as a great man, and he proved to be such an adept debater in favor of his views that in 1950 he was elected president of Oxford's Labour Club.

Meanwhile, as the elder Murdoch remained seriously ill, a few of his subordinates conspired to relieve him of his ownership of the *Melbourne Herald* and other newspapers. After his father's death in 1952 the young Murdoch found that Australia's enormous death taxes had taken away most of the rest of his father's holdings. When he returned to Australia in 1954 Murdoch immediately began striving to build the circulation of a small Adelaide newspaper. Other publishers regarded him as a lazy, foolish young man and treated him with contempt—even into the 2000s Murdoch was chronically underestimated by his opposition. Yet he devoted himself to the publishing business with a passion and learned the details of every aspect of newspaper production. With sensational news stories and a punchy prose style, Murdoch's small holdings made money; he took risks by buying small newspapers that were losing money and then turning them around.

FOUNDATIONS OF EMPIRE

In July 1959 Murdoch bought his first television station, Channel 9 in Adelaide, calling it Southern TV. Throughout his life he would be on the lookout for new communications technologies, constantly trying to integrate them into his existing businesses. In 1960 he bought the *Daily Mirror* (Sydney) and its accompanying Sunday edition for $4 million; the publications quickly became notorious for bizarre and sensational headlines and stories about sex and mayhem. Perhaps in an effort to change his image as a purveyor of prurience, Murdoch established the *Australian*, a national newspaper that began publication in the capital of Canberra on July 14, 1964. The *Australian* was a serious publication featuring in-depth discussion of social issues and government policy and won the admiration of journalists.

In April 1967 Murdoch married for the second time, to Anna Torv, a reporter for the *Daily Mirror*. She would be his counterweight for over 30 years, pulling him back to his family when his work threatened to consume him. By 1968 Murdoch's Australian holdings were worth $50 million. He harbored resentment of the English upper class from his days in Oxford; they had made him feel like an outsider, as if they regarded Australians as inferior beings, and he wanted to strike

back at them. In late 1968 he learned that London's Sunday publication *News of the World* was available. After a battle with other potential buyers, in January 1969 he bought 40 percent of the newspaper's shares, soon increasing the amount to 49 percent and instating himself as the newspaper's chief executive officer. In June 1969 he was elected chairman of the board for the newspaper.

In October 1969 he purchased the *Sun* (London), which had a circulation of 600,000 but was losing $5 million per year. When he announced that he would turn the *Sun* from a broadsheet to a tabloid, some of the newspaper's printers said the switch could not be made because the newspaper's printing machine could not be adjusted; Murdoch climbed on top of one of the huge machines, opened a cabinet, and pulled out a bar that when placed properly would convert the machine to a printer of tabloids. This was an important lesson for observers of Murdoch: he knew everything about running his businesses, down to the nitty-gritty of everyday production. On November 17, 1969, the first tabloid version of the *Sun* was published. On November 17, 1970, the first photograph of a half-naked woman was published; she and others would become known as Page 3 Girls. The *Sun*'s circulation rose to four million, and for the first of seemingly innumerable times, England's Press Council censured Murdoch for appealing to low-class readers—which were the very readers Murdoch wanted to appeal to. Further, the *Sun* tweaked the upper classes with tales of their infidelities, crimes, and foolishness.

In December 1969 Murdoch and his family were tending to business in Australia, leaving the use of their Rolls Royce in England to an editor's family. Alick McKay, the wife of the editor, took the automobile on a shopping trip and was kidnapped and murdered by men who thought she was Anna Murdoch. From that time onward Murdoch downplayed his dynamic personality and tried to keep himself and his family out of the news, not wanting outsiders to know their whereabouts.

INTO AMERICA

Murdoch wanted to expand his holdings into the United States; he chose to begin with two small, struggling newspapers, buying the *San Antonio Express*, the *San Antonio News*, and their united Sunday paper for $18 million in 1973. He revamped the *News* with his sex and mayhem formula while leaving the *Express* relatively untouched. He then established a national American newspaper, the *National Star* (later just the *Star*), a tabloid that competed with the *National Enquirer* in the field of sensational, bizarre, and scarcely credible stories. Murdoch's formula came to include large photographs, big headlines, and brief stories. In 1974 Murdoch began spending most of his time in the United States; his wife had detested the snobbery in England and was happy to split her time between a 12-room duplex in New York City and a country farmhouse in rural New York.

On November 19, 1976, Murdoch bought the *New York Post* from Dorothy Schiff for about $50 million. He edited the *Post* personally for awhile, then hired the *Time* magazine editor Edwin Bolwell to do the job. The *Post* became a tabloid that revealed Murdoch's changing political sentiments. Previously known as Red Murdoch, he was shifting his views away from socialism; the *Post* began attacking liberal politicians who opposed Murdoch's expansion into the United States, especially the Massachusetts Senator Edward Kennedy, whose infidelities were covered in detail. On January 7, 1977, Murdoch bought the New York Magazine Company, publisher of *New York*, *Village Voice*, and *New West*, in a hostile takeover. *New York* would thrive; *Village Voice* would return to its gritty antiestablishment roots after years as a tepid social-life paper; and *New West* would fold after losing money, although it was regarded as a great magazine, comparable to *New York*.

In 1978 newspaper unions went on strike at New York's *Times*, *Daily News*, and *Post* production offices. Murdoch told the unions that if they returned to publishing the *Post*, he would later accept whatever terms they reached with the other two newspapers; thus the *Post* returned to full publication months before its rivals did. Meanwhile, Murdoch's newspapers in London were making large profits, and in February 1981 he used these profits to purchase the *Times* (London), creating a stir because of his existing possession of the lowbrow *Sun* and his status as a foreigner—he was seen as unfit to own the venerable English publication. In November 1983 he bought the *Chicago Sun-Times* for $90 million, creating similar worries in Chicago because the *Sun-Times* was considered a highbrow newspaper. Murdoch worked his usual magic, sensationalizing the *Sun-Times* and thereby expanding its circulation. "I don't run anything for respectability," Murdoch was quoted as saying in William Shawcross's biography, *Murdoch* (1992). By 1984 Murdoch's holding company News Corporation owned 80 newspapers and magazines.

FOX

In early 1985 Murdoch bought half of Fox for $250 million, and on May 6, 1985, Twentieth Century Fox bought Metromedia's seven television stations for $2 billion. By then Murdoch's assets were worth $4.7 billion, with annual revenues of $2.6 billion—but he was borrowing heavily to expand into the American television market. In the United States, only an American citizen could hold a majority interest in a television station, which meant the Metromedia stations could not be owned by Murdoch; Australia had a similar rule. Murdoch obtained an exception in Australia, and on September 4, 1985, he became a U.S. citizen. The rest of his family remained Australian citizens.

In 1985 Murdoch instituted sweeping production changes in all of his London newspapers. He wanted to change from double keystroking (wherein an editor creates a page, and then a printer resets it) to single keystroking (wherein a computer is used, and the typesetting is done entirely by the editor), which would cut labor costs. British labor unions had long enjoyed special privileges at London newspapers. For instance, whenever a newspaper introduced new technology, the union printers would be paid as if there were more printers than there actually were; at the *Times*, it was possible for 10 workers to be paid the wages of 17. In secret, Murdoch built huge printing plants in Wapping and Glasgow, and on January 25, 1986, he began printing all his London newspapers in these plants. A long, violent strike ensued, featuring a pair of riots in Wapping. Murdoch offered a series of compromises that were rejected; the union workers eventually lost their jobs and most of their benefits, with the strike ending in January 1987. By then Murdoch owned about 30 percent of British newspapers. That same month Murdoch bought his father's old newspaper, the *Melbourne Herald*. On March 1, 1987, Murdoch launched the Fox television network. American rules forbade a motion picture studio from owning a television network, so the Fox network at first ran only 14 hours of national programming—one hour less than the legal definition for a network. It took persistent and skillful politicking by Murdoch to have the rules changed so that Fox could expand its programming.

TROUBLED TIMES

In 1988 Senator Kennedy exacted revenge against Murdoch by slipping a small amendment into an appropriations bill that forced Murdoch to sell the *Post* because he also owned a television station in New York. Companies were not supposed to own a television station and a newspaper in the same city, but the Federal Communications Commission (FCC) had granted Murdoch an exemption; Kennedy's amendment ended that exemption. In England, Murdoch had tried to launch a satellite-television service in 1983 but had failed, losing $20 million. In February 1989 he started Sky Television, a satellite service with four channels. He initially lost money on the venture as a result of providing satellite boxes for free; the investment would later pay off when he was able to offer over four hundred channels to subscribers.

In 1990 Murdoch's News Corporation was worth $19 billion, but it was $8.1 billion in debt, and most of the debt was due. Murdoch had to restructure his debts, in part by issuing new stock that diluted the percentage of shares he owned, weakening his control over the businesses. Exercising his persuasive powers to their fullest, he convinced American banks to give him extensions to 1993 to pay what he owed them. Without these extensions he might have lost News Corporation altogether.

In 1991 the Murdoch family moved to Los Angeles. Anna had felt like an outsider in New York; in the Los Angeles home she was the happiest that she had been since leaving Australia. Fueled by profits from his London holdings, Murdoch quickly bought back control of his businesses. In February 1992 his personal wealth was estimated at $2.7 billion. In 1993 he took one of the most breathtaking risks of his career, buying Asia's Star Television, a satellite service that covered southern Asia from the Middle East to Japan. With the laws of many different countries involved, Murdoch would spend much of the next decade negotiating deals with various governments. By 2000 Star Television would have over 300 million subscribers. Also in 1993 the *New York Post* went bankrupt; the FCC granted Murdoch a special exemption to save the newspaper, arguing that either Murdoch would be allowed to own the newspaper or it would die. Thus, he regained what Kennedy had taken from him.

MORE RISKS, MORE GROWTH

In 1994 Murdoch dropped the BBC from Star Television amid protests that he was bowing to complaints from China's dictators, who said the BBC portrayed them badly. Murdoch's response was that he personally disliked the BBC, which was true; he regarded the BBC as an elitist organization that helped prevent the United Kingdom's society from becoming fully free and democratic. The accusation that he was unethically catering to China's dictators would return with more justification when in 1998 his book-publishing firm HarperCollins broke its agreement to publish the memoirs of the last governor of Hong Kong, Chris Patten, supposedly because Patten was overly critical of Chinese communists.

In 1994 Fox bought the rights to broadcast National Football League games for $1.58 billion over five years, meaning that the network would lose $100 million per year. Murdoch averred, however, that his local stations would make up the $100 million in advertising revenues. In 1997 he bought Major League Baseball's Los Angeles Dodgers for $350 million, the International Family Entertainment religious cable network for $1.9 billion, Heritage Media for $1.41 billion, and 40 percent of Rainbow Media Sports Holdings for $850 million. The last of these deals gave Murdoch part ownership of the National Basketball Association's New York Knicks and the National Hockey League's New York Rangers. Murdoch planned to use his sports holdings for overseas broadcasts, noting that the Dodgers in particular had a globally recognizable brand name. On September 21, 1998, Murdoch's British Sky Broadcasting bought British soccer's Manchester United, the most popular sports team on the planet, for $1.5 billion.

In June 1999 Murdoch divorced Anna, worrying many colleagues who saw her as an essential, stabilizing influence on his life. Only three weeks later, in an unpublicized ceremony, he married Wendi Deng, a Chinese employee of Star Television. Those in attendance did not know they were attending anything other than a party on Murdoch's boat until the ceremony began.

In 2000 News Corporation was worth $38 billion, with annual sales of $14 billion. It bought Chris-Craft's 10 television stations for $5.3 billion in stock. By 2002 Murdoch owned more than 750 businesses in more than 50 countries. In December 2003 Murdoch made one of his most daring purchases when his News Corporation paid $6.8 billion for the controlling interest in DIRECTV, an American satellite-television service. This purchase would enable Murdoch to broaden the reach of his existing television services as well as to profit from the dissemination of other television services that would be required to pay him to carry their shows. For 2003 News Corporation netted $1.1 billion and grossed $17.5 billion.

News Corporation was first incorporated in Australia; in 2004 Murdoch reincorporated his company, shifting it from Australia to the United States. By that year Murdoch's 35 American television stations reached 40 percent of America's population. Murdoch himself had come to be regarded by many as an extreme right-wing ideologue; he seemed to have changed his thinking about socialism, which he saw as a poison embodied in government regulatory agencies. He never escaped from bitter criticism that he published vulgar newspapers that demeaned society by emphasizing sex and mayhem at the expense of reasoned discussion. It was Murdoch's view that he was an entertainer, not an informer, and that he merely sold entertainment to his readers, most of whom were lower-class workers and middle-class women. He was unapologetic about his influence on public discourse. Amid complaints that Fox slanted the news in favor of government policies that he advocated, he insisted that he saw no such slant. To his credit, his response to criticism was exclusively verbal; he did not sue or otherwise try to silence his critics, even when they accused him of being a liar or a criminal. He allowed them the same freedom to express their opinions that he wanted for his own publications.

Although regarded as an evil genius by some, Murdoch did not seem to have regarded himself as any sort of genius, but rather as a hardworking taker of risks. In that respect he was extraordinary, continually bouncing back from failures to find new ventures to conquer. He loved to build businesses, and he regularly worked 16-hours days into his 70s, asserting that he would never quit, noting that his mother was in her 90s. He seemed to take the greatest pleasure in turning around failed businesses, which he did without initially overanalyzing or worrying about profit and losses. Instead, he focused on seizing opportunities, confident in his ability to build and motivate goal-oriented teams and in his own extraordinary persuasive powers, with which he convinced employees and bankers of the vitality and potential for success of his enterprises.

See also entries on British Sky Broadcasting Group plc, Fox Entertainment Group, Inc., News Corporation Limited, and Twentieth Century Fox Film Corporation in *International Directory of Company Histories*.

SOURCES FOR FURTHER INFORMATION

Fallows, James, "The Age of Murdoch," *Atlantic Monthly*, September 2003, pp. 81–96.

Grover, Ronald, and Tom Lowry, "Rupert's World: With DirecTV, Murdoch Finally Has a Global Satellite Empire; Get Ready for a Fierce Media War," *BusinessWeek*, January 19, 2004, pp. 52–59.

Shah, Diane K., "Will Rupert Buy L.A.?" *Los Angeles Magazine*, December 1997, pp. 108–114.

Shawcross, William, *Murdoch*, New York, N.Y.: Simon & Schuster, 1992.

—Kirk H. Beetz

■■■
N. R. Murthy
1946–
Chairman and chief mentor, Infosys Technologies

Nationality: Indian.

Born: August 20, 1946, in Karnataka, India.

Education: University of Mysore, BTech, 1967; Indian Institute of Technology, Kanpur, MTech, 1969.

Family: Son of Nagavara Ramarao and Padmavathamma Rao; married Sudha Kulkarni, 1978; children: two.

Career: Indian Institute of Management, Ahmedabad, India, 1969–1971, chief systems programmer; SESA, Paris, 1972–1974, systems engineer; Systems Research Institute, Pune, India, 1975–1977, project leader; Patni Computer Systems, Mumbai, India, 1977–1981, head software group; Infosys Technologies, Bangalore, India, 1981–2002, chairman and chief executive officer; 2002–, chairman and chief mentor.

Awards: World Entrepreneur of the Year, Ernst & Young, 2003; corecipient of Asia's Businessmen of the Year, *Fortune*, 2003; named one of "Global Influentials," *Time*, 2002; Padma Shri, Republic of India, 2000; named one of "Entrepreneurs of the Year," *BusinessWeek*, 1999; J.R.D. Tata Corporate Leadership Award, All India Management Association, 1996–1997.

Address: Infosys Technologies, Plot No. 44 and 97A, Electronics City, Hosur Road, Electronic City, Bangalore, Karnataka 560 100, India; http://www.inf.com.

■ N. R. Murthy, longtime leader of the software-development company Infosys Technologies, became one of India's, and the world's, most highly esteemed managers. Though a wealthy man and a prime mover in India's booming software-outsourcing industry, he continued to live modestly and practice "compassionate capitalism," a philosophy that used free-market systems to create a better life for society as a whole.

N. R. Murthy. *AP/Wide World Photos.*

FROM SOCIALIST STUDENT TO CAPITALIST ENTREPRENEUR

Born in 1946, N. R. Murthy grew up one of eight children in a middle-class family of high caste but meager means. His father was a math teacher, and both parents taught him strong values, such as working hard and serving the public good. Murthy grew up a socialist, which was typical at the time in India. He studied electrical engineering, earning a master's degree at the prestigious Indian Institute of Technology in Kanpur.

During the 1970s he worked for a computer company in Paris, France. In 1974 Murthy decided to return to India, first touring the socialist countries of Eastern Europe. The harsh conditions there made Murthy realize that capitalism was not a sin. Before wealth could be dispersed, it must be created.

Back in India, Murthy began working in the software industry. There he saw how his country could harness its large pool of English-speaking, highly trained technical personnel who worked for a fraction of U.S. salaries. An Indian firm could supply Western companies with low-cost custom software by writing it in India. Murthy also wanted to contribute to his country, and by providing jobs locally large numbers of technicians would not have to leave India to find work. In 1981 Murthy and six other software engineers pooled their savings of about $1,000, and started Infosys in a Mumbai apartment. Murthy was the new company's chairman and CEO.

THE RISE OF INFOSYS

Infosys Technologies designed custom software for companies worldwide. But in 1981 the tightly regulated business environment of India made that difficult to accomplish. The company had to wait nearly a year for its first telephone line to be installed. It took over two years and 25 trips to Delhi to obtain import licenses for the company's first computers. Without computers at their Indian offices, employees had to travel abroad to work, often waiting weeks for travel permits and foreign currency. Despite these problems Infosys landed major accounts, including Reebok International, and managed to stay afloat.

Following the collapse of the Soviet Union and Communism in Eastern Europe, the Indian government liberalized its attitude toward capitalism and instituted free-market reforms in 1991. This made it possible for Indian companies to move goods, services, people, and currency more freely across national borders. The impact on Infosys was direct and rapid. It experienced annual growth rates of 27 percent to 106 percent during the 1990s, and acquired over three hundred new clients, many of them American giants like Citigroup, Aetna, Gap, Dell, and Cisco Systems. In March 2000 Infosys became the first Indian firm traded on an American stock exchange, the NASDAQ. Infosys continued to grow even in periods of stagnation and downturn for the American software industry. In 2004 Infosys was one of India's top three information-technology services firms, along with Wipro and Tata Consultancy Services. It had over 25,000 employees and earned record profits of $270 million on sales of $1 billion.

COMPASSIONATE CAPITALIST

Even though Murthy became one of India's most successful entrepreneurs, he remained committed to what he called "compassionate capitalism," spreading wealth to employees and Indian society in general, not just senior executives. Infosys paid high wages for the local market and was the first Indian company to offer stock options to its employees. The company built a 42-acre campus in Bangalore with employee exercise and relaxation facilities and cafeterias that were partly subsidized by the corporation.

"We all wanted to do something for our country," Infosys cofounder Nandan Nilekani told *Newsweek International* (September 27, 1999). By creating opportunities for people who previously thought the only way to get ahead was to migrate to the United States, Infosys helped establish an entire industry. India's National Association of Software and Service Companies estimated the country's software and service industry by 2003 had grown to 3,000 companies employing 600,000 people, earning total annual revenues of $12.2 billion.

Murthy also believed in contributing to his country as a whole. He told the *New York Times*, "In this country, people have to start putting the public ahead of the personal good" (December 16, 1999). Murthy served on several academic and government boards and established the Infosys Foundation in 1996. Headed by his wife, Sudha, the foundation established vocational training, science centers, hospital wards, and libraries in underprivileged and rural areas. Murthy won numerous national and international honors, including the Padma Shri in 2000, one of India's highest civilian awards for distinguished service to the nation, and Ernst & Young's World Entrepreneur of the Year in 2003.

In 2002 Murthy stepped down as CEO, but he retained the chairmanship and created the position of chief mentor. Although the original stock he owned in Infosys made him India's second-wealthiest person, Murthy continued to live modestly in a Spartan three-bedroom house. With no housekeeper, he began each day scrubbing the toilet, while his wife did all the family's cooking. He continued to dress simply and drive locally made cars, and by 2003 drew only a $44,000 annual salary. "If we want to sell capitalism to the people," Murthy explained to the *New York Times*, "we have to practice a lifestyle that does not seem unattainable. We want more and more people to become entrepreneurs. If the tea stall owner in a small village can say, 'Hey, these guys can do it; so can I,' and get his business into the next orbit, then our job is done" (December 16, 1999). He told the *Ivey Business Journal*, "Great leaders make people believe in themselves" (September/October 2001).

See also entry on Infosys Technologies Ltd. in *International Directory of Company Histories*.

SOURCES FOR FURTHER INFORMATION

Bernhut, Stephen, "Interview: N.R. Narayana Murthy, CEO, Infosys Technologies," *Ivey Business Journal*, September–October 2001, pp. 52–55.

Chandler, Clay, "They Get IT: The Dynamic Duo at the Top of Infosys Have Done Well— and Good," *Fortune International* (Asia edition), February 17, 2003, p. 38.

Dugger, Celia W., "India's High-Tech, and Sheepish, Capitalism; A Sheepish Capitalism Grows In India's High-Technology Triangle," *New York Times*, December 16, 1999.

Mazumdar, Sudip, "The Pride of Bangalore: Infosys is a Software Success and Not Just in India," *Newsweek International*, September 27, 1999, p. 52.

—Kris Swank

■■■
A. Maurice Myers

1940–

Former chairman, Waste Management

Nationality: American.

Born: May 20, 1940, in Long Beach, California.

Education: California State University at Fullerton, BA, 1964; California State University at Long Beach, MBA, 1972.

Family: Son of Walter R. Myers and H. Priscilla Larsen; married Elizabeth Jean Ashburn, 1960; children: three.

Career: Ford Motor Company, 1964–1972, financial manager; Merrill Lynch, 1972–1975, financial consultant; Continental Airlines, 1975–1982, Passenger Marketing director; On TV, 1983, vice president of operations; Aloha Airgroup, 1983–1993, president and CEO; America West Airlines, 1993–1995, president; Yellow Corporation, 1996–1999, chairman, CEO, and president; Waste Management, 1999–2004, CEO and president; 2004, chairman.

A. Maurice Myers. *AP/Wide World Photos.*

■ After a successful 10-year stint with the Hawaii-based Aloha Airgroup, A. Maurice Myers was widely known as an efficient leader who specialized in improving the viability and fortunes of troubled companies. After Aloha, Myers moved on to lead a team of troubleshooters in stabilizing America West Airlines; he then oversaw the reorganization of Yellow Corporation, the major ground-transportation company. His final challenge would be to reorganize Waste Management; he carefully guided the company out of a turbulent period of acquisitions and complicated upheaval, bringing order, stability, and profitability to the enlarged entity as its president and chief executive officer. Once he had achieved his basic overall goals, Myers decided to retire and enjoy his accumulated wealth while still relatively young.

With an energetic, hands-on management style, throughout his adult career Myers consistently promoted the maximal use of high-quality computer technology in improving external customer relations and internal management. Myers was known as "Maury" by coworkers and some analysts, who described his efforts to make systemic technical improvements in corporate culture and operations as generally successful.

ORGANIZATION AND CUSTOMER SERVICE

Myers first acquired important business skills while enrolled in the financial-management training program at Ford Motor Company. He continued his development on the job, earning an MBA and becoming a consultant for Merrill Lynch. He began developing his talents on a greater scale when he became a senior director in the Passenger Marketing department of Continental Airlines. Emphasizing public relations and good service, he learned much about the workings of the transportation industry during a flurry of government deregulation.

In what became his first major test, Myers moved to Hawaii to become the chief executive officer of Aloha Airgroup. He instituted a frequent-flyer program and experimented with an increase in international route expansion before concentrating on the intra–Hawaiian Islands passenger and freight market.

Aloha thereby survived the fallout of deregulation while rivals perished. His methods incorporated a careful focus on procurement and maintenance, the building of a more reliable communications infrastructure, and an emphasis on customer satisfaction. After his success with Aloha, Myers provided much the same leadership for the Phoenix-based America West Airlines when he became the company's president.

Having established a reputation as an executive who could turn around slumping companies, Myers next moved on to head Yellow Corporation, where he used his by then well-tried methods—again successfully and again on a grander scale. Myers embraced Internet-based commerce, developing and expanding its capabilities as a customer-relations tool and for accurate, quick-response tracking of goods and services. Myers emphasized that excellent information services, including accounting and information-management systems, were an essential element in corporate infrastructure. He would later tell London's *Economist* in a basic but telling philosophical formulation, "If you cannot measure it, you cannot manage it" (June 30, 2001).

MR. FIX-IT

For his last hurrah Myers took the reins of Waste Management in the chaotic wake of its huge merger with USA Waste Services and additional acquisitions. He organized an efficient and energetic management team to build a new infrastructure that would be managed from corporate headquarters in Houston. Though, as he told a staff reporter for the *Houston Chronicle*, he enjoyed "taking on fix-it jobs," he made clear relatively early in his tenure that the position would be his last before retirement (November 9, 1999).

The recovery task was formidable, but Myers carefully laid out and began implementing a strategy to develop a new companywide information system, improve customer service in all areas, investigate in detail suitable locales for careful market

development, and improve procurement and maintenance methods and choices. As he observed in an interview with *Waste Age*, his vision was to create a successful "transition from a roll-up or consolidation business model to a model based on operational excellence," embracing "initiatives finally integrating all of the 1,400 acquisitions we've made over the years into a single operation" (January 2002).

Having gone far in setting up and implementing his ideas for new economies of scale and instituting cultural changes in the use of information technology and in Waste Management's commitment to customer relations, Myers promoted members from his management team and selected his own replacement. In March 2004 he stepped back to serve as chairman of the board of directors as a prelude to his retirement in November. Waste Management had gained new footing and was able to improve its profit margins.

See also entries on Aloha Airlines, Incorporated, America West Airlines, Waste Management, Inc., and Yellow Corporation in *International Directory of Company Histories.*

SOURCES FOR FURTHER INFORMATION

"Business: Cleaning Up the Mess," *Economist*, June 30, 2001, p. 64.

Fickes, Michael, "A $12 Billion Start-Up," *Waste Age*, January 2002, pp. 28–35.

Goldberg, Laura, "Dealing Itself a Pile of Problems: Waste Management Pins Rebound Hopes on New Leaders, End to Acquisition Binge," *Houston Chronicle*, February 6, 2000.

————, "Trash Firm Picks New Top Officer: Trucking, Airline Veteran Takes Job," *Houston Chronicle*, November 9, 1999.

—Erik Donald France

∎∎∎
Kunio Nakamura
1939–
President, Matsushita Electric Industrial Company

Nationality: Japanese.

Born: July 5, 1939, in Shiga, Japan.

Education: Osaka University, 1962.

Career: Matsushita Electric Industrial Company, 1962–1965, various posts; 1985–1989, director of Tokyo Special Sales Office, Corporate Consumer Sales Division; Panasonic Consumer Electronics Company (U.S.), 1989–1992, president; Panasonic UK, 1992–1993, president; Matsushita Electric Corporation of America, 1993–1996, president, director, chairman of the board, and director of the Corporate Management Division for the Americas; 1996–1997, managing director; AVC Company, 1997–2000, senior managing director and president; Matsushita Electric Industrial Company, 2000–, president and CEO.

Awards: Businessman of the Year for Asia, *Forbes*, 2003.

Address: Matsushita Electric Industrial Company Ltd. (MC), 1006, Kadoma, Kadoma City, Osaka, 571-8501, Japan; http://www.mei.co.jp.

∎ Kunio Nakamura took over in 2000 as president and CEO of Matsushita Electric, best known for its Panasonic brand name and a worldwide leader in the development and manufacture of electronics products for consumer, business, and industrial needs. Many doubted whether Nakamura could revitalize the stodgy company into a fleet-footed megacorporation in the new technology age. Nevertheless, within three years Nakamura had led Matsushita to the number one spot in the electronics business, outperforming Sony, one of its leading competitors, in terms of sales and profits. Analysts observed that Nakamura achieved this feat partially by revitalizing Matsushita's creaky, overly bureaucratic management system. Colleagues and analysts noted that the media-shy Nakamura, unlike many Asian business leaders, focused on rewarding talent and achievement in management rather than age or seniority. At the same time, he kept in line with the company's traditional philosophy of emphasizing that business must operate for the public good.

Kunio Nakamura. *AP/Wide World Photos.*

TAKES COMMAND

After graduating from Osaka University in 1962 with a degree in economics, Nakamura joined Matsushita Electric. Over the next 25 years he would hold a number of management posts, primarily working in the area of marketing. Little public information is available about Nakamura's early career with Matsushita. In November 1985 he was appointed director of the Tokyo Special Sales Office, Corporate Consumer Sales Division. Two years later he came to America to serve as president of Panasonic Consumer Electronics Company in the United States. Except for one year heading Panasonic UK in Great Britain in 1992–1993, Nakamura would spend about eight years in the United States, gaining a stellar reputation for building strong businesses through massive restructuring of companies. From 1993 to 1997 he served as CEO of Matsushita Electric Corporation of America.

Nakamura returned to Japan in 1997 to head AVC Corporation, which was Matsushita's largest in-house electronics company. During his time at AVC he also was a senior managing director of the company and oversaw turning around its Chinese subsidiaries from money-losing to profitable businesses in less than two years.

Throughout his career, Nakamura had been acquiring extensive experience, especially in the United States. It was his overseas and technological expertise that caught the attention of corporate headquarters as consumer electronics moved into interactive services and Internet-related devices. Matsushita, founded by Konosuke Matsushita in 1918, was still essentially a family company. The company's development of a lightbulb socket that also had a plug for other devices set Matsushita on its course. In 2000 the company's chairman, Masaharu Matsushita, made ready to step down at the age of 87, and the company began looking for a new direction in management.

Matsushita's son, Masayuki Matsushita, was working in the company and was considered a potential candidate to become the new president, his father having moved up to become chairman of the board. But not all analysts were surprised when the board bypassed family tradition. Instead, Nakamura was named company president, a move that industry insiders and analysts saw as greatly reducing the influence of the Matsushita family over the company's day-to-day operations and strategic planning. The *AsiaPulse News* quoted the retiring Matsushita as saying, "Mr. Nakamura has an excellent record as a person in charge, both in Japan and abroad. It is my opinion that he will be a man of action capable of carrying out changes quickly" (April 26, 2000).

Although analysts had given the company's former president, Yoichi Morishita, overall good marks for his performance as president, many thought that the company lacked a clear strategic vision. They pointed out that top rivals—Sony, Hitachi, and Toshiba—had all forged new strategies for the Internet age while Matsushita lagged behind. Furthermore, unlike Sony, with its Walkman portable audio player, Morishita never had an overwhelming hit. The company's operating profit fell 18 percent to $1.8 billion in 1999, and Morishita was struggling to keep up with Sony, the world's number one electronics firm at the time. Matsushita's stock also underperformed in 1999 compared to the broad market and the electronics sector.

While serving as a managing director, Nakamura had spearheaded a drive to compete head on with Sony, and Morishita valued Nakamura's vast knowledge of the U.S. computer and consumer electronics markets. First, however, industry analysts noted that Nakamura had to fix the company's creaky bureaucracy by restructuring its vast number of business divisions, which totaled 140 in Japan alone. The consumer electronics analyst Kazushige Hata told *BusinessWeek*, "He carried out drastic restructuring in the U.S. and China. He should be able [to] do it here, too" (August 7, 2000).

INTENDS TO LEAD

Nakamura wasted no time in establishing his leadership role. The day after he took over, he made a videotaped speech to employees in which he pledged to "empower" them by rewarding proven talent rather than age or seniority. But Nakamura also expected hard work. He gave five hundred senior executives Net-ready cell phones so that they could be reached at any time. The *AsiaPulse News* also quoted him as saying, "Young talented people tend to dislike being controlled. I would like to run the company in such a way that my staff voluntarily tackle assignments, without feeling they are being told to do so by the boss" (April 26, 2000).

But Nakamura needed to do more than make speeches and hand out cell phones. He had to make changes. An encounter with an engineer egged on a quick change. With his vast experience in marketing, Nakamura was astounded when he asked why Matsushita's televisions lacked flat screens, and a technician replied that the middle part of the picture looked sunken in. Competitors like Sony had a growing market for their flat-screen televisions, and here was an engineer telling Nakamura that the market was wrong. He quickly transferred the product planning power to marketers and away from engineers. In the process, Matsushita redesigned its televisions.

Nakamura also kept his promise to the young, up-and-coming workers. For example, he transferred much of the power in the company's designing efforts to women designers and other employees in their thirties and forties. He reasoned that women could best design home appliances used by other women.

Nevertheless, Nakamura had to trim the company's sails. By December 2000 he had announced that the company was closing 30—or 23 percent—of its domestic factories in Japan, including major battery and television factories. In the process he cut one thousand marketing jobs and sold a huge portion of the company's assets. Matsushita had not lost money, but its profit margins were considered thin for a large company. Analysts noted that its return on equity for the year ending March 31, 2000, was 2.9 percent, far under the 15 to 20 percent returns most American companies were recording.

With investors and others looking closely over his shoulder, Nakamura wasted no time in giving senior executives a deadline for completing a massive restructuring plan. They had until the end of November 2000. Even though consumer electronics had been falling, Matsushita gave investors high expectations; the stock rose about 20 percent from early June 2000, when the announcement was made, to that November.

The restructuring would eventually lead to the elimination of 13,000 of 290,000 employees, primarily middle managers in Japan. (Industry analysts noted that they received generous early retirement packages.) In the process, Nakamura also shrank the company's management pyramid from 13 layers to three. Going back to his early experience, Nakamura paid special attention to the marketing divisions and consolidated them under two roofs—one for Panasonic brand electronics and the other for national brand products, such as refrigerators, in the Japanese and Asian market. Nakamura told Peter Landers of the *Wall Street Journal*, "The marketing divisions were so complicated that a lot of time was spent in internal company coordination" (December 1, 2000).

THE TORTOISE AND THE HARE

Despite the company's doing all the right things, analysts noted that Matsushita's stock had nearly halved from January to July 2001, falling below its book value and hitting an all-year low of ¥1,674 in late July. Like his competitors at Sony, Fujitsu, and NEC, Nakamura was facing an economic slowdown in the consumer market as well as dampening profits. Nakamura responded by moving into service-oriented businesses, including elderly medical care, selling such devices as a toilet that measures body fat. He also led the company's cellular phone subsidiary to be the first to offer mobile video phones. Nevertheless, Nakamura was quick to acknowledge that these efforts would not help the bottom line until 2002. In fact, in March 2002 the company announced its fiscal results and, for the first time in its history, had gone into the red by $3.4 billion, the company's biggest net loss on record.

Nakamura remained steady at the helm and organized a massive restructuring designed to cut redundancies and concentrate on the company's primary resources. He reorganized five group companies into 100 percent subsidiaries in order to run a more efficient operation. Nakamura told Yoshiko Hara of *Electronic Engineering Times*, "When the economy was growing rapidly, independent operations in the group encouraged good competition, but now we need to cut redundancy to cope with a digital consumer electronics era that requires a huge R&D cost" (January 14, 2002).

Industry analysts, however, pointed out that many of the markets on which Matsushita was focusing—including home electronics, such as plasma display panel TVs, DVD recorders, and cellular phones—were highly competitive markets. After a painful year of restructuring, Nakamura came out with more bad news. According to Nakamura, business was down so far that the parent company was taking control of five of its listed subsidiaries, including its star cell phone company, Matsushita Communication Industrial Company.

Three of the company's four main divisions—consumer electronics, home appliances, industrial equipment, and devices—lost money in 2001. Nakamura stood firm and said he was slashing costs by centralizing research, development, and marketing. Despite the difficulties, many analysts still liked Nakamura's reforms and thought that the company's future looked brighter. They noted that the initial hit taken by re-

structuring costs would lead to modest recovery, with $1.8 billion in savings in 2002 because of the reforms. One industry analyst was quoted in *BusinessWeek* as saying, "His strategy is to use any means possible to increase revenue in the coming year" (April 1, 2002).

SUCCESS AT LAST

Nakamura's emphasis on job cuts and business reorganization, as well as a change in the corporate culture, produced results far beyond many industry analysts' expectations. By September 2003 Matsushita had regained the leading spot as the world's biggest consumer electronics company. Overall it posted half-year sales for the 2003–2004 fiscal year of $32.3 billion and profits of $717 million, compared to the former number one Sony's respective numbers of $29.6 billion and $306 million.

Several strategic victories in sales helped spur the turnaround. Panasonic quickly mass-produced large, thin plasma displays at prices and quality levels that no one else matched. Matsushita also dominated new product categories, such as DVD recorders with hard disk drives. Industry analysts noted that Nakamura appeared to have turned the tide. For many years Matsushita had jokingly been called "maneshita," a pun translated as copysonic, referring to the company's tendency to follow Sony and others as they created new technologies rather than pioneering new technology itself. But, according to *Forbes*, the seasoned marketer Nakamura had helped the company regain its edge primarily through its flagship brand, Panasonic, and by taking over 50 percent of the new product category in DVD players. In 2003 *Forbes* magazine named Nakamura its global businessman of the year for Asia.

MANAGEMENT STYLE

Known for his lightning-fast makeovers of company operations by eliminating deadwood and creating new businesses, Nakamura never hesitated to shake up corporate structure through mergers, acquisitions, and layoffs. His emphasis on cutting the workforce and giving rewards based solely on merit largely dismantled the company's renowned lifetime-employment system, which was started by Matsushita's legendary founder and introduced to Japan before World War II.

Although Nakamura had earned this reputation for speedy makeovers for his work in the United States, he did not lose his touch as president of the Japan-based parent corporation. For example, over the first three years of his tenure, he invested a hefty $1 billion to boost Matsushita's information technology capacities. His cuts included top executive salaries, saving the company $385 million in 2002. He even forced his management teams, including the most senior, to summarize their reports in a few words or a sentence for faster communication and decision making.

Nakamura's approach to management at Matsushita also included completely changing the company's corporate culture, which was based in Japan and still clung to Asian corporate philosophies of rewarding people for seniority and age. Performance was king to Nakamura. He continually worked on the mentality of his management team and workers, telling Benjamin Fulford of *Forbes*, "We must never think we are the champions. We must always be the challengers" (February 2, 2004).

Nakamura not only rewarded younger employees who exhibited drive and new ideas, but he also emphasized the role of women. Nakamura once said that the best lesson he learned while heading Matsushita's American operations was that young people and women should have more responsibility. He immediately stopped the traditional practice of women serving tea at meetings. And he told Peter Landers of the *Wall Street Journal*, "These are simple things, but unless you get them right, you're going to fail as a leader" (July 26, 2000). He also told he *AsiaPulse News* that he wanted to run the company so that younger employees did not feel controlled and would "voluntarily tackle assignments, without feeling they are being told to do so by the boss" (April 26, 2000).

Despite the fact that much of his style incorporated the Western approach to business, Nakamura believed that capitalism in the United States had serious flaws. He noted that a corporation should be run for the public good and for the good of its employees. He told Fulford of *Forbes*, "The best-paid employee should not earn more than ten times more than the lowest-paid employee" (February 2, 2004).

SETS A GOAL

Despite Nakamura's success in guiding Matsushita to the top spot in the consumer electronics business, competition remained fierce. In 2004 Nakamura remarked that he would not step down from the company until he had reached a goal of improving the group's operating profit margin from around 2 percent for the 2003–2004 fiscal year to 5 percent. The *Knight Ridder–Tribune Business News* quoted Nakamura as saying, "We will definitely achieve it" (January 22, 2004). Nakamura also kept a keen eye on restructuring and setting new goals for his management teams. In 2004 he announced a plan that would shift the company's performance stage from, as he termed it, "creating" to "leaping ahead." He called the plan "Leap Ahead 21" and announced that the plan's ultimate goal was to achieve an operating profit ratio of 5 percent or more before he retired.

Nakamura continued to institute corporate reforms designed to streamline the business hierarchy. Always tinkering with the corporate structure, he announced that the purview of the board of directors and executive officers was changing in 2004, with the board focusing more on corporate strategy and supervision of business domain companies and the executive officers taking complete control of day-to-day business affairs. Nakamura also continued to consolidate efforts, as when he made Matsushita Electric Works Company a subsidiary, thus creating the biggest electronics and electrical equipment maker in Japan in terms of consolidated sales.

Little is known about Nakamura's activities outside of the company. Surprisingly, he liked to leave work early so that he could pursue his voracious reading habits. According to Fulford, writing in *Forbes*, Nakamura normally read around 200 books a year, most of them on history.

See also entry on Matsushita Electric Industrial Co., Ltd. in *International Directory of Company Histories*.

SOURCES FOR FURTHER INFORMATION

"A Bold Mechanic for a Creaky Machine," *BusinessWeek*, August 27, 2000, p. 58H.

Fulford, Benjamin, "The Tortoise Jumps the Hare," *Forbes*, February 2, 2004, p. 54.

Hara, Yoshiko, "Japanese Giant to See Red Ink for First Time in over 50 Years," *Electronic Engineering Times*, January 14, 2002, p. 12.

Landers, Peter, "Matsushita Electric New Official Starts with 'Simple' Steps," *Wall Street Journal*, July 26, 2003, p. 1.

———, "Matsushita to Restructure in Bid to Boost Thin Profits," *Wall Street Journal*, December 1, 2000, p. A13.

"Matsushita Elec Industrial Names Kunio Nakamura President," *AsiaPulse News*, April 26, 2000, p. 0240.

"Matsushita Electric to Achieve Profit-to-Sales Ratio Goal, President Says," *Knight Ridder–Tribune Business News*, January 22, 2004, p.ITEM04022022.

"Matsushita's Long March," *BusinessWeek*, April 1, 2002, p. 18.

—David Petechuk

Robert L. Nardelli

1948–

Chief executive officer and chairman, Home Depot

Nationality: American.

Born: May 17, 1948, in Old Forge, Pennsylvania.

Education: Western Illinois University, BS, 1971; University of Louisville, MBA, 1975.

Family: Son of GE plant manager and homemaker/real estate agent; married Susan (maiden name unknown); children: four.

Career: General Electric, 1971–1988, manufacturing engineer, various management positions at GE Appliances, GE Lighting, and GE Transportation Systems; Case Corporation, 1988–1991, executive vice president and general manager of Case Construction Equipment; General Electric, 1991–1992, executive vice president and chief executive officer of Canadian Appliance Manufacturing subsidiary; 1992–1995, president and CEO of GE Transportation Systems; 1995–2000, president and CEO of GE Power Systems, senior vice president of GE; Home Depot, 2000–, CEO, 2002–, chairman.

Awards: Distinguished Pennsylvanian Award, Gannon University, 1995; Distinguished Alumni Award, Western Illinois University College of Business and Technology, 1997; Alumni Fellow, University of Louisville, 1999; Executive of the Year, *Capital District Business Review*, 2000; Executive of the Year, Schenectady County Chamber of Commerce, 2000; Honorary Doctorate of Business Administration and Alumnus of the Year, University of Louisville, 2001; Honorary Doctorate of Laws, Siena College, 2001; Honorary Doctorate of Humane Letters, Western Illinois University, 2002.

Address: Home Depot, 2455 Paces Ferry Road, Atlanta, Georgia 30339; http://www.homedepot.com.

Robert L. Nardelli. *AP/World Wide Photos.*

■ After losing the competition to become CEO of General Electric (GE), Robert Nardelli was recruited by Home Depot—the world's largest home-improvement retailer—as CEO and later chairman. He overhauled the company's decentralized management structure and replaced its freewheel-

ing, entrepreneurial culture and its exuberant—some would say rowdy—atmosphere with "Six Sigma" managerial procedures. Utilizing GE's classic business strategies, Nardelli installed processes and systems, streamlined operations, moved into new markets, and grew Home Depot through acquisitions.

Robert Louis Nardelli was born on May 17, 1948, in Old Forge, Pennsylvania. His parents, who had grown up during the Depression, instilled in him a strong work ethic. His father had started at GE as an hourly worker and rose to plant manager. His mother kept the home for the two children and worked as a real estate agent. Nardelli was a mediocre student but a star athlete, altar boy, Boy Scout, class officer, yearbook editor, and ROTC cadet. He earned a football scholarship to Western Illinois University and worked summers paving highways. Nardelli was built too small to fulfill his dream of becoming a professional football player and rejected a coach's career as too unpredictable. He joined GE as an entry-level manufacturing engineer—its lowest salaried position. At night he worked on his MBA at the University of Louisville.

AMBITION WAS TO HEAD GE

By the late 1970s Nardelli was asking CEO Jack Welch to analyze his job performance. In 1988, after Nardelli had risen to a manufacturing vice presidency, he asked Welch for a general management job. Welch refused, and Nardelli quit. When Welch tried to talk him into coming back, Nardelli made it clear that his ambition was eventually to become CEO of GE. Instead, Nardelli became an executive vice president of the Case Corporation, an industrial-equipment manufacturer in Racine, Wisconsin. He headed the company's worldwide parts and components division and was promoted to general manager of Case Construction Equipment, its global business.

Nardelli returned to GE in 1991 as chief executive of CAMCO, GE's Canadian Appliance Manufacturing Company, based in Toronto. The following year he became president and CEO of GE Transportation Systems in Erie, Pennsylvania. There he oversaw the change in basic technology from AC to DC, doubled the size of the division, and took it global. He modernized product lines, expanded services, pacified angry unions, and more than doubled the division's profits.

In 1995 Nardelli was named a GE senior vice president and head of GE Power Systems in Schenectady, New York. The hundred-year-old manufacturer of gas and steam turbines and generators was in deep trouble. The division was considered an "old economy" backwater with almost no potential for growth. Its regional workforce had shrunk from 29,000 in the mid-1970s to only 4,600, with another 28,000 employees worldwide. The division's deserted factories were scattered throughout an alienated community.

OVERHAULED GE POWER SYSTEMS

To cope with energy-industry cycles and government turmoil around the world, Nardelli broadened the company's base. He took advantage of opportunities created by industry deregulation and increased power demands. He turned outdated manufacturing facilities into high-tech service centers for global customers. Nardelli helped formulate a strategy called the "metamarket view" to develop different ways for the company to serve a single customer. Nardelli reinvested in the core products of GE Power Systems, extended its product line, and acquired more than 50 energy-related businesses. He shifted from selling products to selling services, including long-term contracts to operate facilities.

In 1996 Nardelli instituted Six Sigma Quality Improvement Training at GE Power Systems. Pioneered at GE, Six Sigma aimed for the statistical near-perfect variation of 3.4 defects per million. It was a business process that relied on data rather than individual opinion. Six Sigma companies analyzed their processes to discover where defects could occur, measured those defects, and attempted to eliminate them.

GE Power Systems became one of GE's most profitable divisions and one of the biggest success stories in the company's history. In five years Nardelli increased profits almost sevenfold, with half of the division's revenue coming from new products. In addition, Nardelli repaired relationships with employees and the local community. Old factories were transformed into ball fields and green space. He initiated annual worker training and continuing education.

PASSED OVER FOR CEO

In an intense three-way competition to become CEO of GE, Welch chose Jeffrey Immelt. Nardelli was devastated. At GE he was known as "Little Jack." He had worked extraordinarily hard, and Welch had put him through many difficult tests. In June 2002 he told Patricia Sellers of *Fortune*: "There was always this rap against me about being functionally proficient but not very strategic." Nardelli also had a reputation for being somewhat inarticulate.

Nardelli had promised Welch that he would not talk to other companies until Welch had made his decision. Within minutes of the announcement, Nardelli was offered the presidency of Home Depot. He demanded the CEO's job. The Home Depot board was convinced that the company needed a sophisticated leader from the outside. In December 2000, after 27 years at GE, Nardelli moved to Atlanta with a compensation package amounting to $24 million in 2001. Although Home Depot cofounders Bernie Marcus and Arthur Blank continued on as cochairmen, Nardelli and the board soon asked Blank to leave, and Marcus later retired.

Marcus and Blank had a simple business strategy: continuous expansion. In 24 years they had grown Home Depot from a single warehouse store to a 1,155-store giant with $46 billion in annual sales. But costs were out of control, same-store (stores open for at least a year) sales were flat, profit growth had slowed, and the share price had dropped. Lowe's, Home Depot's major competitor, was doing far better.

BROUGHT SIX SIGMA TO HOME DEPOT

After the announcement that Home Depot had hired a CEO with no retail experience, Nardelli tried to squelch concerns. In January 2001 he told *Fortune* that his personal management style fit in with Home Depot's corporate culture and that of all the companies he had looked at "Home Depot most mirrored the way I like to operate." In answer to a question about imposing GE-style management on Home Depot, Nardelli replied that "to move from one social architecture and operating system and assume it's 100% portable and the platform of understanding is there at the new place—that's a terrible mistake." In response to a question about GE executives who were unsuccessful as outside CEOs, Nardelli told Patricia Sellers in a March 2001 *Fortune* story that those executives "didn't realize they were in a different environment. They did not have the respect of the culture and weren't sensitive to the pride of the employees." Nevertheless, most of the 250,000 Home Depot employees had never heard of Bob Nardelli, and some company veterans were openly hostile.

His first day on the job, Nardelli was astonished to discover that Home Depot lacked the infrastructure to send a companywide e-mail. Its stores did not have automated inventory systems; shipments were logged with clipboard and pencil. Home Depot stores were run-down and had a reputation for poor customer service.

Nardelli believed that better processes led to better quality and higher profits. He increased information technology spending by 20 percent. In 2003 he spent $400 million on inventory shipping and tracking systems. He substituted 157 different employee evaluation forms with two. Salaried personnel from the CEO down were to be rated by coworkers, above and beneath them, and salaries were based on the scores. At a time when Home Depot was planning to hire about 100,000 new employees, Nardelli did not necessarily fire those with poor scores. He first sought the advice of others and told underperformers exactly what they were doing wrong. Nardelli created a leadership institute, modeled on GE's, to groom high-potential managers, teaching them all aspects of merchandising, management, and, of course, Six Sigma. Although Home Depot had tried to implement Six Sigma earlier, it rarely had been used for retail businesses.

RESTRUCTURED THE COMPANY

Although efficiency had never been a big priority at Home Depot, it was Nardelli's operating principle. The company had outgrown its laissez-faire "do-it-yourself" management style. Nardelli replaced Home Depot's decentralized structure of local store managers with a technologically sophisticated command center. In his first six weeks he eliminated an entire management layer. He combined divisions and reassigned or eliminated group presidents, with all U.S. division presidents reporting directly to him. Of the 39 senior managers, 24 left and were replaced by managers—many of whom came from GE—with no retail experience.

In January 2004 Nardelli told *Institutional Investor* "We've gone from 1,600 separate businesses under one banner to one brand with 1,600 stores. We went from nine buying offices to one." Centralized management meant better supplier prices

and increased margins. Orders were routed from central purchasing in Atlanta, through transfer centers, to stores. Local suppliers were squeezed out, and Nardelli began buying out wholesalers. However, the new shipping systems required lower inventories, leaving some stores sold out of popular merchandise, such as electronics. Cutting inventories while pushing managers to move products resulted in fewer reorders. Home Depot's regional managers, used to cutting their own deals with suppliers, resisted their loss of control; many opted out and took early retirement.

Analysts began worrying that the company was changing too fast. Nardelli was criticized for dismantling the decentralized structure before investing in the information technology required for centralized management. However, between 2000 and 2002 annual earnings increased 30 percent to $3.7 billion. By June 2002 Home Depot was 18th on the Fortune 500, valued at $53 billion—the largest American retailer after Wal-Mart.

Upon his arrival, Nardelli immediately instituted cost-cutting measures. He slashed the number of new Home Depot stores scheduled to open in 2001 from 225 to 200. He cut full-time jobs, capped wages, and recruited former military officers to run the stores. Staff morale and customer service began to collapse under the new regime. The number of part-time employees skyrocketed from 26 percent to as high as 50 percent in 2002. Nardelli argued that additional part-timers were needed to increase weekend staff, since the stores were now open on Sundays. In addition, for the first time Home Depot offered benefits to part-time workers and included them in its bonus program. Employee tuition reimbursements also were increased. Meanwhile, Lowe's kept full-time employment at 80 percent, resulting in better customer service. Nardelli eventually reversed direction, and the stores began to hire more full-timers.

Nardelli changed Home Depot's trademark open-return policy and began requiring receipts for cash returns, saving the company $10 million annually. He ended Home Depot's traditional—but costly—promotional sales. After eliminating more than $1 billion in inventory in 2002, there was no need for inventory-clearance sales.

CONCENTRATED ON CUSTOMER SERVICE

In 2001 Nardelli introduced his Service Performance Initiative, which called for increased night restocking to avoid forklifts in the aisles and freed up personnel for customer service. Employees began to spend 70 percent of their time on customers rather than on restocking. "Racetrack managers" at each store circulated through the high-volume aisles to improve service.

Nardelli spent $250 million refurbishing Home Depot stores. Self-checkout systems were installed in 800 stores to reduce customer lines and free up salespeople. Two-way cordless scanners allowed products to be price-scanned in the shopping cart, thereby shortening lines. Nardelli began eliminating low-turnover items and permitted stores to tailor their offerings to local markets. Lowe's was considered to be more "female-friendly" than Home Depot, so Nardelli upgraded stores and merchandise to appeal to women. Design Place home-decor departments opened in more stores, and small appliances, lighting, and lamp selections were expanded in an attempt to attract more female customers.

EXPANDED THE BUSINESS

Supplying professional builders and contractors—who spend three times as much as do-it-yourselfers—became a top priority for Nardelli in 2002. He introduced "pro desks" and PRO stores to compete with independent wholesalers. Centralization enabled Home Depot to service corporate accounts. It began selling to Disney and gained exclusive rights to carry Disney furnishings and paints.

In 2003 Nardelli greatly increased Home Depot's services, adding carpet-laying, siding installation, heating, ventilation, installation of air-conditioning systems, high-end landscaping, appliance repair, pest control, home security, and tool rental. He expanded appliance sales, adding more brands and increasing appliance showrooms. Nardelli also launched an in-store campaign that promoted energy-efficient products.

Nardelli concentrated new stores in urban areas with apartment dwellers. Home Depot came to downtown Chicago and Brooklyn, New York. Two Manhattan stores opened in 2004. However, some experiments with new-format stores failed and were replaced with traditional Home Depots. Nardelli acquired Total Home, Mexico's second-largest home-improvement retailer. By the end of 2003 Home Depot had a new store opening in Canada, the United States, or Mexico virtually every 43 hours. In 2004 Nardelli began to expand the business into China.

MANAGEMENT STYLE

Nardelli brought to Home Depot his strong personality, aggressiveness, and GE discipline. In 2001 the analyst Donald Trott told Jennifer Pellet of *Chief Executive*: "With Bernie and Arthur, the approach culturally was, 'We're part of the troops like you guys and we're going into battle with you.' But Nardelli does not look comfortable in that orange apron. His body language is more 'I am the general up on the hill with the binoculars; you guys go take on the enemy.'" Calling his executives in for weekend meetings, Nardelli reminded them that it was not a job but a life. Whereas Blank and Marcus had motivated employees with hugs and cheers, Nardelli sometimes motivated them by instilling fear.

Whereas the 10 people who had reported to Blank were brought together for a quarterly business review, Nardelli had 21 individuals reporting directly to him at Monday-morning meetings or two-hour "market intelligence" conference calls. He demanded their data and action plans. In November 2001 Dennis M. Donovan, who came from GE with Nardelli as his number-two person, told *BusinessWeek*: "Never show him a number you don't want to deliver, because he will remember." Some Home Depot veterans quit, while others felt respected and valued by Nardelli.

Nardelli had learned from Welch that teaching was a big part of a CEO's job. He met with employees considered to be on the way up. In November 2000 Lonnie Edelheit, a senior adviser at GE, told *Capital District Business Review*: "He is very open and positive. He's intense. He demands a lot from people, but he gives a lot too." Although he was thought of as an extremely serious person, Nardelli was famous for throwing lavish parties.

Nardelli was known for his directness. He held town hall-style meetings, sent out biweekly company-wide e-mails, and made a habit of visiting individual stores. He sometimes gave pay raises on the spot, as well as frank assessments of employee performance and future prospects with the company.

In March 2001 Nardelli told Sellers at *Fortune*: "What I'm known for is transferring best practices. That's particularly important in this economic environment, when you have to maximize revenues through existing assets." He summed up his philosophy in a June 2002 *Fortune* interview: "There is an infinite capacity to improve upon everything you do."

THE BOTTOM LINE

Nardelli's transition proved to be much more difficult than expected. By January 2003 Home Depot's stock price was down 50 percent from its December 2000 level. Analysts questioned Nardelli's ability to transform and run a large retail business and worried that he was trying to impose manufacturing-type processes on a retail business. Some analysts worried that the home-improvement market was saturated. Others blamed customer dissatisfaction with a new, overly ambitious inventory and staff changes that disrupted service. Nardelli blamed a poor economic and retail climate and deflated lumber prices that accounted for 15 percent of Home Depot's sales.

However, by the end of 2003 Home Depot was operating more than 1,750 stores in the United States, Canada, Puerto Rico, and Mexico and had posted a net income of $4.3 billion on $64.8 billion in sales, with a 162 percent increase in profits. By January 2004 cash reserves were at a record $5.3 billion, compared with minus $800 million when Nardelli arrived. Home Depot, with more than 300,000 employees, planned to open 185 new stores in 2004 and was buying up abandoned Kmart properties. However, at Home Depot's 2004 annual meeting shareholders objected to Nardelli's extravagant compensation package and continued to complain about poor customer service.

In 2003 Nardelli served as a director of the Coca-Cola Company and was a member of the President's Council on Service and Civic Participation. He also served as a member of the board of councillors of the Carter Center, a leadership-advisory group.

See also entry on General Electric Company and The Home Depot, Inc. in *International Directory of Company Histories.*

SOURCES FOR FURTHER INFORMATION

"A Do-It-Yourselfer Disaster: Home Depot," *Economist,* January 11, 2003, p. 57.

"The Fixer-Upper: The Former GE Exec Is Finally Getting Credit for Doing the Kind of Bold Renovations at Home Depot That the No. 2 U.S. Retailer Promotes Among Do-It-Yourselfers," *Institutional Investor,* January 2004, pp. 18–19.

Foust, Dean, and Brian Grow, "What Worked at GE Isn't Working at Home Depot," *BusinessWeek,* January 27, 2003, p. 40.

"Home Depot Mirrors the Way I Operate," *Fortune,* January 8, 2001, p. 87.

Pascual, Aixa M., "Tidying Up at Home Depot," *BusinessWeek,* November 26, 2001, p. 102.

Pellet, Jennifer, "Mr. Fix-It Steps In," *Chief Executive,* October 2001, pp. 44–47.

"Robert Nardelli, GE Power Systems," *Capital District Business Review,* November 6, 2000, p. 10.

Sellers, Patricia, "Exit the Builder, Enter the Repairman: Home Depot's Arthur Blank Is Out. New CEO Bob Nardelli Is In. His Job: To Tackle the Company's Renovation after Two Decades of Nonstop Expansion," *Fortune,* March 19, 2001, pp. 86–88.

———, "Something to Prove: Bob Nardelli Was Stunned When Jack Welch Told Him He'd Never Run GE. 'I Want an Autopsy!,' He Demanded," *Fortune,* June 24, 2002, pp. 88–94.

—Margaret Alic

■■■
Jacques Nasser

1947–

Nonexecutive chairman, Polaroid Corporation

Nationality: Australian.

Born: December 27, 1947, in Amyoun, Lebanon.

Education: Royal Melbourne Institute of Technology, business degree.

Family: Son of Abdo Nasser (independent businessman); married Jennifer (homemaker and philanthropist; maiden name unknown), 1970 (divorced 2000); children: four.

Career: Ford of Australia, 1968–1973, financial analyst; Ford Motor Company, North American Truck operations, 1974–?, financial staff; Asia-Pacific and Latin American operations, 1970s–1987, financial staff; Ford of Brazil and Ford of Argentina Autolatina, 1987–1990, vice president for finance and administration; Ford of Australia, 1990–1993, president and chief executive officer; Ford of Europe, 1993–1996, chairman; Ford Motor Company, 1993–1996, vice president; Ford of Europe, 1996–1999, chairman; Ford Motor Company, automotive operations, 1996–1999, executive vice president; 1999–2001, president and chief executive officer; Polaroid Corporation, 2002–, nonexecutive chairman; One Equity Partners, Bank One Corporation, 2002–, senior partner; Allianz, 2002–, international adviser.

Awards: Automobile Industries Man of the Year, Retail Motor Industry Organization, 1999; National Order of the Cedar, Lebanon, 2002; Order of Australia, Governor-General of Australia, 2002.

Address: Polaroid, 1265 Main Street, Waltham, Massachusetts 02451; http://www.polaroid.com/index.jsp.

■ Jacques Nasser spent 1999 to 2001 as president and chief executive officer of Ford Motor Company, the automobile maker founded by Henry Ford and one of the best-known companies in the world. Nasser planned to transform Ford by changing its focus from automotive products to consumer goods while emphasizing global competitiveness. He was un-able to reverse Ford's steady loss of market share in its core business and could not save the company from a product safety scandal. Nasser's harsh human resources policies antagonized Ford workers and their family members and contributed to his dismissal.

OUTSIDER

Born in Lebanon, Nasser moved with his family to Melbourne, Australia, at the age of four. His olive skin marked him as an outsider in an Australia unfriendly to immigrants. The experience of prejudice reinforced Nasser's ambition to succeed while imbuing him with a resistance to being bound by tradition. It would also later make him sensitive to the problems of women and minorities. Despite the difficulties in Australia, Nasser began to thrive as an entrepreneur. He spent his teenage years starting businesses, including a bicycle-making operation and a discotheque. His first professional experience came as a student intern at Ford of Australia. After being graduated from the Royal Melbourne Institute of Technology with a degree in business, Nasser joined Ford as a financial analyst.

ON THE MOVE

Gregarious, energetic, and persistent, Nasser moved rapidly through the ranks of Ford. He held positions in Australia, Thailand, the Philippines, Venezuela, Mexico, Argentina, Brazil, and Europe by displaying wizardry with cost cutting. This global experience and leadership strength made Nasser an appealing choice for a company looking to expand its reach around the world. To almost universal acclaim, Nasser in 1999 was named president and chief executive officer of Ford Motor Company. Robert A. Lutz, vice chairman of rival Chrysler, categorized Nasser as a "brilliant automotive executive and unconventional thinker" before adding, "They'd be crazy not to give him the top job" (Zesiger, June 22, 1998). At the time Ford had 370,000 employees in two hundred countries, sales and revenues of $143 billion, record earnings of $6.6 billion, and a stock price of $65 per share.

PASSION FOR CHANGE

Despite its success Ford had lost a considerable amount of market share by the 1990s. Nasser immediately began to streamline the company in an effort to create a giant that responded quickly to consumers. Nasser closed money-losing plants, discontinued models that did not generate adequate profits, sold unprofitable operations, and weeded out executives. He also instituted a human resources policy mandating that 10 percent of workers receive a "C" grade that could lead to termination. Nasser argued that new people, new philosophies, and new technologies were required to assure Ford's success in the new economy. Ford employees unflatteringly gave Nasser the nickname "Jac the Knife."

Contrary to later complaints that he spent little time on the core car business, Nasser aimed to reinvigorate Ford's passenger car market. But Ford made most of its profits from trucks, and Nasser struggled to hold market share in the face of stiff Japanese competition. During his reign, Nasser oversaw the growth and acquisition of Jaguar, Aston Martin, Volvo, Land Rover, and Hertz. He added strength to Ford's light truck and sport utility vehicles and oversaw successes with the introduction of the Ford Ka and the Ford Focus as well as the sporty, two-seater Thunderbird.

Along with brand and product development, Nasser focused on global competitiveness, closer connections to the consumer, increased diversity, and leadership development. He envisioned Ford not only as the potential leader in the world car market but also as a provider of rental vehicles, auto repair, and satellite radio. To facilitate communication and market awareness, Nasser instituted a program that provided home computers and Internet access to employees. Workers gained the power, in a very hierarchical company, to make decisions both small and large. Nasser also launched his own affirmative action program, ensuring that 30 percent of new employees came from minority groups.

PRODUCT RECALL AND PERSONNEL DISASTERS

Nasser's greatest challenge came in 2000 when Ford's flagship four-wheel-drive sport utility vehicle, the Explorer, was involved in numerous rollover accidents. Two hundred deaths were ultimately linked to the Firestone Wilderness AT tires that were standard issue on the vehicle. Firestone recalled 6.5 million tires, and Ford committed itself to replace millions more. Nasser defended the integrity of Ford, even appearing in television commercials to protect the long-term corporate reputation of the company and its employees. In the short term, the company reported its first consecutive quarterly losses in nearly a decade.

While the Explorer debacle soured Ford's fortunes and contributed to Nasser's removal in October 2001, plummeting employee morale was the factor that ensured his dismissal. The Ford family controlled 40 percent of the company stock and had a paternal attitude toward employees. The family had serious disagreements with Nasser over his draconian personnel evaluation methods and the resulting employee lawsuits. When he replaced Nasser as CEO, William Ford Jr. announced that his first task would be healing the company.

Although he was fired, Nasser regarded his Ford days as a positive experience because of the friends he made and lessons that he learned. In 2002 Nasser became a senior partner in One Equity Partners, the private equity business of Bank One Corporation. He bore responsibility for identifying, evaluating, and implementing direct equity investments in various industries around the world. An affiliate of One Equity acquired Polaroid, the instant-imaging camera giant, in July 2002, following the company's voluntary bankruptcy filing in 2001. Nasser became the nonexecutive chairman of Polaroid. He also served on the boards of a number of companies, including Allianz, British Sky Broadcasting Group, and BuyTV.

See also entries on Ford Motor Company and Polaroid Corporation in *International Directory of Company Histories.*

SOURCES FOR FURTHER INFORMATION

Collins, Luke, "Out But Not Down," *Australian Financial Review,* July 11, 2003, pp. 34–38.

Nasser, Jacques A., "Next Frontiers of Globalization," in *Wisdom of the CEO,* edited by G. William Dauphinais, Grady Means, and Colin Price, New York: John Wiley & Sons, 2000.

Shaw, Robert, "A Passion for the Business: An Interview with Jacques Nasser," in *On High-Performance Organizations,* edited by Frances Hesselbein and Rob Johnston, San Francisco, Calif.: Jossey-Bass, 2002.

Zesiger, Sue, "Jac Nasser is Car Crazy," *Fortune,* June 22, 1998, pp. 79–81.

—Caryn E. Neumann

■ ■ ■

M. Bruce Nelson

ca. 1945–

Chairman and chief executive officer, Office Depot

Nationality: American.

Born: ca. 1945.

Education: Idaho State University, BA, 1968; Stanford University Executive Program, 1984.

Family: Married LaVaun (maiden name unknown); children: two.

Career: Boise Cascade, 1968–1990, senior management; BT Office Products USA, 1990–1994, president and chief executive officer; Viking Office Products, 1995, executive vice president and chief operating officer; 1996–1998, president and chairman; Office Depot International, 1998–2000, president; Office Depot, 2000–, CEO and president; 2001–, chairman.

Awards: Honored by the Greater Miami Chamber of Commerce as Hispanic marketer of the year, 2003; given the Applause Award by the Women's Business Enterprise National Council, 2003; named one of the best managers of 2002 by *BusinessWeek* magazine; named entrepreneur business leader of the year by Florida Atlantic University, 2001.

Address: Office Depot, 2200 Old Germantown Road, Delray Beach, Florida 33445-8299; http://www.officedepot.com.

M. Bruce Nelson. *Joel Stah/Getty Images.*

■ As CEO of Office Depot, M. Bruce Nelson came on board at a crucial time for the company. Among his first initiatives was closing unprofitable stores while at the same time opening others in expanding markets. He also worked to give the ailing company a morale boost after a failed merger with Staples by making the company a more attractive place to work. His strategy repositioned Office Depot for success in the competitive business of office products, even as retail sales continued to lag.

EDUCATION AND EARLY CAREER

After completing his bachelor's degree in business accounting at Idaho State University in 1968, M. Bruce Nelson began his career at Boise Cascade Office Products in Itasca, Illinois. He remained with the company for 22 years, leaving in 1990 to become president and chief executive officer of BT Office Products USA. Five years later, in 1995, Nelson moved to Viking Office Products as executive vice president and was soon promoted to chief operating officer. In January 1996 he became president and in November 1996 was elected the chairman of the board of directors. When Viking merged with Office Depot in 1998, Nelson remained as president and CEO of Viking, became president of Office Depot International, and was elected to the board of directors at Office Depot. Nelson became CEO of Office Depot in July 2000 and was named chairman on December 30, 2001.

REDEFINING OFFICE DEPOT

At the time Nelson took over as CEO, Office Depot ranked first among U.S. retailers of office products, had an extensive presence overseas, operated a lucrative business services division, and enjoyed brisk Internet sales. Yet the company was struggling. Nelson assumed control of Office Depot in the wake of a Federal Trade Commission antitrust ruling that had ended a four-year effort to merge with Staples, another office supply company. Calling himself "an agent of change" in *Retail Merchandiser* (May 2001), Nelson immediately set about restoring company morale. He made the success of Office Depot the responsibility of every employee and introduced a new set of values to guide the company: "Respect for the Individual," "Fanatical Customer Service," and "Excellence in Execution." He also removed Shawn McGhee as president of North American operations and Barry J. Goldstein as chief financial officer.

LESS IS MORE

Lagging sales in U.S. retail stores, however, lowered operating profits and marred the recovery. To address the problem Nelson, who had little experience in retail, undertook decisive but painful measures. In January 2001, after only six months at the helm, Nelson announced that Office Depot was closing 70 of its 855 stores, 67 in the United States and three in Canada. He also revealed plans to spend $60 million to renovate stores to make them more attractive to customers and to stock items that small business owners, the core of Office Depot's customer base, purchased regularly and often. Nelson hoped that these initiatives would lure customers into Office Depot stores, improve lackluster sales, and increase profits.

In the meantime, Nelson focused on expanding the number of Office Depot stores abroad, planning to add between six and 10 stores to the seven the company had already opened in Japan and between eight and 10 to the 22 already doing business in France. Additionally, Office Depot constructed new warehouses in Germany and the United Kingdom. "The business is going to grow quicker outside the United States," Nelson explained in *DSN Retailing Today* (January 22, 2001).

A PARTIAL TURNAROUND

Office Depot showed marked improvement in performance during the fiscal year 2001–2002. Nelson could at last begin to savor his accomplishments 20 months into his tenure as CEO. Operational profits increased from $316 million to $747 million, with e-commerce alone soaring by 58 percent to $1.6 million. No other company except Amazon.com did more business over the Internet than Office Depot. International sales boomed, accounting for 27 percent of the company's operating income. The sale of computer software and of-

fice furniture in the North American market, though improved, again failed to show a profit. As a consequence, Nelson became committed to reducing North American retail sales to less than 50 percent of Office Depot's business.

THINK PEOPLE FIRST

Despite the resurgence that Nelson's various strategies had effected, he continued to emphasize the importance of people to the success of any business. As the keynote speaker at the annual Office Products International conference in 2000, Nelson told his audience that leadership in business did not depend on implementing strategic visions but rather on putting the right people in the right positions and then allowing them the freedom to make mistakes, learn, and grow. Too many CEOs, Nelson complained, believed that leadership involved only managing a balance sheet and executing a system. Effective administration, on the contrary, required human understanding, empathy, encouragement, tolerance, patience, and loyalty.

Nelson practiced what he preached. Under his direction Office Depot earned recognition from the National Association for Female Executives as one of the top 30 companies for treatment of women executives and won international renown from *Fortune* magazine as one of the "great places to work" in Germany and Austria.

RECURRING PROBLEMS

The positive financial trends of 2001 and 2002 reversed themselves in 2003, when Office Depot's profits fell from $310.7 million to $276.3 million, and net income declined by 11 percent. Even at stores that had been in business for over one year, sales had declined for consecutive quarters, and the company fell into second place among the retailers of office products. After profits had risen by $109.7 million in 2002, the board of directors had rewarded Nelson with a $1.87 million bonus. In the wake of the dismal news of 2003, the board responded in kind. Although Nelson's base salary remained $1 million, the board reduced his total compensation package by 59 percent, from $7.05 million in 2002 to $2.91 million in 2003.

See also entries on Boise Cascade Corporation and Office Depot Incorporated in *International Directory of Company Histories*.

SOURCES FOR FURTHER INFORMATION

"Leaders: Forget Strategy, Think People," *Office Products International*, December 2002, p. 59.

Libbin, Jennifer, "Office Depot CEO Outlines Future," *DSN Retailing Today*, May 21, 2001.

———, "Office Depot Takes Steps to Offset Soft Sales," *DSN Retailing Today*, May 1, 2001.

Masters, Greg, "Making a Difference," *Retail Merchandiser*, May 2001, p. 19.

"Office Depot Discloses CEO Pay Cut," *Miami Daily Business Review*, April 2, 2004.

Prior, Molly, "Office Depot's Nelson: Rebound is Under Way," *DSN Retailing Today*, May 6, 2002.

Troy, Mike, "Change Is in the Air at Office Depot," *DSN Retailing Today*, August 7, 2000.

———, "Office Depot CEO Outlines Plan to Fix Performance," *DSN Retailing Today*, January 22, 2001.

Vogel, Mike, "Full Nelson," *Florida Trend*, December 2000, p. 78.

—Meg Greene

■■■
Yoshifumi Nishikawa
1939–
President and chief executive officer, Sumitomo Mitsui Financial Group and Sumitomo Mitsui Banking Corporation

Nationality: Japanese.

Born: 1939, in Japan.

Education: Osaka University.

Career: Sumitomo Bank, 1997–2001, president; Sumitomo Mitsui Banking Corporation, 2001–, president; Sumitomo Mitsui Financial Group, 2002–, president and chief executive officer.

Address: Sumitomo Mitsui Financial Group, 1-2 Yurakucho 1-chome, Chiyoda-ku, Tokyo 100-0006, Japan; http://www.smfg.co.jp/english/index.html.

■ Yoshifumi Nishikawa was the president and chief executive officer of Sumitomo Mitsui Financial Group and of its Mitsui Banking Corporation division. He successfully saw the bank through Japan's recession in the late 1990s, earning the admiration of his peers in the banking industry.

Yoshifumi Nishikawa. © *Haruyoshi Yamaguchi/Corbis.*

CHALLENGES AS PRESIDENT OF SUMITOMO

Nishikawa became president of Sumitomo Bank in 1997. In 2001 Mitsui Banking merged with Sakura Bank to become Sumitomo Mitsui Banking, with Nishikawa as its new president. In December 2002 Sumitomo Mitsui Financial Group was formed, and Nishikawa became president and CEO of the group. His ascension was not easy.

In 1998 Sumitomo lost $4.5 billion. In a recovery effort, the bank received money from the government, considered an embarrassment. Nishikawa closed 40 branches of the bank, cut two thousand jobs, and sold off several executive recreational facilities. He combined these cost-cutting measures with a plan to focus the bank's efforts on small and mid-sized corporations, wholesale securities and services, and affluent individuals. To accommodate these goals, Nishikawa split the company into two: one division to focus on the corporations and one

to focus on the retail customers. The most striking departure in these goals was removing the focus from large corporations and placing it on small and mid-sized corporations. The government money combined with Nishikawa's clear strategy paid off: The bank's stock nearly doubled in six months.

CONTINUED SUCCESS

Other savvy decisions led to Nishikawa's success. He did not believe his securities subsidiary could compete with the U.S. and European markets, and he had to make his company more competitive. In 1999, in an effort to expand the bank's offerings, the newly created Sumitomo Securities division and the established Daiwa Securities Trust Company formed a joint venture, Daiwa SB Capital Markets, in which Sumitomo held a 40 percent stake. Sumitomo would provide cash to

Daiwa, and Daiwa would provide Sumitomo with expertise. Such a venture would allow Sumitomo to continue to serve its corporate customers and to pull in customer base from Daiwa. It was a win-win situation for both companies.

Nishikawa was able to reach many of his goals, such as reducing the number of loans that were not providing enough profit. He also changed the location of many of Sumimoto's offices to areas where there would be high potential for new customers. The company offered many financial services to small and medium-sized companies to further expand their business. Nishikawa continued to focus on consumer banking needs as well as business needs. Sumitomo offered insurance products, home mortgages, and investment trusts to customers. In 2003 Goldman Sachs invested $1.26 billion in Sumitomo Mitsui. In exchange, Sumitomo Mitsui agreed to provide loans in the billions to Goldman Sachs for investment-grade clients. As in the previous venture with Daiwa, Goldman Sachs and Sumitomo Mitsui agreed "to enhance and develop business cooperation between the two organizations" wrote Fiona Haddock in *Asiamoney*. Investors believed Goldman Sachs had purchased a customer base in Japan, perhaps for its own means. However, with the government bank loans fresh in its memory, Sumitomo Mitsui welcomed private investments.

REACHED GOAL AHEAD OF SCHEDULE

Six months ahead of goal, in February 2004, Sumitomo Mitsui Banking had reduced its bad loan ratio 50 percent. In addition, the bank reduced its outstanding bad loans to less than JPY3 trillion, another goal reached six months ahead of schedule. The poorly performing loans were restructured in a new venture with Daiwa Securities and Goldman Sachs.

Nishikawa said the move was intended to serve companies attempting to turn around and would further assist Sumitomo Mitsui in cleaning up its bad loans. The bank also strove to cut its shareholdings to minimize risk from the stock market. Like many companies, Sumitomo Mitsui Banking planned aggressive moves into China and other Asian countries. Those regions were poised for growth for years to come.

Nishikawa was raised in the Nara prefecture in western Honshu, the largest island of Japan, and in the 1960s graduated from Osaka University. He enjoyed gardening and was an avid fan of the Hanshin Tigers baseball team from Osaka.

See also entry on Sumitomo Mitsui Banking Corporation in *International Directory of Company Histories.*

SOURCES FOR FURTHER INFORMATION

Haddock, Fiona, "Goldman/Sumitomo Mitsui Deal Shifts Landscape," *Asiamoney*, February 2003, p. 4.

"SMFG to Set Up Corporate Rehab Firm in November," Asia Africa Intelligence Wire, October 8, 2003.

Smith, Charles, "Asia's Most Influential Bankers," *Institutional Investor* (international edition), August 1999, p. 41.

"Sumitomo Mitsui Banking to Halve Shareholdings by End of FY 2005," Knight-Ridder/Tribune Business News, December 19, 2003.

"Yoshifumi Nishikawa, President, Sumitomo Bank, Japan," *BusinessWeek*, June 14, 1999, p. 94.

—Deborah Kondek

■■■
Hidetoshi Nishimura

1942–

Chief executive officer and president, Sojitz Holdings Corporation

Nationality: Japanese.

Born: 1942, in Japan.

Education: Kyushu University, BS, 1965.

Career: Nissho Iwai Corporation, 1965–2003, eventually CEO and president of American subsidiary, then president; Nissho Iwai-Nichimen Holdings Corporation, 2003–2004, co-CEO and president; Sojitz Holdings Corporation, 2004–, CEO and president.

Address: Sojitz Holdings Corporation, 1-23 Shiba 4-chome, Minato-ku, Tokyo 108-8408, Japan; http://www.sojitz-holdings.com/eng.

■ Hidetoshi Nishimura joined the trading house Nissho Iwai Corporation after graduating from Kyushu University with a degree in economics in 1965 and eventually worked his way up to the position of president. In April 2003 Nissho Iwai merged with Nichimen Holdings Corporation to form Nissho Iwai-Nichimen Holdings Corporation, of which Nishimura was named president and co-CEO. In 2004 that group was renamed Sojitz Holdings Corporation. Nissho Iwai had traded in ferrous and nonferrous metals, steel, industrial machinery, textiles, lumber, and grain.

GOAL TO INVEST IN SUBSIDIARIES AND EXPAND GLOBALLY

In 2000, serving as the president and chief executive officer of Nissho Iwai American Corporation, Nishimura addressed the company in the annual report, outlining his strategy to adapt to quickly changing markets both domestically and abroad. His plan for growth included significant investment in subsidiaries in the company's target markets of new technology, energy, automotive, retail, and finance. With only one-third of his parent company's business being done in Japan and the majority coming from the Americas, Nishimura

stressed expansion into global opportunities through Nissho Iwai's network of subsidiaries. He also pushed for more investment in areas outside the company's trading businesses.

In the next two years Nishimura oversaw integration and mergers with numerous companies. Nissho Iwai spun off its information business division to form the company ITX. The LNG business was integrated under a 50-50 joint venture with Sumitomo. In 2002 Nissho Iwai joined Sumitomo Metal Mining Company, Mitsui & Company, and Rio Tuba Nickel Mining Corporation to form a joint-venture company, with construction of a new plant begun in 2004. In January 2003 Nissho Iwai partnered with Xelo, the developer and supplier of document-related software, to promote sales of Xelo's products in the United States through Nissho Iwai American.

With respect to his business style and remoteness from his employees, Nishimura had been chided by business commentators for remarking in the *Japan Times*, "I want you to challenge difficulties with the attitude of devising methods that would realize goals before you utter reasons why the goals appear impossible to attain" (January 7, 2003).

FORMED HOLDING COMPANY NISSHO IWAI-NICHIMEN HOLDINGS CORPORATION

On April 1, 2003, Nissho Iwai Corporation joined forces with the equally large trading company Nichimen Corporation to form Nissho Iwai-Nichimen Holdings Corporation, a firm wholly owned by both companies. The two companies transferred their respective stocks to the new holding company, which would consolidate management, subsidiaries, and affiliates. The new company would then oversee the subsidiaries and general restructuring, cut debt and jobs, and reduce selling, general, and administrative (SG&A) expenses. Hidetoshi Nishimura, the president of Nissho Iwai, was named president of the new company, while Nichimen's president Toru Hambayashi became chairman. Both men would serve as co-CEOs.

Nishimura and Hambayashi immediately laid out plans for the new holding company. Expecting to save ¥80 billion during the following year, they would cut the number of jobs from 21,000 to 17,000 and reduce the number of subsidiaries from 430 to three hundred. Reduction of SG&A would save ¥110 billion by the end of fiscal 2005 by eliminating overlapping subsidiaries.

Nissho Iwai, the sixth-largest trading house in Japan in terms of sales, and Nichimen, the eighth-largest, amassed combined sales of ¥7.5 trillion in fiscal 2001 and had a combined ¥162.4 trillion in equity capital. Together the two companies also had a high level of interest-bearing debt, topping ¥2.75 trillion. Nevertheless, the two trading houses agreed that they would not ask financial institutions to forgive what they owed.

Critics questioned why two giant, debt-swamped trading houses would join to form a new holding company. During the time of Japan's economic bubble companies made bad investments and stretched their businesses too thin. Then during the country's economic slump companies like Nissho Iwai and Nichimen had difficulty adjusting to deflation, the weak stock market, and the global economic slowdown. They abandoned healthy assets but held on to high-risk assets for fear that losing the latter would damage their equity capital. Nissho Iwai was one of the few companies that successfully streamlined business interests.

Shiroh Sakawaki, the analyst at the Daiwa Institute of Research, questioned the compatibility of the two companies. In *Japan Inc.* he noted that Nichimen's goal was to select and concentrate, while Nissho Iwai aimed to be a *soga shosha*, or all-around trading company. He suggested that the alliance would work only if Nissho Iwai came more in line with Nichimen's strategy.

MERGER AN EXAMPLE FOR OTHER COMPANIES

In other ways the merger appeared to be a good fit, as very little duplication of businesses or customers existed. Nishimura commented at a joint press conference in Tokyo that Nichimen, which was strong in textiles and raw materials, and Nissho Iwai, with its airplanes and energy interests, were unlikely to encounter conflict, and that their complementary natures would actually encourage cooperation and result in faster restructuring. At the press conference Nishimura and Hambayashi described the "synergy effects" that their integration plans would bring. Industry observers believed that the Nissho Iwai-Nichimen merger would be an example for other trading houses struggling during Japan's economic doldrums.

In a series of steps taken to increase capital Nissho Iwai-Nichimen planned to add up to ¥325 billion. The company floated a combined ¥278 billion in preferred shares to UFJ Bank, Mizuho Bank, and other investors. The merger also attracted the U.S. investment bank Lehman Brothers Holdings; Lehman's offer of ¥50 billion was the first investment of its kind for a foreign bank in Japan. The influx of capital was intended to cover expenses from the trading house's large-scale restructuring program.

Nissho Iwa-Nichimen also sold a combined ¥7 billion in common shares to two hundred individual investors, including

Nishimura himself, after its instatement. *Kyodo News* reported that Nishimura said of his decision to make the purchase, "I have volunteered to subscribe to the common shares and there is no legal obstacle to my subscription" (April 25, 2003).

SUCCESSFUL INTEGRATION OF NISSHO IWAI-NICHIMEN

Six months after the merger of Nissho Iwai and Nichimen, Nishimura described the integration operations as smooth. In a September 6, 2003, interview with *Kyodo News*, Nishimura said that the company was "working well as a medium to fuse" the two firms. The goal of cutting the workforce by 6,200 by the end of fiscal 2005 was on track. Pay cuts of 20 percent for remaining employees were "painful measures," according to Nishimura, but were "paving the way for shifting the seniority-based system to a merit-based system" (September 6, 2003); he explained that Nissho Iwai-Nichimen would introduce a new pay system that would link pay and bonuses to workers' performances. Nishimura further described plans to combine operating subsidiaries into one company under the Nissho Iwai-Nichimen name. With that restructuring Nishimura expected to change the name of the holding company, which he believed to be "too long."

PRESIDENT OF SOJITZ HOLDINGS CORPORATION

In an effort to cut costs and speed up decision making, Nissho Iwai-Nichimen Holdings integrated their central operations into a new entity called Sojitz Corporation. The holding company controlled Sojitz so that it could respond flexibly to economic and business changes and streamline its business lines. Nissho Iwai-Nichimen Holdings was then renamed Sojitz Holdings Corporation effective July 2004. Nishimura remained the corporation's CEO and president.

In a 2004 letter to Nissho Iwai-Nichimen shareholders, Nishimura and Hambayashi announced that the holding company was continuing progress with its integration and its three-year business plan. The creation of Sojitz allowed the initiation of a process of "selection and focus" intended to improve profitability. The company expected to enhance its competitiveness by establishing a multifaceted business structure.

As a sign that the company's debt restructuring and management consolidation were on the right track, Moody's Investors Service placed the B1 long-term debt ratings of Nichimen and Nissho Iwai under review for possible upgrade. Standard & Poor's reduced its long-term rating on Nichimen from B-plus to B but raised its long-term rating on Nissho Iwai to B-pi from B-minus-pi.

BEYOND NISSHO IWAI

In addition to his 40-year career at Nissho Iwai, Nishimura served as the vice chairman of Japan Foreign Trade Council, a private-sector organization that developed international relations through trade. Nishimura was one of 58 business executives around the world to undersign a letter condemning the environmental impact of a coal-fired power plant being built in the Philippines and urging the insurance companies involved to more carefully review the standards and practices of the project.

In 1994 Nishimura, representing the Japan Overseas Development Corporation, advocated investment in infrastructure in the Greater Mekong subregion of Myanmar and Vietnam. He said in the *BKK Post*, "Without infrastructure, it is impossible to do business. But the important point is who should pay. It should be the government which pays for this out of tax revenue" (November 25, 1994). He went on to suggest that trade and investment insurance be made available in the region.

Nishimura traveled to spread economic good will. In March 2004 he met the prime minister of the Union of Myanmar, General Khin Nyunt. Later that year he met Kraisri Chatikavanij, the chairman and executive chairman of Thai Central Chemical Public Company (TCCC). Nyunt thanked Nishimura for Nissho Iwai's continued support, and Nishimura expressed his appreciation for TCCC's recent successes.

See also entry on Nissho Iwai K.K. in *International Directory of Company Histories*.

SOURCES FOR FURTHER INFORMATION

"Japanese Trading Powerhouse to Pad Capital Base by up to 325 Billion Yen," *Kyodo News International*, April 25, 2003.

Kawakami, Sumie, "Goodbye to the Glory Days," *Japan Inc.*, February 2003, pp. 8–10.

Kothandapani, Dharani, "Private Sector Seen as Major Player in Mekong Project," *BKK Post*, November 25, 1994.

"Nissho Iwai, Nichimen to Form Holding Company," *Mainichi Daily News*, December 11, 2002.

"Nissho Iwai, Nichimen Trading Units Set to Merge," *Japan Times*, February 11, 2004.

"Tokyo Holding Company Makes Good Start, President Says," *Kyodo News International*, September 6, 2003.

—Lorraine Savage

■ ■ ■

Uichiro Niwa
President, Itochu Corporation

Nationality: Japanese.

Education: Nagoya University, law degree, 1962.

Career: Itochu Corporation, 1966–1998, various positions; 1998–, president; 2004–, chairman.

Address: 5-1, Kyutaromachi 4-chome, Chuo-ku, Osaka 541-8577 Japan; http://www.itochu.co.jp/.

■ Uichiro Niwa was a man with a radical vision for the Itochu Corporation, a company that was one of the largest in the world and intended to remain so. After Niwa became president of a company that was faltering in 1998, he reevaluated Japanese executive culture and decided that certain attitudes and practices had to change if his company were to be profitable once again. He cut executive salaries, took away such perquisites as reserved elevators, and even went without his own salary for a period of time. Although his approach was radical for Japan, it worked. Itochu was able to improve its bottom line by 2004, mainly because of Niwa's drastic changes.

EDUCATION AND EARLY CAREER

Niwa graduated from Nagoya University in 1962 with a law degree. Instead of practicing law, however, he became an expert in trading foodstuffs and joined the Itochu Company in 1966. At that time Itochu was an internationally integrated company whose operations covered a broad range of businesses with offices in over 80 countries. Itochu's yearly profits positioned it among the world's largest companies of any type. The company had seven business groups: aerospace, electronics, and multimedia; chemicals, forest products, and general merchandise; energy, metals, and minerals; finance, realty, insurance, and logistics services; food; plant, automobile, and industrial machinery; and textiles.

Niwa worked his way up through the company, starting in the food group and then learning about the rest of the company's businesses. He became president of Itochu in 1998. At that point the company was doing rather poorly, with many of its subsidiaries having run deficits for years. Niwa's first action was to cut executive salaries by 30 to 50 percent. He completely disagreed with the prevailing assumption of Japanese business culture that executives should be paid exorbitant salaries and treated like royalty. For example, certain elevators in Itochu's buildings were set aside for the exclusive use of higher-ranking personnel. Niwa did away with this privilege, allowing all employees to use any elevator because he wished them to be able to return to their offices as quickly as possible. His next action was a declaration that any Itochu subsidiary remaining in the red for three years in a row would either be liquidated or have its entire executive group replaced.

In 1999 Niwa accelerated his plans to reduce the company's interest-bearing debts. He cut the number of Itochu board members and focused on a select few of Itochu's core businesses, including information services, clothing, retail financing, oil and gas, engineering, and food resource development. He was preparing the company, he told the *Financial Times*, to become a holding company by April 2001 (January 5, 1999). Niwa also made plans to cut the number of directors from 45 to between 10 and 15 by 2000.

In addition to cutting back on executive frills, Niwa set an example for his company by giving up his own salary. By 2001 he had gone without pay for 18 months, vowing that he would not accept any money from Itochu until its financial situation had improved. In January 2001, however, the company finally turned a profit and Niwa once again drew his salary. "As the leader of the Itochu group with some 1000 companies, I wanted to show that corporate executives should always be first to put their own performance under the microscope and discipline themselves," Niwa said in *The Australian* (January 3, 2001). Forgoing his pay was a radical act, but it showed a dedication to the company that few executives would have been willing to imitate.

EXPANSION IN CHINA

In the early 2000s Japanese companies had come to fear China as an unbeatable competitor in production and exports. Such companies as Sony, however, began moving into China and developing their products there, having decided to benefit from the country's lower costs rather than avoiding competition with Chinese industries. Itochu itself worked with Japan's

Ito-Yokado Company in 2001 to open a department store in Beijing at the Asian Games Village, which had already been constructed in preparation for the 2008 Olympics. Niwa also stated that the company planned to open two more stores in Beijing, including one near the zoo in the downtown area and one near Lizeqiao. He said that Itochu had considered opening between 10 and 15 more stores in Beijing before expanding outside the capital. In addition, Itochu planned to open three thousand FamilyMart convenience stores, with expectations of increasing the number to 10,000 over the next several years. Niwa maintained that the sheer size of the Chinese population meant that Itochu could eventually open almost four hundred thousand convenience stores. "I'm not thinking China is the enemy to Japanese companies anymore," Niwa told a reporter from *Forbes* (December 23, 2002). "It is quite a good thing for us that China might be developing its economy very rapidly in the future."

Niwa also made an agreement in 2002 with the government of Shandong province that committed Itochu to helping the Chinese expand their trading and upgrade their economy. This agreement between a foreign business and a Chinese provincial government was the first arrangement of its kind. Niwa noted that Itochu had invested in businesses in the Shandong area since the 1970s. "The scope of the business opportunities will expand down the track because the province has abundant human and agricultural resources," Niwa told the *Asian Economic News* (May 13, 2002). Around the same time Niwa himself became an economic adviser to the central Chinese government in Beijing.

INVESTING IN THAILAND

The Japanese economy was not doing very well at the beginning of 2003 in spite of reassuring statements from the Japanese government. Niwa was not entirely optimistic, however, and advised caution on the grounds that full economic recovery takes time. He urged Japanese companies to follow their customary pattern of seeking business partners as well as customers in foreign countries by expanding into Thailand. He was quoted as having said, "I would like Japanese companies to invest in Thailand as their second headquarters. I want Thailand to be the most ready in Asia to absorb the expansion of investments of Japanese companies outside Japan" (The America's Intelligence Wire, December 24, 2003). Itochu at that time announced a deficit and appeared to have other difficulties because of the epidemic of severe acute respiratory syndrome (SARS) that was raging all over Asia. Niwa questioned whether his company would be able to pay dividends in mid-2003, as the epidemic had affected Itochu by delaying business meetings and depressing sales.

In mid-2003 Niwa announced Itochu's plans to invest ¥100 billion in its advanced technology and consumer goods businesses as well as its operations in China. Niwa followed up this statement in 2004 by reporting that Itochu would pay $10 million to acquire a 50-percent equity stake in the Tingtong Holding Corporation, a Chinese distribution company. Niwa told the press that the agreement was important because "... the distribution network in China may make the country a core base for its delivery business in the future" (Asia Africa Intelligence Wire, March 29, 2004).

NEW RULES AND DEVELOPMENTS

By 2004 Itochu had become one of several relatively untroubled Japanese companies that began to include such fixed assets as real estate and factories to improve their balance sheet under a new rule scheduled to take effect in 2005. The new rules force companies to claim their losses on fixed assets—such as buildings and equipment—that are losing value. By claiming things early the costs are disseminated over a number of years. Niwa told the Asia Africa Intelligence Wire, "We decided to introduce the new rules early in order to get rid of future burdens as soon as possible" (April 5, 2004).

In 2004 Niwa was asked to chair a subcommittee of the Japanese government's Commission on Policy Evaluation and Evaluation of Incorporated Administrative Agencies. It was then announced in March 2004 that Niwa would assume the position of chairman of Itochu with representative rights, which enabled him to make decisions he had as president. And for someone who had brought his company out of the red during a very difficult period, it was certain he would use them.

See also entry on ITOCHU Corporation in *International Directory of Company Histories*.

SOURCES FOR FURTHER INFORMATION

"Government to Reform Ministry Project Evaluation System," Asia Africa Intelligence Wire, May 2, 2004.

"Growth Prospects Seen Unclear," Asia Africa Intelligence Wire, August 14, 2003.

Haisma-Kwok, Constance, and Tsukasa Furukawa, "Asia Watch: Dropping Lingerie... New Underwear... Boosting Output," *Women's Wear Daily*, March 16, 2004.

"Itochu Agrees to Aid China's Shangong in Trade, Development," *Asian Economic News*, May 13, 2002.

"Itochu Chief Lauds Thailand over China," The America's Intelligence Wire, December 24, 2003.

"Itochu to Assist Beijing with Distribution Infrastructure," *AsiaPulse News*, December 11, 2002.

"Itochu to Invest 100 B. Yen in Tech, China, Life Goods," Asia Africa Intelligence Wire, April 22, 2003.

"Itochu to Own 50 Pct of Chinese Distributor Tingtong," Asia Africa Intelligence Wire, March 29, 2004.

"Itochu's Group Net Profit Down 32.4 Pct," Asia Africa Intelligence Wire, May 9, 2003.

"Japan Trader Itochu Names Managing Director as President," *Knight Ridder/Tribune Business News*, March 5, 2004.

"Japan's Ito-Yokado, Itochu Expand China Presence," *China Online*, December 19, 2001.

"Japan's Itochu to Invest US$1.3 Bln in Priority Areas Over Next 2 Yrs," *AsiaPulse News*, April 10, 2001.

Lunn, Stephen, "New Pay Dawns for the Boss Who Gave It All Up," *The Australian* (Sydney, Australia), January 3, 2001.

Meredith, Robyn, "If You Can't Beat 'Em," *Forbes*, December 23, 2002, p. 84.

Nakamoto, Michiyo, "Asia-Pacific: Itochu Steps Up Pace of Restructuring Programme," *The Financial Times*, January 5, 1999.

"SARS Looming as Threat to Japan Trading Houses," Asia Africa Intelligence Wire, May 9, 2003.

Shimbun, Asahi, "Uichiro Niwa," Asia Africa Intelligence Wire, January 28, 2003.

"Some Japan Firms Adopt Asset Impairment Rules 2 Yrs Early," Asia Africa Intelligence Wire, April 5, 2004.

"Trading in Knowledge," *Forbes.com*, 2004, http://www.forbes.com/specialsections/japan/27_niwa.html.

—Catherine Victoria Donaldson

■■■
Gordon M. Nixon
1957–
President and CEO, Royal Bank of Canada

Nationality: Canadian.

Born: June 25, 1957, in Montreal, Quebec, Canada.

Education: Queen's University, Bachelor of Commerce, 1979.

Family: Son of Melbourne Nixon and Elizabeth (maiden name unknown); married Janet (maiden name unknown); children: three.

Career: Dominion Securities, 1979–1986, Fixed Income and Corporate and Government Finance; RBC Dominion Securities, 1986–1989, Global Markets and Investment Banking (Tokyo); 1989–1995, managing director of Investment Banking; 1995–1998, head of Global Investment Banking; 1998–2001, head of Global Banking Division; Royal Bank of Canada, 2001–, president and CEO.

Awards: Innovator of the Year, *American Banker*, 2001.

Address: Royal Bank of Canada, 200 Bay Street, Floor 8, S Tower, Toronto, Ontario M5J 2J5; http://www.rbc.com.

■ At age 44 Gordon M. Nixon became the youngest-ever chief executive of a major Canadian financial institution when in August 2001 Royal Bank of Canada (RBC) named him as CEO. In 2002 RBC was in fact Canada's largest financial institution, with 12 million customers worldwide, C$413 billion in assets and a market capitalization in excess of C$41 billion. With Nixon at the helm RBC aggressively pursued a U.S. expansion plan; between 2001 and 2003 the bank announced 10 acquisitions in the United States, including the purchases of Centura Bank, Liberty Life Insurance Company, and the Dain Rauscher brokerage firm. The C$5.3 billion spending spree saw RBC's U.S. brokerage business outstrip its Canadian operations by a third and reinforced Nixon's reputation as a dealmaker, a tough competitor, and the man widely expected to be at the forefront of the bank merger push in Canada.

MANAGEMENT STYLE

The descendant of an affluent Montreal family (his grandfather was a director at RBC), Nixon paid his way through university by tending bar during the school year and pushing paper during the summer at a Montreal investment firm. An average student, Nixon distinguished himself on the rugby pitch where he made first team and played on the varsity side for each of his four years at Queen's. Gavin Reid, a former coach and Queen's professor, remembered Nixon as a prize player: "fast and a very good tackler and a good team man" (*Kingston Whig-Standard,* July 28, 2001).

Such terms were also used to describe Nixon's leadership style at RBC. Nixon acknowledged that the team-player mentality fostered on the rugby field served him well: "I personally believe, particularly in the financial services sector, that your most important aspects ride the elevator with you each day; that you are as good as the people who work with and for you" (*Kingston Whig-Standard,* July 28, 2001). Teammates and competitors alike described Nixon as a skilled communicator, outgoing, patient, and a good listener—an affable team player genuinely interested in the people around him. He also evidenced a sense of humor. During an interview following his promotion to RBC's top job, Nixon was asked how he spent his spare time at university. Noting that he "hung out" at two of Kingston, Ontario's more notorious watering holes, Nixon was quick to add, "for the interview, you have to throw in the Queen's library as well" (*Kingston Whig-Standard,* July 28, 2001).

BUSINESS STRATEGY

Under Nixon's leadership RBC's quest for North American expansion accelerated. An ardent believer in the irreversibility of globalization, Nixon looked to markets outside Canada, specifically in the United States, for growth. Like any good rugby player, Nixon could spot an opening and saw the U.S. market for what it was: the largest global economy and a geographically contiguous region with a banking sector offering good potential for growth. When asked about RBC's particular expansion strategies, Nixon said, "We know we have to grow outside Canada if we're going to flourish as a global or even Canadian financial services company" (*The Globe & Mail,* February 22, 2002). The "platform extension" plan adopted by Nixon meant that RBC's foray into the U.S. market would be "measured" and would serve to establish a beachhead for future growth. Acquisitions were focused, at least initially, on U.S. banks with strong retail, personal, and commercial operations—traditional areas of strength and expertise for RBC in Canada.

RBC's strategy was not an unqualified success. While the U.S. acquisitions increased its international revenues, the costs associated with the acquisitions along with the relatively weak profitability of the American banks undermined RBC's overall performance and share price. Shareholders who had seen stock values move from C$15 to C$51 under Nixon's predecessor were not pleased with the lackluster returns. Growing pains were short-lived, however, and in 2003 RBC became the first bank in Canadian history to earn more than C$3 billion in a single year.

COMMUNITY INVOLVEMENT

Nixon served as a director of the Canadian Council of Chief Executives and co-chaired that council's committee on national policy. He was chairman of the United Way of Greater Toronto and a director of the North York General Hospital.

See also entry on The Royal Bank of Canada in *International Directory of Company Histories.*

SOURCES FOR FURTHER INFORMATION

Armstrong, Frank, "Average Queen's Grad Rises to Banking Pinnacle," *Kingston Whig-Standard*, July 28, 2001.

Kalawsky, Keith, and Derek Decloet, "Royal to Cut Staff, Sell Assets," *National Post*, October 23, 2001.

Nixon, Gordon, "We Can't Sit Back and Allow All of Our Industries to Become Globally Insignificant," *The Globe & Mail*, July 3, 2001.

"Royal Bank CEO Wins 'Innovator' Award," *The Globe & Mail*, December 10, 2001.

Yakabuski, Konrad, "Merger Ambitions Thwarted: Royal Bank Has Quickly Sewn Up a Little American Empire," *The Globe & Mail*, February 22, 2002.

—Timothy J. Wowk

■■■

Jeffrey Noddle

1947–

Chairman, president, and chief executive officer, Supervalu

Nationality: American.

Born: 1947.

Education: University of Iowa, BA, 1969.

Career: Supervalu, 1976–1982, director of retail operations, merchandising director, and vice president of marketing, JM Jones division; 1982–1985, president, Fargo and Miami divisions; 1985–1988, corporate vice president, merchandising; 1988–1992, senior vice president, marketing; 1992–1995, corporate executive vice president and president; 1995–2000, chief operating officer, Distribution Food Companies; 2000–2001, president and chief operating officer; 2001–2002, president and chief executive officer; 2002–, chairman, president, and chief executive officer.

Address: Supervalu, PO Box 990, Minneapolis, Minnesota 55440; www.supervalu.com.

■ Jeffrey Noddle may have been born with supermarkets in his blood and the lyrics of "food, glorious food" from the musical *Oliver* on his brain. He certainly believed in the local touch. Noddle grew up in Omaha, Nebraska, and two of his brothers preceded him into the supermarket business with a regional supermarket chain in the Omaha area. His older brother later became an executive with a supermarket firm in the Midwest before starting his own real-estate development company. Jeff and his other brother stayed in the food industry, with the brother being an executive of another major U.S. food retailer.

During the early 1970s Noddle worked for a company that operated discount retail supermarkets alongside discount department stores, worked in Miami, ran a store in Louisiana, and was a sales director in Los Angeles. He joined Supervalu in 1976, rising to president and CEO in 2002, succeeding former CEO Mike Wright. Noddle felt that as the sixth largest company in the grocery channel, Supervalu clearly had established itself as an industry leader.

Supervalu, indeed, is a major force in the supermarket business. "We're not always well understood, simply because we operate many different banners in different niches in the grocery industry—but Supervalu today is a $20-billion-plus company" (*Wall Street Transcript*), said Noddle, noting that the company was one of the most successful, and certainly the most profitable, in wholesale distribution and in retailing. Supervalu conducts its retail operations under three formats: extreme-value stores under the retail banner Save-A-Lot; price superstores under the regional banners of Cub Foods, Shop 'n Save, Shoppers Food Warehouse, and Bigg's; and full-service supermarkets under the regional retail banners of Farm Fresh, Scott's, and Hornbacher's. Supervalu holds leading-market-share positions with some 1,400 retail-grocery locations, including licensed Save-A-Lot locations. Through its Save-A-Lot format, the company holds the leading market position in the extreme-value retailing sector.

Noddle decided that the company would be better served by accelerating the growth of its extreme-value format Save-A-Lot chain. As in other competitive retail businesses, the company wanted to strengthen its market position as well as exit less profitable markets. "Rather than spreading [the company's capital] over a large network, we're targeting our capital toward fewer markets that offer the best opportunities," noted Noddle (*Wall Street Transcript*). In another strategic change, he added, Supervalu would revamp its distribution business to position itself as a fully integrated supply-chain business. Noddle saw that the company had previously operated primarily as a food marketer, supporting some of the top independents, ranging from single-store niche operators to multistore regional operators. Supervalu recognized this business as having reached its growth potential, with slow growth predicted in the future, Noddle added. "We're focusing on repositioning ourselves within the supply chain, rather than just operating as a food marketer in support of others in the retail food business," (*Wall Street Transcript*), he said, pointing to a strategy of cutting costs, incorporating new technologies, and reorganizing many company functions.

CEOs of food-distribution companies worry increasingly about the tremendous competition in the field, particularly as Wal-Mart expands its massive supercenters and the number of retailers entering the grocery business continues to grow. Finding and keeping good workers is another challenge. Supermarket CEOs are faced with the difficult task of wringing positive results out of an environment full of negative influences. "We believe there's going to be a battle for consumers, and those who can execute right at the local level are going to ultimately win, whether it's a supercenter or anyone else," Noddle said (*Progressive Grocer*, January 1, 2004). Noddle kept a close eye on the growth of aggressive competitors, but he felt that new challenges were a permanent feature of the food-retailing business.

"We've put a lot of stress on delivering our retail business and in support of the independents we serve on the distribution side being very local in our merchandising and marketing," he said (*Progressive Grocer*, January 1, 2004). He added that Supervalu believed very strongly in the local touch and that consumers would respond to those companies that did the best job within their markets. "The decisions as to what people are going to buy, how to price goods in the market, what to advertise, what to display—those kind of decisions, we believe, you leave in the local market," he added (*Wall Street Transcript*).

Noddle was also involved in many industry and community activities. He served on the boards of the Food Marketing Institute, Food Distributors International, Donaldson Company, IGA, and General Cable Corporation. He served on the board of trustees for the Boys and Girls Club of the Twin Cities and chaired the major-firms division of the Twin Cities United Way campaign.

See also entry on Supervalu Inc. in *International Directory of Company Histories*.

SOURCES FOR FURTHER INFORMATION

Fosse, Lynn, "Interview with Jeffrey Noddle," *Wall Street Corporate Reporter*, July 9, 2001, http://www.highbeam.com/library/docO.asp?docid=1P1%3A46791600&refid=ink-g5sk.

"Jeffrey Noddle, Supervalu Inc.," *Wall Street Transcript*, http://www.twst.com/perl/profile.pl?file=consum/PAA211.

Major, Meg, "The Bold and the Embattled," *Progressive Grocer* 83, no. 1, January 1, 2004, p. 38.

Weir, Tom, "What's on Your Worry List?" *Progressive Grocer*, January 1, 2004, pp. 12–15, http://www.progressivegrocer.com/firc_new/article-display.jsp?vnu-co.

—Peter Collins

■■■
Tamotsu Nomakuchi

1940–

President and chief executive officer, Mitsubishi Electric Corporation

Nationality: Japanese.

Born: November 18, 1940, in Kagoshima, Japan.

Education: Kyoto University, postgraduate studies, 1965; Osaka University, M.S., 1975, PhD, 1978.

Career: Mitsubishi Electric Corporation, 1965–1997, researcher in the Central Research Laboratory; 1995–1997, director of information technology; 1997–2001, senior vice president and vice president of the Corporate Research and Development unit; 2001–2002, executive vice president and vice president of the Information Systems & Network Services unit; 2002–, president and chief executive officer.

Address: Mitsubishi Electric Corporation, Mitsubishi Denki Building, 2-22-3, Marunouchi, Chiyoda-ku, Tokyo 100-8310, Japan; http://www.global.misubishielectric.com.

■ Tamotsu Nomakuchi was a scientist who specialized in miniaturization and miniature machines; during his career at Mitsubishi Electric Corporation, he was sometimes the company's representative at scientific conferences, serving on panels or delivering short talks about the details of measuring high-technology equipment with small, hypersensitive instruments. Mitsubishi Electric was typically run by people with advanced degrees in engineering or physics, and it was probably a sign of Nomakuchi's ambition to advance within the company that he studied to earn a doctorate in physics while still working as a researcher at Mitsubishi Electric. After Mitsubishi Electric saw a downturn in its fortunes, Nomakuchi was selected by the board of directors to lead the company out of its doldrums. By cutting wasteful businesses and forming mergers and alliances with onetime rivals, even while pursuing an environmentalist policy, Nomakuchi helped Mitsubishi Electric to the most profitable years in its history.

ORIGINS OF MITSUBISHI ELECTRIC

Mitsubishi Electric was part of the enormous Mitsubishi Corporation, Japan's largest company. Mitsubishi Corporation was begun in 1870 when a young nobleman descended from samurai, Yataro Iwasaki, leased three ships and began a shipping company. He created the symbol for his company of three diamonds touching at a point, the source for the name Mitsubishi, which means "three diamonds." He and his successors spun off new companies and purchased others, uniting them all through family ownership; such a gathering of companies tied together by family ownership was called a *zaibatsu*.

In 1921 the part of the Mitsubishi shipbuilding company that specialized in manufacturing electrical systems for ships was spun off and incorporated into Mitsubishi Electric Corporation. By Nomakuchi's era, Mitsubishi Electric would manufacture electronic equipment, communications equipment, components for automobiles, and machines for construction, transportation, and energy industries. Before and during World War II, the parent company, Mitsubishi Corporation, was deeply involved in the buildup and support of Japan's military, and many in Japan as well as outside Japan blamed Mitsubishi Corporation and Japan's other powerful *zaibatsu* for encouraging Japan's militarism in order to profit from Japan's wars. After Japan's defeat in 1945, the Allies broke up the *zaibatsu* into many smaller companies. Mitsubishi Corporation was broken up into more than one hundred companies, but almost immediately Mitsubishi Electric began to recover by producing consumer electronics, such as radios, in 1945.

During the 1950s and 1960s many of the former members of Mitsubishi Corporation formed ties by buying shares in one another, and the holding company Mitsubishi Corporation was reborn as a *keiretsu*, a group of companies tied together through cross-ownership and traditional association. Traditionally, members of a *keiretsu* were expected to work together and consult with one another about business plans. As president and chief executive officer of Mitsubishi Electric, Nomakuchi showed an independence of mind, insisting that members of the Mitsubishi *keiretsu* were like members of a family who were independent of each other—implying that cooperation with one another was not required.

RESEARCHER AND LEADER

Nomakuchi joined Mitsubishi Electric in April 1965, following postgraduate studies in engineering at Kyoto University. He worked in Mitsubishi Electric's Central Research Laboratory, remaining fairly obscure except for occasional attendance at a scientific convention. In 1975, he received his Master's degree in engineering from Osaka University; in 1978 he received his doctorate in physics from Osaka University. In 1993 Mitsubishi Electric introduced Factor X. This Factor X was a numerical measurement of the level of environmental friendliness of Mitsubishi Electric products, figured by comparing the materials and energy used and the toxic products released of a new version of a product with the same parameters as its predecessor. As president and CEO, Nomakuchi used Factor X to motivate researchers to improve the environmental friendliness of company products. In 1997 Nomakuchi was named to Mitsubishi Electric's board of directors and became a corporate senior vice president and vice president in charge of the Corporate Research and Development unit.

In June 1998 Ichiro Taniguchi became president and CEO of Mitsubishi Electric; at the time, there was no official chairman of the board—the CEO had the responsibilities of a chairman of the board. In that year Mitsubishi Electric began manufacturing residential photovoltaic cells in its Iida factory in Nagano. In October 1999 Mitsubishi Electric and the American company Space Systems/Loral won a joint contract to build the *Optus C1* satellite for SingTel Optus, Australia's second-biggest communications company. This was the first time a Japanese company had won a satellite contract to be delivered overseas.

In April 2001 Nomakuchi became corporate executive vice president for Mitsubishi Electric and vice president in charge of the Information Systems & Network Services unit. His elevation came in an atmosphere of crisis. The company grossed $33 billion for the fiscal year that end March 31, 2001, but it lost $58 million. It had assets of $33.1 billion, but its debt was $27.3 billion. In late 2001 Mitsubishi Electric contributed $1 million to disaster relief for recovery from the September 11, 2001, terrorist attacks on the United States.

PRESIDENT AND CEO

In 2002 Mitsubishi Electric had businesses in 35 countries, and its electric components were found worldwide, from televisions to communications satellites. On March 5, 2002, Mitsubishi Electric established the Corporate Strategy & Management Office to absorb the Associated Companies Department, the Corporate Strategic Planning Office, and the Public Relations Department, in the hope of centralizing cooperation among Mitsubishi Electric's numerous subsidiaries at home and overseas. This heralded a general restructuring of the company's management. On April 1, 2002, Taniguchi was given the newly created office of chairman of the board, while Nomakuchi was made president and CEO for Mitsubishi Electric, with powers over corporate governance greater than Taniguchi had enjoyed.

Nomakuchi introduced the "Changes for the Better" campaign, saying that he envisioned a company that emphasized the manufacture of high-quality products, with a worldwide brand image that was respected by customers, employees, and shareholders. He put his hopes in Mitsubishi Electric's technical expertise, in which he had much pride. In addition, he took a classic American approach to returning Mitsubishi Electric to profitability by working to reduce procurement and operations costs. This cost savings eventually helped Mitsubishi Electric make a profit in the next year (2003), even though Mitsubishi Electric's worldwide sales dropped 6 percent in 2003.

All Japanese semiconductor manufacturers were losing money in 2002. Hoping that by consolidating their resources they could compete with American, Korean, and Taiwanese manufacturers who were underselling them, in March 2002 Mitsubishi Electric and Hitachi merged their semiconductor manufacturing operations to manufacture chips. The new venture was called Renesas Technology. Later in 2002 Mitsubishi Electric contracted with Boeing to manufacture antennas to allow passengers in aircraft to access the Internet while in flight. This was part of Nomakuchi's broad ambitions for Mitsubishi Electric to expand its satellite business, because the antennas would contact satellites.

In July 2002 Nomakuchi was worried that falling stock prices in the United States would hurt the value of Mitsubishi Electric's stock, lowering the market value of the company, which would affect its ability to obtain loans at good interest rates. One of the notable aspects of his tenure as president and CEO was the furious rate at which Mitsubishi Electric paid down its debts. Meanwhile, he reorganized Mitsubishi Electric into five business areas: electronic devices, consumer appliances (such as washing machines), industrial electronics, communications and information products, and heavy equipment (such as electric turbines).

A RECORD PROFIT

Even though Nomakuchi had made cuts in Mitsubishi Electric's holdings, at the end of the fiscal year on March 31, 2003, the company still had more than 110,000 employees around the world, with 74 factories, 15 research laboratories, and 132 offices in 35 countries. In April 20, 2003, in another alliance with a longtime rival, Mitsubishi Electric combined its manufacturing of automation systems with that of Toshiba Corporation, cutting costs for each by sharing them.

In May 2003 Nomakuchi believed that the war in Iraq and an epidemic of a virus called SARS (severe acute respiratory syndrome) had hurt Mitsubishi Electric's export sales; a drop in the company's overseas sales corresponded with an overall decline in Japan's economy for April and May as well as the economy of Southeast Asia. Even so, he forged ahead with forming new alliances. On May 29, 2003, Mitsubishi Electric joined the Blue-ray Disc Founders industry group, which was devoted to developing the use of blue lasers for reading and writing DVDs and CDs. Members included most of the major electrical manufacturing companies of Japan, but Mitsubishi Electric was thought to give the group the additional muscle it needed to make its technology standard in Japan for DVD and CD drives. On June 12, 2003, the *Optus C1* satellite was finally launched. After Mitsubishi conducted tests on it, the satellite became operational on July 18, 2003; its success became part of a marketing effort by Nomakuchi to find buyers for more satellites to be built by Mitsubishi Electric. That month, Nomakuchi revealed a new chip set for radar in automobiles that would allow automobiles to automatically adjust their speed as well as their distance from other vehicles.

Crucial to Nomakuchi's efforts to establish Mitsubishi Electric as an environmentally friendly company were the company's innovations in solar power. On October 21, 2003, Mitsubishi Electric's lead-free photovoltaic cells won United Laboratories' certification as safe, enabling Mitsubishi Electric to sell its cells in the United States. In December 2003 Mitsubishi invested $27.5 million to upgrade its residential photovoltaic-cell production capacity with a goal of producing 90 megawatts' worth in 2004 and 135 megawatts' worth in 2005. Nomakuchi hoped to power homes throughout Japan with solar energy from Mitsubishi Electric's cells.

Nomakuchi wanted innovation, and 2004 looked like a great year for Mitsubishi Electric's innovations. On February 17, 2004, the company introduced a liquid crystal display that could be viewed from both its front and its back; it could be used in mobile phones to allow the screen to be viewed while the phone was closed. On March 5, 2004, Mitsubishi introduced the Face-to-Face Video Call Center System that allowed people to see each other and simultaneously to see each other's documents when teleconferencing; the system would be im-

portant to medical people, who could consult with one another at great distances. On May 30, 2004, Mitsubishi Electric introduced a 7.42-millimeter-thick high-resolution camera to be used in mobile phones. Samples shipped in July 2004, and full production began in September 2004. Meanwhile, Nomakuchi urged new employees to eliminate old-fashioned ways of doing business. For the fiscal year ending March 31, 2004, Mitsubishi Electric made a record-high profit of $112 million. The fly in the ointment was another member of the Mitsubishi *keiretsu*, Mitsubishi Motors, which was bleeding money; rocked by scandal and mismanagement, the company was losing hundreds of millions of dollars per year. Mitsubishi Electric sold about 20 percent of its automobile components to Mitsubishi Motors; when Mitsubishi Motors asked members of the *keiretsu* to give it financial help, Nomakuchi promised that Mitsubishi Electric would do so, provided that he approved of Mitsubishi Motors' recovery plans.

See also entry on Mitsubishi Electric Corporation in *International Directory of Company Histories.*

SOURCES FOR FURTHER INFORMATION

"Corporations Racked Up Record Profits in Fiscal '03: More Needed to Lift Nation's Economy Out of Doldrums," *Japan Times*, June 1, 2004, http://202.221.217.59/print/business/nb06-2004/nb20040601a1.htm.

Kunii, Irene M., "Japan Hits the Panic Button: Once-Proud Chipmakers Are Merging for Dear Life," *BusinessWeek Online* May 27, 2002, http://www.businessweek.com/magazine/content/02_21/b3784129.htm.

"Mitsubishi Electric Announces Consolidated and Non-Consolidated Financial Results for Fiscal 2004," Kensei News and Information Services, April 28, 2004, http://www.kensei-news.com/cgi-bin/bizdev/exec/view.cgi/20/23096.

—Kirk H. Beetz

■■■
Indra K. Nooyi

1955–

President, chief financial officer, and director, PepsiCo

Nationality: Indian.

Born: October 28, 1955, in Madras, India.

Education: Madras Christian College, BS, 1976; Indian Institute of Management, MBA, 1978; Yale University, master of public and private management, 1980.

Family: Married Raj K. Nooyi (management consultant); children: two.

Career: Johnson & Johnson and Mettur Beardsell, product manager; Boston Consulting Group, 1980–1986, director of international corporate strategy projects; Motorola, 1986–1988, member of automotive division development team; 1988–1990, vice president and director of corporate strategy and planning; Asea Brown Boveri, 1990–1994, senior vice president of corporate strategy and strategic marketing; PepsiCo, 1994–2001, senior vice president of corporate strategy and development; 2001–, president.

Awards: Named one of the "most powerful women in business" by Fortune magazine.

Address: PepsiCo, Inc., 700 Anderson Hill Road, Purchase, New York 10577; http://www.pepsico.com.

Indra K. Nooyi. © Najlah Feanny/Corbis SABA.

■ As of 2004 Indra Nooyi was the number two executive at the world's number two soft drink maker—a multinational firm that generated nearly $27 billion in sales in 2003. As the highest-ranked Indian American woman in corporate America, Nooyi led some of PepsiCo's most significant strategic moves. The crowning glory in her career was serving as lead negotiator of PepsiCo's $13.8 billion acquisition of the Quaker Oats Company, which led to her being named one of the top five officers at her company. Intensely competitive, the always unique Nooyi helped to position PepsiCo one day to overtake the longtime market leader and PepsiCo's bitter rival, the Coca-Cola Company.

DEFYING EXPECTATIONS

Raised in a middle-class family in India, Nooyi seldom did what people expected of her. Most young girls in India spent their time learning household chores; Nooyi played in an all-girl rock band and on a women's cricket team. She completed the MBA program at one of only two business schools in India and worked at Johnson & Johnson and Mettur Beardsell in India. Around the same time, a magazine advertisement for Yale School of Management caught her eye, and she impulsively applied. Much to her surprise, she was accepted. Even more surprising was the fact that her parents let her immigrate to the United States. Said Nooyi, "It was unheard of for a good, conservative, south Indian Brahmin girl to do this. It would make her an absolutely unmarriageable commodity after that" (*Financial Times*, January 26, 2004). After working in planning strategy at Boston Consulting Company, Motorola, and Asea Brown Boveri, she joined PepsiCo as senior vice president of corporate strategy and development in 1994.

BRINGING FOCUS TO A CONGLOMERATE

Nooyi worked directly with PepsiCo's then CEO Roger Enrico and was involved in every major strategic decision that Enrico made as CEO. One of the key executives behind the company's transformation into a focused food and beverage entity, Nooyi persistently argued for the spin-off of the company's struggling restaurant division, which included Kentucky Fried Chicken, Pizza Hut, and Taco Bell. Enrico was skeptical, but he finally relented. Enrico said that "Indra is like a dog with a bone" (*Forbes Global*, January 20, 2003).

A rabid sports fan, Nooyi spent hours studying videotapes of the final championship games that the basketball great Michael Jordan played with the Chicago Bulls; she reviewed the tapes for lessons on teamwork. Because of her desire to win, Nooyi fought hard for PepsiCo's successful $3.3 billion acquisition of Tropicana in 1998, eyeing the transaction as a vehicle to increase PepsiCo's earnings and enhance its image as a premium brand for convenient foods and drinks. A devotee of the company's orange juice, Nooyi understood before others Tropicana's brand potential, both to increase PepsiCo's earnings and to enhance the company's developing portfolio of convenience and "functional" foods and drinks. Nooyi said, "When other PepsiCo executives continued to question the $3.3 billion acquisition at a final meeting, Roger and I just told them, 'We are going to do it'" (*Contra Costa Times*, December 10, 2000).

In 2000 Nooyi was promoted to CFO and finished the year with four continuous quarters of uninterrupted growth—in revenues, profits, and return on capital. In December of that year, the company's stock price was up 40 percent from the year before. Nooyi described her job—and her commitment to leaving behind a lasting corporate legacy—as an "obsession." Said Nooyi, "I love my family, but PepsiCo's also my child. So really I don't look upon it as a chore. In fact, I find work very therapeutic" (*Business India*, January 8, 2001).

WINNERS HAVE FUN AND TAKE STOCK OF LIFE

Two of Indra Nooyi's bosses at PepsiCo had significant health issues, both of which impacted Nooyi. PepsiCo CEO Wayne Calloway was diagnosed with terminal cancer in 1996. Nooyi's own mentor and boss, Roger Enrico, had a history of heart trouble, which led to his retiring at age 57. Though a self-professed workaholic, Nooyi preferred to keep the mood light. "You must have fun in whatever you do. Your work takes up so much of your life that if you're not having fun, what's the point in it?" (*Business India*, January 8, 2001). She was known to sing around the corporate offices and keep a karaoke

machine at home. Highlighting the on-the-go lifestyle that fuels demand for her company's products, she once commented that she had not realized how precious time was until she noticed a driver on the highway flossing his teeth. A devout Hindu, Nooyi went to temple and prayed regularly.

A CAREER-SHAPING MERGER

In August 2001 PepsiCo purchased the Quaker Oats Company. On the morning that the acquisition was announced, Nooyi went to temple and prayed. During the arduous negotiations, she demanded a limit on the stock price of no more than $105 a share for Quaker shareholders. According to Steven Baronoff, cohead of mergers at Merrill Lynch, which represented PepsiCo, "Throughout the whole process, she was disciplined and held very firm" (*Contra Costra Times*, December 10, 2000).

Adversaries underestimated Nooyi at their peril. Financial professionals greatly admired her strengths and focus. Andrew Conway, a beverage analyst with Morgan Stanley Dean Witter, noted that "Indra is extraordinarily financially detailed. . . . With Tropicana, she was willing to take a lower-return-on-asset business because she saw a way to improve it to get strong margin growth. Her ability to find value in an acquisition is very high" (*Contra Costra Times*, December 10, 2000).

Integrating the two companies was an even tougher challenge—one that would be crucial to determining Nooyi's prized legacy. The integration did not go smoothly at first. The merger of the Gatorade and Tropicana sales forces resulted in a botched sales promotion, and a key Quaker Oats executive left the company. Supermarket sales of Gatorade, Quaker's crown jewel, were up only 7 percent in the last quarter of 2001 compared to the 15 percent pace set by its market peers.

But Nooyi stayed the course, and no obstacle appeared to prevent the acquisition from ultimately succeeding. PepsiCo's total sales grew nearly 7 percent in 2002, boosting the company's annual revenue growth over its historical 6 percent growth rate. In 2003 the company announced that it was on track to realize its goal of achieving $400 million in synergies by the end of fiscal year 2004. Nooyi's next move was unclear as of early 2004. Some industry insiders predicted that she would be moved to another area of the company to gain experience running her own business division. Rather than a step down, the move could ultimately catapult her to a takeover at the top. Even as one of the few women in corporate America's highest echelons, and the only Hindu woman in 2004, Nooyi had an unbeatable attitude: "I'm sure a glass ceiling exists, but it's both transparent and fragile so you can break it" (*Business India*, January 8, 2001).

See also entries on Motorola, Inc. and PepsiCo, Inc. in *International Directory of Company Histories*.

SOURCES FOR FURTHER INFORMATION

McKay, Betsy, "PepsiCo's Nooyi to Add Top Job; After the Acquisition of Quaker Oats Co, the PepsiCo Chief Financial Officer Will Take on More Responsibilities," *Contra Costra Times*, December 10, 2000.

Murray, Sarah, "From Poor Indian Student to Powerful U.S. Businesswoman," *Financial Times*, January 26, 2004, p. 3.

"PepsiCo's Indian Icon," *Business India*, January 8, 2001.

Wells, Melanie, "A General in Waiting?" *Forbes Global*, January 20, 2003, p. 19.

—Tim Halpern

■■■
Blake W. Nordstrom
1961–
President, Nordstrom, Incorporated

Nationality: American.

Born: 1961, in Washington.

Education: University of Washington, 1982.

Family: Son of Bruce Nordstrom (chairman of Nordstrom, Incorporated).

Career: Nordstrom, Incorporated, 1974–1983, stockperson, then salesman in the women's shoe division; 1983–1987, buyer; 1987–1988, merchandise manager for women's shoes for Nordstrom Rack, the Place Two division, and the Alaska stores; 1988–1991, merchandise manager for women's shoes for stores in Washington and Alaska; 1991–1995, vice president and general manager of the Washington and Alaska region, overseeing operations for eight full-line stores, two Nordstrom Rack stores, and the Place Two division; 1995–2000, copresident (along with five brothers and cousins) with responsibilities including operations, the shoe division, and Nordstrom Rack; February–August 2000, president of Nordstrom Rack; August 2000–, corporate president.

Awards: Named one of the 50 most powerful people in Washington, *Washington CEO*, 2004.

Address: Nordstrom, 1617 Sixth Avenue, Seattle, Washington 98101; http://www.nordstrom.com.

■ When Blake Nordstrom took the helm of Nordstrom, Incorporated in the summer of 2000, he represented the fourth generation of the Nordstrom family to run the Seattle-based department store chain. Blake had grown up with the company, and some employees and analysts thought that it was only natural for him to eventually lead it. When he became president, however, Nordstrom was struggling with sagging sales and lowered stock prices. Blake launched an aggressive new strategy that introduced newer computer technology for tracking sales and inventory while reviving the company's long-standing commitment to customer service. Within four years he had not only improved Nordstrom's profitability but had also made plans for expansion.

A FAMILY BUSINESS

Blake Nordstrom was the great-grandson of John W. Nordstrom, a Swedish immigrant who invested the $13,000 he'd made from a gold mine stake in a Seattle shoe store that eventually grew into a nationwide chain of department stores. Even though Blake was a member of the Nordstrom family, however, he did not receive preferential treatment. He worked in the stockroom of the shoe department in Nordstrom's flagship Seattle store at the age of 13, along with several other Nordstrom children. Blake swept the floor and restocked merchandise. "[The Nordstrom children] paid their dues. They worked really hard," said Betsy Sanders, a former Nordstrom vice president, speaking of Blake and his siblings (*BusinessWeek*, July 30, 2001).

By working hard at the lower levels of the company's hierarchy, Blake rose quickly through the ranks from salesman and buyer to merchandise manager and store manager. In 1991 he was named vice president and general manager of Nordstrom's Washington and Alaska region. Four years later he shared the position of president with five other family members—a management experiment in dividing responsibilities. Blake then became president of the Rack Group—a discount store unit—in February 2000, when Nordstrom was reorganized into five separate units. Blake succeeded in raising the sales of the Rack Group by nearly 20 percent within the first few months of his presidency.

THE FAMILY IS BACK IN BUSINESS

As the 21st century dawned, however, Nordstrom was in trouble. Its sales had slowed down and its stock prices had declined. Nordstrom's board of directors even considered merging with another retailer or selling the company. Instead, the long-time chairman John Whitacre resigned—or was ousted, according to some analysts. Whitacre had been with Nordstrom since 1976, when he started out selling shoes while still a student at the University of Washington. He eventually rose to the chairman and CEO position. Although he made great strides in modernizing the company, he shifted away from the traditional customer-focused philosophy and began focusing more on Nordstrom shareholders. When Whitacre resigned as CEO, Blake took the position of president and his father became chairman. The company left the CEO position open and has not since filled it. The board hoped that reinstating the Nordstrom family at the executive level would turn the company around.

Although some managers and salespeople were pleased by the return of Nordstrom family members to executive positions, others wondered whether Blake had sufficient experience at the age of 39 to handle the job of president. Blake and his father assured the analysts, however, that they were carefully reviewing every aspect of the business and were determined to make it profitable once again. When Blake assumed the presidency, he was quoted as saying, "My name's on the door. Every penny I have is in Nordstrom stock" (*Puget Sound Business Journal*, September 29, 2000).

Blake slowed the pace of new store openings in order to focus on Nordstrom's existing stores. He also improved the company's use of technology by investing in speedier cash registers and a computerized inventory system; trimmed the company's inventory; and reemphasized Nordstrom's personalized service culture to bring back disenchanted customers. "We know by giving good service we sell more," Blake told *BusinessWeek* (July 30, 2001). "It's the heart and soul of our business." But even while catering to Nordstrom's customers, Blake also remembered the company's shareholders. He was as serious about raising the price of Nordstrom's stock as he was about improving service.

A NEW BEGINNING

Nordstrom did experience a turnaround over the next three years. Its sales and stock prices had risen measurably by 2004,

which allowed Blake to turn his attention once again to expanding the chain into new locations.

Blake attributed his success to his policy of listening to and supporting his sales force rather than ordering them to perform. "We believe in an inverted pyramid where management is on the bottom and salespeople and customers are on the top," he told *Women's Wear Daily* (March 15, 2002).

In addition to Blake's role in his family's company, he served as president of the Downtown Seattle Association, an organization dedicated to preserving the city's business district.

See also entry on Nordstrom, Inc. in *International Directory of Company Histories*.

SOURCES FOR FURTHER INFORMATION

"The Corporation: Strategies: Can the Nordstroms Find the Right Style?" *BusinessWeek*, July 30, 2001, p. 59.

Spector, Robert, "Nordstrom Is More Than a Name, It's a Culture," *Puget Sound Business Journal*, September 29, 2000, p. 63.

Young, Kristin, "New Nordstrom Blows in L.A.," *Women's Wear Daily*, March 15, 2002.

—Stephanie Watson

■ ■ ■
Richard C. Notebaert

1947–

Chief executive officer and chairman of the board, Qwest Communications International

Nationality: American.

Born: 1947, in Montreal, Quebec, Canada.

Education: University of Wisconsin, BA, 1969; MBA, 1983.

Family: Married Peggy (maiden name unknown); children: four.

Career: Wisconsin Bell, 1969–1983, in marketing and operations; Ameritech Communications, 1983–1986, vice president of marketing and operations; Ameritech Mobile Communications, 1986–1989, president; Indiana Bell Telephone Company, 1989–1992, president; Ameritech Services, 1992, president; Ameritech Corporation, 1993, president, chief operating officer, and vice chairman of the board; 1994–1999, president, chief executive officer, and chairman of the board; Tellabs, 2000–2002, president and chief executive officer; Qwest Communications International, 2002–, chief executive officer and chairman of the board.

Awards: Distinguished Alumnus Award, University of Wisconsin–Milwaukee, 1999.

Address: Qwest Communications International, 1801 California Street, Denver, Colorado 80202; http://www.uswest.org; http://www.qwest.com.

Richard C. Notebaert. *AP/Wide World Photos.*

for Qwest when the situation appeared hopeless. Although he was visionary in terms of what he foresaw his companies providing in services, his business techniques were classic: anticipate developments in the marketplace, cut costs, and organize a company around its customers' needs.

THE COMPANY MAN

Notebaert's career began while he was in college, when he took a job washing trucks. While in college he married Peggy, who was one of the anchors of his life throughout his sometimes tumultuous career. He worked in both marketing and services during the first decade of his career at Ameritech; he began his rapid rise up the corporate ladder when he received his MBA in 1983. It was an opportune time to have earned an MBA because AT&T, which had long held a monopoly on

■ Richard C. Notebaert (pronounced *note*-a-bärt), who was born in Canada but raised in Columbus, Ohio, was a happy warrior, eager to take on new challenges and to mingle with workers, shareholders, and customers to show them his vision of a bright future even during the most miserable of times. A low-key personality, he had the common touch and would converse as easily with blue-collar workers as he did with corporate executives. He was responsible for making Ameritech one of the most successful "Baby Bells" (companies spun off from AT&T in an antitrust settlement), he was credited with saving Tellabs from dissolution, and he staved off bankruptcy telephone communications in the United States, was being broken up into a long-distance carrier and five new local phone companies. One of the new local companies was Ameritech Corporation, which received the states of Illinois, Indiana, Michigan, Ohio, and Wisconsin as its territory. Notebaert quickly became the vice president of marketing and operations for Ameritech Communications, one of the divisions of Ameritech Corporation.

When Notebaert became president of Ameritech Mobile Communications in 1986, the cellular communications industry was just beginning to catch on; through aggressive marketing, he built the customer base of Ameritech's cellular telephone division to 950,000. Near the end of Notebaert's tenure as president of Indiana Bell Telephone Company, in February 1992, William Weiss, Ameritech's chief executive officer and chairman of the board, held a special meeting of the company's management. He had asked each attendee to write about what Ameritech should be doing in the future and then had each read aloud his views during the meeting. Notebaert's presentation caught Weiss's attention with its expansive view of Ameritech's possibilities, advocating that the company develop video conferencing; blend the Internet, telephones, and televisions into one vast interactive service; and offer "quality of life" services, such as safety and security.

At age 45 Notebaert was considered young by the standards of Ameritech executives, but in 1992 Weiss promoted him to president of Ameritech Services, where Notebaert put his ideas to work, beginning a security monitoring service that would have 340,000 customers by 1999. Notebaert proved to be an excellent motivator of employees, communicating with and inspiring even the lowest ranks through open communications and easy accessibility. In January 1993 Weiss and the board of directors of Ameritech named Notebaert vice chairman of the board, and in June 1993 they named him president and chief operating officer of Ameritech, leaping him past many more senior executives. During this period, Notebaert helped expand Ameritech's international operations, including Telecom Corporation in New Zealand and Belgacom in Belgium. Ameritech played a crucial role in the creation of Belgacom, which was the first of Belgium's government monopolies to be privatized.

When Notebaert became president and CEO of Ameritech in January 1994, he took charge of a company that had 12 million local phone customers, 2.5 million cellular customers, and $14.9 billion in annual revenue. Notebaert wanted Ameritech to have a share in the long-distance phone call market, but a court ruling and government regulators, both federal and state, forbade the Baby Bell from selling long-distance services where it had a monopoly on local phone service. Weiss and Notebaert had worked closely together to reorganize Ameritech's corporate structure from five divisions by state to one in which the state operations were merged into a whole and then divid-

ed by product lines, such as local telephone services and cellular services. When Weiss retired on April 20, 1994, Notebaert added chairman of the board to his other offices.

Notebaert hired marketing specialists to run the new divisions of Ameritech, and he changed Ameritech's stodgy style of advertising that emphasized its stability and long heritage to one that targeted specific aspects of the marketplace, such as small businesses, emphasizing Ameritech's high-tech new services. He worked with government regulators as partners, not foes, in opening the marketplace to competition. Notebaert pressed hard to have Ameritech's local telephone territories opened to Ameritech's long-distance telephone services, and he took the daring step of opening Ameritech's five-state territory to local telephone competition. AT&T leaped at the chance and almost immediately began competing for the lucrative Chicago local market. Notebaert hoped that the move to set aside Ameritech's local telephone service monopoly in exchange for a competitive marketplace would encourage regulators and the courts to allow Ameritech to compete for long-distance services. This plan put rural telephone users at a disadvantage because urban telephone income had traditionally subsidized the low-profit rural markets. Notebaert proposed a "universal service fund" that would help keep down rural telephone costs to consumers by having all American telephone companies contribute to it. In spite of these efforts and proposals, regulators refused to allow Ameritech to offer long-distance services in the five-state territory. By the end of 1994 Ameritech had 48,000 employees and had operations in all 50 states and in 40 countries.

In 1995 Notebaert targeted economic development, education, and quality of life for Ameritech's marketing. He hoped to develop services that helped businesses process their sales electronically, that helped people commute electronically by working at home and using telephone lines to connect them to their offices, that helped students attend classes from home through a blend of telephones and computers, and that enhanced the security of people through electronic alarms and swift contact of support and emergency services. Further, he foresaw "electronic government" in which government business could be done with Ameritech Internet services—for example, allowing lawyers to file court briefs electronically. He also wanted voice-activated telephones that allowed a caller just to say a name and have the telephone automatically dial the appropriate phone number; when he found that the Ameritech research and development team was trying to create a voice-activated telephone with a capacity to understand 40 names but already had an inexpensive one that recognized 10 names, he trimmed the research and sent the 10-name telephone to market. During 1995 he cut about 6,000 jobs, saving Ameritech $350 million. He asked regulators to allow Ameritech to keep the savings because regulations at the time forced such savings to be passed on as lower telephone rates—a practice that discouraged corporate efficiency and encouraged bloated corporate bureaucracies.

In spite of Ameritech's inability to offer long-distance services to its local customers, the company's fortunes boomed during Notebaert's tenure, and he became a very rich man. Always busy in local affairs in Chicago, where Ameritech was based, he even donated $5 million to help build the Peggy Notebaert Natural History Museum in 1998; it quickly became a prime destination for visitors to the city. When Ameritech was sold to SBC Communications in 1999, Notebaert received a severance bonus of approximately $21 million. Ameritech had had five straight years of growth under Notebaert's leadership, with a 45 percent growth in revenues. Its market capitalization tripled to $70 billion. Notebaert sold Ameritech to SBC for $72 billion, a windfall for Ameritech's shareholders.

MAKING PROFITS AMID DISASTER AT TELLABS

Notebaert promised his family that he would take some time off from work and spend it with them, but there seemed little doubt that he would take a job again. In August 2000, only 10 months after the sale of Ameritech, the board of directors of Tellabs offered him the offices of president and CEO, and he accepted. The management had hopes of tripling its revenues in the next three years, and the board of directors thought Notebaert had what was needed to guide the company through expansion. Notebaert was known for his combination of creativity and steady leadership, and Ameritech had been a customer of Tellabs, which meant that Notebaert was familiar with Tellabs' products.

Tellabs manufactured parts for communications systems. In 2000 its revenues were $3.3 billion. The dot-com revolution had spawned numerous companies that needed equipment for communications and for hosting Web sites, and the possibilities for electronics communications seemed limitless. But in 2000 the dot-com collapse began, with hundreds of communications and Internet companies going out of business. Surviving companies found themselves with overcapacity—more room for business than there was business to be had. The decline in business meant that many Tellabs customers had already purchased more Tellabs products than they could use, which in turn meant that Tellabs lost business it had counted on.

Tellabs was in danger of going out of business almost as soon as Notebaert settled into his new positions. During the first eight months of 2001, he cut 1,000 jobs at Tellabs, including managers, with 50 employees taking early retirement and the others being laid off. They represented 12 percent of Tellabs' workforce. The labor cuts saved Tellabs $120 million. Notebaert himself cut his pay for 2001 by 26 percent and took no bonuses. Revenues for the year were $2.3 billion, down $1

billion from the year before. In 2002 Notebaert continued to cut jobs, reducing the workforce by a total of 38 percent from 8,900 when he first joined Tellabs to 5,500. "It was awful. You hate firing people—nobody enjoys it—but we did what we had to do," he asserted in 2002 (*Knight Ridder/Tribune News Service*, June 17, 2002).

During Notebaert's tenure at Tellabs, the company's stock dropped from $50 to $10 per share, yet when he left the company, he was praised by those who worked with him, and he was credited not only with saving Tellabs from extinction but also with making it profitable in 2002. He had done "what's right for the business as a whole," he said (*DenverPost.com*, June 23, 2002), and he left the company in sound financial condition, although much smaller than it had been, with $1 billion in cash reserves in the bank. He had accomplished his goals in part by focusing Tellabs on two profitable lines of products: the Titan optical products that helped networks interact and the Cablespan line of cables used in electronic communications. He aggressively pursued sales of Tellabs products globally in 80 countries. When it was announced that he was leaving Tellabs, the company's stock fell 6.76 percent in one day.

THE CHALLENGE OF QWEST

Qwest was America's fourth-largest telephone company, but it was in poor shape. In 1999 it had purchased the local phone service provider U.S. West, nicknamed U.S. Worst for its bad customer service, at a cost of $38 billion. Thereafter, the company was beset by problems, although the true extent of the problems became known only after Notebaert took over control and had the company's financial records examined.

During 2000 and 2001 Qwest's stock price fell 92 percent. It had revenues of $20 billion in 2001, but it also had $26 billion in debt. It was being investigated by the U.S. Department of Justice, the Federal Bureau of Investigation, and the Securities and Exchange Commission (SEC) for falsifying financial reports and perpetrating underhanded schemes that made it look like it was earning money when it was not. In one scheme Qwest sold access to its telephone network to companies that then sold Qwest access to their networks for the same amount of money, meaning that no one actually made a profit; however, Qwest entered the bogus sales into its financial books as income to inflate its reported revenues to fool investors into thinking Qwest was doing better than it really was. CEO Joseph P. Nacchio began fishing around Qwest's Yellow Pages business to potential buyers to bring in enough money to stave off disaster. Qwest was on the verge of bankruptcy when Notebaert joined it.

Nacchio was a flamboyant leader who drew publicity to himself and his company and who had pursued an audacious expansion of Qwest. When the company's board of directors looked for a replacement, they favored the low-key manner and traditional economics represented by Notebaert. The board of directors offered Notebaert $1.1 million in salary plus bonuses that would increase his annual income to $1.69 million, and the directors offered him a $14 million bonus if he remained leader of the company until age 65. In May 2002 rating agencies relegated Qwest's bonds to junk bond status. Yet Notebaert may have relished taking leadership of a huge corporation and the challenge of setting it straight. Still, it is unlikely that he realized just how badly off the company was when he became CEO and chairman of the board on June 17, 2002, and relocated to Denver, Colorado, home of Qwest's headquarters. The company was in danger of collapse at any time during 2002. Its fiber-optics network alone was losing more than $500 million annually.

Qwest stock rose 20 percent the day Notebaert was hired. In July 2002 he removed five Qwest executives from their posts and brought in three executives who had worked with him at Ameritech: Oren G. Shaffer, CFO at Ameritech from 1994 to 2000, was made vice chairman at Qwest; Joan H. Walker, vice president of corporate communications at Ameritech from 1996 to 1999 and senior vice president of global affairs for Pharmacia in 2002 when hired by Notebaert, became senior vice president of corporate communications; and Gary R. Lytle, leader of Ameritech's Washington office from 1992 to 2000, became vice president of policy and law. Shaffer went quickly to work, mending fences by visiting the SEC accountant in charge of the SEC's investigation of Qwest and by auditing the company's books. He found $1.1 billion in phony income listed for 2002.

Notebaert found himself in charge of a company of 56,000 U.S. employees that saw a 14 percent decline in revenue from January to September 2002 and therefore might not be able to meet its payroll. *Fortune* called Qwest "one of the biggest wrecks in America" (January 20, 2003). Notebaert began campaigning among the rank-and-file workers that summer, traveling to meet them in groups, usually small, to tell them of the future he saw for Qwest and to enlist their help, asking wage earners to cut back on the hours they worked. The company's 27,000 union members agreed to forego their scheduled 3 to 4 percent pay increases in exchange for performance bonuses in 2003. Notebaert opened permanent communication between himself and his employees. On the basis of his good name, Notebaert persuaded Bank of America to pull lenders together to lend Qwest $750 million to stave off immediate bankruptcy.

In an action that Notebaert later said he had never done before and hoped never to do again, he pressed Qwest bondholders to forgive much of the debt owed to them. He did this by noting that Qwest could go bankrupt and that those who agreed to exchange their bonds for bonds worth 40 percent less would be placed at the head of the line of investors who would

be paid first from Qwest's assets, implying that those bondholders who did not exchange their notes might get nothing at all if the company died. This tactic angered bondholders, but enough of them accepted the offer to reduce Qwest's bonded debt from $5.2 billion to $3.3 billion. In 2003 some bondholders sued Qwest over the bond restructuring.

By the end of 2002 Notebaert had reorganized Qwest's corporate structure into three units: business customer services, general consumer services, and wholesale marketing. He tried to extend Qwest's long-distance services to the old U.S. West local service territories, but as at Ameritech, regulators refused the plan. As 2003 began Qwest had 25 million customers in 14 states, a formidable customer base if Qwest could dig out from under its debts, but the company lost 4.9 percent of its customers from June 2002 to June 2003. Due in May were $3.2 billion in debts that Notebaert and Shaffer managed to persuade debt holders to restructure into longer-term payments. In 2003 Notebaert sold Qwest's Yellow Pages for $7 billion, which was applied to debts. Both Qwest's $16 billion fiber-optics network of 190,000 miles of lines and its long-distance network (in areas where Qwest offered no local phone service) were losing money, and financial analysts suggested that Qwest should sell them, but Notebaert saw them as part of a profitable future and insisted that Qwest hang on to them. He reduced the fiber-optics network from 14 servers to seven because the network was not receiving enough customers to use more than seven; he then moved the fiber-optics network into the jurisdiction of the corporation's business unit. Notebaert shaved off costs even further by cutting 3,500 jobs during 2003. By the end of 2003 Qwest had lost perhaps $470 million for the year on $14.3 billion in revenue but had reduced its overall debt to $16 billion.

These results were achieved not only by cuts but also by new strategies. Notebaert changed the focus of business services from large corporations to midsize businesses, exploiting a new (for Qwest) market. He formed a partnership with Sprint for national wireless service, giving Qwest a big share of the cellular phone market. Part of his strategy rejected the possible sale of Qwest and rejected the possible acquisition of smaller companies; Notebaert pursued alliances such as that with Sprint to expand Qwest's markets without incurring more debts. He placed emphasis on good customer relations and would pose as a consumer to call Qwest customer service representatives to make sure they were delivering good service. Overall, he gave his employees the impression that he was always involved in the company's day-to-day business and that he cared about them and their work.

During 2003 Notebaert was appointed by President George W. Bush to the National Security Telecommunications Advisory Committee, where he worked to establish standards for new communications technologies and to find ways to secure America's communications networks from sabotage by terrorists. When Notebaert accepted his appointments at Qwest, he and his wife moved from Chicago to Denver, although they kept an apartment in Chicago so that they could visit with family and friends. In Denver they were active in the United Way and other local charities.

See also entries on Ameritech Corporation, Qwest Communications International, and Tellabs, Inc. in *International Directory of Company Histories.*

SOURCES FOR FURTHER INFORMATION

Gilbert, Nick, "The Best Defense: Ameritech Plans to Keep Home Field Advantage as the Free Market Comes to Phone Service," *Financial World*, October 11, 1994, pp. 48–51.

Griffin, Greg, "Qwest Woes Dwarf Past Challenges," *DenverPost.com*, June 23, 2002, http://www.denverpost.com/Stories/0,1413,36%257E689404,00.html.

Mehta, Stephanie N., "Now the Honeymoon's Over: Dick Notebaert Pulled Qwest Back from the Brink of Bankruptcy. Here Comes the Hard Part," *Fortune.com*, January 20, 2003, http://www.fortune.com/fortune/ceo/articles/0,15114,405981,00.html.

Patch, Kimberly, "Ameritech's Goal: Anything Customers Want," *PC Week*, February 13, 1995, pp. 103–104.

Samuels, Gary, "A Meeting at the Breakers," *Forbes*, June 20, 1994, pp. 51–55.

Van, John, "Tellabs Won't Waver Without Notebaert, Chairman Says," *Knight Ridder/Tribune News Service*, June 17, 2002.

—Kirk H. Beetz

■■■
David C. Novak
1953–
Chairman, president, and chief executive officer, Yum! Brands

Nationality: American.

Born: 1953.

Education: University of Missouri–Columbia, BA, 1974.

Career: Tracey-Locke BBDO, ?–1986, various positions leading up to executive vice president; PepsiCo, 1986–1990, senior vice president of marketing for Pizza Hut; 1990–1992, executive vice president of marketing and national sales for Pepsi-Cola; 1992–1994, COO of Pepsi-Cola North America; 1994–1996, president and CEO of KFC North America; 1996–1997, group president and CEO of KFC and Pizza Hut; Tricon Global Restaurants, 1997–1999, vice chairman and president; 1999–2001, CEO and president; 2001–2002, chairman, CEO, and president; Yum! Brands, 2002–, chairman, CEO, and president.

Address: Yum! Brands, 1441 Gardiner Lane, Louisville, Kentucky 40213; http://www.yum.com.

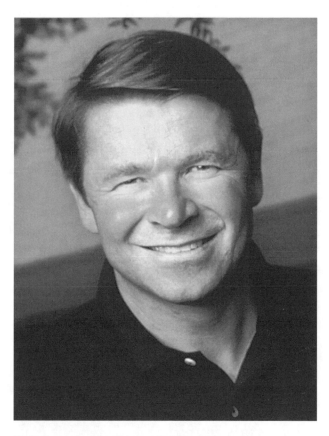

David C. Novak. *John Chiasson/Getty Images.*

■ David C. Novak was the chairman and CEO of Yum! Brands, an independent, publicly owned fast-food franchiser that in 2004 was made up of six subsidiaries organized around five core restaurants: Pizza Hut, KFC, Taco Bell, Long John Silver's, and A&W All-American Food. Pizza Hut, KFC, Taco Bell, and Long John Silver's were the global leaders in the quick-service pizza, chicken, Mexican, and seafood categories, respectively. Serving its signature frosty-mug root beer drinks since 1919, A&W All-American Food was the longest-operating quick-service U.S. franchise chain. Due greatly to Novak's creative management and organizational style, Yum! Brands' global sales totaled more than $24 billion in 2002.

FROM PEPSICO TO TRICON TO YUM! BRANDS

Novak started his career in the advertising field, holding leadership positions over a 20-year period primarily with the advertising agency Tracey-Locke BBDO (now TLP Tracey Locke Partnership). There he eventually reached the position of executive vice president, as which he supervised client relationships, including those with PepsiCo and Frito-Lay. Novak later held similar positions at Pizza Hut, PepsiCo, and KFC. Starting in 1986 he became senior vice president of marketing at Pizza Hut, reaching the same position at PepsiCo in 1990. In 1992 he became chief operating officer of Pepsi-Cola North America. Novak became president of KFC's North American operations in 1994 and group president and CEO of the North American operations of both KFC and Pizza Hut in 1996. He became president and vice chairman of the board at Tricon Global Restaurants when it came into existence on October 7, 1997, as a result of a spin-off from PepsiCo, which had owned and franchised the KFC, Pizza Hut, and Taco Bell brands worldwide. Novak served in these capacities until December 1999.

NOVAK AT THE HELM

Novak was named the chief executive officer of Tricon Global Restaurants in January 2000, succeeding Tricon's first CEO Andy Pearson; a year later, on January 1, 2001, Novak became Tricon's chairman. During Pearson's time as CEO, he and Novak worked together closely in focusing on three main goals: to correct the management problems left over from the company's time under PepsiCo, to increase the competitiveness of its four operating companies, and to capitalize on opportunities for multibranding, international growth, and increased scale.

During this time span, first under Pearson and later under Novak, Tricon's performance dramatically increased with respect to profit and sales growth, debt payment, margin improvement, return on investment, and employee commitment. In fact, Novak's excellent grasp of the nature of the CEO position allowed Pearson to bring him up to the top management spot earlier than had been expected. Pearson called Novak a driving force behind Tricon's great performance—with a remarkable grasp of the company's business, outstanding skills as a conceptual management leader, and superior operating expertise. Appropriately, in a 1999 press release, upon stepping down from the top position, Pearson said of Novak, "David is the most effective leader I have ever worked with" (November 15, 1999).

UNITING A NEW COMPANY

Novak immediately faced an ominous challenge in uniting the global fast-food brands of KFC, Pizza Hut, and Taco Bell. The three individual companies were floundering and, just as seriously, were mutually suspicious of each other's management styles. By utilizing the same people-friendly attitude, quality-service standards, comprehensive vision, and product innovations that he had used to help turn KFC around in the mid-1990s, Novak took and molded the three restaurants into a cohesive partnership with division leaders who cooperated with rather than competed against one another.

Novak was able to transform the company with regards to its franchisee relationships; in retrospect, Novak was considered to be the mastermind and architect of Tricon's successful and profitable one-system company. In the first five years following the spin-off, Tricon increased systemwide sales by 8 percent, more than doubling operating earnings per share, and improved return on invested capital by 10 percentage points.

HYPERCOMPETITIVE AND GENEROUS

Novak's skillful management tactics were credited with influencing the cultural shift that was eventually incorporated into Tricon. He was characterized as wearing many hats during the changeover: those of captain, friend, mentor, politician, and team player. Novak was described by many observers as a man so hypercompetitive that he frequently went "for the jugular" when urgency called for such action. As quoted in an article in *Brandweek*, John Neal, the president of JRN who operated one hundred KFC units, said of Novak, "He is one of the most competitive leaders that I have ever sat across the table from. He will beat you whether in golf, poker, or basketball. He just isn't going to lose" (October 11, 1999).

Novak's competitiveness, however, was grounded in a leadership style that was also generous when it came to recognizing and rewarding individuals who had performed well. Rather than dictating the manner in which work should be done, Novak used a "buy-in" approach to accomplish projects with a team attitude. In 1995, when he was working exclusively for KFC, he used one thousand autographed rubber chickens to generate employee, supplier, and manager support around a new employee-recognition program. Pizza Hut and Taco Bell then instituted their own employee-recognition programs centered around the Big Cheese and the Royal Order of the Pepper Awards, respectively.

Such concepts, according to Novak, helped company employees create positive experiences each and every time a customer entered their restaurants. Novak remarked that these tactics, which he constantly reinforced, had far greater long-term impact on brand perceptions than even television advertisements. In general Novak called this approach "Customer Mania," saying that it improved the method with which each restaurant interacted with its customers and "put a 'Yum' on their faces all around the world" (YUM.com).

YUM! BRANDS CREATED

In March 2002 Tricon declared that it would be acquiring the Lexington, Kentucky–based Yorkshire Global Restaurants as well as its two brands: Long John Silver's and A&W All-American Food. At that time Novak announced the company's intention to change its name to Yum! Brands in order to better reflect its expanding portfolio of restaurants as well as its New York Stock Exchange ticker symbol, YUM. On May 7, 2002, the Yorkshire acquisition was finalized, showing the extent to which Novak and the company were committed to multibranding. On May 16, 2002, a vote during the company's annual shareholders meeting officially changed the company's name from Tricon Global Restaurants to Yum! Brands. In 2002 the company's U.S. sales totaled $7.78 billion, as produced by a workforce of 244,000 employees.

LONG-TERM STRATEGY

Novak's Yum! Brands, a Fortune 300 company, had become one of the largest quick-serve restaurant companies in the world, trailing only McDonald's in sales. Yum! Brands did eventually grow to the point where it outnumbered its hamburger competitor in terms of system units, with nearly 33,000 units in more than one hundred countries and territories. The company owned and operated about one-fifth of its stores, franchising the remainder.

Under Novak's direction the company's long-term strategy built on Yum! Brands' foundation as a worldwide brand franchiser. Novak's five areas of long-term focus, which were considered essential to the company's growth and progress, included multibrand expansion, international expansion, the company's portfolio of category-leading U.S. brands, worldwide franchise fees, and strong cash generation and returns.

MULTIBRANDING

Novak instituted multibranding, a concept that provided consumers with more choices and convenience at a single location hosting a combination of KFC, Taco Bell, Pizza Hut, A&W All-American Food, or Long John Silver's restaurants. Under Novak, Yum! Brands became the worldwide leader in multibranding with over 1,800 domestic multibranded restaurants, representing nearly 10 percent of total traditional U.S. units. Over two thousand multibranded restaurants worldwide generated nearly $2 billion in annual sales, and in 2002 Yum! Brands was opening three new restaurants outside the United States each day. In addition Novak bought into a portion of Yan Can, the start-up casual, quick-service Asian restaurant chain.

Novak directed the development, operation, licensing, and franchising of a system of both traditional and nontraditional units in each of the company's brands. Nontraditional units included kiosks and express units that had a more limited menu and operated in nontraditional locations like airports, amusement parks, colleges, gas and convenience stores, and stadiums, where traditional, full-scale outlets would not be efficient or profitable.

STRESSING DIVERSITY

Under Novak's direction Yum! Brands was named one of *Fortune* magazine's 50 Best Companies for Minorities for its comprehensive adherence to key diversity measures. This honor was bestowed upon Yum! Brands based on the survey that appeared in *Fortune*'s July 7, 2003, issue. The authors of the article described how surveyors measured minority representation throughout organizations in such categories as the

board of directors, the 50 highest-paid executives, purchasing from minority firms, diversity training, recruitment and retention, and charitable contributions to minority organizations.

The results showed that Yum! Brands led all companies for managerial diversity and was ranked among the top 10 companies having the highest percentage of African American employees. In all, 54 percent of the company's U.S. workforce, including 53 percent of recent hires, comprised minorities. Novak remarked in a press release that "Yum! Brands' commitment to diversity helps drive all aspects of our business" (June 26, 2003). He further stated that the company's diversity strategy included leadership development, purchasing, franchising, and community involvement.

PHILANTHROPY EFFORTS TARGET MINORITIES

Novak was actively involved in Yum! Brands' philanthropy efforts targeting minorities. In 2002 the company almost tripled its charitable contributions to minority communities and the volunteer involvement of its employees through initiatives such as the Dare to Care Food Bank, based in Louisville, Kentucky. Yum! Brands committed one million dollars annually to the Food Bank; two-thirds of that total would help the Food Bank in supporting upwards of 46,000 undernourished children in minority communities lacking in resources.

Novak, through Yum! Brands, also supported charitable organizations such as the National Association for the Advancement of Colored People, the League of United Latin American Citizens, the National Urban League, the National Council of LaRaza, the National Minority Supplier Development Council, the MultiCultural Foodservice and Hospitality Alliance, the National Minority Franchising Initiative, the American Indian College Fund, and the U.S. Pan Asian American Chamber of Commerce.

See also entry on Yum! Brands Inc. in *International Directory of Company Histories*.

SOURCES FOR FURTHER INFORMATION

Howard, Theresa, "Quick-Serve Artist: David Novak's Fast-Food Empire," *Brandweek*, October 11, 1999.

"Message from Andy Pearson Announcing David Novak's Promotion to CEO," November 15, 1999, http://www.yum.com/news/111599.htm.

"Yum! Brands Recognized in Fortune's Top 50 'Best Companies for Minorities' and Takes Number-One Spot for Managerial Diversity," June 26, 2003, http://www.yum.com/news/062603.htm.

—William Arthur Atkins

Erle Nye

1938–

Former chairman and chief executive officer, TXU Corporation

Nationality: American.

Born: June 1938, in Fort Worth, Texas.

Education: Texas A&M University, BS, 1959; Southern Methodist University, JD, 1965.

Family: Son of a veterinarian (name unknown); married (wife's name unknown).

Career: Texas Utilities Company, 1960–1987, various management positions; 1987–1995, president; 1995–1997, chief executive officer and president; 1997–1999, chairman and CEO; TXU Corporation, 1999–2004, chairman and CEO; 2004–2005, chairman.

Awards: Honorary Doctorate, Baylor College of Dentistry, 1997; Distinguished Citizen Award, Longhorn Council of the Boy Scouts of America, 1998; Dallas Father of the Year Award, 1998; Humanitarian of the Year, American Jewish Committee, 1999; C. W. Conn Distinguished New Venture Leader Award, Mays College and Graduate School of Business, 2001; Robert G. Storey Award, Southern Methodist University, 2002; Distinguished Leader Award, Texas Association of Business, 2002.

Address: TXU Corporation, Energy Plaza, 1601 Bryan Street, 33rd Floor, Dallas, Texas 75201-3411; http://www.txucorp.com.

■ Erle Nye rose to become the chairman and chief executive officer of TXU Corporation (formerly Texas Utilities Company), the diverse energy company based in Dallas, Texas. Under Nye's reign TXU at one time served the energy needs of customers not only in Texas but in England and other European countries as well as parts of Australia. Optimistic and confident in his outlook, Nye's vision was to integrate gas and electrical utilities when possible, with the goal of consolidating energy generation, delivery, and service.

Nye attended Texas A&M University in College Station, Texas, where he earned a bachelor's degree in electrical engi-

neering; he then earned a degree in law at Southern Methodist University in Dallas, Texas. As soon as he graduated in 1960, he took an entry-level engineering position with Texas Utilities (TU). The son of a veterinarian, Nye had a love of horseback riding and ranches. He worked hard to succeed at his company by focusing his energies on a wide variety of issues, including finance, law, operations, and regulatory guidelines.

EXPANDING BEYOND THE BORDERS OF TEXAS

When Nye started working for Texas Utilities, the company operated strictly on a regional basis, delivering electricity to customers in the state of Texas. TU was the umbrella company for both TU Electric and Southwestern Electric Service. In 1996 Nye was instrumental in merging TU with the natural gas company Enserch Corporation and its subsidiaries, which were involved in the processing and marketing of natural gas as well as in independent power production. After the merger TU became the primary utility company in northern Texas.

As the 1990s progressed Nye initiated an expansion program at Texas Utilities—which changed its name to TXU Corporation in 1999—leading to the purchase of utility companies throughout Europe as well as one in Australia. TXU doubled the value of its assets between 1996 and 2000, from $20 billion to $40 billion; in the same period of time the company tripled revenues from its gas and electric divisions. Nye also saw opportunities in telecommunications, and TXU expanded to include the company Lukin-Conroe in its operations. TXU's successful expansion across three continents pleased Nye, who believed his company had the opportunity to grow even further and become one of the most prosperous international energy firms in the world.

However by 2002 Nye's grandiose plans began to fall apart. In 2001 wholesale prices declined sharply in Britain due to newly introduced regulations, leading TXU to reduce its profits forecast. In addition to its pricing problems TXU fought to keep customers who were being given a greater number of choices for energy providers. Nye initiated aggressive money-saving plans that entailed restructuring the company, ending development, and laying off some employees. Unfortunately these measures proved ineffective at halting the UK division's problems; TXU agreed to sell that division to the German-owned company Powergen in October 2002 to ease its debts.

PULLING IN THE REINS

By February 2003 Nye's plans were completely in ruins. The UK operation had been forced to file for bankruptcy in late 2002. Shareholders saw their dividends get cut by nearly 80 percent, from $2.40 to $0.50. TXU was forced to report $4.2 billion in losses for 2002, whereas only two years earlier the company had reported a profit of $655 million. Nye's words to Sudeep Reddy of the *Dallas Morning News* revealed the effect that the company's failure had on him: "It's painful. I will always remember it. But I think it provides us a clear path ahead and a promising one" (February 6, 2003). In response to the company's dismal peformance Nye took a cut in compensation of more than $5.5 million.

In early 2003, having survived the company's worst-performing years, Nye announced his plans for retirement and his intention to handpick his successor. Unlike several contemporary energy-company CEOs who found themselves caught up in investigations for fraud, Nye had steered TXU through turbulent times and emerged with his own and the company's reputations intact. Hoping to finish his career on an upbeat note, Nye summed up his desire to pick the next chief executive in a statement made to Mitchell Schnurman of the *Fort Worth Star-Telegram*: "It's my last opportunity to do something really good for the company" (May 7, 2003).

In early 2004 Nye named John Wilder, formerly the chief financial officer at Entergy Corporation in New Orleans, Loui-siana, to be his replacement as president and CEO. Nye's tenure as chairman of the board for TXU ended in 2005. As of his departure TXU was the gas and electricity provider for 2.6 million customers in North Texas as well as one million customers in Australia.

SOURCES FOR FURTHER INFORMATION

Koo, Carolyn, "Texan Stands Out among Energy Firm CEOs," *Houston Chronicle*, July 12, 2002.

Piller, Dan, "TXU Chairman to Get 75 Percent Cut in Compensation Pay," *Fort Worth Star-Telegram*, February 16, 2003.

Reddy, Sudeep, "After Nearly $5 Billion Loss, TXU Corp. to Concentrate on Core Texas Business," *Dallas Morning News*, February 6, 2003.

———, "A Year after Stock Dive, the Chairman Reports a 'Sense of Renewal,'" *Dallas Morning News*, September 13, 2003.

Schnurman, Mitchell, "Retiring TXU Chief Executive Seeks Own Replacement, Repair to Tarnished Legacy," *Fort Worth Star-Telegram*, May 7, 2003.

—Eve M. B. Hermann

■■■

James J. O'Brien Jr.

1955–

Chairman and chief executive officer, Ashland Inc.

Nationality: American.

Born: 1955, in Circleville, Ohio.

Education: Ohio State University, BBA, 1976.

Career: Ashland Chemical Company, 1976–1992, management positions of increasing responsibility in Foundry, Specialty Polymers, and General Polymers; 1992–1994, executive assistant to the chairman and CEO; Ashland Petroleum Company, 1994–1995, vice president and general manager of branded marketing; Ashland Inc., 1995–2001, president of Valvoline and vice president of Distribution and Specialty; 2001–2002, senior vice president and group operating officer; 2002, president and COO; 2002–, chairman and CEO.

Address: Ashland Inc., 50 East River Center Boulevard, P.O. Box 391, Covington, Kentucky 41012-0391; http://www.ashland.com.

■ The transportation and chemical-materials executive James J. O'Brien Jr. was the CEO and chairman of the Covington, Kentucky-based Ashland. O'Brien was employed by the company beginning in 1976 and during his 28-plus years there gained an enormous amount of experience in most of Ashland's operations, including petroleum, chemicals, and motor-oil marketing.

ASHLAND

Ashland, a Fortune 500 company, was an oil-products and specialty-chemical company that provided services, products, and solutions for the chemical, construction, energy, and transportation industries. The company operated in the United States and in over 120 countries around the world through four wholly owned divisions: Ashland Paving and Construction (APAC), which paved streets and built bridges, mostly in the midwestern and southern United States, and supplied as-

phalt and highway materials to the construction and transportation industries; Ashland Distribution, which bought plastics and chemicals, then mixed and repackaged them for distribution in North America and Europe; Ashland Specialty Chemical, which produced specialty adhesives, chemicals, and polymers and resins for water treatment; and Valvoline, which operated an oil-change chain comprising over 600 outlets and marketed Zerex antifreeze and Valvoline motor oil.

BACKGROUND WITH ASHLAND

O'Brien began his employment with what was then known as Ashland Chemical Company in 1976. During the next 16 years he took on managerial assignments of increasing responsibility within the Foundry, Specialty Polymers, and General Polymers divisions. In 1992 O'Brien was named executive assistant to John R. Hall, then Ashland's chairman and CEO; for two years O'Brien left the well-known operations side of Ashland's business in order to assist Hall through what was a globally unstable political and economic period for the petroleum-refining industry.

In 1994 O'Brien was hired as the vice president and general manager of branded marketing for Ashland Petroleum Company. At this time he took on the difficult assignment of revitalizing Ashland's branded gasoline-marketing operations. In 1995, when the company changed its name to Ashland, O'Brien was promoted to president of Valvoline, the smallest division, as well as corporate vice president. With sales having fallen below projected performance rates over the preceding few years, O'Brien refocused Valvoline's operations and developed an improved and very successful brand strategy that entailed building a competitive management team to concentrate on enlarging the product line into new, expanding markets. Specifically, O'Brien guided the branded-product line into the European and Chinese markets, purchased the Eagle One brand of waxes and car-care products, and launched a new development laboratory responsible for products such as Valvoline Max Life motor oil.

In November 2001 O'Brien was named senior vice president and group operating officer for two of Ashland's divisions: Distribution and Specialty Chemicals. As group operating officer he was responsible for developing new initiatives that would revise the Distribution division's business model

214

with the goals of bettering efficiency, increasing revenues, and restoring returns. At the same time O'Brien sharpened the Specialty Chemical division's market focus in order to achieve more growth from its existing product lines.

In October 2002 O'Brien began to serve as president, chief operating officer, and member of the board of directors for Ashland. In these positions O'Brien's areas of responsibility included chemical operations and their related support units, such as the European shared-services center. He also supervised corporate functions, including business-development, environmental, health-and-safety, and human-resources operations. Within the month O'Brien became CEO, succeeding Paul Cheligren. In November 2002 he became chairman.

FOCUSING A TURNAROUND

When he took over its leadership position, O'Brien decided to transform Ashland into a better-focused, more energetic company so that it could once again deliver reliable results to shareholders and superior products to customers. At this time many financial analysts who covered the company were hopeful that O'Brien would turn Ashland around as he had done with Valvoline—which had gone from being Ashland's smallest divisions to one of its best performers.

TROUBLING TIMES

However, as O'Brien began his reign at Ashland, troubling times were plaguing the company as well as the oil industry in general. The possibility of war with Iraq had brought the supplies and prices of oil and all of its derived products into a state of uncertainty. With this global uncertainty came a disappointing 2002 fiscal year, in which Ashland's sales fell 2 percent to $2.1 billion and net earnings fell 61 percent to $47 million. Disappointments continued into the first quarter of 2003, when O'Brien announced a loss of $92 million.

Ashland shareholders were also troubled for some time with regards to asbestos litigation that had hampered Ashland over recent years. After an analysis was performed on past insurance claims, O'Brien increased the amount of money within the company's asbestos reserves by $95 million in order to relieve those concerns. O'Brien was happy with the company's management of its asbestos liability over the preceding 15 years but admitted that estimates on future claims could prove to have been low.

PROFITABILITY-IMPROVEMENT PLAN

During his first couple of years at Ashland's helm, O'Brien transformed the company from one whose business revolved strictly around oil to one involved in a wider array of transpor-

tation, chemical, and oil businesses. Its products and services were far ranging, encompassing Valvoline motor oil, water-purification chemicals, and highway construction along with a joint venture with Marathon Ashland Petroleum. However, management at Ashland had been unable to get these various groups of products and services to work together smoothly. O'Brien remained optimistic when he detailed a profitability-improvement plan at the company shareholders' meeting in January 2003. He assured listeners that he would direct the company to sharpen its focus, increase efficiency, and deliver greater value to its shareholders. With the help of movements in the right direction that had been made by his predecessor, O'Brien aimed to further restructure the company so that Ashland could realize its full potential.

After his statement to the board O'Brien cut about 450 jobs from Ashland's global workforce of 24,300 employees. He also restricted future commitments to the Ashland Foundation, a project initiated to improve the communities in which offices were based, although he promised to continue with the commitments to which the company had previously agreed.

REDUCING DEBT

O'Brien aimed to reduce the company's debt-to-capital ratio from 45 to 35 percent, mostly through the discontinuation of acquisitions. His profitability plan entailed research on whether portions or the entirety of the Distribution unit, along with particular assets of the Specialty Chemicals and APAC divisions, would need to be sold in order to improve profitability and allow the company to become more focused on processes within existing markets.

O'Brien directed a major restructuring of Ashland's distribution business in order to bring marketing activities together into regional territories and place businesses such as the North American and European Plastics Distribution operations under one management team. In August 2003 O'Brien completed the sale of Ashland's Electronic Chemicals business group to the Allentown, Pennsylvania–based Air Products and Chemicals in a cash transaction valued at approximately $300 million. In addition the Brenntag and Solvadis companies were sold from within the Distribution division.

O'Brien next sold the company's stake in its joint venture with Marathon Oil Corporation. The 38 percent interest that Ashland had controlled in Marathon Ashland Petroleum, the country's fifth-largest refiner and marketer of petroleum products, was sold for about $3 billion in 2004. The action ended Ashland's involvement in oil refining and gasoline retailing, the latter of which had included the company's line of Speedway gasoline stations. O'Brien also completed the sales of two other businesses to Marathon Oil, including 61 Valvoline Instant Oil Change centers in Michigan and northwest Ohio and operations concerning maleic anhydride, the starting material used in the formulation of resins within the chemical, paint, plastics, and food industries. As a result of these last major actions—which were expected to be finalized at the end of 2004 with cash inflows of about $2.7 billion—O'Brien was able to concentrate solely on Ashland's primary businesses of road construction, specialty chemicals, lubricants, car-care products, chemicals and plastics distribution, and transportation fuels. The company's brands included Eagle One appearance products, Pyroil performance products, Valvoline motor oils, and Zerex antifreeze. The last sale eliminated the vast majority of Ashland's outstanding debts of $2 billion and gave the company cash credit of about $500 million.

2004 RESULTS

Due to O'Brien's measures in cutting costs and refocusing core businesses, Ashland's stock price rose about 75 percent in 2003. O'Brien decided it would then be appropriate to add complimentary businesses in order to expand the company's core chemical, transportation, and construction divisions. O'Brien hoped to focus on creating a balanced mix of interrelated operations in order to improve profitability among all of its wholly owned businesses. He wished to achieve growth while delivering a more predictable and stable overall performance throughout the company.

VOLUNTEERING AND SERVING

O'Brien served his alma mater, Ohio State University, as a member of the Dean's Advisory Council for the Fisher Graduate College of Business. He was a volunteer big brother with Big Brothers/Big Sisters of the Bluegrass in Lexington, Kentucky; he also served on the organization's national board of directors. He was a member of the American Chemistry Council, the American Petroleum Institute, and the National Petroleum Refiners Association. He was a member of the board of directors for Fifth Third Bank and the Cincinnati Zoo; chairman of the board of trustees for Midway College in Midway, Kentucky; and a member of the Association of Governing Boards of Universities and Colleges. O'Brien was a graduate of the 1994 class of Leadership Kentucky, a nonprofit educational organization that brought together people possessing a variety of leadership abilities, career accomplishments, and volunteer expertise in order to gain insight into the issues facing the state.

See also entry on Ashland Inc. in *International Directory of Company Histories.*

SOURCES FOR FURTHER INFORMATION

"Directors and Officers," Ashland Inc. Web site, http://www.ashland.com/ashland/directors_officers.asp?selid=4.

"Our Milestones," Ashland Inc. Web site, http://www.ashland.com/ashland/our_milestones.asp?selid=2.

"Vision, Mission, and Values," Ashland Inc. Web site, http://www.ashland.com/ashland/mission_vision.asp?selid=1.

—William Arthur Atkins

■ ■ ■
Mark J. O'Brien
Chief executive officer and president, Pulte Homes

Nationality: American.

Career: Pulte Homes, 1984–1997, employee; 1997–1998, COO; 1998–2002, president; 2002–, CEO and president.

Address: Pulte Homes, 100 Bloomfield Hills Parkway, Bloomfield Hills, Michigan 48304; http://www.pulte.com.

■ Mark J. O'Brien worked his way up through the Pulte Homes organization to become the president and chief executive officer of the large builder in 2002. He steered Pulte Homes into new markets, helping the company that had yet to show a loss throughout its existence continue to grow. Under his leadership the company ranked as one of the top three companies in the J. D. Power and Associates customer-satisfaction poll year after year, and O'Brien was constantly looking for new ways to increase Pulte's rating.

O'Brien joined Pulte Homes in 1984, which was founded in the early 1950s and incorporated in 1956; by 2004 the company was the largest home builder in the United States. After 13 years with Pulte, O'Brien became chief operating officer in 1997 and then president in 1998. In January 2002 he took over the additional role of chief executive officer. A top analyst noted in the *Wall Street Transcript*, "I think he will do an outstanding job as CEO of Pulte. All indications so far are that O'Brien is going to be a very capable replacement for Robert K. Burgess and a very capable CEO for Pulte" (March 14, 2002).

In 2000 O'Brien worked to acquire two retirement communities in Banning and Brentwood, California, for Pulte to develop. These gains were expected to raise the profits from the retirement home portion of Pulte by 25 percent or more and brought the company into a prominent position in a new market. In 2001 Pulte Homes merged Del Webb into its operations, forming the biggest, most lucrative home builder in the United States. Meanwhile Pulte received the highest marks for customer satisfaction in four out of 10 markets by the J. D.

Power and Associates New-Home Builder Customer Satisfaction Study of 2001. The company was voted number one in Charlotte, North Carolina; Denver, Colorado; and Las Vegas, Nevada and placed second in Houston, Texas; Chicago, Illinois; and San Diego, California. Together with the newly acquired Del Webb, Pulte Homes ranked as one of the top three home builders in seven of the 10 markets surveyed.

After the J. D. Powers report was released, *Realty Times* reported O'Brien as saying, "Exceeding customer expectations and providing a quality product remain the foundation of Pulte Homes' 'Homeowner for Life' strategy. Our goal is to ensure that a similar standard of customer satisfaction, as reflected in the J. D. Power and Associates results, is achieved throughout our operations" (September 27, 2001). In 2001 O'Brien was asked to join the National Advisory Council of Fannie Mae.

After the terrorist attacks of September 11, 2001, some of the top builders in the country, including Pulte Homes, conferred and resolved to each donate $1 million to a Home Builders Care Victims Relief Fund. The fund was set up to assist all of the victims of the attacks, including families, rescue workers, and others disturbed by the tragedy.

In 2002 business was looking slower for the home-building industry as a whole. O'Brien was optimistic, however, telling *Builder* magazine, "Even before the slowdown, it was clear that the size of the industry itself isn't really growing. We have a dominant position in all our markets. We want to get larger market shares in larger markets" (December 2001). On February 25, 2002, O'Brien tried something at Pulte that not many builders had done at the time: he held a Webcast of the company's Investors' Conference, sharing information with anyone who was interested in domestic home building, retirement communities, housing-market opportunities, and Pulte's growth strategies; O'Brien hoped that Pulte's openness would win them more clients.

In 2002, thanks to low interest rates, the building market for Pulte Homes boomed. O'Brien told the *Detroit News*, "We're obviously enjoying good times. If we've done our work effectively, we'll continue to return the benefits to shareholders" (November 29, 2002). Pulte Homes was the only publicly traded company in Michigan to garner an A+ grade in *Detroit News* 2002 Serving the Shareholders report. That year Pulte was also named Builder of the Year by *Professional Builder* magazine, and O'Brien and his colleagues Anne Mariucci and Henry DeLozier were collectively named among the top 10 people or groups of people with the most influence over the golf industry. As the trio was listed alongside such golfing greats as Tiger Woods and Jack Nicklaus, the recognition showed how important Pulte's role in building and designing golf courses was to the sport—something O'Brien had been emphasizing ever since his ascendancy to the position of president.

Through 2003 Pulte Homes had shown a profit for 51 straight years, a record of which O'Brien noted few companies could boast. The company as a whole was credited with always being willing to change, pushing into new markets, new states, and new kinds of constructions. O'Brien stated in the *Detroit News*, "At the end of the day, we're a big-ticket consumer-products company. It's our absolute belief that if we don't deliver quality products and have happy customers, we'll vanish. We intend to be relevant" (November 29, 2002).

Mainly because of his entrepreneurial attitude O'Brien was called "the new number one among the Giants" of the home builders by Heather McCune on the HousingZone Web site (April 1, 2003). That year Pulte was named one of the top three builders in 17 of the 21 market areas polled by J. D. Power and Associates. By 2004 Pulte had become the leading builder of retirement communities and also owned a mortgage corporation that was committed to meeting consumers' financial needs, offering a large assortment of loans as well as top-quality customer service. Pulte operated in over 40 markets across the United States, Argentina, Puerto Rico, and Mexico. In the latter half of 2004 O'Brien intended to work on further expanding Pulte Homes, adding an extra tier of management and increasing the company's operational geographic areas from six to 11. As of 2004 Pulte was building around 23,000 homes a year.

See also entry on Pulte Homes, Inc. in *International Directory of Company Histories.*

SOURCES FOR FURTHER INFORMATION

Brown, Lori, "Pulte Homes Dominates J. D. Power Customer Satisfaction Poll," HoustonHomeCenter.com, 2001, http://www.houstonhomecenter.com/centers/news/stories/story5.asp.

Dobbs, Lou, and Richard Wagoner, "Focus on the Fundamentals: Housing, Auto, and Energy Executives Assess Their Industries," *Money*, February 1, 2002, p. 59.

Dreier, R. Chad, "From the Top: Big Builders' Take on the Year Ahead," *Builder*, December 2001, p. S11.

Dybis, Karen, "Pulte Stands Alone with A+ Grade," *Detroit News*, November 29, 2002, http://www.detnews.com/2002/business/0211/29/h08-22282.htm.

Guido, Daniel Walker, "O'Brien Rules," *Builder*, March 2002, p. 27.

"Hires and Fires: Dec. 31, 2001–Jan. 4, 2002," *Forbes.com*, January 5, 2002, http://www.forbes.com/2002/01/05/0105hires_print.html.

"Industry Movers and Shakers," *Builder*, March 2001, p. 16.

"Mark J. O'Brien Was Assigned to the National Advisory Council of Fannie Mae," *Multi-Housing News*, August 2001, p. 7.

McCune, Heather, "Beyond the Numbers," HousingZone, April 1, 2003, http://www.housingzone.com/topics/pb/management/pb03da001.asp.

"Meet the 25 People Who Have the Clout—and Will Shape the Future of the Industry," KemperSports, June 2002, http://www.kempersports.com/media/press/golfinc/July_2002.htm.

"Nation's Largest Home Builders Announce $10 Million Fund to Aid Those Affected by Terrorist Attacks," PR Newswire, September 24, 2001, http://ir.centex.com/ReleaseDetail.cfm?ReleaseID=103902&RELTYPE=General.

"Off the Record: A Top Analyst Praises Pulte Homes' Management Team," *Wall Street Transcript*, March 14, 2002, http://www.twst.com/notes/articles/pab700c.html.

"People," *Crain's Detroit Business*, January 14, 2002, p. 13.

Perkins, Broderick, "Pulte Wins New Satisfaction Survey," *Realty Times*, September 27, 2001, http://realtytimes.com/rtnews/rtcpages/20010927_survey.htm.

"Pulte Acquiring Two Communities," *National Mortgage News*, March 13, 2000, p. 27.

"Pulte Homes to Webcast Investor Conference," *Business Wire*, February 22, 2002.

"Pulte Names O'Brien CEO," *Business Journal–Phoenix*, January 3, 2002, http://www.bizjournals.com/phoenix/stories/2001/12/31/daily25.html.

Richmond, Iris, "Added Tier: Pulte Restructures for Growth," *Builder Online*, July 1, 2002, http://www.builderonline.com/Industry-news.asp?channelID=59&sectionID=66&articletype=1&articleID=1000025351.

Smith, Jennette, "Pulte Chief to Retire: President to Be New CEO," *Crain's Detroit Business*, January 29, 2001, p. 53.

"The Straight Dope," *Builder*, March 2001, p. 54.

—Catherine Victoria Donaldson

Robert J. O'Connell

1943–

Chairman, chief executive officer, and president, Massachusetts Mutual Life Insurance Company

Nationality: American.

Born: May 16, 1943, in New York City, New York.

Education: Fordham University, BA, 1965; University of Pennsylvania, MA, 1966.

Family: Married Claire M. Costantini; children: two.

Career: Fairfield University, 1966–1970, assistant professor of economic history; New York Life Insurance Company, 1970–1986, vice president; 1986–1989, senior vice president; American International Group (AIG), 1989–1991, senior vice president in group-management division; 1991–1999, CEO and president of AIG U.S. Life Companies and senior vice president; Massachusetts Mutual Life Insurance Company, 1999–2000, CEO and president; 2000–, chairman, CEO, and president.

Address: Massachusetts Mutual Life Insurance Company, 1295 State Street, Springfield, Massachusetts 01111-0001; http://www.massmutual.com.

■ Robert J. O'Connell served as chairman, chief executive officer, and president of Massachusetts Mutual Life Insurance Company (MassMutual), a diversified financial-services firm. He utilized his background in economics to understand the forces surrounding the financial and insurance industries and apply them to MassMutual's advantage. O'Connell was known for his ability to make excellent management decisions, keeping MassMutual profitable even during the financial downswing and mutual-fund scandals of 2003. He was described by employees and managers as a strong, experienced executive who rewarded innovative ideas.

STUDYING MARKET FORCES

Before entering the corporate world, O'Connell intensively studied the historic underpinnings of economics at the Univer-

sity of Pennsylvania, where he obtained a master's degree in European economic history. His studies helped him develop a keen ability to analyze the multiple forces affecting the financial and insurance markets. Through his examination of the historical events that altered long-standing institutions, O'Connell learned that technological changes often drove social progress, which knowledge led him to welcome innovation and new technologies as they emerged in the financial industry. Additionally, through study of the long-term effects of economic policies, O'Connell learned that a leader—whether king, president, or chief executive officer—must always look at the potential ramifications of any and all policy decisions.

CAREER BUILDING

After finishing his studies, O'Connell began his career as an assistant professor of economics at Fairfield University. He taught for several years then chose to stop simply analyzing companies and market forces and join the corporate marketplace. He used the very principles he had taught to his students to spend the next 30 years successfully moving up the corporate ladder in the insurance business. His combination of corporate experience and economic knowledge would eventually make him an excellent candidate to run a large insurance and financial-services company such as MassMutual.

EVALUATING THE BENEFITS OF CHANGE

Upon becoming the CEO of MassMutual in 1999, O'Connell created a business plan designed to keep the company profitable and evaluated corporate structural changes as they arose. In 2003 the CEOs of other financial-services companies—such as John Hancock Financial Services—believed that their companies needed to become publicly traded and increase in size in order to compete in the growing industry. O'Connell did not feel it necessary to either become a holding company or go public to be successful; rather he felt that going public would divide the company's loyalties between policyholders and shareholders, leading to confusion with respect to goals and strategic planning.

O'Connell also believed it to be important for the 150-plus-year-old company to retain both its name and its reputation by avoiding mergers for the sake of growth. He did not rule out mergers and acquisitions as tools to enter global markets but did avoid engaging in mergers simply to increase MassMutual's size. O'Connell's aversion to such mergers was commended by Arthur Fliegelman, the senior vice president at Moody's Investor Service, who remarked in the *Boston Globe* that he felt MassMutual to be "plenty big for most reasonable purposes. It is clear that the biggest companies are not always the most effective or best-run companies" (October 1, 2003). As an alternate strategy O'Connell focused on the basic economic principle that if one builds a good, solid product that customers want, one can compete effectively against even the largest of companies. O'Connell created growth at MassMutual through the provision of new products and innovative services.

INTERNATIONAL GROWTH

In order to expand into the overseas insurance and financial businesses, O'Connell did acquire several small, successful international insurance companies. He felt that uniting his firm with a foreign market's known companies would ease entrance into the international market and maximize early profits. MassMutual expanded into Southeast Asia in 2000 by acquiring the Hong Kong-based CRC Protective Life Insurance Company, covering Malaysia, Thailand, and the Philippines. O'Connell worked toward global expansion as opportunities arose instead of following a short-term plan for rapid growth. By 2003 MassMutual had developed operations in Bermuda, Chile, Hong Kong, Japan, Luxembourg, and Taiwan. As evidence of the success of O'Connell's approach, during 2003 MassMutual's worldwide insurance sales increased by 7 percent.

LEADING THROUGH INDUSTRY SCANDAL

In 2003 the mutual-fund industry was rocked by a scandal centered around the financial benefits or commissions received by agents for leading clients to certain funds. There were also several high-profile cases of insider trading. In order to counter the industry's bad press, O'Connell supported a change in regulations that would provide consumers with more information about mutual funds, fees, and brokering commissions. Additionally O'Connell required that MassMutual brokers not invest more than $50 million in any one company, such that the mutual funds would not be so severely impacted by the one company's fortunes. Evidence of the wisdom of this strategy could be seen in the 2003 annual report: MassMutual's major businesses achieved substantial growth and profitability, with the value of total assets under management increasing by 19 percent. O'Connell was able to keep his firm's core values of integrity, trust, and community support strong while provid-

ing new products, expanding globally, and avoiding large mergers. In fact in 2003 MassMutual moved up the Fortune 500 list to number 84 from 104 and advanced to number two in its industry category in the magazine's list of the Most Admired Companies in America.

CLIENT-CENTERED EDUCATION

In addition to his support of increasing transparency industrywide, O'Connell ensured that MassMutual created a series of programs, resources, and brochures to educate the company's own current and potential clients. He formed partnerships with 60 major colleges and universities to create local family-business centers and a Family Business Enterprise that provided networking and resources for clients who ran such businesses. In addition to its sponsorship of those centers MassMutual produced guides, workbooks, videos, and an interactive CD-ROM on the intricacies of running family businesses. Through such educational programs O'Connell increased MassMutual's presence in clients' day-to-day financial lives and enhanced their understanding of insurance options.

REACHING OUT TO THE COMMUNITY

Under O'Connell's direction MassMutual focused on community outreach, also largely through educational programs. In 2002 O'Connell developed a program that moved beyond educational materials and into more direct community support: the innovative LifeBridge program offered eligible working parents of low-income families free 10-year life-insurance policies. The goal of the program was to protect the children's abilities to obtain education by insuring the lives of their parents. If a parent were to die during the term of the policy, the death benefits would be paid into a trust to be used for the child's education. In addition to the LifeBridge program O'Connell and MassMutual continued to promote education through the creation and support of academic-achievement programs and through new educational models promoting success in public schools.

MANAGEMENT SKILLS

In his role as MassMutual's CEO, O'Connell became known as a strong, experienced manager who was not afraid to implement innovative ideas. He used his experience and economic knowledge to make excellent management decisions that protected MassMutual's reputation during scandals and kept the firm profitable during fragile economic times. He led his employees to focus on clients and develop ideas that would assist those clients in understanding their own insurance and financial needs. O'Connell emphasized core principles of ethical conduct for himself and for all others in the company. On the whole O'Connell's management skills kept MassMutual strong and competitive in a time when the financial-services industry was undergoing many fundamental changes.

See also entry on Massachusetts Mutual Life Insurance Company in *International Directory of Company Histories*.

SOURCES FOR FURTHER INFORMATION

Bailey, Steve, "Steve Bailey Downtown: Taking Another Look at the Road Not Taken," *Boston Globe*, October 1, 2003.

O'Connell, Robert, "MassMutual Financial Group—CEO Interview," *Your World with Neil Cavuto*, January 7, 2004.

—Dawn Jacob Laney

■■■
Steve Odland
1959–
Chairman, chief executive officer, and president, AutoZone

Nationality: American.

Born: 1959, in Minneapolis, Minnesota.

Education: University of Notre Dame, BA; Northwestern University, MA.

Career: Quaker Oatmeal Cereals, 1995–1996, general manager of U.S. Food Division; Sara Lee Corporation, 1996–1998, senior vice president of snacks division; 1997–1998, president of bakery foods service division; Tops Markets, 1998–2000, CEO and president; Ahold USA, 2000–2001, COO; AutoZone, 2001–, chairman, CEO, and president.

Address: AutoZone, 123 Front Street, Memphis, Tennessee 38103; http://www.autozone.com.

■ Steve Odland was the chairman, chief executive officer, and president of AutoZone, the largest auto-parts and accessories retailer in the nation, with more than $5 billion in sales and 45,000 employees throughout the United States and Mexico as of 2004. One of the first orders of business for Odland when he took control of AutoZone in 2001 was to institute tougher ethical standards and practices throughout the corporation. Odland stressed to all company employees the importance of conducting business with honesty and integrity, whether dealing with the board of directors or customers.

EDUCATION AND EARLY CAREER

Odland and his family moved to Denver when he was six years old. While attending high school, Odland worked as a stocker for King Soopers, a local grocery store chain. He also spent a summer interning in the accounting department for the *Rocky Mountain News*. In 1976 Odland left to attend college at Notre Dame where he earned a degree in business administration. After earning a bachelor's degree from the University of Notre Dame and a master's degree from the J. L.

Kellogg School of Management at Northwestern University, Odland continued to work at a variety of jobs in the grocery business. He served as vice president and general manager of the U.S. Food Division of Quaker Oats Cereals between 1995 and 1996; general manager of the snacks division for Sara Lee Corporation between 1996 and 1998; and CEO and president of the Tops Markets chain between 1998 and 2000. From 2000 to 2001 Odland was chief operating officer of Ahold USA, the U.S. subsidiary of Royal Ahold, the Dutch conglomerate that operated supermarkets and specialty food shops around the world. In 2001 Odland joined AutoZone as chairman, chief executive officer, and president.

APPLES, ORANGES, AND AUTO PARTS

Odland assumed control of AutoZone when the United States was in the midst of a sluggish economy, which weakened sales and lowered profits. The increasing complexity of automobiles also hurt AutoZone, since larger numbers of potential customers lacked the expertise to work on their own vehicles. Undaunted by these difficulties, Odland seemed the perfect fit to revive AutoZone's fortunes. The fast-paced, ever-changing grocery industry offered little time for deliberation and less room for error; Odland's ability to adjust quickly, efficiently, and purposefully to fluid market conditions served him well as the head of the auto-parts retailer.

Odland dismissed concerns about the complexity and improved quality of modern automobiles, noting that people were keeping their cars longer and driving them more; extensive age and mileage made them ripe for repair. Upon taking the helm at AutoZone, Odland immediately sought to change the company's merchandising strategy. He cited statistics revealing that the average AutoZone customer visited the store only six times a year, spending less than $100 in that time period. On average 80 percent of customers purchased only one or two items per visit; 20 percent left the store without having made a purchase at all. Odland set out to increase the numbers of both customer visits and transactions per visit.

Where some saw only problems, Odland saw merchandising opportunities. At a Lehman Brothers' retail conference held in May 2001, he outlined five proposals to improve sales: first, remind customers of the safety risks involved in not performing basic maintenance; second, emphasize products that improved the appearance of older vehicles; third, appeal to customers' pride of ownership by aggressively marketing accessories that enabled them to customize their vehicles; fourth, advertise products designed specifically for the owners of light trucks, minivans, and sport-utility vehicles, which tended to be driven harder than automobiles and required more extensive repairs using more expensive parts; and fifth, prominently display such items as air fresheners, tools, and sunglasses that consumers often bought on impulse. Odland wanted each store to "micromerchandise"—that is, to carry slightly different products suited to its particular clientele. He insisted that stores unfailingly provide excellent customer service and that sales personnel be knowledgeable about the products on the shelves and auto repair in general so as to supply expert advice.

Odland raised AutoZone's annual advertising budget to approximately $20 million in an effort to create strong national brand identification in a generally regional and fragmented market. In an interview with Jeffrey Kutler of *Institutional Investor* Odland noted, "We can double the size of this industry simply by reminding people through advertising to do more maintenance" (February 2003). He introduced a new slogan for the company that had a special appeal for younger customers who thought of their vehicles as extensions of themselves and who considered themselves to be trendy, capable, and smart: "Get into the zone—AutoZone!"

IN THE ZONE

Two years into Odland's tenure at AutoZone's helm, the company showed a total revenue increase of 11 percent, to $5.3 billion. The value of AutoZone stock tripled, as the company acquired a 12 percent share of a crowded market; none of AutoZone's thousands of competitors even approached a double-digit market share. In fiscal 2002 alone profits soared 68 percent. In *Institutional Investor* John Lawrence of the brokerage firm Morgan Keegan & Company remarked, "AutoZone has been one of the best performers in all of retail. Its stores' productivity is up, returns on capital are impressive, and it has plenty of leverage to keep moving forward" (February 2003). Even Odland marveled at the success enjoyed by the company. In addition to the overwhelmingly positive financial news and stock forecasts, the business seemed impervious to recession and depression. During hard times, Odland noted, people would tend to retain their vehicles even longer, and millions turned to AutoZone to keep them running. By 2003, 50 percent of the 225 million motor vehicles on American roadways were seven years old or older—an increase of 33 percent since 1983. Odland called them "OKVs," short for "Our Kind of Vehicles" (*Institutional Investor*, February 2003).

Odland further bolstered AutoZone's success by ridding the company of unprofitable subsidiaries. Shortly after taking control he sold the struggling truck-parts division and reduced the number of new-store openings. Still, in each of 2001 and 2002 AutoZone added one hundred new stores; in 2003 that figure was increased to 150. Besides looking after the financial welfare of his company, Odland anticipated changes in corporate governance. Months before the accounting scandals at Enron and MCI became public knowledge, Odland instituted a strict code of business ethics for executives, managers, and general employees alike at AutoZone.

BUSINESS ETHICS 101

Odland emphasized the ethical obligations of salespeople, managers, executives, and the board of directors to both customers and shareholders, believing that the only sure way to guarantee a company's continued value was by upholding honesty and integrity in its business practices. As such Odland averred that effective and trustworthy corporate governance required the implementation of five key elements.

First was the development of clear and consistent guidelines to spell out what was expected of employees, explain how the company was to operate, and determine how the board of directors was to conduct business and monitor its activities. To that end Odland instituted a confidential, toll-free hotline at AutoZone for employees to report theft or other improper behavior in the workplace. He also assured them that they faced no reprisals for lodging complaints, even against superiors.

The second of Odland's key elements was the creation of an independent board of directors. He restructured the 10-member board by removing four AutoZone executives and replacing them with people who had no connection to the company outside of the required ownership of stock. Odland himself remained the only insider. Third was the establishment of a group of officers to verify company finances; fourth was the "regular, frequent, and rigorous" reviewing of company finances; and fifth was the hiring of employees at every level of company operations who adhered to the standards of conduct stated in company guidelines. In an interview with *BusinessWeek* Odland told David Liss, "You must hire the right people. If you hire crooks, they'll steal"; Odland also saw leadership as vitally important, noting that employees needed to "be led from the top of the company to do the right thing and to behave with the highest ethical standards" (May 16, 2003).

A CULTURE OF SHARED RESPONSIBILITY

Odland spared no effort in making the success and integrity of AutoZone the personal responsibility of every employee. Financial accountability fell upon all company executives, not only those in the accounting department. Every month vice presidents, senior vice presidents, and the CEO met to review the books; weekly conferences of the executive committee supplemented the monthly meetings. Similarly if one division within the company faltered, Odland involved everyone in finding the cause of and rectifying the problem. He told Liss that the company was "dependent on the success of the business as a whole, not on the success of individual parts" (May 16, 2003).

The emphasis on honesty, integrity, and responsibility may not have directly affected the financial success of AutoZone, but such an attitude certainly did not hurt the company's performance. As of 2003 AutoZone's sales growth was approximately four times higher than that of the auto-parts industry as a whole. Odland estimated that the company could still build and operate thousands of additional stores at a profit. Moreover AutoZone conducted $500 million worth of annual business in the sale of auto parts to commercial dealerships and repair shops. Already first in the retail sale of auto parts to consumers, by 2003 AutoZone occupied third place in the commercial auto-parts market, behind Napa and Carquest. With an annual growth rate of between 5 and 6 percent from 1994 to 2004, the auto-parts business presented an ideal environment for economic expansion. By all accounts Steve Odland positioned AutoZone to take full advantage of that opportunity.

See also entries on AutoZone, Inc. and Tops Markets LLC in *International Directory of Company Histories.*

SOURCES FOR FURTHER INFORMATION

"AutoZone Names Odland CEO/Chairman," *Automotive Marketing*, February 2001, p. 9.

"AutoZone's Trendsetting Governance," *Corporate Board*, July–August 2002, p. 32.

Battle, John, "AutoZone's New CEO Brings 'Super' Marketing Expertise to Job," *Aftermarket Business*, 111/2, February 2001, p. 8.

Liss, David, "AutoZone's '40-Headed CEO,'" *BusinessWeek Online*, May 16, 2003, http://www.businessweek.com/bwdaily/dnflash/may2003/nf20030516_8961.htm.

"Odland Presents AutoZone as Solutions Source," *Aftermarket Business*, June 2001, p. 1.

"Pedal to the Metal: Regardless of Economic Conditions, America's Top Auto-Parts Dealer Stays in the Fast Lane," *Institutional Investor*, February 2003, pp. 23–24.

—Meg Greene

Adebayo Ogunlesi

1953–

Head of global investment banking, Credit Suisse First Boston

Nationality: Nigerian.

Born: 1953, in Nigeria.

Education: Oxford University, BA, 1976; Harvard University, MBA, 1978; LLB, 1979.

Family: Married Amelia Quist (optometrist); children: two.

Career: U.S. Supreme Court, 1980–1983, clerk; Cravath, Swaine & Moore, 1983, associate; First Boston, Incorporated, 1983–?, associate; ?–1993, head of project finance group; 1993–1997, managing director of global energy group; Credit Suisse First Boston, 1997–2002, managing director of global energy group; 2002–, head of global investment banking and company director.

Awards: Seventh Most Powerful Black Executive, *Fortune*, 2002; International Center of New York Award, 2003.

Address: Credit Suisse First Boston, Incorporated, 11 Madison Avenue, New York, New York 10010; http://www.csfb.com.

■ Adebayo Ogunlesi was an innovative investment banker who arranged financing for $20 billion worth of industrial projects in a career that spanned over 20 years with Credit Suisse First Boston (CSFB). Many of his clients were governments and firms developing energy resources in emerging markets. In 2002 Ogunlesi became the head of CSFB's global investment banking division with 1,200 bankers and $2.8 billion in assets under his supervision.

BREAKING BARRIERS

Adebayo Ogunlesi, called "Bayo" by family and friends, was born in Nigeria in 1953, the son of the first Nigerian-born professor of medicine to earn tenure at a medical school in his own country. Ogunlesi went to England in the 1970s to study philosophy, politics, and economics at Oxford University,

where he earned a bachelor's degree with honors. He was accepted by Harvard Law School as one of three foreign students in his class, even though the school did not usually admit students who had been born and educated outside the United States at the time. At Harvard, Ogunlesi and W. Randy Eaddy became the first two editors of African descent to serve together on the prestigious *Harvard Law Review*.

Ogunlesi also enrolled at the Harvard Business School at the same time that he was studying law. Although he did not intend to pursue a business career, he thought that courses in finance would help him overcome his fear of numbers. He finished his MBA program in 1978 and earned his law degree *magna cum laude* in 1979. Ogunlesi then served as a law clerk for U.S. Supreme Court Justice Thurgood Marshall from 1980 to 1983. He was the first non-American ever to clerk at the nation's highest court.

In 1983 Ogunlesi became an associate of the prestigious New York law firm Cravath, Swaine & Moore after having worked for the firm as an intern. He had been practicing law for only nine months, however, when he was called by First Boston, an investment bank. The bank was helping the Nigerian government finance a $6 billion liquefied natural gas project. Its contact in Nigeria was a personal friend of Ogunlesi. The bankers at First Boston asked Cravath, Swaine if they could borrow Ogunlesi for three months to facilitate the deal.

MOVING TO FIRST BOSTON

Three months at the investment bank turned into 20 years. Ogunlesi's superiors at First Boston were pleased with his work and offered him a permanent position even though his homeland was in turmoil. He told the *New York Times* on one occasion, "Six months after I got here, there was a coup in Nigeria, the government got tossed out and my friend almost went to jail" (March 14, 2002). He rose through the ranks at First Boston from associate to head of the project-finance group. Ogunlesi spent much of his time traveling through countries regarded as emerging markets, where he brokered deals among lenders, governments, and firms developing such large projects as oil refineries, natural gas plants, and mines. The lenders recovered their investments from the proceeds of the projects funded.

Ogunlesi built First Boston's project-finance business into the world's largest by using "money-spinning innovations"

(*New York*, May 27, 2002) such as off-balance sheet financing and raising money through public debt markets. In off-balance-sheet financing, companies use sources other than equity or debt offerings to raise money; these sources can include joint ventures, operating leases, and research and development partnerships in which two companies, or a company and a university, share costs and resources to develop new products. Off-balance-sheet financing subsequently gained popularity in the 1990s. By raising money through public debt markets, companies could borrow money for longer terms than they would get from commercial lenders.

Ogunlesi was soon promoted to managing director of the project-finance group at First Boston. Over time his team absorbed several others, including the power, oil and gas, and chemicals groups. In 1993, this amalgamated unit was officially renamed the "Global Energy Group," but was informally dubbed "The Bayosphere." Known for his competitive spirit, Ogunlesi installed a foosball table in his office and had his name painted on one of the goalies—his way of saying that he was taking on the competition.

KEY PROMOTION

In 1997 First Boston was acquired by the Credit Suisse Group and renamed Credit Suisse First Boston, or CSFB. Ogunlesi became the head of the new firm's global investment banking division in 2002 at the age of 48. At that time global investment banking was one of CSFB's most influential divisions, employing 1,200 bankers and managing $2.8 billion in assets. Ogunlesi was also given seats on the bank's board of directors and its powerful 15-member operating committee. The chief executive of CSFB, John J. Mack, praised the new appointee in a press release. "Bayo Ogunlesi is a banker of powerful intellect, integrity and innovation. He has a broad global perspective and keen understanding of complex financial transactions. Our clients worldwide have benefited greatly from his strategic insight" (February 20, 2002). Another colleague put it more simply, "He's the smartest guy in the room" (*New York Times*, March 14, 2002).

Other accolades quickly followed the news of Ogunlesi's appointment. *Time* magazine named Ogunlesi to its "2002 Global Influentials" list of the 15 most-promising young executives, while *Fortune* ranked him as the "Seventh Most Powerful Black Executive" in the United States.

Ogunlesi's first task after his promotion was to cut costs in the investment banking division, which had lost nearly $1 billion the previous year. The division was overstaffed as well as ineffective. Ogunlesi furloughed 300 bankers and 50 managing directors in the first few weeks of his new job. He also asked the remaining staff to accept pay cuts and reduce expenses. His economy measures showed some success when the bank's revenues in the following quarter increased by 25 percent.

NEW CHALLENGES

The early years of the twenty-first century brought more difficult challenges. First, a bear market that started in 2000 made new financing difficult to find. Next, off-balance-sheet financing lost public favor when the energy company Enron abused the technique in order to hide its debts and risky investments, which contributed to its collapse in the winter of 2001. Still another scandal erupted in 2002, when some analysts at CSFB and other large brokerage firms were accused of openly giving some stocks a "buy" rating while secretly telling their larger clients to steer clear of them. CSFB and nine other firms eventually paid out $1.4 billion in 2003 to settle the charges without admitting guilt. Ogunlesi told New Zealand's *Dominion Post* that new rules had been enacted to create a "very clear separation" between equity market research and investment banking functions. Those rule changes would limit future conflicts of interest and "help restore confidence" in broker recommendations (May 13, 2003).

In addition to Ogunlesi's work at CSFB, he served as cochair of the Global Economic Forum's 2003 Africa Economic Summit and as an informal adviser to the President of Nigeria, Olusegun Obasanjo. Ogunlesi also raised funds for education and African charities.

SOURCES FOR FURTHER INFORMATION

"CSFB Names Tony James Chairman of Global Investment Banking and Private Equity; Adebayo Ogunlesi to Become Head of Global Investment Banking," press release, February 20, 2002, http://www.csfb.com/news/html/2002/february_20_2002.shtml.

Gregory, Sean, "Adebayo Ogunlesi: CSFB's Global-Banking Chief. His Road from Nigerian Doctor's Son to Wall Street Boss Has Crossed Oil Fields, the Supreme Court and a Rifle or Two," *Time*, December 2, 2002, pp. 56–57.

Sorkin, Andrew Ross, "Accidental Investment Banker Shakes Up Credit Suisse Unit," *New York Times*, March 14, 2002.

Thomas, Landon Jr., "The New Color of Money," *New York*, May 27, 2002, pp. 32–35, 50.

Weir, James, "World Markets May Be on the Way Up," *Dominion Post* (Wellington, New Zealand), May 13, 2003.

—Kris Swank

■■■
Minoru Ohnishi
1925–
Fuji Photo Film Company

Nationality: Japanese.

Born: October 28, 1925, in Japan.

Education: Tokyo University.

Family: Sokichi Ohnishi and Mitsu (maiden name unknown); married Yaeko Yui, 1951; children: two.

Career: Fuji Photo Film Company, 1948–1964, employee; 1964–1968, executive vice president of U.S. subsidiary; 1968–1976, manager of export-sales division; 1976–1980, managing director, then senior managing director; 1980–1996, president; 1996–2003, chairman and CEO; 2003–, chairman.

Awards: Honorary Doctorate, Clemson University; Hall of Fame, International Photographic Council; Cruzeiro do Sol, Order of Orange-Nassau; and Leadership Award, National Association of Photographic Manufacturers in the United States.

Address: Fuji Photo Film Company, 26-30, Nishiazabu 2-Chome, Minato-Ku, Tokyo 106-8620, Japan; http://www.fujifilm.co.jp.

Minoru Ohnishi. © *Tom Wagner/Corbis SABA.*

■ Minoru Ohnishi first joined the Fuji Photo Film Company in 1948. During his long, successful career with Fuji, Ohnishi rose through a variety of managerial positions in both the United States and Japan. In 1980 he became president of Fuji Photo Film and was eventually credited with turning the company into a global leader in the photography and imaging industry. Ohnishi was born on October 28, 1925, in Hyogo, Japan. He graduated from the School of Economics at Tokyo University. After beginning his career with Fuji in 1948, he married Yaeko Yui in 1951. They had two sons.

STANDS UP TO AMERICANS

Ohnishi's first major career challenge came in 1964 when he was chosen to be the executive vice president of Fuji's first U.S. branch in the Empire State Building in New York City

where he was one of only six employees. During the 1960s Eastman Kodak Company dominated the American photography market; Ohnishi was credited with helping to open that market to Fuji. His time in America was formatively important, as the knowledge he gained with regard to Eastman Kodak and American politics and economics proved very beneficial when he moved up the corporate ladder.

One situation in which the knowledge gained by Ohnishi proved particularly helpful was in the court case Eastman Kodak filed against Fuji through the World Trade Organization (WTO) in 1993. Ohnishi mounted a blunt, impassioned criticism of Kodak's contentions that Fuji, in cooperation with the Japanese government, had set up unfair import policies to ensure Fuji's near monopoly of the Japanese film market. Although Ohnishi's public rebuke of Kodak was seen by many as un-Japanese in its forcefulness, he was ultimately vindicated when the WTO ruled that Fuji had committed no infractions, thus allowing Fuji to maintain a strong lead in its domestic Japanese market.

In 1980, after being promoted through the managerial ranks of Fuji—he served as manager of the export-sales division from 1968 to 1976 and also as director, then managing director, then senior managing director between 1972 and 1980—at age 55 Ohnishi was appointed president of Fuji, as which he implemented a visionary strategy to make the company a global force while expanding its line of products and services. During Ohnishi's first year Fuji saw unprecedented growth, including a 400 percent increase in consolidated sales over the prior year.

TECHNOLOGICAL VANGUARD

One of Ohnishi's greatest successes was his recognition—long before many other corporate leaders—of the impending industry shift to digital photography at the end of the 20th century. Ohnishi pursued a somewhat dangerous strategy, furthering the market for digital photography and thus potentially decreasing the market for Fuji's best-known product: film. While many of his colleagues disagreed with his emphasis on digital imaging—instead advocating a loyal reliance to the company's established lines of photosensitive products—Ohnishi was steadfast and funneled billions of dollars into the research and design of digital cameras, analog-to-digital hybrids, and imaging technologies.

During his presidency Fuji successfully repositioned itself as a digital—not just film-based—company and eventually grew to be considered one of the major forces in digital photography and imaging. One of the groundbreaking technologies that emerged from the company's research was the Super CCD, a small image-capturing chip employing octagonal pixels, which provided a dramatic increase in resolution over standard rectangular pixels and decreased the overall size of devices.

REACHES THE TOP

From 1996 to 2003 Ohnishi served as chairman and chief executive officer of Fuji Photo Film Company. During his 23 years of leadership as president and then as CEO, Fuji continuously experienced laudable growth and profitability; the company's growth was especially impressive when measured against Japan's economic depression and the increased tax rates of the late 1990s. By 2003 Fuji had secured 70 percent of the Japanese film market and had made dramatic gains in shares in a variety of international markets—most notably Europe, the United States, Brazil, and China. Ohnishi stimulated Fuji's necessary evolution from a film- and camera-based company into a holistic information-management and imaging company.

Indeed, in Fuji's 1998 shareholders report Ohnishi called his general strategy an Imaging and Information (I&I) philosophy. He stated that the I&I philosophy "presents us with two challenges: that of continuing to improve our image-capturing, recording, and reproductions systems, and that of creating systems that combine electronic imaging and computer technologies, facilitating the quick and easy manipulation, transmission, and utilization of high-quality images in a range of applications" (1998).

From 1980 to 2003 Ohnishi made a variety of large-scale strategic moves in order to realize what he perceived to be Fuji's full potential, initiating a number of key acquisitions and ventures. In 1987 he established Fuji Magnetic in Germany; in 1988 Fuji Photo Film in South Carolina; in 1990 Fujifilm Microdevices Company; in 1995 Fujifilm Imaging Systems in China; in 1996 Fujifilm Electronic Imaging in England; and in 1997 Eurocolor Photofinishing in Germany. Under his direction Fuji bought a majority share in Fuji Xerox Company, furthering Fuji's ability to tap the document-management market. In 2002 Fuji outbid Kodak to acquire Jusphoto Company, one of Japan's leading film-processing chains, further solidifying Fuji's stronghold in its domestic market.

By 2003 Ohnishi had successfully manifested his transformative vision. Fuji boasted a diverse, high-tech product line that enabled image production, dissemination, and management for individual, scientific, and corporate ends. In addition to traditional photosensitive materials Fuji produced digital cameras, digital printers, minilab systems for the developing of film and paper, medical-imaging products, motion-picture film, software, and nanotechnologies. Ohnishi's leadership facilitated and necessitated innovation, research, globalization, and efficiency, resulting in a substantial increase in profits—between 1980 and 2003 Fuji more than quadrupled yearly sales; between 1997 and 2004 productivity increased by 50 percent; and by 2004 Fuji employed over 70,000 people worldwide. During his tenure Ohnishi also showed a commitment to environmental protection. The International Organization of Standardization certified many of Fuji's production facilities around the world, including all four of its Japanese facilities, as environmentally sound.

OUT OF THE DARK ROOM

In 2003 Ohnishi retired as Fuji's CEO and retained the job of chairman of the board of directors, a nonvoting position. While the position was viewed by many as honorary, Ohnishi hoped to maintain some influence with upper-level management while leaving all other aspects of Fuji's production and marketing to succeeding executives. At the time of Ohnishi's stepping down Fuji had grown to be the world's second-largest producer of photographic film and supplies. Despite the company's position and growth Ohnishi's detractors believed that he spent too much of the company's profits on research and design at the expense of shareholder returns.

In 1991 Ohnishi was awarded an honorary doctoral degree from Clemson University in recognition of his business skills and in appreciation for his selecting South Carolina as the site for one of Fuji's film-production plants. In 2004 Ohnishi's notable contributions to the photographic industry were recognized by the International Photographic Council when he was inducted in to the organization's hall of fame. Ohnishi served as the chairman of the Photographic Society of Japan and as the president of the Tokyo chapter of the Photosensitized Materials Manufacturers Association of Japan. He was awarded the Cruzeiro do Sol, the Order of Orange-Nassau, and the Leadership Award from the National Association of Photographic Manufacturers in the United States.

See also entry on Fuji Photo Film Co., Ltd. in *International Directory of Company Histories.*

SOURCES FOR FURTHER INFORMATION

Kunnii, Irene M., "Fuji: Beyond Film," *BusinessWeek,* November 22, 1999.

Ohnishi, Minoru, and Masayuki Muneyuki. "A Message from the Chairman and President," *Fuji Photo Film Company 1998 Shareholders Report,* July 1998, http://home.fujifilm.com/info/share/repo_98.html.

—Jim Fike

■■■

Motoyuki Oka
Chief executive officer and president, Sumitomo Corporation

Nationality: Japanese.

Born: In Japan.

Career: Sumitomo Corporation, circa 1998–2001, managing director; 2001–, CEO and president.

Address: Sumitomo Corporation, Harumi Island Triton Square Office Tower Y, 8-11 Harumi 1-chome, Chuo-ku, Tokyo 104-8610, Japan; http://www.sumitomo corp.co.jp/english/index.htm.

■ Motoyuki Oka was a handsome man with a strong lower jaw and a piercing gaze. He was a tough-minded and determined leader. His company, Sumitomo Corporation, was an old institution that survived wars and revolutions and endured dramatic revisions of its corporate focus during economic changes, including the arrival of Western ways of conducting business and the losses of power and prestige after World War II. Oka may have undertaken one of the most dramatic changes in corporate outlook in the company's history when he tried to transform Sumitomo Corporation from a Japanese firm into a global firm; he envisioned prosperity in the embracing of local economies around the world.

HISTORY OF SUMITOMO

Sumitomo was an ancient company, having been founded in the early 1600s when Masatomo Sumitomo (1585-1652) established a shop to sell medicines and books in Kyoto. He wrote a business guide called *Founder's Precept*, the principles of which came to be known as the "Sumitomo Spirit." The corporate culture was barely modified over four centuries before Oka made significant modifications to reflect not only changes in Japanese society but in Sumitomo's global ambitions, which required the company to interact with many different cultures. Riemon Soga (1572-1636), the brother-in-law of Masatomo Sumitomo, was an innovator in copper mining who discovered a method for separating silver from copper ore. The technique was passed along to other copper smelters,

binding them to the Sumitomo family and beginning a *zaibatsu*, or family-owned trading company, of which the Sumitomo family was the head. Thus metal production was the lifeblood of the early Sumitomo *zaibatsu*, which would be reflected in dealings with both North America and China in Oka's era. The *zaibatsu* would expand to become a *keiretsu*—a vast holding company composed of numerous interrelated smaller companies that did business with and owned shares in each other.

Collectively the Sumitomo *zaibatsu* became a dominant manufacturer of copper in the 1600s, opening its most important facility in 1691: the Besshi copper mine, which operated continuously for 283 years. For this mine the *zaibatsu* imported Western technologies, especially during the 1800s and 1900s, helping to prepare Sumitomo for Japan's industrialization and giving the group a global outlook. The Sumitomo *zaibatsu* became a *keiretsu* after expanding into warehousing and manufactured retail metal goods; but not until the initiation of expansion into finance did Sumitomo have a significant presence in the United States. In Osaka the *keiretsu* established a financing business called a *Namiai-gyo*, which in the early 1900s became a banking business like those familiar to Westerners. The legacy from this business manifested itself in Sumitomo's U.S. banking operation, which included Union Bank of California.

The Sumitomo *keiretsu* was one of several very powerful *keiretsu* that dominated Japan's economy, and the metals business was very important in the wars Japan waged against its neighbors and the United States, culminating in World War II. In November 1944 the Sumitomo Building Company merged with Osaka Hokko Kaisha, which had been incorporated on December 24, 1919. The new company, Sumitomo Real Estate and Building Company, went back into the trading business in November 1945. Sumitomo and other *keiretsu* were blamed by many for promoting Japan's militarism for profit; the United States curtailed their powers after World War II, and over a decade passed before Sumitomo restabilized itself. In June 1952 the *keiretsu* changed its name to Sumitomo Shoji Kaisha. In December 1962 it reorganized itself into nine divisions spanning the *keiretsu*'s vast interests in metals, farming, fuels, retailing, and real estate. In July 1978 the *keiretsu* gave itself an English name, Sumitomo Corporation.

Not until February 1998 did Sumitomo Corporation try to significantly reform itself; a new company mission statement was created that tried to redirect the efforts of the firm's employees to incorporate a modern outlook on social issues such as environmentalism and cultural diversity. By then Oka was a managing director of the company, and he became responsible for explaining the company's new policies. He probably played an important role in the formulation of the "Reform Package" that was introduced in October 1998, which included one of his favorite ideas: "integrated business enterprise." The plan was a response to Japan's flat economy and reflected Oka's view that Sumitomo Corporation needed to think of itself as a global company rather than strictly as a Japanese one if it wished to survive.

OKA'S EMERGENCE

Perhaps the earliest point at which Oka showed up in the English-language press was in November 1998, when he attended a conference on Asian investments in Africa. Sumitomo was an exporter of African goods for sale overseas, especially to the United States; when asked about what Africa needed to do to improve its economic situation, Oka produced an answer that varied from those of other delegates, who mentioned their concerns about the stability of African governments. Oka told delegates that he was worried more about the physical infrastructure of African nations and the skill levels of African workers. At the time he was a managing director at Sumitomo but not well known outside of his company.

By 1998 Sumitomo had been organized into five major divisions: metals, traditionally the most important, which consisted primarily of manufacturing in steel and iron; transportation and construction equipment, which comprised complete transportation systems as well as a vast array of construction vehicles, ships, aerospace materials, and construction and factory machinery; information technology and electrics, which Oka thought of as a knowledge-based business; electricity, comprising complete electrical systems with power plants and energy resources; and consumer goods and retail services, from foods to textiles. Each of these divisions was composed of numerous companies, each with its own management and all of which belonged to the *keiretsu*; over 700 such companies existed.

By 2000 Oka was becoming publicly prominent as Sumitomo's representative in international affairs. In October 2000, in his capacity as the chair of the International Market Committee of the Japan Foreign Trade Council, Oka asked the Japanese government to negotiate a free-trade treaty with Mexico before Mexico's Maquiradora system of duty-free exports and imports expired in January 2001. Oka foresaw chaos for Japanese businesses in Mexico if tariffs and other duties were to be imposed on companies that had historically operated without them; but he faced a Japanese government that for years had opposed free trade by protecting local businesses from outside

competition with its own byzantine tariffs and regulations. Efforts to lower trade barriers would be one of the hallmarks of Oka's leadership of Sumitomo.

Oka was a strong advocate of the "Step Up Plan" that was launched at Sumitomo in April 2001. The plan was intended to make the company quicker to react to economic and social changes by giving individual managers more power to make decisions. Oka emphasized the importance he attributed to making the leaders of each business unit autonomous in an essay of July 2001. Perhaps in response to managers being too slow to accept the changes in corporate culture that he wished to institute, he later pressed division managers to conform to his guidelines liberalizing the treatment of employees and demanding strict respect for the laws—especially environmental laws—of the countries in which Sumitomo's companies did business.

The Step Up Plan also introduced rewards for profitability. For all of Japan's *keiretsu* the volume of business had been more important than the value of that business—which was one reason why major *keiretsu* such as Sumitomo Corporation had become so huge: acquiring businesses to increase sales volume had been deemed more crucial than making businesses profitable. When Japan's economy flattened in the 1990s, the *keiretsu* found themselves with huge debts and various companies producing goods that were not being sold. Oka wanted a system whereby managers would be encouraged to make profits; yet he was not as liberalizing as Mitsubishi Corporation's Mikio Sasaki, who eliminated the tradition of promotion based solely on seniority and replaced it with a system whereby promotion was based on employees' earning of profits.

PRESIDENT AND CHIEF EXECUTIVE OFFICER

On June 22, 2001, Oka became president and chief executive officer of Sumitomo Corporation, replacing Kenji Miyahara, who became chairman of the board. On that very day Oka launched what would be one of his most important efforts as president and CEO: he established a set of environmental regulations for Sumitomo's *keiretsu* mandating more efficient use of energy resources as well as the incorporation of renewable resources. Oka wanted to break with the past; he envisioned turning Sumitomo Corporation into a company that was constantly renewing itself, looking for new and better ways to conduct business. He believed that globalization and information technology would generate profound changes in Japan's society and economy and wanted to transform Sumitomo into a major global company. In the Sumitomo Business News he said, "What I have in mind is a company whose corporate vision, management principles, and activity guidelines reach across all the barriers of culture and language to be shared as common values by all employees across the globe, each of whom implements them with confidence and pride" (October 2001).

In explaining how he wanted Sumitomo Corporation to achieve his goals, Oka ventured into the realm of the metaphysical: he boiled his notions down to "dreams." He wanted to reform Sumitomo Corporation into a company that fulfilled the dreams of each individual employee as well as each individual client. He asserted that this would entail ensuring that Sumitomo Corporation met people's cultural needs while earning their trust through services that were not only the best but individually appropriate. Throughout his tenure as president and CEO Oka was bothered by the bad reputation Japanese companies had among the Japanese themselves for corruption; this translated into an enduring resolve to earn trust everywhere.

Oka wanted to incorporate a particular American notion into Sumitomo's corporate culture: providing for the needs of shareholders. To do this he introduced and then reworked throughout his tenure the idea of risk management. In 2002 he created the Credit Rating System for quantifying the risks of business ventures and calculating those risks against returns on shareholder investment. Oka remarked in the Sumitomo Business News, "It is not an exaggeration to say that risk management is at the core of our business" (July 2003); by 2003 however he was ready to admit that some risks could not be quantified—including those of natural disasters and political upheavals—and thus worked on developing strategies for every business unit that incorporated flexibility in responding to unquantifiable emergencies.

As another element of his plans for making Sumitomo the ideal global company, Oka wished for his firm to be a good corporate citizen, paying attention to the well-being of the people with whom it worked as well as maintaining a healthy global environment. In addition he wanted Sumitomo to uphold a positive working environment for its employees, in which ingenuity would be encouraged and employees would feel enthusiastic about their work and would be willing to work as a team. These ideas were paramount in Oka's vision of making Sumitomo a *sogo shosha*, or trading company, for which people would be proud to work. He noted that many corporations were moving into global commerce and believed that as a *sogo shosha* Sumitomo would be ideally situated to take advantage of the opportunities brought forth by globalization.

Throughout Oka's writings the words "integrated corporate strength" recurred; the phrase came across as somewhat vague, perhaps because of difficulties in translating from Japanese to English. Nevertheless Oka explained that he saw "integrated corporate strength" as the essence of Sumitomo; for him the phrase connoted strong ties binding all of Sumitomo's disparate companies into a coherent unit—which in turn suggested that Oka was ambivalent about some of the changes he

made to corporate governance and culture. That is, the binding of the *keiretsu* was an old idea, not one of the new ideas that he advocated, suggesting that he held the view that the companies of the *keiretsu* were obligated to support one another even if they were failing—which would suggest that risk assessment and realizing value for shareholders were not as high among Oka's objectives as his pronouncements suggested. Therein he met a problem that many Japanese business leaders faced: they could not stop being Japanese altogether and abandon the core cultural values of cooperation. Letting a failing company just fail was not really an option; Sumitomo Corporation was obliged to help its weak members. Indeed, in Oka's view the obligation was to turn the weak companies into strong ones.

In the Sumitomo Business News in 2002 Oka remarked, "The most important theme of the Step Up Plan is rapidly expanding our earning base. We are actively replacing low-return assets with those of higher return and strategically allocating management resources" (July 2002). As such Oka was working his way through a quagmire, from the long-held tradition that productivity was more important than earnings to the realm of focusing on profits. In practice he did not drop outright a losing company and replace it with another, but instead merged companies or expanded them into areas of higher returns, often by following Sumitomo's old practice of acquiring new companies. On the other hand he also formed partnerships with companies outside of Sumitomo's *keiretsu*, which proved effective in broadening his company's dealings in foreign countries.

In 2002 Oka pressed Sumitomo Corporation to find ways to use the Internet to enhance business opportunities. He had created a "Plan—Do—See" process in which managers were responsible for formulating strategies and following through on them; the development of an electronic medical record process that used the Internet to help hospitals share medical data was an example of the company's putting the Internet to use while implementing Oka's ideals of benefitting people through ethical business practices. Yet 2002 was a tough year: Sumitomo Corporation grossed $75 billion, down 1.8 percent from 2001, and netted $230 million, down 36 percent from 2001.

The year 2003 saw a turnaround in Sumitomo Corporation's fortunes, with a 43 percent increase in its net income over that of 2000, the year before Oka was elevated to president and CEO. Oka was making tough choices; he cut loose Sumitomo's U.S. farms, its golf-course business, and much of the e-commerce business that Oka himself had treasured but that was losing money. During that year Oka further refined Sumitomo's risk-management strategy, which he broke up into categories such as credit risk and investment risk. He introduced the Approach for Achievement Plan, the goal of which was to improve returns on risk to 7.5 percent, which would, Oka figured, cover the investment risks of company shareholders. At the time returns were 5 percent.

In April 2003 Oka tried to regenerate the Sumitomo Spirit with the Sumitomo Corporation Corporate Governance Principles, which laid out his mission statement for employees, demanding an awareness of legal requirements for doing business and promoting the ideal of helping people realize their dreams. Oka also reduced the size of the board of directors, cutting the number of insiders. He increased the use of outside auditors and corporate advisors in efforts to make corporate governance transparent for insiders and outsiders alike; the strategy was borrowed from American companies, who—caught up in grievous scandals of their own—reformed governance by ensuring that independent outsiders took part in overseeing the management process. At Sumitomo, Oka hoped that the changes he instituted would provide managers with a greater sense of their obligations to help others and with a greater passion for fulfilling Sumitomo's goals. He further hoped that outside observers would encourage sound business practices.

The success of Sumitomo Corporation's electronic medical record process led to greater involvement in medicine, and Oka emphasized biotechnology and information technology as areas in which his company could prosper. He also identified clean energy and nanotechnology as significant industries in which Sumitomo could be a pioneer. On January 29, 2003, Oka met with Indonesia's president Megawati Soekarnoputi to discuss Sumitomo's taking over the construction of a Javanese power plant, which had been initiated in 1997 but had been stalled by the Asian economic crisis that began that year. Sumitomo had been only a contributor to the project, but Oka proposed taking over the entire effort; he believed that the project could be a model for the responsible energy production he advocated. Postwar Iraq provided further opportunities for Sumitomo to put Oka's management principles to work. He pulled together a task force to formulate ways to assist in Iraq's reconstruction and to form lasting ties with the country. He noted in the Sumitomo Business News that his immediate goal was "to help stabilize the lives of the people there" (July 2003). By 2004 Oka was optimistic that Japan's economy was improving and that he had pointed Sumitomo Corporation and its 720 companies and 31,000 employees in the best direction for the future.

CHINA

Oka often said that Sumitomo Corporation's future was in China. In the company's business news he noted, "Geographically, China will be positioned as our chief strategic region both as a production base and an expanding market" (July 2003). Practically any businessperson could recognize that China's gradual transformation into a free economy would result in enormous business opportunities; yet, despite their proximity to China, the Japanese encountered special problems doing business there—even fifty years after the end of World War II the Chinese remembered Japan's depredations

against them, and Japan's military's killing of tens of millions of Chinese civilians was unlikely to be forgiven. Oka saw China's joining the World Trade Organization as a key moment in the opening of the country's economy, and Sumitomo used its considerable logistical resources to take advantage of the situation, establishing a delivery service in Shanghai, forming a partnership in 2002 with the Chinese electric company TCL Group, and assisting in the construction of an industrial park in Wuxi.

On April 15, 2002, Oka met with Beijing's mayor Liu Qi. Oka was looking for Sumitomo to help the city of Beijing manage its logistics, which would be a true challenge, because Beijing's economy was rapidly becoming ever more complicated; Oka knew that the hiring of a Japanese corporation by the Chinese civil government would be a great achievement. His efforts to overcome Chinese apprehension over one of the old *keiretsu* investing heavily in their country was directed to forming partnerships with Chinese companies. Such partnerships would assure Chinese participation in Sumitomo's activities and help bring about the transparency in corporate governance that he was striving to achieve. In what may have been his greatest accomplishment in China, on May 14, 2003, Oka signed an agreement to form a joint venture between China Steel Corporation, Sumitomo Metal Industries, and Sumitomo Corporation—to be called East Asia United Steel Corporation—which would produce slabs of steel to be used by both China Steel and Sumitomo Metal.

See also entry on Sumitomo Corporation in *International Directory of Company Histories.*

SOURCES FOR FURTHER INFORMATION

Oka, Motoyuki, "Message from the President & CEO," *Sumitomo Business News*, July 2002, http://www.sumitomocorp.co.jp/english/company_e/message/message2002_e.shtml.

———, "Message from the President & CEO," *Sumitomo Business News*, July 2003, http://www.sumitomocorp.co.jp/english/company_e/message/index.shtml.

———, "Thoughts on the 21st Century," Sumitomo Business News, October 2001, http://www.sumitomocorp.co.jp/english/company_e/message/pdf/message01.pdf.

"Sumitomo Corporation Invests Jointly with Walden International in China's United Platform Technologies," TelephonyWorld.com, March 31, 2003, http://www.telephonyworld.com/cgi-bin/news/viewnews.cgi?category=all&id=1049162259.

—Kirk H. Beetz

■ ■ ■
Tadashi Okamura
1938–
Chief executive officer and president, Toshiba Corporation

Nationality: Japanese.

Born: July 26, 1938, in Tokyo, Japan.

Education: University of Tokyo, Faculty of Law, 1962; University of Wisconsin, MBA, 1973.

Family: Married Hiroko (maiden name unknown); children: two.

Career: Toshiba Corporation, 1962–1973, held general positions within the company; 1973–1989, worked in instrument and automation division; 1989–1994, general manager of marketing and planning; 1994–2000, vice president and director; 2000–, president and chief executive officer.

Address: Toshiba Corporation, 1-1 Shibaura 1-chome, Minato-ku, Tokyo 105-8001 Japan; http://www.toshiba.co.jp.

■ Before entering the world of the computer age, Tadashi Okamura studied under the prestigious Faculty of Law at the University of Tokyo. He came to work at Toshiba in various positions before heading to the United States to earn a master's degree in business administration from the University of Wisconsin in 1973. He received praise in his early years with the company for overseeing several shifts in the technology market. When he was appointed the chief executive officer of Toshiba in 2000, the company was facing many difficulties. Okamura took over and continued the efforts of the former CEO. However, he also began making drastic decisions to raise profits and remain current in the ever-changing technology market. The economic downturn in the industry impacted Toshiba's profit margins, but with Okamura's efforts at diversification and opening up production outside of Japan, some of the downward trends were averted.

BUILDS CAREER IN MARKETING AT TOSHIBA

Okamura moved up the ranks at Toshiba over four decades before earning the top slot of chief executive officer. One of

his first positions with Toshiba involved overseeing a shift from analog to digital technology in a gear control for heavy manufacturing. His success earned him the position of communications director as that division turned from telecom to Internet-based devices.

As vice president Okamura headed the Information and Industrial Systems division, a very high-profile section of Toshiba. Industry insiders placed Okamura in the category of business leaders in Japan who had learned the electronics business in the 1960s and 1970s, when Japan ruled the electronics market.

When CEO Taizo Nishimuro began planning for his retirement in early 2000, he asked Okamura, then vice president, to take over for him and to continue his plan for restructuring the company. Nishimuro fought for four years to institute the plan. A high-profile lawsuit in 1999 brought troubles to the company and left Nishimuro struggling for support for the reforms resisted by the older managerial employees of the company.

As a result of the lawsuit, Toshiba suffered a net loss of $262 million, partially because of the $1 billion settlement with a U.S. company on a class action suit over defective disk drives in laptops sold in the United States. In two years the company lost nearly $400 million because computer memory prices dropped and Toshiba's share in the worldwide laptop market plummeted.

Okamura and Nishimuro hoped that the latter's retirement would push some of the more resistant managers also to retire, leaving Okamura the freedom to implement the changes. Almost immediately after taking over, Okamura began cutting costs and focusing Toshiba on investments for the future to sustain growth.

Okamura took the negative profit statements and the negative press coverage in stride. He credited his predecessor with having set the course for him to follow. He told *Forbes* magazine, "It is like driving a big limousine. [Nishimuro] had the slow job of turning it around; all I had to do was put my foot on the accelerator" (January 8, 2001).

IMMEDIATE CHANGES MADE

When Okamura was appointed by the board of directors in 2000, he told *BusinessWeek*, "In each area, I was in charge when there was a major shift, so I'm not worried by the changes I see today" (July 24, 2000).

With such competitors as NEC and Fujitsu already ahead of Toshiba in slashing costs and forging ahead with new acquisitions, Okamura looked forward to the challenge of making Toshiba an equal competitor in the marketplace.

The first change Okamura made at Toshiba headquarters symbolized what he hoped the company portrayed to the world. He had employees dismantle satellite and fast-breeder reactor models that had greeted visitors to the Tokyo headquarters since 1984. Okamura told *BusinessWeek*, "Power plants and satellites are no longer symbols of where Toshiba is headed" (July 24, 2000).

As Okamura took over Toshiba, Japan was in an economic upswing after a lengthy recession. Toshiba's profits had been dwindling for three years, unlike those of its Japanese competitors. However, Toshiba was still overcoming its payout of $1 billion to disgruntled customers. As a result, Okamura moved decisively to bring the company into competition with rivals who had been paring down inefficient divisions while Toshiba fought the lawsuit. Okamura began his changes by revamping the computer chip portion of the company.

In 2000 sales of cell phones and chips were booming, and Okamura moved quickly to take advantage of the upswing in the market. Analysts noted that Toshiba was already ahead of its competitors with its memory chip, which retained data even when electricity might be lost. Even though other companies offered the same type of chip, Toshiba was one step ahead because its chip was specially suited to large memory items, such as the photographs in digital cameras or the music downloads on an MP3 player. The ownership of this patent put Toshiba in an advantageous position as Okamura took over leadership because other companies wanting to use the large-memory chip would have to pay a licensing fee to Toshiba. Analysts predicted that owning this license would put Toshiba in a very strong position in the market, particularly with the upsurge in sales of digital cameras and MP3 players.

Okamura also kept to the plan set before him to reform the company. His predecessor had begun slashing spending in the year before Okamura took over. Nishimuro cut areas such as energy and heavy equipment, emphasizing instead the smaller technologies in the information sector. Just months before Okamura became CEO, Nishimuro directed 80 percent of the company's research and capital spending to mobile Internet phones, personal computers, chips, and computer monitors. Okamura, sensing the shift in the economic outlook for technology industries, stuck to the plan already instituted.

Within a year of his appointment, Okamura laid off nearly 20,000 Toshiba employees and moved the company away from the commodity chip business. He also invested $2.5 billion in Internet services. He opened negotiations with Time

Warner over the installation of Internet content through cell phones. Industry insiders noted that Okamura would have to begin selling off portions of the conglomerate and pointed to Okamura's appointment as an adviser to a special interest group as an indicator that he understood very well the steps necessary to lessen Toshiba's diversification. In 2000 Okamura breakfasted with the former U.S. president George H. W. Bush, who wanted Okamura's guidance for the Carlyle Group with a $750 million fund instituted to buy up pieces of Japanese businesses.

BACK ON TOP AGAIN

Within the first half of Okamura's first fiscal year at the head of Toshiba, the company earned $1 billion in profits, beating out such industry giants such Sony and Matsushita. Toshiba came in second behind Hitachi. Okamura credited Nishimuro's 1999 restructuring plan as the driving force behind the comeback.

Okamura protected the company from too much dependence on one source of profit, even as he continued to get rid of unprofitable sectors. He set up new divisions, which allowed alliances with rivals to reduce risk in the development of technologies. An industry insider compared the system to banks making syndicated loans. The new divisions allowed resources to be shared between the companies, thus reducing the risk of overly investing in one area that might not pan out in the marketplace.

However, analysts predicted in 2001 that Toshiba still faced obstacles in keeping on top of the game because it relied too heavily on Japanese factories, which cost more and kept product prices high within Toshiba. Okamura's plan of attack was not to lower prices but to offer products that came with more product features. In addition, Okamura opened Toshiba's own laptop factory in Shanghai in 2001 and contracted out laptop production to a Taiwanese company.

Analysts criticized Okamura for keeping some of Toshiba's unprofitable divisions, such as the Dynamic Random Access Memory (DRAM) chip sector. They pointed to Okamura's reluctance to lay off employees as being harmful to profits, predicting that his lack of ruthlessness would not help the company achieve higher profits.

TECHNOLOGY SLUMP HAS LITTLE EFFECT ON TOSHIBA

By the end of 2001 the global marketplace had hit a slump in the sale of chips, cell phones, and notebook computers—all items heavily marketed by Toshiba. So even though Okamura started as CEO with a solid upswing, when Toshiba's business year ended in March 2002, the company posted $2.1 billion in losses. As a result, Toshiba fell to 317 on the *BusinessWeek* list of top global technology firms, down from 254 in 2001.

Okamura expressed confidence despite the dismal figures. He continued to close plants and cut costs. He also cited the increased sales of memory flash chips, LCD panels, DVD players, and laptops—all strongholds in Toshiba's production line.

Okamura asserted that the profits would begin to change because of all the measures he had taken, including pulling out of the DRAM business, despite critics' claim that Okamura had not closed enough of these profit losers.

Although Okamura insisted that Toshiba would continue to draw in profits, analysts refused to give him their full support. In 2002 the yen strengthened while the U.S. dollar weakened considerably. Analysts predicted that if the U.S. economy continued its downward spiral, then Toshiba's sales to that country would also be in danger of weakening.

Okamura worked to balance the uncertain economy in a foreign nation by continuing the restructuring of Toshiba at an even faster rate. At the very beginning of the slump in 2001, he began combining manufacturing units within the company, setting a goal to reduce Toshiba's Japanese plants by 30 percent in two years. Jobs were also cut at the domestic level with a reduction of 12 percent during the same time period.

In addition, Okamura began selling approximately $7 billion of the company's assets. The sale of stocks and real estate impressed analysts as they watched the company make strides in increasing profits.

Akira Minamikawa, a senior analyst with WestLB Securities Pacific in Tokyo, told *BusinessWeek Online*, "Toshiba is finally changing, and that will help it survive" (August 9, 2002).

Analysts credited Toshiba with doing more than any other electronics company in Japan to cut costs by the end of 2002. Okamura reduced the company's capital outlay to the semiconductor business and continued to outsource basic production duties to factories in Malaysia and Thailand.

PRESSURE BUILDS TO REVAMP JAPANESE INDUSTRY

By 2003 the giants in the Japanese technology industry were facing a market that demanded a change from the way things had been done ever since Japan had emerged as a leading industrial nation, particularly in the years that some viewed as the glory days of the 1980s and 1990s. In those decades Japan won nearly every battle with global competition.

With the old style no longer working by the 21st century, Okamura endeavored to focus and streamline the giant that Toshiba had become. Analysts agreed that out of all the corporations in Japan, Toshiba had made the most strides in overhauling its operations, which ranged from the manufacture of chips to the operation of nuclear reactors. However, there still remained the worry among industry insiders that the taint of history remained stuck to Toshiba and its counterparts.

Peter Kirkman of J. P. Morgan Fleming Asset Management voiced his concern to the *New York Times*: "I am reasonably skeptical about the electronics conglomerates because they have lost competitiveness to other Asian countries and their balance sheets are impaired," he said. "They cannot implement restructuring when they employ as many people as the U.S. Army" (August 21, 2003).

Toshiba's falling share of the chip market remained a major concern in 2003. Toshiba's market share dropped from 50 percent to 22 percent in 2003. Companies in other Asian nations and in the United States began outselling Toshiba as costs for manufacturing technological products kept rising within Japan.

With high debts and low stock prices, industry insiders noted that the electronics business in Japan remained just a notch above junk-bond status, a situation that put companies like Toshiba in a difficult position as they still had to remain competitive. Okamura's answer to the dilemma came in a plan to spend ¥350 billion, or $2.9 billion, from 2003 to 2007 on the expansion of next-generation chip production.

Okamura sought to change Toshiba's image from its reputation for a particular product line to that of a company that could do everything associated with electricity. He continued to invest heavily in flash memory chips as demand for the products associated with these items grew. Toshiba partnered with Sony to produce the next-generation chip for the popular PlayStation game console. Analysts predicted that Okamura had made a wise decision as the market for this type of chip continued to soar.

Toshiba also met the growing demands of the 21st-century information age by continuing to produce state-of-the-art laptops rather than venturing into the desktop model computer. Toshiba's laptops remained some of the most reliable on the market, despite competition from Dell and Hewlett-Packard.

Okamura's goal was to shed Toshiba's old-fashioned and conservative image and instead keep the company current with the times and abreast of the potential growth of certain items in a changing age.

Despite Toshiba's efforts to be viewed as a modern company, analysts still criticized the company's insistence on maintaining older lines, including lightbulbs, air conditioners, elevators, and turbines. Instead, analysts believed that Toshiba should dump these sectors, which were viewed as low-margin divisions, letting other manufacturers deal with them.

Okamura ignored those who doubted the wisdom of selling home appliance items in China and in developing countries throughout the world. He determined that sales were strong enough in these places to justify the continued manufacture of domestic goods.

Other strategies in 2003 showed that Okamura kept a strong focus on the future as Toshiba pursued research into developing memory chips that use magnetism to read data faster and consume less energy as well as producing new fuel cells using methanol for laptop computers. Okamura also pursued nanotechnology, a process that changes atomic and molecular particles to create lighter and more durable products. This technology added more memory to many of the products manufactured by Toshiba, such as cell phones and digital cameras. Okamura committed $3.6 billion to research these new technologies over a two-year period beginning in 2003.

Again Okamura's actions were viewed skeptically by analysts, who said that it did not matter how much money Toshiba spent on the research if the company could not recoup the costs almost immediately.

However, Okamura continued to pursue his plan throughout 2003. He explained that he was following the model set by General Electric by getting rid of any sector not performing at the top of its game.

As 2003 drew to a close, Okamura said that he had achieved only 80 percent of the goals set forth in his four-year plan in 1999. He reiterated that he was committed to the plan because not to follow through would mean the end of Toshiba, given the amount of global competition and the changing demands of a fluctuating economy.

MANAGEMENT STYLE

Okamura often depended on the cultural heritage of Japan to guide him through the changes he oversaw while at Toshiba. In particular, the 19th-century Meiji era inspired him most. The medieval sword fighters of this time fought the status quo in Japan in a rebellion that helped create the first industrial power outside of the Western world. Okamura told the *New York Times* that the stories of these rebels needed to be remembered. "After being isolated so long, these young people had the spirit and energy to go out into the huge world," he said. "The most important thing is that we get back that spirit and energy now" (August 21, 2003).

Okamura was described as a gentle, grandfatherly type who never felt comfortable with the task of laying off employees to increase profits. Whenever he found that he had to cut jobs, he did so with minimal impact on his workers. He offered early retirements rather than layoffs as one measure to remain

a benevolent employer. However, analysts said that this type of soft management would not bring Toshiba out of the economic slump, which continued to be a concern in 2003.

A *New York Times* reporter described Okamura as having "a soft smile and gentle eyes," noting that "he hardly looks like a hatchet man" (August 21, 2003).

VOTE OF CONFIDENCE

In 2003 Toshiba revamped the governance of its management level within the company by instituting the committee system. Goals included operating transparently while redefining managerial and supervisory job descriptions. Also established was a nominating committee that had jurisdiction over appointments within Toshiba.

As a result, the three-member committee nominated Okamura to lead Toshiba for one more year beginning in January 2004. The committee explained that it made the nomination because of Okamura's past record of renovating the company and placing it in a good position to make continued sustained growth.

See also entry on Toshiba Corporation in *International Directory of Company Histories*.

SOURCES FOR FURTHER INFORMATION

Belson, Ken, "Japan Inc. Now Just a Memory, Toshiba Retools Its Image," *New York Times*, August 21, 2003, p. C1.

Fulford, Benjamin, "Gadget Colossus," *Forbes*, January 8, 2001, pp. 238–239.

Gutil, Robert A., "Toshiba Plans Strategic Shift to Fast Growth," *Wall Street Journal*, February 17, 2000, p. A1.

Kunii, Irene M., "Can Okamura Recharge Toshiba?" *BusinessWeek Online*, August 9, 2002, pp. 1–2.

"Toshiba Tries to Reboot," *BusinessWeek*, July 24, 2000, p. 26–27.

—Patricia C. Behnke

Jorma Ollila

1950–

Chairman and chief executive officer, Nokia

Nationality: Finnish.

Born: August 15, 1950, in Seinäjoki, Finland.

Education: Atlantic College; University of Helsinki, MS, 1976; London School of Economics, MS, 1978; Helsinki University of Technology, MS, 1981.

Family: Married Liisa Annikki Metsola; children: three.

Career: Citibank, 1978–1980, account manager at N. A. Corporate Bank; 1980–1982, account executive; 1982–1985, member of management board; Nokia, 1985–1986, vice president of international operations; 1986–1989, senior vice president of finances; 1989–1990, deputy board of directors; 1990–1992, president of Nokia Mobile Phones; 1992–, chairman and CEO.

Awards: Order of the White Star, Estonia, 1995; Order of Merit, Hungarian Republic, 1996; Order of Merit, Federal Republic of Germany, 1997; Commander's Cross of the Order of Merit, Republic of Poland; Commander of the Order of Orange-Nassau and Commander, First Class, of the Order of the White Rose, Finland; CEO of the Year, *Industry Week*, 2000; 9th Most Powerful Business Leader Outside the United States, *Fortune*, 2003.

Address: Nokia, PO Box 226, Espoo, Finland 00045; http://www.nokia.com.

■ When Jorma Ollila went to work for Nokia in 1985 the company manufactured a diverse line of products that included televisions, toilet paper, and rubber fishing boots; mobile telephones made up only a small portion of the business. After taking over as president and CEO in January 1992, Ollila extricated Nokia from debt and transformed the company into one of the world's leading manufacturers of cellular telephones. His daring, unorthodox, innovative management not only saved Nokia but revived the Finnish economy, which had fallen into a severe recession during the early 1990s after the collapse of the Soviet Union. Known for taking risks and toler-

ating mistakes, Ollila insisted that maximum flexibility and continuous adaptation to both market conditions and consumer needs should govern research and development, manufacturing, and sales.

EDUCATION AND PROFESSIONAL LIFE

Born in the Finnish coastal town of Seinäjoki on August 15, 1950, Ollila earned a scholarship to Atlantic College in Wales in 1967. He earned a master's degree in political science from Helsinki University in 1976, a second master's in economics from the London School of Economics in 1978, and a third master's in engineering from the Helsinki University of Technology in 1981.

Between 1978 and 1980 Ollila worked as an account manager for the Citibank N. A. Corporate Bank in London before transferring to Helsinki, where he served as an account officer from 1980 to 1982. Ollila rose quickly though the corporate hierarchy, joining Citibank's board of management in 1982, a position that he occupied for three years; in 1985 he accepted an offer to become vice president for international operations at Nokia.

HISTORY OF NOKIA

Founded in 1865 as a lumber mill, in time Nokia came to diversify its activities. The company entered the manufacture of paper products and after merging with Finnish Cable Works and Finnish Rubber Works in 1967 turned out phone lines, power-transmission cables, radio telephones, televisions, personal computers, tires, and fishing boots.

In 1988, three years after Ollila had come to Nokia, Kari Kairamo, the company's capable and ambitious but erratic CEO, committed suicide. Kairamo's death was the first in a series of misfortunes to befall the company. The 1991 collapse of the Soviet Union had a disastrous effect on the Finnish economy, as the USSR had provided a market for 25 percent of Finnish exports. As a consequence Finland's gross domestic product declined 6.1 percent while a staggering 13 percent of the workforce became unemployed. Like virtually every other Finnish company Nokia soon felt the impact of the recession, reporting an annual net loss of 211 million markka. Nokia teetered on the abyss of financial ruin.

REINVENTING NOKIA

Following a prolonged and bitter struggle, the board of directors ousted Kairamo's successor Simo Vuorilehto as well as his heir apparent Kalle Isokallio and appointed Ollila president and CEO. Ollila had garnered a reputation for efficiency by reviving the troubled mobile-phone division, of which he had taken control in February 1990. Once he had transformed the mobile phone division into a profitable enterprise, against all advice and common business opinion Ollila insisted that Nokia retain it. His affection for the division he had salvaged was no mere expression of sentiment; Ollila foresaw that as cellular telephones became less expensive to manufacture and sell, they would become more popular among consumers. He set out to make cell phones not only useful tools but also fashionable accessories.

As president and CEO Ollila thus concentrated his efforts on expanding the company's business in mobile telecommunications. Much to the chagrin of stockholders, executives, and employees past and present, Ollila sold other company assets and interests as quickly as possible. While his strategy may have been unpopular, it paid off. In 1993, before Nokia turned exclusively to the manufacture of cell phones and related products, profits totaled $2 billion. By 1999 profits topped $10 billion, a 57 percent increase over 1998, and total revenues totaled nearly $20 billion. Gains in 2000 were even more impressive: operating profits soared 56 percent to $3.45 billion and net sales jumped 57 percent to nearly $18 billion. Growth was slower but solid in 2001, when Nokia registered operating profits of $4.8 billion. Between 1995 and 2000 the price of Nokia shares traded on the New York Stock Exchange rose 2,000 percent. As early as the mid-1990s Nokia was positioned to challenge the industry leaders Ericsson and Motorola for the lead in the worldwide cell-phone market.

ACCOMPLISHMENTS AND ACCOLADES

Nokia sold 140 million cell phones in 2001 and controlled 37 percent of a nearly saturated and highly competitive market. Anticipating and even creating trends was critical to Nokia's success; the Finnish company preceded Ericsson and Motorola in adapting digital technology to mobile communication, marketing a dual-function personal organizer and telephone, producing phones specifically designed for Asian customers, using changeable cover plates, and incorporating text messaging. The Communicator 9210, a combination mobile telephone and handheld personal computer, proved to be an especially popular item.

Much of the credit for reviving Nokia belonged to Ollila, whose extraordinary business acumen brought him international renown. The number of awards he received were legion; among them were the Order of the White Star from Estonia (1995), the Order of Merit of the Hungarian Republic (1996),

and the Order of Merit of the Federal Republic of Germany (1997). He also held the Commander's Cross of the Order of Merit of the Republic of Poland, was an honorary citizen of Beijing, and was Commander of the Order of Orange-Nassau and Commander, First Class, of the Order of the White Rose of Finland. *Industry Week* magazine named him CEO of the Year in 2000, and in 2003 *Fortune* listed him ninth among the 12 most powerful business leaders outside the United States.

MANAGING PEOPLE, MANAGING RISK

Along with president and CEO, Ollila added the title chairman of the board of directors to his résumé in 1999. Fearing complacency as the fatal weakness of successful companies, Ollila consistently encouraged Nokia employees to think independently and to take chances. He welcomed and seemed to thrive on multiple points of view and a diversity of opinions. In promoting creativity and innovation, he was willing to live with mistakes and to accept the occasional failure. He also wanted employees at all levels and in all divisions to work as an integrated team; cooperation rather than competition defined the corporate culture at Nokia during Ollila's tenure. He regularly shifted the jobs and responsibilities of his senior executives, so that they could not only acquire a comprehensive overview of company operations but also understand the work that other positions entailed.

Generous and tolerant, Ollila sought to empower workers but was not afraid of making hard and even unpopular decisions. Ollila did not permit the company, its employees and executives, or himself to become self-satisfied, lazy, careless, arrogant, or to rest on the laurels of past achievements. To survive, Nokia had to adapt to constantly changing economic circumstances; Ollila believed that the company had to perennially move forward, exploring, creating, and taking advantage of new trends, new markets, new partnerships, and new opportunities. Unlike the CEOs of other corporations, Ollila eagerly allied with such rivals as AT&T and IBM, pursuing joint ventures that were mutually beneficial. Ollila told Janet Guyon of *Fortune* magazine, "This isn't a business where you do one, big strategic thing right and you're set for the next five years. It's a big orchestration task" (March 4, 2002).

PROBLEMS AND PROSPECTS

Part of the remarkable success that Nokia enjoyed during the second half of the 1990s rested on the steadfast loyalty displayed by customers to the company's products. Manufacturing sleek, stylish phones that were easy to use, Nokia succeeded in wedding form to function. By 2002 approximately 32 percent of the 930 million cell-phone subscribers in the world relied on Nokia phones. Industry research suggested that between 80 and 90 percent of those clients would return to Nokia when they needed to replace their phones.

Ollila's overall approach continued to work well into the 2000s, but the future was by no means assured. Ollila admitted that Nokia faced new challenges in the saturated global telecommunications market; prices, profits, and sales had begun to decline as early as 2001. Especially disappointing was consumer response to wireless access protocol phones. By 2001 an estimated 40 companies, including the established electronics giants Samsung, Siemens, Panasonic, and Alcatel, had the technological capacity to produce cell phones. A market saturated with so many competitors meant lower shares and diminished profits all around, and Nokia clearly felt the strain of the increased competition. In June 2000 Nokia stock was valued at $62.50 per share, and at $290 billion the company had the largest market capitalization in Europe; by March 2001 stock values had plummeted 70 percent, or $190 billion in total.

As always Ollila came out fighting. Nokia flooded the market with a record 40 new products in 2003 and launched a similar number in 2004. In an article published in the *Nordic Business Report* Ollila noted, "Our product portfolio will continue to be very competitive and will offer mobile devices that change the way we work, play, and stay connected to the people and information that matter to us" (March 25, 2004). Ollila's announced goal for Nokia was to capture a full 40 percent of the mobile-phone market, although the research firm Gartner calculated that Nokia's share had diminished to 28.9 percent by the first quarter of 2004. Still Nokia remained the market leader, and most analysts agreed with Janet Guyon of *Fortune* magazine, who stated, "If any cell-phone maker can thrive in this new world, Nokia can" (March 4, 2002). Thanks to Jorma Ollila, Nokia had reinvented itself once before, and the company certainly had the potential to do so again.

See also entry on Nokia Corporation in *International Directory of Company Histories.*

SOURCES FOR FURTHER INFORMATION

"Biography of Jorma Ollila," Nokia Company Web site, June 1, 2004, http://www.nokia.com/nokia/0,,53691,00.html.

"CEO of Nokia Outlines Company Strategy for 2004," *Nordic Business Report*, March 25, 2004, online: http://web5.infotrac.galegroup.com/itw/infomark/26/562/51595805w5/purl=rc1_ITOF_0_A114602959&dyn=18!xrn_1_0_A114602959?sw_aep=va0036_011.

"CEO of Nokia to Leave His Position in 2006," *Nordic Business Report*, April 8, 2003, online: http://web5.infotrac.galegroup.com/itw/infomark/26/562/51595805w5/purl=rc1_ITOF_0_A99748926&dyn=20!xrn_1_0_A99748926?sw_aep=va0036_011.

"A Finnish Fable," *The Economist*, October 14, 2000, p. 83+.

Guyon, Janet, "Nokia Rocks Its Rivals," *Fortune*, March 4, 2002, p. 115+.

"Jorma Ollila," *Current Biography Yearbook 2002*, pp. 441–445.

"Making the Call: How Nokia's Chief Turned Cell Phones into a Necessity—and Took the Market," *Time*, May 29, 2000, pp. 64–65.

Mason, Joanne, "The Labours of Ollila," *International Management*, July–August 1992, pp. 52–54.

McClenahen, John, "CEO of the Year," *Industry Week*, November 20, 2000, p. 38+.

Morais, Richard C., "Damn the Torpedoes," *Forbes*, May 14, 2001, p. 100.

"Nokia Unveils Five New Phones," *Forbes.com*, June 14, 2004, http://www.forbes.com/technology/feeds/infoimaging/2004/06/14/infoimaging01087224062397-20040614-074500.html.

—Meg Greene

■ ■ ■
Thomas D. O'Malley
1942–
Chairman and chief executive officer, Premcor

Nationality: American.

Born: 1942.

Education: Manhattan College, BA, 1963.

Family: Son of a customs inspector and a nurse; married Mary Alice Lucey; children: four.

Career: Philipp Brothers, 1963–1966, mailroom employee; 1966–1975, commodities trader, Europe; Salomon, 1975–1986, performed various executive roles at Salomon Inc. and its predecessor companies, Philbro/Salomon and Philipp Brothers, including vice chairman of Salomon, chief executive of the oil-trading division, chairman of Phibro Energy, and membership on the parent company's board of directors and executive committee; Argus Resources, 1986–1988, chairman and chief executive officer; Comfed Bancorp (a holding of Arugs), chairman, 1988–1989; Tosco Corporation, 1989–1990, president; 1990–1993, chairman and chief executive officer; 1993–1997, president, chairman, and chief executive officer; 1997–2001, chairman and chief executive officer; Phillips Petroleum, vice chairman, 2001–2002; Premcor, 2002–, chairman and chief executive officer.

Address: Premcor, 8182 Maryland Avenue, St. Louis, Missouri 63105; www.premcor.com.

■ Thomas O'Malley built a fortune as a commodities trader and created the modern, independent refining industry. But he did so without a pedigree. O'Malley's toughness served him well in the refinery business. After transforming Tosco into one of the most successful trading firms in the industry and the largest independent refinery in the United States, O'Malley took Premcor public in 2002 and began work on a strategy to turn around the debt-laden firm through a series of earnings-boosting acquisitions. Revered by Wall Street investors for his Midas touch in the oil industry, his work at Premcor was widely watched.

A WORKING-CLASS BACKGROUND

O'Malley was raised in New York City. "I did not grow up with a silver spoon in my mouth," he said. "I grew up with a stickball bat in my hand." He paid for college by driving a taxi on weekends and a school bus for a private school on weekdays. "I drove the rich kids for four years," he said (*New York Times*, February 11, 2001).

After college, a friend's uncle helped him get a job working in the mailroom of Philipp Brothers, a commodities-trading company. From there he quickly landed a job trading, in which he dealt with "just about every commodity the company handled" (*New York Times*, December 1, 1988). After 10 years in the company's European operations, he successfully ran the company's energy business, a stint that formed the foundation for his climb up the executive ranks. He described how all the crucial executive skills he learned came from his earliest jobs as follows: "Do everything right. Make no mistakes. Pay attention to cost, cost, cost. Constantly review the commercial viability of something. See if you could buy something cheaper, and sell it for more" (*New York Times*, February 11, 2001).

In 1981 Philipp Brothers engineered a merger with Salomon, the investment-banking firm, and O'Malley served as vice chairman and chief executive of the Salomon's oil-trading division. O'Malley left Salomon in 1986 and founded Argus Investment. The 1987 stock-market crash allowed him and his Argus partners to buy 26 percent of Tosco Corporation, a large independent refinery on the West Coast that also held a stake in Comfed Bancorp, a Massachusetts savings and loan firm. When Tosco's chairman announced his retirement, O'Malley stepped in as chairman and chief executive officer (CEO). He also later became chairman of Comfed.

THE MIDAS TOUCH

O'Malley was chairman and CEO of Tosco from January 1990 to January 2001. With 2000 sales of $24.5 billion, Tosco was the leading independent U.S. oil refining and marketing company, ahead of Ultramar Diamond Shamrock and Sunoco. Tosco operated more than 4,500 service stations and convenience stores throughout the United States under the BP, 76, Exxon, and Mobil brands.

At Tosco, O'Malley perfected an acquisitions strategy that involved buying refineries at a fraction of their replacement cost, increasing operating efficiencies, cutting costs, and consistently generating the highest return on capital of all of the independent U.S. refineries. Also while at Tosco, O'Malley forged his reputation for being tough. When Tosco bought Unocal's refining and marketing business in 1997, employees at a Unocal refinery in Trainer, Pennsylvania, were dismissed. Accused of bullying unions for concessions, O'Malley refuted the charges vigorously. "The Trainer plant was losing money. Playing hardball is not going to make everybody happy, and sometimes you just have to" (*New York Times*, February 11, 2001).

A RESPONSIBLE EXECUTIVE

In February 1999 an accident at a Tosco refinery in Avon, California, killed four workers and injured one. As a result, Tosco paid criminal fines and made donations that totaled $2 million. In an unusual step for O'Malley, indeed any chief executive, he appeared at a public meeting near the refinery shortly after the accident. He said: "I went out there and apologized and accepted responsibility. It was the most difficult experience in my life and one that I absolutely will never forget" (*New York Times*, February 11, 2001). In early 2001, after building Tosco into the largest independent refinery in the United States, he sold it to Phillips Petroleum for $7.36 billion and became a vice chairman of Phillips. Under his watch, Tosco was one of the most successful trading firms in the industry and a favorite of Wall Street investors.

CAN SUCCESS BE REPLICATED?

O'Malley resigned from Phillips in 2002 and two weeks later agreed to become chairman and chief executive officer of Premcor, a privately owned refinery based in St. Louis. He immediately began replicating the low-cost business model he perfected at Tosco. In April 2002 he announced a layoff involving one-third of the 273 employees at Tosco's administrative offices in St. Louis and the relocation of the company's commercial division to executive offices in Greenwich, Connecticut.

Premcor was formerly known as Clark USA, a St. Louis company that in 1997 was the seventh-largest direct operator of gasoline and convenience stores in the United States, with 800 retail outlets in 10 midwestern states. That year, the company's revenue exceeded $4 billion. In 1997 the Blackstone Group bought a 65 percent controlling stake in Clark USA from the Trizec Hahn Corporation for about $135 million. Although Blackstone identified a solidly discounted deal, it lacked experience in energy and oil investing. Said one analyst, "Although Blackstone made a timely investment, they lack the oil market trading savvy that it takes to maximize the return on these assets. With Mr. O'Malley on board, Wall Street will look for him to turn them into the next Tosco" (*IPO Reporter*, April 22, 2002).

It proved to be a tough challenge. The company lacked the diversity of assets that O'Malley built at Tosco, which was a top refinery and retailer on the East and West Coasts, as well as a significant force in Gulf Coast refining. Premcor was also highly leveraged and laden with debt. At the end of the third quarter of 2001, the company had long-term debt of $1.53 billion against total assets of $2.59 billion. There were also concerns about whether the company could generate enough capital to upgrade its assets to comply with U.S. environmental regulations. In 2000 Clark officially changed its name to Premcor, an acronym for "premier corporation."

THE O'MALLEY LEGEND

Despite the challenges, O'Malley's mere presence in the company provided an instant lift. Premcor was on the verge of an initial public offering (IPO) when he accepted the position, and investors expected his presence to automatically increase the worth of the offering. Said Tom Kloza, publisher of *Opis*, an oil-trade newspaper based in Rockville, Maryland: "He is to oil refining what Bill Parcells is to football coaching. He has [a lot of respect] on Wall Street with very good money connections. The union people might not like him because he cuts costs at refineries, but among investors, he's the gold standard" (*St. Louis Business Journal*, February 8, 2002).

Indeed, the spring 2002 IPO was a resounding success. Thanks to strong demand for the stock issue, Premcor increased the size of its IPO from 15 million to 18 million shares, and it priced the offering at $24 per share—the peak of its expected range. The company raised $432 million from the IPO, which accounted for about 36.4 percent of the company's 53.35 million outstanding shares. The stock closed at $27.80 on May 3, 2002, giving Premcor a market capitalization of more than $1.4 billion. Said John S. Herold analyst Louis Gagliardi, "The market obviously took a liking to this one. It was oversubscribed and the shares made a nice gain on the first day. I think O'Malley had a lot to do with that. His name is carrying a lot of cachet" (*International Petroleum Finance*, May 6, 2002).

TRUE TO FORM

After the IPO was completed, the industry waited for O'Malley to lead the company through a series of acquisitions, much as he did with Tosco. In December 2002 he made his first move, acquiring the Williams Companies' Memphis refinery for $455 million. In January 2004 Premcor bought the assets of a Delaware City refinery from the Shell-Saudi Motiva Enterprises joint venture, paying about $900 million. The refinery had performed poorly for Motiva. The success of the acquisition, which boosted Premcor's total refining capacity by 30 percent and gave it access to the northeast U.S. market, depended on O'Malley's ability to manage the plan better than its former owners. O'Malley called the facility "the most technologically complex refinery on the East Coast." Delaware had a primary advantage over other East Coast refineries because of its high production rates. O'Malley expected the refinery to generate $112 million in net earnings for 2004, adding: "We're confident in stating that this refinery acquisition will be immediately and significantly accretive to Premcor's after-tax earnings per share and cash flow" (*Octane Week*, January 19, 2004). As of 2004 Premcor comprised four refineries with the potential of processing 790,000 barrels of crude oil per day.

See also entry on Premcor Inc. in *International Directory of Company Histories.*

SOURCES FOR FURTHER INFORMATION

Cuff, Daniel, "Comfed Bancorp Chief Heads Investor Group," *New York Times*, December 1, 1988.

"Investors Gobble Up Tasty Premcor IPO," *International Petroleum Finance*, May 6, 2002.

"'Midas-Touch' O'Malley Leads Premcor," *St. Louis Business Journal*, February 8, 2002, p. 1.

O'Connor, Colleen Marie, "Premcor Prays For JetBlue Kind Of Success," *IPO Reporter*, April 22, 2002.

Wakin, Daniel J., "From Black Monday to Black Gold," *New York Times*, February 11, 2001.

—Tim Halpern

■■■
E. Stanley O'Neal
1951–
Chairman, chief executive officer, and president of Merrill Lynch

Nationality: American.

Born: October 7, 1951, in Roanoke, Alabama.

Education: Kettering University, BS, 1974; Harvard University, MBA, Finance, 1978.

Family: Married Nancy A. Garvey (economist and former controller of Allied-Signal); children: two.

Career: General Motors Corp., pre-1978, assembly-line employee; 1978–1986, entry-level analyst, assistant treasurer, treasurer of GM's Spanish division in Madrid; Merrill Lynch, 1986, director in investment banking; 1986, managing director of investment banking; 1997, head of Global Capital Markets; 1998, executive vice president and co-head of the Corporate and Institutional Client group; 1998–2000, executive vice president and CFO; 2000–2001, president of U.S. Private Client Group; 2001–2002, chief operating officer; 2001–, president; 2002–, CEO; 2003–, chairman.

Address: Merrill Lynch, 4 World Financial Center, North Tower, New York, New York 10080; http://www.ml.com.

E. Stanley O'Neal. *AP/Wide World Photos.*

■ O'Neal was named CEO February 12, 2002, succeeding David Komansky. He was one of the first nonbrokers to run Merrill Lynch in the company's 80-year history, the first African-American to head a major Wall Street firm, and one of only four black CEOs of Fortune 500 companies. While O'Neal had faced a lifetime of adversity due partly to race, he quickly adapted and never let social barriers dull his ruthless, competitive edge. O'Neal faced enormous challenges, particularly in terms of repairing the firm's damaged reputation. He unapologetically revamped the firm, cutting costs and boosting profits, while leaving behind a trail of enemies and critics.

With $27.7 billion in revenues for 2003, Merrill Lynch was one of the world's leading financial management and advisory companies. As an investment bank, it was the top global underwriter and market maker of debt and equity securities and

a leading strategic advisor to corporations, governments, institutions, and individuals worldwide. The firm has three divisions: the Private Client Group, which offers brokerage, mutual funds, and life insurance and annuities to individuals; the Corporate and Institutional Client Group that provides investment banking and capital market services to corporations, institutions, and governments; and the global Asset Management Group.

GM SHAPES A LIFE

O'Neal grew up in poverty on a farm in the Deep South. He was educated in a schoolhouse built by his grandfather, who was born a slave. His grandmother, mother, and aunts picked cotton. Much of O'Neal's life was guided by his association with General Motors. Too poor to properly support his family, O'Neal's father eventually moved the family to Atlanta, where they lived in a housing project, so he could work at a newly integrated GM assembly plant. O'Neal worked the night shift at the same plant as a teenager. GM sent the young O'Neal to the GM Institute (now Kettering University), where he earned a bachelor's degree in industrial administration. He later received a scholarship to Harvard from GM and spent the first 10 years of his career there. Finally, he met his wife at GM because she was an economist who worked with him in GM's treasury office.

ON THE FAST TRACK FOR SUCCESS

His first job after graduating from Harvard Business School was with GM, where he began his career in 1978 as an entry-level analyst. In just three years he moved to director level in the treasurer's office. According to John D. Finnegan, chairman of General Motors Acceptance Corp. and a former colleague: "That's about as fast as you can do it." He next worked for GM in Madrid, Spain, as treasurer of GM's Spanish division. Sandy Robertson, founder of the investment bank Robertson Stephens, who dealt with O'Neal during his time at GM, stated: "He was proud of the fact that he had started at the bottom" (both *BusinessWeek*, November 12, 2001).

ARRIVING ON WALL STREET

O'Neal resigned from GM in 1987 and changed over to a career in finance, joining Merrill Lynch's investment banking division. His move showed foresight. GM's finance division was losing its influence and O'Neal had his doubts about the future of the entire company, worrying that its success would lead to complacency. "I was concerned I would wake up 10 years hence and be very successful in a context I was not entirely happy with" (*BusinessWeek*, November 12, 2001)

Just three years after arriving at Merrill Lynch he was appointed head of its lucrative junk-bond unit, where he coached a team of young vice presidents in an effort to win new clients. Under his watch, Merrill Lynch rose to number one and remained first or second in junk bonds until O'Neal was promoted to head of global capital markets in 1995. After he left, the company fell to number eight. Bennett Rosenthal, who worked with O'Neal at the time, stated: "I never took Stan on a pitch where we didn't win the business. He was obsessed with being No. 1" (*BusinessWeek*, November 12, 2001).

RESTORING CALM FOLLOWING A CRISIS

In 1997 O'Neal was appointed co-head of Merrill Lynch's corporate and institutional client group, while also working in other areas such as real estate and private placements. In 1998 he was appointed CFO, but within his first few months Merrill Lynch suffered a $164 million loss when the hedge fund Long Term Capital collapsed. Losses for the hedge fund totaled more than $4 billion—rocking the financial markets. O'Neal was instrumental in putting measures in place that would ensure Merrill Lynch was not financially crippled by the LTC Management debacle. The firm contributed $300 million to a fed-brokered bailout fund.

A CASE OF FINANCIAL COMPLACENCY

When O'Neal was handed the CFO title, he inherited a fiscally irresponsible firm. In 1996 Merrill Lynch's profit margins sank an average of 5 percent below its competitors; by 1998 the gap had doubled. Between 1996 and 1998 revenues grew by $3 billion; yet only $100 million was realized in profits. Money was wasted on lavish perks, such as chauffeured cars for low-level managers and concierge services for investment bankers.

As one of his first tasks as CFO, he created an assessment of the bank's financial well-being and presented it to the firm's management committee. According to O'Neal: "What was supposed to be a 45-minute presentation turned into about two and a half hours. What was easy to see was the cost structure. It was incredibly visible. The question was how does one get at it. But I was not in a position to do anything about it" (*New York Times*, November 2, 2003).

Testing a strategy that he hoped to implement across the entire firm, O'Neal received board approval for cost-cutting measures in the struggling retail brokerage division. With the help of a former McKinsey consultant, he analyzed the division's nine million retail accounts, segmenting them according to profitability. The bottom-of-the-barrel accounts—those with less than $100,000—were transferred to low-cost call centers, while teams of wealth-management aficionados were assigned to the firm's biggest accounts. Compensation was changed to affect the new strategy: brokers were no longer paid for trades they made in accounts worth less than $100 thousand. His changes worked. Merrill Lynch doubled the amount of revenue per dollar of assets in its accounts and cut operating costs by $800 million.

A PRESSURE-PACKED PROMOTION

O'Neal's promotion to president of the firm in 2001 was the confirmation he needed to take his strategy company-wide. In the process he irritated many of Merrill Lynch's rank-and-file employees. His decision to continue a restructuring process begun before September 11 irked many employees and created the perception that he was using the tragedy as an excuse to fire people.

O'Neal's decision, however, may have been the result of panic. Not long after the attacks, Guy Moszkowski, Salomon

Smith Barney financial-services analyst, predicted that Merrill Lynch's board would push O'Neal to sell the company if he couldn't bring profit margins in line with competitors. O'Neal dismissed the talk as "crap" (*BusinessWeek*, November 12, 2001).

THE RACE CARD HE'D RATHER NOT PLAY

Even though O'Neal was one of the highest ranked executives in the financial services field, institutionalized racism regularly presented itself. When he became president, O'Neal was more visible on the social circuit. He lost his relative anonymity and was frequently the recipient of oblivious, inappropriate comments. According to O'Neal: "I would meet people socially and they asked what I did for a living. I would say I worked at Merrill. 'And what do you do there?' they would ask. When I said I was CFO, there inevitably would be a pause, followed about 75 percent of the time by: 'Of the whole company?' It's not malicious at all, but there's an unspoken expectation that's embedded in that exchange" (*New York Times*, October 29, 2000).

ENGINEERING A TURNAROUND

O'Neal pressed on, announcing a plan to increase profit margins from 17 percent in 2001 to 24 percent in 2003. (He ended up beating his own goal by about four percentage points.) He was the first Wall Street executive to move his company back to the location that had been torn apart by terrorist attacks, basing his decision on the fact that "at the end of the day, we're about the business of conducting business. This is where we do it" (*BusinessWeek*, November 12, 2001).

Abandoning the company's long-held mission of bringing its services to the demographics of the market—from small-time investors on Main Street to individuals of substantial net worth—O'Neal concentrated resources on the company's most lucrative accounts, leaving unprofitable businesses behind. According to him, "That means being properly positioned in the markets we want to be positioned in. It also means not expending resources on those things that will not ultimately produce the growth and profits we want to achieve" (*BusinessWeek*, November 12, 2001). He froze salaries, slashed bonuses, and made it clear that the business culture would be based on meritocracy and not the sense of entitlement that had pervaded the company.

AN UNLIKELY LEADER

O'Neal, the company's 11th CEO, represented a radical departure from his predecessors. Not only was he African-American (most of the former leaders had been of Irish descent), but he didn't begin as a broker. O'Neal wasn't worried

about fitting in; his priority was turning the company around. After posting record quarterly earnings of $1.04 billion in April 2000, the firm announced a $1.3 billion loss in the fourth quarter of 2001. The company's stock, which once enjoyed a high of $80 a share, hit a 52-week low of $33.50 on September 21, 2001.

By O'Neal's estimate, the firm had become too comfortable. Commenting on the firm's nickname of "Mother Merrill," he argued that "people interpret it in different ways. I interpret it as a club. If you are part of the club, we take care of you. But this is a 47,000-person organization, and not everyone can be part of that club. I think clubs have their place, but not in modern commerce" (*New York Times*, November 2, 2003).

A MOMENT OF TRUTH

O'Neal led a difficult restructuring, including a complete overhaul of its overseas business. David Komansky, his predecessor, had made aggressive investments overseas, acquiring 33 retail brokerage branches in Japan alone. The operations were crippled by an ailing economy and ended up losing about $100 million a year; Komansky later conceded that his timing had been terrible. In January 2002 O'Neal shut down 20 Japanese branches and fired 1,200 employees. A similar approach was taken in Australia. O'Neal commented: "Even if we're successful beyond our wildest imagination in Australia in the wealth-management space, it's not going to make a big difference to Merrill Lynch overall" (*Money*, March 2002).

Apart from undoing the mistakes of his predecessor, O'Neal faced competition from firms like Morgan Stanley, Goldman Sachs, and large, well-capitalized banks whose massive balance sheets won them underwriting assignments by linking investment-banking work with lending. All of this continued to fuel speculation that Merrill Lynch would have to merge or sell out to a larger financial player.

James Gorman, head of Merrill Lynch's retail brokerage division, commented: "Stan was made CEO at the ultimate moment of truth. Our world was imploding, and he had the courage to make difficult decisions. If that's not heroic, I don't know what is" (*Fortune*, April 5, 2004).

HARSH MOVES SEND A MESSAGE

Not everyone considered O'Neal's decisions heroic. In the summer of 2003 he bumped his second in command, Vice Chairman Thomas H. Patrick. Next Arshad R. Zakaria, the president of Merrill Lynch's investment-banking unit, resigned abruptly. The message to company employees was clear: the old Merrill Lynch died with the appointment of the new CEO.

At the center of O'Neal's falling out with Patrick was the latter's decision to go behind O'Neal's back in an attempt to convince the board to appoint Zakaria, his protégé, as president. According to company insiders, Patrick and O'Neal had made a deal. Patrick would support O'Neal for chief executive if O'Neal agreed to choose Zakaria as president. When O'Neal decided he wasn't ready to appoint a president, Patrick took matters into his own hands.

In the fall of 2003, Winthrop H. Smith Jr., the son of a company founder and a former president of the firm's international Private Client Group network, who had left Merrill Lynch after O'Neal took over, doubted whether his former boss could live up to the legacies of his predecessors. "Stan is a relative newcomer to Merrill Lynch. He is an extremely bright and able person who like Charlie Merrill came from a humble background and did not receive a traditional education. But, I am not sure that he has heard or yet fully appreciates the Merrill Lynch stories and may not be able to embrace the culture in the same fashion as his predecessors. Time will tell" (*New York Times*, November 2, 2003).

SCANDALS PLAGUE A COMPANY

Besides his own image, O'Neal also had to contend with the company's reputation. Merrill Lynch and its primary rivals were being investigated to determine whether their analysts' stock recommendations were influenced by the quest to retain and attract new investment-banking customers. Stocks were recommended by brokerage houses that sought to distribute those firm's shares, so that the brokerages could win lucrative investment-banking fees from the companies. Doing so meant that the small investor was frequently given biased research that led to their losing money. In 2003 New York State found that the 10 brokerage houses had corrupted the stock-research process. As part of a historic settlement, Merrill Lynch ultimately paid $100 million to settle charges that the investment-banking business had influenced research. The 10 brokerage houses had to put a total of $432.5 million into an independent-research fund to finance free research over a five-year period for small investors. As part of the agreement, Merrill Lynch agreed to implement changes that would further separate its research department from its investment-banking unit.

Next followed allegations by a Senate subcommittee that the firm's investment bankers had helped Enron lie about profits (through a mysterious Nigerian barge deal) and that 96 Merrill Lynch employees had invested $16.6 million in a partnership with the now infamous Andrew Fastow of Enron.

Meanwhile, the securities firm was drawn into the Martha Stewart insider-trading accusations and had to contend with charges of pension-fund mismanagement by its London-based subsidiary. In each case Merrill Lynch vehemently denied any wrongdoing. O'Neal commented: "Ensuring integrity at our firm has always been a top priority and will continue to be" (*USA Today*, July 25, 2001).

SUBSTANCE OVER STYLE

Within three years after taking over Merrill Lynch, O'Neal had eliminated 24,000 jobs, including 20 percent of all investment-banking and analyst posts. He closed more than 300 offices, wiping out operations in South Africa, Canada, Australia, New Zealand and Japan. He also retooled the company's executive management committee, firing nearly every member hired by his predecessor. The new group was diverse, consisting of one African-American male, one Korean, one Egyptian, and two American women.

Merrill Lynch started 2004 on a positive note. It had posted a record profit in 2003, with earnings that reached a best-ever $4 billion—better than even the prosperous quarters of the late 1990s. Merrill Lynch was generating more income per broker than any of its competitors; its investment-banking division touted more fees in 2002 than Goldman Sachs or Citigroup. Shareholders watched the company's stock increase 100 percent. O'Neal pocketed a compensation package worth $28 million, making him one of the highest-paid executives in the field of financial services.

Some company insiders have nicknamed O'Neal's new followers in the company the "Taliban" because of their blind faith. Critics have even referred to O'Neal as "Mullah Omar." Less vitriolic is the perception that he's simply an aloof executive who was more interested in profits than people. O'Neal has responded: "People say all these things about me. They say I'm a bean counter. I'm not. I spend so little time thinking about numbers they wouldn't believe it. But if people want to say that, I can't do anything about it. I have a job to do, and it has nothing to do with worrying about what people call me" (*Fortune*, April 5, 2004).

See also entry on Merrill Lynch & Co., Inc. in *International Directory of Company Histories*.

SOURCES FOR FURTHER INFORMATION

Knox, Noelle, "Merrill Lynch Names New President, COO," *USA Today*, July 25, 2001, p. 3B.

McGeehan, Patrick, "Poised to Take Merrill by the Horns," *New York Times*, October 29, 2000, Section 3, p. 1.

Rynecki, David, "Putting the Muscle Back in the Bull," *Fortune*, April 5, 2004, p. 162.

Thomas, Landon, Jr., "Dismantling a Wall Street Club," *New York Times*, November 2, 2003.

Thornton, Emily, "Shaking Up Merrill," *BusinessWeek*, November 12, 2001, p. 96.

Woolley, Suzanne, "A New Bull At Merrill Lynch," *Money*, March 2002, p. 82.

—Tim Halpern

David J. O'Reilly

1947–

Chairman and chief executive officer, ChevronTexaco Corporation

Nationality: Irish (became naturalized American citizen in 1973).

Born: January 1947, in Dublin, Ireland.

Education: University College, Dublin, BS (chemical engineering), 1968.

Family: Son of a menswear buyer for department store and a homemaker (first names unknown); married Joan Gariepy (a nurse), 1970; children: two.

Career: Chevron Research Company, 1968–1971, process engineer; 1971–1975, process engineer, operating assistant, and supervisor; Chevron Corporation, 1976–1979, adviser, Foreign Operations Staff; Chevron Chemical Company, 1979–1980, planning manager, Fertilizer Division; Chevron Chemical Company, 1980–1983, manager of agricultural chemicals plant; 1983–1985, manager of Salt Lake City refinery; 1985–1986, manager of manufacturing, Olefins Division; 1986–1989, general manager of El Segundo Refinery; 1989–1991, senior vice president; Chevron Corporation, 1991–1994, vice president, strategic planning and quality; Caltex Petroleum Corporation, 1992–1994, director; Chevron Products Company, 1994–1998, president; Chevron Corporation, 1998–2000, vice chairman; 2000–2001, chairman and CEO; ChevronTexaco Corporation, 2000–, chairman and CEO.

Awards: Named 2001 Executive of the Year by *San Francisco Business Times*, 2002; Secretary of State's Award for Corporate Excellence, U.S. Department of State, 2003.

Address: ChevronTexaco Corporation, 6001 Bollinger Canyon Road, San Ramon, California 94583; http://www.chevrontexaco.com.

David J. O'Reilly. *AP/Wide World Photos.*

■ Less than a year after taking office as the new chairman and chief executive officer (CEO) of Chevron Corporation, David J. O'Reilly in late 2000 engineered his company's merger with Texaco Inc. The merger created the second-largest integrated U.S. oil company, a far-flung international enterprise with interests in more than 180 countries. O'Reilly, who took over the reins of the newly created ChevronTexaco Corporation as chairman and CEO, presided over one of the world's most competitive energy companies. In addition to its primary concentration in oil and gas, including exploration, production, refining, marketing, and transportation, ChevronTexaco was heavily involved in energy generation and the manufacturing and marketing of chemicals. The company, second only to ExxonMobil in the United States, in early 2004 boasted worldwide reserves of nearly 13 billion barrels of oil and gas equivalent and daily production of approximately 2.5 million barrels.

Despite the pressures of worldwide economic recession and the resultant softening of oil prices in the early 2000s, O'Reilly managed to steer the newly created ChevronTexaco to creditable financial performance. However, after the company's bottom line took a big hit in 2002 from $3.3 billion in special charges, higher pension expenses, and weak margins for refining and marketing, O'Reilly laid out his strategy for turning things around. That strategy focused on four key areas of the company's operations: (1) operational excellence, that is, running of operations safely, reliably, efficiently, and with sound environmental stewardship; (2) lowering of the company's cost structure; (3) maintaining a highly focused capital spending program, directing outlays to projects that could best deliver long-term value; and (4) actively managing the corporate portfolio to develop strongly competitive businesses with solid growth potential, low cost structures, and an ability to generate robust returns.

DECIDES TO STUDY CHEMICAL ENGINEERING

O'Reilly, the son of a department-store menswear buyer and a homemaker, was born in Dublin, Ireland. He attended Willow Park School and its senior counterpart, Blackrock College, in the Irish capital. While at Blackrock, O'Reilly took up the sport of running. To build himself up to compete as a middle-distance runner on his school track team, he lugged sacks of flour up and down a flight of stairs, urged on by his coach, who was also involved in the bakery business. He credits another of his teachers at Blackrock—Mr. Fleming—with first awakening his interest in business. "I will always remember [Fleming], because he took the class to see different businesses in action," O'Reilly told the *San Francisco Chronicle* in 2003. "We went to canneries. We went to fertilizer parties. We went to a brewery—a Guinness brewery." In the end, after viewing all sorts of businesses, O'Reilly found himself particularly drawn to the chemicals and petroleum businesses. After completing his secondary education, he enrolled in a chemical engineering program at University College, Dublin (UCD), part of the National University of Ireland.

An honors student throughout his four years at UCD, O'Reilly was also active in student affairs. After taking his final exams in 1968, his senior year at UCD, he gathered financial support for and edited the first volume of what was called the *Journal of the Chemical Engineering Student Society.* The UCD professor John Kelly, introducing O'Reilly at a 2002 ceremony during which he received an honorary doctorate degree from UCD, observed that, sadly, there was never another volume. Although student unrest swept colleges around the world in 1968, O'Reilly wrote in his introduction to the journal that UCD had not yet been touched by student rebellion against academic authority. He questioned, however, how much longer Irish students could bear the deteriorating educational system. He went on to single out the overemphasis on pure academics and high staff-student ratios as among the biggest problems at Ireland's postsecondary institutions. As Kelly pointed out, not long after O'Reilly left Dublin for a career in the United States, his alma mater underwent the so-called Gentle Revolution of UCD.

RECRUITED BY CHEVRON

During O'Reilly's final year at UCD, a recruiter from the Chevron Oil Company visited the Dublin Campus. After interviewing a number of job candidates, Chevron promised jobs to O'Reilly and two of his classmates—Brian O'Connell and Brendan Sheehan. O'Reilly began his career with Chevron in the fall of 1968, working as a process engineer for Chevron Research Company in Richmond, California. Although his Irish classmates worked for Chevron for a few years and then returned to their homeland to pursue their careers, O'Reilly decided to stay in the United States.

One factor in O'Reilly's decision very likely was his marriage in 1970 to Vermont-born Joan Gariepy. O'Reilly and Gariepy met in 1969 at San Francisco International Airport when Joan flew in from her hometown of Burlington to move in with her sister and look for a nursing job in the Bay Area. O'Reilly went to the airport with his roommates, one of whom was dating Joan's sister. Of that first encounter, recounted by Nancy Boas in an article for *Encore,* a quarterly newsletter for ChevronTexaco retirees, Joan recalled, "I got off the plane, and there was David. He seemed like a nice guy" (January–March, 2000). O'Reilly was immediately smitten. Within a month the two were dating. They were engaged two months after their first meeting and eventually married and had two daughters.

From his earliest days with Chevron, working in the company's research center in Richmond, O'Reilly quietly rebelled against the oil industry's hierarchical approach to personnel relations. He was quickly singled out as a new-style manager for both his good sense of humor and his total lack of status consciousness.

O'REILLY POSTED TO NEW JERSEY

After roughly three years with Chevron Research in Richmond, O'Reilly moved to a research facility in Perth Amboy, New Jersey. Over the next five years in New Jersey, he was promoted from process engineer to operating assistant and, finally, to supervisor. It was during this period, in 1973, that O'Reilly became a naturalized U.S. citizen. In 1976 he was named an adviser in Chevron Corporation's Foreign Operations Staff, in which position he remained until 1979, when he was appointed planning manager for Chevron Chemical Company's Fertilizer Division. A year later O'Reilly took over as manager of Chevron Chemical's agricultural chemicals plant in Richmond, California. Beginning in 1983 he served for two years as manager of the company's Salt Lake City refinery.

During the late 1970s and 1980s O'Reilly established his unique management style. Shortly after taking over as manager of Chevron's agricultural chemicals plant in Richmond, O'Reilly found himself confronted with a strike. To learn more about the grievances of the plant's workers, he went directly to the picketing workers, introduced himself, and inquired, "What's up, lads?" Security guards at the Richmond plant also vividly recall the new manager arriving for work on a number of occasions in a battered 15-year-old Cadillac he had bought from a friend.

From Salt Lake City, O'Reilly moved in 1985 to Houston, where he took over as manager of manufacturing of Chevron Chemical's Olefins Division. A year later he was named general manager of the company's refinery in El Segundo, California. In El Segundo, O'Reilly revolutionized the operation's dress code by handing down an edict directing managers to "lose the ties," the wearing of which distinguished those in the ranks of management from workers. In 1989 Chevron Chemical named O'Reilly senior vice president, a post he held until 1991, when Chevron Corporation pulled him back to headquarters to serve as a corporate vice president with responsibility for strategic planning and quality.

INITIATES TALKS FOR KAZAKHSTAN VENTURE

The early 1990s saw the collapse of the Soviet Union and its subsequent breakup into independent republics, one of which was Kazakhstan. As Chevron's point man for strategic planning, O'Reilly initiated negotiations for a promising, but high-risk venture in Kazakhstan. These talks culminated in Chevron's purchase of a 50 percent interest in the super-deep, giant Tengiz oil field near the Caspian Sea that had estimated reserves of six billion to nine billion barrels but was far from any existing pipeline. With its 50 percent interest in the newly formed Tengizchevroil (TCO) joint venture, Chevron in 1993 became the first Western oil company to operate in Kazakhstan. TCO began to develop the Tengiz and Karachaganak oil fields, both of which had been discovered in 1979. In 1997 Texaco separately purchased a 20 percent stake in the Karachaganak oil field. A major problem remained regarding how to get the oil to market. After the merger of Chevron and Texaco, the newly combined company, along with 10 private and public partners, in 2001 opened the $2.6 billion Caspian Pipeline Consortium (CPC) pipeline from the Tengiz field to the Black Sea port of Novorossiysk. Two years later a separate 395-mile pipeline linking the Karachaganak field to the main CPC pipeline went into operation.

In March 1992 O'Reilly was named a director of Caltex Petroleum Corporation, a 50-50 joint venture of Chevron and Texaco with refining and marketing operations in the Eastern Hemisphere. He continued to sit on the Caltex board as well as to serve as Chevron's vice president of strategic planning and quality until September 1994, when he was named president of Chevron Products Company, responsible for Chevron's U.S. refining and marketing operations. In his new post O'Reilly began to emerge as a force to be reckoned with in the petroleum industry. Struggling just to break even when O'Reilly assumed its presidency in 1994, the company, under his direction, steadily increased its profitability. In November 1998 O'Reilly moved another step up the corporate ladder at Chevron when he was named vice chairman of Chevron Corporation. It was widely reported at the time of O'Reilly's appointment as vice chairman that he had been selected by Chevron's chairman, Kenneth Derr, to be groomed as his successor following Derr's planned retirement at the end of 1999.

CHEVRON'S INITIAL BID FOR TEXACO FAILS

Under Derr, Chevron was first caught up in the merger craze sweeping the global oil industry in the spring of 1999. Only months earlier, in December 1998, Exxon Corporation announced plans to buy Mobil Corporation, and British Petroleum Company of London purchased Chicago-based Amoco Corporation. In April 1999 the newly merged BP Amoco agreed to acquire Atlantic-Richfield Company of Los Angeles. In early May 1999 Chevron began negotiations on a possible merger, but the talks were short-lived. On June 2, 1999, the two companies announced that negotiations had broken off, reportedly because Texaco was dissatisfied with Chevron's offer of $70 per share, hoping for at least $80. Derr defended Chevron's offer as competitive and said his company would look elsewhere for a merger partner.

On January 1, 2000, O'Reilly took over as chairman and CEO of Chevron, succeeding Derr, who had retired at the end of 1999. It soon became apparent that Chevron's interest in Texaco was still very much alive. The intervening months since Texaco's rejection of Chevron's 1999 offer had not been particularly kind to the oil company, based in White Plains, New York. Its stock had languished, underperforming the industry average, and by mid-2000 it was willing to talk again with Chevron. According to several oil industry insiders, the new round of merger negotiations was given further impetus by better chemistry between Texaco's chairman, Peter Bijur, and O'Reilly than had existed between Bijur and Derr. On October 16, 2000, the two companies announced that they had reached an agreement to merge. Under the provisions of that agreement, Texaco shareholders received 0.77 share of Chevron's common stock for every share of Texaco common they held. This amounted to just under $65 per share, lower than the offer Texaco had found unacceptable in mid-1999.

In announcing the merger plan, O'Reilly said the combined company would create a significantly stronger U.S.-based energy producer that would be better able to contribute to U.S. energy needs. "That's good news for the country because the United States will have an additional top-tier energy company better positioned to compete effectively with the international majors," he added, according to a company press release (October 16, 2000). Both O'Reilly and Texaco's Bijur said the merged company would be stronger in a number of key respects, thanks to lower costs, a leadership upstream competitive position as well as a world downstream platform, strength and scale in chemicals operations, broad technology portfolio, and superior organizational capability.

O'REILLY BECOMES CEO OF MERGED COMPANY

Under the terms of the merger agreement, O'Reilly became the chairman and CEO of ChevronTexaco, while Bijur was to serve as vice chairman. However, in February 2001, before the merger was finalized, Bijur retired as Texaco's chairman and CEO and was succeeded by Glenn F. Tilton. When the ChevronTexaco merger took effect in October 2001, Tilton became the new company's vice chairman but served less than a year before leaving in September 2002 to become the chairman, president, and CEO of UAL Corporation, the parent company of United Airlines.

On November 19, 2001, a little over a month after the merger of Chevron and Texaco was completed, O'Reilly laid out in detail for security analysts his short-term goals for the new company. He reaffirmed the company's commitment to achieving $1.2 billion in synergies by mid-2002 at the latest. For the longer term, O'Reilly was even more ambitious, promising that by March 2003 recurring synergies would be running at an annual rate of $1.8 billion. He told analysts that he expected a bigger increase in synergies than originally predicted from ChevronTexaco's downstream sector. O'Reilly said in a company press release that "even without overlap we've found considerably more synergies by integrating on a global basis businesses that were previously operated regionally" (November 19, 2001). He said that the company had also set ambitious goals for improving its return on capital employed, projecting growth of 2 to 3 percent in the 2003–2004 timeframe, with even bigger gains expected in the years beyond that period. O'Reilly also predicted that the company's production of oil and gas would expand at an annual rate of 2.5 to 3 percent in the five-year period from 2002 through 2006.

In its first full year of operations, ChevronTexaco in 2002 posted a profit of only $1.1 billion, down sharply from net income of $3.9 billion in 2001. Much of the decline could be attributed to special charges absorbed by the company to cover merger costs and losses connected with the collapse of Dynegy, in which ChevronTexaco held a 26.5 percent stake. Nevertheless, O'Reilly made clear that he considered the company's performance unacceptable and vowed to turn things around. He delivered on that promise a year later, when the company posted net earnings of $7.2 billion for 2003. In announcing the dramatic rise in earnings, O'Reilly noted on January 30, 2004, that the company had also made significant strides in advancing its longer-term objectives, singling out Chevron-Texaco's formation of two new business units. He said that

one of the units would concentrate on commercializing the company's extensive worldwide gas resources while the other would focus on identifying and developing major investment opportunities around the world.

CALLS MERGER "VERY SUCCESSFUL"

Interviewed by the *San Francisco Chronicle* in December 2003, O'Reilly was asked to evaluate the merger of Chevron and Texaco, a little more than two years after it was completed. "Very successful," he replied, citing the merged company's total stockholder return (stock appreciation plus dividends reinvested), compared with that of other major oil companies, in the period from October 16, 2000, when the merger was announced, through November 19, 2003. The numbers for all companies were down, because the stock market had been higher in the fall of 2000, but ChevronTexaco had declined less than 1 percent, compared with declines of 4.7 percent for BP, 5.4 percent for ExxonMobil, and 7.5 percent for Royal Dutch/Shell. In its 2001 profile of O'Reilly, *San Francisco Business Times* observed that his personal secret to success in the oil business "isn't getting the most out of the ground. It's getting the most out of people."

In addition to his responsibilities with ChevronTexaco, O'Reilly was active in both industry and civic affairs. A longtime member of the American Petroleum Institute, he served as the organization's chairman in 2003. He was also a member of the National Petroleum Council, the World Economic Forum's International Business Council, Business Roundtable, Business Council, American Society of Corporate Executives, and the JPMorgan International Council. On the civic side, O'Reilly sat on the boards of the San Francisco Symphony, Leon H. Sullivan Foundation, and Bay Area Council.

See also entry on ChevronTexaco Corporation in *International Directory of Company Histories.*

SOURCES FOR FURTHER INFORMATION

Banerjee, Neela, and Mary Williams Walsh, "1 New Oil Company, 2 Corporate Cultures," *New York Times*, October 17, 2000.

Boas, Nancy, "An Irish Original," *Encore*, January–March, 2000, http://www.chevrontexacoretirees.org/archive/Q12000/0001encore07a.html.

Calvey, Mark, "Executive of the Year 2001: ChevronTexaco CEO David O'Reilly Runs Well-Oiled Machine," *San Francisco Business Times*, December 28, 2001.

"Chevron and Texaco Agree to $100 Billion Merger Creating Top-Tier Integrated Energy Company," *PR Newswire*, October 16, 2000. Also available at http://www.chevrontexaco.com/news/archive/chevron_press/2000/2000-10-16.asp.

"ChevronTexaco Establishes Financial and Operational Goals to Achieve Industry-Leading Performance and Top Shareholder Return," company press release, *PR Newswire*, November 19, 2001.

Ivanovich, David, "Texaco-Chevron Deal Took More Than a Year to Complete," *Houston Chronicle*, October 17, 2000.

"On the Record with Dave O'Reilly," *San Francisco Chronicle*, December 21, 2003.

Rocks, David, "In Business This Week: Texaco-Chevron: Undone Deal," *BusinessWeek*, June 14, 1999.

Stein, George, "Oil Giants Talk Merger: Chevron, Texaco Mull Big-League Deal," *Los Angeles Daily News*, May 8, 1999.

—Don Amerman

■■■
Amancio Ortega
1936–
Chairman, Industria de Diseño Textil

Nationality: Spanish.

Born: March 1936, in León, Spain.

Family: Son of railroad worker and maid (names unknown); married (wife's name unknown); children: three.

Career: Zara, 1975–1985, owner; Industria de Diseño Textil, 1985–, chairman.

Address: Industria de Diseño Textil, Edificio Inditex, Avenida de la Diputación, 15142 Arteixo, La Coruña, Spain; http://www.inditex.com.

Amancio Ortega. *Getty Images.*

■ Amancio Ortega was the founder and chairman of the Spanish company Industria de Diseño Textil (Inditex), the parent company of a number of chain stores including the internationally successful clothing retailer Zara. Ortega came from humble beginnings to turn himself into Spain's richest man in 2001 when Inditex first offered shares to the public. Ortega acquired a reputation as a private and down-to-earth person; he rarely made public appearances and shunned the trappings of the wealthy.

EARLY CAREER

The son of a railroad worker and a maid, Ortega received no formal higher education. He began his remarkable career as a teenager in La Coruña, Spain, the traditional center of the Iberian textile industry. When he was 13 years old he worked as a delivery boy for a shirtmaker who produced clothing for the rich. He later worked as a draper's and tailor's assistant. In seeing firsthand how costs mounted as garments moved from designers to factories to stores, Ortega learned early on the importance of delivering products directly to customers without using outside distributors. He would later employ such a strategy with great success at Zara, attempting to control all of the steps in textile production in order to cut costs and gain speed and flexibility.

In the early 1960s Ortega became the manager of a local clothing shop, where he noticed that only a few wealthy residents could afford to buy the expensive clothes. Thus he started producing similar items at lower prices, purchasing cheaper fabric in Barcelona and cutting out pieces by hand using cardboard patterns. Ortega then sold his items to local shops; he used the profits to start his first factory in 1963 at the age of 27.

THE ZARA PHENOMENON

In 1975 Ortega opened his first Zara shop across the street from La Coruña's most important department store; he would become renowned for choosing the best locations for his outlets. Zara was soon reputed for selling quality designer fashions at reasonable prices. The formula had been used successfully by Gap in the United States and Next in Great Britain but was entirely new in Spain; the large Corte Inglés and Cortefiel had controlled the midrange clothing market, but neither appealed to youthful fashion sense. The company's first annual report, which would be produced in 1999, outlined Ortega's goal, stating, "Zara's aim was to democratize fashion. In contrast to the idea of fashion as a privilege, we offer accessible fashion that reaches the high street, inspired by the taste, desires, and lifestyle of modern men and women" (Nash, October 27, 1999). By 1989 Ortega had opened nearly one hundred stores in Spain.

Zara became so successful that advertisement was almost never necessary, as word of mouth sufficiently maintained sales; the chain especially depended on frequent repeat customers. Julian Vogel of the public-relations firm Modus told the *Guardian*, "The girls in the office know that new stock comes in on Tuesday and Thursday and off they go. It's a guilt-free high" (October 28, 2002). Zara merchandise even became acceptable in the world of high fashion. Susie Forbes of British Vogue admitted to the *Guardian*, "My everyday Vogue life is spent in Zara; 70 percent of my wardrobe is from the store" (October 28, 2002).

INDITEX

Ortega's business ventures eventually led to the formation of Inditex, the holding company he created in 1985 to represent his well-known Zara clothing chain along with other smaller chains. Inditex became the biggest multinational textile company in Spain and among the largest in the world; in the late 1990s only Gap and Sweden's HM were larger. The company employed more than 12,000 workers worldwide. Zara and other Inditex chains operated branches in Italy, Great Britain, the United States, Latin America, Japan, and Kuwait.

Inditex's success was based on the fast-fashion model, bringing clothing from the design stage to the store in a matter of weeks. Inditex spotters surveyed designs at fashion shows; in-house designers then copied the most promising ideas. The company's manufacturing base and distribution network was capable of pushing new clothes into stores within weeks—up to 12 times faster than the competition. Inditex shipped fewer pieces, in greater variety, and more often, avoiding high inventory costs and the frequent clearance sales common among most fashion retailers. The whole system was computerized, helping Ortega determine when to restock or drop a design; the company produced only what was needed to sell in its shops. The Inditex CEO José María Castellano told *Newsweek*, "Our structure gives us tremendous advantages over our competition" (September 17, 2001).

Ortega's model seemed to go against the forces of globalization. In the post–World War II era manufacturers increasingly utilized low-wage workers in developing countries. Ortega,

however, kept jobs in Spain and showed that speed, flexibility, and low inventories could be just as important in keeping expenses down: while Ortega spent up to 15 percent more on labor costs than did his third-world-employing competitors, he saved by doing almost no advertising, quickly adjusting to fashion trends, and minimizing shipping costs by keeping production close to markets. As such Inditex largely avoided criticism from human-rights activists, since the company did not exploit workers in developing countries.

The Inditex model came to be taught in many business schools, replacing the model that had called for complex global networks that could take nine months to get clothing from the design stage to the store. Observers noted that such a model had the potential to end the losses of jobs in the developed world. John Thorbeck of the consulting firm Supply Chainge commented in *Newsweek*, "Zara has proven that speed and flexibility matter more than pure price. They've turned the old way of doing business on its head" (September 17, 2001).

PRIVATE AND DOWN-TO-EARTH

Ortega had a reputation as a private and secretive man. He never granted interviews to the media, and the company released very little personal information about its founder and chairman; some in the press referred to the Inditex chief as a "publicist's nightmare." For decades there was only one known photograph of Ortega in circulation. When the company issued its first annual report in 1999, a new photograph finally appeared. Ortega rarely attended official events. When the Spanish Prince Felipe called on Inditex headquarters, the royal visitor was received by one of Ortega's representatives.

Ortega was also known for being a down-to-earth boss. He never wore a tie to work; indeed his wedding was reportedly the last time he had donned one. He hated working with investment bankers in preparation for the initial public offering of Inditex stock. One banker told the *Financial Times*, "We could see it was absolute torture for him" (April 28, 2001). Even on the first day of the sale of Inditex stock in 2001, when Ortega became the richest man in Spain, he did not celebrate in grand style. Rather he went to work, watched the news on television for 15 minutes to find out that he had just earned $6 billion, and then ate lunch in the company cafeteria.

SOURCES FOR FURTHER INFORMATION

Crawford, Leslie, "Spanish Recluse Tailors New Way to Do Business," *Financial Times*, April 28, 2001.

Mcguire, Stryker, "Fast Fashion," *Newsweek*, September 17, 2001, p. 36.

Nash, Elizabeth, "The Discreet Mogul Fashioning an Empire," *Independent* (London), October 27, 1999.

Roux, Caroline, "The Reign of Spain," *Guardian* (London), October 28, 2002.

Wilkinson, Isambard, "Amancio Ortega Has Just Become Spain's Richest Man," *Sunday Telegraph* (London), May 27, 2001.

—Ronald Young

Marcel Ospel

1950–

Chief executive officer, United Bank of Switzerland

Nationality: Swiss.

Born: February 8, 1950, in Basel, Switzerland.

Education: School of Economics and Business Administration, BS, 1977.

Career: Swiss Bank Corporation, 1977–1980, member of Department of Planning and Marketing; SBC International, 1980–1984, member of capital markets division; Merrill Lynch Capital Markets, 1984–1987, managing director; Swiss Bank Corporation, 1987–1995, director of securities trading and sales; 1995–1996, chief executive officer; 1996–1998, president and group chief executive officer; United Bank of Switzerland, 1998–2001, group chief executive officer; 2001–, chairman of the board and director.

Address: United Bank of Switzerland, Bahnhofstr.45, 8021, Zurich, Switzerland; http://www.ubs.com.

Marcel Ospel. *AP/Wide World Photos.*

■ Marcel Ospel began his banking career with the Swiss Bank Corporation (SBC) in 1977. He spent the next few years working on the international banking scene before leaving SBC in 1984 for a position with Merrill Lynch, where he remained for three years before coming back to the Swiss bank, where he rapidly moved up the ranks within the company. He spent five years overseeing securities and trading before becoming a member of the executive board in 1990. His success with mergers brought him the title of chief executive officer in 1995. Ospel was credited with turning around SBC. When SBC and Union Bank of Switzerland merged in 1998 to form United Bank of Switzerland, Ospel became the CEO and received criticism for not making a smooth transition in uniting these two very different banks. Analysts continued to watch Ospel closely as turnover among top executives became a regular occurrence and as industry insiders blamed Ospel's management style for problems within the largest of Switzerland's banks.

RISING TO THE TOP JOB

When Ospel turned 16, he was given two choices for the next stage of his life: he could continue with his schooling, or he could take a job with a small bank in Basel, Switzerland. He decided to take advantage of Switzerland's apprentice program, in which he worked for the bank for three years while attending school.

His first job in the late 1960s consisted of going every day to the stock exchange, where he learned firsthand about the stock market from the bottom up. He ran around the exchange floor with pieces of paper to aid in his company's arbitration with foreign exchanges. When his three years ended, he went to Geneva and worked in the trading division of a private bank. He decided after a short time that he should attend school, so he went back to Basel and completed a three-year degree at the School of Economics and Business Administration before beginning his career at SBC in 1977.

Ospel worked at SBC for seven years before leaving for a position with Merrill Lynch, where he received much of his training in the American style of banking. He returned to SBC 10 days before the stock market crash of 1987. He was in Hong Kong on the day of the actual crash and learned of such risk management strategies as derivatives at that time. Ospel began to restructure SBC's decentralized operation to include a risk management sector, and he started to develop relationships with companies that would later play an important role in his rise to the top of SBC's management.

In 1990 SBC held the unfortunate title of being the weakest of the three top banking firms in Switzerland, with a less-than-average international operations sector. Under Ospel's guidance as the director of securities trading, SBC began a program to turn its image around.

In 1992, when SBC bought O'Connor, an American options trading firm, Ospel oversaw the selection of O'Connor's partners as top managers in SBC. At the time, Ospel ran securities trading and hoped that the placement of people he called "O'Connorites" would help SBC increase its expertise in derivatives. Ospel wanted the O'Connorites to transform the lagging international sector of the company.

However, analysts thought that Ospel had acted with little thought as to whether the partners from O'Connor could handle a beast as large as SBC. They did create a strong derivatives sector but did not understand the nature of luring clients to SBC. By 1994 SBC showed weak revenues when the market hit a slump. Analysts blamed the problems on the O'Connorites' lack of experience and understanding of the market. However, these difficulties did not stop Ospel from looking for another merger.

Ospel studied the markets in both the United States and Europe and at first believed that a move on an American company would make the most sense. However, Ospel began receiving reports that Wall Street looked unstable for the future while Europe seemed poised to enter into a period of privatization and corporate restructuring. When S. G. Warburg, a British investment bank, quit negotiating a deal for a merger with Morgan Stanley, Warburg became Ospel's choice in 1995 for acquisition.

Industry insiders said that the move was risky because of the size of the merger, which brought together 11,000 employees, a feat never before attempted. Ospel was also criticized for not attempting to merge the differing cultures of the two banks. Warburg emphasized the client rather than the deal while SBC focused on the deal rather than on the client. Ospel responded to those claims by stating that the differences were not so great, and he moved to complete the integration as quickly as possible. He stressed that a change of culture could

not be forced, allowing the Warburg staff to acclimate at its own pace.

Ospel announced the immediate dismissal of one thousand staff, with most of the layoffs in the equities and settlements departments. Ospel completed the dismissals quickly and had determined which staff to keep before the finalization of the merger. He and his management team conducted interviews and kept to a format to minimize subjective criteria as a basis for the layoffs. This move generated a reaction from the Warburg staff, with three hundred leaving within the first months of the merger, a circumstance Ospel downplayed by stating that such activity was normal after a merger of this type.

However, with the merger came success for SBC and notoriety for Ospel. By 1996 SBC ranked number one in certain areas of the Swiss banking world and had become a major player in derivatives in both European corporate finance and international equities.

RECEIVES THE NOD AS CEO

Ospel's appointment as CEO of SBC came with both controversy and success. In 1995, less than six months after he had persuaded SBC to purchase Warburg, Ospel replaced George Blum as CEO.

Industry insiders said the move indicated that SBC wanted to focus on its international banking operations since Swiss opportunities remained limited in an oversaturated market. Ospel's background with Merrill Lynch put him in a strong position to fit with the new emphasis.

Within three years Ospel announced another major merger. Analysts applauded the move because it combined two Swiss banks, SBC and Union Bank of Switzerland (UBS), into one entity. Analysts hailed the deal as positive because it lessened the glut of banking institutions in a saturated market. The new company became known as United Bank of Switzerland.

This merger also received praise because it took the weakest of Swiss banks, UBS, and combined it with one of the most vital of Swiss banks, SBC. Analysts said that the merger represented a move to make headway into the large profits enjoyed by English banks. The merger cut the costs of the banks' retail networks while allowing them to share the costs of a global banking operation. Industry insiders predicted that UBS would become a major presence in the world of international banking. Ospel was named CEO of the newly merged bank because of his success in turning SBC into a powerhouse among European banks.

The merger created a balance sheet of $625 million, forming a situation for Ospel that he had not yet encountered. Ospel was further challenged by the differing cultures of the two institutions and excessive overlap of divisions, which would require trimming to keep down costs.

Ospel announced that problems would not have time to develop because he planned to integrate the two banks fully on a 12-month schedule for the investment banking and institutional asset management divisions. He estimated one to two years for the integration of the private sector part of the corporation. Analysts noted that Ospel's success depended on the qualities of the management team he assembled to deal with the transition. Ospel chose the former CEO of Union Bank of Switzerland, Mathis Cabiallavetta, as chairman of the new bank. It was reported in *Institutional Investor* that Ospel wanted Cabiallavetta because he was "a fast-taking, no-nonsense manager who headed his bank's trading and sales, risk management, and group treasury functions for five years before becoming CEO in 1995" (January 1998). Ospel saw Cabiallavetta as someone who could integrate people and company structures. It was also noted that the two men were close personal friends who enjoyed playing chess.

A MERGER CREATES A CLASH OF DIFFERENT CULTURES

The praise for Ospel's genius in creating UBS was short lived. Within two years analysts were declaring that the merger had failed and so had Ospel. It was reported in 2000 that some analysts and investors in London wondered whether UBS could even continue, citing the large number of giant European financial institutions. They announced that breaking apart UBS might be the best strategy.

The investment and private banking operations showed poor performance by 2000, and stock prices had dipped 1 percent from 1999's level.

Chief among the criticisms of Ospel was his inability to combine the two very different banking cultures involved in the merger. Union Bank had strong ties to the Swiss Army elite while SBC's top management held less privileged backgrounds. Fights began as soon as the merger occurred.

As a result, Ospel announced a restructuring of the bank in early 2000, particularly because of the dismal reports from the private banking sector. He fired managers who clashed with others within the company, including Rodolfo Bogni, an Italian who did not meld into the Swiss culture. Analysts said that Ospel was making moves in the right direction but predicted that he did not have much time to realize the benefits of the restructuring.

Business Week reported that a Swiss analyst "gives Ospel six months to show progress. Otherwise, he says, shareholders will demand Ospel's ouster, maybe even the bank's breakup" (March 6, 2000).

Even though Ospel's goal in 1997 had been for the private banking sector to run the profits machine at UBS, by the third quarter of 1999, reported in March 2000, earnings from private banking had fallen by $397 million from the previous year. The losses grew, and Cabiallavata resigned. Even though UBS was considered one of the world's largest banks, with $1 trillion in assets under management, its losses in the private banking section took a beating. In July 2000 UBS announced that it had dropped 18 percent in the quarter ending June 30, 2000. However, its overall operations in 1999 showed that net income had doubled from $3.9 billion, despite a 39 percent decrease in profit in private banking and the loss of many large clients in the asset management division.

Ospel's critics accused him of being unable to make decisions, causing the share price to drop considerably. They said that he had rested on the praise heaped upon him early on, and even though he was only 50 years old in 2000, some felt he was acting as if he were ready for retirement. However, Ospel did take immediate measures by firing the head of the private banking division and implementing a major restructuring of that unit.

Morale dropped among employees as a result of the dire predictions for UBS in the media. Many of the sectors feared that they would be either sold or closed. In 2001, when some of Ospel's strategies had begun to pay off, he commented on the dark days of 2000 to *Euromoney* magazine: "The last four months of last year were obviously a very difficult period," he said. "As well as merging the businesses and running them, we had to overcome these new types of shocks which created disappointments both internally and externally" (June 2, 2001).

Ospel announced in 2001 that the international portion of the merger was completed and that the final touches on the Switzerland integration would be finished in mid-2001. Ospel viewed the markets according to the definitions he had learned while working for Merrill Lynch. Asset management, private banking, and securities and capital markets became separate and distinct divisions within the large corporation. The purchase of PaineWebber Group for $12 billion in 2000 also boosted the company's place in the banking world in the United States. However, not all analysts saw this move as one that would help UBS since PaineWebber was not one of the top institutions for an American acquisition.

Ospel also repeated a strategy that had been successful with SBC in the 1990s. He announced plans to shrink the loan book from Sfr 270 billion to Sfr 60 billion, which emphasized the move away from UBS's classification as strictly a commercial bank. Ospel said that making loans to clients was not the driving force behind a bank such as UBS.

MANAGING THE MANAGERS

Ospel again made the news late in 2001, when he fired UBS's British president, Luqman Arnold, because of a difference of opinion. Industry insiders said that Arnold had been unable to offer a bridge between his bosses in Switzerland and executives on Wall Street.

The *New York Times* reported that major dissension came when Arnold went against Ospel's wishes and did not approve a loan to Echostar Communications, even after advising the client to go ahead with a lucrative acquisition. The paper reported, "It was Mr. Arnold who opposed making the loan, executives at the bank said, despite support for the deal from the UBS chairman, Marcel Ospel. In an embarrassing twist for UBS, Echostar won the bidding, but ended up giving the financing to two archrivals of UBS" (December 19, 2001).

Some industry insiders blamed Arnold's quick dismissal after only seven months on rumors that had surfaced about Arnold's desire to take over Ospel's position on the board. Investors expressed surprise at the announcement as shares dropped 3 percent. One investment banker with UBS said that not even rumors had been whispered about the firing in a business in which gossip is easily spread.

Ospel received much criticism for a decision he made in 2002 regarding a rescue package for Swissair. Analysts said that Ospel and the head of Credit Suisse, Lukas Muhlemann, interfered with a process that led to a quick downfall for the Swiss airline. They were blamed for not balancing their international aspirations with local obligations.

Ospel in particular was blamed for making a commitment to bail out Swissair with a rescue package of $860 million late in 2001. Industry insiders said that he should have gone to the board. It was reported that the board chastised him for failing to keep his directors informed of his actions.

MANAGEMENT STYLE

Ospel broke the rules not only in Swiss banking circles but also with his own management style and personal characteristics. While working with Merrill Lynch, he established a style resembling that of a U.S. investment banker.

While Ospel loved a nontraditional style of dress and office accoutrements, his colleagues sometimes described him as quietly thoughtful. In his first years as CEO of SBC, he was described as a leader who delegated and encouraged his employees. Ospel believed that in a corporation as large as SBC, an autocratic, centralized management style would be impossible to maintain. He also said that as the CEO, he was not skilled in every area of the business; therefore, placing key individuals with the proper experience was key to running a company like SBC.

His policy of no dress code at SBC earned the bank and the banker the reputation of having a unique style in the more conservative banking culture. Ospel said that a dress code added nothing to the company except to make employees uncomfortable by requiring them to wear a tie.

However, it was his knowledge of the inner workings of financial markets and an emphasis on strategies and management that received much of the attention in the late 1990s.

When *Euromoney* interviewed him in 1997, Ospel said he knew that his life would change after the Warburg deal. He had worked hard at analyzing the market before suggesting the merger but had finally determined that the European market looked better in the future than Wall Street. Ospel said in the interview, "So we were primed to do some type of a corporate deal, either in the States or in Europe. I knew that would completely change my professional and personal life. I might have ended up in London or New York. But I'm a mobile person and flexible about these sorts of things" (April 1997).

Despite agreeing to the interview with *Euromoney*, Ospel maintained that bankers should always keep a low public profile, leaving a high-profile lifestyle to the politicians. He also stressed intellectual honesty as the attribute most important to him in an employee, surrounding himself with successful individuals with strong ethics.

By 2000 Ospel had begun losing his reputation as a fair employer and delegator. The press criticized him as being an active president and not clearly defining other positions within the company. He was accused of surrounding himself with people who agreed with him without considering their abilities in international banking.

Euroweek painted an unflattering picture of Ospel as a leader who filled positions at UBS with his friends and admirers, reporting that dissension was not allowed, and "when you pass the great man, you no longer say, 'guten morgen, Herr Ospel,' but 'Hail Caesar!'" (February 22, 2002).

Industry insiders hinted that Ospel did not enjoy sharing power and that his desire for control led to many of the problems with management from 2000 to 2002.

See also entry on Swiss Bank Corporation in *International Directory of Company Histories.*

SOURCES FOR FURTHER INFORMATION

Andrews, Edmund L., "International Business; Swiss Acquirer Has Had Plenty of Its Own Problems," *New York Times*, July 13, 2000.

———, "UBS Ousts President After 7 Months in Job," *New York Times*, December 19, 2001.

Evans, Garry, "The Ospel Interview," *Euromoney*, April 1997, cover story.

Kerr, Ian, "A Week in the Markets," *Euroweek*, February 22, 2002, p. 10–12.

Lee, Peter, "The Race Is on for Europe's Nouveaux Riches," *Euromoney*, June 2, 2001.

"Time Is Running Out for UBS," *BusinessWeek*, March 6, 2000, p. 46.

"Under New Management: SBC Warburg," *Economist* (U.S.),
November 11, 1995, p. 79.

"Why It's Ospel's United Bank of Switzerland," *Institutional
Investor*, January 1998, pp. 14–15.

—Patricia C. Behnke

◼◼◼
Paul Otellini
1950–
President and chief operating officer, Intel Corporation

Nationality: American.

Born: October 12, 1950, in San Francisco, California.

Education: University of San Francisco, BA, 1972; University of California, Berkeley, MBA, 1974.

Family: Son of David Otellini (butcher; mother's name unknown); married Sandy; children: two.

Career: Intel Corporation, 1974–1980, programmer, marketer, financial analyst; 1980–1987, account manager; 1987, general manager, peripheral components operation; 1988, operating group vice president; 1989, technical assistant to president and chief executive officer; 1990, general manager, microprocessor products group; 1991–1993, corporate executive officer; 1993–1996, senior vice president; 1996–1998, executive vice president, sales and marketing; 1998–2002, executive vice president, architecture business group; 2002–, president and chief operating officer.

Address: Intel Corporation, 2200 Mission College Boulevard, Santa Clara, California 95052; http://www.intel.com.

Paul Otellini. *AP/Wide World Photos.*

◼ Paul Otellini joined Intel Corporation straight out of business school and rose through the company's ranks as a result of his marketing savvy and leadership in product development. During the 1980s he cultivated a key strategic relationship between Intel and International Business Machines (IBM), and during the 1990s he presided over the development of Intel's flagship computer chip, the Pentium. Elected president and COO of Intel in 2002, Otellini became second in command of the world's leading producer of microprocessors.

EARLY LIFE AND EDUCATION

Born and raised in San Francisco, California, Otellini grew up in a working-class Italian American family with deep roots in the Bay Area. He began working at an early age, delivering newspapers while in grammar school and stocking shelves and selling suits at a men's clothing store while in high school. As a child Otellini took an interest in chemistry and mathematics. His lack of engineering ability, however unusual among Intel executives, was reflected in a humorous anecdote from his adolescence. While swinging from an ill-designed pulley system constructed with his brother and cousin, he plunged into a rocky bluff near Lake Tahoe.

Otellini's devoutly Catholic father urged his sons to join the priesthood—a call that Otellini's brother heeded. Otellini resisted, instead attending the University of San Francisco, a Jesuit institution. As an undergraduate Otellini developed an interest in finance and majored in economics. He completed his degree in 1972 and enrolled in the business school at the University of California, Berkeley, where he studied finance and earned a master of business administration degree in 1974.

JOINS INTEL AND MANAGES IBM ACCOUNT

With his formal education behind him, Otellini sought employment in the burgeoning computer technology industry in Silicon Valley, then a mostly agricultural region south of San Francisco. Otellini considered Fairchild Semiconductor and Advanced Micro Devices but ultimately choose Intel, the semiconductor company founded in 1968 by the computer pioneers Robert Noyce and Gordon Moore. In 1971 Intel introduced the world's first microprocessor, a powerful miniature circuit that revolutionized computing by integrating and rapidly speeding up multiple information-processing functions.

Hired in 1974 Otellini began working in the finance department, where he programmed a cost system for the company on a primitive computer. During the next six years Otellini was involved in various finance and marketing roles related to Intel's new microprocessor division. In 1980 he was placed in charge of Intel's account with IBM, at the time Intel's largest customer of memory, rather than microprocessor, products. Otellini persuaded IBM to use Intel's microprocessors in its new computers, a sales triumph with tremendous consequences. The world's first personal computer, introduced by IBM in 1981, was powered by an Intel microprocessor. Over the next two decades Intel's chips would serve as the brains behind IBM's groundbreaking 286, 386, 486, and 586 series computers.

RISE TO TOP MANAGEMENT

In 1987 Otellini advanced as general manager of the peripheral components operation and was sent to manage Intel's new plant in Folsom, California. During this time he was recognized as an inspiring leader for his compassion in handling grief-stricken workers in the wake of two unrelated employee suicides within a six-month period. Otellini brought in counselors and personally engaged employees at the plant, exhibiting a gentle strength that impressed the Intel president, Andrew Grove.

In 1988 Otellini was promoted to operating group vice president, and in 1989 he served as technical assistant to Grove, who sought to groom Otellini for a top management position. In 1990 Otellini was tapped to head Intel's microprocessor products group, which included managing the development of the Pentium chip. Although harried by minor calculating glitches on its release in 1993—a public relations crisis that Otellini successfully weathered—the Pentium set the standard for fifth-generation, or 586, microprocessors and became one of the most recognized trademarks in the world.

Otellini was named a corporate executive officer at Intel in 1991 and, with the launch of the Pentium, advanced to senior vice president in 1993 and executive vice president in 1996. In 1998 he was placed in charge of the Intel Architecture Group, taking on overall responsibility for Intel's $21 billion microprocessor business, which accounted for 80 percent of Intel's total business.

PRESIDENT AND COO OF INTEL

After 28 years at Intel, Otellini was elected president and COO of the company in 2002. The move signaled that Otellini was Intel's heir apparent, because the company's presiding chief executive officer, Craig R. Barrett, then 62 years old, was three years away from the company's mandatory retirement age. Otellini's ascendance was presumed to represent the first stage of a gradual succession plan in which Barrett and Otellini shared leadership of the company. Barrett focused on Intel's broad corporate strategy, and Otellini continued to oversee internal operations such as product development and manufacturing.

Otellini assumed the presidency in a year that Intel reported precipitous financial losses as the personal computer market matured and Intel's efforts to diversify its business in consumer electronics and web-hosting ventures failed to meet expectations. Otellini, who viewed himself as a "product guy" despite his lack of engineering credentials, helped turn the company back toward its core business in silicon microprocessors. Instead of merely working to produce faster chips, Otellini touted the importance of developing multifunctional chips with integrated communication features and reduced external power requirements. New products such as the Centrino laptop chipset, introduced in 2003, and Intel's XScale processors, used in an array of handheld devices such as personal digital assistants, mobile phones, and MP3 players, embodied Otellini's vision of lightweight, highly mobile technology.

Otellini's success as an executive was attributed to his superior marketing ability and light touch as a manager. He motivated rather than dictated. In contrast to Barrett, who reportedly wielded a baseball bat at meetings, Otellini was soft-spoken and encouraged his subordinates to push themselves through his own quiet confidence, described by Cliff Edwards of *BusinessWeek* as "Zen-like." Otellini's appointment as Intel's president, which came at a time when the company was attempting to reposition itself as the world's premier chipmaker, reflected the respect with which he was viewed by Intel insiders as a tested leader and pitchman.

See also entry on Intel Corporation in *International Directory of Company Histories.*

SOURCES FOR FURTHER INFORMATION

Clark, Don, "Intel Promotes Veteran Paul Otellini to President, Chief Operating Officer," *Wall Street Journal,* January 17, 2002.

Paul Otellini

Detar, James, "Pervasive Intelligence: Pervasive Intel Networks That Can 'Think'," *Investor's Business Daily*, November 29, 2002.

Edwards, Cliff, "No Nerd at the Top? Heresy! Intel's CEO-in-Waiting, Paul Otellini, Is a Master Marketer," *BusinessWeek*, November 4, 2002, p. 78.

Kirkpatrick, David, "At Intel, Speed Isn't Everything," *Fortune*, February 9, 2004, p. 34.

Morrow, Daniel S., "Paul Otellini Oral History," Computerworld Honors Program International Archives, April 30, 2003, http://www.cwheroes.org/oral_history_archive/paul_otellini/Otellini.pdf.

Taylor, Chris, "The Salesman of Silicon Valley: Paul Otellini," *Time*, December 1, 2003, p. 75.

—Josh Lauer

■ ■ ■
Mutsutake Otsuka
1932–
President and chief executive officer, East Japan Railway Company

Nationality: Japanese.

Born: January 5, 1932, in Beijing, China.

Education: Tokyo University, received degree, 1965.

Career: Japan National Railways, 1965–1987, various positions; East Japan National Railway Company (JR East), 1987–1997, managing director; 1997–2000, vice president; 2000–, president and chief executive officer.

Address: JR East, 2-2, Yoyogi 2-chome, Shibuya-ku, Tokyo, 151-8578, Japan; http://www.jreast.co.jp.

■ In 2000 Mutsutake Otsuka, the son of a Southern Manchuria Railway executive, became president and chief executive officer of East Japan Railway Company (JR East), the largest railway company in the world. Otsuka joined Japan National Railways in 1965. Following a loss of $14 billion in 1985, Japan National Railways was privatized and divided, which led to the establishment of JR East in 1987. Otsuka became the managing director of the new firm. Privatization enabled Japan's railroads to employ fewer workers and charge lower fares. Otsuka was a hands-on manager who took a close interest in the completion of projects. He also had an eye for future innovations for JR East. "In today's business world, management must plan in several time frames at once," he said in *Forbes.com.* "And you need to roll forward your goals to absorb the impact of new conditions and technologies."

To further increase passengers and revenue, Otsuka looked to foreign tourists. "Only five million tourists visit Japan annually, about one-third the number of Japanese visiting abroad," he said (*Forbes.com*). To increase tourism, the Ministry of Land, Infrastructure, and Transport began a campaign aimed at doubling the number of foreign tourists who visited Japan by 2010, and Otsuke expected that these tourists would also become railway users.

Otsuka also initiated a plan to make JR East a leading provider of services by transforming railway stations into centers for shopping, dining, and other leisure activities. In 2002 Union East became the first of the stations to be renovated and expanded. Otsuka planned to renovate the Tokyo station by 2010; the plans included restoring the station to its original three-story design, renovating the plaza in front of the station, and adding a shopping center and office-building complex.

Other innovations from Otsuka included the Suica, a smart card that functioned as an electronic train pass. Instead of waiting in line at a ticket machine, a person could get to the train by simply touching their Suica card to the gate. The card was designed to reduce the number of ticket offices, vending machines, and employees. Otsuka said that it would promote spontaneous and use of trains.

Environmental concerns also were a component of Otsuka's strategy. JR East announced a plan to reduce emissions of carbon dioxide by 2006 to 80 percent of their 1990 levels. He also pursued mergers and acquisitions; in 2002 JR East acquired Orangepage, a magazine publisher that collects and analyzes consumer trend statistics and information, as well as Tokyo Monorail.

See also entry on East Japan Railway Company in *International Directory of Company Histories.*

SOURCES FOR FURTHER INFORMATION

Nikkei kaisha jinmeiroku (Nikkei Who's Who of Corporate Executives and Managers), Tokyo, Nihon Keizai Shinbunsha.

"Otsuka to Become President of JR East," Jiji Press English News Service (Tokyo), April 25, 2000, p. 1.

"Working on the New Frontier: Mutsutake Otsuka," *Forbes.com*, http://www.forbes.com/specialsections/japan/13_otsuka.html.

—Lucy Heckman

■ ■ ■
Lindsay Owen-Jones
1946–
Chairman and chief executive officer, L'Oréal

Nationality: Welsh.

Born: March 17, 1946, in Wallasey, Wales.

Education: Oxford University, BA, 1968; INSEAD, Fontainebleau, France, 1969.

Family: Son of an engineer and professor; married; children: one.

Career: L'Oréal, 1969–1976, product manager in France and Belgium; 1976–1978, marketing director of Consumer Division; 1978–1984, chief executive officer of Italian subsidiary and chairman and CEO of U.S. subsidiary; 1984–1988, executive vice president and chief operating officer; 1988–, chairman and CEO.

Awards: Global Corporate Achievement Award, Economist Intelligence Unit, 2002; named one of the "25 Most Influential Names and Faces in Fashion," *Time Magazine*, fall/winter 2002.

Address: L'Oréal, Centre Eugène Schueller, 41, rue Martre, 92117 Clichy, France; L'Oréal USA, 575 Fifth Avenue, New York, New York 10017; http://www.lorealv2.com/.

Lindsay Owen-Jones. © *Stephane Cardinale/People Avenue/ Corbis.*

■ Lindsay Owen-Jones skillfully developed L'Oréal into the largest beauty-products company in the world through global marketing, product-line diversification, and customer savvy. He spent his entire corporate career at the company, becoming chairman and chief executive officer (CEO).

A GLOBAL REACH FROM THE START

After finishing business school in Paris in 1969, Welshman Owen-Jones started out with L'Oréal as a sales representative in Normandy, France, selling Dop shampoo. Even at the beginning of his career in cosmetics he displayed enthusiasm and sales acumen. Owen-Jones quickly ascended the ranks of this French company. He moved up to the position of junior prod-

uct manager in Belgium in the early 1970s and went on to hold other management positions in Italy, the United States, and France. Working in the United States in the early 1980s, Owen-Jones competed successfully with Estée Lauder and Revlon. In 1988, after under 20 years with L'Oréal, he became chairman and CEO.

By 2004 L'Oréal had acquired dozens of product lines and brands that were sold to both women and men in 150 countries: perfume, color cosmetics, makeup, and hair and skin care. Successful brands included Ralph Lauren fragrances, Preference hair color, Maybelline, Lancôme, Vichy, Garnier, and Redken hair-salon products. Dubbed "The United Nations of Beauty" by Owen-Jones, L'Oréal became a global force in beauty products. After high sales in Europe and the United States, Owen-Jones looked to expand into China, the

Russian Federation, and Japan. Emerging consumer markets with growing middle classes were always compelling for him.

Owen-Jones consistently diversified his products to appeal to women and men around the world. He worked to appeal to widely differing tastes and demonstrated that he knew how to create a need for products previously unknown in a country. To achieve his dream of putting lipstick into the hands of every Chinese woman, for example, Owen-Jones reached across boundaries of culture, race, and income in his advertising and product development. He would sell a style, be it New York street smarts or French chic, always conscious to increase international sales and make each product line stand out for consumers.

Rather than homogenize the company's products across countries and socioeconomic backgrounds, Owen-Jones focused on the cultural specificities of each product line and company. This approach gave L'Oréal the reputation for acknowledging many different perceptions of beauty around the world. In 1997 L'Oréal became the first company to sell a hair color other than black in India. Looking to expand into sub-Saharan Africa, Owen-Jones established a research and development center in Chicago to study African hair types.

SUCCESS STORY

When Owen-Jones joined L'Oréal in 1969, 90 percent of its sales were in Western Europe. By 2003 the company's revenues had reached $14 billion, after 18 consecutive years of double-digit sales and earnings growth. By 2004 L'Oréal had 50,500 employees worldwide.

Risk-taking was central to L'Oréal's growth. Against the better judgment of some, Owen-Jones acquired ailing Maybelline for $758 million in 1996 and completely revamped the brand with a new urban American look. As a result, Maybelline's sales doubled in three years and as of January 2003 it was the top makeup brand in the world.

L'Oréal also set an example, under Owen-Jones's direction, for rival cosmetic companies in the areas of research and development. Owen-Jones ramped up L'Oréal's traditional focus on research and development and set an example for rival companies with increased yearly budgets for technological development and long-term success. This emphasis enabled L'Oréal to develop a varied brands and technology portfolio for stockholders interested in these areas.

Owen-Jones was infamous for acquiring small companies in Asia, the South Pacific, South America, and Africa, a habit that was central to his success. His frequent acquisitions followed a similar routine: Owen-Jones bought out local cosmetics brands, changed their product lines and marketing approach to fit the goals of L'Oréal, and reintroduced the new product lines to both the local market and larger regional mar-

ket. Owen-Jones was not afraid to create competition within his own company, as he showed when he introduced a new line of Redken hair products that competed directly with L'Oréal's Preference line. Owen-Jones believed in the wisdom of selling through retail outlets as well as by direct marketing. He applied a diversified approach to sales and distribution, placing L'Oréal products in mass-market venues, upscale retail stores, and salons.

DEMANDING, YET PERSONABLE

Owen-Jones was known as a perfectionist. He told *Business Week* in 1999, "I am never satisfied and never convinced we are winning." He was known to be demanding in meetings with his own executives, but colleagues and employees affectionately called him "O-J." Company insiders reported that Owen-Jones encouraged female representation and ethnic diversity in the company's leadership ranks. He visited department stores regularly to observe and question customers. He was known to approach women on the street, inquire about their choice of hair color, and march them into a store for free boxes of L'Oréal hair dye.

In 2004 Owen-Jones was named one of twenty "builders and titans" on *Time* magazine's list of the one hundred most influential people in the world. *Time* called him "the man who globalized beauty" and made L'Oréal "into the world's largest cosmetics company."

See also entry on L'Oréal in *International Directory of Company Histories.*

SOURCES FOR FURTHER INFORMATION

"The Best Managers: Lindsay Owen-Jones," *BusinessWeek Online*, http://www.businessweek.com/magazine/content/03_02/b3815621.htm.

Edmonson, Gail, "L'Oréal: The Beauty of Global Branding," *BusinessWeek Online*, http://yahoo.businessweek.com/1999/99_26/b3635016.htm.

James, Jennie, "Lindsay Owen-Jones: Dreams of Beauty," Time Magazine's 2004 Builders and Titans, http://www.time.com.

"L'Oréal's Owen-Jones: 'I Strive for Something I Never Totally Achieve,'" *BusinessWeek Online*, http://yahoo.businessweek.com/1999/99_26/b3635021.htm.

"The Stars of Europe: Managers—Lindsay Owen-Jones," *BusinessWeek Online*, http://www.businessweek.com/magazine/content/02_24/b3787607.htm.

—Alison Lake

Pae Chong-yeul

1943–

President and chief executive officer, Samsung Corporation

Nationality: Korean.

Born: February 18, 1943.

Education: Seoul National University, BA, 1965.

Family: Married; children: four.

Career: Bank of Korea, 1969–1976, junior economist in research department; 1973–1975, assistant advisor on economic policy in the office of the president; Samsung Corporation, 1976–1983, manager, planning department; Samsung Pacific International, 1983, president; Samsung America, 1983–1987, president; Samsung Electronics, 1988–1990, senior executive managing director, sales and marketing, semiconductor division; Samsung Group, 1991–1993, vice president, chairman's office; Joong-ang Daily News, 1994–1998, executive vice president; Cheil Communications, 1998–2001, president and chief executive officer; Samsung Corporation, 2001–, president and chief executive officer.

Address: Samsung Corporation, Samsung Plaza, 263 Seohyeon-dong, Bundang-gu Songnam, Kyonggi 463-721, South Korea; http://www.samsung.com.

■ Pae Chong-yeul was president and CEO of the advertising and media agency Cheil Communications before being appointed in 2001 to the same positions at the Korean conglomerate Samsung, then under the chairmanship of Lee Kun-hee. Samsung was established in 1938 and immediately targeted the global electronics market. In 1975 the Korean government designated it the country's first General Trading Company (GTC), a title that designates an officially recognized import and export trading company. By 2002 the Samsung industrial group employed 175,000 people worldwide and posted revenues of $116.8 billion.

ALL IN THE FAMILY: A SAMSUNG STORY

A major transition took place in 1996 when Samsung Corporation merged with Samsung Engineering and Construc-
tion. Following the merger Samsung added retail to its existing business portfolio of trading and apparel products, and a joint venture with Tesco of Great Britain saw it consolidate its three major business groups in trading, construction, and housing development. Samsung built the 92-story KLCC Petronas Tower complex in Malaysia, then the world's tallest buildings, and was the top maker in the world of dynamic random-access memory (DRAM) and other memory chips. Its venture into information technology endowed it with Korea's largest online shopping mall and industry-specific global e-markets for the export of industrial goods and commodities. Two of its original e-markets were in chemicals and seafood products.

Pae's graduation from Samsung's in-house advertising company Cheil Communications to Samsung Corporation's president and CEO may be interpreted as a shift in the Samsung Group's global strategy. After a period of expansive growth in the 1990s, Samsung moved to consolidate its gains after 2001 by selling off unproductive assets and cutting costs while emphasizing developmental work in media and marketing. A focus on emerging markets, notably in Brazil, Russia, India, and China, was accompanied by Cheil Communication's steady acquisition of Samsung accounts in those countries. In 2004, for example, Samsung's advertising budget in India alone was some 1 billion rupees, making Cheil an obvious choice as Samsung's advertising agency. The shift in emphasis toward marketing thus created a stable client-partner relationship between Cheil and its parent company Samsung.

SPEAKING FOR SAMSUNG: A VOICE HEARD AROUND THE WORLD

Pae cut his executive teeth at Cheil Communications, which was established in 1973. Under Pae's direction Cheil Communications was transformed into one of Korea's largest advertising agencies, with over 856 employees and a market capitalization of more than 5 billion won. The company expanded into the international market and had branches in London, Barcelona, Beijing, Frankfurt, Hong Kong, Moscow, Tokyo, and Vienna, and two branches in Korea, at Seoul and Pusan. Its American partner, Cheil Communications America, was headquartered in New York and had branches in Miami and Los Angeles. Another partner, Cheil Bozell, based in Korea, was a joint venture with Bozell USA. When Pae assumed control in 1998, the company billed 686.1 billion won.

The business philosophy that Pae set for Cheil was simple and direct: number one in strategy and number one in creativity. Its strategy focused on three main business sectors: television and radio, which accounted for 40.4 percent of total business activity, promotion (25.3 percent), and print media (23.7 percent). Other activities accounted for the remaining 10.6 percent.

An idea of the diversity of Cheil's market share under Pae can be gained from its client list, which included Ace Bed Company, Dae Woong Pharmaceutical Company, Dongsuh Foods Corporation, Hanil Synthetic Fiber Company, Hotel Shilla, Korea Mobile Telecom, Lamy Cosmetics Company, Koreana Cosmetics Company, Pigeon Corporation, Pizza Hut Korea Company, Pulmuwon Foods Company, Samsung Aerospace Industries, Samsung Corporation, Samsung Life Insurance Company, Samsung Engineering & Construction Company, Samsung Electronics Company, and Sun Kyung Business Group.

Pae expanded Cheil's client list when it merged with the American advertising giant FCB. FCB Worldwide was the largest advertising agency in the United States and the fifth-largest agency worldwide, with 1999 billings of $8.8 billion. With more than 200 offices servicing clients in 96 countries, FCB Worldwide's client roster included S. C. Johnson, DaimlerChrysler, Compaq, AT&T, Dockers, Quaker Oats, U.S. Postal Service, Coors, and Beiersdorf. Pae Chong-yeul was personally credited with raising Cheil Communications stock value eight-fold. In 2004 Cheil had become the 18th-largest marketing agency in the world, with $182 million in revenues.

MARKETING A NEW BRAND OF CAPITALISM: CHAIRMAN LEE'S PHILOSOPHY

In 1993 Samsung's chairman Lee Kun-hee launched his New Management Initiative, whose key element was ethics. Lee stipulated that a business that lacked a sense of ethics could not make good products. The guiding principles laid down by Lee emphasized the "three virtues" of humanity, ethics, and good manners.

Referred to as "chairman and chief ethics officer" by the group's key members, Lee stated the Samsung philosophy as follows: "Profit for profit's sake does not make sense. . . . In the new century, businesses must sell their philosophy and culture in addition to products" Korea Herald, September 16, 2003). Pae summarized the chairman's position by noting that Lee firmly believed that good-quality management and products could be expected from good-quality people.

If Lee set the moral tone for his affiliates and employees, he has also set the cultural tenor at Samsung. His personal style was as simple as his philosophy: "Stick to business." His belief in the virtues of corporate discipline can be seen in a comment

he made to his counterpart at Daewoo, Kim Woo-choong, then contemplating a bid to run in the upcoming Korean Presidential election: "Why don't you withdraw that bid?" A major rift between the two companies ensued. Pae, who was then vice president of the chairman's office at Samsung, apologized on behalf of Lee and explained that the chairman only meant that a businessman should remain a businessman (Korea Herald, July 24, 2003).

The chairman's remark also marred Samsung's good relations with the government, which had used the group to educate its secretarial staff under the New Management Initiative. Ranking bureaucrats, including Interior Minister Choi Hyung-woo and provincial governors, also underwent educational courses provided by Samsung's Human Resource Development Center. The government took offense at the chairman's implied criticism of politicians and bureaucrats. Relations soured and the government put Samsung under considerable pressure, including investigations concerning alleged real-estate speculation.

At this trying time, Pae expressed Samsung's position that businessmen and politicians needed to cooperate for the good of the country and, on behalf of Chairman Lee, stressed the need for a unified effort by the people, the government, and businesses to build national competitiveness. The controversy eventually died down.

PLAYING THE GAME

Lee's management philosophy was said to have been inspired by golf and other sports. He believed that golf teaches self-discipline, obedience to rules, and gentlemanly behavior; baseball teaches one how to be a star player and a team player; and rugby teaches the spirit of fortitude. Pae interpreted Lee's remarks about the proper way to swing a golf club as meaning that an organization must be flexible and agile if it is going to succeed. In response to his employee's sluggish response to his call for innovation, Lee imposed a 7 a.m. to 4 p.m. workday. Although the group's actual business started at 8:30, the hour and a half between 7:00 and 8:30 was designed to make employees feel the need for drastic change through a break in routine. This shock was an attempt to awaken employees from their lethargy. The move met with some controversy, and some employees did not understand the reason for changing the workday. Pae explained the new system had several intentions: it allowed Samsung employees to reduce the time for commuting, which in turn was expected to increase efficiency, and—because the workday was now ending earlier than in the past—it allowed employees to study after work and spend time with their families.

A SLOGAN FOR SAMSUNG: COUNTRY, COMMUNITY AND COMPANY

Perhaps nobody affiliated with Samsung better embodied Lee's corporate philosophy and personal style than Pae. At Cheil, Pae was already concerned about public relations and the company's role in community affairs. For example, he organized a benefit concert with Michael Jackson in 1995 on behalf of the World Peace Forum for Children in response to the famine in North Korea. Lee himself repeatedly stated that a company must be held responsible to its community and must participate in charity functions and benefits.

As a spokesman and representative for Chairman Lee and Samsung, Pae helped to redefine the Samsung image while introducing products to the marketplace. The emphasis on employee self-improvement, good community relations, and corporate transparency played a role in supporting the creation of a management system that could garner large annual profits even under unfavorable business conditions. In 2004, three years after Pae became president and CEO, Samsung surpassed Hyundai to become Korea's largest corporate group.

See also entries on Samsung Electronics and Samsung Group in *International Directory of Company Histories.*

SOURCES FOR FURTHER INFORMATION

Kim Sung-hong and Woo In-ho, "Going to Work at 7: Wake Up Call for Sleeping Samsung; 7-to-4 Workday Scheme Marks Starting Point of Lee's Bold Reform for His Business Empire," *Herald Business,* June 5, 2003.

———, "Korea Should Change as well as Samsung," *Korea Herald,* July 24, 2003.

"Learning Management on Green," *Korea Herald,* June 19, 2003.

"Lee's Principle: 'Politics Is Not My Cup of Tea,'" *Korea Herald,* July 24, 2003.

"Samsung Puts Corporate Ethics First," *Korea Herald,* September 16, 2003.

—John Herrick

■ ■ ■
Samuel J. Palmisano
1951–
Chairman of the board, chief executive officer, and president, International Business Machines Corporation

Nationality: American.

Born: 1951, in Baltimore, Maryland.

Education: Johns Hopkins University, BA, 1973.

Family: Married Gaier Notman (homemaker); children: four.

Career: International Business Machines Corporation (IBM), 1973–1989, sales representative; 1989–1991, executive assistant to chief executive officer John Akers; IBM Japan, 1991–1993, senior managing director, operations; Integrated Systems Solutions Corporation, January 1993–1996, president; October 1993–1996, CEO; 1995–1997, head of strategic outsourcing; Personal Computer Company, 1996–1997, managing director; Personal Systems Group, 1997–1998, senior vice president; IBM Global Services, 1998–1999, corporate senior vice president and manager; Enterprise Systems Group, 1999–2000, senior vice president; IBM Corporation, 2000–2002, president and chief operating officer; 2002–, president and CEO; 2003–, chairman of the board.

Awards: Alumni Hall of Fame, Calvert Hall College High School, 1999; Distinguished Alumni Award, Johns Hopkins University, 2003.

Address: International Business Machines Corporation, New Orchard Road, Armonk, New York 10504; http://www.ibm.com/us.

■ Samuel Palmisano was charismatic and likable; he was also decisive, passionate about his work, and very competitive. When he ran Integrated Systems Solutions Corporation, a subsidiary of the International Business Machines Corporation (IBM), he was said to have kept a list of a rival company's clients and checked names off the list as his sales force won them for IBM. His usually relaxed demeanor belied a fiery temperament and a strong personality that drove him to micromanage almost every project he directed. Those who worked for him

gave him high marks for honesty and candor; they liked him even though he often generated high anxiety levels in his subordinates with demands for almost daily updates on what they were doing. Palmisano's leisure activities included reading history books, skiing, golfing, and jogging to stay in shape. He brought optimism and exceptional self-discipline to his leadership of IBM.

RANK AND FILE

Palmisano was born into an old family that had its roots in eighteenth-century America. Its members had spread their influence across the United States as physicians, politicians, and business leaders. Palmisano's father owned an automobile repair business in Baltimore, Maryland, where young Palmisano learned his street smarts among the rough-and-tumble laborers of Baltimore's docks. He attended a Roman Catholic college preparatory school, Calvert Hall, in Towson, Maryland, where he distinguished himself as an honors student and an outstanding football player. He played center and tackle for the school and was noted for his intelligent and unselfish conduct on the playing field as well as for his toughness. Palmisano was also a gifted musician who joined Baltimore's musicians' union while he was in high school. He once had a weeklong professional engagement playing the saxophone in a backup band for the Temptations, which paid him a thousand dollars. He used his earnings to buy himself a car. Palmisano remembered his youth as a happy one with loving parents and siblings. He lived in a disciplined household where he was taught to behave well and work hard.

In 1969 Palmisano entered Johns Hopkins University, where he became a popular student. His nickname was "Baloo," the name of the jolly bear in the Disney animated feature *The Jungle Book*. He played football for Johns Hopkins and was considered an outstanding scholar-athlete. When he graduated with a bachelor's degree in history in 1973, he was invited by the Oakland Raiders to try out for their professional football team. Palmisano saw little future in physical collisions with men who outweighed him. Apparently a career in music did not appeal to him either, because he went to IBM's Baltimore office to apply for a job. He was hired as a sales representative and sent to an IBM training school; there he met Gaier Notman, who became his wife.

SELLING

Palmisano found IBM to be an exciting place to work in the 1970s. The company's employees referred to themselves as IBMers, meaning that they shared a special corporate culture. To Palmisano, IBM was more than a money-making enterprise; it was a corporation that stood as a model for other companies to emulate, a firm that gave women and minorities jobs and equal pay 28 years before the law required fair treatment. His winning personality, intelligence, and drive made him a successful salesman; he hated meetings, however, and was noted for finding excuses to be with his clients rather than attend what were supposed to be mandatory sessions with colleagues and supervisors.

IBM focused on building behemoth mainframe computers and inviting software developers to write programs for them through the 1970s and most of the 1980s. In 1988, however, Palmisano changed the way IBM sold computers. He had been assigned to a team formed to sell a new giant computer called the AS/400. His assertive approach to sales set the pattern for IBM's future. On his own initiative, Palmisano took the AS/400's specifications to numerous software companies and persuaded them to write programs for it before the computer was ready to market. The result was that when the AS/400 was launched, there were already over one thousand programs available for it. Potential customers had a multitude of applications to choose from if they purchased the computer—a powerful attraction that made the AS/400 one of IBM's most successful products. This achievement made Palmisano a rising star at IBM.

Palmisano became John F. Akers' executive assistant in the spring of 1989. Akers, who was then IBM's CEO, later recalled Palmisano as the best executive assistant he had ever had—always ready with what Akers needed when he needed it. In 1991 Palmisano was sent to direct the operations of IBM Japan. During this period, Palmisano gained a reputation for being a maverick who challenged the decisions of upper-level managers while frequently introducing innovations that kept IBM Japan's balance sheet healthy. He was instrumental in bringing the ThinkPad®, a laptop computer, to the Japanese market and making it a success.

A NEW FOCUS FOR IBM

IBM was doing less well in its home country, however—it lost $5 billion in 1992. Akers wanted to break up IBM into 13 loosely affiliated smaller companies, as some financial analysts saw such a breakup as the best hope for regaining profits. The press was already depicting the old IBM—the company that Palmisano had loved because it stood for technical excellence and moral integrity—as dead in the water. In 1992, however, IBM's board of directors replaced Akers with Lou Gerstner, a manager from R.J. Reynolds, the well-known tobacco company. Gerstner chose to shift IBM from being a company that produced commodities to one focused on services to clients, and he recognized Palmisano as someone who shared his long-term goals for the company.

Gerstner made Palmisano president of Integrated Systems Solutions Corporation in January 1993. Integrated Systems had an interesting history within the IBM network. It had been formed in the 1980s when Eastman Kodak asked IBM to take over some of its information technology chores. The corporation was created to meet Eastman Kodak's needs; it was made a subsidiary of IBM, with headquarters in Tarrytown, New York, 20 miles from IBM's corporate headquarters in Armonk and about 330 miles from Eastman Kodak's headquarters in Rochester. At the time that Palmisano was put in charge of Integrated Systems, the corporation provided networking and information technology services. It was also a maverick unit within IBM, making its own rules and encouraging employees to take initiatives. This approach was congenial to Palmisano, who listened to employees and clients as he learned the ropes of IBM's services business. In October 1993 he moved up to become the CEO of Integrated Systems Solutions Corporation.

Palmisano met with his managers for two days each month, examining every services contract that IBM held around the world. He wanted Integrated Systems to grow, and he pressed his sales force to target the clients of rival services companies. IBM's management had long believed that services contracts were for long-term profits, taking possibly as long as several years to enter the black. Palmisano, however, challenged the notion that services could not boost short-term earnings and insisted that new contracts make money from the very start. He led by example; he was noted for hopping on an airplane at a moment's notice to meet a potential client in person. His employees caught his fire—whereas the parking lot at IBM's headquarters was nearly empty at night and on weekends, the lot in Tarrytown was filled seven days a week, long after five o' clock. In 1993 Integrated Systems Solutions Corporation grossed $14.9 billion; by 1996 it made $22.9 billion.

PREPARATION

The flow of money generated by Palmisano's division helped Gerstner keep IBM intact while Palmisano's emphasis on service fit well with Gerstner's plans for the company's future. Gerstner consequently appointed Palmisano managing director of IBM's Personal Computer Company on April 1, 1996. The Personal Computer Company was a $10 billion per year business that allowed Palmisano to gain experience in running some of IBM's hardware units. That year, Gerstner combined Integrated Systems Solutions Corporation with other smaller service groups to form IBM Global Services, which accounted for 29 percent of IBM's total revenue.

Palmisano's responsibilities were expanded in 1997 when he became senior vice president of the Personal Systems Group, which put him in charge of IBM's personal computer business. He was a rigorously goal-oriented leader who expected his managers to meet their promised goals. In December 1997, however, he found himself falling behind his own goals for the fourth quarter. Beginning on December 26, he held conference calls with his sales representatives at 7 a.m. and 9 p.m. every day through December 31, pushing them hard but finally meeting his sales goal.

IBM's various businesses were booming, but Gerstner wanted to take IBM's services to a higher level. In January 1998 he made Palmisano a senior corporate vice president in charge of IBM Global Services, which was the world's largest provider of information technology with 135,000 employees. Palmisano was then put in charge of IBM's Enterprise Systems Group. There he began IBM's acceptance of the free open-source-code Linux operating system in late 1999. Open source code allowed anyone to read and modify the operating system code to work with other programs. Palmisano advocated open-source software standards rather than proprietary standards as a way to unify all of IBM's hardware and software offerings. Such unification would allow clients to pick and choose what they wanted with the assurance that every component would work with all others without any special proprietary programs that might be difficult to learn. In October 1999 Palmisano introduced "Project Pain," in which IBM's servers were offered to customers at discounts as high as 70 percent.

In 1999, IBM's computer business declined as part of a slump that affected high technology businesses worldwide, and the company's growth flattened. In spite of the downturn, IBM grossed $85.9 billion while netting $7.7 billion. IBM's services—particularly IBM Global Services—accounted for 41 percent of the company's revenues, and were largely responsible for IBM's business decreasing only slightly while competitors saw double-digit drops in income. Moreover, IBM had a market capitalization of $186 billion, providing it with enormous resources not only for weathering the downturn in business but also for readying itself for its next phase of development.

IBM'S NEW PRESIDENT

Palmisano maintained that he was completely surprised when he was informed that he was the new president of IBM. Nevertheless, he became the company's president and chief operating officer on September 1, 2000, responsible for its day-to-day operations as well as being Gerstner's heir apparent. Palmisano had acquired a nickname, "The Closer." The name was apt because he had, perhaps without realizing it, compiled the best sales record in IBM's history. His skills in closing deals with clients had sometimes made the difference between profit and loss on a division's bottom line. In addition to Palmisano's negotiating skills, he had also emphasized the importance of cultivating high-end clients and pressured his subordinates to pursue multimillion-dollar contracts.

As president, Palmisano quickly established weekly operations conferences—even though he disliked meetings—in place of monthly ones, and asked for weekly reports from his managers detailing what business plans they had for the coming week. That year, IBM Global Services hired 19,000 new employees and grossed $33.2 billion of IBM's total income of $88 billion. Global Services's nearest competitor earned only $19.2. In addition to increasing sales, Palmisano strove to improve cooperation among IBM's various units. In January 2001 he made public IBM's intention to invest $1 billion in Linux; he wanted to give IBM's units a unifying goal to create hardware, software, and services that worked together seamlessly.

CRISIS AND RESPONSE

Palmisano's resourcefulness was tested on September 11, 2001, when terrorists demolished the twin towers of the World Trade Center. The attack destroyed the offices of Fiduciary Trust's subsidiary Franklin-Templeton, one of IBM's clients. Palmisano saw to it that Fiduciary Trust received all the technological materials it needed to restart Franklin-Templeton—an IBM employee even checked local hospitals for a missing Franklin-Templeton worker. Palmisano's response to the emergency showed that he was reshaping IBM into a service company that cared about the well-being of its clients. He wanted to form a corporate culture in which employees could again say "I'm an IBMer," confident that they stood for something good. Further, he wanted his employees to understand that they were recognized by management for their good work. To do this, he took his personal touch to employees.

For instance, in the fourth quarter of 2001, the IBM factory in Poughkeepsie, New York, shipped its mainframe computers to customers two weeks early. Palmisano visited the factory's floor, chatting with workers and buying them coffee while telling them, "You guys saved the quarter. You're the heroes" (*BusinessWeek Online*, February 11, 2002). One of his goals was to foster a sense of commitment to IBM's standard of excellence on the part of every employee, regardless of position.

ON-DEMAND COMPUTER SERVICES

Palmisano became CEO of the IBM Corporation on March 1, 2002, the eighth in the company's history. He won few friends, however, when he laid off 15,000 employees, mostly in manufacturing, in an effort to eliminate operations he believed would be money losers for the present and future. He sold IBM's hard drive manufacturing unit to Hitachi in June 2002. In July he purchased PricewaterhouseCoopers' consulting business for $3.5 billion, making IBM the world's largest consulting firm. He wanted IBM to focus on selling solutions to clients—to show clients how the company could help them make money by fixing problems before the problems even arose. His new employees from Pricewaterhouse-Coopers were essential to reaching that goal. IBM then paid $2.1 billion for Rational Software Corporation, a manufacturer of software-development tools. The full significance of this purchase did not become clear until October 2002.

Business journalists had been abuzz for months about Palmisano's new strategy for IBM, but his speech at the American Museum of Natural History in New York City on October 30, 2002 still took them by surprise in terms of the grand scope of IBM's new plans. Palmisano announced his intention to make IBM a computer services-on-demand company; that is, the company would function like a utility, charging its customers for the use of data-centered web sites. IBM would create software capable of fixing clients' software problems automatically online. The clients would pay only for the amount of services they used, in the same way they presently paid for water or electricity. The image of a drop of water became the symbol of Palmisano's goal for IBM.

According to Palmisano's announcement, IBM planned to commit $5 billion to create a single integrated system of computers, software, and other electronic devices that would allow anyone to purchase any part of IBM's services and use it with any other part. One of Palmisano's goals was already partly achieved when IBM created open-source software that altered a company's need for servers dedicated to only one task. For example, a server dedicated to computing accounts might become overloaded, causing delays of hours or even days. IBM's new software was designed to recognize when a server had reached its capacity and automatically redirect the excess work to other servers with available space. A key part of this strategy was that if the servers at the client's company had no excess space, the overflow workload would be sent to IBM's own computers, which would recognize any program that accessed them and silently perform the client's work. Palmisano hoped to take this service to the next level, which would allow IBM's computers to check the client's computers for flaws automatically and fix them before anyone could notice them.

This level of service was part of a grand strategy that Palmisano believed would keep American jobs from continuing to flow to other countries—a phenomenon called "off-shoring." Most off-shoring involved electronic services, especially "outsourcing," a practice in which a company referred some of its work to another company. Palmisano argued that IBM's ideas for future services would encourage companies to outsource to an American company like IBM rather than to foreign busi-

nesses. By using Linux, an operating system that was free to the public, American firms could then make it easy for anyone to write software programs that would work with their systems.

Some observers in the business community expressed doubts about the sheer scale of Palmisano's objective. His concept seemed straight out of science fiction, a dream that would take hundreds of years to fulfill. The technical difficulties were indeed daunting. IBM's researchers said that they had only 10 percent of the technology necessary to turn the company into a technology utility. Palmisano, however, committed $5 billion to research and development for "e-business on demand" and launched an $800 million advertising campaign in 2003. He hoped to convince other corporate leaders that by buying into IBM's idea, they would save themselves money by not having to invest in different proprietary technologies or train personnel to understand those technologies. They would also save by paying only for what they needed instead of an entire system. They could focus on what made them money while IBM handled their computational needs. Palmisano estimated that IBM's new strategy would take five to seven years to implement. In the meantime, he had a vast company in which every employee had a common goal—an inspiring one worthy of the company's proud tradition.

RESTRUCTURING IBM

In spite of the grand scale of Palmisano's strategy, he kept his staff small, preferring to do without the executive assistant that other CEOs had employed. He surprised many in his company when he disbanded the 12-member Executive Management Committee on January 23, 2003. The committee had been in existence for 92 years and had served as a filter for high-level planning, but was much too slow for the new century. Palmisano replaced the committee with a new system of three teams, one focusing on operations, the second on strategy, and the third on technology. Instead of filling each team with top-level executives, he drew members from all divisions of the company and all levels of employment. One immediate effect of this restructuring was to draw a new generation of young men and women into the heart of IBM's operations. Just as Gerstner had been careful to groom a generation of leaders to follow his time, Palmisano seemed to be doing the same. Besides, he was still a maverick at heart who thrived on fresh ideas.

Palmisano became IBM's chairman of the board on January 1, 2003, when Gerstner retired after helping smooth the transition in leadership. That month, IBM's plans for the future received a significant boost when the large investment bank J.P. Morgan Chase contracted to pay the company $5 billion dollars to handle its information technology needs for seven years. In January 2003 Palmisano asked the board of directors to take about half his annual bonus—$3 to $5 million—and use it to reward IBM's top 20 managers for teamwork. He said that he wanted the entire company to behave as a team, and that he should therefore set the example.

See also entry on International Business Machines Corporation in *International Directory of Company Histories*.

SOURCES FOR FURTHER INFORMATION

Ante, Spencer E., "The New Blue: Lou Gerstner Saved Big Blue: Now It's Up to New CEO Sam Palmisano to Restore It to Greatness," *BusinessWeek*, March 17, 2003, pp. 80–88.

Ante, Spencer E., and Ira Sager, "IBM's New Boss," *BusinessWeek Online*, February 11, 2002, http://www.businessweek.com/magazine/content/02_06/b3769001.htm.

Kirkpatrick, David, "IBM: Inside Sam's $100 Billion Growth Machine Sam Palmisano Has Two Huge Goals: To Get This Giant Growing Again—and Return IBM to Greatness," *Fortune.com*, June 14, 2002, http://www.fortune.com/fortune/subs/article/0,15114,644257,00.html.

Koudsi, Suzanne, "Sam's Big Blue Challenge: Sam Palmisano Helped Build IBM Global Services into the Company's Growth Engine: Now, As He Prepares to Succeed Lou Gerstner, Can He Keep It Revving?" *Fortune* August 13, 2001, pp. 144–148.

Strout, Erin, "Blue Skies Ahead?: IBM Is Transforming the Way Its Sales Force Does Business: Can New Management Strategies Catapult this Notoriously Bureaucratic Organization to the Top of a Fiercely Competitive Industry?" *Sales & Marketing Management*, March 2003, pp. 24–29.

—Kirk H. Beetz

■ ■ ■
Helmut Panke
1946–
Chairman of the board, BMW

Nationality: German.

Born: August 31, 1946, in Storkow, Kreis Fürstenwalde, Germany.

Education: University of Munich, BSc, 1968; MS, 1972; PhD, 1976.

Career: Swiss Institute for Nuclear Research, 1976–1978, researcher; University of Munich, 1976–1978, lecturer; McKinsey & Company, 1978–1982, consultant; Bayerische Motoren Werke (BMW), 1982–1985, head of planning and control, research and development division; 1985–1988, head of corporate planning; 1988–1990, head of corporate organization; 1990–1993, head of corporate strategy and coordination; BMW (US) Holding Corporation, 1993–1995, chief executive officer and chairman of the board; BMW AG, 1995–1996, executive director; 1996–1999, head of personnel and information technology; 1999–2002, chief financial officer; 2000–2002, head of the sales division; 2002–, chairman of the board.

Awards: *Wall Street Journal Europe*, Customer Value Champion of the Year, 2003; Cannes Lions International Advertising Festival, Advertiser of the Year, 2004.

Address: BMW AG, Petuelring 130, 80788 Munich, Germany; http://www.bmw.com.

■ Helmut Panke had an intense gaze and a forceful personality. He relished and encouraged debates during staff meetings, and he was admired for his penetrating questioning. He would spend hours one-on-one with a manager, working out in detail what the manager was to do, and then he would let the manager work without further interference. It was Panke's belief that working for Bayerische Motoren Werke (BMW; Bavarian Motor Works) should be fun, and he created an atmosphere in which employees could enjoy their work. Eloquent, Panke spoke flawless English.

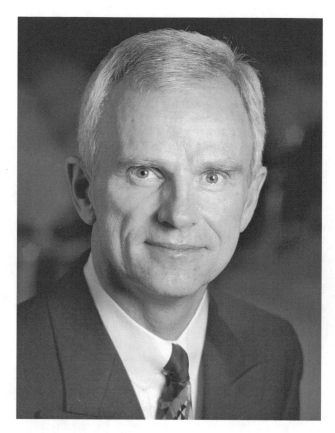

Helmut Panke. *AP/Wide World Photos.*

PHYSICS

In Germany in the 1950s young people were expected to know if they were destined for higher education or something else by the time they were 14 years old; Panke seemed to have known by age 11 when he entered Klenze Gymnasium in Munich, leaving with the equivalent of a high-school degree in 1966. He interrupted his studies at Klenze in 1964 when he received a scholarship from the American Field Service to study at the Philips Exeter Academy in Exeter, New Hampshire, where he received the equivalent of an American high-school diploma in 1965.

After leaving Klenze, Panke attended the University of Munich, receiving a bachelor of science degree in physics in 1968. He continued his studies at the University of Munich, receiving a master's degree in physics in 1972 and a doctorate in nuclear engineering in 1976. Panke then held two jobs from

1976 to 1978, one as a researcher in nuclear physics for the Swiss Institute for Nuclear Research, and the other as a lecturer in physics for the University of Munich. Panke would later hint that the attraction of free enterprise lured him to become a consultant in 1978 for McKinsey & Company, working in Düsseldorf and Munich. While working for McKinsey, Panke was assigned as a consultant to BMW.

At the time BMW was primarily a local manufacturer of niche automobiles designed for and sold to small groups of people with special demands for exceptional performance. In 1977 BMW had begun manufacturing its 6 Series coupe, which by 1982 was BMW's most successful model ever, selling 86,000 units by the time it ceased production in 1989 and broadening BMW's appeal in the United States. On January 1, 1982, Panke was hired by BMW to lead the planning and control office of the division for research and development. BMW's corporate culture, which offered the freedom to be creative, attracted Panke. Employees were responsible for their own work, and managers could make decisions without having to pass them through committees.

THE LEADER

About 47 percent of BMW was owned by the Quandt family, which ran BMW as a family business, favoring longtime employees and stability. In the 1970s there had been an attempt to kidnap the children of the family, and as a consequence they became very secretive and remained so decades later. This secretiveness seemed to pass on to BMW's corporate leaders. Panke distinguished himself for his understanding of the complexities of BMW's engineering research and manufacturing, and in 1985 he was made leader of BMW's division for corporate planning. This would make him a key figure in BMW's expansion in the 1980s and beyond. While leading the division for corporate planning, he was instrumental in pushing the idea that BMW should build a factory in the United States. In 1988 he became the leader of organization, responsible for coordinating the activities of BMW's different divisions. In 1990 Panke became leader of group planning for BMW, taking a hand in developing BMW's long-term strategy.

Panke and colleagues visited the United States, searching for a place to build an assembly plant. Panke drove through much of the eastern United States, visiting many towns. After much fuss and debate, he and his superiors settled on Spartanburg, South Carolina. Fluent in English and well versed in American business practices, Panke was an obvious choice to lead BMW's U.S. expansion, and in April 1993 he took charge of BMW (US) Holding Corporation as its chief executive officer (CEO) and chairman of the board. Under Panke's leadership, the United States became BMW's largest market, and the Spartanburg factory manufactured the Z3 roadster for the

United States and for export to Europe. Initially the Z3s were so badly put together that they had to be scrapped, but eventually the problems were fixed and the Z3 roadster became popular. In July 1995 Panke was appointed BMW AG's *Generalbevollmäächtigten*, a word often translated as CEO in the English-speaking press, although Panke's duties were more like those of an American chief operating officer and lacked some of the authority that a CEO would be expected to have.

In 1994 BMW had acquired the United Kingdom's ailing automobile manufacturer Rover Group from British Aerospace for $1.27 billion. BMW's chairman of the board, Bernd Pischetsrieder, hoped that Rover's line of midsized automobiles would give BMW entry into the automobile mass market; BMW had been the subject of takeover rumors, and BMW's executive committee hoped that by increasing the company's size, it would be able to remain independent. The German press dubbed Rover Group the "English patient" because it always seemed unhealthy.

UPPER MANAGEMENT

On July 4, 1996, Panke was elected to the executive committee of BMW, placing him among the company's elite. There, he worked with the Quandt family's representatives, as well as other shareholder and management representatives. He had toured part of the United States with Pischetsrieder, and the two were close allies as Pischetsrieder tried to expand and reorganize BMW to become a truly global corporation. Panke's duties were to supervise human resources and information technology. He proved to be a wizard with the computers that became essential to the manufacturing of BMWs, and his sheer enthusiasm for BMW's automobiles helped make him a success with personnel.

In 1998 another English institution became part of BMW when the company purchased Volkswagen's rights to the name "Rolls-Royce," and BMW began to set up shop in West Sussex to build new Rolls-Royces. In 1999 BMW's Spartanburg factory began manufacturing BMW's first sport-utility vehicle, the X5; it had the sharp handling that BMWs were famous for, and in spite of some misgivings among industry analysts that the X5 would dilute the BMW brand by not being a luxurious coupe, it became popular. Yet 1999 was a difficult year for BMW. Having already lost $3.6 billion on Rover Group, BMWs finances continued to be dragged down by its British subsidiary. To fix Rover Group, Pischetsrieder had assigned scores of BMW's engineers, including some of the best of BMW's next generation of future leaders, to the United Kingdom, but only the Land Rover off-road vehicle sold well.

By the start of 1999 BMW's executive committee had had enough. The Quandt family exerted its control of corporate affairs, and on February 5, 1999, Pischetsrieder was fired. The executive committee then surprised just about everyone when it named committee member Joachim Milburg as the new chairman of the board. Milburg had begun as an apprentice factory laborer, worked his way up to become a college professor of engineering, and then accepted a position with BMW in 1993. BMW's second in command, Wolfgang Reitzle, quickly resigned after being passed over for the position. Milburg accepted his new position, understanding that it was an interim job because he would reach BMW's retirement age of 60 in 2003. He quickly moved to rebuild BMW's upper management and appointed Panke chief financial officer on March 18, 1999.

Panke proved to be a wizard at finances, but he could not help Rover Group, which lost another $1 billion during 1999. Although Milburg was full of ideas to make Rover Group profitable, Panke viewed the company as a lost cause. When Rover Group was finally sold, journalists believed that Panke was primarily responsible for the sale. In 2000 the Land Rover was sold to Ford Motor Company for $3 billion. The rest of Rover Group was sold on March 16, 2000, to Alchemy Partners, a group of venture capitalists, for £10. BMW quickly became the subject of takeover bids, because by dropping Rover Group its annual sales would fall by about 400,000 vehicles, thus reducing its gross sales and ability to compete in the mass market. Yet Milburg defiantly maintained that BMW would remain independent. He took on responsibilities for marketing, and to help him with this he made Panke his codirector of marketing.

BMW had lost many of its most promising engineers and managers in the Rover Group disaster, but neither Milburg nor Panke panicked. Panke was especially gifted at attracting promising young leaders, and BMW retained its corporate culture of allowing employees great latitude in making decisions, maintaining a creative atmosphere that attracted young talent. Regardless of his job titles, Panke was plainly second in command at BMW. His outgoing style complemented the quiet, reticent Milburg, and the two formed a good relationship.

RECOVERY

Milburg and Panke emphasized BMW's brand name in advertising, noting the brand's reputation for building sharp-handling cars for automobile enthusiasts. They set about reorganizing BMW, putting aside aspirations to enter the mass market in favor of satisfying niche groups of customers. This involved reorganizing and in some cases retooling BMW factories to make them flexible enough to shift rapidly from manufacturing one model to another as market demands fluctuated. Further, the two men planned to expand BMW's offerings from a few models, each with several variations, to several models, each customizable to a customer's specifications. Panke would eventually push this to its limit by offering per-

sonalized automobiles. For 2000 BMW grossed $31 billion and netted $940 million.

By 2001 BMW had plans to spend $23 billion to expand its offerings, hoping to increase sales 40 percent by 2008. It opened an engine plant in Birmingham, England, to manufacture four-cylinder engines. In Oxford, England, BMW began manufacturing the Mini, a luxury small car. There was nattering in the press about a small car diluting the BMW brand name, but the Mini had all of BMW's special-handling traits. In July 2001 BMW announced its intention to build a new factory in Leipzig, which would begin manufacturing the 3 Series in 2005. The German government promised to help fund the building of the factory because it would help the economy of the former East Germany. Then the X5 off-road BMW sport-utility vehicle was launched, becoming a hit in the United States. BMW spent $350 million to upgrade its U.S. dealerships.

The introduction of the 7 Series line of high-end luxury vehicles in November 2001 was crucial to BMW's future. The 7 Series competed with and was intended to take a share of the U.S. market from Lexus and Mercedes. The iDrive computer system was introduced. It displayed data on a screen on the 5 Series and 7 Series dashboards, synthesizing data on weather conditions, radio preferences, telephone communications, and navigation, and was controlled by a knob near the gearshift. Automobile reviewers declared the iDrive a confusing mess, but Panke defended it as a valuable feature. The iDrive suffered numerous glitches, causing buyers to return their automobiles to dealers for repairs. Panke had a team of engineers rework and simplify the iDrive's software, and by 2002 it functioned well. In 2001 two-thirds of BMW owners were repeat buyers, and the company netted $2.8 billion, more than the combined nets of DaimlerChrysler and General Motors.

CHAIRMAN OF THE BOARD

On December 5, 2001, Milburg announced that he would retire early in May 2002 because of an ailing back. He and the other executive committee members knew already who they wanted to be the new chairman of the board, and Panke was named Milburg's replacement almost immediately.

The 7 Series was designed by an American, Chris Bangle. It included a large trunk that some reviewers thought was too chunky, but it gave the 7 Series a muscular look, which went well with its powerful engine and road-hugging ability. The engine was part of an effort to be more efficient at BMW. Panke felt that buyers were not choosing different models of BMW because of the engine differences, and so the V-6 engine was installed in several different models. On the other hand, Panke thought that interior design mattered very much to consumers. He said that he wanted people to be able to sit blind-folded in a BMW and know by the smell and feel that they were in a BMW and no other kind of automobile. He was selling high-quality engineering and style, and the 7 Series retained the feel of a BMW while offering an up-to-date look.

On May 16, 2002, Panke became chairman of the board. Though he was often referred to in the English-speaking press as a CEO, technically he chaired the board, which at BMW carried the authority that both chairman of the board and CEO would carry in an American company. He strove to develop a corporate culture that was fun, even exciting, which was even spelled out in BMW's code of corporate behavior: "Rule 7 states that it's the responsibility of any manager to create an atmosphere of fun in the organization," said Panke (*BusinessWeek online*, June 9, 2003). Flexibility was an important part of the culture. Not only would BMW factories be able to shift from manufacturing one model to another according to consumer demand, but the factories would be able to tailor individual vehicles to individual consumers with a multitude of options, some of which were developed out of the creative atmosphere Panke promoted. For example, BMW developed keys that were individualized for different drivers of the same automobile. Each individual key would automatically set the radio, driver's seat, climate control, steering wheel, and other options to the driver's preset preferences.

All BMWs sold at the high end of their classes in 2002, with the sporty 3 Series starting at $28,495, the medium-sized 5 Series at $38,205, and the luxury 7 Series at $69,195, and with all usually selling for much more because of numerous options added by purchasers, giving BMW the highest profit margins in the industry. Panke rejected the idea that to survive BMW had to penetrate the mass market. Instead, he emphasized qualities that set BMWs apart from other automobiles to attract people willing to pay more for a vehicle that could be customized to suit them in just a few weeks. A somewhat awkward consequence of the drive for flexibility was that BMW had over three hundred different time schedules for employees, varying with the factory and the model being manufactured.

Panke and BMW reached an agreement with Toyota Motor Corporation to jointly manufacture diesel engines, even as BMW overtook Toyota's Lexus in sales in the United States. While the automobile-manufacturing industry as a whole was in a slump, BMW's worldwide sales grew 17 percent, reaching 1.05 million vehicles. BMW was ranked 81st on the *Forbes* list of the world's top 500 companies. In a tough market, Panke warned, "We have to remain hungry and to keep up our desire to outperform others" (*Forbes.com*, July 22, 2002).

Few people could have been happier in their jobs than Panke was in his. The pleasure he took in his work was evident to insiders and observers alike. In 2003 BMW finished building a new factory in Britain for Rolls-Royce Motor Cars and

began producing Phantoms, which sold for $320,000. The Phantom featured a 12-cylinder engine designed and built by BMW. A new version of the 5 Series was introduced, with longer bodies and an upgraded iDrive system. Safety features included standard side-door air bags. The 6 Series and the X3 Baby sport-utility vehicle were introduced in 2003. Panke took to calling customers "investors," probably to emphasize the high resale value that BMWs typically carried. The worldwide decline in automobile manufacturing affected BMW, however, and even though BMW upped its manufacturing total to 1.1 million vehicles, most of the increase in sales came from its small-car series. Its gross for the year declined 2.1 percent, and its net declined 3.6 percent, although at $2.3 billion the net was enviable.

In May 2004 BMW opened a factory in Shenyang, Liaoning province, China. The factory was owned jointly with Brilliance China Automotive Holdings and produced 3 Series and 5 Series automobiles. Panke hoped the Chinese factory would do for BMW in China what the factory in Spartanburg had done for BMW in the United States. On June 7, 2004, Panke was named the leading foreign "star manager" by *BusinessWeek*, and on June 26, 2004, he was named Advertiser of the Year at the Cannes Lions International Advertising Festival. He had big plans, including the launch of a new luxury 6 Series coupe and the launch of the 1 Series, a small BMW for young customers who would one-day be able to buy bigger BMWs. "When people work in a fun atmosphere it's very motivating. I love my job," Panke told an interviewer in 2003 (*BusinessWeek online*, June 9, 2003). He had created a culture in which people throughout the corporate ranks could send questions all the way to the top, in which debate and new ideas were encouraged. Panke dealt with the tough questions that arose, but he insisted that "My biggest challenge is saying 'no' to projects that are exciting but don't fit BMW's strategy" (*BusinessWeek*, June 7, 2004). His strategy was to make sure every BMW fit the brand's image.

See also entry on Bayerische Motoren Werke in *International Directory of Company Histories*.

SOURCES FOR FURTHER INFORMATION

Edmondson, Gail, "BMW's Shifting Strategy," *BusinessWeek online*, June 9, 2003, http://www.aol.businessweek.com/bwdaily/dnflash/jun2003/nf2003069_6720_db053.htm.

Holloway, Nigel, "The Best-Driven Brand," *Forbes.com*, July 22, 2002, http://www.forbes.com/global/2002/0722/024.html.

"Performance Driver: Helmut Panke Chief Executive, Bavarian Motor Works, Germany," *BusinessWeek*, June 7, 2004, p. 40.

Tierney, Christine, Joann Muller, Katharine A. Schmidt, and
    Heidi Dawley, "BMW: Speeding into a Tight Turn: Will
    Its Expanding Line Survive this Economic Skid?"
    BusinessWeek online, October 29, 2001, http://
    www.adinfo.businessweek.com/magazine/content/01_44/
    b3755140.htm.

—Kirk H. Beetz

■■■
Gregory J. Parseghian
ca. 1961–
Former chairman, Federal Home Loan Mortgage Corporation

Nationality: American.

Born: ca. 1961, in Philadelphia, Pennsylvania.

Education: University of Pennsylvania, BS; MBA, c. 1982.

Family: Son of John Parseghian; married; children: two.

Career: Credit Suisse First Boston, 1987–?, managing director; BlackRock Financial Management, partner; Salomon Brothers, ?–1996, managing director; Federal Home Loan Mortgage Corporation (Freddie Mac), 1996–2003, senior vice president and chief investment officer; chief executive officer, 2003–.

Awards: Ranked first on *Institutional Investor* magazine's fixed-income and mortgage strategy polls, six times.

Gregory J. Parseghian. © *Reuters NewMedia Inc./Corbis.*

■ Gregory J. Parseghian became head of the Federal Home Loan Mortgage Corporation (Freddie Mac), the publicly traded, U.S. government-chartered, guaranteed-mortgage and lending institution, in a management reshuffling in June 2003. The previous head, Leland Brendsel—along with chief operating officer David Glenn and chief financial officer Vaughn Clarke—resigned on June 9 at the board's request because of revelations of accounting problems that had underreported the company's profits. Parseghian lasted two months in his new position before pressure from the Office of Federal Housing Enterprise Oversight (OFHEO), which regulates Freddie Mac and its sister organization, Fannie Mae, and the Securities and Exchange Commission (SEC) persuaded the board to replace him as well. The law firm of Baker Botts LLP, hired by Freddie Mac's board of directors to investigate the financial problems, determined that the company had been changing its records solely to improve its standing with investors. On August 22, 2003, Parseghian departed under a cloud, having been tainted by the same accounting irregularities as his predecessors.

PROBLEMS AT FREDDIE MAC

Parseghian's departure from the leadership of Freddie Mac was significant because of the institution's standing as a government-sponsored enterprise (GSE). Freddie Mac was created in 1970 by the U.S. government as a means of putting home ownership and rental housing in the hands of people who could neither afford nor qualify for conventional mortgages. The corporation made funding available to lenders, bought mortgages and mortgage-related securities, and paid for them by putting securities and debt instruments in capital marketplaces. By doing this Freddie Mac helped keep mortgage rates down and maintained a stable American home-lending system. "Over the years," explained a press release located on the corporate Web site, "Freddie Mac has opened doors for one in six homebuyers and more than two million renters in America" (December 7, 2003).

At the same time, however, Freddie Mac differed from other publicly traded lending institutions because stockholders believed that its loans were underwritten by the U.S. Treasury. The corporation also had special advantages given to it, known as the "implicit guarantee," because of its status as a quasi-governmental organization. Freddie Mac paid no state or local corporate income taxes. Its securities could be used as collateral for loans. Should the institution fail because it made too many risky or bad loans, which nearly happened to Fannie Mae in 1981, investors expected that the government would intervene to protect the corporation, using public money if necessary to protect their investments. In fact, at one point the charters for Freddie Mac and Fannie Mae stated specifically that the U.S. Treasury maintained a line of credit for the institutions so that it could finance $2.25 billion dollars worth of debt. In essence, the federal government guaranteed Freddie's debt, and Freddie helped keep the market stable and provided low-cost loans for low-income families to buy houses.

Freddie's problem was that its public-service duties conflicted with the interests of its stockholders. In order to maximize their own profits, stockholders encouraged Freddie's management to take risks that other corporations would not dare to take. Freddie Mac and Fannie Mae together maintained a debt load that, according to Jason Thomas in a report on the U.S. Senate's Republican Policy Committee's Web site, was worth almost 40 percent of the entire U.S. public debt in 2003. The two corporations together also had financial assets at that time worth about 44 percent more than the assets of the largest U.S. bank, Citibank. "The scandal at Freddie Mac," Thomas stated, "is a direct product of a strategy, well underway at both firms, to leverage their 'implicit guarantee' to accumulate larger and larger mortgage investment portfolios and increase returns to shareholders" (September 9, 2003). In other words, because stockholders believed that the risks the corporation took fell not on the stockholders themselves, but on U.S. taxpayers, they pressed Freddie Mac's managers to take greater risks, assume greater debts, and make more loans than corporations without the backing of the U.S. government could possibly do. In some ways, stated Bill Mann on the *Motley Fool* Web site, the "implicit guarantee" gave Freddie and its big sister Fannie monopoly status in the mortgage-lending business.

PARSEGHIAN'S ROLE

Gregory Parseghian came to Freddie Mac in 1996 with a reputation he had already earned as a successful bond trader. His early career was spent in banking and financial services firms in the private sector, including Credit Suisse First Boston, BlackRock Financial Management, and Salomon Brothers. He joined the GSE in 1996, working as a senior vice president in investing. He earned a reputation as an aggressive, risk-taking trader in 1998, when Russia repudiated its debts.

Parseghian responded to the financial crisis by instructing his buyers to purchase mortgage bonds held by the hedge-fund corporation Long Term Capital Management. In the last quarter of 1998 Parseghian oversaw the acquisition of about $38 billion in mortgage bonds alone.

ACCOUNTING IRREGULARITIES

When the market for these bonds recovered in 2002, Freddie Mac earned big profits for its stockholders, but not for the American public, who underwrote the risks involved. The profits, however, disturbed Freddie Mac's planned performance reviews. The accounting company that audited Freddie Mac, Arthur Anderson LLP, the same firm that helped Enron Corporation conceal its true financial position, suggested changing the books to underreport the amount received. That income could be reported later in the year, to smooth out Freddie Mac's earnings and help it keep the nickname it had earned over the previous forty-odd years, "Steady Freddie." The reality of the company's practices increased shareholder value, but at the cost of increased volatility in the market, something that Freddie Mac, as a quasi-federal institution, was supposed to help suppress.

Arthur Anderson was not the only firm involved in concealing Freddie Mac's earned income until a future date. Two banks that also traded on the New York Stock Exchange, CSFB and Goldman Sachs, helped hide assets from one year to the next. According to Bill Mann of the *Motley Fool* Web site, Goldman Sachs alone was responsible for creative accounting that put away $400 million in 2001 earned income to a different year. Other companies, including Microsoft and General Electric, had in the past also resorted to creative accounting to smooth out their earnings and increase their ratings on the stock exchange. Although the practice had been widely condemned, it had not been made illegal.

Further investigations indicated that corporate management had underreported the company's income by as much as $5 billion averaged over the previous three years, 2000 through 2002. This was despite the fact that in 2001 management actually overstated the company's earnings by nearly $990 million. "Traders in Mr. Parseghian's unit who were executing the deals," explained the *Wall Street Journal*, "acknowledged they were involved in an accounting gambit that might draw criticism if it surfaced publicly" (June 11, 2003). Employees were warned to keep the news about the underreporting quiet in order to preserve the company's conservative reputation. After the scandal broke in June 2003, three of the top executives at Freddie were forced to resign. Their practices had threatened the stability of the entire mortgage market in the United States in order to keep their rates of growth high, benefiting stockholders and generating bonuses for the corporate executives.

MANAGEMENT SHAKE-UP

Parseghian was appointed to the head position in the company that same June after the former chairman, Leland Brendsel, left the company under the cloud of those accounting irregularities. Before that he had managed Freddie Mac's entire loan portfolio, worth an estimated $600 billion. Company sources portrayed Parseghian as a relatively innocent insider, one who knew the markets (and therefore could calm Wall Street worries about Freddie's future) but at the same time who opposed the practice of managing earnings. From the beginning of his tenure Parseghian openly expressed his intention to create perfect financial clarity in the ongoing audit of Freddie's accounts and practices. In an interview with Janet Reilley Hewitt published in the industry magazine *Mortgage Banking*, he declared that among his chief aims as Freddie's head were to institute new accounting practices and deliver "accurate, comprehensive restatement results to the financial community" (August 2003).

Yet Parseghian was himself tainted by the accounting scandal, and the people who appointed him knew it. In July, only one month after Parseghian had been selected, the law firm Baker Botts LLP released a report explaining the irregularities. Baker Botts's officials had been among the people who had examined Parseghian before he was appointed and pronounced him fit to hold the post of chairman. However, in the report issued by the law firm, Parseghian was fingered as someone who either knew, or should have known, about the manipulation of information provided to shareholders. Jerry Knight, writing in the *Washington Post*, succinctly identified the central issue in the controversy surrounding Parseghian's role: "How can an executive who knew of and participated at least peripherally in efforts to mislead investors restore Freddie's credibility?" (September 1, 2003).

QUESTIONABLE STOCK SALES

Compounding the problem were stock sales Parseghian had made in January 2001 and June 2002. A lawsuit filed in West Virginia in August 2003 accused the executive of profiting inappropriately from the sales of these stocks because he had been at the time in possession of information about the company's improper accounting records. After news about the underreporting emerged, Freddie's stock dropped over 20 percent, and the executive profited by about $3 million. Parseghian argued that the stock sales had been arranged weeks in advance and were a direct result of the compensation agreement he had signed when he first joined the company in 1996. At that time he was provided with stock options that vested after five years, in his case, January 31, 2001. When he signed his new contract in 2001, Parseghian explained, he was given further options that vested in June 2002 and in 2005. It was the sale of these vested stocks that gave his actions the appearance of insider trading, an illegal activity. In fact, the executive declared, he had done nothing either illegal or wrong.

Among the casualties of the creative accounting measures was the trust that had been placed in Freddie Mac's board of directors and OFHEO, the federal office charged with regulating the safety and soundness of Freddie's activities. Hoping to quell stock market fears, Freddie's board announced Parseghian's appointment without first investigating his possible involvement in the accounting issue. Parseghian was an insider with a proven record of achieving growth, and by naming him the successor to Brendsel the board hoped to keep the company's profitability in the stock market. It was only after OFHEO pressured the board that it finally asked Parseghian to step down.

CONGRESSIONAL ACTION

At the same time the OFHEO had, critics complained, been lax itself in allowing the board to appoint Parseghian in the first place. Freddie's lack of accountability, its freedom to maintain debt-to-credit ratios that other banks were not allowed to match, and its tax breaks were also cited as contributing to the problem. As a result, three Republican senators—Chuck Hagel of Nebraska, John Sununu of New Hampshire, and Elizabeth Dole of North Carolina—introduced legislation to take the OFHEO's function away from the department of Housing and Urban Development and turn it over to a different office, the Office of Federal Enterprise Supervision, in the Treasury Department. Similar bills were introduced in the House of Representatives and the Senate at the same time. All of these bills took the lack of oversight of the GSEs seriously and recommended steps to bring Freddie and Fannie's behavior more in line with that of other, privately held institutions. Some sponsors of bills recommended that Freddie and Fannie be totally privatized in order to relieve the Treasury from the responsibility of underwriting their debts and to keep taxpayers from having to bail out the companies in case of a failure.

AFTERMATH FOR PARSEGHIAN

Parseghian emerged from the scandal without his job but with his reputation largely intact. Although company documents showed that in 2001 he had signed onto a plan, with other executives, to recalculate the values of some of Freddie Mac's contracts, in general his fellow professionals felt that he was doing his job. He was being held accountable for practices that, in a less politically charged company, would never have been revealed in the first place. In December 2003 the outsider Richard Syron replaced Parseghian as chairman and CEO. Freddie's lead director, Shaun O'Malley, expressed the board's gratefulness to Parseghian for developing Freddie Mac's "premier risk management strategies and capabilities that remain today as the core of the company's safety and soundness regimen" (December 7, 2003).

See also entry on Freddie Mac in *International Directory of Company Histories.*

SOURCES FOR FURTHER INFORMATION

Barta, Patrick, "Leading the News: Freddie Mac CEO Defends Stock Sales," *Wall Street Journal*, August 18, 2003.

Barta, Patrick, and Gregory Zuckerman, "New Top Officer at Freddie Mac Praised as Pro," *Wall Street Journal*, June 11, 2003.

Barta, Patrick, John D. McKinnon, and Gregory Zuckerman, "Freddie Mac Ready to Oust CEO over Role in Accounting Scandal," *Wall Street Journal*, August 22, 2003.

"Finance and Economics: Off with Another Head: Freddie Mac," *Economist*, August 30, 2003, p. 61.

"Freddie Mac Board of Directors to Replace Chief Executive Officer," *Freddie Mac*, August 22, 2003, http://www.freddiemac.com/news/archives/corporate/2003/parseghian_082203.html.

"Freddie Mac Loses Another Chief Exec as Falcon Gives Verdict on Parseghian," *Euroweek*, August 29, 2003, p. 1.

"Freddie Mac Names Richard Syron Chairman and Chief Executive Officer," *Freddie Mac*, December 7, 2003, http://www.freddiemac.com/news/archives/corporate/2003/syron_120703.html.

"Freddie Mac Ousts Parseghian amid Accounting Errors," *Bloomburg.com*, http://quote.bloomberg.com/apps/news?pid=10000103&sid=aVMfxDwrERwk&refer=us

"Freddie Ousts CEO," *GSE Report*, August 25, 2003, http://www.gsereport.com/2003/July%2029%20-%20August%2025.pdf.

Hewitt, Janet Reilley, "Meet Freddie's New CEO," *Mortgage Banking*, August 2003, p. 55.

Knight, Jerry, "The Next Dramatic Exit at Freddie Mac Should Be O'Malley's," *Washington Post*, September 1, 2003.

Lofton, LouAnn, "Our Take: Freddie's New Head(ie)," *Motley Fool*, December 8, 2003, http://www.fool.com/News/mft/2003/mft03120813.htm.

Mann, Bill, "Our Take: Freddie Mac's Summer of Love," *Motley Fool*, September 26, 2003, http://www.fool.com/News/mft/2003/mft03092613.htm.

———, "Our Take: Freddie Smack," *Motley Fool*, November 21, 2003, http://www.fool.com/News/mft/2003/mft03112109.htm.

———, "Our Take: Knife the Mac," *Motley Fool*, August 25, 2003, http://www.fool.com/news/mft/2003/mft03082503.htm.

O'Malley, Shaun, "Chairman Supports CEO in Letter to *The Washington Post*," http://www.freddiemac.com/news/in_the_news/omalley_letter.html.

Parseghian, Greg, "Freddie Mac CEO Greg Parseghian Comments on Stock Trades," *Freddie Mac*, August 15, 2003, http://www.freddiemac.com/news/archives/corporate/2003/parseghianstocktrade_081503.html.

"Prepared Remarks: Greg Parseghian, CEO and President, Freddie Mac," *Freddie Mac*, August 18, 2003, http://www.freddiemac.com/speeches/parseghian/gp081803.html.

Sonnenfeld, Jeffrey, "Hit the Road, Mac," *Wall Street Journal*, August 26, 2003.

Thomas, Jason, "Problems at Freddie Mac and Fannie Mae: Too Big to Fail?" *U.S. Senate Republican Policy Committee*, September 9, 2003, http://rpc.senate.gov/_files/bk090903.pdf.

—Kenneth R. Shepherd

■ ■ ■

Richard D. Parsons

1948–

Chairman and chief executive officer, Time Warner

Nationality: American.

Born: April 4, 1948, in New York City, New York.

Education: Bachelor's degree, University of Hawaii; Albany Law School, JD.

Family: Son of Lorenzo L. Parsons (electronics technician) and Isabelle J. Parsons (homemaker); married Laura Bush (child psychologist); children: three.

Career: Governor Nelson Rockefeller (New York), 1974–1976, counsel; President Gerald R. Ford's domestic policy office, 1974–1976, senior White House aide; Patterson Belknap Webb & Tyler, 1977–1988, managing partner; Dime Savings Bank, 1988–1995, chairman and chief executive officer; Time Warner, 1995–?, president; ?–2002, co-chief operating officer; 2002–, chief executive officer; 2003–, chairman.

Address: Time Warner, 75 Rockefeller Plaza, New York, New York 10019; http://www.timewarner.com.

Richard D. Parsons. *AP/Wide World Photos.*

■ Richard Parsons was one of four African American CEOs of a Fortune 500 company in 2004. He led Time Warner, a media company that was facing some of its most challenging times in its history, struggling to overcome a $165 billion failed merger with America Online (AOL) in 2001. Parsons established himself as a skilled conciliator who could mend rifts and rally forces. Parsons was also a reluctant symbol of the positive changes transforming corporate America.

As of 2004 Time Warner had five basic divisions: cable networks, publishing, music, filmed entertainment, and cable. Its movie, publishing, music, and cable television portfolio included Time, the number one U.S. magazine publisher; Warner Brothers, a producer and distributor of movies, television programs, and videos; Warner Music Group; Home Box Office, the number one paid cable network; Time Warner Cable, the number one cable delivery system; Warner Books; and the Book-of-the-Month Club. Time Warner also owned cable

television networks (CNN, TBS, and TNT), the WB Television Network, and properties ranging from *Mad* magazine to the Atlanta Braves. Its struggling AOL unit continued to hurt the bottom line. The unit has suffered from drastically lower advertising revenues and slowing subscriber growth. AOL lost 2.2 million subscribers in 2003 as customers defected to rival high-speed and discount Internet services.

LAYING THE FOUNDATION

Parsons surfaced from the hardscrabble Bedford-Stuyvesant section of Brooklyn, New York, to earn the top score among all 3,600 law school graduates who took the New York State Bar exam with him. He earned his degree while working nights as a janitor. Early in his career, Parsons worked as an assistant counsel to Governor Nelson Rockefeller (New York). He later moved to Washington, D.C., and worked for the then vice president Rockefeller and President Gerald R. Ford's domestic policy office, traveling in circles that would come in handy later in his corporate life. Next Parsons practiced law for Patterson Belknap Webb & Tyler from 1977 to 1988 in New York, handling free speech, product liability, and banking cases.

By 1988 Parsons had become CEO of Dime Savings Bank, just as the Northeast's real estate market collapsed. He engineered a massive restructuring, unloading $1 billion in bad loans while cutting the workforce from 3,500 to 2,000. The bank stayed afloat. Parsons kept employees informed, creating quarterly videotapes to discuss earnings and the restructuring process.

A LIKABLE MANAGER

While leading Dime Savings Bank, Parsons assumed several corporate and civic directorships, including joining the board of Time Warner in 1991. This move would be pivotal to his career. In February 1995 Parsons joined Time Warner as the company's president. He worked closely with the former chairman and CEO Gerald Levin, cleaning up the company's balance sheet and doggedly driving the Time Warner message to Wall Street.

Over time Parsons developed a reputation as the best executive to resolve sticky situations. When controversy erupted in the media community following Time Warner's refusal to carry the Fox News Channel and the Disney Channel on its cable system, it was Parsons who diplomatically settled the disputes. Time Warner understood the value that Parsons's skills conveyed to the investment community and played upon it. Said David Joyce, an equity analyst at Guzman & Company, "My sense is that Parsons is truly a statesman. He's got a really even keeled, witty temperament about him" (*Black Enterprise*, February 2002).

Unlike CEO Gerald Levin, who was seen as reluctant media mogul, Parsons was viewed entirely differently by the Time Warner family. Known to mingle easily with employees, Parsons once flew to Barcelona, Spain, for a record industry bash. Recalls Roger Ames, chairman and CEO of Warner Music Group, "Dick was still dancing when I left at 6 in the morning. Yet he was there when the plane left at 7." (*BusinessWeek*, May 19, 2003).

THE MERGER THAT MADE HISTORY

In January 2000 the announcement of a merger between AOL and Time Warner made headlines. With the specter of the 1999 failure of a similar proposed merger between USA Networks and Lycos hanging over them, AOL and Time Warner worked diligently to reassure investors that the companies' combination made strategic sense, meeting with top shareholders, extolling the virtues of the deal to the press, and promising more details about linkups between the two companies soon.

Following the merger, Parsons and Robert Pittman became co-COOs at AOL Time Warner. Parsons was given responsibility for overseeing Time Warner's filmed entertainment and music businesses as well as all corporate staff functions, including financial activities, legal affairs, public affairs, and administration. He was also the principal executive responsible for supervising the interaction and coordination of the company's operating divisions. He oversaw Time Warner's efforts in New York City to rescue Harlem's financially troubled Apollo Theater. From the beginning the merger seemed destined for failure, and Parsons spent much of his early tenure allaying the concerns of angry shareholders. Ultimately every executive who led AOL Time Warner, other than Parsons, was forced out as the merger failed. In 2001, with the media industry hurting from a slump in advertising spending, AOL Time Warner suffered financially after the terrorist attacks of September 11. In December 2001 Gerald Levin abruptly retired, and Pittman resigned his post at AOL Time Warner in late July 2002.

MEDIA EXECUTIVE SURVIVES AS NEW MEDIA FAIL

Although Parsons was part of the team that orchestrated the AOL merger with Time Warner, the reality was that once AOL Time Warner's board made the decision to distance itself from the merger, it needed a senior executive from the original Time Warner to run the company. Parsons was named CEO in May 2002, and at that time his in-the-trenches managerial style, along with a track record running a global business and contacts in Washington, D.C., drove his ascension. Parsons described the differences between his predecessor and himself: "I'm kind of a lunch-pail manager. Where Jerry Levin was more cerebral and strategically focused as a CEO, I will tend to demonstrate more of an in-the-trenches style of leadership. I like to be with the troops" (*Black Enterprise*, February 2002).

The 2002 fiscal year was rough for the company, with its stock price falling to around $9 per share—a record low—and the price of its bonds falling to the levels of junk. One of Parsons's early struggles came in June 2002, when the Securities and Exchange Commission (SEC) alleged that AOL had inflated its premerger revenues. Parsons defended the company before CFO Wayne H. Pace had completed his investigation. In August, AOL Time Warner embarrassingly disclosed dubious transactions totaling $49 million. An additional disclosure of $190 million followed. (As of early 2004 the company had yet to settle with the SEC.) What is more, the investigation hampered the company's ability to spin off its cable division as a separate business. "This is an overhang on the company," Parsons conceded (*Washington Post*, January 7, 2004).

AN AFRICAN AMERICAN TRAILBLAZER

Parsons's CEO appointment placed him in the spotlight for more reasons than his company's immense power. He had also become one of the top African Americans in Corporate America. He said of the distinction, "It's an annoyance. Of course your priority is the shareholders and 90,000 employees. But there are also countless numbers of people outside who, for whatever reason—race being the biggest—are rooting for you. And not" (*Fortune*, July 22, 2002). However, Parsons did not turn his back on the African American community. He said that one of his objectives was to transform his workforce, to better reflect the customers and community it serves. "We need to make more progress in our senior management ranks" (*Black Enterprise*, February 2002).

ORCHESTRATING A TURNAROUND

Effective September 2003 AOL Time Warner's directors voted to rename the company Time Warner, marking a symbolic end to the ambitions of the Internet boom. The name change process—including the adoption of the "TWX" ticker symbol on the New York Stock Exchange—was completed in late 2003. Also during 2003 Parsons proved willing to make tough moves. Time Warner sold a controlling interest in its principal music operation, Warner Music Group, for $2.6 billion to an investor group led by Thomas H. Lee Partners and Edgar Bronfman Jr. This sale was expected to reduce Time Warner's reported net debt by approximately $2.6 billion. Parsons said, "I'm very pleased that we are putting our music company in such capable hands. Despite my personal fondness for the music business as well as for all of our wonderful managers and music group employees, I believe that this transaction is clearly in the best interests of our company's shareholders. Not only will it greatly enhance our financial flexibility, it also will enable us to pursue higher growth opportunities in our other lines of business" *Business Wire*, November 24, 2003).

By the end of 2003 Parsons had managed to elevate both his company's stock and his reputation. His strategy was to understate the goals of a company that had been crippled by hype. For the nine months that ended September 30, 2003, the company's revenues rose 5 percent to $31.15 billion. Net income from continuing operations and before accounting changes totaled $2.01 billion, up from $331 million, reflecting growth in the company's cable subscriptions and increased gross profit margins.

Once Parsons had turned the company around, he began looking for possible new merger partners. "We're now in a position to play," said Parsons (*Newsweek*, December 22, 2003). He added that the company could pay for a deal worth up to $8 billion in cash, with the goal to expand Time Warner's cable operations.

See also entries on Dime Savings Bank of New York, F.S.B. and Time Warner Inc. in *International Directory of Company Histories*.

SOURCES FOR FURTHER INFORMATION

Bianco, Anthony, and Tom Lowry, "Can Dick Parsons Rescue AOL Time Warner?" *BusinessWeek*, May 19, 2003, p. 86.

Daniels, Cora, "Most Powerful Black Executives in America," *Fortune*, July 22, 2002, p. 60.

Dingle, Derek, and Alan Hughes, "A Time for Bold Leadership," *Black Enterprise*, February 2002, p. 76.

Roberts, Johnnie, "Prime Time for Parsons," *Newsweek*, December 22, 2003, p. 4.

Time Warner, "Investor Group Led by Thomas H. Lee Partners, Edgar Bronfman Jr., Bain Capital, and Providence Equity Partners to Purchase Warner Music Group," *Business Wire*, November 24, 2003.

Vise, David, "Time Warner Is Ready To Grow, Parsons Says" *Washington Post*, January 7, 2004.

—Tim Halpern

■■■
Corrado Passera
1954–
CEO, Banca Intesa

Nationality: Italian.

Born: December 30, 1954, in Como, Italy.

Education: Bocconi University, BA; Wharton School,
University of Pennsylvania, MBA.

Family: Married.

Career: McKinsey and Company, 1980–1985, senior
engagement manager; CIR, 1986–1990, chief
operating officer; Arnoldo Mondadori Editore,
1990–1991, chief operating officer; Gruppo Espresso-
Repubblica, 1991–1992, deputy chairman and CEO;
Olivetti, 1992–1996, managing director and co-CEO;
Banco Ambrosiano Veneto, 1996–1998, managing
director and CEO; Poste Italiane, 1998–2002,
managing director and CEO; Banca Intesa, 2002–,
managing director and CEO.

Address: Via Monte di Pieta, 8, Milano 20121, Italy; http:/
/www.bancaintesa.it.

■ During the 1990s and early 2000s Corrado Passera became
one of Italy's best-known and most successful executives despite his young age. His claim to fame was his ability to rescue
failing companies and restore them to profitability and efficiency. He successfully revitalized such companies as Olivetti,
an IT firm; Poste Italiane, the country's postal system; and
Banco Intesa, Italy's largest bank. Such was his reputation that
when a company was in need of help, Passera's name inevitably
came up as the person to save it.

EARLY CAREER

Passera was born in Como, Italy, in 1954 and obtained a
degree in business administration from Bocconi University in
Milan, graduating with first-class honors. He later received his
MBA from the prestigious Wharton School of the University
of Pennsylvania in Philadelphia. He began his career in 1980
with the consulting firm McKinsey and Company, where he
served as a senior engagement officer. Passera then went on to

become chief operating officer at CIR from 1986 until 1990.
He then held the same post at Arnoldo Mondadori Editore
from 1990 until 1991.

After 1991 Passera worked as CEO at several Italian companies. From 1991 to 1992 he was chief executive at Gruppo
Espresso-Repubblica. In 1992 he left that post to take the co-
CEO position at Olivetti, which had become Italy's leading
information technology company. Olivetti was suffering
though difficult financial times, and Passera was charged with
turning the company around. Along with Olivetti's chairman,
Carlo DeBenedetti, Passera drew up a recovery strategy for the
troubled firm. Among the problems he faced at Olivetti was
the creation of a single European market and ever-changing
technology, which made it difficult for the company to define
what it should do. He would soon develop a reputation as an
expert in turning around companies in trouble.

In a speech at the 1995 World Economic Forum, Passera
outlined the problems of companies like Olivetti. In the presentation, which the *Economist* (May 20, 1995) called a "brilliant analysis," Passera proposed a three-part strategy to reen-
gineer the company. First, he wanted to restructure the
company by cutting the workforce by 40 percent and removing layers of management. Second, Passera sought to refocus
Olivetti by expanding in selected businesses, such as ink-jet
printers. In the past the firm had tried to do too much in too
many different areas. Third, he sought to reinvent Olivetti by
moving in new directions, such as cellular telephones. The
company had once focused on making manual typewriters and
later moved into producing computers. Passera wanted to
make Olivetti into a more service-oriented company, focusing
on Omnitel, its cellular phone division.

PASSERA TAKES OVER AT POSTE ITALIANE

In 1996 rumors circulated that Passera had received another job offer and that he might leave Olivetti. The company initially denied the reports but eventually admitted that Passera
had received an offer from Banco Ambrosiano Veneto, one of
Italy's largest private banks. Passera decided to accept the position as managing director and CEO at the bank.

In 1998 the Italian government began to overhaul the
country's postal system, which was costly and inefficient. The
government transformed the postal service from a public sector

department to a shareholding company. The government still was the only shareholder, but the legal change opened the door for private investment in the postal system. Also, for the first time, Poste Italiane would have a CEO. Italian Prime Minister Romano Prodi and Treasury Minister Carlo Azeglio Cianpi decided to offer the job to Passera. Passera recounted to the *Financial Times* that he "had just set up an Internet bank and could have made a fortune. But then I received a conference call from Cianpi and Prodi offering me this job. I couldn't say no. Sometimes one has to make idealistic choices" (March 1, 2002).

When Passera took over the postal system, it was losing large amounts of money. In 1997 losses amounted to $441 million. It was the most inefficient postal system in Europe, known for its slow delivery times. Passera admitted to the *Financial Times* that the job would be "very difficult and demanding" (March 2, 1998). He quickly announced layoffs, the use of automation, and the addition of electronic services. Passera told *BusinessWeek* that "we will reorganize like any private-sector company" (August 17, 1998). It would be his ability to transform an extreme case such as Poste Italiane that would give Passera his reputation for corporate turnarounds.

Passera told the *Financial Times* that "when I got there we had two months' worth of cash for salaries, negative net equity and no technology. No one believed in the future. I had to make sure the government was behind us and start investing in people" (March 1, 2002). He implemented a five-year business plan for Poste, and he hired tough managers from outside the postal service. Passera invested in information technology and modern sorting equipment, and he trained employees in the use of computers. He even began to offer banking services, taking advantage of customers who were unhappy with traditional Italian banks. The postal service began offering savings accounts, debit cards, and credit cards.

Perhaps the most difficult part of Passera's tenure at Poste was cutting jobs. The postal system was once known for its cronyism, a system in which jobs were exchanged for votes. Despite cutting large numbers of jobs, Passera was able to gain the support of union leaders. As Ciro Amiore, a union leader, told the *Financial Times*: "You sense that postal workers have regained a certain amount of pride. A few years ago they were considered to be do-nothings and there wasn't much to defend them against that charge" (March 1, 2002). Postal workers came to realize that an efficient, profitable company could mean jobs for them.

PASSERA LEAVES FOR BANCA INTESA

In March 2002 Passera left his job at Poste Italiane to take on the challenge of another company experiencing difficulties.

There was some talk in government circles that Passera should be made head of Eni, the oil-and-gas company. Instead, he was named CEO of Bank Intesa, Italy's largest bank. The bank was going through a process of restructuring. Over the previous five years, Intesa had made many acquisitions, but management had struggled to efficiently incorporate the new additions. Intesa had hoped to create a large bank that would play a role throughout Europe. However, the various parts of the bank failed to unify. Furthermore, Intesa lost money in its Latin American operations and to loans to troubled companies such as Enron.

When Passera took over, Intesa was losing $1 billion annually. It had unusually high operating costs. Powerful unions made it difficult to cut jobs, although most workers were demoralized. Passera was expected to cut costs and improve efficiency as he had done with the postal system. His goal was to make Intesa into Italy's best-performing bank. To do so, he cuts jobs and added new services. By measuring and evaluating employees based on performance, he was able to cut 25,000 jobs. He also added a new financial services unit that contributed 40 percent of revenue. Intesa also began to offer branches in post offices for customer convenience, and the bank became the country's number-three seller of life insurance. Overall, Passera did what he was asked to do: rescue another Italian company on the brink of collapse.

See also entries on Compagnie Industriali Riunite S.p.A., McKinsey & Company, Inc., and Olivetti S.p.A. in *International Directory of Company Histories.*

SOURCES FOR FURTHER INFORMATION

Blitz, James, "Italy to Overhaul Postal Service," *Financial Times*, March 2, 1998.

Echikson, William, "Posts with the Most," *BusinessWeek*, August 17, 1998, p. 18.

Hill, Andrew, "Olivetti Chief Poised to Leave," *Financial Times*, June 27, 1996.

Kapner, Fred, "Intesa Starts Revamp with Passera Move," *Financial Times*, March 28, 2002.

——— "Pushing the Envelope," *Financial Times*, March 1, 2002.

"Olivetti on the Ropes," *Economist*, May 20, 1995, p. 60.

—Ronald Young

■ ■ ■
Hank Paulson

1946–

Chairman and chief executive officer, Goldman, Sachs & Company

Nationality: American.

Born: March 28, 1946, in Chicago, Illinois.

Education: Dartmouth College, BA, 1968; Harvard Business School, MBA, 1970.

Family: Son of a wholesale jewelery business owner; married Wendy J. Paulson (naturalist and volunteer bird educator in New York City schools); children: two.

Career: Pentagon, 1970–1972, aide; Nixon White House, 1972–1973, assistant to John Ehrlichman; Goldman, Sachs, 1974–1988, investment banker; 1982–, partner; 1988–1994, co-head of Investment Banking; 1994–1998, COO; 1998–1999, co-chairman and co-CEO; 1999–, director; 1999–, chairman and CEO.

Address: Goldman, Sachs & Company, 85 Broad Street, New York, New York 10004; http://www.gs.com.

Hank Paulson. *AP/Wide World Photos.*

■ Unlike other major financial-service firms in the new millennium that offered one-stop shopping for corporate financial needs, Goldman, Sachs resisted this trend. Henry M. "Hank" Paulson, its leader since May 1999, was one key reason why. He embraced a strategy to make Goldman, Sachs a leader in pure-play investment banking—the "go to" firm for major corporations, governments, and individuals with a high net worth. He also stood out for his public crusade against corporate malfeasance, the climax of which was his push for the ouster of Richard Grasso as chairman of the New York Stock Exchange. Depending upon whom one trusted, Paulson was either a paragon of virtue in the den of iniquity or a hypocrite seeking an easy scapegoat.

With 2003 revenues of $23.6 billion, Goldman, Sachs was a major player in global investment banking, securities, and investment management. Despite the economic downturn in the United States and a lackluster demand for deal making, the company had long enjoyed a position as the global leader in mergers, acquisitions, and initial public offerings. Founded in

1869, its services fall into two segments: Global Capital Markets, which includes trading, principal investments, and investment banking; and Asset Management and Securities Services, which comprises institutional brokerage, investment management, and merchant banking.

PLANS TO BECOME A FOREST RANGER

Paulson's upbringing on a farm outside Chicago led to his love of animals. As he recalled: "I wanted to be a forest ranger right up until the time I went to college" (*Fortune*, January 12, 2004). Instead, he went to Dartmouth College and then on to Harvard Business School. But he eventually returned to his roots, buying five acres of his family's farm and building a house for himself and his new bride. In addition to his two children, the family also included raccoons—which had free run of the house—flying squirrels, alligators, mice, birds, dogs, cats, turtles, frogs, lizards, a tarantula, and a few snakes.

Another major influence on Paulson as a child was religion. His parents were devout Christian Scientists, a belief system that he felt had nurtured his self-confidence: "Christian Science is a religion in which you emphasize love as opposed to fear. I think fear in young kids is the biggest inhibitor to success" (*Fortune*, January 12, 2004).

FROM PUBLIC SERVICE TO PRIVATE SECTOR

Paulson studied English literature at Dartmouth College, earning a Phi Beta Kappa key, and was an honorable mention All-American as offensive lineman on the football team. Following graduation from Harvard Business School, he was drawn to a political career, which included a stint at the Defense Department and (later) a job as an aide to the Nixon White House. Hoping to avoid the stress of Wall Street, in 1974 he accepted a job as an investment banker in Goldman Sachs's Chicago office.

Paulson spent two decades as an investment banker in Chicago, priding himself on his avoidance of the spotlight, later claiming that "clients don't want to read about their investment bankers" (*New York Times*, June 16, 2002). But he was a known entity within the walls of his firm, distinguished by his fierce work ethic. A CEO once confided to another Goldman, Sachs banker: "If I don't give the business to Goldman, Paulson will call all my board members" (*Newsweek*, June 7, 2004).

THE SPOTLIGHT'S GLARE

Ultimately, Paulson could not avoid the lure of New York City. He moved there in 1988, becoming co-head of investment banking. In 1994 he was appointed the number-two executive at the firm and in 1998 he was appointed co-CEO, sharing the title for seven months with Jon Corzine, the bond trader-turned-U.S. senator. However, they failed to develop the close working relationship necessary to make a shared power arrangement work. The main issue dividing them was whether—and how—Goldman, Sachs should end its partnership and go public. Paulson, who had been a vice chairman and COO reporting to Corzine, was a longtime dissenter on the IPO and pledged his support only when Corzine agreed to make him his equal. Another issue that divided them was whether Goldman, Sachs should use as much as $350 million in proceeds from the IPO to establish a charitable foundation, a cherished goal of Corzine. Ultimately Corzine left the firm and Paulson emerged on top. While some claimed that Paulson "ousted" Corzine, the average retirement age at Goldman, Sachs was 50 and Corzine, aged 52, left the firm with more than $50 million.

LEADING A LONG-ANTICIPATED IPO

In 1999 the Goldman, Sachs IPO went forward, with Paulson deciding to distribute the financial rewards more broadly. He required partners to give up $5 billion, which was distributed among the firm's 13,000 employees. The idea was to retain the firm's best employees during a tumultuous period and to promulgate a sense of loyalty throughout the organization. Employees received stock worth half of their previous year's compensation. According to Joan Zimmerman, a Wall Street headhunter with G. Z. Stephens: "It certainly is something that has never been done on the Street before" (*BusinessWeek*, March 29, 1999).

The transition to a publicly held corporation was not easy. During Goldman Sachs's first annual meeting in March 2000, Paulson and his executive team came under fire for a security breach involving a temporary employee of the firm who had stolen and sold information about merger deals. Evelyn Y. Davis, a well-known corporate activist, criticized Paulson by asking: "Which idiot in this company is responsible for hiring a temp to work on mergers?" Paulson had no regrets about taking the company public; it was a necessary step toward raising the money needed to compete. Nevertheless he conceded: "Was it easier to be private? You betcha" (both *New York Times*, June 16, 2002).

WORKING CAPITAL FUELS GROWTH

After the company went public, Paulson spent more than $7 billion to expand the business. It was the first time in its history that the company had made major acquisitions. His biggest transaction was the $6.5 billion acquisition of Spear, Leeds & Kellogg, the largest share dealer, or specialist firm, on the New York Stock Exchange and the number-three market maker on the NASDAQ stock market. Market makers buy and sell shares from investors and pocket the difference between the asking and bidding prices. Paulson also spent lavishly to bulk up the executive ranks with talent; between 1999 and 2001 the staff tripled, growing to 25,000.

A TRANSITIONAL YEAR

In 2002 Paulson resisted the industry-wide trend of acquiring commercial banks and using lending as an entrée into accounts with investment-banking needs. Instead he held firm to his belief that the company's future lay in dominating the investment-banking market: "We want to be the premier global investment-bank, securities, and investment-management firm. We want to have a disproportionate share of the business of the most important clients in the most important markets" (*BusinessWeek*, March 4, 2002).

Skeptics wondered whether Paulson could execute his grand vision in the midst of a slump in the markets. A global recession started in 2001, merger-and-acquisition (M&A) activity had tapered off, and the Enron debacle had cast a long shadow across the entire industry. Another challenge to Paulson's plan to stay independent was his own employees, who in 2000 owned 55 percent of the company. At the time Guy Moszkowski, a financial-services analyst with Salomon Smith Barney Holdings Inc., remarked: "If Goldman's employees feel that preservation of their wealth requires affiliation with a commercial bank, I don't think they'd hesitate to do it, and I think they'd move very quickly" (*BusinessWeek*, March 4, 2002).

PROVING HIS CRITICS WRONG

Goldman, Sachs put an end to any speculation about the viability of Paulson's strategy in 2003, when the firm held on to the top spot in global-equities underwriting and M&A advisory. The trading unit that included fixed income, currency, and commodities generated record net revenues of $5.6 billion, while equities trading added another $1.74 billion. The company generated an annual profit of more than $3 billion, nearly surpassing its earnings at the height of the bull market.

Paulson also found a way to compete with the megabanks that had been using discount lending to attract investment-banking business. An arrangement with Sumitomo Mitsui Financial Group allowed Goldman, Sachs to offer bigger loans to its marquee clients while protecting itself with $1 billion in first-loss insurance. According to Paulson: "The challenge for us was to be able to meet our clients' needs and, at the same time, be able to do so in a prudent manner" (*Investment Dealers Digest*, January 19, 2004).

MAINTAINING A STRONG CULTURE

Another competitive advantage was the intense loyalty and dedication its employees felt toward Goldman, Sachs. It was a culture that encouraged teamwork and discouraged independence. Instead of being measured solely on their individual performance, compensation was also based on divisional and overall company performance. Paulson commented at the time: "We've always stayed away from a star system. We've got very good people, but we're part of a team, and people work here because they like working with the other people at Goldman, Sachs" (*Investment Dealers Digest*, January 19, 2004). Paulson insisted that public ownership also contributed to the firm's unity.

A SERIES OF SCANDALS AND QUESTIONS OF FAITH

In 2002 Wall Street came under fire for a host of allegedly unethical business practices. Unlike his peers, who claimed the industry was taking the fall for a few unscrupulous players, Paulson called for reforms in the financial industry to guard against future transgressions. In a speech entitled "Restoring Investor Confidence: An Agenda for Change," delivered at a 2002 meeting of the National Press Club in Washington, D.C., he said American business was facing its largest crises in more than 50 years.

Ironically, former foe Corzine, by then a New Jersey senator, was one of the first people to commend Paulson's willingness to take a public stand on the issue. While leading Goldman, Sachs, Paulson continued to be a person who professed strong Christian values: "My wife and I try to begin every day by affirming Jesus. Sound ethics and morals have got to be the underpinning—the basis—of everything we do" (*Christian Science Journal*, May 2000).

MOTIVES CALLED INTO QUESTION

Paulson's position nevertheless raised a few eyebrows. Goldman, Sachs was the leading underwriter of new-economy companies in the heady years leading up to the market bust. Paulson insisted that "if you don't speak out on these things, it could be construed as tacit approval" (*New York Times*, June 16, 2002).

At the time of his speech, Goldman, Sachs and its primary rivals were being investigated to determine whether their analysts' stock recommendations were influenced by the quest to retain and attract new investment-banking customers. Stocks were being recommended by brokerage houses seeking to distribute those firm's shares in order to win lucrative investment-banking fees from the companies. Doing so meant that the small investor was frequently given biased research, which often led to their losing money. In 2003 New York State found that the 10 brokerage houses had corrupted the stock-research process. As part of a historic settlement, Goldman, Sachs ultimately paid $110 million—less than its main competitors—to settle charges that the investment-banking business influenced research. The 10 brokerage houses had to put a total of $432.5 million into an independent-research fund to finance free research ("Goldman CEO on Enron Effect" (*CNNMoney*, February 4, 2002).

Paulson's desire to speak out about corporate governance was intensified by the 2001 Enron scandal. Once the largest U.S. buyers and sellers of natural gas, Enron estimated that the collapse of its stock would cost all investors in the firm at least $25 billion. Paulson, who considered Enron a bellwether that could irrevocably change the industry's accepted business practices, argued: "We've all got to work to restore business confidence . . . but I believe that longer term we may look at Enron as being a positive as opposed to a negative. It may lead to greater transparency" (*CNNMoney*, February 4, 2002). He also insisted that greater visibility in earnings, along with a clearer picture of a corporation's financial health, could become a catalyst for increased M&A activity in the future.

THE DESTABILIZATION OF CAPITALISM

In 2003 Richard Grasso, longtime chairman and CEO of the New York Stock Exchange (NYSE), resigned following several weeks of intense criticism over his $139.5 million compensation package. Paulson played a central role in the scandal, which threatened to have a profound impact for years to come. The NYSE, generally considered the most prominent symbol of the capitalist economy, is a nonprofit, member-owned entity originally founded in 1792. It is the world's largest and most lucrative securities exchange. However, the NYSE had historically been accused of being too insular, self-referential, unrepresentative of its membership, and lacking input from investors. Having led the NYSE since 1995, Grasso oversaw the most significant period of growth in its history. He relaunched the NYSE following 9/11 and dealt with the fallout and embarrassment of the corporate scandals being highlighted on Wall Street.

Grasso's fate was sealed with the disclosure of an employment contract, struck in August 2003, that provided payments totaling $139.5 million in deferred compensation, savings, and pension benefits. Although NYSE officials claimed that Grasso had accumulated the sum by deferring significant components of his pay during his 20 years as an executive at the exchange, he was forced to resign when details about his pay package emerged. Nevertheless, he left with the $139.5 million in his pocket. Federal regulators, politicians, and investors insisted that Grasso's leadership of a quasi-public organization—one where he was supposed to be regulating the financial markets—meant that his pay was inappropriate and unethical. Jeffrey A. Sonnenfeld, associate dean of the Yale School of Management, remarked that this represented the first time in American history that a person was considered to have done a good job but was fired because the board was paying him too much. Sonnenfeld considered the board's accountability to be a secondary, but important, issue.

SAINT OR SNAKE?

In 2004 New York State Attorney General Eliot Spitzer announced that he would sue Grasso to recover the $100 million of pension allowance he had received. Grasso filed a $48 million countersuit. He threatened to make Paulson's board service at the NYSE a key issue, claiming that Paulson had never objected to the size of his pay when he was on the compensation committee. Grasso also said Paulson helped him handle the controversy, suggesting he release details of his pay package close to Labor Day 2003 because "the press won't be around" (*Newsweek*, June 7, 2004). Paulson never disputed his account. For his part, Grasso repeatedly called Paulson a "snake" and said he looked forward to watching him "squirm" during cross-examination.

The merits of Grasso's pay can be debated ad infinitum. What was thought to be central to the Grasso case is the fact that he was paid proportionally to what members of the NYSE compensation committee earned, such as Paulson and Richard S. Fuld Jr. of Lehman Brothers. Fuld served on the committee in 1999 and 2000, while Paulson was on it in 2002. In 2001 Paulson received a total award of over $12 million. In 2000 Fuld received over $20 million in stock and cash.

Whether Paulson participated in the initial deliberations of Grasso's contract became a subject of debate. Paulson contended that he had arrived late at the crucial meeting and was only briefed on the pay package a full month later. Other directors on the NYSE said Paulson did participate and wondered why he had not spoken up when the issue was first presented to the board. Former NYSE director Kenneth Langone, billionaire founder of Home Depot, vigorously defended Grasso and attacked Paulson. Langone was also sued by Spitzer in 2004. According to one former director: "Hank was the most aggressive in getting Dick out. But people questioned his loyalty: Was he looking out for the exchange or for his own company?" (*New York Times*, November 23, 2003).

In addition to helping orchestrate Grasso's ouster, Paulson called for a removal of conflicts of interest in the NYSE, expressing a desire to see it devoid of any director who also headed a Wall Street firm. Paulson suggested that a more appropriate way for Wall Street members to voice their opinions on NYSE issues would be through the creation of a separate advisory committee. In 2004 the publicity fallout from the Grasso scandal threatened Paulson's career. If it were to intensify, the consequences could be deadly. Paulson's number-two executive was said to be angling for his job, and the likelihood that he would succeed was only increased by the possibility of a highly publicized lawsuit.

ENVIRONMENTAL ACTIVIST

In his private life Paulson devoted a great deal of time to conservation. In 2004 he served as vice-chair of the board of governors for the Nature Conservancy, then the world's biggest nonprofit environmental organization. The group established partnerships with companies to encourage and help them make decisions that would not harm the environment. According to Paulson: "It compromises to achieve its goals, and it collaborates with business. That bothers some people. It attracts me" (*Fortune*, January 12, 2004). Paulson's passion for what he has called the "ultimate global issue" resulted in tireless fund-raising; as of early 2004 he had raised $7 million for Asian projects.

Although Paulson's motivations were charitable—a byproduct of his childhood upbringing on a farm—he insisted that his nonprofit work paid off in the for-profit arena: "It helps me do my job better because I learn about cultures and people in a way that you can't when you're just getting them financing." His work involving the environment has made people "see me in a different light" (*Fortune*, January 12, 2004). For example, when Paulson traveled to China to pitch a deal, he talked to executives about conservation efforts, not simply investment banking. Paulson even considered leaving Goldman, Sachs for a full-time career in environmental protectionism. The Nature Conservancy was searching for a new CEO in 2001 and asked Paulson whether he would consider leaving his job. Although he told the group that the timing was not right, claiming that he was bonded to his mission at the company, he nevertheless added: "Whenever I do finish here, I have no doubt that I'll do something with the environment" (*Fortune*, January 12, 2004).

See also entry on Goldman, Sachs & Co. in *International Directory of Company Histories*.

SOURCES FOR FURTHER INFORMATION

Celarier, Michelle, "For the Prize: Navigating Risky Waters, Goldman Is Named IDD's Bank of the Year," *Investment Dealers Digest*, January 19, 2004.

Gasparino, Charles, "Power Play," *Newsweek*, June 7, 2004, p. 39.

"Goldman CEO on Enron Effect," *CNNMoney*, February 4, 2002, http://money.cnn.com/2002/02/04/news/davos_goldman.

McGeehan, Patrick, "An Unlikely Clarion Calls for Change," *New York Times*, June 16, 2002.

Nathans Spiro, Leah, "Goldman's Quiet Man Gets His Shot," *BusinessWeek*, March 29, 1999, p. 178.

Plitt, Todd, "Economy Has Turned Around, but Look for Yellow Flags," *USA Today*, February 1, 2002, http://www.usatoday.com/money/companies/management/2004-02-01-insana_x.htm.

Sellers, Patricia, "Hank Paulson's Secret Life," *Fortune*, January 12, 2004, p. 121.

Shippey, Kim, "Heading True North," *Christian Science Journal*, May 2000,

Thomas, Landon, Jr., "The War between the Street and Floor," *New York Times*, November 23, 2003.

Thornton, Emily, "Wall Street's Lone Ranger," *BusinessWeek*, March 4, 2002, p. 82.

—Tim Halpern

■■■
Michel Pébereau
1942–
Chairman, BNP Paribas

Nationality: French.

Born: January 23, 1942, in Paris, France.

Education: École polytechnique, 1961; École nationale d'administration, 1967.

Family: Brother of French financier Georges Pébereau; married Agnès (maiden name unknown).

Career: Ministry of the Economy and Finance, 1970–1974, Inspecteur Général des Finances; Ministry of the Economy and Finance, 1971–1982, representative subdirector, assistant director, and head of service at the Treasury Directorate; Ministry of the Economy, 1978–1981, director of the cabinet and representative; Crédit commercial de France, 1982–1987, managing director; 1987–1993, chairman and chief executive officer; Banque nationale de Paris (BNP), 1993–2000, chairman and chief executive officer; Paribas, 1999–2000, chairman; BNP Paribas, 2000–2003, chairman and chief executive officer; BNP Paribas, 2003–, chairman.

Awards: Honored as the European Banker of the Year, Group 20+1, 1994; named Strategist of the Year, *La tribune*, 2001; named Financier of the Year, ANDESE, 2001; made a Commander in la Légion d'honneur, French government, 2004.

Address: BNP Paribas, 16, boulevard des Italiens, 75009 Paris, France; http://www.bnpparibas.com.

Michel Pébereau. *AP/Wide World Photos.*

POISED FOR BECOMING THE WHO'S WHO OF FRENCH BANKING

Michel Pébereau was born in Paris, France, on January 23, 1942. He and his older brother, Georges, were both destined for lucrative careers in the finance industry. Their father drilled mathematics into them at an early age, forcing Pébereau to sneak his favorite diversion, reading, past his mother at bedtime. Reading remained a passion for Pébereau throughout his life. He especially enjoyed the science fiction of Eastern European writers and even wrote science fiction reviews for *La Recherche* magazine. He told *Financial News* that science fiction "allows my imagination to go into a different world which is such a change from the day-to-day realities" (June 18, 2001).

As teenagers the brothers attended the École polytechnique, an elite private school known for guaranteeing a high-profile career. Pébereau praised the school for offering unlimit-

■ Michel Pébereau was the CEO of BNP Paribas, one of the world's largest banks and the second largest in the Eurozone. Pébereau made headlines in the late 1990s for attempting to accomplish what his predecessor could not, creating the largest bank in France through acquisitions and mergers. In particular, Pébereau sought a cross-border candidate to create the world's largest bank. With a background in the Ministry of Finance, Pébereau was poised to combine business acumen with a diplomatic twist.

ed career opportunities following graduation. When he joined the rugby team, Pébereau found a spirit of unity among his teammates. In addition to science, language, and humanities courses, Pébereau said he had a great deal of spare time that allowed him to further himself and pursue other interests. This included reading the classics, especially the works of Honoré de Balzac. In order to return to the school something of what he believed it had given him, Pébereau later taught seminars in economics and international politics at École polytechnique and became a member of the board of regents. He believed strongly in the values that the school instilled in students, remarking, "The preparation for the entrance exam and the studies at Polytechnique have always given students invaluable qualities: the ability to quickly absorb new concepts, the capacity to work hard and fast, and the ability to formulate a precise analysis and synthesis of a question or problem" ("Alumni Interview: Michel Pébereau, X1961: BNP Paribas President"). Upon graduating from École polytechnique, Pébereau entered the École nationale d'administration, positioning him for a lucrative career in government.

LEARNING THE INS AND OUTS OF THE FINANCE MINISTRY

After graduating from École nationale d'administration in 1967, Pébereau became an inspector with the Ministry of Finance. After three and a half years, he joined the cabinet of Valery Giscard d'Estaing as financial minister. His tenure became a trial by fire; three years into the position, during an economic crisis, Pébereau was given the tasks of integrating the treasury and taking charge of the CIASI (the Interministerial Committee for Improving Industrial Structures), which negotiates between financially struggling companies and their creditors to avoid liquidation. The negotiating skills he learned during this period served him well during his later merger and acquisition activities.

When d'Estaing was elected president of France, Pébereau held various positions in the treasury department, including directing the service of monetary and financial affairs. From 1978 to 1981 he was the principal private secretary of the cabinet member and economic minister René Monory. Pébereau was set to become a treasury minister, but the 1981 election of a socialist government thwarted those plans. "I was 40 and I knew that I had to make a choice—either stay in the civil service and wait for one of the top jobs, or move into the private sector," Pébereau told the *Financial News* (June 18, 2001).

In 1982 the president of the Crédit commercial de France (CCF) appointed Pébereau a general director. The CCF was privatized in 1987, and Pébereau was promoted to president. At CCF Pébereau learned about the efficiencies of technology. In collaboration with the French technology specialist Minitel

and France Telecom, he started the first home banking program in the world.

FROM GOVERNMENT TO PRIVATE SECTOR

In 1993 Pébereau's cost-cutting initiatives at CCF earned him the post of president of the Banque nationale de Paris (BNP). Here Pébereau spearheaded privatization by streamlining operations, creating what the *Financial News* called the "most efficient retail network in Europe" (June 18, 2001). He was credited with revolutionizing back-office technology.In 1997 BNP won the right to operate in New Zealand, bought Laurentian Bank and Trust of the Bahamas, enhanced its joint venture with Egypt's Banque du Caire, and opened a subsidiary in Brazil. BNP expanded to China in 1998 with the purchase of Peregrine Investment's Chinese operations. Further expansion included new offices in Peru, Algeria, Uzbekistan, and India. BNP also bought Prudential's Australian stock-brokerage operations. Pébereau avoided scandals during the real estate crisis in the early 1990s, and he also emerged unscathed from the 1998 emerging-markets setbacks in France. In addition to his leadership at BNP Paribas, Pébereau served as a director of Lafarge and Saint Gobain, a member of the supervisory boards of AXA and Dresdner Bank AG, and president of the French Banking Federation.

CHANGING THE FACE OF FRENCH BANKING

In 1999 France's two other large banks, Société Générale and Paribas, announced plans to merge. Pébereau, seeing that BNP's position would be weakened by this potential merger, made an unprecedented double counteroffer to merge Société Générale, Paribas, and BNP into a "tres grande banque" or superbank. The bank was to be dubbed BSP for each company's initials. Pébereau urged the formation of a French bank strong enough to compete with firms from Switzerland, Germany, Great Britain, and the United States, especially in terms of market capitalization. Pébereau's initiative was met with criticism and skepticism, reminding some analysts of other grand schemes in France that had not fared well.

Pébereau's move ruffled many feathers, especially since he did not consult with regulators or the leaders of Paribas and Société Générale, as was customary in French banking. Soon he was being compared to a cowboy and frowned upon by the old guard; however, the hostile counteroffer marked a new era in the French banking world. "France has been lagging behind other countries," Laurent Treca, BNP's director of strategy and development, said in *Newsweek International*. "For years French banks weren't governed by the market, but by the state. . . . So this is a big, big change" (March 22, 1999).

To the younger banking generation, Pébereau became a hero for braving the French authorities and marking "the end of 'Papa's capitalism'" (March 22, 1999). The *Financial News* reported, "His plans to create France's biggest bank so upset the status quo that the governor of the Bank of France, Jean-Claude Trichet, finally blocked the deal even though 43 percent of SocGen's shareholders had agreed to the takeover" (June 18, 2001).

Société Générale had proven elusive for Pébereau's brother a decade earlier. While Pébereau designed avenues leading toward privatization, Georges made headlines for his involvement in a 1988 takeover bid of Société Générale. The financier received amnesty during a lawsuit accusing George Soros and others of insider training, a charge for which Soros was convicted in 2002.

PEACE RESTORED

BNP finalized its merger with Paribas in 2000. When the merger was announced, 900 Paribas staff members quit, and senior Paribas managers were openly opposed to the bid. However, Pébereau's firm yet loyal management style won over the Paribas camp, and peace was restored. In Pébereau's view the merger between BNP and Paribas was very successful. He believed that despite the different cultures of the two organizations, the merger was truly one of equals. Moreover, services for both the domestic and international customers were greatly expanded.

The combination of the two companies gave BNP Paribas more than 2,200 retail branches in France and combined operations in more than 85 other countries. The company focused on three business units: corporate and investment banking; private banking, asset management, and insurance; and retail banking. The successful integration won critics over and made BNP Paribas Europe's second most profitable bank by return on equity. Its cost-to-income ratio ranked it as one of the most efficient banks in Europe.

TOWARD A GLOBAL SUPERBANK

Globally, rankings were not as high, but Pébereau said he would expand on his business units by acquiring specific niche businesses and hiring top talent. BNP Paribas controlled the consumer lender Cetelem and purchased the U.S.-based Banc-West in 2002. During this time *CFO Magazine* described Pébereau as "ambitious and micromanaging. Pébereau may describe himself as risk averse, but he's not afraid to put his money down on a deal" (June 11, 2002).

In January 2002 *La tribune*, a daily business paper, named Pébereau the Strategist of the Year for 2001. The award, voted on by *La tribune* readers, honored the head of the French company whose strategy produced the best performance during the year. ANDESE, the national association of doctors of economics, named Pébereau Financier of the Year of 2001, honoring him as the person who had done the most to contribute to the growth of financial activity in France during the year.

Shunning French players altogether after losing Société Générale, Pébereau focused on cross-border mergers. "We are advancing rapidly towards the euro and it is a very exciting time," he told the *Financial News*. "But who will take the lead and what shape that will take, I don't know. I think there will be about 12 big global players of which six to eight banks will be European. And, yes, I think we will see this before I retire" (June 18, 2001).

Pébereau stepped down from the position of CEO in 2003 and handed leadership over to Baudoin Prot. Although speculation arose over whether Pébereau might be appointed president of the European Central Bank, he insisted that his only ambition was to remain chairman of BNP Paribas. In 2004 Pébereau was made a commander of la Légion d'honneur, France's highest civilian award. Prot continued Pébereau's legacy by strengthening BNP Paribas's coverage in Germany, Italy, and the United Kingdom. In October 2003 BNP Paribas was ranked eighth in equity capital in Europe, the Middle East, and Africa, and ninth in market share. Globally BNP Paribas ranked third in mergers and acquisitions in the media sector in 2003.

See also entry on BNP Paribas Group in *International Directory of Company Histories*.

SOURCES FOR FURTHER INFORMATION

"Alumni Interview: Michel Pébereau, X1961: BNP Paribas President," *École polytechnique*, http://www.polytechnique.edu/interview.php?id=21.

Calabro, Lori, and Alix Nyberg, "The Global 100: Bankers," *CFO Magazine*, June 11, 2002, http://www.cfo.com/Article?article=7292.

"Hard Study and Little Sleep Give Big Advantage to France's Top Banker," *Financial News*, June 18, 2001.

Leroy, Pierre-Henri. "A Freely Changing Opinion on the BNP—Société Générale-Paribas," *Proxinvest*, July 1, 1999, http://www.proxinvest.com/actualites/bnpsocpar.htm.

Manière, Philippe, "Michel Pébereau, le grand calculateur," *LExpansion*, December 18, 2002, http://www.lexpansion.com/art/91.0.64467.0.html.

Nadeau, Barbie, "Commence Firing! (European Takeover Bids)," *Newsweek International*, March 22, 1999.

—Maike van Wijk

■ ■ ■
Roger S. Penske
1937–
Chairman of the board and chief executive officer, Penske Corporation and its subsidiary, United Auto Group

Nationality: American.

Born: February 20, 1937, in Shaker Heights, Ohio.

Education: Lehigh University, BA, 1959.

Family: Son of Jay (vice president of metal fabrication company) and Martha (housewife and community volunteer); married Kathryn; children: five.

Career: Alcoa Aluminum, 1959–1963, sales engineer; George McKean Chevrolet, 1963–1965, general manager and, later, owner; 1965–1969, owner of several automobile dealerships, a truck-leasing operation, and two racing-tire distributors; Penske Corporation, 1969–, president and CEO; United Auto Group, 1999–, chairman and CEO.

Awards: Named SCCA Driver of the Year, *Sports Illustrated*, 1961; named Driver of the Year, *New York Times*, 1962.

Address: Penske Corporation, 8801 North Haggarty Road, Ann Arbor, Michigan 48107; United Auto Group, 2555 Telegraph Road, Bloomfield Hills, Michigan 48302-0954; http://www.penske.com; http://www.united auto.com.

Roger S. Penske. *Photo courtesy of Penske Motorsports, Inc.*

■ In 2004 the transportation executive and auto-racing legend Roger S. Penske was the chairman of the board and chief executive officer (CEO) of Penske Corporation, which he founded in 1969. Penske discovered his niche in life early, when, as a teenager, he began refurbishing and racing cars and selling them for profit. Basing his achievement on his stringent guidelines for setting goals, Penske made race-car driving an obsession that eventually earned him a driving record held by only a few talented drivers. After retiring from driving, Penske became one of the most successful and best-known car and track owners in the history of motor sports.

A KNACK WITH CARS

Even from an early age, Penske had a knack for fixing automobiles. As a teenager in the 1950s, he would buy "junker" cars, make repairs on them, and sell them at a profit from his parents' home in suburban Cleveland, Ohio. Over the next 10 years, Penske raced and sold 32 cars, among them a Chevrolet, Corvette, Jaguar Cooper, Maserati, MG TD, MG TC, Oldsmobile, Porsche, and the Zerex Special. The experiences learned from these early ventures became the hallmark for Penske's later successes in the automobile world, both as a race-car driver and as a transportation businessman. Finding early in life what he liked to do, Penske was able to seize on opportunities that led him to legendary status as a race-car driver and, later, helped him accumulate a transportation empire, record-setting racing teams, and a successful truck-leasing company.

RACE-CAR LEGEND

Almost from the start, racing cars was an obsession for Penske, who first drove at the Akron (Ohio) Speedway. In 1958 he entered his first official race in the Sports Car Club of America (SCCA) National at Marlboro Motor Raceway in Maryland. After consistently running behind the leader, his car eventually overheated, and Penske had to withdraw from the race. His first win came in 1959 when, driving an F-Modified Porsche RS, he beat the competition at the SCCA Regional at Lime Rock, Connecticut. Unwilling to stay with a proven but older car, Penske bought an RSK and used it later for an SCCA class title.

In the same year as his first racing win, Penske also graduated from Lehigh University with a business degree (industrial management) and went to work as a sales engineer for Alcoa Aluminum. Continuing his racing career, Penske won the F Modified in 1960. In 1961 he bought a Cooper and a Maserati, rebuilt a Cooper-Climax with an aluminum body, persuaded Zerex to sponsor him, and started to race professionally. Penske's first professional win was at Vineland, New Jersey, in a Maserati nicknamed the "Telar Special." He also set a race speed record with his win at Road America. Penske then won three nationals in a row in 1961, the year he became the SCCA National D Modified champion and was named *Sports Illustrated*'s SCCA Driver of the Year.

In 1962 Penske was named the *New York Times* Driver of the Year when he became the United States Auto Club champion, driving in Monaco with the Cooper-Climax and in Sebring, Florida, with a Cunningham. In 1963 Penske won the National Association for Stock Car Auto Racing (NASCAR) Grand National Series race. In 1964 he won five races; two of them were the Nassau Tourist Trophy, when he drove a Chaparral Corvette Grand Sport, and the Nassau Trophy, when he beat Bruce McLaren, A. J. Foyt, and Dan Gurney. The race that established Penske as one of the world's best was the 1964 Governor's Trophy race in the Bahamas, where he confronted Foyt and Wait Hansgen, beating Foyt on the last lap.

FROM DRIVER TO OWNER

Much to the surprise of the racing community, Penske announced in 1965 his retirement as a driver in order to devote all his time to the business component of racing. Penske purchased a Chevrolet dealership in Pennsylvania, where he had been general manager since 1963. As his first dealership grew, Penske branched into other automobile dealerships. In 1969 Penske bought a small truck leasing operation along with two racing-tire distributors. The dealerships, truck leasing operation, and racing-tire distributors formed the foundation for his future business empire. For example, the truck leasing operation Penske bought in the late 1960s was converted to Penske Truck Leasing Company. In 1970 Penske moved to the Detroit area after buying a Chevrolet dealership in the Detroit suburb of Southfield.

During this time, he teamed up with the engineer and driver Mark Donohue , and the pair launched Penske Racing, with Team Penske as their new racing team. Within two years Team Penske won the United States Road Racing Championship with Mark Donohue driving a Lola T70 MKIII chassis with Chevrolet power. In 1972 Penske's team appeared in its first NASCAR Winston Cup Series race, and one year later, it won the first Winston Cup race of their second season.

In 1975 Mark Donohue was killed while practicing for the Austrian Grand Prix Formula One race. Nonetheless, Penske continued to enter cars during the next two years, with the drivers John Watch in 1976 and Tom Sneva in 1977. From 1978 to 1991 Team Penske continued to win races with such drivers as Rick Mears, Rusty Wallace, Bobby Unser, Al Unser, and Danny Sullivan. In fact, between 1977 and 1983 Team Penske won the national points championship in six of the seven seasons. In 1991 Penske teamed up with his driver from 1980, Rusty Wallace. Driving for Penske, Wallace won 37 times, with over half of those wins occurring between 1993 and 1994.

Penske directed one of the best-known and successful organizations in the sports world while breaking most racing records. Penske Racing, which as of the early 2000s held 225 major race titles, maintained records for most race poles (135), wins (110), 500-mile wins (22), Indy Car National Championships (11), Indianapolis 500 poles (11), and Indianapolis 500 wins (11). Penske Racing also has more than 30 victories in the NASCAR Winston Cup Series. By this time Penske owned the California Speedway, Michigan Speedway, Nazareth (Pennsylvania) Speedway, and North Carolina Motor Speedway.

PENSKE CORPORATION AND ITS SUBSIDIARIES

As a businessman, Penske owned the private company Penske Corporation, which was the parent of four business groups: Penske Performance, Penske Automotive, Penske Capital Partners, and Penske Transportation Services. As a group, the Penske Corporation was a closely held diversified transportation-services company that directed, through its subsidiaries, a number of businesses, including Penske Truck Leasing, Penske Automotive Group, United Auto Group, Penske Logistics, Penske Capital Partners, Truck-Lite, Davco, Penske Performance, FER, and Penske Racing. Penske actively supervised the Penske Corporation and its subsidiaries, which managed and operated businesses with annual revenues of more than $11 billion and employed 35,000 people at over three thousand worldwide locations.

Penske took on the chairmanship of the board of Penske Truck Leasing in 1982. He developed the global transportation-services provider, which specialized in commercial truck-rental operations, so that as of 2004 it had more than 206,000 vehicles serving customers at about one thousand locations in the United States, Canada, Mexico, South America, and Europe. The company, with annual revenues of about $3.4 billion, provided product lines in such areas as full-service leasing, contract maintenance, commercial and consumer rental, integrated logistics services, and supply-chain management.

Penske also directed Penske Automotive, which grew into a company that in the early 2000s operated several car dealerships in Southern California and sold over 44,000 cars, among them, the brand names Toyota, Lexus, Honda, Mercedes-Benz, Jaguar, and Aston Martin. His Longo Toyota dealership in El Monte, California, became the top-selling Toyota dealership in the United States. He also became the chairman of the board and CEO of the United Auto Group Inc. (UAG) in 1999 and turned the company into the second-largest publicly traded automobile retailer (auto dealer) in the United States (as measured by total revenues). As a member of the Fortune 500, the UAG, under Penske's direction, owned and operated, according to its website, 134 franchises in the United States and 83 franchises internationally, primarily in the United Kingdom but also in Puerto Rico and Brazil. UAG dealerships sold new and used vehicles, operated service and parts departments and collision-repair centers, and sold various after-market products and services, including extended service, finance, warranty, and other insurance contracts.

Penske made Penske Logistics into the company that provided logistics and custom-designed supply-chain solutions in order to cut costs, reduce cycle time, improve service, and help integrate technology into the operations of Penske's customers. In addition, Penske Capital Partners was a partnership venture organized by Penske, along with J. P. Morgan Partners, GE Capital, and Aon Corporation, to focus on making strategic acquisitions in the transportation industry.

Truck-Lite, of which Penske was a majority owner, manufactured lighting products, harness systems, and accessories for transportation industry such as safety lights for boats, buses, cars, commercial trucks, construction equipment, and recreational vehicles. Moreover, Penske operated several automotive-related racing businesses through Penske Performance. Its teams held numerous all-time racing records, and Penske Performance, as a company, was the second-largest shareholder of International Speedway Corporation, the leading U.S. motor-sports company. Within Penske Performance was Penske Racing, as of the early 2000s the most successful Indy car-racing team in history. Penske was a founder of Penske Racing Inc., along with Penske Racing South Inc.

SUPER BOWL XL IN 2006

Penske faced one of his biggest challenges with a time-critical repair job to the city of Detroit, Michigan, in preparation for its hosting of Super Bowl XL at Ford Field on February 5, 2006. Detroit had a deteriorated downtown area with abandoned buildings and was subject to poor building-code enforcement and ineffectual municipal bureaucracy. Bill Ford Jr., chairman and CEO of Ford Motor Company, handpicked Penske to coordinate the massive facelift.

As chairman of the Detroit Super Bowl XL host committee, Penske, who personally pledged to raise $12 million for the event, was coordinating efforts to prepare Detroit for the worldwide event that as of the early 2000s consistently drew 100,000 fans, thousands of sports journalists, 800 million television viewers, and millions of dollars in advertising. With his usual well-organized style, Penske assembled a 41-member committee, identifying downtown problem areas, raising donations, meeting with National Football League officials, and working to gather local support for the event. The *Detroit News* quoted Bill Ford Jr. as saying of his new chairman, "Penske is the most impressive businessman in the city. Everything he touches works because of his personal drive and because his attention to detail is so exquisite. I just love being around that guy."

A hands-on administrator, Penske recommended a long list of improvements, totaling $100 million, to Kate Beebe, president of the Greater Downtown Partnership. Requiring that only concrete renovations be made to the city in order to initiate long-lasting progress, Penske gathered momentum for the project. The planned upgrade to the city included an offer of loans or matching grants to property owners to renovate their buildings, major replacement of three main roads, installation of new sidewalks, and addition of plush landscaping.

As an example of a renovation already credited to Penske's work, the $146.8 million renovation of the Book-Cadillac Hotel helped put Detroit back in the game in time for the Super Bowl in 2006. The *Detroit News* quoted Penske's wife, Kathryn, as saying, "Roger and I didn't grow up here, but this is our home now, and we both want to help Detroit succeed. I can tell you he doesn't like to lose, so he's looking to win people over during the Super Bowl and show them Detroit is a great city." With friends and business associates describing him as tenacious, a workaholic, a perfectionist, seemingly tireless, and focused on detail, Penske was not the type of leader simply to lend his name to the event; he actively worked to make Detroit's Super Bowl a success for the state and the city.

See also entry on Penske Corporation in *International Directory of Company Histories.*

SOURCES FOR FURTHER INFORMATION

King, R. J., "Racing Legend Roger Penske Steers Super Bowl Drive," *Detroit News*, October 19, 2003.

—William Arthur Atkins

▪▪▪
A. Jerrold Perenchio
1931–
Chairman and chief executive officer, Univision

Nationality: American.

Born: 1931, in Fresno, California.

Education: University of California, Los Angeles, BA, 1954.

Family: Son of a winemaker (name unknown); married and divorced twice; married (third wife's name unknown); children: three.

Career: Music Corporation of America, 1958–1963, talent agent; 1963–?, independent talent agent; Embassy Communications, ?–1985, partner; Perenchio Television, 1985–1992, partner; Univision, 1992–, chairman and CEO.

Address: Univision, 1999 Avenue of the Stars, Suite 3050, Los Angeles, California 90067; http://www.univision.com.

▪ By the 1990s A. Jerrold Perenchio had become one of the richest persons in America, having amassed a fortune worth some $3 billion. His wealth came from many different sources: He was a talent agent in Hollywood in the 1950s and 1960s, representing some of the most well-known movie stars; by the 1970s he was also involved in promoting sporting events. In the 1970s and 1980s he enjoyed great success in the television industry, further increasing his personal wealth. In the 1990s he made a bold and extremely successful move into the Spanish-language television market in the United States—though he did not speak Spanish. Perenchio earned a reputation as an excellent negotiator with a knack for finding the right deals. He was extremely private, never granting interviews and rarely making public appearances.

EARLY CAREER

Perenchio was born in 1931 in Fresno, California, to an Italian winemaker. He graduated from UCLA in 1954 and later served as an Air Force flight instructor. In 1958 he joined

A. Jerrold Perenchio. *AP/Wide World Photos.*

Music Corporation of America (MCA) as a talent agent, becoming the protégé of the Hollywood mogul Lew Wasserman. In 1963 Perenchio formed his own talent agency through which he represented many famous Hollywood actors, including Marlon Brando and Elizabeth Taylor. In 1971 he helped to promote the heavyweight boxing match between Muhammad Ali and Joe Frazier, charging U.S. viewers $25 to watch the fight on closed-circuit television, where earlier bouts had cost only $5 to $10.

Perenchio later teamed up with Norman Lear to form Embassy Communications, which played an important role in the television industry; Perenchio also became a key player in syndicated and pay-per-view television. In 1985 he and Lear sold Embassy to Coca-Cola for $485 million. After the sale Perenchio began to look for new investment opportunities, including Spanish-language television in the United States.

BUYS UNIVISION

In 1992 Perenchio used his Los Angeles–based Perenchio Television to buy a group of television stations—including the Univision Spanish-language network—from Hallmark cards. Univision provided Spanish broadcasts in the United States and was in fact the key to the deal. The network had been founded in 1961 as the Spanish International Network, with most of its financing coming from Emilio Azcarraga, a wealthy Mexican media executive. In 1986 the government claimed that Univision was in violation of foreign ownership rules and forced Azcarraga to sell the network. Perenchio tried to buy Univision at that time, but the asking price was too high, and Hallmark purchased the network instead. Univision performed poorly under Hallmark ownership, however, and the card company decided to sell the station in 1992.

There was some public opposition to the sale because in addition to Perenchio, Azcarraga's Televisa company and the Venezuelan television network Venevison each bought 12.5 percent of Univision. Opponents claimed that Perenchio was simply acting as a front man for the Latin American investors. Yet the Univision president Ray Rodriguez told the *Wall Street Journal*, "No one has strings on Jerry Perenchio" (August 13, 1999). The Federal Communications Commission (FCC) found no legal violations since Perenchio was a U.S. citizen and the portion of the station owned by foreign investors did not exceed 25 percent. Nevertheless opponents argued that Azcarraga would remain in control of Spanish-language programming in the United States; many U.S. Hispanics feared that if a Mexican network dominated programming, Spanish-language production in the United States would be stifled. The lawyer for the national Hispanic Media Coalition commented in the *New York Times*, "Once again, the FCC has been duped" (October 1, 1992).

After the purchase Perenchio became the chairman and CEO of Univision, and the network enjoyed great success. Between 1992 and 1998 viewership grew by 14 percent annually—faster than any other network in the country. By 1997 Univision had 1.4 million prime-time viewers, ranking fifth among all networks. In the late 1990s Univision controlled more than 80 percent of the Spanish-language market. Univision's success led to piqued interest in Spanish-language television in the United States; with the Hispanic population growing faster than the general population, major companies were looking for effective opportunities for marketing to Hispanics. Univision was able to deliver a large audience to those advertisers.

Perenchio himself would profit greatly from the purchase. In the original transaction he committed about $50 million; in 1998 he sold only half of his shares in the company for $700 million, after which he still owned 20 percent of Univision and controlled 78.5 percent of the voting shares.

Furthermore he remained the chairman and CEO of the network.

MANAGEMENT STYLE

Perenchio utilized a list of 20 maxims that he called "road rules" in running Univision. He distributed the rules, which reflected his no-nonsense management style, to all company executives; he especially became associated with the first rule, which the *Wall Street Journal* reproduced: "Stay clear of the press: no interviews, no panels, no speeches, no comments. Stay out of the spotlight—it fades your suit" (August 13, 1999). Perenchio explained that individual publicity hurt both business and teamwork. He strictly enforced his no-comment rule at Univision; when the president of the network gave an interview to *Broadcasting and Cable* magazine, Perenchio fined him $25,000.

Some argued that in addition to the reasons Perenchio commonly gave for staying away from the media, he also remained silent because he was not Hispanic and never even learned to speak Spanish. Thus he was perhaps shying away from resentment among the Spanish-speaking community over the fact that Hispanics did not control their own media. Furthermore some Hispanics criticized Perenchio's support of Republican politicians in California who took anti-immigrant stances. In his defense Perenchio also contributed large sums to Democrats; he gave $1.5 million to oppose a proposition that would have ended bilingual education in California.

Following his own rules, Perenchio stayed out of the spotlight. Peter Nolan, the investment banker who once worked with Perenchio, told the *Wall Street Journal*, "I always tell people that Jerry is the most important guy in Hollywood you've never heard of" (August 13, 1999).

Those who knew or worked with Perenchio described him as intense and persistent. He understood and liked numbers and was detail oriented. He was renowned for relying on his gut instinct—and usually being right; many analysts pointed to the fact that he had managed to enter the Spanish-language market at precisely the right time. One film producer remarked in the *Wall Street Journal*, "I've never come across anybody who seemed to be so intuitive" (August 13, 1999). Perenchio demanded loyalty and cooperation from all of his employees; in return he established a reputation for paying quite well.

See also entry on Univision Communications Inc. in *International Directory of Company Histories*.

SOURCES FOR FURTHER INFORMATION

Andrews, Edmund, "FCC Approves Hallmark's Sale of Univision Network," *New York Times*, October 1, 1992.

A. Jerrold Perenchio

Pollack, Andrew, "The Fight for Hispanic Viewers: Univision's Success Story Attracts New Competition," *New York Times*, January 19, 1998.

Wartzman, Rick, and Lisa Bannon, "Silent Treatment," *Wall Street Journal*, August 13, 1999.

—Ronald Young

■■■
Peter J. Pestillo

1938–
Chariman and chief executive officer, Visteon Corporation

Nationality: American.

Born: March 22, 1938, in Bristol, Connecticut.

Education: Fairfield University, BS, 1960; Georgetown University, LLB, 1963.

Family: Son of Peter Pestillo and Ruth Hayes; married Betty Ann Barraclough, 1959; children: three.

Career: General Electric Company, 1968–1974, various industrial-relations positions, including manager of union-relations planning; B.F. Goodrich Company, 1974–1980, vice president of corporate and employee relations; Ford Motor Company, 1980–1985, vice president of labor relations; 1985–1986, vice president of employee relations; 1986–1990, vice president of employee and external affairs; 1990–1993, vice president of corporate relations and diversified businesses; 1993–1999, executive vice president of corporate relations, then chief of staff; Visteon Corporation, 2000–, chairman and CEO.

Address: Visteon Corporation, 17000 Rotunda Drive, Dearborn, Michigan 48120; http://www.visteon.com.

■ The automotive-parts executive and lawyer Peter J. Pestillo became the first CEO and chairman of the Dearborn, Michigan–based Visteon when it was spun off from Ford Motor Company at the end of June 2000. The new company was created in an effort headed by Pestillo to make Visteon a leading independent automotive-systems supplier. The spin-off came less than three years after Ford management first organized the automotive-systems integrator in September 1997. Pestillo was named to be Visteon's chairman and CEO in November 1999 and officially assumed the positions on January 1, 2000. Through Visteon's first year of independent operations Pestillo oversaw near-constant restructuring, as he faced growing pressure from Ford to cut costs.

Peter J. Pestillo. *George Waldman/Getty Images.*

NUMBER TWO

Visteon Corporation was the world's second-largest full-service automobile-parts manufacturer and supplier, behind General Motors Corporation's spin-off of the Troy, Michigan–based Delphi Automotive Systems Corporation. Visteon had a global operations and delivery system comprising 182 total facilities, including manufacturing, assembly, technical, service, engineering, and aftermarket facilities, located in 25 countries on six continents. Among these facilities were 104 manufacturing locations, 14 regional assembly facilities, 25 customer-service centers, and 39 technical, engineering, aftermarket, and general offices. Although Visteon made and sold products in many foreign countries, sales in the United States accounted for more than 70 percent of total sales as of 2004.

Visteon had nearly 81,000 employees working in three business segments: dynamics and energy conversion; comfort, communication, and safety; and glass. The company's work-force made and marketed a wide range of automotive products, including air conditioners, automotive glass, climate-control systems, instrument panels, power-train control systems, steering wheels, and suspension systems.

CAREER HIGHLIGHTS

Before joining Ford and Visteon, from 1968 to 1974 Pestillo held several industrial-relations positions, including manager of union-relations planning, with General Electric Company in New York City. From 1974 to 1980 Pestillo was vice president of employee relations for B.F. Goodrich in Akron, Ohio, during which time he distinguished himself as a talented labor negotiator.

In 1980 Pestillo joined Ford Motor Company in Dearborn, Michigan, as vice president of labor relations. He was later named vice president of employee relations in 1985 and then vice president of employee and external affairs in 1986. In 1990 Pestillo became vice president of corporate relations and diversified businesses, where he assumed responsibilities for managing and later divesting the company of its aerospace, steel, and tractor operations. Pestillo was selected on January 1, 1993, to become Ford's executive vice president of corporate relations. He was promoted later to vice chairman of the board of directors and chief of staff—both of which positions were created especially for him. As vice chairman and chief of staff Pestillo had responsibilities for managing the Ford departments of governmental affairs, human resources, the office of the general counsel, and public affairs as well as for overseeing Visteon, Hertz Corporation (the car-rental business that was later spun off in 1997), and Ford Motor Land Development Corporation, a leading provider of comprehensive, integrated real-estate services.

FIRST VISTEON CEO

In November 1999 Ford management publicly announced that Pestillo would become chairman and CEO of the soon-to-be-spun-off Visteon Corporation. He assumed the position on January 1, 2000—about half a year before Visteon became fully independent. As noted on the company Web site, when Pestillo took charge of the new company, he declared, "Visteon has global reach, strong electronic expertise, systems capabilities, and technologies that help our customers differentiate their brands. We'll build on these strengths to become the global leader among integrated systems suppliers. Our goal is to be fast, flexible and flawless."

Before assuming control of Visteon, Pestillo played a key role in separating the company from its longtime parent employer Ford. During this time Ford management desired to reduce its asset base, while Visteon sought independence in order to more effectively sell to automobile manufacturers other than Ford. In addition Pestillo negotiated a promise from Ford management that Ford would match any competitors' bids over the next three years in exchange for overall price reductions of 5 percent for all Visteon products. Pestillo also received a commitment from Ford management to appoint four or five members to Visteon's board of directors. Ford personnel agreed to permit union representatives from the United Automobile Workers (UAW) to be placed on the Visteon board.

Pestillo aggressively led the fledgling Visteon—which had 1999 sales of $19.36 billion and earnings of $735 million—into the very price-sensitive automobile-parts industry. In 2000, Visteon's first year, revenues stood at $19.5 billion, up about 1 percent from the company's performance as part of Ford in 1999, with earnings of $270 million. Although the earnings figure was significantly below that of 1999, the difference was more than accounted for by the effects of the one-time 5 percent price realignment that followed Visteon's separation from Ford.

CONCERNS FOR THE NEW CEO AND COMPANY

Pestillo faced many uncertainties in his first year as CEO. When Visteon was spun off, he was burdened with many underperforming businesses to turn around. Visteon was forced to rely on Ford to a much greater extent than Delphi relied on its own parent company—nearly 90 percent of Visteon's 2000 sales went to Ford, while 80 percent of Delphi's first-year sales went to GM. Although Visteon had strong experience with products involving heating, ventilation, and air conditioning, the company had not amassed as much technical knowledge as Delphi in other areas, hurting Pestillo's ability to keep Visteon competing at Delphi's level. Also the Visteon separation was pushed much faster than the separation of Delphi from GM had been, which led to concerns for Pestillo from a planning and organizational standpoint.

A few months after Visteon was spun off, the automobile industry along with the rest of the U.S. economy fell into recession. With an uncertain future, Visteon's workforce grew worried about the effect that the spin-off would have on profit-sharing checks, pensions, and employee-discount plans. Pestillo had to contend with some of the most expensive labor contracts in Visteon's industrial sector; one-fourth of the company's employees were represented by the UAW. As part of Visteon's separation plan 22,000 UAW members who worked at Ford parts plants were reassigned to Visteon—Ford paid the workers, with Visteon reimbursing the automobile manufacturer.

POSITIVES ON ITS SIDE

Because the separation from Ford had been so amicable, Pestillo was able to retain all of Visteon's existing supply contracts with its parent company. Pestillo intended to use Ford's technologies and systems strategies in order to expand Visteon into a global giant while also reducing Visteon's reliance on Ford to 85 percent in its first year of operations and further to 80 percent by 2002.

Pestillo was in fact able to reduce Visteon's reliance on Ford to 79 percent by the end of fiscal 2003 in securing contracts with other automobile manufacturers, especially those overseas. He wanted to show the world that Visteon would be a credible player in the automobile-parts industry and would not just be "little Ford"—which many people had called Visteon after its initial separation. Pestillo was especially concerned about Visteon's presence in Europe, where it held less than a 10 percent market share as of the mid-2000s. Pestillo primarily pursued acquisitions and joint ventures in order to achieve his expansion goals.

EARLY STRATEGIC ACTIONS

Pestillo directed his new management team to expand the parameters and traditional roles of the automotive supplier as well as to strengthen and redefine the relationships between Visteon and its customers. As such Pestillo realized that the company needed to enlarge its customer base, cut costs, and remove unprofitable parts of the product line in order to distinguish itself in the marketplace. Pestillo sold Visteon's non-core seating business in Chesterfield, Michigan, without which Pestillo felt Visteon would be able to better focus its resources on growth-oriented businesses.

DRIVING ITS OWN FUTURE

After losing about $1.7 billion between 2001 and 2003—including $1.2 billion in 2003 alone—Pestillo expected Visteon to earn $65 to $130 million in 2004, the year in which he hoped Visteon would break out of its fledgling mediocrity. As of 2004 Pestillo believed that Visteon had evolved from a simple processor of orders for Ford into a fully independent corporation; it was no longer a supplier but was a "systems integrator." Pestillo built relationships with other suppliers—some of which were competitors—in order to make use of expertise that would have been otherwise unavailable. For instance, Pestillo used digital-radio technology from Texas Instruments in order to extend Visteon into the field of microelectronics.

Pestillo also applied the systems-integrator tag when speaking of the company's assembly process. In some cases Visteon was a tier-one supplier, meaning that it assembled entire sections of cars. In other cases it was a tier-two supplier, providing only parts. Pestillo preferred that the company be a tier-one supplier but was willing to accommodate all of his customers' needs.

Pestillo reported in 2003 that Visteon had made drastic expansions throughout its product lines. The company ventured into the production of automotive cockpits, which comprised everything in the dashboard from instrument gauges to the glove box, along with air-conditioning systems, axles, audio and entertainment systems, drive shafts, headlights, and interior-door trim. According to Pestillo, what most helped Visteon enlarge its market share and raise sales during 2002 and 2003 was the company's ability to innovate. Some of Visteon's unique products included rear-seat DVD players, voice-activation technology for hands-free cell-phone use, and plastic fuel tanks. A high-end audio system that Visteon helped develop was supplied to several of DaimlerChrysler's Chrysler Group vehicles. These products and others helped Visteon continually attract new customers.

Pestillo moved forward aggressively in solving the problems that he had inherited when Visteon was spun off. Although many other problems remained, Pestillo seemed to be well equipped to deal with them and to continue to transform Visteon into a successful independent company.

MEMBERSHIPS

Pestillo was the director of the American Arbitration Association. He was also a member of the advisory board of the United Foundation in Detroit, Michigan; the labor-relations committee of the U.S. Chamber of Commerce; the Washington, D.C. Bar, having passed the exam in 1964; the Labor Policy Association; the Business Roundtable; and the National Association of Manufacturers. Pestillo served on the boards of directors of Rouge Industries, the Michigan Manufacturers Association, and Sentry Insurance.

SOURCES FOR FURTHER INFORMATION

"Executives: Peter J. Pestillo," Visteon, http://www.visteon.com/newsroom/executives/pestillo.shtml.

—William Arthur Atkins

■■■
Donald K. Peterson
1949–
Chairman and chief executive officer, Avaya

Nationality: American.

Born: 1949, in Worcester, Massachusetts.

Education: Worcester Polytechnic Institute, BS, 1971; Dartmouth College, MBA, 1973.

Family: Married Maureen Mack; children: two.

Career: State Mutual Life Assurance Company, 1973–1976, senior analyst; Northern Telecom, 1976–1994, financial and sales positions, then CFO; Nortel Communications Systems, 1994–1995, president; AT&T Communications Services Group, 1995–1996, CFO; Lucent Technologies, 1996–2000, executive vice president and CFO; Avaya, 2000–2002, CEO and president; 2002–, chairman and CEO.

Awards: CEO of the Year, Frost & Sullivan, 2001.

Address: Avaya, 211 Mount Airy Road, Basking Ridge, New Jersey 07920; http://www.avaya.com.

Donald K. Peterson. *AP/Wide World Photos.*

■ The telecommunications-equipment executive Donald K. Peterson was the first CEO and president of Avaya, based in Basking Ridge, New Jersey. Avaya—which had been called the Enterprise Networks Group under its parent company—was spun off from the Murray Hill, New Jersey–based Lucent Technologies in October 2000. When conceiving a name for the soon-to-be-spun-off company, Peterson had thought that the made-up word "Avaya" sounded appropriate for an open-minded company that would provide smooth communications among people and businesses.

AVAYA

Avaya's history could be traced back to 1869 through the storied predecessor companies of Western Electric Manufacturing Company, AT&T, Bell Labs, and Lucent Technologies. As of 2004 Avaya designed, built, and managed communications networks for more than one million businesses world-

wide. It used its communication software, hardware, and solutions to link voice and data networks for enterprises of all sizes, including government agencies and more than 90 percent of Fortune 500 companies. The company also made network-cabling products and provided consulting and outsourcing services.

Avaya held about half a million service-maintenance contracts worldwide, with 24 network-operations centers and 13 technical-support centers. It employed more than 15,000 people, including about 2,500 research-and-development professionals.

ENGINEERING AND BUSINESS DEGREES

Born in Worcester, Massachusetts, Peterson attended Worcester Polytechnic Institute, earning his bachelor's degree in mechanical engineering in 1971. He graduated with a master's degree in business administration from the Amos Tuck School of Business at Dartmouth College in Hanover, New Hampshire, in 1973. Peterson's professional qualifications included his status as a Chartered Financial Analyst and a Chartered Life Underwriter.

BEGINNING TELECOMMUNICATIONS CAREER

In 1973 Peterson began his professional career as a senior analyst at State Mutual Life Assurance Company in Worcester. He started his telecommunications career in 1976 when he was hired at Northern Telecom, headquartered in Brampton, Ontario. Over the next 18 years Peterson moved through a series of increasingly important sales and financial positions within Northern Telecom's offices in both the United States and Canada. His advancements at that company concluded with his assignment to the position of chief financial officer.

In 1994 Peterson was selected to be president of the Nashville, Tennessee–based Nortel Communications Systems. As such he was responsible for direct sales to customers involving private branch exchange (PBX), packet-switch, key, and broadband products in the United States, and PBX and key products in Canada. Peterson next served, beginning in September 1995, as the chief financial officer of AT&T Communications Services Group, where he was responsible for the supervision of all of the company's financial operations. In 1996 Peterson was selected to be the executive vice president and chief financial officer at Lucent Technologies, where he became responsible for executive management and supervision of all of the company's information systems and financial operations.

SHOWING AVAYA THE WAY

Peterson led Avaya through its October 2000 spin-off from Lucent. At Lucent he had logged a great deal of experience with regards to business communications, enterprise internet-working units, and government solutions. According to Peterson, Avaya management brought two major strengths away from Lucent: relationships with customers, 78 percent of whom were Fortune 500 companies, and technology, most importantly including converged voice and data networks, customer-relationship management software, and call-center applications. Peterson believed that Avaya's commitment to providing technology solutions that could be incorporated into companies' existing technology would prove to be the key distinction between Avaya and its competitors.

On the negative side Lucent had known that Avaya needed to be completely restructured. Lucent management had decided not to spend the time that would have been required to accomplish such restructuring so as to develop the company into a wholly owned subsidiary. In fact, when Avaya was spun off, Lucent did not even retain an investment in the company. Peterson knew that Avaya was considered a slow-growth castoff and that its prospects did not look very good. He would have a huge job ahead of him.

JITTERY EMPLOYEES

During the unsettling times of Avaya's newfound independence, long-term employees were uneasy about the company's future. Peterson insisted that he would not tolerate those who refused to adapt to changes but realized that the best way to deal with unrest was through communication. He established a routine of either going himself or sending one of his management team to each of the company's offices in order to explain to the staff in a straightforward manner actions that were being taken. He and his team also made themselves available to answer employees' questions. Peterson believed that in such a critical time it was essential to take all of his employees' concerns seriously; on the other hand he admitted that if employees could not accept the direction in which the new company was going their services would no longer be needed.

RESTRUCTURING PLAN

Peterson knew that he needed to totally restructure the new company—which was in fact made from several old parts of Lucent—and completely alter its products in order to achieve the potential growth that had never been fully realized at Lucent. Unfortunately, at the time of the spin-off the technology market collapsed—especially in the area of telecommunications equipment—causing further problems for Peterson.

By the end of 2001 Peterson saw a small downward trend in revenues, which decreased by about 10 percent, but found that earnings were up. He felt that these results were in accordance with the cost reductions he had instituted, the operational problems he had begun to correct, and the reductions in the workforce he had made—from 34,000 employees at the time of spin-off to less than 24,000, saving the company $600 million. With regards to cost reductions Peterson reduced sales, general, and administrative costs into the 25 percent range, with further reductions of several percentage points expected to follow. Within a year of Avaya's spin-off Lucent was in terrible shape, while the fledgling company looked to be at least able to hold its own—which would not have been the case had it stayed with its sinking parent.

OVER THE NEXT TWO YEARS

During 2002 and 2003 Peterson continued to execute his business plan according to the required budget. He began to position the company as an expert link between the areas of networking and telecommunications with such Internet protocol (IP) telephony technologies as VoIP (voice-over Internet protocol, which converted telephone conversations into data packets that could be transmitted more easily and economically over communication networks), SIP (session initiation protocol, which played a key role in realizing the full potential of IP-converged networks), and VPN (virtual private networks, which provided security solutions). IP telephony was a term used to describe the transfer of voice communications—such as voice, video, data, facsimile, and voice-messaging applications—all over the same IP-based packet-switched network (the Internet) rather than over traditional circuit-based, public-switched telephone networks.

Peterson believed that companies would increasingly switch over from traditional circuit-switched telecommunications-system technologies to IP-based integrated voice and data network technologies. Part of his plan was to preserve as much of customers' existing communications investments as possible while making transitions to and adding the benefits of IP telephony. Peterson stated that customers could save up to 85 percent of existing investments through Avaya, since the company's solutions were designed to work with older systems.

Avaya touted extensive voice experience, end-to-end customer solutions, and a services organization that could design and manage the IP-telephony networks that customers wanted; Peterson made sure that all of the unique technology needed to support Avaya's customers was maintained within the company's knowledge database. Peterson worked to bring these technologies to clients either directly or through distributors and value-added resellers.

Through the end of 2002 the economy remained sluggish, especially in the telecommunications industry. Peterson saw Avaya's revenues drop 120 percent as a direct result of the economic slow-down. He was forced to lay off additional employees and implement additional cost savings; nevertheless, he continued to spend money on technical improvements, which he knew would always be critical in the high-technology environment of the telecommunications-equipment supply industry.

During 2003 Peterson held to the cost structure that he had put forth in his business plan, continuing Avaya's financial commitment to research and development of about 9 percent of total revenues, or $400 million a year. He introduced a comprehensive communications center inside Avaya's messaging business as well as a new software core for its call center, which improved its Multivantage Communications Manager—the core software that ran all of the company's equipment and systems.

By the end of 2003 Peterson had reduced Avaya's workforce to fewer than 17,000 full-time employees, with slightly more than 1,000 part-time and contract employees. On a more positive note, at that time Avaya was considered a leader in call-center technologies, having signed deals that would expand its IP-telephony and wireless-connectivity businesses.

AVAYA UNIVERSITY

Because Peterson worked under an aggressive schedule of new-product introductions in conventional communications networks and particularly in converged communications, including IP telephony, Peterson decided to rebuild training—based on a cost-efficient model—in order to meet the many work-related needs of Avaya's global workforce and its customers. Through an outsourced operation, the training curriculum was redesigned to combine the company's existing facilities and laboratories with online training.

The entire program, called Avaya University, produced a mixed-learning curriculum in which self-paced online programs were combined with problem-solving exercises managed by teachers in laboratory-style classrooms. Available to 50,000 employees and customers in 90 countries, Avaya University supported all of Avaya's product and service-training requirements. With courses delivered through the Internet, employees could access lessons wherever they were, at their own pace, and with monitored support from online instructors. By the end of 2003, 50 percent of all training was conducted online.

IN THE YEAR 2004

By the first quarter of 2004 Peterson had restructured Avaya for financial stability, invested in key growth areas, and led a successful project to increase market leadership by building a new, global brand. In April 2004 Peterson reported Avaya's fourth-consecutive profitable quarter as the company continued to expand its IP-telephony business. As other companies began to convert to IP telephony, Peterson felt that Avaya's position would allow it to capitalize on the changeover and generate profitable growth. Peterson said that the business plan that he had developed over the previous four years was proving effective, with the balance sheet showing increased strength during that period. For the fiscal quarter ending March 31, 2004, Peterson reported earnings of $125 million, as compared to the $41 million loss of a year earlier. Revenues for the quarter rose to $1.01 billion, from the $950 million of the previous year.

FOR THE FUTURE

Peterson transformed Avaya's operations and its products and services such that it emerged from its 2000 spin-off financially stronger and better-positioned to help its customers improve their businesses by integrating IP-telephony applications, appliances, and services into their processes. Peterson developed an Avaya team that could deploy applications throughout customers' businesses in order to improve productivity; such deployments entailed ensuring that customers could export applications from headquarters to branch offices and to employees who worked from remote stations. Peterson stated that the overall combination of the company's infrastructure, strong suite of application products, underlying services support, and strong IP telephony allowed Avaya to stand apart from its competition.

CEO OF THE YEAR

In 2001 Peterson was named CEO of the Year in the enterprise market by the strategic-market consulting and training firm Frost & Sullivan. The award recognized Peterson for lead-

ing Avaya through an outstanding year while the telecommunications industry as a whole was contracting dramatically. Peterson was a member of the boards of trustees of Worcester Polytechnic Institute and the Committee for Economic Development and a board member of Reynolds & Reynolds Company, a leading information manager headquartered in Dayton, Ohio.

SOURCES FOR FURTHER INFORMATION

"Leadership," Avaya Web site, http://www.avaya.com/ac/common/index.jhtml?location=M1H2G2F1021&&rec_id=Leader_Ship_Bios

—William Arthur Atkins

Howard G. Phanstiel

Chairman, president, and chief executive officer, PacifiCare Health Systems

Nationality: American.

Education: Syracuse University, BS; Maxwell School of Public Administration, Syracuse University, master's degree.

Family: Married Louise (maiden name unknown).

Career: Illinois Bureau of Budget, Office of Fiscal Affairs, division chief; Wisconsin Bureau of Planning and Budget, executive budget officer; U.S. Department of Health, Education, and Welfare, Office of Management and Budget and the Health Care Financing Administration, director; Prudential Bache International Bank, Prudential Bache Securities, Marine Midland Banks, Sallie Mae, Citibank, the Illinois Bureau of Budget, and the Wisconsin Bureau of Planning and Budget, executive and management positions; WellPoint Health Networks, executive vice president, finance and information services; ARV Assisted Living, chairman and chief executive officer; PacifiCare Health Systems, 2000, executive vice president and chief financial officer; 2000–2004, president and chief executive officer; 2004–, chairman, president, and chief executive officer.

Awards: Recognized for significant achievements and contributions to the managed-care sector of Who's Who in Managed Care; honored at the third annual American Heart Association Corazones Unidos/Hearts United Gala for dedication and support provided to the Latino community.

Address: PacifiCare Health Systems, 5995 Plaza Drive, Cypress, California 90630; http://www.pacificare.com.

■ In 2000, just two weeks after California-based PacifiCare Health Systems, a managed-care company, issued a third-quarter profit warning of anticipated lower earnings and watched its stock value drop by half, its chief executive officer (CEO) said he was leaving the position. Robert O'Leary, who had held the job for only three months, was replaced on an interim basis by the former chief financial officer (CFO), Howard Phanstiel, who was also named to the board. O'Leary

said the company's short- and long-term priorities had changed substantially from what he perceived when he took the job. His skills and background were not a good fit for a company that needed a leader well grounded in the fundamentals of managed care.

They found such a leader in Phanstiel, whose background in financial management, information technology, and managed care made him a perfect replacement for O'Leary. Phanstiel had joined PacifiCare as executive vice president and CFO in July 2000. As CFO, Phanstiel was responsible for the company's corporate finance and accounting, treasury, and investor-relations departments. In October 2000 the company's board of directors appointed him to be president and CEO; he was also named to the board of directors. In 2004 he was elected chairman of the board.

Phanstiel had solid health-care and management experience prior to joining PacifiCare. He had been chairman and CEO of ARV Assisted Living of Costa Mesa, California, a $150 million company with 60 assisted-living communities nationwide serving eight thousand residents. He led ARV's expansion, acquiring 12 communities with two thousand residents, opening four new communities of six hundred residents, and reducing ongoing corporate overhead by 5 percent.

Before joining ARV, Phanstiel was executive vice president for finance and information services at Wellpoint Health Networks in Woodland Hills, California. He led efforts to complete Wellpoint's $3.5 billion recapitalization and acquire two major indemnity companies that doubled its membership and revenue. He also held various executive management positions with Prudential Bache International Bank and Prudential Bache Securities, Sallie Mae, and Citibank. Phanstiel also gained health-care and management experience in the public sector at both state and federal levels. He served as a director of the Health Care Financing Association of the U.S. Department of Management and Budget, division chief at the Office of Fiscal Affairs at the Illinois Bureau of Budget, and executive budget officer at the Wisconsin Bureau of Planning and Budget.

Phanstiel was well suited for the job at PacifiCare, the nation's largest health-maintenance organization (HMO), which was reeling financially when he took the reins. The company faced numerous problems, including shareholder and patient litigation, and Phanstiel acknowledged that he confronted "a couple of very tough years before we can get the company straightened out" (*BusinessWeek online*). For example, the Texas attorney general's office was considering whether to demand that the company pay an estimated $100 million in past-due medical claims. If such litigation came to pass, the company would have had to divert money to create adequate cash reserves. Stock-market experts said that Phanstiel's main challenge was to reduce PacifiCare's reliance on Medicare for its revenues and draw commercial customers to its more profitable healthcare plans, including behavioral health, dental, and vision coverage.

As for the company's low earnings, PacifiCare attributed its shortfall to a jump in medical costs that forced it to curtail Medicare enrollment in some areas. The costs were driven higher, in part, by the ongoing conversion of fixed-payment (or capitated) hospital contracts to shared-risk contracts. Under the capitation system, managed-care companies pay a predetermined fee to hospitals and doctors regardless of the cost of the care. Under the shared-risk contract, the insurance companies pay fees after medical costs are incurred. Stock-market analysts claimed that PacifiCare was having difficulties in estimating the shared-risk costs as it was used to paying a fixed fee, and that the company then underestimated the medical cost reimbursements. Higher medical costs were blamed for the bulk of its problems—conversion from capitation to shared-risk contracts ended up costing PacifiCare $70 million to $75 million more than expected.

The company, with its four million members in nine states, faced such problems as a consequence of its 1990s push into the Medicare market. The move, said one expert, had quadrupled the number of older members on PacifiCare's roster, but it also saddled the HMO giant with one million members on Medicare. Medical expenses for those patients rose 10 to 11 percent annually during this time, but premiums increased only about 2 percent, resulting in an earnings shortfall. To get a better handle on rising costs, Phanstiel had the company take several major steps, including new restructuring efforts and outsourcing its information technology. The moves were expected to save the company $90 million annually.

Phanstiel announced a strategy aimed at increasing earnings and shifting PacifiCare's reputation from an HMO-focused organization to a company that would focus on diversifying its services to its members. He expected to restore higher earnings, offer Medicare supplemental options, expand pharmacy benefit management, and delve into clinical drug trials. Phanstiel said in June 2002 that the company was about halfway through its turnaround plan. "From now on, it is a brand new day at PacifiCare," he told investors (*Business Week online*). Phanstiel admitted that PacifiCare had made mistakes, particularly in Texas, but said it was correcting the problems; PacifiCare, he said, had been "a bit naïve" in not changing its business model (*BusinessWeek online*).

Despite the steps taken to put PacifiCare on a better financial footing, Phanstiel faced major hurdles. For example, PacifiCare committed to supporting the federal government's effort to provide a comprehensive, affordable prescription-drug program for seniors. "As the most sweeping legislative reforms in the Medicare program's 38-year history come to fruition, we believe PacifiCare is well positioned as a leader in serving the health care and prescription drug needs of America's seniors," Phanstiel noted, adding that the company had the expertise and experience to provide affordable and flexible prescription benefits that seniors seek (*BusinessWeek online*).

Phanstiel pointed specifically to the company's Medicare Choice plans and its fee-for-service Prescription Advantages program. In 1985 PacifiCare's Secure Horizons became one of the first Medicare health plans to be awarded a Medicare+Choice contract by the federal government. In 2004 Secure Horizons reached some 700,000 members through its Medicare+Choice, Medicare Supplement, and drug-benefit programs and its caregiver services. Seniors need prescription drug options, he said, and the private sector can offer Medicare beneficiaries more options and flexibility.

Despite being somewhat dependent on future government actions, Phanstiel saw cause for optimism, but he also saw a "potential gathering storm ahead for managed care." He felt that his job was "to set the course, batten down the hatches, so PacifiCare can outrun the storm." He saw the managed-care industry facing pressure from decreasing bed capacity nationwide and rising pharmaceutical costs. The industry also had to grapple with "adverse selection," in which members who use more health-care services enroll in HMOs, which can drive up costs for health-care plans (*Hoover's Online*).

On the positive side, Phanstiel felt that new legislation overhauling Medicare would pump money into the health-care system. Further, the U.S. Supreme Court had effectively capped excessive damage awards, while consumer-directed health plans and lower-cost HMOs seemed to be gaining wider acceptance. Also, employers were increasingly willing to pay for preventative-care and disease-management programs, and there had been some shift back from employer-funded insurance to managed-care plans.

Phanstiel said that PacifiCare would try to focus on its successful businesses while building complementary businesses, such as pharmacy benefit-management services. The company aimed to aggressively manage its administrative costs and make incremental technology investments. With health-plan members sharing more premium costs, PacifiCare hoped to build a leading consumer brand, with a focus on customer service. Under Phanstiel's experienced leadership, PacifiCare transformed itself into a leading consumer-health organization offering a variety of consumer-driven programs that aimed to provide more affordable and flexible health insurance and related products.

Howard G. Phanstiel

See also entry on PacifiCare Health Systems, Inc. in *International Directory of Company Histories.*

SOURCES FOR FURTHER INFORMATION

Grover, Ronald, "This HMO Needs Resuscitating: Low Premiums from Medicare have Pacificare on Life Support," *BusinessWeek online,* http://www.businessweek.com/bwdaily/dnflash/dec2002/nf2002126_5895.htm.

"PacifiCare CEO Optimistic Despite Industry Woes," press release, June 11, 2004.

"PacifiCare Expects to Participate in New Medicare Prescription Drug Program," *Assisted Living Success,* http://www.alsuccess.com/hotnews/37h248573.html.

"PacifiCare Health Systems, Inc.," *Hoover's Online,* http://www.hoovers.com/subscribe/co/, June 15, 2004.

Weintraub, Arlene, "PacifiCare's Iffy Prognosis," *BusinessWeek online,* http://www.businessweek.com/bwdaily/dnflash/dec2002/nf2002126_5895.htm.

—Peter Collins

■■■
Joseph A. Pichler
1939–
Retired chairman and chief executive officer, Kroger Company

Nationality: American.

Born: October 2, 1939, in St. Louis, Missouri.

Education: University of Notre Dame, BBA, 1961; University of Chicago, MBA, 1963; PhD, 1966.

Family: Son of Anton Dominick Pichler and Anita Marie Hughes; married Susan Ellen Eyerly, December 27, 1962; children: four.

Career: University of Kansas, 1964–1968, assistant professor of business; 1968–1973, associate professor of business; 1973–1978, professor of business; 1974–1980, business school dean; U.S. Department of Labor, 1968–1970, special assistant to the assistant secretary for manpower; Dillon Companies, 1980–1982, executive vice president; 1982–1986, president; Kroger Company, 1985–1986, executive vice president; 1986–1990, president and chief operating officer; 1990–2003, chief executive officer; 2003–2004, chairman.

Awards: Horatio Alger Award of the Horatio Alger Association, 1998; William Booth Award, Salvation Army, 1998; Distinguished Service Citation, National Conference for Community and Justice, 2000; Greater Cincinnati and Northern Kentucky Business Hall of Fame, 2001.

Publications: *Inequality: The Poor and the Rich in America* (with Joseph W. McGuire), 1969; *Creativity and Innovation in Manpower Research and Action Programs*, 1970; *Contemporary Management: Issues and Viewpoints*, 1973; *Institutional Issues in Public Accounting*, 1974; *Ethics, Free Enterprise, and Public Policy: Original Essays on Moral Issues in Business*, 1978; *Co-Creation and Capitalism: John Paul II's Laborem Exercens*, 1983.

■ As CEO and chairman of the Kroger Company, Joseph A. Pichler maintained Kroger's position as the nation's number one grocery store chain, despite increasingly fierce competition from discount superstores. He expanded Kroger's product line

Joseph A. Pichler. *AP/Wide World Photos.*

and services. His many acquisitions included Fred Meyer, a West Coast chain of grocery and general merchandise stores. As president and COO in the late 1980s, Pichler formulated and implemented strategies to protect Kroger from hostile takeovers by corporate raiders. Unlike most supermarket executives, Pichler did not work his way up in the business. Rather he earned a PhD in business and spent 15 productive years in academia, including six years as dean of the University of Kansas School of Business. Pichler was a financial expert and a proponent of long-range planning.

ENTERED BUSINESS VIA ACADEMIA

Pichler was born in St. Louis, Missouri, on October 2, 1939. He earned a bachelor's degree in business from the University of Notre Dame in Indiana and a master's degree in business administration from the University of Chicago. While finishing his PhD at the University of Chicago, Pichler worked as an assistant professor at the University of Kansas School of Business. He was awarded a Woodrow Wilson fellowship, a Ford Foundation fellowship, and a Standard Oil Industrial Relations fellowship. Between 1968 and 1970 he also served as a special assistant to the U.S. Labor Department's assistant secretary for manpower. He was chairman of the Kansas Manpower Services Council from 1974 until 1978.

Prior to becoming a business leader, Pichler worked his way up the academic ladder at the University of Kansas. He became dean of the business school in 1974. His research focused on various issues, including studies of the adjustments made by laid-off workers following plant closures. Pichler authored numerous articles for professional journals and wrote and edited several books on business topics.

While still at the University of Kansas, Pichler joined the board of directors of the Dillon Companies of Hutchinson, Kansas, an operation that included grocery and convenience stores as well as manufacturing facilities. He left the University of Kansas in 1980 to become executive vice president and later president of Dillon. When the Kroger Company acquired the Dillon Companies in 1985, Pichler became an executive vice president of Kroger, which was based in Cincinnati, Ohio. He became president and COO in 1986, when his predecessor left because of long-standing disagreements with Chairman Lyle Everingham over the company management.

Founded in Cincinnati by Barney Kroger in 1883, the Kroger Company had become the largest retail food chain in the United States, with about 3,500 stores. Neighborhood Kroger supermarkets were so ubiquitous in the Midwest that "Krogering" came to mean grocery shopping at any food store. Neighborhood Kroger stores depended on the loyalty of their customers, who generally came from within a 2.5-mile radius of the store. Kroger store careers often lasted 40 years.

LEVERAGED KROGER TO THWART CORPORATE RAIDERS

It was a scary time at Kroger. Corporate raiders were going after chain-store companies, and Kroger was seen as a prime target. First the Dart Group drugstore chain and then Kohlberg Kravis Roberts & Company attempted to buy it out.

In 1986, in response to the possibility of a hostile takeover, Pichler and Everingham undertook a major restructuring of Kroger. They sold off the company's nonsupermarket assets and refocused and strengthened local management, giving regional managers more independence. They also stonewalled labor union demands and moved out of some areas in which labor costs could not be kept down.

In response to the 1988 attempt by Kohlberg Kravis Roberts to buy out the company for $4.64 billion, Pichler initiated

an even bolder restructuring and recapitalization plan in hopes of increasing Kroger's value. Prices were slashed, store formats were updated, unprofitable stores were closed, and many employees were laid off. Pichler's riskiest move was to leverage the company by issuing $5.3 billion in junk bonds and paying shareholders a onetime dividend of $40 per share.

Ultimately Pichler's strategy proved to be a major success, and he was heralded as a corporate hero. Kroger became one of the very few multiregional chains to survive the breakups of the 1980s. However, in the process Kroger took on enormous amounts of debt. More than one-third of companies that carried out leveraged recapitalizations between 1985 and 1989, borrowing against future earnings to pay a large, onetime stockholder dividend, ended up defaulting on their debt.

FACED NEW COMPETITION

When Pichler became CEO of Kroger in 1990, the company was facing new crises. Kroger's unionized stores were affected by labor strikes and found it increasingly difficult to compete with Wal-Mart, Kmart, and other nonunionized one-stop superstores. Furthermore, these warehouse stores sold groceries at a loss, relying on higher-margin merchandise to make up the difference, although the price wars started by the superstores affected independent stores far more than Kroger.

In response to such competition, Pichler began to move Kroger toward a combination store format, adding higher-end cosmetics and perfumes, one-hour photo processing, video rentals, florists, bakeries, and delis. In an interview with David Merrefield of *Supermarket News* (May 28, 1990), Pichler said, "We spend a lot of time trying to read the tea leaves of lifestyle and demographic changes and asking ourselves 'what are the implications of this in shopping patterns and for consumer needs, and what departments do we need to develop and grow?'"

However, Pichler relied primarily on customer loyalty to neighborhood Kroger stores and committed the company to community relations. He invested in older stores in poorer inner-city neighborhoods and became involved with numerous local and national business initiatives for education. Pichler created a program for Kroger employees to volunteer at local schools. He told Michael Sansolo of *Progressive Grocer* in December 1991, "We, as an industry, are suited for this. We have to deal with people. We have to motivate and educate. This industry is so competitive that you can't afford to be arrogant or the market would eat you. We are a service industry."

"CASH FLOW JOE"

Although under Pichler costs were controlled and Kroger gained market share, its huge debt kept company profits at the bottom. In order to compete with the increasing numbers of food clubs and discount retailers, in 1992 Pichler announced major cost-cutting measures.

Pichler stressed efficiency but not efficiency at any cost. Instead he tried to take full advantage of Kroger's size. He updated Kroger's Peyton distribution center in Lexington, Kentucky. From there, general merchandise, including drugs and seasonal goods—among Kroger's fastest-growing product lines—was distributed to all 1,263 Kroger stores nationwide. Improved purchasing and distribution efficiency enabled Kroger's multidepartment stores to decrease floor space while increasing sales. Pichler invested heavily in information systems. Scanning technology at receiving docks yielded huge savings in labor costs. Pichler made full use of Kroger's manufacturing and food-processing plants to produce more private-label goods, including health and beauty products, which often could be sold for as much as 50 percent less than name brands.

By selling off stores and wholesale warehouses and postponing expansion, Pichler saved the company $333 million. The strategy proved to be fortunate since most of Kroger's competitors were overbuilding, only to be hit with a recession. Pichler reduced Kroger's corporate staff from 1,400 to four hundred and gave operating divisions more freedom in merchandising, purchasing and pricing, advertising, and labor. In addition, Pichler stood firm in the face of union demands. Productivity enhancements cut $142 million per year from Kroger's operating costs.

Above all, Pichler ordered managers to generate cash in every way possible, and he became known in the industry as "Cash Flow Joe." The plan worked. The increased cash flow, along with declining interest rates, enabled Pichler to begin repaying the company's debt and to increase stockholder dividends. The new cash flow also enabled Pichler to open new stores and remodel older ones. By 1994 Kroger was increasing total store floor space by almost 5 percent per year, up from 2.5 percent in previous years.

STRATEGY FOR GROWTH

In 1998 Pichler announced a major three-year growth plan. He invested in new systems and technologies to reduce costs and operating expenses and increase profits while allowing local managers enough flexibility to compete with the superstores. Pichler's plan included maintaining a high level of investment in Kroger stores, opening new stores and relocating, expanding, or remodeling older stores. Instead of moving into new markets, new Kroger stores were added in existing markets, resulting in more efficient distribution and advertising. With more stores in a given locale, Kroger took customers away from its competitors rather than from its existing stores.

Although Pichler centralized more of Kroger's purchasing and increased its emphasis on national promotions, according to an April 1998 article by Steve Weinstein in *Progressive Grocer*, Pichler told a group of analysts, "We are not in the business of buying centrally and telling our KMAs [Kroger marketing areas] what they can sell. Rather, they have come to us and asked what we could do on coordinating deals and street money."

Pichler's biggest acquisition came in 1999, when Kroger bought Fred Meyer, a chain of multidepartment stores based in Portland, Oregon. Kroger—which had briefly lost its position as the nation's largest supermarket chain to Albertson's—regained its number one spot. Kroger now had a total of 2,200 stores in 31 states, a 50 percent increase. It was first or second in market share in 33 of the nation's largest markets. The Fred Meyer merger enabled Kroger to move into major, fast-growing West Coast markets and greatly increased its purchasing power.

Pichler and Fred Meyer CEO Robert Miller had been sharing ideas and strategies for about five years prior to the acquisition. However, the integration of Kroger and Fred Meyer was complicated because Fred Meyer stores had a variety of different formats in different locations. Nevertheless, the merger facilitated the addition of general merchandise to many of Kroger's combination food and drug stores. Fred Meyer also served as a springboard as Kroger began to launch its own multiformat stores. More Kroger stores added photo processing services and pharmacies as well as jewelry and clothing departments, bank branches, and gas pumps. In turn Kroger provided Fred Meyer with manufacturing facilities for private-label products.

MANAGEMENT STYLE

In May 1990 Pichler told Merrefield of *Supermarket News*, "I think management style should reflect the organization in which the individual is operating . . . So Kroger operates with a great deal of discussion. . . . Things happen as people agree, and then they say: 'here we go.'"

Associates consistently described Pichler as a modest, low-key leader who spoke simply and clearly and listened well. He carried on lengthy conversations with customers while shopping at his neighborhood Kroger store. He was known for his superb negotiating skills. As head of the Cincinnati Business Committee, Pichler acted as a diplomatic mediator between vying interests. He told Jennifer Bjorhus of the *Oregonian* (Portland), "As long as people keep eating chocolate chip cookies, they all stay, and no one gets mad" (October 25, 1998).

As Pichler acquired other supermarket chains, he made relatively few changes, maintaining local control. The chains usually continued to operate under their own names. Kroger developed positive employee relationships by paying union wages with good benefits. Under Pichler, Kroger had a reputation as a good corporate citizen with strong community ties.

COMMUNITY INVOLVEMENT

Pichler was known for his civic involvement. Between 1983 and 1996 he served on the national board of directors of Boys Hope. Pichler was a member of the fellowship advisory committee of the Woodrow Wilson Foundation from 1990 to 1993. Between 1994 and 2000 he was a member of the advisory board of the Salvation Army School for Officers' Training. Pichler served on the boards of directors of Tougaloo College and the Cincinnati Opera. In addition, he served on the board of the Cincinnati Center City Development Corporation and as chairman of its Over-the-Rhine working group, dedicated to revitalizing a historic but blighted Cincinnati neighborhood. In 2000 Pichler and his wife donated $1 million to Cincinnati inner-city Catholic elementary schools.

A board member of the National Alliance of Business between 1988 and 1996, Pichler served as its chairman from 1991 until 1993. He also chaired the Cincinnati Business Committee in 1997 and 1998 and served as a trustee of the Greater Cincinnati Chamber of Commerce and a member of the Business Roundtable. Pichler was a member of the board of directors of Cincinnati Milacron and Federated Department Stores.

THREATENED BY WAL-MART

By the end of 2001 Kroger was forced to begin slashing prices to compete with Wal-Mart and other superstores. Pichler announced a new strategic growth plan, investing in pricing, promotion, and acquisitions of additional chain stores. He further increased Kroger's pharmacy business, and the company became the world's largest florist.

However, Kroger continued to lose market share to Wal-Mart. In 2002 Pichler again undertook major cost cutting, further centralizing procurement and distribution and eliminating some 1,500 jobs. His budget-trimming strategy enabled Kroger to lower prices on some goods and to maintain or increase market share against superstore competitors.

In 2004 Kroger remained one of the biggest grocery store chains in the country, with fiscal 2003 sales of $58.3 billion and 2,530 supermarkets and department stores in 32 states. In addition to grocery and multidepartment stores, the company owned convenience stores and mall jewelry stores. Kroger operated under nearly two dozen different banners, including Quality Food Centers, Food 4 Less, Fred Meyer, and Kwik Shop. The company was first or second in sales in 41 out of the 48 major American markets it operated in.

Pichler consistently made *Forbes* magazine's list of corporate America's most powerful people. In 2003 he received $6.3 million in compensation in addition to stock options. Pichler retired as CEO of Kroger in 2003. As he approached the mandatory retirement age of 65, he worked on long-term planning and instituting a smooth leadership transition. He retired as chairman and board member on June 24, 2004, and was replaced by CEO David Dillon.

See also entry on The Kroger Company in *International Directory of Company Histories*.

SOURCES FOR FURTHER INFORMATION

Berss, Marcia, "Cash Flow Joe," *Forbes*, June 6, 1994, p. 47.

Bjorhus, Jennifer, "Alliance Born of Friendship: The Kroger–Fred Meyer Merger CEOs Began Sharing Ideas and Strategies Five Years Ago," *Oregonian* (Portland), October 25, 1998.

Byrne, Harlan S., "Kroger: Bigger Is Better," *Barron's*, February 28, 2000, p. 22.

Epstein, Joseph, "Forced March," *Financial World*, August 12, 1996, pp. 39–41.

Merrefield, David, "Kroger's New Chief," *Supermarket News*, May 28, 1990, pp. 1–4.

Sansolo, Michael, "'We Can Do Something,'" *Progressive Grocer*, December 1991, pp. 16–17.

Ward, Leah Beth, "Kroger Sees a Shadow Lurking over Aisle 3," *New York Times*, April 7, 2002.

Weinstein, Steve, "The Missing Link," *Progressive Grocer*, April 1998, pp. 79–81.

—Margaret Alic

William F. Pickard
1941–

Chairman and chief executive officer, Global Automotive Alliance

Nationality: American.

Born: January 28, 1941, in La Grange, Georgia.

Education: Flint Mott College, AS, 1962; Western Michigan University, BS, 1964; University of Michigan; MSW, 1965; Ohio State University, PhD, 1971.

Family: Son of William H. Pickard and Victoria Woodyard; married Vivian (maiden name unknown); children: one.

Career: Cleveland Urban League, 1965–1967, director of education; National Association for the Advancement of Colored People, 1967–1969, executive director; Wayne State University, 1971–1974, professor; McDonald's, 1971–, franchise owner; Cleveland State University, 1971–1972, associate director of urban studies; Wayne State University, 1972–1974, associate professor; Global Automotive Alliance, 1985–, chairman and chief executive officer.

Awards: National Institute of Mental Health Fellowship, 1964; Haynes Fellowship, National Urban League, 1965; Honorary Doctorate in Business Administration, Cleary College, 1980.

Address: Global Automotive Alliance, 211 West Fort Street, Detroit, Michigan 48226.

■ William F. Pickard was the founder, chairman, and chief executive officer of Global Automotive Alliance, one of the country's leading minority-owned businesses. Under his leadership the business became the first minority-owned group of plastic-parts suppliers to service the top three U.S. automakers. On several occasions the company was on *Black Enterprise*'s list of the top 100 industrial/service companies. Pickard was honored numerous times for his business acumen, actions to assist African Americans and other minorities in the business world, and commitment to teaching and mentoring others.

LEARNING TO DREAM BIG

Pickard caught his first glimpse of the automotive world in the 1950s when his parents moved the family from Florida to Flint, Michigan, a city built on the car industry. While his parents worked on the assembly line at General Motors, the young Pickard attended school, where he was treated as an outcast for being both new to the neighborhood and African American. He struggled in his schoolwork until an English teacher encouraged him to work to his fullest potential. Pickard considered this teacher his first mentor and the person who introduced him to the importance of helping others to achieve their best.

With his new ambition in place, Pickard pushed ahead to earn an associate's degree at Flint Mott College in 1962 and a bachelor's degree at Western Michigan University in 1964. He then earned a master's degree in social work at the University of Michigan.

STARTING A CAREER, HELPING OTHERS

Armed with his training, Pickard began his good works. He started his career in 1965 as the director of education at the Cleveland Urban League and then, in 1967, joined the National Association for the Advancement of Colored People as executive director. In 1969 Pickard returned to school to earn a PhD in psychology at Ohio State University in Columbus. On completing his studies he worked in several professorial positions at various institutions in southeastern Michigan and northern Ohio. At the same time he started on a new path into the world of entrepreneurship, allowing his business and investment skills to emerge—skills that would be tested through several ventures and eventually lead him to success.

FROM GOOD DEEDS TO GREAT SUCCESS

Soon after a chance meeting with a McDonald's corporate executive, Pickard began his first business endeavor as the owner of several McDonald's franchises. He was also investing, not too successfully, in car dealerships around that time. Later, a lunch with Henry Ford II led him from dealerships to the automotive supply industry. Ford told him, "We need black suppliers," and Pickard took that to heart (*Detroit News*, May 21, 2002). Soon he began investing in minority firms that produced automotive parts. This move led to his creating the Global Automotive Alliance (Alliance), one of the country's leading minority-owned companies.

Pickard created the Alliance when he gained 51 percent ownership of six firms and combined them to form his own group of suppliers. In establishing this new business, he followed a trend in consolidation set by other major automotive suppliers that had formed joint ventures. "Joint ventures allow established businesses to provide mentoring for new minority companies, to assist in their development," said Pickard (*Plastics Technology Online*, July 1999). At the Alliance nearly 50 percent of the employees and more than 30 percent of management were minorities. The Alliance became the first minority-owned group of tier-one and tier-two suppliers of plastic parts to the top three U.S. automakers. By 2004 the firm employed 1,275 people and had sales of $235 million.

SHARING THE WEALTH

With the means to help others on a larger scale, Pickard created a companywide internship program to recruit the next generation of minority employees in plastics processing. In 1990 President George H. W. Bush appointed him to the Federal Home Loan Bank Board in Indiana. Shortly after, the president appointed him to the National Advisory Committee on Trade Policy Negotiations. In addition, he served on numerous boards, continued teaching, was an avid volunteer and donor to charities, and mentored many colleagues. In 2001 the *Detroit News* honored him as a Michiganian of the Year for his accomplishments as an entrepreneur, teacher, and mentor to future leaders.

See also entry on McDonald's Corporation in *International Directory of Company Histories.*

SOURCES FOR FURTHER INFORMATION

Carney, Susan, "Entrepreneur Extends a Helping Hand as a Mentor," *Detroit News* May 21, 2002.

Knights, Mikell, "Partnerships Open Doors in Detroit for Minority-Owned Plastics Group," *Plastics Technology*, July 1999.

—Jeanette Bogren

Harvey R. Pierce

1942–

Chairman and chief executive officer, American Family Insurance

Nationality: American.

Born: 1942, in Hutchinson, Minnesota.

Education: Attended Casper Community College.

Family: Married Delores (maiden name unknown); children: four.

Career: American Family Insurance, 1963–1990, various positions including agent, district sales manager, state director, regional vice president, and executive vice president of field operations; 1990–1998, president and chief operating officer; 1998–, chairman and chief executive officer.

Publications: A Box of Treasures (children's book), 2000.

Address: American Family Insurance Group, 6000 American Parkway, Madison, Wisconsin 53783-0001; http://www.amfam.com/.

■ Harvey R. Pierce climbed the corporate ladder at American Family Insurance Group from the position of agent in 1963, to president and chief operating officer in 1990, and to chairman of the board and chief executive officer in 1998. Through his career at the top positions in the company, his leadership allowed American Family to continue growth despite difficult periods involving heavy losses due to claims as well as an unstable stock market. An avowed family man, Pierce was actively involved in numerous civil and charitable organizations. In 2000 he also penned a children's Christmas book.

CLIMBS THE LADDER IN AMERICAN FAMILY

Pierce's life and career were relatively stable, given his rapid rise through the ranks at American Family Insurance. He was born in 1942 in Hutchinson, Minnesota, and grew up in nearby Willmar, which is located in the center of the state, west of St. Paul–Minneapolis. He married his high school sweetheart, Delores, and for a time attended Casper Community

College in Casper, Wyoming. He joined American Family as an agent in Minnesota in 1963 at age 20.

Over the next 14 years Pierce moved to several cities in Minnesota, including Chaska, Windom, Fairfax, and Willmar. At one stop his family moved to St. Joseph, Missouri. He held several positions at American Family during his early years, rising from agent to district sales manager, state director, regional vice president, and, eventually, executive vice president of field operations. In 1987 he moved to Madison, Wisconsin, where the headquarters of American Family was located.

Rising the corporate ladder to a leadership position within American Family Insurance is not unusual. In 1990 Dale Mathwich, then the president and chief operating officer at American Family, was elected as board chairman and chief executive officer, replacing Robert Koch. Like Pierce, Mathwich had begun his career as an agent and had risen through the ranks to the top position in the company. When Mathwich was elected CEO and chairman, the board chose Pierce to become the new president and chief operating officer.

ASSUMES DUTIES AS PRESIDENT AND CHIEF OPERATING OFFICER

Pierce assumed his new duties after American Family had experienced several years of growth. Between 1984 and 1990 the company's assets had grown from $1.6 billion to $3 billion. Its policies had risen from 3.2 million in 1984 to 4.6 million in 1990, and the total amount of life insurance in force had more than doubled from the previous five years. When Pierce took over as president and chief operating officer, American Family was doing business in 14 states.

In Pierce's first year as president and COO, American Family announced that it had experienced a net loss, which was not unusual for insurance companies. At that time Pierce maintained that the company had continued to expand its business. Subsequent years were more successful while Pierce was president. In 1995 the company announced an income of $363 million, an increase of nearly $200 million from the previous year. Two years later, in 1997, the company posted record sales and revenues, based in large part on high returns on stock investments.

Pierce's years as president and chief operating officer did not come without controversy. In 1995 it was revealed that top executives within American Family had received double-digit raises even though the company had announced that certain agent commissions would be reduced significantly over a 10-year period. Four American Family agents were fired after raising complaints against the insurance company's management, including Pierce. In January 1996 a group of agents sought to oust the board of directors, which then included Mathwich, Pierce, Albert Nicholas, and Richard Renk. Although the agents cast about 1800 proxy votes against the incumbent board members, the board remained intact by receiving a high majority of the overall votes.

The following year, Pierce, along with Mathwich and others, was named in a lawsuit against the company filed by two former American Family agents. The agents reportedly supported a bill in Minnesota that would have banned sales quotas imposed by insurance companies. American Family did not support the law, and when the agents voiced their support for the legislation, they were fired. American Family settled with the agents out of court in 1998.

Despite the controversies, under the leadership of Mathwich and Pierce, American Family increased its total policies from 4.6 million to 6.8 million from 1990 to 1998. The company tripled its total assets during this period to $9.2 billion and became the 11th-largest insurance company in the United States.

ELECTED CHAIRMAN AND CHIEF EXECUTIVE OFFICER

When Mathwich retired in 1998 after having served 42 years with the company, American Family recognized Pierce's leadership, naming Pierce chairman of the board and chief executive officer. Fittingly, the *Capital Times* referred to Pierce as an "avowed family man" as he took the reins of the company (August 12, 1998). Pierce's style complemented that of Mathwich, who was known as a "nice guy" within an industry that is often known for cutthroat tactics (*Capital Times*, January 21, 1999).

In March 1999, when Pierce presided over the annual meeting of American Family Insurance, his first after his election as CEO and chairman, the company had stumbled through a difficult year. Record storm claims of $583 million hurt the company's income that year, which fell from $251.6 million in 1997 to $39.6 million in 1998. Despite the bad news, Pierce "kept smiling" when he borrowed Mathwich's favorite company motto, "We're still strong, growing, and friendly" (*Capital Times*, March 3, 1999).

Pierce's first five years as chairman and CEO involved something of a roller-coaster ride. In 2001 the company paid a record $834.9 million in storm and catastrophe losses, though company profits were $100.4 million during that year.

During the following year, losses fell to $309.3 million, but the company's total income fell by 42 percent to $58.2 million due to a weak stock market. The company rebounded in 2003, when net income increased by 167 percent to $155.4 million. Pierce remained optimistic, noting in 2004, "Building and maintaining an appropriate level of equity is part of what makes us a strong, stable company. Our growth equity lets customers know they can count on us to keep our promise to be there when they experience a loss" (March 2, 2004).

As American Family celebrated its 75th anniversary in 2002, Pierce said that the company he led maintained values that were present from its origins as Farmers Mutual Insurance Company in Madison in 1927. In a guest column for the *Wisconsin State Journal*, Pierce wrote, "We remain committed to the same values that Wittwer [the company founder] established 75 years ago: integrity, strong, personalized consumer service, quality products, and a dedication to our company's hometown" (September 29, 2002). By 2004, under Pierce's leadership, American Family had expanded its areas of operations to 17 states, with plans to continue expansion in later years.

FAMILY COMES FIRST

In keeping with the family atmosphere that the former chairman and CEO Mathwich favored, Pierce maintained that his top priority remained his family. His wife, Delores, described him as a "very kind, gentle, patient man" in an interview with the *Wisconsin State Journal* (August 16, 1998). In this same interview Pierce noted of himself and Delores, "We're pretty basic people. I think I'm very family oriented, but when it comes to business, I'm very task oriented." Two of Pierce's children served as agents for American Family Insurance.

ACTIVE IN PROFESSIONAL AND CIVIL GROUPS

Throughout his career, Pierce remained highly active within his community and in professional associations. In 2003 he was elected first vice chairman of the board of directors for the National Association of Independent Insurers. He was appointed to the board of the Insurance Institute for Highway Safety and became its chair in 2004. He participated on the University of Wisconsin Children's Hospital Advisory Board and the Founders Club of Southwest Missouri State University Insurance Chair. He also served on the boards of the United Way of Dane County, Competitive Wisconsin, the Greater Madison Chamber of Commerce, and Family Services in Madison. In addition, he was a member of the Wisconsin Governor's Economic Growth Council, a member of the Key Club Committee in Madison, and a trustee of the American

Institute of Charter Property Casualty Underwriters–Insurance Institute of America.

In addition to his positions in various organizations, Pierce was visible in his community. In 1994, while he was president and chief operating officer at American Family, he personally delivered 300 stocking hats to the Madison Police Department to be distributed to children in need. American Family also made several sizable donations in the community, such as a $20,000 gift in 1997 to a local housing project in Madison as well as a $10 million gift in 2003 that allowed American Family to claim naming rights to a new children's hospital. After the company donated the money, Pierce was named to the hospital's advisory board.

In 2000 Pierce added a rather unusual entry on his resume: author of a children's book. In his spare time he wrote a Christmas tale entitled *A Box of Treasures,* which was sold at several locations in Madison. The book told the tale of a box of ornaments awaiting placement on a family Christmas tree. The book also included a family recipe for shortbread. Proceeds from the book's sale benefited the United Way of Dane County.

SOURCES FOR FURTHER INFORMATION

"American Family Board Resists Agent Takeover," *Wisconsin State Journal,* January 20, 1996.

"American Family Reports Strong Gains in 2003," Press Release, American Family Insurance Group, March 2, 2004, http://www.amfam.com/media/news_releases/2004/ann_op_03.asp.

Ivey, Mike, "Am. Family Weathers Stormy '98," *Capital Times,* March 3, 1999.

———, "American Family Taps New Chief Executive," *Capital Times,* August 12, 1998.

———, "Nice Guy Mathwich Bids Am. Fam. Farewell," *Capital Times,* January 21, 1999.

Pierce, Harvey R., "American Family Commitment Still Strong," *Wisconsin State Journal,* September 29, 2002.

Simms, Pat, "New CEO Says He's 'Pretty Basic,'" *Wisconsin State Journal,* August 16, 1998.

—Matthew C. Cordon

Mark C. Pigott

1954–

Chief executive officer and chairman, PACCAR Inc.

Nationality: American.

Born: 1954.

Education: Stanford University, BS, 1976; MS, 1984; BA, 1998.

Family: Son of Charles McGee Pigott (CEO of PACCAR Inc. until 1997) and Yvonne Flood.

Career: PACCAR Inc., 1977–1988, internal auditor, along with various later positions at several divisions; 1988–1990, vice president; 1990–1993, senior vice president; 1993–1995, executive vice president; 1994–, member of the board of directors; 1995–1997, vice chairman; 1997–, chief executive officer and chairman.

Awards: Honored by the government of Great Britain with the Order of the British Empire, 2003; named CEO of the Year by *Washington CEO* magazine, 2004.

Address: PACCAR Inc., 777 106th Avenue NE, Bellevue, Washington 98004; http://www.paccar.com/.

■ Truck manufacturing executive Mark C. Pigott was the CEO and chairman of the Bellevue, Washington-based PACCAR. As the leader of this diversified, multinational company, Pigott was responsible for maintaining the consistently high standards of quality that PACCAR had historically guaranteed in all of its products. Pigott ensured that his lines of well-engineered, highly customized, and exceptionally performing products were sold efficiently throughout its global markets. In fact, in 2003 Pigott was awarded the Order of the British Empire in recognition of outstanding services that were directed toward strengthening business relationships between the United Kingdom and the United States. In 2004 Pigott was named CEO of the Year by *Washington CEO* magazine. In that same year PACCAR won the International Stevie Business Award based on the company's consistently producing the highest-quality products in their sector, along with maintaining strong cost controls and developing new and original technological applications.

PACCAR

As a global technology company, PACCAR was the world's second-largest manufacturer of big rig trucks, with sales in North America, Europe, Africa, and the Middle East. (DaimlerChrysler's Freightliner subsidiary was the largest such maker.) Because PACCAR had consistently been a leader with regards to technology, Pigott maintained that PACCAR should rightfully be called a technology company that made trucks, not a truck company that used technology. PACCAR designed and manufactured exclusive lines of light-, medium-, and heavy-duty trucks that included the Kenworth, Peterbilt, DAF, Leyland, and Foden nameplates. In addition, the company also provided customer support and aftermarket parts for its products. PACCAR's other products included Braden, Carco, and Gearmatic industrial winches. Except for a few company-owned branches, PACCAR's trucks and parts were sold exclusively through independent dealerships. The company's PacLease and PACCAR Financial Corporation subsidiaries sold PACCAR products in many countries worldwide, along with truck leasing and financing services. In the early 2000s PACCAR employed about 17,000 people in 11 factories, nine distribution centers, and various regional offices around the world.

FOUR GENERATIONS OF PACCAR LEADERS

In 1905 William Pigott Sr. (1860–1929), the son of Irish immigrants and great-grandfather of Mark Pigott, founded the Seattle Car Manufacturing Company—as PACCAR was originally known—in West Seattle, Washington, where it made logging equipment and trucks. The company was incorporated on February 11, 1905. It merged with a Portland, Oregon, company, Twohy Brothers, in 1917 and was renamed the Pacific Car and Foundry Company, where it expanded into making rail cars. The company was sold to American Car and Foundry in 1924 and went through several difficult periods during the Great Depression as demand decreased for rail cars. The Pigott family did not have control of the company from the late 1920s to the early 1930s.

Paul Pigott (1900–1961), William Pigott's son and Mark's grandfather, reacquired the company in 1934 and ran it as chairman and CEO until his death in 1961. The company manufactured Sherman tanks for use during World War II. At the war's end, however, in 1945, the company migrated its business into truck manufacturing when it acquired the Kenworth Motor Truck Company in Seattle, Washington, and later the Peterbilt Truck Company, based in California. Charles M. Pigott (1929–), Paul Pigott's son and Mark's father, became president in 1965 and added the titles of chairman and CEO three years later. On January 25, 1971, Pacific Car and Foundry Company changed its name to PACCAR to better describe the businesses it owned and operated. Charles's son, Mark Pigott, the company's chairman and CEO in the early 21st century, succeeded him in 1997.

CAREER WITH PACCAR

Pigott worked at the company during the summers while he was in high school. During summer breaks from Stanford University, Pigott was employed at PACCAR dealerships. Those early experiences, which included welding, painting trucks, operating forklifts, and assembling chassis (main frames of trucks), helped Pigott learn almost all aspects of the business. After college he was hired in 1977 as an internal auditor. Pigott advanced in several positions at a number of divisions including Peterbilt Motors, headquartered in Denton, Texas, and Foden Trucks in the United Kingdom. Pigott was hired as vice president of PACCAR in October 1988 and was promoted in January 1990 to the position of senior vice president. In December 1993 he was selected to be PACCAR's executive vice president. Pigott became a director beginning in 1994 and was promoted to vice chairman in January 1995. Pigott became CEO and chairman in January 1997.

Pigott was a low-key leader, avoiding interviews and the high-profile lifestyles often led by his corporate peers. In fact, Pigott was opposed to the publicity-seeking headlines that were all too often prominent in corporate management. On the other hand, he was very lively and informative when speaking with pride, for example, about his aerodynamic truck bodies and various custom-made accessories inside the cabs. An enthusiastic, detail-oriented leader, Pigott gained a reputation as one of the most respected world authorities in the trucking industry. People who knew the tall, lanky Pigott frequently commented about how dedicated he was to the company and its people. No doubt part of that passion for PACCAR came from the long family heritage of building vehicles to transport freight.

PACCAR IN THE 1990S

During the 1990s Pigott continued the consistent, customer-oriented philosophy that had been adopted by his predecessors within the company. Pigott also maintained a strong leadership style for PACCAR. Consequently, PACCAR was not as negatively affected as other large companies during periodic operational and economic upheavals in the industry.

Pigott spent much of his time in the 1990s supporting new technologies within PACCAR. He was proud of the fact that PACCAR was one of the few truck manufacturers that incorporated technology in its designing, manufacturing, and marketing processes. For example, Pigott introduced computer technology when bringing parts into PACCAR factories. This just-in-time process (a set of computer techniques to improve the return on investment by reducing in-house inventories and their related costs) dramatically reduced the amount of storage space needed for PACCAR, area that was eventually turned into additional manufacturing surfaces. Application of this and other innovative technologies meant that PACCAR was able to develop new truck lines in months, not years, like other companies. In fact, the company was recognized by *PC Week* magazine in 1999 for the quality of its information technology systems.

According to Pigott, such investments in technology gave PACCAR a three-to-five-year lead over its competition with respect to overall ability to design, manufacture, and market products, serve customers, and manage finances. With very little debt to restrict its operations, Pigott was able to invest more money in the business for quicker production of its goods. Such actions yielded greater profits, higher market share, and better name recognition, all of which resulted in PACCAR's winning quality awards from around the world. Stock analysts who regularly followed PACCAR agreed that Pigott's focus on operational excellence would continue to increase the company's share of this key manufacturing market.

In 1992 PACCAR's Parts Division opened a new headquarters building in Renton, Washington. The building occupied part of the company's historic Pacific Car and Foundry site. The 1990s were also an important growth period for PACCAR Financial Corporation, which offered in-house financing for Kenworth and Peterbilt and for PACCAR's leasing corporation, which became one of the 10 largest full-service leasing companies in North America. By 1995 PACCAR marketed trucks in more than 40 countries and was one of the largest exporters of capital goods in North America. By the end of the 1990s Pigott had overseen the inception of several capital projects, including a 24,300 square-foot research and development center at its Kenworth truck plant in Renton; an expansion project that nearly doubled the size of its customer call center, also in Renton; and new parts distribution centers in Atlanta, Georgia, and Leyland, England.

During the late 1990s Pigott focused on communication and management systems for its truck dealers and owner-operators. Pigott had PACCAR's Dealer Management Consulting arm offer services for human resources, insurance and financial planning, dealership operations and management, and computer systems management. Pigott directed PACCAR's Driver Board and Dealer Councils to let Kenworth and Peterbilt drivers and dealers share customer feedback with the

PACCAR management team. As a result of Pigott's innovations, especially with new computer technologies, improved design features and greater product quality were incorporated into all of the company's products.

DRIVING SUCCESS

Net income in the first quarter of 2004 at PACCAR rose 64 percent to $182.2 million compared with $110.8 million just one year earlier. At the same time, revenue rose 32 percent to $2.37 billion from $1.8 billion. Pigott announced that all of PACCAR's segments had strong results, with 2003 being the company's second-best year in its history.

Pigott also participated in various activities outside of PACCAR. He was a member of the Washington State Roundtable, the Business Council in Washington, D.C., the World Economic Forum in Davos, Switzerland, and the Society of American Engineers, and he was active in numerous local charitable organizations in the Pacific Northwest.

A TRADITION OF EXCELLENCE

The four generations of Pigott men who led PACCAR achieved quality results for decades, earning a net profit and paying a dividend every year since 1941. With Pigott's technological innovations and attention to customer services, PACCAR continued to show consistent profits even though the trade and transportation industry went through a dramatic downturn at the beginning of the 2000s. Mark Pigott, along with his forebears, pursued nearly a century of quality that led to PACCAR's being a strong business leader in the northwestern United States and a major global corporation.

Pigott credited the creative contributions of PACCAR's employees and coordinated efforts by management to expand market share overseas and to invest in facilities, new products, and information technology for the company's outstanding performance in the 1990s and early 2000s. PACCAR was well positioned in the early 21st century to extend its string of profitable years.

See also entry on PACCAR Inc. in *International Directory of Company Histories.*

SOURCES FOR FURTHER INFORMATION

Becker, Paula, "Seattle Car Manufacturing Co. Opens a Railcar Manufacturing Plant in Renton on February 1, 1908," *HistoryLink.org: The Online Encyclopedia of Washington State History*, http://www.historylink.org/_output.CFM?file_ID=4271.

Groner, Alex, *PACCAR: The Pursuit of Quality*, Woodinville, Wash.: Documentary Book Publishing, 1996.

Wilma, David, "Kenworth Motor Truck Corporation Incorporates in Seattle in January 1923," *HistoryLink.org: The Online Encyclopedia of Washington State History*, http://www.historylink.org/_output.CFM?file_ID=3192.

———, "Pacific Car and Foundry Co. Becomes PACCAR, Inc. on January 25, 1972," *HistoryLink.org: The Online Encyclopedia of Washington State History*, http://www.historylink.org/_output.CFM?file_ID=3194.

———, "Pigott, Paul (1900–1961)," *HistoryLink.org: The Online Encyclopedia of Washington State History*, http://www.historylink.org/_output.CFM?file_ID=3193.

———, "Pigott, William (1860–1929)," *HistoryLink.org: The Online Encyclopedia of Washington State History*, http://www.historylink.org/_output.CFM?file_ID=3177.

———, "Seattle Car Manufacturing Co., Precursor to PACCAR, Incorporates on February 11, 1905," *HistoryLink.org: The Online Encyclopedia of Washington State History*, http://www.historylink.org/_output.CFM?file_ID=3189.

———, "Seattle Steel Co. Begins Manufacturing Steel Products on May 4, 1905," *HistoryLink.org: The Online Encyclopedia of Washington State History*, http://www.historylink.org/_output.CFM?file_ID=3175.

—William Arthur Atkins

■■■
Bernd Pischetsrieder
1948–
Chief executive officer, Volkswagen

Nationality: German.

Born: February 15, 1948, in Munich, Germany.

Education: Technical University of Munich, diplom-ingenieur, 1972.

Family: Son of an insurance executive.

Career: Bayerische Motoren Werke (BMW), 1973–1975, production planning engineer; 1975–1977, head of operations control department; 1978–1981, head of work preparation division of the Dingolfing factory; BMW South Africa, 1982–1985, director of production, development, purchasing, and logistics; 1985–1987, head of quality assurance; 1987–1990, head of technical planning; 1990–1993, department member, board of management and production; 1993–1999, chairman of the board and CEO; Rover Group Holdings, 1994–1995, chairman of the board; Volkswagen, 2000–2003, chairman-elect; 2003–, chief executive officer.

Awards: Man of the Year, *Automobile Industries*, 1995.

Address: Volkswagen Aktiengesellschaft, P.O. Box 1864/1, 38436 Wolfsburg, Germany; http://www.volkswagen-ag.de.

Bernd Pischetsrieder. *AP/Wide World Photos.*

■ Bernd Pischetsrieder, the only person ever to head two separate major car-manufacturing companies, became head of Volkswagen (VW) through a series of unexpected turns of events. He began his career with the luxury car maker Bayerische Motoren Werke (BMW) and spent the first 20 years of his career designing, building, and assuring the quality of premium automobiles aimed at a wealthy public. Pischetsrieder lost his position with BMW in 1999, after his attempt to acquire another automaker backfired. After he joined Volkswagen in 2000, the engineer-turned-manager began to change the image cultivated by decades of lowest-common-denominator "people's car" advertising. Pischetsrieder pushed for the introduction of luxury lines into a company that had made its reputa-

tion building small cars for ordinary people. His new car models, some inherited from his predecessor Ferdinand Piech, included the Phaeton, which ranged in price up to $95,000.

Pischetsrieder's management style proved to be a marked contrast to that cultivated by his former boss—and the man who had hired him after BMW terminated his contract—the legendary Ferdinand Piech. Industry analysts were surprised by Pischetsrieder's early assertion of his independence from Piech. They had expected him to follow Piech's orders even after his predecessor had been moved up to chairman of the supervisory board of VW. Piech had been described as "autocratic," a man whom it was not wise to cross. Under Piech, VW had been a corporation driven from the top down. Executives who argued with Piech ended up in dead-end jobs or (in some cases) were summarily dismissed. Pischetsrieder, however, had "an almost zen like calming effect" on VW, according to Herbert

Shuldiner in *Chief Executive* (March 2004). He tended to delegate assignments much more frequently than Piech, while freeing up his time to concentrate on major decisions.

START IN LUXURY CARS

Although his early education had emphasized modern languages, Pischetsrieder began his career as a mechanical engineer at BMW in 1973. He had family connections with the automotive industry—his grandfather had designed cars for the British automaker Austin, including the famous Mini—but his rapid rise at the German luxury car maker had little to do with his family's reputation. Only 20 years after he entered the company, he became chief executive officer. Soon, according to Christine Tierney and Katharine Schmidt, writing in *BusinessWeek* (February 19, 2001), "he helped turn the small Bavarian luxury car maker into one of the world's most advanced and flexible auto manufacturers."

Under Pischetsrieder, BMW expanded in many ways, most notably, through acquisitions. Early in 1994, less than a year after he became head of the luxury car maker, Pischetsrieder launched a takeover bid of the British manufacturer Rover Group for $1.3 billion. Rover, best known for its line of SUVs, seemed an attractive partner for BMW, since the German automaker had no SUVs in its catalogue. Although BMW successfully bought the British company, the acquisition was not a happy one. Rover marketed its cars to a lowest-common-denominator market, very different from the elite auto buyers cultivated by BMW. The two companies did not share a common culture, and their products used very different parts, meaning that manufacturing for the two brands had to be kept separate as well. The difficulties involved in trying to merge the two companies cost BMW huge amounts of money—$1 billion in 1998 alone—and in 1999 the BMW board asked Pischetsrieder to step down as CEO.

A GOOD FIT WITH VOLKSWAGEN

Enter Ferdinand Piech, chairman of Volkswagen, one of most established and best-known European automakers. Piech had earned a reputation as a hard taskmaster and a successful businessman soon after being appointed head of VW. He brought the German automaker out of a severe sales slump in the 1990s by introducing an updated version of VW's most famous car: the New Beetle. He also launched VW on a course that would lead the company to compete with luxury cars made by companies like Mercedes-Benz and Pischetsrieder's own BMW. Piech introduced luxury models into VW's catalogue, including the Phaeton, priced between $60,000 and $90,000, and the company's first SUV, the Touareg.

Piech had encountered Pischetsrieder while the latter was still heading BMW and the two of them were rivals bidding

for control of the British luxury auto maker Rolls-Royce. Pischetsrieder outmaneuvered the VW chair for possession of Rolls-Royce, and he favorably impressed Piech at the same time. Piech ended up with the British Bentley brand name, several Italian luxury sports car builders (Bugatti and Lamborghini), and a desire to bring Pischetsrieder into VW as a co-worker. The two were compatible; they both had engineering backgrounds and were interested in creating new models for existing markets.

Piech originally gave Pischetsrieder the assignment to bring VW's brand-name Seat under control. Pischetsrieder quickly came to understand that Seat and VW's other brands—Skoda and Audi, in addition to Bentley, Bugatti, and Lamborghini—needed to appeal to niche markets, in part because many models across the company were built on the same frameworks with the same parts. By allowing customers to distinguish between the different models, niche marketing would improve sales. Pischetsrieder used his position at Seat to show how this could be done. He upgraded Seat's image, changing it from a manufacturer of relatively sedate cars into a company that made primarily sporty, performance-oriented automobiles. When Piech stepped down from the leadership of the company in 2002, Pischetsrieder filled his newly vacated shoes. The former BMW head had thus become the only person to have headed two different German car companies.

The new VW head was faced with a number of difficult decisions that came with Piech's legacy. Piech had been a very top-down manager; Pischetsrieder preferred to delegate and work through subordinates. He also put plans into effect to preserve the automaker from the cyclical market that has plagued the industry for decades. One way of doing this was to expand VW's product line to appeal to other markets. Introducing the Touareg, for example, gave the German company an inroad into the lucrative SUV market in the United States, where the light trucks accounted for more than half of all automotive sales. Other models did not fare as well. A new version of VW's classic Passat, boasting an innovative engine known as the W8, sold well below its expected levels in the United States, despite the fact that industry journals compared its handling to that of the much more expensive Mercedes.

THE PEOPLE'S CARMAKER

By supporting the move into luxury vehicles, Pischetsrieder was fighting VW's long history as a people's car manufacturer. The company was created in 1937 to build a vehicle originally designed by Ferdinand Porsche. That car was, as the company's name implied, a functional car intended for ordinary people. During World War II the company factories worked to produce arms and armor for the German war machine. The Nazis provided VW with slave labor from forced-labor camps, concentration camps, and prisoner-of-war camps. About

20,000 such laborers worked for VW during the war. Late in Piech's term in office, VW dealt with these unsavory aspects of its past by establishing a fund for survivors of the camps. In 1999 the company became a founding member of Germany's national remembrance group that dealt with the problem of forced labor during the war. By 2001, according to the company's Web site, the company's own fund had made payments to more than two thousand people. VW also created a memorial for their unwilling workers at its historic Wolfsburg factory, where many of the abuses had taken place.

The end of the war marked a new era for Volkswagen, changing the way it did business and allowing it to expand its operations beyond Germany and Europe. Exporting Volkswagens took place under Dutch oversight in 1949. That same year the British military government of Germany transferred trusteeship of VW to the federal government of West Germany. The German state of Lower Saxony took over administration of the company at the same time, ending up with 18 percent ownership of VW's shares. That state ownership influenced the development of VW's corporate culture, in part because the government was more interested in protecting jobs than in improving profitability and in part because public ownership prevented a hostile takeover of the company—giving the automaker a security that many other German companies did not have. Volkswagen was partially privatized in 1960, when 60 percent of its shares were offered for sale to the public. The federal and state governments together retained 40 percent ownership in the corporation.

During the 1950s and the 1960s VW began to expand its production overseas, beginning with the creation of Volkswagen of Canada in 1952. In 1955 the corporation added plants in Brazil and the United States; in 1956 it entered South Africa, and in January of 1964 it began making both parts and finished cars in Mexico. Volkswagen also acquired several independent European firms in the 1960s. Audi, formerly part of Daimler-Benz, was purchased in 1965, and VW broke into the Swedish market in 1968 when the subsidiary Svenska Volkswagen AB opened its doors. Early in 1970 Volkswagen entered the rental-car business by purchasing Selbstfahrer Union, the ancestor of the modern Eurocar Group, which became a wholly owned subsidiary of VW in 2000. In 1982 VW entered the Chinese market with a factory in Shanghai. Coowned with the Chinese government, the Shanghai plant became the largest passenger-car factory in China.

VW passed a milestone in 1972 when the legendary Beetle became the most-produced car model of all time, surpassing Henry Ford's Model T. The following year production of the Beetle stopped at most facilities, and the model was replaced by the subcompact hatchback sedan known as the Golf in January 1974. (The Beetle's record was broken by the Golf in June of 2002.) In 1973 Volkswagen also introduced the Passat, the first of the standardized-component cars whose parts could be used in a variety of models. The Jetta was introduced several years later. These three models basically defined VW's car product line for most of the next quarter-century. While changes were made to the cars' power trains and other interior systems in what were known as "generational" upgrades, the basic design of the cars remained the same. It was this cult of sameness that Piech and Pischetsrieder tried to break with the introduction of the New Beetle, the establishment of a luxury-car line, and the acquisition of the Bentley, Lamborghini, and Bugatti model names.

INTO THE 21ST CENTURY

By the time Pischetsrieder took over the reins from Piech at the beginning of the 21st century, Volkswagen had become the fifth-largest automaker in the world. At the same time, VW had become a pioneer in sustainable management and other environmental and worker-friendly practices. It created and enforced common environmental standards on all four continents where its cars were built, set global standards for job security and employee salaries, established flex-time options for all its employees, and changed management standards across continents so that it would not have to fire employees during economic downturns. The company was also listed on three different stock market indexes of sustainable growth, and, according to the company's Web site, it led the entire automotive industry on one of them, the Dow Jones Sustainability Index STOXX.

When he came to lead VW, Pischetsrieder declared that he had several objectives in mind. He wanted to make the company less Eurocentric, to change its corporate culture to make the company more transparent to investors, and to make its product line more appealing to non-Europeans. He also wanted to improve the company's profitability and increase sales worldwide. In meeting these objectives, Pischetsrieder was partly successful. China, which had become VW's largest market outside Germany, saw sales increase by 43 percent in 2003 alone, but sales dropped at the same time in Germany, Brazil, and the United States. He regrouped the VW family of models into a traditional model group (VW) and a sporty model group (Audi) and made individual brands responsible for developing marketing strategies to keep from competing with one another. He also introduced fiscal transparency into VW management to make it more attractive to financial markets—a move that Piech and previous heads had not felt pressed to make, because VW was partly owned by the German state and federal governments. "Analysts say VW has become more communicative, holding regular conference calls," said Janet Guyon in *Fortune* magazine (October 13, 2003), "and its financial statements are less opaque."

Pischetsrieder's future influence on VW's corporate culture, however, remained unclear. Piech had gotten his way, stated Gail Edmondson in *BusinessWeek* (May 12, 2003), largely through ignoring middle management and bullying anyone who dared to disagree with him. Pischetsrieder's less autocratic management style allowed "VW's traditional civil service "like bureaucracy" to reassert itself. One result was a proliferation of committees to make and review decisions and thereby delay or bury the changes Pischetsrieder needed to make. VW's mixed legacy as a state-owned corporation continued to dog the number-five automaker into the 21st century.

See also entries on Bayerische Motoren Werke A.G. and Volkswagen Aktiengesellschaft in *International Directory of Company Histories.*

SOURCES FOR FURTHER INFORMATION

"BMW Ex-Chairman to Join Board of Volkswagen AG," *Wall Street Journal*, December 16, 1999.

"Business: The Curse of Pischetsrieder; Volkswagen," *Economist*, February 28, 2004, p. 75.

Edmondson, Gail, "Volkswagen Needs a Jump: Does Its Secretive Boss Have a Strategy up His Sleeve?" *BusinessWeek*, May 12, 2003, p. 48.

Guyon, Janet, "Getting the Bugs out at Volkswagen," *Fortune*, October 13, 2003, p. 145.

Kelly, Kevin, "VW's Big Gamble," *Ward's Auto World*, May 2002, p. 22.

Miller, Scott, "Incoming VW Chief to Lead Revamping on a Broad Scale," *Wall Street Journal*, November 26, 2001.

———, "New VW Chief Assumes Post at Key Time—Stronger Rivals and Shadow of Piech May Make Life Hard for Pischetsrieder," *Wall Street Journal*, September 7, 2001.

———, "Volkswagen to Give More Weight to Return-on-Investment Measure," *Wall Street Journal*, January 28, 2002.

———, "VW's Chairman-Elect Signals New Route—Pischetsrieder Hints Strategy toward Truck Business, Auto Groups May Change," *Wall Street Journal*, September 11, 2001.

Shuldiner, Herbert, "VW and Luxury?" *Chief Executive*, March 2004, p. 43.

Tierney, Christine, and Katharine Schmidt, "Will This Man Drive Volkswagen? A Onetime BMW Boss Is Emerging as a Likely Successor to Piech," *BusinessWeek*, February 19, 2001, p. 53.

—Kenneth R. Shepherd

Fred Poses

1942–

Chief executive officer and chairman, American Standard Companies

Nationality: American.

Born: 1942, in Yonkers, New York.

Education: New York University, BA, 1965.

Family: Married Nancy (maiden name unknown); children: two.

Career: Peace Corps, 1967–1969, volunteer; Allied Corporation, 1969–1977, financial analyst; 1977–1985, general manager of Home Furnishings division; AlliedSignal, 1985–1986, president of Plastics and Engineered Materials division; 1986–1988, president of Fibers division;1988–1998, executive vice president of company and president of Engineered Materials division; 1998–1999, president and chief operating officer; American Standard Companies, January 2000–, chief executive officer and chairman.

Address: American Standard Companies Inc., One Centennial Avenue, Piscataway, New Jersey 08855-6820; http://www.americanstandard.com.

■ Engineering executive Frederic M. "Fred" Poses was the CEO and chairman of Piscataway, New Jersey-based American Standard Companies. During Poses's transition from AlliedSignal to American Standard, the outgoing CEO, Emmanuel A. Kampouris, said of Poses, "We are delighted to have Fred Poses lead American Standard into the new century. Fred has a strong track record of driving business performance and enhancing shareowner value. He also has an intense focus on growing businesses and developing people. His global leadership abilities, coupled with broad management experience, will enable American Standard to profitably grow its businesses around the world" (*peacecorpsonline.org*, October 7, 1999). During the same time, Lawrence A. Bossidy, the chairman and CEO of AlliedSignal, stated that Poses was "A strong, experienced, innovative leader with a wonderful will to win. He will make American Standard a great place" (*peacecorpsonline.org*, October 7, 1999).

AMERICAN STANDARD

American Standard was a leading manufacturer of a wide range of air-conditioning systems, plumbing products, automotive braking systems, and medical diagnostics equipment. In 1999, the year before Poses took over, American Standard had total sales of $6.7 billion, while operating 116 manufacturing facilities in 50 countries and employing 60,000 people worldwide. As of 2004 American Standard derived 62 percent of its $8 billion in annual sales from its air-conditioning business, 24 percent from plumbing (bath and kitchen), and 14 percent from vehicle-control systems. About 43 percent of those sales occurred outside the United States.

The three divisions of American Standard were Bath and Kitchen, Air Conditioning Systems and Services, and Vehicle Control Systems. American Standard sold its plumbing fixtures under the American Standard, Ideal Standard, and Porcher brand names, among others. It was the world's largest seller of fixtures and faucets. The air-conditioning group made commercial, institutional, and residential products under the Trane and American Standard brand names; moreover, it was the world's number-one producer of chiller equipment and a leading provider of commercial air-conditioning systems in the United States. Through its WABCO (Westinghouse Air Brake Company) subsidiary, American Standard made electronic braking systems and air suspension systems for vehicles, which it sold mainly to original equipment manufacturers such as Volvo (Sweden), DaimlerChrysler (Germany), and Scania (Sweden), as well as to the secondary market. American Standard was the world's leader in electronic control systems for braking, stability, suspension, and automated transmissions for heavy-duty trucks, buses, and trailers. In the early 2000s it expanded its sales into systems for luxury cars and sport utility vehicles.

CAREER HISTORY

Poses spent two years, from 1967 to 1969, on voluntary assignment in Peru with the Peace Corps. He joined Allied Corporation as a financial analyst in 1969 and was named general manager of the company's Home Furnishings division in 1977. In 1985 Allied Corporation merged with the Signal Companies to form AlliedSignal. At that time Poses became president of the Plastics and Engineered Materials division. In

1986 Poses was selected to become president of the Fibers division and was promoted in 1988 to president of the Engineered Materials division and executive vice president of the company. He became a member of AlliedSignal's board of directors in 1997, a position he held until 1999. Poses was appointed president and COO in June 1998. He was targeted to become the CEO of AlliedSignal until the company merged with Honeywell International in 1999. Poses terminated his relationship with AlliedSignal on December 31, 1999, and assumed the position of chairman and CEO of American Standard Companies on January 1, 2000, upon the retirement of his predecessor, Kampouris.

WORK WITH AMERICAN STANDARD

Poses began to build on the work of Kampouris, who had reengineered the company's manufacturing operations around Demand Flow Technology (DFT). The operational strategy of DFT was to bring in raw materials and products to be manufactured through a process that relied on actual customer demand, resulting in much more efficient operations. Kampouris's efforts had transformed American Standard into what industry experts considered one of the best manufacturing companies in the world. Kampouris gave American Standard a strong operational performance, an experienced and well-coordinated management team, a high profit statement, and good cash flow. However, even though the company saw increased sales from its strong brand names and enviable market positions, its profit margins were not increasing. Poses identified this problem and strengthened the already strong company by focusing on this variable.

"CALL ME FRED" ATTITUDE

Poses directed his new company based on a self-improvement method of operations, complete with his management style of "Call me Fred" and his teamwork logo of "Raise the Standard." Early on Poses saw that many of the company's operations needed much more focused programs based on improvement, such as those with which he was familiar while working at AlliedSignal. Poses also disliked such words as "fault," "blame," and "boss," but he liked the phrase "we could be better" and the word "leader." Poses concentrated on an improvement strategy that included consolidating the ways raw materials were bought, improving productivity, and decreasing manufacturing errors. He also relied heavily on the widely accepted corporate improvement program called Six Sigma, which is an integrated, disciplined strategy aimed toward efficiently improving measurable parts of an organization based on historical information and data. (Sigma is a term used to represent standard deviation; that is, how far from the average [mean] is some measurable quantity. One sigma means that 68 percent of all measured quantities are at a distance of one standard deviation from the mean, while six sigma means that no more than 3.4 errors will occur in one million chances.)

PRODUCING IMPRESSIVE RESULTS

When Poses assumed the leadership of American Standard in 2000, he raised the goals for financial performance, specifically targeting growth for earnings per share in the range of 13 to 17 percent each year. Within his first 12 months with the company, Poses began to take market share away from the company's competition, which included Kohler, Robert Bosch, and York International. He also began to produce impressive results by cleaning up the company's balance sheet through reducing debt, which also decreased interest payments; reducing operating expenses; streamlining operations; increasing productivity; and expanding globally, including into China. The company still carried billions of dollars of debt, but the amount was far less than at the height of its burden in 1988. One of Poses's most impressive projects was a materials-management program involving office supplies. In the past various company branches had purchased these items from a total of 81 vendors. Poses consolidated purchasing under a single vendor, saving the company 28 percent over what it had spent the previous year.

Due to the economic downturn that occurred from 2000 to 2002, Poses was forced to lay off employees (about 1,700 people in 2001) and administer additional cost-cutting measures, such as relocating plants to places that would incur lower costs. Poses continued to lay people off only as a last resort, preferring to transfer employees to other locations. He also preferred to move production plants to locations near local markets if conditions permitted. Poses reorganized his management team as well. Within two years of taking over, Poses had removed seven of 10 people who reported directly to him and had created three new positions to supervise global supply management, communications, and marketing.

Poses moved to American Standard during troubled economic times. Under his leadership, however, the company's stock gained nearly 2.1 percent from January to August 2002, as compared to a decline of almost 25 percent in the Standard & Poor's 500-stock index, which added American Standard to its roster in May 2002 due to its rising performance and financial strength.

Poses announced in March 2004 that first-quarter total sales were $2.185 billion, up 12 percent from the previous year, with net income rising to $84.6 million, up 33 percent for the same period. Bath and Kitchen unit sales increased 11 percent to $601.4 million, and net income rose 43 percent to $50.3 million. Poses said that gains were the result of better productivity numbers, better foreign exchange rates, increased sales from its Champion toilet line, and fewer operating issues that had plagued this division during the previous year.

Sales from the Air Conditioning Systems and Services unit were $1.16 billion, up 7 percent, and net income was $93 million, up 12 percent from the previous year. Poses noted that growth in U.S. residential systems, global commercial equipment, and global commercial parts, services, and solutions contributed most to the growth. Sales from the Vehicle Control Systems unit were $420.3 million, up 30 percent, and net income was $58.9 million, up 26 percent in one year. Poses declared that increases were due to larger global sales areas, higher sales volumes, and additional physical features sold on trucks. With a strong first quarter behind him, Poses predicted a solid growth in sales, earnings, margins, and cash flow for the entire year of 2004 from each of American Standard's three business segments.

Besides his work as a CEO and chairman, Poses also served on the boards of Raytheon Company, Centex Corporation, the National Center for Learning Disabilities, and the 92nd Street Y in New York City. Additionally, he served on the Duke University Board of Visitors.

See also entries on AlliedSignal Inc. and American Standard Companies Inc. in *International Directory of Company Histories.*

SOURCE FOR FURTHER INFORMATION

"Fred Poses Spent Two Years in the Peace Corps in Peru," *Peace Corps Online*, October 7, 1999, http://peacecorpsonline.org/messages/messages/467/3001.html.

—William Arthur Atkins

■■■
John E. Potter
1956–
Postmaster General, United States Postal Service

Nationality: American.

Born: 1956, in New York City, New York.

Education: Fordham University, BA; Sloan Fellows Program, Massachusetts Institute of Technology, MA.

Family: Married; children: two.

Career: United States Postal Service, 1977–1988, started as distribution clerk and moved into operations management, serving in a number of positions, including supervisor of Washington–Baltimore–Northern Virginia field operations; 1998–1999, senior vice president of labor relations; 1999–2000, senior vice president of operations; 2000–2001, executive vice president and COO; 2001–, postmaster general.

Awards: Board of Governors Award, U.S. Postal Service, 1999; J. Edward Day Award, Association for Postal Commerce, 2003; Zumwalt Legacy Award, Marrow Foundation, 2003.

Address: United States Postal Service, 475 L'Enfant Plaza SW, Washington, D.C. 20260; http://usps.com.

John E. Potter. *AP/Wide World Photos.*

■ Postmaster General John (Jack) E. Potter, a lifelong postal employee well acquainted with both the strengths and weaknesses of the U.S. Postal Service (USPS), faced the daunting challenges of terrorist attacks in 2001 and of transforming the massive USPS into a viable business operation ready to cope with the unique demands of the 21st century.

21ST-CENTURY CHALLENGES FACING THE U.S. POSTAL SERVICE

Less than four months after taking office as postmaster general on June 1, 2001, Potter had to confront the problem of ensuring that the nation's post–September 11 mail would be delivered safely. The postal veteran managed to keep the mail moving in the face of a suddenly all-too-real terrorist environ-

ment. He also led the USPS, albeit not without considerable criticism, in coping with anthrax contamination through the mail.

Potter became the sixth career employee to hold the position of postmaster general. Although his experience and familiarity with the postal service were essential in his efforts to reform the USPS, the sheer size of the operation made the transformation task formidable. With more than 750,000 employees as of the early 2000s, the USPS was the second-largest civilian employer in the United States and the eleventh-largest U.S. enterprise on a revenue basis. As of 2004 the postal service generated an annual operating revenue of roughly $66.5 billion while delivering more than 200 billion pieces of mail each year.

Potter took on the challenge of transforming this enormous industry when the U.S. Senate in 2001 asked the postmaster general and his staff to map out a plan to arm the USPS for the demands it would face in the 21st century. On April 5, 2002, Potter unveiled before the National Press Club in Washington, D.C., a transformation plan that he said would "help us secure the future of universal mail service at affordable rates and give us the tools to protect regular mail and ensure a sound national system well into the future" (USPS press release, April 5, 2002).

Besides his responsibilities for spearheading the postal service's own internally generated transformation plan, Potter was charged with integrating recommendations from the Presidential Commission on the U.S. Postal Service into the reform process. Created by an executive order from President George W. Bush in December 2002, the nine-member bipartisan commission was asked to study the economic and structural challenges facing the USPS and to come up with suggestions for possible solutions. The commission issued its final report to the president in July 2003.

In addition to managing the overall nationwide operations of the USPS, Potter needed to streamline the postal service to function in an era when more and more communications are being sent electronically. Even within the frequently disgruntled customer base of the postal service, Potter had a number of champions who seemed confident that the postmaster general could make the USPS more responsive to changing consumer needs and improve its mail service. For example, the Directing Market Association (DMA), the largest American trade association for businesses involved in database and interactive marketing, supported Potter. H. Robert Wientzen, DMA president and CEO, said: "We are confident that Potter's background qualifies him to lead the effort as the Post Office works to solve its present problems" (DMA press release, May 24, 2001).

POTTER'S PROFESSIONAL AND EDUCATIONAL BACKGROUND

Potter began his career with the postal service in 1977 as a distribution clerk in Westchester County, New York. He soon was drafted into the USPS operations-management structure and rose quickly through the ranks. In his various positions, Potter played a key role in the postal service's rate-reclassification efforts and the nationwide integration of letter-mail automation. During his field leadership of the Washington–Baltimore–Northern Virginia postal region, the area improved its performance in the nationwide system from the worst to the best. Along the way, Potter earned a bachelor's degree in economics from Fordham University in the Bronx, New York, and a master's degree in management from the Sloan Fellows Program at the Massachusetts Institute of Technology.

In January 1998 Potter was named USPS senior vice president for labor relations. Under his leadership, the postal service reached negotiated settlements—the first in more than a decade—with the America Postal Workers Union and the National Postal Mail Handlers Union, both of which are member unions of the AFL-CIO. In recognition of his accomplishments in leading all parties to an agreement, Potter received the Board of Governors' Award. In February 1999 Potter was named senior vice president of operations, in which position he was responsible for overseeing USPS operations planning and processing; network operations management; field retail operations; and quality, engineering, delivery, and facilities.

In his last job before becoming postmaster general, Potter served as executive vice president and COO of USPS. After taking over this position in October 2000, he oversaw the operations of the 10 USPS area offices as well as the postal service's nationwide delivery, network, transportation, facility, and engineering operations.

USPS RESPONSE TO THE SEPTEMBER 11 ATTACKS AND ITS COSTS

A little more than 100 days after becoming postmaster general, Potter faced the difficult aftermath of the September 11 attacks on the United States. Having determined that no postal employees had been injured, he ordered the USPS workforce near the World Trade Center to join the rescue efforts. The New York Post Office provided trucks and drivers for carrying much-needed medical supplies, while elsewhere postal workers mapped strategies to keep mail moving throughout the crisis, a challenge made even more difficult when the Federal Aviation Administration (FAA) suspended all passenger aviation operations. In an effort to resolve the dilemma, Potter used cargo flights, including those flown by Federal Express.

Only weeks later, unidentified persons began mailing letters containing anthrax spores. Although the full implications of this crime were not immediately grasped, Potter, with the full backing of the U.S. homeland security apparatus, took various steps to protect postal workers. Nonetheless, two postal workers died, and still others were infected with anthrax but survived. USPS employees believed to be at greatest risk were provided with antibiotics known to help combat anthrax, and some postal facilities contaminated by anthrax-tainted mail were closed until they could be made safe for both workers and the public.

The anthrax attacks proved to be a one-two punch to the USPS bottom line. Testifying before a subcommittee of the Senate Appropriations Committee on November 8, 2001, Potter estimated that the combined costs of the attacks could climb as high as $5 billion. The costs were divided into two categories: $3 billion to cover the attacks' damage to facilities and operations, medical testing and equipment, treatment for employees exposed to anthrax, purchase of sanitizing equipment, disrupted operations, implementation of security procedures, and communication and education of employees and $2 billion to cover declines in both mail volume and revenue.

POTTER'S USPS TRANSFORMATION PLAN

In reshaping USPS to face the future, Potter had to address a fundamental change taking place in the way Americans communicate with one another. In the early 2000s, the postal service's principal source of revenue was first-class mail, a big part of which consisted of mailings containing bills and payments. This type of communication was increasingly conducted electronically. Many consumers chose to receive their bills by e-mail and paid these bills by electronic means, mostly through credit card or checking account debit authorizations. This growing move to electronic communications among Americans contributed to a decline in first-class mail, a drop estimated to total 1.3 billion pieces of mail in the 2004 USPS fiscal year, which ended September 30, 2004. To compensate for losses in first-class mail revenues, Potter's transformation plan called for a combination of stepped-up promotion of other USPS services, cost reductions, and improved first-class service.

The anticipated fiscal 2004 decline in first-class mailings was expected to be balanced in part by an increase of nearly 4.2 billion pieces in standard mailings, which produce less revenue. In releasing his fiscal 2004 projections, the USPS CFO, Richard Strasser, said that he expected revenue to remain flat because of increases in standard mailings and cost reductions of $1.4 billion. The USPS planned to cut costs by lowering its costs of operation, including trimming 25 million employee work hours, largely through attrition, and by expediting debt repayment to reduce interest costs.

Other steps being taken under Potter's transformation plan were initiatives to improve the quality of first-class service, such as careful monitoring of consumer-satisfaction levels and a revamping of the National Postal Forum. In August 2003 USPS announced that for the second consecutive quarter, overnight first-class mail maintained a 95 percent on-time delivery performance. Independent assessment of first-class delivery performance was carried out by the IBM Business Consulting Services division. The IBM unit calculated the lapsed time between the moment a piece of first-class mail was deposited in a USPS collection box and its arrival at one of the 140 million households, businesses, and postal office boxes in the United States that receive deliveries six times a week.

In addition to the IBM measurement of first-class delivery performance, the Gallup Organization has conducted periodic surveys of customer satisfaction with the services provided by USPS. Its Customer Satisfaction Measurement (CSM) survey released in August 2003 showed that 93 percent of all surveyed households rated USPS service as good, very good, or excellent. This finding marked the seventh consecutive quarter in which the CSM rating held at 93 percent.

In 2004, under the USPS transformation plan, the National Postal Forum, which since 1990 had been meeting twice a year at various locations nationwide, began meeting once annually. The content of the forums in the future were to be relevant to a wider range of individual customers and those in the mailing industry. To make the forums more meaningful, workshops would explore ways in which USPS services might be used more efficiently, and more of the postal service's in-house experts on postal sales, marketing, and operations would be available to offer specific advice for customers.

Thanks to its ongoing transformation efforts under Potter, the USPS managed to weather the impact of terrorism and changing customer needs while still turning in a strong financial performance. In fiscal 2003 total mail volume declined a little less than 1 percent, although the number of addresses in the mail-delivery network increased by 1.7 million. Nevertheless, USPS ended fiscal 2003 with net income of $3.9 billion, exceeding its financial plan for the year by $300 billion. The USPS also enjoyed its fourth consecutive year of productivity gains in fiscal 2003. In announcing USPS financial results, CFO Strasser said that Potter's continued emphasis on implementing all aspects of the transformation plan had resulted in another $2 billion in cost reductions.

AWARDS FOR POTTER

Outside his responsibilities at the helm of USPS, Potter was active in civic affairs. On October 1, 2003, he became the second recipient of the Marrow Foundation's Zumwalt Legacy Award, established in 2000 and named for the late Admiral Elmo R. Zumwalt, the foundation's first chairman. Recognized for his efforts in helping patients in need of marrow and stem-cell transplants, Potter said he was deeply honored to receive the award, "named after someone I highly admire—someone whose deeds have left an enduring impact on all of us" (USPS press release, September 30, 2003). Potter in 2003 also received the Association for Postal Commerce's J. Edward Day Award in recognition of "outstanding service rendered on behalf of the postal community and the nation."

See also entry on United States Postal Service in *International Directory of Company Histories.*

SOURCES FOR FURTHER INFORMATION

"Appointment of John Potter as Postmaster General," DMA Press Release, May 24, 2001, http://www.pgh-metro.net/bulletin5_2001.html.

Del Polito, Gene A., "Who Is Jack Potter?," *Direct*, November 15, 2001.

"How Adaptable Is the USPS?," *Circulation Management*, July 1, 2002.

Jacobson, Louis, "Special Delivery," *National Journal*, June 9, 2001.

Keane, Angela Greiling, "Modernizing USPS: Postmaster General Calls for Rate-Setting Flexibility, Labor, and Accounting Changes," *Traffic World*, June 9, 2003.

Knill, Bernie, "How the Mail Went Through," *Material Handling Engineering*, November 1, 2001.

"PMG Unveils USPS Transformation Plan Today at the National Press Club," U.S. Postal Service press release, April 5, 2002, http://www.usps.com/news/2002/press/pr02_trans0405.htm.

"Postmen Die—and Anthrax Suspected," *Seattle Post-Intelligencer*, October 23, 2001.

"President's Commission on the United States Postal Service," http://www.treas.gov/offices/domestic-finance/usps.

"Remarks by Postmaster General John E. Potter: Presidential Commission of the U.S. Postal Service," *Regulatory Intelligence Data*, January 8, 2003.

Stropel, Leslie, "Postal Service Cuts Loss to $676 Million," *AP Online*, December 10, 2002.

"Transformation Plan Progress Report," http://www.usps.com/strategicdirection/tpprogressreport.htm.

"Zumwalt Legacy Award: The Marrow Foundation Honors Postmaster General John E. Potter," U.S. Postal Service press release, September 30, 2003, http://www.usps.com/communications/news/stamps/2003/sr03_059.pdf.

—Don Amerman

Myrtle Potter

1958–

Executive vice president, commercial operations, and chief operating officer, Genentech

Nationality: American.

Born: 1958, in New Mexico.

Education: University of Chicago, AB, 1980.

Family: Daughter of a restaurant owner and a social worker; married; children: two.

Career: Merck 1980–1996, vice president of Northeast Region Business Group, 1993–1996; Bristol-Myers Squibb, 1996–2000, vice president for strategy and economics, vice president of Worldwide Medicines Group, vice president for sales, president of U.S. Cardiovascular/Metabolics Group; Genentech, 2000–, chief operating officer.

Awards: Bristol-Myers Squibb Leadership Development Award; Woman of the Year Award from Healthcare Business Women's Association, 2000; *Fortune* magazine, no. 18 on list of Most Powerful Black Executives in America, 2002.

Address: Genentech, 1 DNA Way, South San Francisco, California 94080-4990; http://www.gene.com.

■ In 2000 Myrtle Potter was offered a million-dollar bonus to join Genentech, the world's number two biotechnology company. At two major pharmaceutical companies, Potter had gained a reputation as a leader who could bring good drugs to market and turn them into blockbuster success stories. She joined Merck right from college and moved from sales to marketing and business-planning roles during her 14 years with the company. At Merck she succeeded in making a struggling ulcer remedy (Prilosec, marketed by AstraZeneca since 1998) one of the best-selling drugs on the market. Potter joined Bristol-Myers Squibb in 1996 as vice president and advanced to senior vice president and then to president of a major group. With that company she brought a high-cholesterol drug (Pravachol) to the billion-dollar mark on the market.

DRIVE AND DETERMINATION STARTED EARLY

Myrtle Stephens Potter grew up in a large family in Las Cruces, New Mexico. She later attributed her team-building business skills to living and coping in a home with five siblings. Potter told *Time* writer Chris Taylor that with "six kids in a two-bathroom home, if you don't work in shifts and make trade-offs, you can't get out of the house in the morning" (December 2, 2002). She also developed a focus and a competitiveness that materially contributed to her rise from an entry sales position to top management.

Potter's professional drive can be traced to her early experiences in Las Cruces. Her father, retired from the military, started a small business that became successful. The family moved to a new neighborhood when Potter was in her early teens, and she found herself one of only four African American students in a school of five hundred. It was not a comfortable environment for the family. Potter's parents told their children to ignore the racial problems and to focus on studies and extracurricular activities. Myrtle Potter excelled academically and convinced her father that she should go to college. She was accepted to the University of Chicago, and he remortgaged the family home to help her.

MOTIVATED TO SUCCEED

At the University of Chicago, Potter took a part-time job at the university hospital and became interested in medicine. She also persuaded the university's Business School to let her take an internship in business at IBM that was generally reserved for MBA students. The rewarding experience at IBM convinced her she wanted a career that combined business and medicine. On graduation from the University of Chicago, she took a job as a drug representative for Merck. She was soon promoted to an analyst position, but after a bit more than a year her managers told her she did not have the intellect to do the job and that they planned to demote her.

Potter disagreed with the managers and asked them to show her what they wanted. She also went to the human resources department. After that the managers did not question her abilities again. "As an African-American woman I was really going against the grain," she said to Cora Daniels, author of the "Most Powerful Black Executives" article in *Fortune* (July 8, 2002). Daniels described African American women executives, including Potter, as of necessity fiercely competitive and more openly ambitious than their male counterparts.

Potter pressed for more responsibilities at Merck, even accepting lateral moves to broaden her experience. In 1991 she was put in charge of a $4-billion joint venture between Astra and Merck to design a business plan and to do it within six months. The appointment met with skepticism within Merck, but in just eight weeks Potter designed a business plan that led Prilosec to become the world's best-selling ulcer medicine.

RECOGNITION CAME WITH SUCCESS

In 1996 Potter went to drug giant Bristol-Myers Squibb, where she started as a vice president of strategy and economics and soon moved up to senior vice president of sales, U.S. Cardiovascular/Metabolics. She was then promoted to president of the $3-billion sales unit, making her the first black woman to lead a major pharmaceuticals business unit. She was hired by Bristol-Myers Squibb to reengineer their drug-development pipeline and worldwide commercialization of products. Her successes in making billion-dollar drugs out of Pravachol (for high cholesterol) and Glucophage (for diabetes) attracted the attention of Genentech executives, who enticed her to join the company in 2000 as executive vice president of commercial operations, chief operating officer, and member of the executive committee.

Myrtle Potter credited her success to her ability to leverage high-performing teams—which, she told Noel Tichy (*The Cycle of Leadership*, 109), "nine times out of ten gets you ten times further than doing it by yourself." Colleague Claudia Estrin described Potter as not an easy person to work for, although Estrin noted that Potter freely gave credit to someone else when it was due. Noel Tichy wrote that Potter put people "out of their comfort zone."

See also entries on Bristol-Myers Squibb Company, Genentech Inc., and Merck & Co., Inc. in *International Directory of Company Histories*.

SOURCES FOR FURTHER INFORMATION

Bell, Ella, L. J. Edmondson, and S. M. Nkomo, *Our Separate Ways: Black and White Women and the Struggle for Professional Identity*, Boston: Harvard Business School Press, 2001.

Daniels, Cora, "Most Powerful Black Executives," *Fortune*, July 22, 2002, pp. 60–80.

Potter, Myrtle S., as told to Eve Tahmincioglu, "A Deal with Dad," *New York Times*, November 23, 2003.

Taylor, Chris, "Myrtle Potter: COO Genentech," *Time*, December 2, 2002.

Tichy, Noel M., and N. Cardwell, *The Cycle of Leadership: How Great Leaders Teach Their Companies to Win*, New York: Harper Business, 2002.

—Miriam Nagel

Paul S. Pressler

1956–

President and chief executive officer, Gap

Nationality: American.

Born: 1956, in New York.

Education: State University of New York at Oneonta, BA, 1978.

Family: Married Mindy (maiden name unknown); children: two.

Career: New York City, late 1970s, urban planner; Remco Toys; Mego Toys; Kenner-Parker Toys, 1982–1987, vice president of marketing and design; Walt Disney Company, 1987–1990, senior vice president for product licensing; 1990–1992, senior vice president for consumer products; Disney Stores, 1992–1994, executive vice president and general manager; Disneyland Parks and Hotels, 1994–1998, president; Walt Disney Parks and Resorts, 1998–2000, president; 2000–2002, president and chairman; Gap, 2002–, president and chief executive officer.

Address: Gap, Two Folsom Street, San Francisco, California 94105; http://www.gapinc.com.

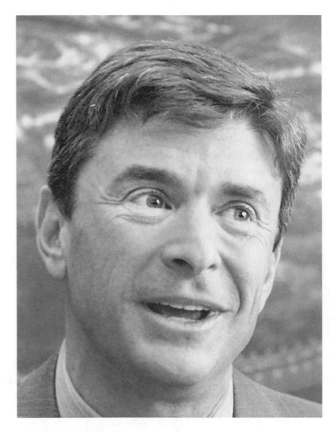

Paul S. Pressler. © *Reuters NewMedia Inc./Corbis.*

■ Having proved himself a competent and successful leader in several positions at the Disney Corporation, Paul S. Pressler made a controversial move to take over operations at Gap. Because of his lack of fashion experience, some doubted his ability to change the direction of the retailer that had experienced 29 straight months of sales losses. However, Pressler used his open management style and innovative ideas based on market research and the expertise of his employees not only to turn the company around but to add new chances for growth into Gap's future plans.

FROM TOYS TO THEME PARKS

Born in 1956, Paul Pressler grew up on Long Island. He graduated from the State University of New York at Oneonta in 1978 with a bachelor's degree in economics. His first foray into the business world was as an urban planner for New York City. He stayed there for a short time before he moved over into the toy business. He worked for both Remco Toys and Mego Toys before he was hired by Kenner-Parker Toys as the vice president of marketing and design in 1982. At Kenner-Parker he made his mark by guiding the company successfully in its marketing of the popular Care Bears line.

Pressler's achievements with the Care Bears marketing campaign were noticed by Disney, which offered him a position as the senior vice president for product licensing in 1987. Pressler accepted the job, starting his 15-year relationship with the company. He held a multitude of positions with Disney over the years, including senior vice president for all consumer products and executive vice president and general manager of Disney Stores. While Pressler held the latter position, the number of Disney Stores increased and sales steadily improved, largely because of Pressler's idea of making each store a mini-Disneyland, giving each customer a fantastical shopping experience. In 1994 Pressler was chosen to head the Disneyland parks and hotels in Anaheim, California, and in 1998 he was promoted to president of Disney theme parks and resorts worldwide. Pressler's success in raising profits and making the Disney brand popular to people of all ages made many analysts think he might one day take over Michael Eisner's position at the top.

A FASHION SENSE

In 2002, however, Pressler made a move that was considered by some to be foolish: he took over the presidency of Gap. In fact, Pressler was criticized when he took over operations at Gap because he lacked fashion experience. Gap Inc. owned The Gap, Banana Republic, and Old Navy chains. The company's previous chief executive, Millard Drexler, was known for his top down style of management: he thought up the ideas and the company followed his word. Pressler came into the company with a different approach, caring much less about his personal tastes and instincts and much more about data from market research. He stated openly that he would not be doing any of the design work; he hired experts to take care of that end of the business for him. He also became known for his willingness to experiment, even holding a fashion show in which actors and actresses dressed in Gap's newest lines and posed on stage at a nightclub. He kept out of the limelight, sharing the credit for the store's turnaround with his entire staff, especially the designers, whose work he began to showcase.

When Pressler took over Gap, the company was in enormous debt, having spent almost two and a half years in sales declines. One of the first things Pressler did as president and CEO was to reestablish the firm's brands. The three stores, the Gap, Banana Republic, and Old Navy, had begun to blur together, losing their distinct personalities. Pressler resolved to sharpen each store's focus. "In Banana Republic, it meant some reinvention.... In the case of Gap, it was clearly going back to our heart and soul, and in the case of Old Navy, it was about driving deeper to take share from our value sector," Pressler was quoted in *Women's Wear Daily* (April 20, 2004). Pressler hoped that his branding efforts would lower the Gap's enormous debt. He began a companywide makeover that would take a year before showing results.

In February 2003 Pressler was named one of the people to watch by *Fortune* magazine. By that time he had managed to reverse Gap's sales decline. Things were looking up for company, and Pressler's one-time critics were beginning to change their opinions about his ability to succeed at Gap. Don Fisher, the chairman of the board of Gap, was quoted by *Women's Wear Daily* as saying, "We've changed a lot in the past year.

We've hired a new CEO, strengthened our board and dramatically improved our performance. Paul Pressler has done a terrific job in his first year as CEO, and I'm more confident than ever about our company's long-term prospects" (December 10, 2003).

The first test of Pressler's success occurred in 2003 when the first line of clothes that his team had come up with hit the stores. The fall line centered on colorful corduroys and had a marketing campaign centered on celebrities like Madonna and Missy Elliott. Pressler got a big break when a picture of Madonna, decked out in Gap clothing, was chosen to be the cover of the September issue of *Harper's Bazaar*. The line was an instant success, and Pressler's fitness for the positions of president and CEO of Gap were no longer derided.

WIDENING THE GAP

In 2004 Pressler and his team researched opportunities for acquiring stores. They were also interested in more international expansion and continued to extend existing brands. In June 2004 Pressler managed to secure popular actress Sarah Jessica Parker to lead Gap's 35th anniversary campaign. At the Credit Suisse First Boston retail conference in New York, Pressler announced that part of Gap's growth plans for the future included pursuing stores that focused on markets different from those in Gap's range.

See also entries on The Walt Disney Company and The Gap, Inc. in *International Directory of Company Histories.*

SOURCES FOR FURTHER INFORMATION

Bermudez, Andrea, Evan Clark, and Dan Burrows, "Can Pressler Revive Gap?" *Daily News Record*, September 30, 2002.

Bhatnagar, Parija, "Gap CEO Talks of New Concepts," *CNN/Money*, June 15, 2004, http://www.moneymag.com/2004/06/15/news/fortune500/gap.

Brady, Diane, "Gap: Dressed to Thrill Investors?" *BusinessWeek*, October 30, 2003, http://www.businessweek.com/bwdaily/dnflash/oct2003/nf20031030_6616_db014.htm.

———, "Trying Not to Be a Fashion Victim," *BusinessWeek*, October 6, 2003, p. 112.

Buckley, Neil, "Snazzy Colours Take Gap into the Black," *Financial Times*, August 18, 2003, p. 38.

Foley, Bridget, and Kristin Young, "Gap, Banana: The Big Makeover," *Women's Wear Daily*, April 20, 2004.

Moin, David, "Handover at Gap Inc.: Fisher to Step Down, Son to Take New Role," *Women's Wear Daily*, December 10, 2003.

"People to Watch," *Fortune*, February 3, 2003, http://www.fortune.com/fortune/peopletowatch/snapshot/0,16431,6,00.html.

Rozhon, Tracie, "Gap's Chief Nurtures Low Profile and High Sales Curve," *International Herald Tribune*, May 4, 2004.

Sellers, Patricia, "Gap's New Guy Upstairs," *Fortune*, April 14, 2003, p. 110.

Smith, Stephanie D., "Changing of the Guard: New Gap CEO Paul Pressler Is Whipping the Flabby Retail Giant Back into Fighting Shape," *Money*, April 1, 2003, p. 61.

Stone, Brad, "Filling in the Gap: Can a Disney Veteran Fix the Troubled Retail Chain?" *Newsweek*, October 7, 2002, p. 48.

"Update 1: Gap's Revving Up the Growth Engine," America's Intelligence Wire, May 20, 2004.

Watters, Susan, "Gap's Fisher Lauds Pressler," *Women's Wear Daily*, May 5, 2003.

Wee, Heesun, "The Challenge in Store for Gap," October 9, 2002, http://www.businessweek.com/bwdaily/dnflash/oct2002/nf2002109_2824.htm.

Young, Vicki M., "Proposal Would Tighten Gap CEO Pay Package," *Women's Wear Daily*, March 31, 2004.

—Catherine Victoria Donaldson

■ ■ ■

Larry L. Prince

ca. 1937–

Chief executive officer and chairman, Genuine Parts Company

Nationality: American.

Born: ca. 1937.

Education: University of Memphis.

Career: Genuine Parts Company, 1958–1977, stock clerk and various other positions; vice president and then group vice president, 1977–1983; executive vice president, 1983–1986; president and chief operating officer, 1986–1990; chief executive officer, 1989–, chairman, 1990–.

Awards: Distinguished Service Citation, Automotive Hall of Fame, 1999; named Notable Georgian, *Georgia Trend*, 2002; named one of America's Most Powerful People, *Forbes*.

Address: Genuine Parts Company, 2999 Circle 75 Parkway, Atlanta, Georgia 30339; http://www.genpt.com.

■ Larry L. Prince spent his entire professional career with Atlanta-based Genuine Parts Company. When he took over as chief executive officer in 1989, he was only the third person in 60 years to hold that position with the company. During his long-term tenure, the Atlanta-based concern was transformed from a local automotive parts distributor to the country's largest auto replacement parts wholesaler and branched out to offer office supplies, office furniture, wire, chemicals, and electronic materials for printed circuit boards. The company was best known for its blue-and-gold National Auto Parts Association (NAPA) trademark outlets, which became its revenue mainstay. Prince played a major role in the growth of NAPA and its classification program as well as in his company's acquisition of the lion's share of NAPA outlets.

CONSISTENCY IN MANAGEMENT

Prince attended the University of Memphis before joining Genuine Parts in 1958 as a stock clerk. He steadily climbed the corporate ladder, becoming vice president and then group vice president from 1977 to 1983 and executive vice president from 1983 to 1986. In 1986 he was named president and chief operating officer, posts he held until becoming chief executive officer in 1989. One year later, in 1990, Prince was named chairman of the board of directors.

Both Prince and the former chairman of Genuine Parts, Wilton Looney, had never worked for any other firm. Moreover, Prince, while he indicated that he had no plans to step down, announced that his choice for successor would be another long-term employee, President Thomas Gallagher. The two had worked together for more than 30 years, and Prince considered them to be almost interchangeable. This consistency in upper management, manifesting in a shared vision, contributed to the overall success of Genuine Parts over the years. In 2004 the company was approaching five decades of annual dividend increases and continued growth while still maintaining a low profile. That year it also sat in the top 10 percent of Standard & Poor's (S&P's) 500, owing to a dividend yield of 3.6 percent.

ACQUISITION AND DIVERSIFICATION

Genuine Parts Company was founded in 1928 to service the automotive replacement parts industry. In the 1970s Prince, as vice president, played a role in the acquisition of the S. P. Richards Company, an office-supply company with sales of $28 million. By 2003 the office-supply group of Genuine Parts was bringing in sales of nearly $1.5 billion. Notwithstanding, Genuine Parts was mostly known for its NAPA parts outlets. Although NAPA was an independent marketing organization that predated the company, Genuine Parts continued over the years to acquire and open NAPA outlets. Through Prince, NAPA distribution stores sprouted up around the country, supplying major repair chains, neighborhood shops, and do-it-yourselfers with quality automobile replacement parts. By the early 2000s almost 90 percent of NAPA's membership was composed of Genuine Parts outlets and jobbers.

Despite the company's steady gains and successes, Prince stayed on top of the market with continually updated market research data that circulated the company's vast computer inventory system. The data was so detailed that on any given day it could advise a NAPA dealer how many new and used Chevrolets or Buicks or Subarus were in his service area and then suggest how many replacement parts he was likely to need for each model. Prince also invested in extensive management marketing and accounting training for NAPA dealers.

Prince told *Forbes* (November 30, 1987) that nasty winters, along with blown head gaskets, dying carburetors, and aging cars, were great for business. Still, he said, "we can't afford to move into the future with a narrow shot." After sprucing up its own outlets, the company began servicing its competitors, such as Sears, Midas, and Pep Boys, with emergency replacement parts service. In mild weather the company relied on its nonautomotive groups to carry the load.

The company also acquired Oklahoma City–based Brittain Brothers in 2000, which had been a longstanding NAPA distributor in four states, with 178 outlets as well as 14 of its own. That same year Genuine Parts announced an alliance with the online auto repair information subsidiary of Snap-On Tools, Mitchell Repair Information Company. The strategy seemed to have worked. In the early 2000s the company enjoyed one of the longest runs for dividend increases in corporate America, with its stock up 40 percent from 1999 and outperforming S&P's 500 stocks for most of the previous five years. In 2004 Prince again directed corporate attention to expansion, planning for the addition of 50 company-owned NAPA outlets and 50 independent ones.

RECOGNITION

Prince was a low-key and private person who did not seek the spotlight. Still, he received several awards and honors for his role in developing Genuine Parts, including a Distinguished Service Citation from the Automotive Hall of Fame in 1999. The award recognized people who had significantly improved their industries or organizations. Prince also remained active on the board of directors for several other companies, including Crawford & Company, Equifax, John H. Harland Company, and SunTrust Banks.

See also entry on Genuine Parts Company in *International Directory of Company Histories*.

SOURCES FOR FURTHER INFORMATION

Byrne, Harlan S., "More Than Autos," *Barron's*, December 18, 2000.

Hannon, Kerry, "Grease Monkey's Dream," *Forbes*, November 30, 1987, p. 193.

Luke, Robert, "Atlanta-Based Auto Parts Maker's Growth Lag Spurs Changes," *Atlanta Journal-Constitution*, January 18, 1999.

McNaughton, David, "At Genuine Parts, Stability Pays Off . . . ," *Atlanta Journal-Constitution*, May 12, 2004.

—Lauri R. Harding

■■■
Richard B. Priory
1946–
Former chairman, chief executive officer, and president, Duke Energy Corporation

Nationality: American.

Born: May 15, 1946, in Lakehurst, New Jersey.

Education: West Virginia Institute of Technology, BS, 1969; Princeton University, MS, 1973; University of Michigan, 1982, graduate utility executive program; Harvard University, 1991, graduate advanced management program.

Family: Son of Joseph Albert Jr. and Betty (Baldwin) Priory; married Joan Ellen O'Rourke, May 30, 1968; children: two.

Career: Union Carbide Corporation, 1969–1972, design engineer and project engineer; University of North Carolina at Charlotte, 1973–1976, assistant professor of structural engineering; Duke Power Company, 1976–1978, design engineer; 1978–1981, principal engineer; 1981–1984, manager, project management division; 1984–1988, vice president, design engineering; 1988–1991, vice president, generation and information services; 1991–1994, executive vice president, generation group; 1994–1997, president and chief operating officer; Duke Energy Corporation, 1997–2003, chairman and chief executive officer.

Awards: Distinguished Service Award, Charlotte Engineers Club, 1998; Ellis Island Medal of Honor, 1999.

■ Using a strategy worthy of a computer gamer, Richard B. Priory transformed Duke Energy from a regional electrical utility company into an integrated energy provider. To achieve his goal, Priory negotiated a number of deals to acquire gas reserves, pipelines, and power plants. A competitive risk-taker, Priory also worked hard to transform the inflexible bureaucratic structure of Duke to keep pace with the constantly changing energy business.

Richard B. Priory. *AP/Wide World Photos.*

RESPONSIBILITY, FAMILY, EDUCATION, AND CAREER

Priory developed early a work ethic and a sense of responsibility. When his parents separated, Priory, who lived with his mother, took a job selling suits after school to contribute to the household income. He also worked as a carpenter and a mason. Just two weeks after his 22nd birthday, on May 30, 1968, he married Joan Ellen O'Rourke. Priory graduated magna cum laude from West Virginia Institute of Technology in 1969 with a degree in civil engineering. Later that year he took his first job as a design and project engineer at the Union Carbide Corporation, where he remained until 1972.

Priory returned to school, earning a master's degree in engineering from Princeton University in 1973. Between 1973 and 1976 he served as an assistant professor of structural engineering at the University of North Carolina at Charlotte and simultaneously operated a consulting firm. Among his largest clients was Duke Power. Eventually Priory left academics and consulting and went to work for Duke Power full-time, rising steadily through the corporate hierarchy. He became president and chief operating office of Duke Power in 1994 and chairman of the board and chief executive officer of the Duke Energy Corporation in 1997, following the merger with PanEnergy.

Although a talented engineer and a capable administrator, Priory nearly realized his dream to play professional baseball. During the mid-1960s he had a tryout with the New York Mets, but to fill the last spot on the minor league system team, officials selected the outfielder Ron Swoboda instead of Priory. Never losing his competitive spirit, Priory played fast-pitch softball in his forties and remained an avid golfer.

ENERGIZING DUKE POWER

Vince Sorrentino, one of Priory's former colleagues, recalled that when Priory came to work at Duke Power, "most of Duke's engineers were still using slide rules, and in comes Rick knowing how to write computer code in Fortran" (*BusinessWeek Online*, November 5, 2001). Even while he was a design engineer and product manager at Duke, Priory understood that the energy industry was changing and that the company was not prepared to compete in the approaching deregulated environment. As Priory's responsibilities increased, especially after he became vice president of design engineering in 1984 and then executive vice president for power generation in 1991, he slowly began to alter the corporate culture at Duke. By the middle of the 1990s Priory had become the consensus choice to succeed William H. Grigg as CEO. Once he became CEO in 1997, Priory began easing out senior managers who had what he described as a "civil-service mentality" (*BusinessWeek Online*, November 5, 2001): they believed that if they stayed with the company long enough, they would eventually but inevitably be promoted. In time Priory replaced 33 percent of Duke managers with administrators who had experienced deregulation in telecommunications and banking. The departure of executives marked the first phase of Priory's strategy to transform Duke Power from a regional utility company into the industry behemoth he thought it had the potential to become.

Priory soon learned, however, that there were only so many managers he could replace and only so many positions he could eliminate. After reducing the workforce from 25,000 to 10,000 employees, Priory found himself at the helm of a slightly more efficient regional utility company that was still posting single-digit annual earnings growth. Rate increases, he knew, would do little to solve the basic problem. By the late-1990s it was clear that the traditional model of operating a power company needed further revision. Priory rose to the challenge with imagination and aplomb.

UNCONVENTIONAL WISDOM AND AN UNORTHODOX APPROACH LEAD TO SUCCESS

Priory devised a business formula elegant in its simplicity. Instead of trying to boost profits by acquiring power plants in underdeveloped countries or investing in unrelated industries, as other power companies were doing at the time, he decided to apply vertical integration to the energy market. Outdated, discredited, and abandoned among most manufacturing firms, the creation of an integrated portfolio of fuel and power assets proved a boon to the energy industry. Priory's original strategy focused on the "convergence" of the markets for electricity and natural gas.

Because he was an engineer as well as a businessman, Priory understood that in the near future natural gas would replace coal and even nuclear material as the fuel of choice in new power plants. Priory thought that if it were somehow possible to merge Duke with a company that produced natural gas, the new company would enjoy a market environment that was virtually limitless in its flexibility. When the price of natural gas rose, Duke Power could adjust by selling more of it and buying electricity. On the other hand, when the price of natural gas fell, Duke Power could readjust by purchasing natural gas and selling electricity. The key for Priory was to own or control assets in all facets of the business from production to delivery to sales. Vertical integration facilitated such opportunities. "To play the convergence game well," he explained, "you had to integrate along the energy value chain . . . . And you had to be good at every part of that energy value chain, from gas gathering and processing to selling electricity" (*Electric Light & Power*, April 4, 2000).

His strategy in place, Priory began the search for a partner. He found one in Paul Anderson, CEO of PanEnergy (formerly Panhandle Eastern), a company based in Houston, Texas, that operated a natural gas pipeline. Priory bought PanEnergy for $9.8 billion in stock and the assumption of company debts. Though at the time Wall Street analysts derided the transaction, as a result of the merger Duke Power became a major force in both the natural gas and the electricity industries. Initial results, however, were financially disappointing. Earnings showed only a minor improvement while Duke Power stock continued to perform below the utility industry average for years after the merger.

OPPORTUNITIES, CHALLENGES, ACCOMPLISHMENTS, AND FAILURES

Priory remained unperturbed and optimistic. Developments took longer to unfold than he had anticipated, but in the end, time and effort vindicated his judgment. The acquisition of PanEnergy was only the beginning. Between 1997 and 2001 Priory completed more than 80 similar transactions, most of them successful, bringing under Duke's control natural gas reserves, pipelines, and power plants. Eventually all of the pieces of the energy jigsaw puzzle that he had assembled began to fit together. By 2002 net income of the massive Duke Energy Corporation, into which Duke Power had grown, had increased 37 percent to $2.15 billion. Operating revenue stood at $68.4 billion. Earnings per share of stock rose to approximately 30 percent, doubling the industry standard. "He took a company with a regional franchise," declared Kit Konolige of Morgan Stanley Dean Witter and Company, "and made it into arguably the biggest and best of the integrated energy companies" (*BusinessWeek Online*, November 5, 2001).

Gradually Priory adopted a more complicated business formula to address changes in the energy market. He divested the company of some assets as quickly as he acquired others. He sold the pipelines that Duke had attained from PanEnergy, and when overbuilding in the energy industry threatened profits, Priory sold Duke's interests in power plants in Ohio, Indiana, and Texas at prices higher than the costs of construction. He reinvested a substantial percentage of the profits in other ventures, such as the $8.5 billion purchase of Westcoast Energy, which facilitated the entry of Duke Power into West Coast markets.

In the fast-paced energy industry, accurate information was invaluable. Priory insisted that information at Duke Energy flow freely between one division and another. He encouraged employees and managers alike to communicate with one another regularly on a series of issues vital to the entire company. Information, Priory argued, bred knowledge and understanding; knowledge and understanding bred good decisions; good decisions bred the effective actions that were necessary to success. And Priory, as subordinates often noted, had "a bias for action." He attested, "Information is the very life blood of the business" (*Electric Light & Power*, April 4, 2000). In Priory's view, keeping ahead of market trends, knowing when to buy and sell, and recognizing the moment when the assets of yesterday have become the liabilities of today mark the narrow difference between success and failure.

Throughout his tenure as CEO, the soft-spoken but fiercely competitive Priory was willing to take calculated, rational, and intelligent risks. For the most part he made the right decisions, and his company flourished. But no utility firm, large or small, completely escaped the repercussions that followed the Enron scandal and Enron's ensuing bankruptcy. By the fall of 2003 Duke stock was trading at 50 percent of its 2001 value, and investors feared an imminent reduction in dividend payments. There was nothing Priory could do to reverse the trend or ease shareholders' anxieties. In the wake of the crisis, Priory stepped down as CEO and turned the job over to Anderson, who had been head of PanEnergy when Duke acquired it. Under Priory's guidance, Duke Energy became a global leader in the energy business, ranking among the top 10 energy companies in the United States at the time of his departure.

See also entries on Duke Energy Corporation and Union Carbide Corporation in *International Directory of Company Histories*.

SOURCES FOR FURTHER INFORMATION

"Against the Flow at Duke Energy," *BusinessWeek Online*, November 5, 2001, http://www.businessweek.com/@@D9UJoYQvHuCvRYA/magazine/content/01_45/b3756083.htm.

Burr, Michael T., "Three for the New Millennium," *Electric Light & Power*, April 4, 2000, p. 15.

Fisher, Daniel, "Trading Places," *Forbes.com*, January 21, 2002, p. 52.

Haver-Allen, Ann, "The Thrill of Risk Assessment," *University Quad: The Alumni Magazine of Princeton University*, Fall 2000, http://www.princeton.edu/~seasweb/eqnews/fall00/feature1.html.

Holy, Chris, "Duke Unveils Finance, E-Commerce Ventures, *Energy Daily*, March 8, 2000.

Palmeri, Christopher, "The Integrated Btu," *Forbes*, January 24, 2000, p. 90.

"Richard B. Priory," *BusinessWeek Online*, January 14, 2002, http://www.businessweek.com/magazine/content/02_02/b3765051.htm.

Roman, Monica, "Duke's Chief Ducks Out," *BusinessWeek*, October 20, 2003, p. 56.

—Meg Greene

■ ■ ■
Alessandro Profumo
1957–
Chief executive officer, UniCredito Italiano

Nationality: Italian.

Born: February 17, 1957, in Genoa, Italy.

Education: Bocconi University, BA.

Career: Banco Lariano, 1976–1987, branch clerk and manager, then director; McKinsey and Company, 1987–1989, consultant; Bain, Cuneo, and Associates, 1989–1991, consultant; Riunione Adriatica di Sicurta, 1991–1994, general manager of banking; Credito Italiano, 1994, deputy general manager for planning; 1995–1997, deputy CEO; 1997–1998, CEO; UniCredito Italiano, 1998–, CEO.

Awards: European Banker of the Year, Group of 20+1, 2002.

Address: UniCredito Italiano, Piazza Cordusio 2, 20121 Milan, Italy; http://www.credit.it.

Alessandro Profumo. *AP/Wide World Photos.*

■ Alessandro Profumo became one of Europe's top bankers in the late 1990s and continued in that role into the 2000s. After working his way up through jobs at branch banks, consulting firms, and an insurance company, Profumo took over as CEO at Credito Italiano in 1997. The bank soon merged with other institutions to become UniCredito Italiano, and Profumo proceeded to establish his reputation as a rising star in the financial world. In 2002 the Group of 20+1 awarded him its "Banker of the Year" award. He challenged the modus operandi that were traditional in Italian banking circles, relying on a bold and aggressive style rarely seen in the country; his approach helped him transform UniCredito into one of Italy's best banks. At the same time his brash style alienated many other bankers, sometimes leaving Profumo—and by extension UniCredito—isolated and without allies.

EARLY CAREER

Profumo was born in Genoa, Italy, in 1957. He spent much of his childhood in Palermo on the island of Sicily, then moved to Milan at the age of 19 where he went to work with Banco Lariano at one of its branch outlets. At the same time he attended Milan's prestigious Bocconi University, where he received a degree in economics. Although he humbly told Jo Wrighton of *Institutional Investor*, "My time at university wasn't so brilliant" (September 2000), Profumo in fact graduated magna cum laude. He then rose through the ranks at Banco Lariano, eventually managing the firm's largest branch and becoming the bank's director within a decade.

In 1987 Profumo went to work for the U.S. management-consulting firm McKinsey and Company; two years later he joined Bain, Cuneo, and Associates, a spin-off of McKinsey. With respect to his time at these organizations, Profumo explained to Wrighton, "My consulting period was my equivalent of an MBA. I learned about being flexible and focusing on the big issues rather than wasting time on the small ones"

(September 2000). After leaving consulting, Profumo joined the Italian insurance group Riunione Adriatica di Sicurta in 1991, where he spent three years in charge of asset management and banking.

MOVES TO CREDITO ITALIANO

In 1994 Profumo joined Credito Italiano, the previously state-run bank that was privatized by the government in 1993. The bank had been created in 1870, and Credito Italiano thenceforth became known as a lender to government institutions and large industrial groups. After more than a century of existence the bank had also become very inefficient. Profumo began at Credito Italiano as deputy general manager, later moving up to deputy CEO in 1995; by 1997 he had taken the reins as CEO.

Profumo soon set to work revitalizing the inefficient bank. He introduced performance goals and productivity-based incentives—relatively new tactics in the Italian banking world. He also replaced two-thirds of the bank's top management, promoting many younger managers. Cutting such a large number of jobs was a bold move in a country where many still viewed employment as an entitlement. Profumo centralized many back-office operations and shifted employees to front-office sales positions. He also created a wholesale-banking division with operations in asset management and investment banking. The new division did well, by 2000 producing 15 percent of the bank's profits. One investment banker told *Institutional Investor*, "Profumo understands all the details, which is why he was able to reshape the branch network so successfully" (September 2000).

Profumo boldly confronted the important Italian investment bank Mediobanca in 1998. Mediobanca was led by the 91-year-old Enrico Cuccia, who possessed unrivaled power in Italian banking circles and rarely found either his power or influence challenged. The brash Profumo, however, attempted to take over Banca Commerciale Italiana, a major Mediobanca shareholder. Cuccia successfully blocked Profumo's bid, but the ploy demonstrated that Profumo was not afraid to take on the biggest and most storied Italian banks.

A more successful move in 1998 was Profumo's merger of Credito Italiano with three banks in wealthy regions of northern Italy, increasing his firm's asset base by 60 percent in creating UniCredito Italiano. Yet the merger was not entirely smooth: Profumo soon found himself in a dispute with the charitable foundations of the acquired banks. The foundations had become UniCredito's largest shareholders and demanded to have a majority of the seats on the new bank's board of directors. Profumo insisted that they remain in the minority, as had in fact been outlined in the merger agreement. As a warning that they were serious about their demands, the foundations sold a small stake in UniCredito to the German Deutsche

Bank in 1999; while the German bank had acquired less than 1 percent of UniCredito's shares, the move looked like preparation for a takeover bid. However, Profumo successfully kept his bank's stock price high, deterring Deutsche Bank from making such an attempt.

By 2000 Deutsche Bank had sold its share in UniCredito; Profumo had succeeded in avoiding a hostile takeover. He somewhat sarcastically told *BusinessWeek*, "Perhaps in 10 years, we will buy them" (December 18, 2000). Profumo and the foundations then reached a compromise in which two new board positions were created, with the foundations getting one spot and Profumo choosing for the other. Afterward Profumo downplayed the dispute, telling Wrighton of *Institutional Investor*, "We got married without having an engagement period. But we soon realized we had the same interest—UniCredito's success" (September 2000).

Another of Profumo's goals was to expand UniCredito's presence throughout the rest of Europe. He attempted the first cross-border European bank merger, though that particular endeavor failed. He did prove able to set up an office in Dublin, Ireland, taking advantage of lower taxes there to establish a European presence. He also met with some success in moving into Central and Eastern Europe. However, UniCredito remained too small to become a major player in European banking circles. In order to solve this problem Profumo aimed to find a domestic partner, which would allow UniCredito to compete with the larger banks. While some of his European plans had to be put on hold, elsewhere Profumo managed to purchase the Boston-based Pioneer Group, a U.S. mutual-fund company.

In 1999 UniCredito's board of directors reconfirmed Profumo's status as the CEO of the bank. Despite the occasional problems, such as the tensions with the charitable-foundation shareholders, the board's backing was a reflection of Profumo's successful rise to a position as one of the most respected bankers in Italy and throughout Europe. He was given much credit for turning UniCredito into one of Italy's best-performing banks. UniCredito became fully profitable and efficient under Profumo's leadership; between 1997 and 2000 the bank's net income grew fourfold and its assets doubled. In *Institutional Investor* the Milan investment banker Paolo Braghiero claimed, "UniCredito is the best positioned, best managed, and most efficient of the traditional Italian banks" (September 2000).

MANAGEMENT STYLE AND PERSONALITY

Profumo was by no means a traditional Italian banker. Many colleagues and analysts described him as bold, daring, and aggressive—all of which were rare attributes in Italian financial circles. While these characteristics contributed to Profumo's overall success, they also sometimes left him isolated;

his tactics did not win him many friends. With respect to his business, other bankers worried that if they merged with UniCredito, Profumo would simply wrest control away from them.

Profumo was seen as a direct and demanding boss. He demanded measurable financial results from his employees, whereas most Italian bankers relied more on personal relationships. The management consultant Vittorio Terzi informed Wrighton of *Institutional Investor*, "Profumo is tough. And he's different from the typical Italian banker, who is cautious and diplomatic. He's straightforward, not the type to smile to your face and criticize you behind your back" (September 2000).

Despite Profumo's creating some enemies due to his aggressive style, few denied that he was one of Europe's most successful bankers. Terzi told Wrighton, "Profumo is the most innovative and aggressive banker in the country" (September 2000). The analyst David Serna told *BusinessWeek*, "Profumo ranks as one of the best European bank managers—among the top five in euroland" (December 18, 2000).

SOURCES FOR FURTHER INFORMATION

"Alessandro Profumo: Chief Executive, UniCredito," *BusinessWeek*, June 11, 2001, p. 32.

Ball, Deborah, "Two Men at Opposite Ends of a Deal Show Flood of Changes at Italian Banks," *Wall Street Journal*, March 24, 1999.

Betts, Paul, "Profumo Reconfirmed as Chief," *Financial Times*, January 12, 1999.

Edmondson, Gail, "UniCredito: Powerhouse in the Making," *BusinessWeek*, April 12, 2004, p. 36.

Edmondson, Gail, and David Fairlamb, "An Appetite as Big as Europe," *BusinessWeek*, December 18, 2000.

Galloni, Alessandra, and Marcus Walker, "The Italian Job: Banker Shakes Up Secretive World of Finance in Milan," *Wall Street Journal*, July 22, 2003.

Kapner, Fred, "Power Struggle Takes Shine off Profumo," *Financial Times*, March 18, 2003.

Robinson, Karina, "Smooth Operator Outlines His Ambitions," *Banker*, June 1, 2002.

Wrighton, Jo, "Profumo at the Rubicon," *Institutional Investor*, September 2000, p. 139.

—Ronald Young

■■■
Henri Proglio
1949–
Chairman and chief executive officer, Veolia Environnement

Nationality: French.

Born: June 29, 1949, in Antibes, France.

Education: Haute École de Commerce, 1971.

Family: Married (wife's name unknown); children: two.

Career: Compagnie Générale des Eaux, 1972–1990, various management positions; Compagnie Générale d'Entreprises Automobiles, 1990–1991, chairman and chief executive officer; Compagnie Générale des Eaux, 1991–1997, director; 1997–1999, deputy managing director; Vivendi Universal, 1999–2000, managing director delegate, chairman of Compagnie Générale des Eaux, director and executive managing director of Vivendi Water, chairman of Compagnie Générale d'Entreprises Automobiles; Vivendi Environnement, 2000–2003, chief executive officer; Veolia Environnement, 2003–, chairman and chief executive officer.

Awards: Chevalier de la Légion D'Honneur; Officer dans l'Ordre National du Mérite.

Address: Veolia Environnement, 52 rue d'Anjou, Paris F-75008, France; http://www.veoliaenvironnement.com.

■ Henri Proglio became chairman and chief executive officer of Vivendi Environnement after the parent company, Vivendi Universal, sold its controlling shares in the company. Proglio immediately changed the name to Veolia Environnement to distance the company from the troubled Vivendi Universal. As head of Veolia Environnement, Proglio oversaw the world's largest water company with interests in waste management, energy, and transportation. Analysts noted that Proglio was a respected business thinker, as well as part of France's "old school" network of businessmen.

ENTERING THE WATER BUSINESS

After graduating from the prestigious French business school Haute École de Commerce in 1971, Proglio went to

Henri Proglio. © *Elipsa/Corbis Sygma.*

work for the Compagnie Générale des Eaux (CGE), founded as a water utility company in France in 1853. Little information is available about Proglio's early career, but in 1990 he rose to become chief executive officer of the CGE subsidiary Compagnie Générale d'Entreprises Automobiles, the group's waste disposal and transport company. He became a director of CGE in 1991 and was named deputy managing director in 1997.

Vivendi Universal was the new name given to overall operations in 1998 by CGE's chairman and chief executive officer Jean-Marie Messier after he took over the French media company Vivendi. Meanwhile, the subsidiary specializing in water retained the name Compagnie Générale des Eaux. In 1999 Proglio was named managing director delegate of Vivendi, chairman of CGE, director and executive managing director of Vivendi Water, and chairman of Compagnie Générale d'Entreprises Automobiles. In 2000 he became chairman of Vivendi Environnement, which was created to encompass Vivendi Water, Onyx (waste management), Dalkia (energy services), and Connex (transportation).

LOADED WITH DEBT

As head of Vivendi Environnement, Proglio quickly faced some tough business decisions. Vivendi Environnement had taken on substantial debt from its parent company, Vivendi Universal, as part of a business plan that would allow the parent to focus on merging with the Canadian entertainment and beverage group, Seagram, creating a media and communications giant to rival AOL Time Warner. As a result, Proglio was left to deal with a net debt of 13.1 billion euros at the end of June 2000. Analysts were concerned about the company's high debt and the immediate drop in the company's stock price that resulted.

By September 2000 Proglio admitted that the company was making only modest progress in reducing debt. He pointed out, however, that the company's internal growth, acquisitions in the United States, and water and wastewater contracts abroad were paying off in other ways. Overall operating profits grew to 866.1 million euros ($767.1 million) from a projected 629.6 million euros in the first half of the year, and net profits rose to 104.7 million euros from a projected 38.5 million. Proglio told *Water Industry News* that he had to make investments to develop the business and noted that pursuing profitable growth was more important than "cutting debt for the sake of it" (September 28, 2000).

In September 2001 Proglio was upbeat about Vivendi Environnement being listed on the New York Stock Exchange. He believed the company was on the brink of significant U.S. development, particularly in the growing water services area. By mid-2001, the company owned several water and waste subsidiaries in the United States and posted a net profit of 275 million euros ($252 million), a 62 percent increase from the same period a year earlier. The company's earnings before interest and taxes had also grown 12.7 percent, based largely on growth in water and energy services.

A NEW DIRECTION

Although Proglio was proud of Vivendi Environnement's performance, the parent company headed by Messier was in trouble. Since first taking over Compagnie Générale des Eaux, Messier had embarked on an extravagant acquisition spree in the United States. One of his cash acquisitions, U.S. Filter, was the biggest French acquisition of a U.S. company in history. Another big acquisition that came shortly afterward precipitated the near collapse of the group and would ultimately cost Messier his job. "I was always against the U.S. Filter acquisi-

tion," Proglio told the *Financial Times*. "It did not fit with the company's traditional multi-utility business model, and we were overpaying" (September 25, 2003).

Proglio had little reason to support Messier, who had essentially used Vivendi Environnement as a "cash cow" onto which he could load debt. Messier had built a U.S. group through a series of small-company acquisitions, some 240 in all. Proglio told the *Financial Times* that the company "paid a super goodwill to buy the lot" (September 25, 2003). In fact, barely six months after the acquisition, Vivendi Environnement was spun off from the parent company and, before its flotation in 2000, took a 2 billion euro ($2.3 billion) write-off on the recently acquired U.S. asset. More galling to Proglio was that the utility was loaded overall with about 20 billion euros in debt from its parent, which Messier had renamed Vivendi Universal.

When Messier stepped down and Jean-Rene Foutou took his place in July 2002, the new company chief announced that he would reduce Vivendi Universal's remaining 41 percent stake in Vivendi Environnement and focus on other areas. Proglio quickly moved to distance himself and Vivendi Environnement from Messier's legacy by announcing that he planned to change the company's name. He told the *Wall Street Journal*, "As a superstitious sailor, I say: 'You don't christen a ship with the name of a ship that sank.'" He added that the Vivendi name "doesn't have a particularly flattering track record" (September 25, 2002).

By December 2002 Vivendi Universal held only a 20 percent stake in Vivendi Environnement. In April 2003, Vivendi Environnement was renamed Veolia Environnement, drawing on the Greek name Aeolus for the god of the winds in Greek mythology. Analysts noted that perhaps the name was meant to blow fresh air through the company and represented Proglio's effort to break once and for all the link with the parent company. Many analysts remained cautious, however, noting that the company had to reduce the debt load it inherited from Vivendi. As Proglio sunk 4 million euros ($4.3 million) into rebranding the company, analysts commented that much more was needed than just a name change.

Proglio and his management team quietly began refocusing the group, getting rid of roughly 4.23 billion euros worth of U.S. Filter assets in nonwater activities. Several other measures also helped the group reduce its debt enough to raise analysts' confidence in the company. In response to the overall new direction, the stock market rose Veolia's shares nearly 8 percent following the announcement of the name change. Proglio told the *Financial Times*, "I suppose it is the end of the beginning. I've lived through all the catastrophes" (September 25, 2003).

BUSINESS AND THE ENVIRONMENT

Proglio stated that Veolia Environnement was a business strongly oriented toward the environment. He often attended international environmental meetings, such as the 2002 Earth Summit held in Johannesburg, South Africa. When asked by a correspondent for the French newspaper *Le Figaro* why he went, Proglio replied, "My teams and I didn't come here to meet customers. We came in order to exchange ideas, share experiences, learn and make a contribution on certain subjects, such as water, energy, and waste management, which are subjects without borders" (September 4, 2002).

Proglio admonished the United States for what he perceived to be its poor environmental record. He noted that in 2002, 3 percent of the U.S. water market was in the private sector and that the rest, as he told *Le Figaro*, "was in a sorry state" (September 4, 2002). He believed the U.S. weaknesses in terms of poor environmental management were obvious and that water services and wastewater management would eventually undergo a drastic change in the United States.

Because his company dealt with the finite resource of water, Proglio was a long-time advocate of sustainable development. For Proglio, sustainable development involved improving economic efficiency, protecting and restoring ecological systems and resources, and enhancing the well-being of his customers and the local communities where Veolia Environnement operated. When asked by *Le Figaro* about the cost burdens to companies and taxpayers, Proglio replied, "Yes, protecting the environment costs money, but you have to look at the productivity gains and savings in public health spending. If we neglect the environment, we are likely to see catastrophes that will cost much, much more" (September 4, 2002).

STILL GROWING

In December 2003 Proglio disposed of some of Veolia Environnement's U.S. holdings, including U.S. Filter. The company reported a full-year net loss of 2.05 billion euros ($2.5 billion) in 2003, largely due to the overall failure of its U.S. Filter business. Nevertheless, Proglio was not going to shy away from the right acquisition. In 2004 he started forming a deal to acquire Gelsenwasser, Germany's largest private water company. Setting his sites on other international expansion efforts, Proglio won two water management contracts in China, one in Beijing and the other in the southwestern province of Guizhou, in May 2004. Proglio was optimistic about the company's future in China and told the *China Daily*, "We are willing to conduct new cooperations with more local Chinese governments in the field of waste and water treatment, and we are always ready to provide quality services" (May 21, 2004). In addition to his duties at Veolia Environnement, Proglio was a director and member of the executive committee of Fomento de Construcciones y Contratas, one of Spain's largest construction groups.

SOURCES FOR FURTHER INFORMATION

Betts, Paul, "U.S. Nightmare Becomes Water Under the Bridge," *Financial Times*, September 25, 2003, p. 35.

Carreyrou, John, and Robert Frank, "Vivendi Environnement Is Close to Name Change, End of Links," *Wall Street Journal*, September 25, 2002.

Guillermard, Véronique, and Sixtine Léon-Dufour, "Henri Proglio Stresses Need to Help Developing Countries Get Over Their Complexes," *Le Figaro*, September 4, 2002, http://www.veoliawater.se/pdf/Henri%20Proglio-Figaro.PDF.

Handyside, Gillian, "Vivendi Environmental Moves to Cut Debt," *Water Industry News*, September 28, 2000, http://www.waterindustry.org/New%20Projects/vivendi-8.htm.

Zhiping, Ma, "Veolia Environnement to Increase China Presence," *China Daily*, May 21, 2004, http://www.chinadaily.com.cn/english/doc/2004-05/21/content_332582.htm.

—David Petechuk

David J. Prosser

1944–

Group chief executive and director, Legal and General Group

Nationality: British.

Born: March 26, 1944, in Wales.

Education: University College of Wales, Aberystwyth, BS, 1965.

Family: Married Rosemary (maiden name unknown); children: two.

Career: Sun Alliance and London Assurance Company, 1965–1969, actuary; Hoare Govett & Company, 1969–1973, stockbroker; National Coal Board Superannuation Investments Department, 1973–1981, responsible for stock market activities; CIN Industrial Investments, 1981–1985, managing director for venture capital activities; CIN Investment Management Company, 1985–1988, chief executive responsible for pension fund assets; Legal and General Group, 1988–1991, group director; 1991, deputy chief executive; 1991–, group chief executive and director.

Awards: Achievement Award, British Insurance Awards, 2001.

Address: Legal and General Group, Temple Court, 11 Queen Victoria Street, London EC4N 4TP, United Kingdom; http://www.legal-and-general.co.uk.

David J. Prosser. *Getty Images.*

■ David Prosser emerged from the hills of Wales to become one of the leading financial leaders in London in the 1990s. Prosser studied pure mathematics at University College of Wales, Aberystwyth, and initially became an actuary. He was later employed as a stockbroker before eventually moving to an executive position with CIN Investment Management Company. In 1988 he was hired by Legal and General Group to head its investments division, and by 1991 he had risen to the position of chief executive and director of the company. Known for his modesty and desire to avoid the spotlight, he was also considered a highly effective manager, running a tight ship and weeding out directors and other employees who failed to perform.

A LONG JOURNEY FROM THE WELSH HILLS

One journalist described Prosser as a "stereotypical Welshman—pinched face, thin-rimmed spectacles and no sign of extravagance" (*Scotland on Sunday*, September 15, 2002). His background stemmed from the hills of Wales, where his grandfather worked as a hill farmer. Prosser was an active boy, standing out as a rugby player, though he reportedly was not ambitious in school. Nonetheless, his family history taught him a valuable work ethic. His first job, he said in a company newsletter sent to Legal and General Group workers, involved breaking stones at a rock quarry. Commenting on the experience, Prosser said, "It can be very hard work until you find the technique. I wouldn't want to do it now" (London *Sunday Times,* September 12, 1999).

Prosser credits much of his career success to his father, who veered from the family farming trade and studied to become a mathematics teacher. Prosser said in a union magazine, as reported in the London *Sunday Times,* that his father gave him the best piece of advice. "When I left home to go to university, my father told me to always be true to myself, to always try my best and to remember that a pint of beer eases stress" (September 12, 1999). Prosser followed in his father's footsteps, studying pure mathematics at University College of Wales, Aberystwyth, and earning first-class honors. While he considered teaching as a profession, financial incentive drove Prosser to become an actuary, a career path also chosen by his brother. In 1971 he was appointed a fellow with the Institute of Actuaries.

In 1965 Prosser joined Sun Alliance and London Assurance Company as an actuary. Four years later, in 1969, he moved on to become a stockbroker at Hoard Govett, where he remained until 1973. That year he was hired by the National Coal Board Superannuation Investments Department, where he was the head of a rich pension fund. He rose to an executive position in 1981, when he was hired as managing director of CIN Industrial Investments. In 1985 he was named chief executive of CIN Investment Management Company.

JOINS LEGAL AND GENERAL GROUP

Prosser's career with Legal and General Group began in 1988, when he was hired as group director for investments. Legal and General Group was founded in 1836 by a group of six lawyers. The company expanded throughout the 19th century, survived both world wars, and continued to grow on an international scale for much of the 20th century. However, the company experienced several problems in the 1980s prior to Prosser's arrival. The company was entangled in a scandal involving certain sales of pensions, referred to in British newspapers as "pension mis-selling," in violation of British regulations. The firm's pension fund asset management also performed poorly, with the amount of assets managed by the investment division of the firm falling from £12.5 billion to £11 billion after the U.S. stock market crash of 1987.

Prosser's first year as head of the investment division was a success. Under his guidance, the division's asset pool increased to £14 billion. His success in the investment division led to his appointment as deputy chief executive of Legal and General Group in January 1991. Months later, in September 2001, he was named the group's chief executive and director.

EARLY YEARS AS CHIEF EXECUTIVE

Within months of taking over as chief executive and director, Prosser faced the unenviable task of announcing £84.6 million in losses resulting largely from failed mortgage-indemnity policies that were sold during the 1980s. The loss was reportedly the first sustained by the company in genera-

tions. The company was also required to pay fines and compensation of £600 million as a result of the pension mis-selling scandal.

Prosser turned the company around immediately. He cut costs and redirected the company. Instead of selling expensive insurance policies that were loaded with commissions for agents, the group began to sell simpler and cheaper mass-market products, such as index-tracking funds. Prosser cut commission rates by up to 25 percent, increased distribution, and bulked up considerably the company's spending on marketing. Legal and General Group reduced its self-employed sales force from more than 3,000 in the late 1980s to about 800 in the late 1990s.

Prosser became incensed in 1997 when Treasury Economic Secretary Helen Liddell announced that Legal and General Group had been placed on a "naming and shaming" list for not assisting in a more rapid resolution of the pension mis-selling scandal. Prosser's supporters quickly pointed out that the company had, in fact, done a great deal to correct the problems. According to insiders, as reported in the London *Sunday Times,* Prosser was "ruthless," withholding bonuses from directors when their staff failed to comply with insurance regulations. Said one insider, "People are culpable with David. He holds them accountable, and they are left in no doubt about that" (September 12, 1999).

Despite the controversy surrounding the pension mis-selling, Prosser directed a complete turnaround of Legal and General Group. In January 1997 Prosser announced that the company had experienced a 54 percent increase in new business during 1996. Prosser's goals were to continue to improve each year in terms of performance. According to Prosser, competitive pricing allowed the company to create a "virtuous circle" of growth in sales and profits, which allowed the company to sell competitive products (March 13, 1997).

MAINTAINING COMPANY INDEPENDENCE

Legal and General Group's successes during the 1990s led to speculation that another company, quite possibly a bank, would make an effort to take over the life insurance company. Prosser steadfastly denied the possibility, saying that the company continued to have great promise for expansion as an independent company. The company exceeded expectations in 1997, and company shares had risen considerably. In an interview with *AFX News* in 1998, Prosser pondered, "Why on earth would one want to quit with such a robust strategy, with such potential and with resources to back it up?" (March 12, 1998).

Prosser apparently had a change of plans in 1999, when his company announced that National Westminster Bank would take over Legal and General Group. Much of the attention over the planned merger focused on Prosser, who would have assumed the third-highest position at National Westminster—executive deputy chairman—reportedly to oversee bank operation, insurance and pension products, fund management, and small and medium-size corporate business. National Westminster at the time of the proposed merger was three times the size of Legal and General Group. One rival said of Prosser, "He's the most important Welshman in commerce, and I think that's a position he rather likes" (London *Sunday Times,* September 12, 1999).

Despite speculation that Prosser could eventually take over as chief executive of National Westminster, the deal never came to fruition. Royal Bank of Scotland seized an opportunity and took over National Westminster, thus leaving Legal and General Group as an independent company. After the failed takeover attempt, Prosser formed alliances with several other London-based companies to sell his company's products.

RUNNING A TIGHT SHIP

As the leader of Legal and General Group, Prosser was described as being modest, mild mannered, "staid and unflashy," and "a naturally cautious and reserved man who often seemed uncomfortable in his role as L&G's public figurehead" (London *Sunday Times,* September 30, 2001). Underneath his humble outer presence, however, was a precise manager. One colleague told the London *Sunday Times,* "I think he can be quite frightening to those further down the line. If you don't perform, he will pounce you" (September 12, 1999).

Commentators referred to his qualities as "typically Welsh." On the one hand, Mark Wood of Axa Insurance said of Prosser, "He has all the positive attributes of a Welshman. He is lucid, persuasive and at ease with himself. He is fun to be with" (London *Sunday Times,* September 12, 1999). On the other hand, the London *Sunday Times* commented that Prosser "also has some of that dark Welsh temper and has a disapproving stare that could curdle milk" (September 12, 1999).

Despite the apparent duality of his personality, Prosser earned great respect among his peers. In 2001 he was awarded the prized Achievement Award at the British Insurance Awards, a testament to a decade of success with his company. He survived largely by avoiding controversy and sustained periods of poor performance in the company, and he was cheered for guiding his company through a difficult period following the scandal in the 1980s and for his ability to direct the company after the failed merger with National Westminster. A

humble Prosser told a reporter for the *Sunday Times* (London), "You can't be trained to be a chief executive. It's a team-building and team-leading job, but it's not the same thing as being a team member. You have to be a little bit separate. At the end of the day, the buck stops on your desk. Difficult decisions tend to stop on your desk" (September 30, 2001).

PLANNING RETIREMENT

Prosser initially planned to retire in 2004 at age 60. However, in 2000 he announced that he would remain as Legal and General Group's chief executive through 2006 in order to direct the company through expected consolidations within the insurance industry. In April 2004 the company announced that it had begun a search for Prosser's successor, though some speculated that Prosser could be persuaded to delay his retirement even further. When the company announced its plans to identify a successor, Legal and General had the highest Standard & Poor's credit rating of any insurer in Great Britain.

See also entry on Legal & General Group plc in *International Directory of Company Histories.*

SOURCES FOR FURTHER INFORMATION

Barker, Sophie, "Prosser Stays to Steer L&G Past Consolidation," *Daily Telegraph,* November 17, 2000.

"The British Insurance Awards 2001 Supplement—The Achievement Award—Captain of Industry," *Post Magazine,* July 19, 2001, p. 67.

Durman, Paul, "Insurance Boss Still Ahead after 10 Years," London *Sunday Times,* September 30, 2001.

"Interview: Legal & General's Management Will Defend Its Independence," *AFX News,* March 12, 1998.

Northedge, Richard. "Profile: David Prosser: Making Sure All the Figures Add Up," *Scotland on Sunday,* September 15, 2002.

Rushe, Dominic, "Boy from the Valleys Scales City Peaks," London *Sunday Times,* September 12, 1999.

Smith, Alexander, "Mild-Mannered Prosser May Have More in Mind," *National Post,* September 7, 1999.

Wickham, Chris, "Interview: L&G Chief Says 1996 New Business More Profitable Than 1995," *AFX News,* March 13, 1997.

—Matthew C. Cordon

■■■
Philip J. Purcell III
1943–
Chairman and chief executive officer, Morgan Stanley

Nationality: American.

Born: September 5, 1943, in Salt Lake City, Utah.

Education: University of Notre Dame, BBA, 1964; University of Chicago, MBA, 1966; London School of Economics, MS, 1967.

Family: Married Anne McNamara; children: seven.

Career: McKinsey & Company, 1967–1978, consultant; 1976–1978, managing director; Sears, Roebuck and Company, 1978–1982, strategic planner; Dean Witter, 1982–1986, president and chief operating officer; Dean Witter Discover, 1986–1997, chairman of the board and chief executive officer; Morgan Stanley, 1997–, chairman of the board and chief executive officer.

Address: Morgan Stanley, 1585 Broadway, New York, New York 10036; http://www.morganstanley.com.

■ Philip J. Purcell III took over Morgan Stanley in May 1997, when Dean Witter, which he had led since 1982, bought Morgan Stanley Group for $10 billion. Purcell's route to the top of a major Wall Street corporation was unusual. Unlike most Wall Street chief executives, Purcell lacked experience as a trader, broker, or investment banker. In fact, he began his career as a management consultant and later a retailer before officially joining Wall Street. Purcell's career at Morgan was marked by both triumph and discontent.

In 2003, with sales of about $34.9 billion, Morgan Stanley was one of the world's top investment banks. Morgan Stanley marketed financial services through three separate units. The securities division offered traditional corporate investment banking services, such as underwriting, mergers and acquisitions assistance, full-service retail brokerage, and premium services for wealthy individuals. Its investment management unit provided both individuals and institutions with investment products and services while the credit services division oversaw its Discover credit card business through its subsidiary Discover Financial Services.

Philip J. Purcell III. *AP/Wide World Photos.*

A DISARMING PERSONALITY MASKS OVERACHIEVEMENT

Despite being characterized as having an "aw-shucks" personality, Purcell was also described by his associates as being a "compulsive overachiever" (*BusinessWeek*, October 5, 1992). He was near the top of his class at Notre Dame. At the University of Chicago, where he earned an MBA, he was the only one out of 65 students to get an A, despite the fact that he was part of a four-person team. To prove his point, Purcell kept a diary of his team's progress; the diary emphasized Purcell's contribution and was submitted to the professor. John Jeuck, a retired University of Chicago business professor, recalled, "Basically, the process was managed so that the group's resentment was channeled toward me and not Purcell. I figured he'd be a success. In my 50 years of teaching, Purcell stood out among a lot of bodies and a lot of heads" (*USA Today*, February 6, 1997).

Purcell attended the London School of Economics, where he earned a master's degree. At age 27 he became McKinsey's youngest principal director and the firm's youngest managing director soon after at age 32. One of his biggest clients was Sears, Roebuck and Company. After developing a working relationship with Edward R. Telling, then chairman of Sears, Purcell left his consulting position in 1978 to take a job as a strategic planner for the retailer.

SOCKS AND STOCKS

At Sears, Purcell took the retailer into uncharted territories, planning the purchases of Dean Witter Reynolds and Coldwell Banker, a real estate company. At the time his strategy to sell stocks alongside clothes was referred to mockingly as "socks and stocks." For Purcell, such skepticism was only further motivation. Said Purcell, "It scares me to death if people applaud what you do" (*Salt Lake Tribune*, October 30, 1998).

Sears gave Purcell the responsibility of integrating Dean Witter Reynolds, naming Purcell president and COO of the brokerage in 1982 and chairman and CEO in 1986. At Dean Witter, Purcell launched the Discover credit card—the first card with no annual fee and a rebate based on purchases—when just about everyone in the industry warned him it would fail. At first, it seemed it would. In the first two years, the card, which cost Sears $1 billion, lost an estimated $250 million. But by the time Purcell was done, Discover had 39 million customers with unpaid balances of $32 billion—generating an annual $500 million annually. Purcell remarked, "I never questioned the strategy, but there were lots who did—including at the time people I worked for" (*Salt Lake Tribune*, October 30, 1998).

Purcell gained experience in operating a financial services firm that would later prepare him for Wall Street.

Sears decided to focus on its retail business and spun off Dean Witter in 1993, taking it public through an initial public offering (IPO) underwritten by Morgan Stanley. In the period after the IPO, the company outperformed its peers. By 1997 its sales force included 8,406 brokers and ranked third after Merrill Lynch and Smith Barney. In addition, the Discover Card exceeded expectations.

All three of the company's product lines—stock brokerage, mutual funds, and credit cards—had generated high profit margins. In fact, in 1997 the company had a pretax margin of 15 percent, the highest in the business. By the end of the decade, Dean Witter had earned a reputation as one of the most profitable Wall Street brokerages. Said Thomas P. Facciola, an analyst with Salomon Brothers, "Dean Witter is one of the best run retail brokerage shops in the country. They have a good cost culture, and they don't get carried away with a bull market" (*New York Times*, February 6, 1997).

A WALL STREET ANOMALY

As head of Dean Witter, Purcell was described as a low-profile player who was an outsider on Wall Street. Unlike industry peers who started as traders, brokers, or investment bankers, Purcell's roots were in the consulting business. James F. Higgins,who ran Dean Witter's brokerage operation under Purcell, noted that "Phil is different. He didn't claw his way up the Wall Street ladder" (*New York Times*, March 2, 2003).

Another stark difference was that Purcell was a staunch believer in pay for performance, taking a relatively modest package in 1995 of a $3.5 million base with stock options that paid only if the company succeeded. Jack Keane, dean of the Notre Dame College of Business Administration and a friend, spoke of Purcell's integrity: "He accomplished a great deal, while others were paying public relations firms to get their names here and there" (*USA Today*, February 6, 1997).

A MUTUALLY BENEFICIAL UNION

Purcell's relative anonymity came to an end in February 1997, when Dean Witter bought Morgan Stanley Group for $10 billion. In May 1997 Purcell became chairman and CEO of Morgan Stanley Dean Witter, a firm with $271 billion in assets managed and $10.6 billion in capital, at the time one of the nation's largest securities companies. It was a mutually beneficial match. Dean Witter's brokers received the additional products they needed to sell to their middle-class customers, and Morgan Stanley broadened its customer group beyond the corporate market to individual investors.

The deal was the by-product of strong relationships between the three executives integral to the deal: Purcell; John J. Mack, Morgan's president; and Richard B. Fisher, Morgan's chairman and chief executive. In fact, both Purcell and Mack wanted to run the newly combined firm, but a sacrifice on the part of one of the executives led to a truce. Fisher recalled, "We talked about it a lot, and John just came in one morning and said that this was so powerful a combination that he would take the second slot" (*New York Times*, February 9, 1997).

During this period, Purcell's challenge was creating cohesiveness out of two distinct corporate cultures. He moved slowly at first, allowing each entity to operate separately.

A MERGER HITS SOME SPEED BUMPS

The first year of the merger was a success. But in the summer of 1998, Purcell faced several challenges. For starters, Mack was angling for more power. Encouraged by a trend in the financial services industry in which top executives were sharing power in co-CEO roles, Mack approached Purcell with a similar proposal. He had a good case; after all, Mack's employees were generating revenues and earnings much faster than the Dean Witter retail businesses.

Purcell's initial reaction was not positive, but he agreed to give the suggestion some thought—if his competitors were so eager to embrace the move, Purcell concluded, maybe the structure could work. But Purcell ultimately rejected the idea, and once again, Mack backed down.

WOUNDS NEED HEALING

An even costlier issue was the frustration felt by the Morgan camp about the slow pace of integrating operations. None of Morgan Stanley's senior executives were invited to be part of the new firm's operating committee in the first year of the merger. After Mack aired the concerns to Purcell, the two executives consolidated the company's fixed-income trading operations. In a major concession, Purcell also invited some of the old Morgan Stanley executives who were heading some of the most profitable business units into the company's management committee. The new management committee was also brought together for a group therapy session.

According to the rules, members of the committee were not allowed to bring up any issue in the future that had not been aired at the meeting. Sir David Walker, a British committee member, recalled, "There was something very American about it, and even a religious fervor. I squirmed some. But it was steam-letting, and I have to say that I think in the end it was cathartic" (*Fortune*, April 26, 1999).

Morgan Stanley finished 1998 on a positive note. It generated $3.3 billion in 1998 profits—more than double Merrill Lynch's $1.3 billion. Assets under management increased from $338 billion in 1997 to $462 billion in 1999. Purcell and Mack called the merger a "home run," with Dean Witter's retail brokers aggressively marketing Morgan Stanley's portfolio of corporate financial services (*Fortune*, April 26, 1999). Their next goal was exporting their offerings overseas and finding a way to integrate the Internet into their brokerage operations without making the company's brokers obsolete.

A POWER STRUGGLE COMES TO AN END

However, by January 2001 Mack had finally grown tired of not running his own operation and announced that he was quitting. His departure greatly influenced the path of Morgan Stanley. Richard K. Strauss, a securities industry analyst at Goldman Sachs, said that had Mack stayed with the firm, it "would have focused more on corporate and investment banking" (*BusinessWeek*, June 25, 2001).

But with Mack out of the picture, Purcell embraced a strategy to strengthen credit cards, retail, and asset management. He also crafted a plan to break down the walls between company divisions and provide clients with a complete portfolio of financial services. Instead of the traditional practice of linking

compensation to the dollar amounts of transactions, he implemented new rules that tied pay to the company's share of the total business each client gave to Wall Street. Purcell also appointed a team of newly promoted younger employees to strategize a better way to service corporate clients. Purcell said, "Easily the most important thing I've done is pick people" (*BusinessWeek*, June 25, 2001).

An important win showcasing Purcell's strategy was the $3.6 billion spin-off of Agere Systems, the optical electronics unit of Lucent Technologies. Although Morgan declined to comment on its fees for directing the deal—at the time the fourth-largest IPO in U.S. history—Goldman Sachs estimated that it received $75 million. John T. Dickson, then president and CEO of Agere, remarked, "Like most people, I'm skeptical of bankers. In this instance, they earned the money" (*BusinessWeek*, June 25, 2001). Even competitors were impressed. A top banker at a rival firm noted, "A lot of firms probably could not have pulled that deal off" (*BusinessWeek*, June 25, 2001).

PLAGUED BY CONTROVERSY

Despite his financial performance, the low-key Purcell struggled in the public perception arena—both inside and outside his firm. Key executives departed the firm. With Mack gone, the investment bankers at the firm who remained felt that they commanded little respect. Said a Morgan Stanley banker, who remained anonymous, "No one on the institutional side would think to leave if Purcell left. In fact, they'd probably have a party" (*BusinessWeek*, June 25, 2001).

Morale was further deteriorated by two scandals. The first involved a junior analyst at the firm who filed a $1.78 billion discrimination suit after he was fired for appearing nude in a gay magazine. Morgan settled the suit, making a $1 million donation to the National Urban League. The company insisted that the analyst who brought the suit did not get any money in the settlement, but the press expressed skepticism. One columnist with the *Wall Street Journal* even suggested that Morgan lied about the settlement.

The second controversy mounted when the company paid Bill Clinton $100,000 for a speech. Investors expressed dissatisfaction with the decision, and Purcell apologized, angering some in his ranks. The executive responsible for hiring Clinton later left the firm.

A PARAGON OF MISCONDUCT?

In addition to suffering with the rest of Wall Street through a stiff market decline in 2001, Morgan faced a slew of challenges in the new millennium. Its stock price fell 66.5 percent from its peak in September 2000 to March 2003, proportionally a larger decline than for the stock prices of its competitors.

Most troubling was the intense regulatory scrutiny of Morgan's business practices. In April 2003 Morgan and 10 other large firms agreed to a $1.4 billion settlement resulting from allegations that research analysts had issued biased stock ratings to attract or retain investment-banking clients. Morgan's share of the settlement came to $125 million. Just a day after the agreement was announced, Purcell irked regulators by telling audience members at a conference that the settlement should not worry retail investors.

William Donaldson, the chairman of the Securities and Exchange Commission, responded with a terse letter, reminding Purcell that terms of the settlement prevented him from denying the allegations and scolding him for his hubris. Donaldson wrote, "First, your statements reflect a disturbing and misguided perspective on Morgan Stanley's alleged misconduct. The allegations in the commission's complaint against Morgan Stanley are extremely serious. They include charges that Morgan Stanley paid other firms to provide research coverage, compensated its research analysts, in part, based on the degree to which they helped generate investment banking business, offered research coverage by its analysts as a marketing tool to gain investment banking business and failed to establish adequate procedures to protect research analysts from conflicts of interest. In light of these charges, your reported comments evidence a troubling lack of contrition" (*New York Times*, May 2, 2003).

Purcell's troubles did not end there. In July 2003 the State of Massachusetts issued a complaint against Morgan Stanley, alleging that brokers and managers were paid incentives for pushing proprietary products that in some cases lagged behind their third-party peers. The charge resulted in a $50 million fine. And in a settlement with the National Association of Securities Dealers involving allegations of overcharging third-party fund vendors for shelf space, the firm paid a $2 million settlement.

In November 2003 Purcell responded to the onslaught of legal troubles by announcing at the Securities Industry Association's annual conference that he was launching an investigation into conflicts of interest. Purcell hired a former enemy—Eric Dinallo, who worked with New York State Attorney General Eliot Spitzer investigating Morgan—to lead his efforts.

PURCELL'S FUTURE UNCLEAR

Year-end results for 2003 suggested a possible turnaround at Morgan. For the fiscal year, the firm generated $3.8 billion in net income, compared with $3 billion in 2002. Pretax profits increased by 22 percent. What is more, the company claimed the number two spot in global mergers and acquisitions and the number three position in equity underwriting. In the first quarter of 2004, it beat estimates, with earnings rising by 35 percent.

Still, some wondered whether Purcell, who turned 61 in 2004, had lost his magic touch. The Wall Street analyst Richard Bov stated, "I think Morgan Stanley's ship is going up and down with the tide, as opposed to Purcell's taking control or command of business" (*Primedia Insight Registered Rep.*, April 8, 2004). Throughout the turmoil, Purcell never gave any indication that his job was at risk, telling one reporter that he planned to stay until he was 65, or until 2008. He had reason to make the assertion: support from Morgan's board of directors was strong because the board included several members with long ties to Purcell. Two were consultants with Purcell in the 1970s; another was Purcell's former boss at Sears.

See also entries on McKinsey & Company, Inc., Morgan Stanley Group, Inc., and Sears, Roebuck and Co. in *International Directory of Company Histories*.

SOURCES FOR FURTHER INFORMATION

Boulton, Guy, "Utah Native Built Top Career in Securities," *Salt Lake Tribune*, October 30, 1998.

Dobrzynski, Judith H., "How a Deal Crowned a New King of Wall St.," *New York Times*, February 9, 1997.

Hansell, Saul, "Giant Wall Street Merger: Dean Witter's Chief," *New York Times*, February 6, 1997.

Jones, Del, "Philip Purcell: Boss Thrives as Outsider," *USA Today*, February 6, 1997.

Loomis, Carol J., "Morgan Stanley Dean Witter; The Oddball Marriage Works," *Fortune*, April 26, 1999, p. 92.

McGeehan, Patrick, and Landon Thomas Jr., "No Worry, Even Now, at Morgan Stanley," *New York Times*, March 2, 2003.

Nathan Spiro, Leah, and Julia Flynn, "A Star in the Gloom at Sears," *BusinessWeek*, October 5, 1992, p. 62.

Norris, Floyd, "Morgan Stanley Draws SEC's Ire," *New York Times*, May 2, 2003.

Thornton, Emily, "Morgan Stanley's Midlife Crisis," *BusinessWeek*, June 25, 2001, p. 90.

Warner, Joan, "Trouble in the House that Purcell Built?" *Registered Rep.*, April 8, 2004.

—Tim Halpern

■■■
Allen I. Questrom
1941–
Chairman and chief executive officer, J. C. Penney Company

Nationality: American.

Born: April 13, 1941, in Newton, Massachusetts.

Education: Boston University, BS, 1964.

Family: Married Carol Kelli (former executive at Ralph Lauren).

Career: Abraham & Straus, 1965–1973, began as executive trainee, became division merchandise manager; Bullock's, 1973–1974, vice president and general merchandise manager of the home store; 1974–1977, senior vice president and general merchandise manager for all stores; Federated Department Stores, 1977–1978, executive vice president of Bullocks Division; 1978–1980, president of Rich's Division; 1980–1984, chairman and CEO of Rich's Division; 1984–1988, chairman and CEO of Bullock's/Bullocks Wilshire Division; 1987–1988, corporate executive vice president; 1988–1990, corporate vice chairman; Neiman Marcus Group Inc., 1988–1990, president and CEO, based in Dallas; Federated Department Stores, 1990–1997, chairman and CEO; Barneys New York, 1999–2000, chairman, president, and CEO; J. C. Penney Company, 2000–, chairman and CEO.

Address: J. C. Penney Company, 6501 Legacy Drive, Plano, Texas 75024; http://www.jcpenney.com.

Allen I. Questrom. *AP/Wide World Photos.*

■ Allen Questrom became the first outsider to assume the top position at J. C. Penney in the company's one-hundred-plus-year history in 2000. He brought with him a track record of turning around struggling companies, including Neiman Marcus and Barneys, and an expertise in brand management and customer service. One of the most well-respected executives in the retail industry, he preferred bold moves and jobs that presented enormous challenges. As a manager he was adept at engineering large-scale change in companies that had been mired in outmoded business practices for decades. He took the lead of a troubled company at an age when most of his peers were winding down their careers. Part of Questrom's motivation for continuing to take on such arduous work appeared to have been his driving need to succeed—although he had also felt undercompensated by a previous employer and had sued to prove it.

A PASSION FOR SPORTS TAKES AN UNLIKELY TURN

Questrom grew up in working-class Waltham, Massachusetts, where his father owned a machine shop. After graduating from Boston University, where he majored in finance and played quarterback on the football team, Questrom decided to be a ski bum for a year. But a drought in the Northeast foiled his plans and at his parents' suggestion he looked for a job instead. After answering an ad in the local paper he enrolled as a management trainee with Federated Department Stores'

Abraham & Straus division, partly because he wanted to see what it would be like to work in New York. He eventually rose to executive vice president of Bullock's department stores in Los Angeles, which he transformed with his customer-focused strategy.

A TURNAROUND ARTIST MAKES MANY MARKS

In 1978 Federated moved Questrom to Rich's, a department store in Atlanta that had earned the dubious distinction of being the company's worst performer. Four years later Questrom had turned Rich's into Federated's most profitable division, earning him a position as president and later as chairman and chief executive. As Questrom described in *Chain Store Age Executive*, "Rich's had been run by the family since the beginning. It was a very entrenched organization; they really talked a lot about the past, even though at the present they were not doing well and had not done well for three or four years. It took a lot of time to get people to refocus themselves not on what they did but on what they were doing and who else was doing better than they were at the time" (September 2000).

Questrom's next turnaround project was Neiman Marcus, which was headquartered in Dallas. By the time Questrom took over as chairman and CEO in 1988, Neiman had shed its reputation for exemplary customer service; Questrom made an immediate impact on the company by personally focusing on that realm of the business. Early on, a letter from an angry customer crossed his desk; the woman had received poor customer service and had been obligated to drive 90 miles back to a suburban New York store to pick up her credit card because a clerk had failed to return it after a purchase. Questrom called her and sent her a gift certificate along with a plea to give the company another chance. He circulated her letter to employees, reminding them that the customer always came first.

A CAREER-CROWNING ACHIEVEMENT

When Questrom became chairman and CEO of Federated in 1990 the company was mired in debt. In *Business Week* Questrom said, "At the time, everyone was telling us that the department store was a dinosaur" (November 28, 1994). By cutting costs, adding inventory-tracking technology, and bringing order to the stores, Quelstrom miraculously took the company out of Chapter 11 bankruptcy proceedings. In particular Questrom led Federated to increase the amount of private-label merchandise carried by the stores. Questrom felt it to be important to develop private labels as brand concepts throughout stores and pushed the proportion of private labels in Federated's home-furnishings business from 14 percent to more than 20 percent.

In 1994 Questrom led Federated's successful bid for the debt-ridden R. H. Macy & Company, an acquisition that significantly raised the company's profile. Questrom then engineered the acquisition of the financially troubled Broadway chain, which operated 82 stores, mostly in California. Although the company was left with a hefty debt of about $5 billion as a result of the deals, it also became the nation's largest retailer. Bob Morosky, who briefly ran Federated before being replaced, stated in *Business Week*, "Questrom solidified the organization and boosted morale. I think he's superb—and for me to say that is a big deal since he got the job I wanted" (November 28, 1994).

Questrom abruptly retired from Federated in May 1997, a year earlier than expected, and shocked colleagues by suing Federated for $47 million in back pay, a suit which he consequently lost.

PERFORMANCE, NOT AGE, COUNTS

After a short term as chairman and CEO of Barneys, Questrom was named Chairman and CEO of J. C. Penney Company, which operated J. C. Penney Stores, the J. C. Penney catalog, the Eckerd Drug Store chain, and other Internet retailing businesses. The career move presented Questrom with an opportunity to make his mark on "one of the legendary names in American retailing" (July 27, 2000). J. C. Penney, which had more than 290,000 employees in the United States and Latin America, reported fiscal 2000 sales of $32.5 billion.

Questrom stood apart from many of his J. C. Penney predecessors, not least of all because of his age—he signed his five-year contract with the company at 60, an age when J. C. Penney executives traditionally retired. When asked about retirement in *Chain Store Age Executive*, Questrom remarked, "Even though I have retired on many occasions, I'm not sure there should be any date. As long as the person wants to be interested and excited about the business, they can go on and on" (September 2000).

Questrom's career stamina may have been a product of his well-balanced lifestyle. He was once an avid fundraiser for United Way and he enjoyed ballroom dancing with his wife after hours. In 1984, when his standing with Federated was at an all-time high, he took a sabbatical to travel around the world with his wife. He noted in the *Los Angeles Times*, "It was a terrific sabbatical. It gave me an opportunity to think about retail and get to know my wife" (December 10, 1989).

THE MOUNT EVEREST OF CAREER CHALLENGES

News of Questrom's appointment at J. C. Penney was received favorably on Wall Street, and Jeff Edelman of PaineWebber upgraded his rating of the company from "attractive" to "buy," raising his 12-month price target from $20 to $25. Still, Questrom's job would prove more daunting than his previous turnaround projects. In 1999 operating profit for J. C. Penney department stores and its catalog dropped to $670 million, slightly more than half the $1.275 billion total from 1997. Eckerd didn't fare much better, with $183 million in operating profit in 1999 versus the $347 million of 1997. For the second quarter ending July 29, 2000 (just two days after Questrom was appointed to the top spot), Penney reported a net income of $23 million, versus the $39 million from the year before.

The poor financial statistics were exactly what attracted Questrom to the job. As he described in *Women's Wear Daily*, "I thought Penney's had lots of potential that was not being fully appreciated. It's like climbing another mountain. You look at one and say you want to climb it, and then you want to climb the next mountain. It's the way one looks at life, asking what's the next challenge. I felt this was an interesting one, in the sense that Penney's hadn't done well for several years and it had good brand recognition" (December 12, 2000).

Unlike Federated, which needed nothing more than a financial makeover, J. C. Penney lacked the respect and loyalty of shoppers. It failed to respond quickly enough to competition from trendier outlets, including Kohl's and Old Navy. Simply stated, the company had an image problem. In *BusinessWeek*, Alan Bergstrom, the head of The Brand Consultancy in Atlanta, said, "Questrom's main task is to redefine what the brand is all about" (February 12, 2001).

It would be a job that played to Questrom's strengths. Elliot Cole, the senior partner in the law firm Patton Boggs who sat on the board of Boston University with Questrom, said in *Women's Wear Daily*, "Allen is the most focused guy I have ever met. He doesn't suffer fools and doesn't waste time. No matter where he was and what the brand is, Questrom understands it quickly. The world is talking about branding, whether it's Neiman's or Macy's. Questrom is very malleable into whatever brand it is his job to serve" (July 28, 2000).

A MASTER OF CHANGE

Before developing a strategy for J. C. Penney, Questrom vowed to spend several months in the field discussing key issues with the employees who knew the stores best. When asked how long it took to change a company's culture in *Chain Store Age Executive*, he replied, "The culture change is glacial. If what you think you're going to do is totally change the culture in a company that's been around 98 years in two years you're wasting your time. But you can get people to change attitudes on some things and, as you build on that, people will change. But you have to have a couple of wins. If you don't have a couple of wins, it's impossible to change anybody" (September 2000).

Questrom's charming, selfless personality helped. He believed in lavishing praise on employees, seemed more interested in what others were saying than in his own opinions, and was skilled at effectively delegating. As noted in the *Los Angeles Times*, a sign from his Bullock's days that hung behind his desk underscored his philosophy. It read, "There's no limit to what a person can do if they don't mind who gets the credit" (December 10, 1989).

A buzzword for Questrom was "refocus." He believed that in order to change long-standing beliefs and business practices one had to motivate employees to capitalize on their strengths. He remarked in *Chain Store Age Executive*, "Most always in companies, there are very good people. Just because businesses don't do well, it's not because they are terrible people. It's what's asked of them. It's what you focus on. And the challenge, in my opinion, for any good manager of a company is to get the present cadre of people to refocus" (September 2000).

Once employees knew what was expected of them, Questrom demanded results. In *Women's Wear Daily*, Ron Frasch, the chairman and CEO of Bergdorf Goodman who once reported to Questrom, said, "He's a griller. I'll never forget one executive committee meeting. He was challenging the men's GM on umbrellas, grilling him about black umbrellas, fold-up umbrellas, fashion umbrellas, umbrellas with canes. How many? What was selling? The GM didn't know. Questrom didn't yell or scream. He's not a screamer, but he challenges every assumption. The point is, if you're working for Questrom you better damn well know every detail about your business. And you better know what's going on with the competition. That's how you become a better executive working with Allen—even if you don't know it at the time" (December 12, 2000).

HIRING 101

At J. C. Penney, Questrom set in motion a five-year plan to rescue the embattled retailer that focused on improving marketing, merchandising, profitability, and hiring. He advocated hiring outsiders with fresh perspective who could fill various expertise gaps in the company. Under J. C. Penney's traditional management pipeline, almost 100 percent of executives were developed internally; Questrom hoped to increase the percentage of outside talent to about 20 percent in order to keep new ideas flowing into the company.

Questrom believed in hiring the right person for the job, even when his personal inclinations might have suggested otherwise. At Federated, Questrom once hired Michael Gould (the CEO of Bloomingdale's), who had run Robinson's when Questrom ran archrival Bullock's. Said one executive in *BusinessWeek*, "Allen and Michael don't like each other. That's part of Allen's genius: to hire somebody you've been an enemy with and say, 'Look, we don't have to love each other, but you're the best guy for this job'" (November 28, 1994).

FOCUSING ON CUSTOMERS

The guiding force of Questrom's business strategy was always to focus on the customer. At Barney's he changed a culture where employees had spent more time buying and selecting merchandise than visiting customers and salespeople in the stores. In his view J. C. Penney's management had forgotten about the very people that kept the company in business.

Questrom took a coast-to-coast tour of 60 J. C. Penney stores and competitors, and what he saw didn't impress him. The merchandise was too safe and too conservative and offered little that customers couldn't buy at other stores. As the new CEO he mandated that his employees stock clothes that were both fashionable and price conscious, hiring trend spotters to scour the coasts and translate must-have looks for its target customers: families with annual income between $30,000 and $80,000.

Questrom remarked in *Chain Store Age Executive*, "If it gives a zing to the product and it's reasonably priced, then it works. But if it's just to have a designer name out there, I'm not sure it makes a lot of sense. I think a lot of these designer labels will backfire if they don't continue to give value to the customer" (September 2000). Using Gap as an industry role model, he implemented subtle fashion twists, such as deviating from the standard blue and white colors offered by the company's men's line.

A CLOUDY BIG PICTURE

While Questrom refashioned his team according to his tried and true playbook, the financial future for retail remained far from certain. In 2003 big chains like J. C. Penney accounted for just 11 percent of the nation's retail sales, down from about 20 percent in 1987. On Wall Street the department-store sector hovered at the bottom of the retail pecking order, with companies such as Federated, Saks, and May Department Stores Company posting month after month of disappointing sales.

For the fiscal year ending January 31, 2004, in its fourth quarter J. C. Penney posted a $1.07 billion loss compared to the profit of $202 million from a year earlier. This led the retailer to agree to sell its Eckerd drug store chain to both Jean Coutu Group and CVS Corporation for $4.525 billion in cash. After counting all the costs, J. C. Penney expected to have received proceeds of about $3.5 billion from the sale. Questrom would continue to search for ways to improve the quality of his company.

See also entries on Barney's, Inc., Federated Department Stores Inc., J. C. Penney Company, Inc., and The Neiman Marcus Group, Inc. in *International Directory of Company Histories*.

SOURCES FOR FURTHER INFORMATION

Forest, Stephanie Anderson, "Can an Outsider Fix J. C. Penney?" *BusinessWeek*, February 12, 2001, p. 56.

Groves, Martha, "Bullock's Wizard Trying His Hand at Neiman Marcus," *Los Angeles Times*, December 10, 1989.

Koenig, David, "Pending Eckerd Sale Pushes Penney to Huge Loss," Associated Press State & Local Wire, February 26, 2004.

"Merchant of Panache," *Chain Store Age Executive*, September 2000, pp. 61–64.

Moin, David, "It's Official: Questrom Named Penney's CEO," *Women's Wear Daily*, July 28, 2000, p. 1.

———, "J. C. Penney Co. CEO Allen Questrom on Company's Management," *Women's Wear Daily*, December 12, 2000, p. 1.

Oldham, Charlene, "Questrom Brings Style to Penney: Master of the Turnaround Is Coming Back to Dallas," *Dallas Morning News*, July 28, 2000.

Zinn, Laura, "Allen Questrom's Ultimate Quest," *BusinessWeek*, November 28, 1994, p. 116.

—Tim Halpern

Franklin D. Raines

1949–

**Chairman and chief executive officer,
Fannie Mae**

Nationality: American.

Born: January 14, 1949, in Seattle, Washington.

Education: Harvard College, BA, 1971; Oxford University,
1971–1973; Harvard Law School, JD, 1976.

Family: Son of Delno and Ida Raines (both custodians);
married Wendy Farrow; children: three.

Career: Office of Senator Moynihan, 1969, intern; Seattle
Model Cities Program, 1972–1973, associate director;
Preston, Thorgrimson, Ellis, Holman & Fletcher,
1976–1977, attorney; White House Domestic Policy
Staff, 1977–1978, assistant director; U.S. Office of
Management and Budget, 1978–1979, associate
director; Lazard Frères & Company, 1979–1982, vice
president; 1983–1984, senior vice president;
1985–1991, partner; Fannie Mae, 1991–1996, vice
chairman; U.S. Office of Management and Budget,
1996–1998, director; Fannie Mae, 1998, chairman;
1999–, chairman and chief executive officer.

Address: Fannie Mae, 3900 Wisconsin Avenue NW,
Washington, D.C. 20016; http://www.fanniemae.com.

Franklin D. Raines. *AP/Wide World Photos.*

■ The first African American CEO of a Fortune 500 corporation, Franklin D. Raines was named chairman and CEO of
Fannie Mae on January 1, 1999. Under his leadership, Fannie
Mae—short for the Federal National Mortgage Association—
remained a major player in what Raines called the "American
Dream Business," (*Financial Times*, October 29, 2002) continued its record of double-digit operating income growth, expanded its product and technology leadership, and committed
to invest $2 trillion to finance affordable homeownership and
rental housing for 18 million families.

In 2003, with revenues of $53.8 billion, Fannie Mae was
the number one source for home mortgage financing in the
United States, providing liquidity in the mortgage market by
buying mortgages from lenders and packaging them for resale,
transferring risk from lenders and allowing them to offer mort-

gages to those who may not otherwise qualify. Fannie Mae was
one of several government-sponsored enterprises, which were
stockholder-owned companies created by Congress to carry
out a public-policy purpose with private capital. Fannie Mae
bought home loans from banks and other mortgage lenders,
providing those lenders with a fresh supply of cash to make
new loans. Fannie Mae also invested in mortgage-backed securities. It benefited from low interest rates, tax exemptions,
and an implicit guarantee of federal support.

OVERACHIEVER FROM AGE EIGHT

Named after the famed president Franklin D. Roosevelt,
Raines, one of seven children, was born in Seattle, Washington. His parents, Delno and Ida Raines, both worked as custodians (neither finished high school). After paying the state

$1,000 for a house that was to be torn down, Delno Raines dug a foundation and used the lumber from the ramshackle house to build a new one. Within five years he had put in the drywall and plumbing. When Delno Raines was hospitalized, the younger Raines began working at the age of eight, helping his mother support the family. Raines's parents never earned more than $15,000 a year, yet his father managed to leave behind $300,000 when he died. Raines remarked, "It's a dramatic demonstration of how important access to capital and homeownership are in the lives of working-class people" (*BusinessWeek*, December 9, 2002).

In high school Raines was the classic overachiever. His honors included captain of the football team, statewide debating champ, and student body president. Continuing on that track, he earned a scholarship to Harvard, where he graduated magna cum laude with a BA degree in government. Raines gravitated toward contentious situations, organizing a campuswide strike at Harvard to protest police actions. He became a Rhodes Scholar at Oxford University and earned a law degree from Harvard Law School. His foray into politics was marked by an internship with Senator Daniel Patrick Moynihan's office.

FROM THE WHITE HOUSE TO THE HOUSING MARKET

After college Raines fulfilled his political ambitions, working for President Richard Nixon and then President Jimmy Carter in various economic posts. Throughout the 1980s he was employed with Lazard, Frères & Company, the investment banking firm, where he worked in municipal finance and was named a general partner. In 1991 Fannie Mae recruited Raines, offering him the title of vice chairman.

One of Raines's early contributions to Fannie Mae was promoting the use of technology as a tool for reducing risk and fueling growth, investing massive amounts of money to bring the company up to date with sophisticated automating systems and Internet applications. Two results of that initiative were the "Desk Top Underwriter," an automated underwriting system that allowed lenders to originate mortgages in a cheaper and more efficient manner, and "Desk Top Home Counselor," an electronic system that helped loan counselors repair the credit of prospective buyers so that they could quality for mortgages.

The importance of technology was made apparent to Raines on one of his first days on the job. He needed to cash a check, yet he could not find a place anywhere in the building that could give him money. Said Raines, "What that said to me was: All of the company's billions of dollars are in the computers down in the basement. From there it struck me that our major competitive tool was technology and matching technology to mortgages. It wasn't going to be marketing or hands-on service, because of the kind of product we have—a high-value

product with enormous processing costs" (*American Banker*, January 31, 2001.)

LEARNING HOW TO NEGOTIATE

In 1996 the White House came calling again. President Clinton tapped Raines as a member of his cabinet and as director of the Office of Management and Budget (OMB). Raines was the president's key negotiator in the talks that led to passage of the bipartisan Balanced Budget Act of 1997. Raines was the first OMB director in a generation to have balanced the federal budget. Raines noted, "When you're the OMB director, every day you're dealing with people who want things and conflicts that have to be resolved . . . . Both sides of the aisle found they could trust me" (*American Banker*, January 31, 2001.)

AN AFRICAN AMERICAN ROLE MODEL

In the spring of 1998 Raines announced that he was leaving his position at the White House to become chairman and CEO of Fannie Mae. His appointment marked the first time in history that an African American executive had taken the top position at a Fortune 500 company. Hugh Price, president of the National Urban League, said, "I consider Frank Raines the Jackie Robinson of corporate America" (*Black Enterprise*, August 31, 1998). Not only was Raines setting an important example for fellow African American executives, but he was also doing so at a firm that would be immensely helpful to African American home buyers. One of his goals was to increase the population of African American and Hispanic homeowners.

Raines's position came with a $7 million annual compensation package and instant credibility in corporate circles. Said Raines, "The boards of companies tend to be fairly conservative, and the fact that the Fannie Mae board saw me as the best CEO, I think, will be reassuring to other boards as they seek to promote black executives" (*Black Enterprise*, August 31, 1998).

UNDER ATTACK

Raines became chairman and CEO of Fannie Mae on January 1, 1999. Immediately he had to contend with an unprecedented attack by both industry rivals and government officials. Critics in Congress were pressing for a single influential regulator to replace the two weak agencies that had long monitored government-sponsored entities. Meanwhile, big banks and mortgage insurance companies created a Washington lobbying group called FMWatch to monitor the activities of Fannie Mae and its smaller rival, Freddie Mac.

One of the group's primary concerns was the company's foray—what the group derisively called "mission creep"—into home equity financing and subprime mortgage lending. In response to his critics, Raines showed no intention of slowing down. Raines remarked, "There is a school of thought that if you harass Fannie Mae, maybe they'll pull their punches, maybe they'll slow down, maybe they'll not be as good a company. But anybody who knows me knows that would be a very large tactical error. Anyone who thinks that trying to intimidate us would be productive would be making a mistake" (*American Banker*, January 31, 2001).

POST-ENRON SCRUTINY

In 2002, with investors facing as much as $25 billion in shareholder losses from the Enron debacle, government officials began paying even closer attention to corporate governance. Fannie Mae became a target of this scrutiny. To understand why is to understand Fannie's complex history. President Franklin D. Roosevelt created the company in 1938 as way to free up money in the housing market. In 1968 Congress deemed Fannie Mae a government-sponsored private enterprise, which meant a presumed federal guarantee of the company's debt. In fact, Fannie had a $2.25 billion line of credit with the U.S. Treasury. That benefit enabled the company to obtain a lower-than-average rate on the debt it issued. Banks gave the company loans at rates nearly as low as those paid by the government on its own debt. As a result, the company profited on the difference between the rate of the mortgages it bought and the rate of the money it borrowed.

The Congressional Budget Office said that the company's entitlements as a government-sponsored entity amounted to $6.1 billion in 2000; Fannie put that number at $3 billion to $3.6 billion. The true number most likely lay somewhere in the middle, but the result of the fiscal benefit was undeniable: at least 16 years of double-digit profit growth. Critics warned that during these years of explosive growth, the company had taken on a dangerous level of risk. Industry insiders had long questioned the operations of both Freddie Mac and Fannie Mae, in essence stating that the firms' highly complex financial transactions were created as a shield to hide the volatility of their businesses. For decades stock investors favored Fannie and Freddie for their smooth, predictable earnings growth. That predictability went out the window in 2001, thanks to new accounting rules for derivatives—complex financial contracts that Fannie and Freddie used to protect their earnings against swings in interest rates. The derivatives themselves could have wide swings in value.

A RIVAL'S SCANDAL TURNS UP THE HEAT

In June 2003 Fannie Mae's primary rival, Freddie Mac, fired its chairman and CEO, CFO, and COO following an accounting scandal. The company became the subject of a for-

mal investigation by the Securities and Exchange Commission (SEC) regarding whether Freddie Mac was manipulating its earnings or, worse, attempting to disguise the amount of its credit or other risk.

The Freddie Mac scandal had severe repercussions for Fannie Mae. It generated uncertainty in the capital markets, which led to higher interest rates and an inability on the part of Fannie to do more for its consumers. Raines remarked, "I jokingly said to friends that I now know what the definition of collateral damage is" (*Fair Disclosure Wire*, July 30, 2003). When asked in a press conference if Fannie Mae had used any accounting judgment that either its employees or its auditors considered debatable, Raines responded, "The answer to that is clearly, no. We have not. If we had, I would have violated the law in certifying our financial results. If we had, our auditors would be obligated to publicly do something about that. So I do not think that there is any question on that, of our taking any steps to subvert accounting" (*Fair Disclosure Wire*, July 30, 2003).

Raines responded to the calls for increased scrutiny with the adeptness of a politician campaigning for reelection. He supported plans for stronger regulation of Fannie Mae and other government-sponsored entities while warning of the repercussions of reining in the company's charter. Said Raines in a 2003 speech at George Washington University, "In pursuing positive reform, we believe—and I think most policymakers believe—that Congress needs to be extraordinarily careful to avoid changes that would undermine our mission and stifle the flow of low-cost mortgage capital and mortgage innovations" (*CBS MarketWatch.com*, December 17, 2003).

A SAVVY POLITICAL OPERATIVE

Raines had long used his impressive political connections to defend attacks on Fannie Mae. When Representative Christopher Shays (R-Connecticut) presented legislation to force Fannie Mae to begin registering with the SEC, he came face-to-face with Raines's political power.

Immediately each member of the U.S. House of Representatives was mailed a letter saying that more than two dozen groups, including the National Association of Realtors and the National Council of La Raza, which represented Hispanic Americans, would fight the bill based on the negative effects it would have on consumers. Shays recalled, "I felt like I kicked a hornet's nest" (*BusinessWeek*, December 9, 2002). Fannie Mae ultimately relented and became an SEC registrant.

The extent of confidence in Raines was illustrated in the tepid reaction from government officials in response to Fannie Mae's October 2003 announcement that it had to correct quarterly financial results. An incorrect application of accounting standards led to an adjustment of some figures by more than $1 billion. The day after the announcement, Paul S. Sarbanes of Maryland, a top Democrat on the Senate Banking Committee, brushed off the news as a nonevent. Said Sarbanes, "It didn't affect their financial strength. That's an important consideration" (*Congressional Quarterly Weekly*, April 16, 2004). But others saw such a reaction as further evidence of a problem. Said Representative Richard H. Baker (R-Louisiana), a longtime Raines nemesis, "If this were any other publicly traded corporation of any stature, those statements would be of such enormous consequences in the market that you might have to suspend trading. It has not yet had that kind of effect. . . . So there isn't any market discipline here, and that's what makes them unique" (*Congressional Quarterly Weekly*, April 16, 2004).

UNCLEAR FUTURE

In 2004 the Bush administration, some members of Congress, and several competitors in the housing market continued to raise questions about whether Fannie Mae's size and growth posed a risk to the nation's economy and whether the company and its smaller rival, Freddie Mac, required more oversight.

That year Senator Richard C. Shelby (R-Alabama), chairman of the Banking Committee, introduced a bill proposing a new regulator with significant power to police both Fannie Mae and Freddie Mac. In a particularly controversial aspect of the bill, the new regulator had the power to appoint a receiver to sell assets and pay off creditors in the event that either company faced a financial disaster. The provision challenged the long-standing belief that the government would bail out the company in the case of such an event. In April 2004 the Banking Committee approved the bill, but its long-term prospects seemed dubious. Said Shelby, "I don't see the bill moving. We're up against a powerful lobby" (*Congressional Quarterly Weekly*, April 16, 2004).

Also in 2004 the Office of Federal Housing Enterprise Oversight, an agency in the Department of Housing and Urban Development created in 1992 to regulate Fannie and Freddie, began an investigation into Fannie Mae's accounting to determine potential improprieties in earnings management. Said John Barnett, an analyst at the Center for Financial Research and Analysis in Rockville, Maryland, who had studied Fannie Mae's financial statements, "My main concern is that they're not as well capitalized as the minimum or risk-based capital standards would require them to be" (*Congressional Quarterly Weekly*, April 16, 2004).

BACK TO THE WHITE HOUSE?

Company officials credited Raines with initiatives to make the company's financial transactions more transparent and said that the accounting scandal at Freddie had nothing to do with Raines. But the increased government scrutiny combined with Fannie Mae's lackluster stock performance—between 1998 and 2003 the stock remained flat—spelled potential trouble for Raines.

Raines could find an escape hatch in politics. Some expected he would return to his past as a government official. In a fall 2003 interview with one industry publication, Raines said his career in government service was over. But not everyone was convinced. Said one mortgage executive, who asked to remain anonymous, "Anyone who says that Frank is done with politics is misguided. He has made all the money he will ever need. He is a sincere public servant" (*National Mortgage News*, May 3, 2004).

See also entry on Fannie Mae in *International Directory of Company Histories.*

SOURCES FOR FURTHER INFORMATION

Boland, Vincent, "Why Americans Feel at Home with Fannie Mae," *Financial Times* (London, England), October 29, 2002.

Cohn, Laura, "Protecting Fannie's Franchise," *BusinessWeek*, December 9, 2002, p. 94.

"A Conversation with Franklin D. Raines, Chairman and Chief Executive Officer, Fannie Mae," *Fair Disclosure Wire*, July 30, 2003.

Harris, Hamil R., "Franklin Reigns: Franklin Raines Returns to Fannie Mae as the First Black CEO of a Fortune 500 Corporation," *Black Enterprise*, August 31, 1998, p. 103.

Hughes, Siobhan, "Fannie and Freddie: Too Big to Fail, Too Big to Regulate," *Congressional Quarterly Weekly*, April 16, 2004.

Muolo, Paul, "Analysis: Stock Price a Blemish," *National Mortgage News*, May 3, 2004, p. 1.

Rosenberg, Hilary, "Fannie Mae CEO Poised For Fresh Onslaught," *American Banker*, January 31, 2001, p. 1.

Watts, William L., "Raines Defends Fannie Mae's Charter," *CBS MarketWatch.com*, December 17, 2003.

—Tim Halpern

M. S. Ramachandran

ca. 1944–

Chairman, Indian Oil Corporation

Nationality: Indian.

Born: ca. 1944, in India.

Education: College of Engineering, Guindy (India).

Family: Married Vasundhara (maiden name unknown); children: two.

Career: Indian Oil Corporation, 1969–?, management trainee; 2001–2002, director of planning and business development; 2002–, chairman; government of India, Ministry of Petroleum & Natural Gas, executive director of Oil Coordination Committee; IBP Company and Chennai Petroleum Corporation, chairman; Indian Oiltanking, head.

Address: Indian Oil Corporation, Core–2, SCOPE Complex, 7, Institutional Area, Lodhi Road, New Delhi 110003; http://www.iocl.com.

■ During his stint as head of India's only Fortune 500 company, M. S. Ramachandran managed one of the world's largest petroleum development industries. The India Oil Corporation (IOC) moved up quickly in the Fortune 500 rankings during his tenure. The 17th-largest oil company in the world during Ramachandran's time in office, India Oil met half of all the nation's petroleum requirements, ranked first in oil commodities trading in the Asia-Pacific region, and also ranked 325th in *Forbes* magazine's Global 500 listing and 191st in the Fortune 500 listing. Ramachandran also helped to launch the company's transformation from a government-held public utility to a private-sector, publicly traded corporation after India had completed the deregulation of its petroleum industry in 2002. Under Ramachandran's watch India Oil won many awards for its management and its business acumen, being ranked India's number one company in the business magazines *Businessworld* and *Business India*. Ramachandran's leadership and devotion to nurturing talented management and a healthy corporate culture led *Business Today* to list IOC among India's top 10 employers for 2003.

One change that Ramachandran introduced to IOC was, in the words of Shyamal Majumdar, a contributor to the *Business Standard* (February 16, 2004), to "make the entire organisation take marketing as a religion." Ramachandran articulated his theory of management in his convocation address to the Nirma Institute of Management in March 2003. He encapsulated the basics of management in what he termed "the five mantras of success." These mantras included a clear vision of the future, a sense of social responsibility and the need to return value to society, the need for continual education, the abandonment of cynicism and apathy, and the belief in one person's ability to make a difference in both government and society. Ramachandran also based these management mantras on Indian ideas and concepts rather than on Western ones. "Ancient wisdom," he told the graduates at the Nirma Institute of Management, "teaches us to believe in ourselves. . . . The fundamental truth is 'Ahm Brahma Asmi,' which means, I am the Brahman—the supreme power."

EARLY CAREER

Ramachandran began his career on the fast track to management success. He received his degree in mechanical engineering from the College of Engineering, Guindy, in Chennai. Soon after graduation he was recruited to become part of a management trainee program at the India Oil Corporation. The trainees were placed on fast tracks to advancement; for instance, explained Shyamal Majumdar in the *Business Standard* (New Delhi), all seven members of the original trainee group were promoted within two years—a process that, in the hierarchical world that was Indian management at the time, normally took 10 years. Although the program was later axed, over half the members of the first group went on to hold significant positions in the country's major publicly traded firms.

During the first Gulf War (1990–1991), Ramachandran won praise from the IOC board for the steps he put in place to protect India's oil and gas industry from the threat of attack. He left the IOC briefly to become executive director of the Oil Coordination Committee of India's Ministry of Petroleum and Natural Gas. The position gave the budding young manager both prestige and power. Ramachandran helped oversee the deregulation of India's petroleum and natural gas industry in the years during which he occupied the government office. In 2001, partly as recognition of his accomplishments, he was named a member of IOC's board and director of planning and business development. The following year he was made chairman of the company. He announced his intention to retire from the chairmanship in 2005.

NEW IDEAS AT IOC

The transformation that Ramachandran made in the company he headed was significant. The India Oil Corporation was a political creature from its creation in 1964 through the merger of S. Nijalingappa's Indian Oil Company Ltd. and Firoz Gandhi's Indian Refineries. Nijalingappa was a significant member of India's governing congress. In 1965 Dr. Radhakrishnan, then president of India, opened the corporation's first oil refinery. Eight years later Prime Minister Indira Gandhi broke ground for the corporation's new Mathura refinery. In 1976 the oil industry in India was nationalized and brought under the control of the federal government. The IOC would remain under the guidance of political figures for about two decades.

In fact, Ramachandran's stint as executive director of the Oil Coordination Committee was a stepping stone to his appointment to the IOC board. Majumdar declared in the *Business Standard* (New Delhi) that during the 1990s Ramachandran had been approached by Prabir Sengupta, then serving as petroleum secretary for the Indian government, about a possible position with the governmental committee. The executive director's position was of huge importance at the time because of the deregulation and dismantling of government oversight that was scheduled for the petroleum industry's companies. Although the executive director's job was a "hot seat," as Ramachandran told Majumdar in the *Business Standard* (February 16, 2004), if it was well handled, it could become an opportunity for further advancement. Indeed, shortly after leaving government service, Ramachandran was named to the IOC board, and in 2002 he became the corporation's chairman.

Although Ramachandran introduced many important changes to the IOC's corporate culture, he maintained aspects of work life that had been important characteristics of the corporation since its founding. Some of them dated back as far as 1966, when the corporation signed an agreement with its employees to ensure stable relations between them. In 1971, as a result of a war with Pakistan, the corporation extended dealership privileges to women who had been widowed in the war and to disabled veterans. In particular, Ramachandran maintained policies that rewarded employee loyalty and retarded attrition and employee turnover. When the new chairman arrived in 2002, IOC already had planned "retention strategies" in place to encourage talented and experienced employees to stay with the company. These strategies included distributing shares to employees, offering bonuses linked to performance, and creating fast-track positions for its most talented executives. Housing, transportation, and welfare-related

programs—including medical care following retirement—were also part of the corporation's package. The IOC even had in place a plan to help defer expenses for an employee's funeral. Under Ramachandran the corporation expanded its employee rewards program to acknowledge exceptional group and individual performances.

EXPANSION

Ramachandran also oversaw the expansion of IOC's business interests into areas as geographically distinct as Sri Lanka, Thailand, Iraq, Abu Dhabi, Tanzania, Ethiopia, Algeria, Kuwait, Mauritius, and Iran. The corporation served as a distributor for petroleum products in Sri Lanka and invested in oil exploration in Middle Eastern oil fields in Kuwait and Iran. There were also suggestions that IOC might also be employed as a consultant and in pipeline maintenance and repair in rebuilding the Iraqi infrastructure following Iraq's war with the United States in 2003. Most of IOC's supplies of petroleum come from domestic sources—in *Business India* Ramachandran declared that in 2003 the corporation was pursuing development of about 14 different potential sites, all of them either in India or just offshore—but markets for the products it made from petroleum expanded rapidly overseas, ranging from Sri Lanka to West Africa.

India Oil Corporation's major customer, however, remained the people of India. In 2004 IOC owned about 42 percent of the nation's entire refining capacity, owned 67 percent of pipeline throughput capacity, and supplied over 50 percent of all petroleum products sold in India. Its SERVO brand lubricant accounted for more than 42 percent of the market in India alone, but it was also sold in many other markets, including Sri Lanka, Indonesia, Kyrgyzstan, Bhutan, and Bahrain. In a nod toward traditional Indian retailing methods, India Oil incorporated a process by means of which SERVO lubricants could be sold through bazaars and thereby be placed in the hands of millions who could not get them through retail outlets. It was that kind of function, said Ramachandran in an address to employees on IndianOil day in 2003, placing affordable petroleum and energy products into the hands of common people in India, that defined the corporation's future. "The trust that our customers have bestowed on us," he explained, "will be our biggest accolade."

See also entry on Indian Oil Corporation Ltd. in *International Directory of Company Histories.*

SOURCES FOR FURTHER INFORMATION

"Convocation Address of Mr. M. S. Ramachandran—
   Chairman, Indian Oil, at the Nirma Institute of
   Management, Ahmedabad, India on March 24, 2003,"

www.iocl.com/downloads/Chairman_
Speech_%20Nirma_IM_Mar23%20.doc.

Hille, Alfred, "Indian Oil Taps Burnett, Starcom for
Rebranding," *Media* (Hong Kong), July 25, 2003, p. 3.

"Indian Oil Corporation Limited," *Indian Oil*, http://
www.iocl.com/ourcompany_profile.asp.

"Indian Oil—Reinventing the Future," *Business Today*,
September 14, 2003.

"IOC Chairman's Message On IndianOil Day," *Indian Oil*,
September 1, 2003, http://www.iocl.com/
displayit.asp?pathit=/releases/rel71.txt.

Majumdar, Shyamal, "An Escalator to 'Eighth Heaven,'"
Business Standard (New Delhi), February 16, 2004.

"Making the Elephant Dance," *Business Standard* (New Delhi),
May 1, 2004.

"Our Company: Corporate History," *Indian Oil*, http://
www.iocl.com/ourcompany_cohistory.asp.

"Our Company: Overview," http://www.iocl.com/
ourcompany_overview.asp.

Seli, Yeshi, "A Result of Focused Initiatives," *Business India*
(New Delhi), June 13, 2003.

Tan, Clara, "IOC Aims to Start C2 Work in Apr '04," *Asian
Chemical News*, October 13–19, 2003, p. 24.

"Time to Shine in Oil Industry," *Hindu* (Chennai), January
15, 2004.

—Kenneth R. Shepherd

■■■
Dieter Rampl
1947–
Managing director and chief executive officer, Bayerische Hypo- und Vereinsbank (HVB Group)

Nationality: German.

Born: September 5, 1947, in Munich, Germany.

Career: Societe de Banque Suisse, 1969–1970, collections and foreign-trade finance, Geneva; Bayerische Vereinsbank, 1971–1973, foreign trade and commodity finance, Munich; 1974–1980, senior lending officer, North America Corporation and Credit Department, New York; 1981–1982, senior lending officer, Nordrhein-Wesfalia, Düsseldorf; BHF-Bank, 1983–1984, head of U.S. corporations in Europe and corporations in Belgium and Holland; 1984–1987, senior vice president and manager, New York branch; 1988–1992, general manager, export and trade finance, Frankfurt; 1993–1995, general manager, Corporation Finance, Frankfurt, and member of the board of managing directors; Bayerische Vereinsbank, 1995–1998, member of the board of managing directors; Bayerische Hypo- und Vereinsbank (HVB Group), 1998–2002, member of the board of managing directors; 2003–, managing director and chief executive officer.

Address: HVB Group, Am Tucherpark 16, 80538 Munich, Germany; http://www.hvbgroup.com.

■ Dieter Rampl took over what most banking-industry analysts considered one of the toughest jobs in Europe when he became managing director and CEO in January 2003 of one of Germany's largest banks, Bayerische Hypo- und Vereinsbank, also known as HVB Group. The floundering bank's troubles were amplified by a poor German economy as Rampl set out to win back investors' trust and put the bank back on track. Analysts noted that Rampl firmly established control over the company's many subsidiaries and was able to keep his equanimity throughout the worst financial times in the bank's history.

Dieter Rampl. *AP/Wide World Photos.*

TAKING OVER A TROUBLED BANK

Rampl began his banking career in 1969 at Societe de Banque Suisse in Geneva, working in collections and foreign-trade finance. He joined Vereinsbank in 1971, working in foreign trade and commodity finance in Munich, Germany, before going to New York to work in the bank's North America Corporation and Credit Department subsidiary. After spending seven years in the United States, Rampl was assigned to Düsseldorf as senior lending officer. In 1983 he left Vereinsbank and joined BHF-Bank as head of U.S. corporations in Europe and corporations in Belgium and Holland. He spent the next dozen years at BHF-Bank, where he was appointed to the board of managing directors in 1993. Rampl returned to Vereinsbank in 1995 as a member of the board of managing directors. Through mergers, Vereinsbank became Bayerische Hypo- und Vereinsbank (HVB Group) in 1998, and Rampl continued as a member of the board of managing directors.

Rampl gained a good reputation for his ability to restructure divisions, and HVB soon turned to him for help. By the end of 2002 the company found itself in dire straits, primarily due to the bad debts of German companies that had gone into bankruptcy. In the third quarter of 2002 alone, the company had to make bad-debt provisions of $1.25 billion, which represented more than double its operating profit of $545 million. Overall, analysts were predicting that HVB's loan losses would reach $3.4 billion. Furthermore, Standard & Poor's placed HVB on a "credit watch." The company tapped Rampl to turn HVB around, appointing him managing director and the new CEO beginning in 2003. A managing board member of a rival bank told David Fairlamb of *Business Week*, "I don't think I could sleep if I had [Rampl's] problems. The loan book alone would give me nightmares" (January 20, 2003).

FIGHTS ROUGH SEAS

In fact, Rampl took over the reins five months earlier than expected. His predecessor, Albrecht Schmidt, had originally intended to resign following the next year's annual general meeting, but stepped down earlier with the worsening economic news. Rampl took charge of Germany's second-biggest bank, with more than $730 billion in assets and 8.5 million retail customers. He said he was determined to put HVB back on track and regain the trust of investors. It would not be easy as the bank was hit hard by the poor condition of the German economy. A little more than a month after Rampl took over, the bank announced that it had a net loss before taxes in 2002 of more than EUR 800 million, a far bigger loss than expected. A year earlier HVB had made a profit of EUR 1.5 billion. In an interview with *BBC News* Rampl admitted that the year had been "the most difficult and worst in the bank's history" (February 19, 2003).

Rampl and HVB were not alone, however, as other German banks struggled and investors expressed nervousness over their solvency. Rampl confirmed to the *Evening Standard* of London that HVB had even gone so far as to meet with German Chancellor Gerhard Schroeder to discuss creating a "bad loans bank" to help clean up their balance sheets (February 26, 2003). Nevertheless, Rampl remained optimistic that he could turn around the bank's fortunes, noting that he believed the worst was over. He pointed out that the bank was on track in its "Transformation 2003" program to reduce administrative costs and ultimately improve earnings. The restructuring effort also included plans to sell some of the bank's assets and spin off its entire commercial real-estate business.

According to Rampl, the real-estate move was crucial to HVB's effort to break after a damaging pretax loss of more than EUR 800 million in 2002. Analysts noted that bad loans made by HVB Real Estate Bank caused huge losses in recent years. The decision to spin off the real-estate activities had

been a difficult one for Rampl, who noted that the move greatly diminished the bank's size to the point of threatening its second-place ranking in Germany. Rampl told the *Banker*: "Yes, I agree that it marks a shift from our previous expansionist strategy, but what are we supposed to do after a 821 [million euro] loss?" (May 1, 2003).

TURNS A PROFIT

Analysts were shocked when Rampl maneuvered the bank into turning a quarterly profit of EUR 107 million by November 2003. To shore up core capital, Rampl had sold much of the bank's assets. As reported by *Retail Banker International*, analysts noted that HVB needed "to sell some of the 'family silver' not only because of Rampl's strategic overhaul, but also to replenish the bank's capital reserves" (January 14, 2003).

Yet analysts remained concerned because HVB's domestic unit in Germany accounted for two-thirds of its earnings and was floundering. They noted that the most difficult task, showing that he could make money in its main operating business, still needed to be done. Investment banker Ralph Lau was quoted in *Troubled Company Reporter Europe* as saying, "Rampl needs to turn around the German business and improve its profitability" (October 29, 2003).

Some analysts approved Rampl's early restructuring efforts despite the fact that the company had ended 2002 with a core-capital ratio, which is an important measure of financial stability, of 5.6 percent, somewhat below the 6 percent usually seen as obligatory within the banking community. Bundesbank board member Edgar Meister told *BBC News*, "From the Bundesbank's point of view, HVB has taken appropriate steps to strengthen its business a while ago and is on the right track in my opinion" (February 27, 2003).

Some analysts suggested that the company should seek a merger. When Rampl received the backing of HVB's board to raise at least EUR 3 billion of fresh capital to clean the German bank's balance sheet, many saw this as paving the way for a possible merger with its competitor Commerzbank. However, Rampl quickly put a stop to such speculation and told Vita Bekker of *Bloomberg.com*, "At the moment, the right thing for us to do is to rely on our own strengths and focus on profit growth" (May 27, 2004). Nevertheless, Rampl did not rule out the possibility of a merger at a later date.

MANAGEMENT STYLE: MR. COOL

Analysts generally described Rampl as cool, calm, and confident. For example, a Munich-based money manager commented on Rampl's general joie de vivre even in troubled times by noting that "Dieter would still have been smiling if the HVB ship had sunk with all hands" (*Euroweek*, May 7, 2004).

Reports such as these along with Rampl's style earned him *Euroweek*'s tongue-in-cheek "Most Optimistic Banker of 2003" award (November 7, 2003). Despite his seemingly laid-back approach, analysts praised Rampl for his focus on the bottom line. In one article he was described as one of "a new breed of managers who understand—and not before time—that shareholder value requires 100 percent commitment to performance targets" (*European Banker*, February 2004).

Rampl's easy-going nature was complemented by the skills and personality needed to oversee far-reaching changes in the company, noted Fairlamb in *BusinessWeek*. For example, prior to Rampl taking over, HVB had taken a decentralized approach, with the management of regional banks retaining a great deal of autonomy. Rampl changed that. One market analyst said, "The managerial shift could be compared to a parent who finally realizes the children are all off doing their own thing and not always with the optimum results." Analysts also noted that Rampl was not a micromanager. "His goal is to make sure his lieutenants are on the same page as he is. His aim is to squeeze maximum performance forged by closer ties with Munich, and that is a smart management move" (*European Banker*, February 2004).

See also entry on Bayerische Hypo- und Vereinsbank AG (HVB Group) in *International Directory of Company Histories*.

SOURCES FOR FURTHER INFORMATION

"And More HVB Subsidiaries For Sale," *Retail Banker International*, January 14, 2003, p. 3.

"Cash-Call Fears Hit HVB Shares," *BBC News*, February 27, 2003, http://news.bbc.co.uk/1/hi/business/2805405.stm.

"Down for the Count," *BusinessWeek*, January 20, 2003, p. 42.

"Global News: Spin-off Of HVB Real Estate," *Banker*, May 1, 2003.

"Historic Loss for German Bank Giant," *BBC News*, February 19, 2003, http://news.bbc.co.uk/1/hi/business/2779375.stm.

"HVB GROUP: Analysts Peg Q3 Profit Within EUR100 Million Range," *Troubled Company Reporter Europe*, October 29, 2003, http://bankrupt.com/TCREUR_Public/031029.mbx.

"HVB Left in the Ditch as Commerz Flashes Past," *Euroweek*, May 7, 2004, p. 20.

"HVB Profits: Tell the Pike To Go Take a Hike," *Euroweek*, November 7, 2003, p. 16.

"HVB's Rampl Says Merger Not Priority as Bank Focuses on Profits," *Bloomberg.com*, May 27, 2004, http://quote.bloomberg.com/apps/news?pid=10000100&refer=germany&sid=ab3S_0x4yEM8.

"In Brief: German Banks in State Bailout Talks," *Evening Standard* (London), February 26, 2003.

Skelly, Jessica, "Leading From the Centre at HVB," *European Banker*, February 2003, p. 3.

—David Petechuk

■ ■ ■
Lee R. Raymond
1938–
Chief executive officer, Exxon Mobil Corporation

Nationality: American.

Born: August 13, 1938, in Watertown, South Dakota.

Education: University of Wisconsin, BS, 1960; University of Minnesota, PhD, 1963.

Family: Son of a railroad engineer; married Charlene (maiden name unknown); children: three.

Career: Exxon Corporation, 1963–1972, various engineering positions; 1972–1984, management positions; 1984–1987, senior vice president and director; 1987–1993, president; 1993–1999, chairman of the board and chief executive officer; Exxon Mobil Corporation, 1999–, chairman of the board and chief executive officer.

Address: Exxon Mobil Corporation, 5959 Las Clinas Boulevard, Irving, Texas 75039-2298; http://www.exxonmobil.com.

■ Lee R. Raymond headed one of the most powerful corporations in the world, Exxon Mobil Corporation. He began his career after receiving a PhD in chemical engineering from the University of Minnesota. The son of a railroad engineer from Watertown, South Dakota, Raymond kept his personal life out of the limelight while steering one of the world's largest corporations. Raymond set his course with Exxon early on with innovative moves that cut costs and increased profits, the hallmark of his entire career. With a changing view on petroleum-based products, Raymond defended Exxon against environmentalists and human rights activists while denying the viability of renewable energy sources. He continued to pursue natural gas projects and grew Exxon in other parts of the world, despite war and threats of war in oil-rich countries in the early years of the 21st century. As a result, Exxon continued to grow even though the protests grew louder.

RELUCTANT PUBLIC FIGURE REVEALS LITTLE

Raymond prided himself on the lack of information in the media about his personal life. He was born in Watertown, South Dakota, in 1938 in the Great Plains area of the United States. Watertown sits on the shores of Lake Kempeska, and by 2004 its population had grown to 20,000. Most accounts note that Raymond's father was a railroad engineer, but little is known of Raymond's early years in South Dakota. He began his college career at the University of Wisconsin in Madison, some 400 miles east of Watertown. He completed his education with a PhD from the University of Minnesota in 1963. Both of his degrees were in chemical engineering. Even though Raymond did not venture very far from the Midwest during his early years, his career began in the oil industry in Texas when he was hired by the Exxon Corporation, which is the successor company to John D. Rockefeller's Standard Oil.

EXXON'S RISING STAR

Exxon hired Raymond in 1963 and put him to work as a production research engineer in Tulsa, Oklahoma. For the next 14 years, he received promotions as an engineer, eventually ending up on the island of Aruba in the Caribbean. It was in that tropical paradise that he set the course for his career in the oil company by turning around profits at the refinery on the island. At the time of his appointment, the refinery was losing $10 million a month. By cutting costs and convincing Venezuela to provide extra-heavy crude oil, he had turned the losses into a profit of $25 million per month by 1979.

Executives at Exxon took notice of the major turnaround and named Raymond vice president of Exxon Enterprises in 1981. Raymond said that he received no directives on how to proceed with this diversified company that produced items from solar energy products to a computer chipmaker. After studying the company, Raymond decided to shut down some operations, a move approved by the leadership at Exxon. The company eventually shut down or sold all of the Enterprise businesses in existence. This move garnered Raymond the top slot in Esso Inter-America, a job used to groom future executives for Exxon.

Raymond continued to impress his superiors with his cost-cutting measures, especially after such failures as Enterprise, Reliance Electric, and a shale oil program. As the 1980s began,

Raymond's style fit right in with Exxon's new direction on profit enhancement rather than on growth.

APPOINTED CEO

During the first four years after his appointment as CEO, Raymond increased profits on operations from the company's oil fields, refineries, and convenience stores. He solidly built up the return on capital, which determined for Exxon the measure of profitability. By 1996 Raymond had brought up the return to 14.7 percent, a feat that, according to analysts, other companies had been attempting to achieve for years. However, some analysts believed that Raymond's record was not all that impressive. Some contended that Exxon was ready for a monopoly breakup, but Raymond insisted that such a move would make little sense. The analysts cited the decline in the production of crude oil during the 1990s.

Raymond responded to those critics by buying back stock rather than by starting new oil fields. Without the distraction of exploring for oil fields, Raymond spent nearly five years getting the most out of a barrel of oil. Pinching pennies with the processes of oil production, transportation, and marketing had paid off by 1997, when it was shown that operating costs had been reduced by $1.3 billion annually.

The analyst William Randol told *Fortune* in 1997, "Exxon has proven itself to be very, very stingy. They just don't piss away money the way other integrated companies do" (April 28, 1997).

GROWS COMPANY AGAIN

In 1997 Raymond made a decision to begin growing Exxon once again. When Exxon reported income of $7.5 billion in 1996, Raymond decided to change course after spending his first few years as CEO concentrating on the cost-cutting methods on which his reputation within the company had been founded.

Raymond began by pursuing a new patent that would convert natural gas into a diesel-like fuel or heating oil. He hoped this new method would boost revenues because a barrel of this new fuel could be produced for $20 in 1997, the cost of a regular barrel of oil. The process itself involved simply adding steam, oxygen, and catalysts to natural gas. Even though Exxon owned large gas fields, transporting the gas had been cost prohibitive. With the conversion of natural gas into a liquid form, transportation became less costly and required less extensive plants to process the new fuel. Cooling the natural gas to minus 260 degrees Fahrenheit converts the gas to its liquid form, which takes up much less space. Industry insiders called this new invention a revolution in the oil industry.

Opportunities began arising in Russia, Indonesia, and Africa to develop gargantuan fields at low costs. These countries

had begun settling down politically by the late 1990s, and Raymond took advantage of analysts' predictions that Asia's demand for oil products would begin to expand. Raymond set a goal of increasing Exxon's crude oil output by 3 percent over the next 10 years.

MANAGEMENT STYLE

Noted for his reticence to talk to the press, Raymond kept his own counsel after his appointment as CEO. Industry insiders said that he had no hobbies, nor did he have any colleagues to whom he turned when he needed advice. Public relations officials with Exxon adamantly protected his privacy. In 1997 insiders noted that he was the only Exxon CEO ever to operate without a clear second in command. Some found his lack of an inner circle refreshing. His predecessor, Lawrence Raul, had an intimate inner circle, and many who worked for Exxon found it difficult to judge whom to court and whom leave alone. No such worries existed under the leadership of Raymond.

Raymond was the only Exxon CEO ever to have earned a PhD. Many found his extreme intelligence to be intimidating while others characterized him as arrogant. He was extremely well informed on anything related to Exxon.

BusinessWeek described Raymond's workplace in Irving, Texas, as being located in "a fortress-like building" with his office located at the end of a long row of anterooms (April 9, 2001). His desk was placed under the painting of a ferocious-looking tiger. This interior suite for management at the Exxon headquarters was referred to as "the God pod." A visitor reporting to *BusinessWeek* said that Raymond was always courteous but unmovable. "If he gives his word, which he is reluctant to do, he will keep it. But he is very difficult to deal with" (April 9, 2001).

Even though Exxon ruled as the oil giant, industry insiders described Raymond's management style as centralized. Raymond was noted for his penchant personally to have a hand in all sorts of deals within the company, becoming characterized as a micromanager.

MERGER SUCCESSFUL, BUT NOT FOR EMPLOYEES

When Exxon and Mobil announced a merger in 1998, regulators required the companies to sell some of their assets to allow competition within the oil industry. Bringing together the two major oil companies meant that the new Exxon Mobil Corporation increased its net earnings by $1.2 billion in the first year of the merger, with the potential of bringing a total of $2.5 billion in growth by 2003. When the merger was announced, it immediately became clear that Raymond would lead the combined corporation, giving the Mobil CEO a backseat in the top echelon of Exxon Mobil.

Before the merger was finished, Raymond had cut annual costs by $1.2 billion. After the merger, to increase profits Raymond reverted to his former cost-cutting methods, eliminating 2,000 executive positions out of the 3,000 in place between the two companies. Raymond also made sure that the requirements made by the Securities and Exchange Commission did not hurt the profit sheets either. The sales of such assets as service stations and a refinery brought $3 billion in cash to Exxon Mobil.

In addition to cutting executive positions and selling assets, Raymond began cutting employees throughout the company, bringing a total savings of $3.8 billion a year within four years of the merger. These huge savings came as a result of the elimination of 16,000 jobs. Despite the dire news for employees, Exxon Mobil stock rose to $84.25 on the day of the announcement of the job losses. Analysts applauded the savings and calculated that Raymond's estimates were low, predicting that the corporation would become a moneymaking machine.

When Raymond announced the job cuts, he noted that the entire blueprint for the elimination of 16,000 jobs had not been completed but said that 10,000 cuts would occur within two years, with 6,000 outside of the United States and the remaining 4,000 at U.S. facilities. Some of the job losses, approximately 6,000, came as a result of attrition, and those positions were not refilled. The rest of the employees were laid off, although they were offered a severance package that included four weeks' salary for every year worked at the company plus their highest bonus earned.

With cost-cutting measures in place, Raymond readied the company to become the biggest fish in the ocean, literally. Oil exploration in deep ocean waters beckoned Raymond despite the high costs associated with this type of experiment, especially in the uncharted waters off the coast of Africa and South America.

NEW CENTURY MARKS CRITICAL PERIOD

As the 21st century loomed, Raymond still remained steadfast in his defense of the fossil fuel business, stating at an industry conference in 2000 that Exxon would stay away from renewable sources of energy. He cited Exxon's history of concentrating on oil and said that oil would continue to be the corporation's focus.

The *Oil Daily* reported that Raymond was a "vehement campaigner on behalf of the fossil fuel lobby [and] has argued for years that limiting the greenhouse emissions from fossil fuels believed to cause global warning will have a devastating impact on world economic growth" (February 16, 2000).

Raymond made this announcement despite the entrance into the renewables business of such competitors as BP, Amoco, and Shell. Those companies predicted that renewables would provide half of the world's power within 50 years.

Raymond's adamant stance brought protests from the company's religious shareholders. In 2000 the Dominican Sisters of Caldwell, New Jersey, filed a resolution. According to the *Oil Daily*, the resolution stated that Exxon "has misinformed shareholders about global warming with inaccurate statements and unreliable information" (December 13, 2000).

Further, the group accused Raymond of making false statements based on unreliable sources. They based their findings on a report by Dr. Lloyd Keigwin, a scientist who had completed studies for Exxon on global warming, who said that Exxon had used his information in a misleading way.

Campaign Exxon Mobil, the group of religious shareholders in Exxon, cited Raymond's claim that he had a petition containing signatures of 17,000 scientists who believed that there was no consensus on global warning. Campaign Exxon Mobil argued that the signatures had been obtained from the Internet with no verification, stating that the names included those of TV sitcom characters, the Spice Girls, and the singer James Brown.

Raymond did not respond to the charges. Instead he announced that he would seek out methods to increase Exxon's efficiency while bringing larger returns to its stockholders, but he drew the line at outsourcing to other countries for research and development.

By 2001 Raymond's strategies had made Exxon Mobil one of the world's most powerful corporations. An industry insider told *BusinessWeek* that Exxon had only one way to do things: "the most efficient with the least risk. They want to see the studies. If the studies are yours, they want to redo them" (April 9, 2001).

As Exxon's power base grew, so did resentment over the company's arrogance, which caused analysts to turn skeptical when predicting the future of Exxon. While analysts respected Raymond's leadership, they did not have positive feelings about his methods. These skeptics pointed to Exxon's isolation within the industry as causing its own set of problems. Most of the other large corporations banded together to cut the cost of exploration and development, but Exxon went its own way.

RETIREMENT POSTPONED

When Raymond turned 63 in 2001, Exxon announced that he would stay beyond his official retirement in 2003, when he would turn 65. The company said that it needed time to groom a successor to the CEO. Analysts suggested that the announcement signaled the company's intention to choose a younger CEO rather than someone within the ranks just behind Raymond.

The decision may have been based on some of the difficult situations that loomed in the future for the company as Exxon was awarded gas development projects in Saudi Arabia.

In addition, in 2002 Raymond announced a host of projects in the works regarding natural gas, including the production and exploration of major gas sources in Bolivia, Indonesia, Australia, and Russia. Raymond also assured analysts that Exxon would still be able to produce the 3 percent annual average increase in oil and gas production despite the interference of the Organization of Petroleum Exporting Countries in initiating restraints on production as well as the war and unrest within the countries from which Exxon obtained most of its products.

Raymond continued to push his company on researching the technology that would turn natural gas into a diesel form of fuel. He also said that the company was concentrating on its North American sources through new drilling and seismic technologies.

By 2002 the gains from the merger of Exxon and Mobil showed that early predictions had underestimated the potential growth. The projection of a $4 billion gain in efficiency production by 2002 turned out to be low. Within the first quarter of 2002, the figure was upped to $7 billion, with another $1 billion added in 2003. Raymond said his predictions had proven that he knew how to produce profits despite changes in the economy.

DEFENDING ENVIRONMENTAL AND HUMAN RIGHTS RECORD

Raymond often defended the environmental and human rights record of Exxon against protesters who said that the oil giant did not use accurate research or treat all of its employees across the globe fairly.

Despite his acknowledgment at a 2002 shareholder meeting that there might be a high risk of climate change due to the use of fossil fuels, Raymond still maintained that huge differences of opinion remained among the different researchers in climate science. He asked for further research but also insisted that an initiative in emissions reductions with car manufacturers was still needed.

During this June 2002 meeting, shareholders were asked to vote on two proposals, both opposed by Raymond. One concerned more development of renewable energy sources. The other involved a ban on discrimination against homosexuals.

Amnesty International and Greenpeace both hosted protest rallies in Dallas the day before the meeting, and their representatives also attended the meeting. While advisers on the voting suggested that shareholders support the renewable energy proposal, the motion was rejected by an 80 percent vote.

Raymond continued his campaign to discredit the viability of renewable energy sources. Weekly Petroleum Argus reported that Raymond said "Even 'green' energy has an impact on the environment, noting that large-scale solar and wind farms take up land and can affect wildlife" (June 3, 2002).

To appease the protesters, Raymond did concede that Exxon would report greenhouse gas emissions while cutting the emissions at facilities in an attempt to reduce energy consumption by 15 percent over a several-year period. In addition, Raymond continued to stress Exxon's dedication to work with automobile manufacturers on reducing vehicle emissions. He announced that new methods might include advancement in the internal combustion engine and more dependence on fuel cells.

Raymond told shareholders that the company was committed to work with the new technologies in an effort to remain competitive within the oil industry. He stressed that these new technologies would reduce not only costs but also the impact on the environment. His commitment to this goal was reflected in the $500 million spent by Exxon by 2002 on renewable energy sources research.

In 2003 Raymond maintained that he would remain patient as the project to convert natural gas continued its slow progress to completion. Also the expansion into Russia entered into negotiations in 2003. Analysts speculated that an agreement with Russia remained Raymond's goal before he entered into a discussion about his retirement. Raymond told Petroleum Intelligence Weekly, "I totally recognize I can't shed my Exxon background, and whatever I do reflects on the company, so that's why I'm a lifer. And I'm pleased to be a lifer" (November 10, 2003).

SOURCES FOR FURTHER INFORMATION

"Exxon Turns Its Back on Renewable Energy to Focus on Strengths in Traditional Areas," Oil Daily, February 16, 2000.

"Exxon Unleashed," BusinessWeek, April 9, 2001, pp. 58–66.

"ExxonMobil Goes on the Offensive," Weekly Petroleum Argus, June 3, 2002, p. 3.

"Exxon's Raymond Cites Virtue of Patience," Petroleum Intelligence Weekly, November 10, 2003, pp. 1–2.

Maxon, Terry, "Exxon Mobil Expects to Cut about 16,000 Jobs," Knight Ridder–Tribune Business News, December 15, 1999.

"Shareholders Press Exxon CEO," Oil Daily, December 13, 2000.

Teitelbaum, Richard, "Exxon: Pumping up Profits," Fortune, April 28, 1997, pp. 134–140.

—Patricia C. Behnke

Steven A. Raymund

1955–

Chairman and chief executive officer, Tech Data Corporation

Nationality: American.

Born: November 16, 1955, in Van Nuys, California.

Education: University of Oregon, BS, 1978; Georgetown University School of Foreign Service, MBA, 1980.

Family: Son of Edward Raymund, the founder of Tech Data Corporation, and Annette Leah, a philanthropist and volunteer for Gulf Coast Jewish Family Services; married Sonia (maiden name unknown); children: two.

Career: Manufacturers Hanover Corporation, 1980–1981, employee; Tech Data Corporation, 1981–1984, operations manager; 1984–1986, COO; 1986–, CEO; 1991–, chairman and CEO.

Awards: Entrepreneur of the Year, Arthur Young Entrepreneurial Services, 1988; 25 Most Influential Executives in the PC Industry, Computer Reseller News, 1989–2004; Industry Hall of Fame, *Computer Reseller News*, 1999.

Address: Tech Data Corporation, 5350 Tech Data Drive, Clearwater, Florida 33760-3122; http://www.tech data.com.

■ In 2004 Steven A. Raymund was the chairman of the board of directors and chief executive officer of the Clearwater, Florida–based Tech Data Corporation, one of the industry's leading providers of information technology (IT) products, logistics management, and other value-added services. When Raymund's father, Edward, founded the business in 1974, it was called a "pick, pack, and ship" operation. Raymund developed that small company from a 10-employee, $2-million-in-sales business to a 7,900-employee, integrated supply-chain specialist worth over $15.7 billion and depended on by technology manufacturers and sellers worldwide for outsourcing materials. During his two-decades-plus association with Tech Data, Raymund developed and expanded the company's contributions to such essential industry services as technical support, education, and custom configuration while at the same time expanding into international markets across the globe.

COMPUTER GADGET DEALER

Edward C. Raymund, Steven's father, founded Tech Data in 1974. Although its original purpose was to market data-processing supplies directly to end users of miniature and mainframe computers, the company expanded its markets in 1983, redirecting efforts toward serving microcomputer resellers as a wholesale distributor. Tech Data remained a small organization during its first decade of operations, employing about a dozen people who handled all customer orders from a small office and warehouse building in Clearwater, Florida. The elder Raymund credited his son Steven with expanding distribution well beyond its modest beginnings.

In 2004—thanks to the younger Raymund's drive, intelligence, and abilities—Tech Data was the world's second-largest distributor of computer-related products (behind Ingram Micro). Tech Data provided more than 75,000 different items to more than 100,000 resellers in about 70 countries in North America, the Caribbean, Latin America, Europe, and the Middle East. Its extensive catalog of products and services included computer components (such as keyboards, disk drives, and video cards), networking equipment (such as routers and bridges), peripherals (such as modems, printers, and monitors), software, pre- and post-sale training, technical support, configuration and assembly services, e-commerce solutions, and financing options. The company distributed products from about one thousand manufacturers. Tech Data added to its international operations in early 2003 with the acquisition of the United Kingdom's Azlan Group; sales were then evenly divided between Europe and the United States.

CLEANING UP BEFORE COLLEGE

Raymund was employed as a janitor at the Pasadena Elementary School in California while taking a year off between high school and college. He was able to finish his duties in half of the time needed and so was left with plenty of time to read and study. The janitorial job earned him enough money to travel to Europe and parts of the Middle East, which gave him an urge to do further international traveling. With regard to his professional life Raymund decided that picking up trash and cleaning up after children was not what he wanted to do; he decided to attend college to learn a better profession.

COLLEGE AND EARLY CAREER

Raymund completed his undergraduate work at the University of Oregon in Eugene in 1978, earning a bachelor's degree in economics. He went on to earn a master's degree in international politics in 1980 from Georgetown University's School of Foreign Service in Washington, D.C. After graduation Raymund found a job with the Manufacturers Hanover Corporation in the financial district of New York City. After a short time Raymund realized he was one of about two thousand employees who had master's degrees in business administration within the company. He did not think he would be able to develop his full potential in such an environment. He quit the Wall Street job and returned home to Florida—unemployed and with no career plans.

Raymund's father had started Tech Data a few years earlier and offered him the chance to develop a new retail catalog for the company's rapidly growing telemarketing department. Believing that he would accomplish this task in a couple of months and then look for another job elsewhere, Raymund took the offer. During his first few months at the new job Raymund also assisted in other areas of the company that needed help. At that time, somewhat suddenly, several members of upper management left for promising jobs at a local competitor—taking with them the majority of the business and product lines developed at Tech Data. Seeing the company's business cut to one-fourth of its previous month's revenues, the younger Raymund made a bold move. He convinced his father to begin selling products within the fledgling personal computer (PC) market that IBM and Apple had recently introduced. He also made a commitment to stay on at Tech Data.

JUST YOUR AVERAGE GUY

With 10 employees who were as committed to the struggling company as the owner and his son, the younger Raymund expanded the company with hands-on techniques. Those employees remembered Raymund as being "just your average guy" who was learning the business in the same fashion as they were doing. One of the important ingredients in Tech Data's early success was Raymund's ability to surround himself with smart people who could teach him the PC business. He was known as a good learner and teacher who was very curious about all sorts of things. Most importantly the employees did not construe his inquisitiveness as being intrusive. The comradeship formed during those early years continued into the 2000s.

RECOGNIZING TRENDS AND IMPROVING PROCESSES

Before orders were made electronically, Tech Data's sales associates placed completed order forms in baskets that would be periodically picked up by the distribution department. As an example of Raymund's curious nature he would go through the piles several times a day in order to recognize sale trends. This desire for knowledge helped Tech Data stay on top of the drastically changing computer industry as it grew during those infant years. Later, when the company was fully computerized, Raymund helped to pioneer the creation of "co-location"—that is, the procedure of shipping products to end users directly from a manufacturer's plant—a process that was eventually called integrated distribution.

TRUSTED PARTNERSHIPS FORMED

When Raymund became Tech Data's operations manager, his father went around the country in search of distribution contracts with vendors and further business with small resellers. Both men saw that rival distributors were aiming at large resellers and members of the emerging retail market; thus, in small resellers they found an important and often overlooked niche early in the development of the industry. During this period the senior Raymund instilled a sense of partnership with Tech Data's suppliers, a sense that was not ordinarily present when companies did business with suppliers. This sense of partnership would remain an important aspect of the younger Raymund's dealings with suppliers.

GOING PUBLIC

The younger Raymund directed the company to expand its sales of computer supplies, such as computer monitors, printers, add-on cards, and other accessories new to the burgeoning PC market. He quickly realized that dealing with computer supplies garnered great profits for the company. Tech Data grossed $2.1 million in sales in 1982; that number tripled to $6.3 million in just two years. A huge jump in gross sales in 1985 of $21 million was nothing compared to the continued climb of $38 million in 1986—the year Raymund took Tech Data public on the NASDAQ stock market.

EXPANSION WORLDWIDE

Raymund expertly molded successful operations at Tech Data by using a steady internal-growth model. After becoming convinced that the company had solid, consistent performance in the United States, Raymund ventured into the rest of the world.

Raymund expanded Tech Data operations into Canada in 1989 and founded an export division in Miami, Florida, in early 1993 to serve the computer market of South America. He entered the European market in 1994 through the acquisition of the Paris, France–based Softmart International, which was France's largest distributor of PC products. In 1997 Raymund opened a distribution center in São Paulo, Brazil—Tech Data's first center in South America. In 1998 Raymund acquired a majority interest in the Munich, Germany–based Computer 2000, Europe's foremost provider of IT products to resellers. The purchase gave Tech Data direction into the countries of the Middle East, through the company's office in the United Arab Emirates, and into the South American markets of Argentina, Chile, Peru, and Uruguay. In 1999 Raymund acquired Globelle Canada, doubling Tech Data's presence in the country and giving it an office in Israel through an existing subsidiary. That year Tech Data's revenue grew to $11.5 billion from the $7.1 billion of a year earlier. While much of this growth resulted from the German acquisition, U.S. sales also grew 17 percent in 1999.

EXPANSION INTO NEW MARKETS

While expanding Tech Data geographically through various acquisitions, Raymund also delved into new market segments. The company's original base was value-added resellers (VARs), corporate resellers, and franchisees. Raymund added to this base so that by 2004 Tech Data served more than 100,000 customers including application service providers, internet service providers, VARs, corporate resellers, systems integrators, system builders, government resellers, exporters, retailers, direct marketers, catalogers, and Web resellers. Raymund also developed many other specialized programs and business units to serve specialty niches.

THOUGHT HIGHLY OF

Even Tech Data's competitors thought highly of Raymund, as reported by Computer Reseller News. Jerre Stead, the chairman of the Santa Ana, California–based Ingram Micro, said of archrival Raymund, "Steve is a very good leader, a strategic thinker, and he does a great job making sure Tech Data is focusing on infrastructure." Raymund was also known in the vendor community as a person who helped to shape the industry. Dave Boucher, the general manager of the Armonk, New York–based Advanced Fulfillment Initiative (which was part of IBM Corporation), remarked, "One of the guys who is a thinker and who brings an awful lot of intellect to the whole industry is Steve Raymund. He looks beyond day-to-day and he has a lot of vision. He's steered Tech Data into the success it has realized."

THE THINKER

Raymund was described as a methodical executor in his business dealings with other companies. He was mild-mannered, reserved, and "cerebral"—a thinker who carefully selected the words he was about to say. Raymund was an excellent negotiator, as was his father, always looking for the "win-win" situation. A "laser-like" focus in all facets of his life and attention to detail were other well-known Raymund traits. Yet, he realized that facts and figures were not the only important concepts for a successful business. He also relied on intuition to play a critical role in building successful management teams.

SERVING WITH DISTINCTION

Raymund was a member of the board of directors for Jabil Circuit, the electronics manufacturing-services provider, where he served as chairman of the audit committee. He was inducted into the Computer Reseller News's Hall of Fame in 1999, two years after his father was inducted. Raymund was named one of the 25 Most Influential Executives in the PC Industry, as compiled by Computer Reseller News, each year from 1989 through 2004. Raymund was inducted into the Tampa Bay, Florida, Business Hall of Fame in 2000.

Raymund served on the boards of directors of several local organizations, including the Advisory Board for the Partnership for a Drug Free America, a private, nonprofit, nonpartisan coalition, and the Temple Beth-El, a synagogue serving the reformed Jewish community of Florida's Suncoast. Raymund served as chairman of the executive committee of the Global Technology Distribution Council, an IT industry-advocacy organization. He was a member of the All Children's Hospital board of trustees in Saint Petersburg, Florida. During his off-hours, Raymund liked to fly-fish for snook off his dock in Tampa Bay or for bonefish in the Bahamas, and he enjoyed skiing in the mountains of Colorado.

See also entry on Tech Data Corporation in *International Directory of Company Histories.*

SOURCE FOR FURTHER INFORMATION

Campbell, Scott, "Steve Raymund," *Computer Reseller News,* http://www.crn.com/sections/special/hof/ hof.asp?ArticlcID-11162.

—William Arthur Atkins

■■■
Sumner M. Redstone
1923–

Chairman and chief executive officer, Viacom International; chairman and chief executive officer, National Amusements

Nationality: American.

Born: May 27, 1923, in Boston, Massachusetts.

Education: Harvard University, BA, 1944; Harvard Law School, LLB, 1947.

Family: Son of Michael Rothstein, a salesman then owner of Northeast Theater Corporation, and Bella Ostrovksy; married Phyllis Raphael, a schoolteacher, 1947 (divorced); children: two.

Career: U.S. Court of Appeals, Ninth Circuit, 1947, law clerk; U.S. Justice Department, 1948–1950, special assistant to the Attorney General; Ford, Bergson, Adams, Borkland & Redstone, 1950–1954, partner; Northeast Theater Corporation, 1954–1967, executive; National Amusements, 1967–, president and CEO; Viacom International, 1987–1996, chairman and president; 1996–2003, chairman, president, and CEO; 2003–, chairman and CEO.

Awards: Commendation Medal, U.S. Army and Military Intelligence Division, 1945; 10 Outstanding Young Men in New England, Boston Chamber of Commerce, 1958; William J. German Human Relations Award, American Jewish Committee, 1977; Silver Shingle Award, Boston University Law School, 1985; Man of the Year, Entertainment Industries Division, United Jewish Appeal Federation, 1988; Graduate of the Year, Boston Latin School, 1989; New England Humanitarian Award, *Variety*, 1989; Communicator of the Year, B'nai B'rith Communications and Cinema Lodge, 1991; Pioneer of the Year, Motion Picture Pioneers, 1991; Golden Plate Award, American Academy of Achievement, 1993; Business Excellence Award, University of Southern California School of Business Administration, 1994; Honorary LLD, Boston University, 1994; Stephen S. Wise Award, American Jewish Congress, 1994; Allan K. Jonas Lifetime Achievement Award, American Cancer Society, 1995; Hall of Fame, *Broadcasting and Cable*, 1995; Humanitarian Award, Variety Club International, 1995; Legends in Leadership Award, Emory University, 1995; Expeditioner's Award, New York City Outward

Sumner M. Redstone. *AP/Wide World Photos.*

Bound Center, 1996; Honorary LHD, New York Institute of Technology, 1996; Patron of the Arts Award, Songwriter's Hall of Fame, 1996; Vision 21 Award, New York Institute of Technology, 1996; Trustees Award, National Academy of Television Arts and Sciences, 1997; Robert F. Kennedy Memorial Ripple of Hope Award, 1998; Humanitarian Award, National Conference of Christians and Jews, 1998.

Publications: *A Passion to Win* (with Peter Knobler), 2001.

Address: Viacom International, 1515 Broadway, New York, New York 10036; National Amusements, 200 Elm Street, Dedham, Massachusetts 02026; http://www.viacom.com; http://www.national-amusements.com/home.asp.

Sumner M. Redstone left a lucrative Washington law partnership in 1954 to work for his father's company, Northeast Theater Corporation. The younger Redstone built the company up from a regional operator of drive-in theaters in New England and New York into National Amusements, one of the largest movie theater chains in the United States. In the 1980s, following his recovery from life-threatening injuries suffered in a fire, he made a series of investments in movie studios and other companies and emerged as a powerful figure in the entertainment industry. In 1987 Redstone gained a controlling interest in the communications conglomerate Viacom International. Under his leadership Viacom acquired a wide-ranging collection of entertainment properties, including Paramount Pictures, CBS, Blockbuster Entertainment, and Simon & Schuster. As of 2004 Redstone was believed to be among the 50 wealthiest Americans, with a personal fortune estimated in excess of $8 billion.

BOY GENIUS

The son of second-generation, American-born parents, Redstone grew up in the Charlesbank Homes, a public housing project in the predominantly Jewish West End neighborhood of Boston. In his autobiography he recalled, "Our apartment had no toilet; we had to walk down the corridor to use a water closet we shared with the neighbors. That was all I knew and I never felt less privileged than anyone else" (2001). By the time Redstone was 12 his father had prospered sufficiently to move the family to the Brighton area. Educational achievement was stressed, especially by Mrs. Redstone, who encouraged rivalries between Redstone and his younger brother.

A precocious student, the elder Redstone son graduated with the highest grade point average ever attained at the Boston Latin School, which ranks among the most competitive public high schools in the United States. Admitted to Harvard in 1940, Redstone focused on foreign languages, including German and Japanese. He so impressed his teachers that he was recruited by his Japanese professor, Edwin Reischauer, for a special U.S. Army intelligence unit charged with decrypting Japanese military and diplomatic codes during World War II. Redstone was decorated with several commendations and attained the rank of first lieutenant. Though he had left college in his junior year to join the army, Redstone was not asked to fulfill further graduation requirements and was awarded a bachelor's degree by the university's Board of Overseers in 1944. He was admitted to Harvard Law School the following year.

After receiving his LL.B. degree in 1947, Redstone clerked for the U.S. Court of Appeals in San Francisco and, during evening hours, taught classes in labor-management law at the University of San Francisco. In less than a year he was called to Washington, D.C., by the Truman administration to work for the Justice Department as special assistant to U.S. Attorney General Tom C. Clark, working mainly in tax litigation. Redstone decided to leave government service in 1951 and, though not yet thirty years old, was invited to join the Washington law practice of several former senior Justice Department colleagues who had taken notice of him. While with Ford, Bergson, Adams, Borkland & Redstone, he successfully argued a case before the U.S. Supreme Court that effectively ended the Internal Revenue Service practice of charging citizens with criminal tax evasion based on no other evidence than sudden large increases in personal net worth, forcing the IRS to present specific evidence.

Perhaps a more important case for the young attorney in terms of career development was his representation of United Paramount Theaters (UPT) in its merger negotiations with the American Broadcasting Company (ABC), a process that took place from 1951 to 1953. UPT was a movie-theater chain that had been divested by Paramount Pictures under a 1948 federal antitrust order, and ABC was the weakest of the three national radio-and-television broadcasting networks. The negotiation issues and the antitrust objections to the merger exposed Redstone to the intricacies of both the film and the broadcasting businesses as he helped to cobble together two relatively weak companies into an early prototype of a contemporary integrated multimedia corporation. The trajectory of Redstone's career would take him to the pinnacle of American corporate power as the head of just such a company some four decades later.

In 1954 Redstone made an abrupt decision to withdraw from his law partnership and return to the Boston area to work for his father's company, Northeast Theater Corporation, a chain of drive-in movie theaters. As a result, his annual salary declined from $100,000 to $5,000. Furthermore, television had put the movie business into steep decline during the early 1950s, making the decision even more mystifying to family and friends alike. In his autobiography Redstone explained the unlikely career move in terms of a personal loss of innocence. He had been motivated by social idealism to study law, but his stints at the Justice Department and in private practice had changed his view of the profession: "Law is just a business, not a crusade for humanity. When I reached that conclusion, I decided I was going to go into business" (2001). It is also likely that Redstone learned some important lessons from a former client, Leonard Goldenson of UPT, who became head of ABC after the merger. Goldenson, who sold off many of his theaters to raise capital for more lucrative entertainment projects, demonstrated that the true value of a chain of movie theaters was best understood when considered as a real-estate portfolio, a principle that Redstone would exploit profitably as head of Northeast Theater.

ENTERTAINMENT INDUSTRY TRENDSETTER

Among Redstone's first accomplishments for the family business was his successful antitrust litigation against movie distributors who denied drive-in operators access to first-run films. The company grew steadily under his direction, changing its name to National Amusements in 1967 to reflect its expanding chain of properties, which now included indoor theaters as well as drive-ins and a growing real-estate portfolio.

During the late 1960s Redstone took the company in a radical direction based on his analysis of the changing circumstances under which Americans chose to attend the movies. He concluded that the increasingly suburban, automobile-oriented character of American life demanded a different kind of exhibition venue: a single building holding multiple viewing spaces and a centralized concession area, all surrounded by a large parking lot. The preferred location would not be in a commercial downtown or family neighborhood area but rather at a junction of major roadways. To draw a new generation of moviegoers who were accustomed to watching television in their homes, he emphasized comfort in theater seats. Loudspeaker systems, which had changed little since the introduction of sound cinema in the late 1920s, were replaced by state-of-the-art stereophonic systems. Redstone coined the term "multiplex" to describe this new type of movie theater. With so many spacious drive-in movie locations among its real-estate holdings, the company was particularly well-positioned for multiplex development. Competitors were forced to imitate the model Redstone created.

As the multiplex became the industry standard in the 1970s, Redstone began to invest National Amusement's spiraling profits in the production end of the movie business. From his suburban headquarters in Dedham, Massachusetts, outside of Boston, Redstone bought and sold his way through Hollywood, banking substantial profits on stock deals involving Twentieth Century–Fox (sold in 1981 for $20 million), Columbia Pictures (1982, $25 million), and MGM/UA (1985, $15 million).

In 1979 Redstone miraculously survived a hotel fire in Boston by holding on to a third-floor building ledge with one arm while severe burns covered nearly half his body. Saved by firefighters, he was given little chance of surviving or, if he did, of ever walking again. But after undergoing five major operations and scores of skin grafts during the ensuing months, he made a full recovery. In 1981 he was elected president of the Theater Owners of America and received a thunderous ovation from his industry colleagues at his inaugural address in Los Angeles. It is worth noting that Redstone sued the Copley Plaza Hotel for negligence in the fire and donated the entire settlement to the Burn Center of Massachusetts General Hospital, where his life had been saved. Though he had been a successful businessman by almost any measure up until this time, Redstone's earlier business accomplishments would pale in comparison to his achievements following his recovery. He wrote, "The most exciting things that have happened to me in my professional life have occurred after the fire, but not because of it. Life begins whenever you want it to begin" (2001).

MOGUL

During the 1980s Redstone used his growing war chest of investment profits to prove the wisdom of another of his insights into the changing nature of consumption patterns in the American entertainment business. Recognizing the consequences of the mass diffusion of the videocassette recorder (VCR) and of cable television, he switched his focus from theater development to home entertainment products and services. The principal target of his investing strategy became Viacom International, an integrated communications company that operated local cable franchises in many parts of the country and offered its own cable channels to a national audience. Viacom's premier programming service was Showtime, a pay-cable channel that was the chief competitor of the industry's leader, Time-Warner's HBO. Viacom also held a collection of basic cable services, including MTV, Nickelodeon, and The Comedy Channel.

In 1987 Redstone succeeded in pulling off a leveraged buyout of Viacom, something that other top investors, including Carl Icahn and Ivan Boesky, had been unable to do. Upon acquiring majority stock ownership for a price believed to be more than $3 billion, he became chairman of the board at Viacom and began dividing his work week between his long-time home in Newton, Massachusetts, and Viacom's midtown-Manhattan headquarters. In 1996 he became Viacom's chief executive officer. National Amusements, the parent company of Viacom, remains a privately held company, owned by Redstone and other members of his family. Operating under the brand names of Multiplex Cinemas, Showcase Cinemas, and Cinemas de Lux, National Amusements owns more than 1,400 movie screens in North America, South America, and the United Kingdom.

In the late 1990s Redstone refocused Viacom on the production end of the entertainment industry, de-emphasizing its role as a cable franchise operator and turning it into a brand-name entertainment company. Even the pronunciation of the company's name was changed (from "vie" to "vee") in order to roll more easily off the public tongue. In 1994, following a now-legendary corporate slugfest with another media titan, Barry Diller, Redstone gained control of Paramount Pictures, one of Hollywood's oldest movie studios. Paramount's properties at the time included television stations, theme parks, and two sports franchises—the New York Knicks of the National Basketball Association and the New York Rangers of the National Hockey League—both of which Redstone sold in 1994 for phenomenal profits.

Redstone's 1999 acquisitions of CBS and Infinity Broadcasting, the latter with holdings in radio stations and billboard advertising, were believed to have cost some $46 billion. The additions of these companies put Viacom on solid ground in all four of the areas identified by Redstone as the centers of advertising growth in the early 21st century: cable television, broadcast television, broadcast radio, and outdoor advertising. As the only company so positioned, Viacom could offer large corporations "one-stop shopping" for integrated advertising campaigns. The point was driven home in a 2002 deal in which Procter & Gamble, the household-products giant, purchased a $300 million diversified advertising package from Viacom.

International expansion was also emphasized by Redstone. In 2001 he made a trip to China to personally promote new Viacom satellite-television services, including a new Asian MTV channel. He was warmly received by Chinese President Jiang Zemin, who lauded the opportunities Redstone was creating for better communication between China and the other nations of the world. Through the mid-2000s, Viacom would be able to offer advertisers access to tens of millions of Asian households.

Redstone wrote that his material desires were always minimal, and this remained true despite the size of his personal fortune and the fact that his combined business interests generated more than $10 billion in transactions each year. He enjoyed teaching, an avocation he practiced ever since he led courses at the University of San Francisco's College of Law in the late 1940s. Over the years he served as a visiting professor at the law schools of Boston University and Harvard University and at the International Business School of Brandeis University.

In politics Redstone was an active supporter of the Democratic Party. He contributed heavily to the presidential candidacies of Jimmy Carter, Michael Dukakis, and Bill Clinton, and was an enthusiastic supporter of Edmund Muskie's campaigns to gain the party's presidential nomination during the 1970s. President Jimmy Carter appointed Redstone to the Presidential Advisory Committee of the Arts, John F. Kennedy Center for the Performing Arts; and as a director of the John F. Kennedy Presidential Library Foundation.

A generous philanthropist, Redstone channeled much of his wealth to support medical institutions and other organizations in the Boston area. He was a founder and trustee of the American Cancer Society Foundation and a board officer for dozens of organizations, including the Dana-Farber Cancer Institute; the Will Rogers Memorial Fund; the Corporation of the Massachusetts General Hospital; the Children's Cancer Research Foundation ("The Jimmy Fund"); and the Corpora-

tion of the New England Medical Center. He was also a member of the executive board of the Combined Jewish Philanthropies of Greater Boston and the former chair of its Metropolitan Division.

In his work for the arts Redstone sat on the Board of Overseers of the Boston Museum of Fine Arts, the Board of Directors of the Boston Arts Festival, and the Board of Trustees of the Museum of Television and Radio. In the legal profession he was a member of the American Bar Association, the Massachusetts Bar Association, the Boston Bar Association, the Harvard Law School Association, and the American Judicature Society. He maintained affiliations in the entertainment industry with the National Association of Theatre Owners, as former president; the National Academy of Television Arts and Sciences, as a board member; Theatre Owners of America, as former president; and the Motion Picture Pioneers. The social clubs to which he belonged included the Masons, the University Club, and the Harvard Club.

See also entries on National Amusements Inc. and Viacom International Inc. in *International Directory of Company Histories.*

SOURCES FOR FURTHER INFORMATION

"Joint Statement of Sumner M. Redstone, Chairman and Chief Executive Officer, Viacom Inc., and Mel Karmazin, President and Chief Executive Officer of CBS Corp.," *Federal Communications Law Journal,* 52, no. 3 (May 2000), pp. 499–511.

Kim, Hank, "Sumner Redstone's Global Sprawl," *Advertising Age Global,* July 2002, pp. 12–13.

Koch, John, "Sumner Redstone," *Boston Globe,* October 26, 1997.

Leonard, Devin, "Who's the Boss?" *Fortune,* April 16, 2001, pp. 122–138.

Picker, Ida, "Sumner Redstone Fights Back," *Institutional Investor,* November 1995.

Redstone, Sumner, *A Passion to Win,* with Peter Knobler, New York, N.Y.: Simon & Schuster, 2001.

Villa, Joan, "Redstone Rejects Rev-Share Deals as Being Exclusive," *Video Store,* June 16–22, 2002.

Voss, Gretchen, "The $80 Billion Love Affair," *Boston Magazine,* January 2000.

—David Marc

Dennis H. Reilley

1953–

Chairman, president, and chief executive officer, Praxair

Nationality: American.

Born: 1953, in Oklahoma City, Oklahoma.

Education: Oklahoma State University, BS, 1975.

Family: Married Cindy (maiden name unknown).

Career: Conoco, 1975–1979, pipeline engineer; 1979–1990, executive assistant to the chairman, along with other positions including president and managing director of Conoco Ireland; DuPont Company, 1990–1994, vice president and general manager of titanium-dioxide business; 1994–1995, vice president and general manager of specialty-chemicals business; 1996–1997, vice president and general manager of Lycra business; 1997–1999, executive vice president; 1999–2000, COO; Praxair, 2000–, president, CEO, and chairman.

Address: Praxair, 39 Old Ridgebury Road, Danbury, Connecticut 06810-5113; http://www.praxair.com.

■ Dennis H. Reilley eventually became president, chief executive officer, and chairman of the board of directors of the Danbury, Connecticut–based Praxair, a global leader in the development of processes and technologies involving industrial gases. As of 2004 Praxair was the largest industrial-gases company in North and South America and one of the largest such companies worldwide. Praxair served a wide range of industries, including aerospace, chemicals, energy and refining, food and beverages, health care, refining, semiconductors, manufacturing, and primary metal fabrication.

GASSING UP WITH PRAXAIR

Praxair was a global Fortune 500 company with 2003 revenues of $5.6 billion and a net income of $585 million. The company's primary products were atmospheric gases—such as oxygen, nitrogen, argon, and rare gases (produced when air is purified, compressed, cooled, distilled, and condensed)—and

process and specialty gases—such as carbon dioxide, helium, hydrogen, semiconductor process gases, and acetylene (produced as by-products of chemical production or recovered from natural gas). Reilley oversaw the design, engineering, and construction of equipment that produced industrial gases for the internal use and the external sale of such processes within cryogenic and noncryogenic supply systems.

The company's Praxair Surface Technologies subsidiary applied high-temperature, wear-resistant, and corrosion-resistant metallic and ceramic coatings and powders to metal surfaces. These coatings and powders were supplied mainly to the aircraft, plastics, and primary-metals industries. The surface technologies segment of Praxair also provided aircraft-engine and airframe-component overhaul services.

BACKGROUND IN COLLEGE, CONOCO, AND DUPONT

A native of Oklahoma City, Oklahoma, Reilley received a bachelor's degree in finance from Oklahoma State University (OSU) in 1975. Reilley credited OSU with providing the academic background in business and executive management that he would need and make use of over the next 30 years.

Reilley held numerous earlier positions at the Wilmington, Delaware–based DuPont Company and its former energy subsidiary, Conoco (now called Conoco-Phillips). Reilley joined Conoco in 1975 where he served as a pipeline engineer until 1979, when he was promoted to executive assistant to the chairman. DuPont purchased Conoco in 1981, and Reilley continued to serve in a variety of positions in both upstream and downstream organizations, including as president and managing director of Conoco Ireland.

In 1989 Reilley transferred to DuPont's chemicals and specialty business. From 1990 to 1994 he served as vice president and general manager of its titanium-dioxide business. Between 1994 and 1995 Reilley held the position of vice president and general manager of specialty chemicals. In 1996 he was named vice president and general manager of the Lycra business. Reilley was named an executive vice president of DuPont in 1997 and chief operating officer in 1999, in which position he was responsible for the divisions of pigments and chemicals, specialty polymers, and nylon and polyester. In 2000 Reilley moved over to Praxair.

AT PRAXAIR

Reilley became president and chief executive officer of Praxair in March 2000. He assumed the additional title of chairman on December 1 of that year. Upon joining Praxair, Reilley strenuously promoted the "take or pay" contracts that the company signed with customers before building gas plants next to their factories. These agreements made up about 35 percent of the sales generated within Praxair. The strategy promoted by Reilley strengthened Praxair's focus on critical resources within geographic markets bearing the greatest potential for high-return growth.

WEEKLY VISITS AND ETHICS

Reilley's responsibilities as chief executive officer involved spending around three days a week visiting factories and customers. This approach—which Reilley offered as a countermeasure to the scandals involving corporate-executive misdeeds that had been recently exposed by the media—ensured Reilley's hands-on involvement with the day-to-day details of Praxair's businesses.

While spending a day talking with students at Oklahoma State University's first annual "CEO Day," sponsored by the College of Business Administration, the alumnus Reilley averred that all employers needed to be held to the highest ethical standards in order to dispel the negative impressions left by illegal corporate activities such as insider trading and fraud. Referring to the importance of chief executive officers operating with the greatest possible degree of integrity, Reilly said at the event, "The actions of a few have cast a shadow on everybody else. It's important that the rest of us not only do the right things but let people see that we're doing the right things. That's the only way that we're going to help rebuild the confidence that's been pulled away from the marketplace as a result of what's happened" (April 2003).

EFFICIENCY CRUSADE

Reilley was heavily involved with improving efficiency at Praxair—an effort he sometimes called his "crusade." As of 2001 Reilley adopted the Six Sigma approach at the company, a management-directed, team-based, and expert-led program that he brought over from the DuPont Company. Six Sigma measures quality and strives for near perfection—specifically, a process must not produce more than 3.4 defects per million situations. Reilley emphasized the program's focus on helping employees recognize and avoid behavior that put them at risk (and sometimes in danger of injury and death). Such actions played a large role in the 15 percent improvement in Praxair's worldwide 2002 recordable injury rate as compared to the rate

of 2001. Six Sigma promotes strong compliance to policies and procedures in order to avoid even the potential for injury.

As of February 2003 the prevalence of the Six Sigma methodology in Praxair businesses grew to more than 800 projects throughout the global organization. Savings from Six Sigma activities totaled almost $34 million in 2002, with additional savings expected by Reilley in 2003. Reilley told his employees that many career advancement opportunities within Praxair would go to the employees who not only performed best but also demonstrated success using Six Sigma methodologies.

RETURNS ON CAPITAL AND INVESTMENT IMPROVEMENTS

Reilley was well known within the gas industry as a chief executive officer who constantly pushed for improvements in returns on capital and investments. In 2002 Praxair had $498 million in capital expenditures and $548 million in net income—a decline of about 29 percent from 2000. Yet, the after-tax return on capital climbed, as Reilley noted, approximately 7 percent between 2000 and 2002. Reilley demanded a return on investment of at least 15 percent over the life of any major project.

Priorities for Reilley included developing the petrochemicals and electronics business in China. Worldwide he made the development of hydrogen plants for refineries, electronics, and health care a major priority. He maintained a strong policy of investing in capital for industrial gases, health care, and electronics in order to increase revenues. The Reilley strategy provided a total return of 14.2 percent between 1998 and 2002—a score that ranked Praxair first in all companies within the chemical industry.

As of the end of 2003 Reilley believed that Praxair was on track to continue to achieve improved performance and profitability, thanks to the correct combination of growth platforms and core businesses; products, services, and technologies; and geographic emphasis and global potential. He promised to continue to emphasize earnings growth and return on capital and cash flow. With new opportunities for expansion, strong performance in base businesses, and an active employee team, Reilley saw continued prosperity for Praxair and increased value for its shareholders. Praxair was the only major, fully integrated industrial-gas company with national coverage in the United States, and Reilley took full advantage of its position in sustaining its success.

OTHER FUNCTIONS

Reilley was a member of the U.S. Department of Energy's Electricity Advisory Board as well as the boards of directors of the utility holding company Entergy Corporation and the oil and gas exploration and development company Marathon Oil Company. He was a chairman of the American Chemistry Council, formerly called the Chemical Manufacturers Association.

See also entry on Praxair, Inc. in *International Directory of Company Histories.*

SOURCE FOR FURTHER INFORMATION

Mitchell, Jim, "CEO Day Wins Applause from Students and Alumni," College of Business Administration, Oklahoma State University, April 2003, http://www.bus.okstate.edu/cba/pressreleases/Spring2003/ceo_day_review.htm.

—William Arthur Atkins

■■■
Steven S. Reinemund
1948–
Chairman and chief executive officer, PepsiCo

Nationality: American.

Born: April 6, 1948, in New York City, New York.

Education: U.S. Naval Academy, BS, 1970; University of Virginia, MBA, 1978.

Family: Married Gail (maiden name unknown); children: four.

Career: PepsiCo, 1984–1986, senior vice president of operations of Pizza Hut division; 1986–1991, president and chief executive officer of Pizza Hut division; 1991–1992, president and chief executive officer of Pizza Hut Worldwide; 1992–1996, president and chief executive officer of Frito-Lay North America division; 1996–1999, chairman and chief executive officer of Frito-Lay worldwide division; 1999–2001, president and chief operating officer; 2001–, chairman and chief executive officer.

Address: PepsiCo, Inc., 700 Anderson Hill Road, Purchase, New York 10577; http://www.pepsico.com.

Steven S. Reinemund. *AP/Wide World Photos.*

A TRACK RECORD OF PERFORMANCE

After college Reinemund spent five years in the marines, achieving the rank of captain. He guarded the White House during parts of the Nixon and Ford administrations. Reinemund began his career with PepsiCo in 1984 at the corporation's former Pizza Hut division, where he served as CEO from 1986 until 1992. One of his first decisions was to enter the delivery business dominated by Domino's Pizza. When his staff complained that delivering pizzas was too undignified, he hired a new team. Two years after the 1986 launch of its delivery business, Pizza Hut overtook Domino's as the number one delivery business in the country.

Reinemund's next assignments at PepsiCo's Frito-Lay unit prepared him ultimately to lead the company. PepsiCo's Frito-Lay division accounts for more than 50 percent of PepsiCo's

■ Steven S. Reinemund was only the fourth chief executive in the history of PepsiCo, a multinational that generated nearly $27 billion in sales in 2003. A company man throughout his career in operations, Reinemund earned his rank by leading unprecedented growth of units he commanded. The former marine was the rare executive who was just as effective at making executive decisions as he was working hands on. Chosen by the previous PepsiCo CEO, Roger Enrico, Reinemund was given the mandate to lead a fast-growth company in a notoriously slow industry. After maneuvering the company through an initially painful integration with Quaker Oats, Reinemund continued to chip away at Coca-Cola's market share while positioning his company to capitalize on the health concerns sweeping the country.

company sales. First Reinemund was president and CEO of Frito-Lay North America and then chairman and CEO of Frito-Lay worldwide. During that time, Frito-Lay sales grew an average of 10 percent a year, and profits doubled. In 2000 Frito-Lay achieved greater sales volume growth than any other major U.S. food company. Later, as PepsiCo's president and COO, Reinemund led the company's five operating units to generate respectable growth in a sluggish sector.

At each step of his climb up the corporate ladder, Reinemund earned a reputation as a visionary who knew how to translate the big picture into clearly defined goals. When Eagle Snacks challenged Frito-Lay's market share, Reinemund fought for new ways to become more competitive. He ultimately overhauled logistics to make it easier for route managers to forecast and fill inventories. Said Bill Nictakis, a sales executive who worked with Reinemund at Frito-Lay, "He dives really deep and understands what's going on, but at the same time he has a master plan to figure out how the pieces fit into the mosaic from 30,000 feet" (*USA Today*, December 5, 2000).

A POLISHED EXECUTIVE AT EASE WITH HIS TROOPS

For Reinemund, image was important. As a former marine, he maintained a militaristic preference for a clearly defined corporate uniform. Combining seriousness with formality and polish, he preferred monogrammed shirts and shiny wing tip shoes. Craig E. Weatherup, CEO of Pepsi Bottling Group, described Reinemund's style: "He always looks like he's ready to go on the cover of *Gentleman's Quarterly*" (*Business Week*, January 29, 2001). But Reinemund was no "corporate suit." He relished opportunities to roll up his sleeves and get his hands dirty outside the executive offices. A famous Reinemund story occurred one Christmas Eve. Reinemund was doing family errands, having gone to the store to pick up few things. He found a Frito-Lay delivery driver at work that night, stocking a Colorado convenience store. Reinemund jumped in immediately, helping the worker load chips onto the store's shelves.

As an effective leader, Reinemund knew how to build morale and motivate employees. In 2000 he recruited a team of 50 Pepsi employees to run the New York City Marathon in memory of a coworker's brother. The pregame festivities included a pep rally hosted by Reinemund, a dinner at his home with his wife, Gail, and another dinner at the ESPN Zone in New York City. (The 1999 marathon marked Reinemund's fifth appearance in the race.) Said Enrico of Reinemund, "He goes out of his way to put a very human face on this organization" (*USA Today*, December 5, 2000).

STEPPING INTO THE CEO'S SHOES

In December 2000 Enrico announced PepsiCo's $13 billion deal to buy Quaker Oats, which included the prized Ga-

torade brand. As soon as the deal closed, then CEO Enrico said he would hand over the CEO title to Reinemund, who would be in charge of ensuring that the integration produced shareholder return. Reinemund inherited a recharged company with enough momentum to unnerve Coca-Cola. But while Enrico managed to turn the company around, Reinemund was left with the potentially more difficult task of ensuring its accelerated growth in a painfully slow yet fiercely competitive industry. Tom Pirko, president of BevMark, a beverage marketing consultancy in Santa Barbara, California, noted that "Reinemund's mandate is to go faster" (*Business Week*, January 29, 2001).

Success depended on the company's ability to create pioneering products and to capitalize on the huge opportunity in urban markets. "The day we are not talking about growth at PepsiCo we are no longer in business. We have to be more focused on innovation than ever before," said Reinemund (*USA Today*, December 5, 2000). In order to do just that, Reinemund began broadening the company's management. His goal was to align the rate of retention and promotion of women and minorities. He even tied that objective to senior management performance reviews.

PASSING THE FIRST TEST AS CEO

In order for Reinemund to meet his goals, he would have to ensure the success of the Quaker acquisition. The postmerger transition did not go smoothly at first, and Reinemund's reputation was on the line. The integration of the Gatorade and Tropicana sales forces resulted in a botched sales promotion, and a key Quaker Oats executive left the company. When Reinemund announced the first combined results, it was unclear whether the acquisition could deliver the intended results. Supermarket sales of Gatorade, Quaker's crown jewel, were up only 7 percent in the last quarter of 2001 compared with the 15 percent pace set by its market peers. One grocery store buyer said that he had not even heard from his Gatorade rep in several months. "I kind of think they're in limbo" (*Business Week*, March 4, 2002).

Reinemund remained confident that the problems could be worked out. "I don't know how long it will take, how long that is, but it's not a month or two" (*Business Week*, March 4, 2002). The obstacles did not prevent the acquisition from ultimately succeeding. PepsiCo's total sales grew nearly 7 percent in 2002, boosting the company's annual revenue growth over its historical 6 percent growth rate. In 2003 the company announced that it was on track to realize its goal of achieving $400 million in synergies by the end of fiscal year 2004.

REORGANIZING FOR GROWTH

In late 2003 Reinemund announced a reorganization intended to increase revenues by focusing sales efforts and reducing redundancies. In addition to terminating the employment of 750 people and closing a Frito-Lay factory, he announced the debut of a new "power of one" sales team that would promote and sell Quaker and Tropicana or Frito-Lay and Pepsi together. The initiative was a long time coming and one originally heralded by the former CEO Enrico. The aim was to integrate selling operations and distribution logistics. Even though Pepsi, Tropicana, Frito-Lay, and Quaker delivered their products to the same U.S. stores, each division previously ran separate distribution systems. Reinemund believed that they had to act as a single company.

During a 2003 meeting with financial analysts in which he detailed many changes, Reinemund expressed optimism for 2004 but conceded that the company still faced formidable challenges, not the least of which was Coca-Cola. A week before that meeting, Coca-Cola inked a deal to take over fountain sales in 2005 at the 16,000-store Subway chain, Pepsi's biggest fountain customer.

POSITIONING PEPSI AS HEALTH CONSCIOUS

An early 21st-century consumer trend challenged the very relevance of PepsiCo's products. Consumers began planning their diets with more scrutiny amid concerns that more and more Americans—particularly kids—were wreaking havoc on their bodies with meals lacking any substantive nutritional value. The Centers for Disease Control and Prevention announced that more than half of U.S. adults were considered overweight or obese. Lawsuits linked the McDonald's menu and Oreos to the so-called obesity epidemic, and legislators proposed taxes on fatty foods.

Reinemund turned this consumer trend into a growth strategy—one that he could feel good about. Rather than eliminating the company's hallmark chips and soda, he envisioned a company whose products would mirror a diet based on moderation and balance. He divided the company into three categories. "Fun-for-you" products, such as Doritos and Mountain Dew, represented the biggest piece of the company's portfolio with 62 percent of North American sales volume in 2002. "Better-for-you" products, brands like Baked Lays that have fewer calories and less fat, represented 22 percent of sales. Relatively nutritious "good-for-you" products, like Quaker products and Tropicana orange juice, accounted for 16 percent of sales.

With existing brands such as Tropicana and Quaker giving him a head start, Reinemund expressed an interest in making 50 percent of the company's new products nutritious. "It's one of the few opportunities in my career to promote a set of products I personally believe in, in a way which is good for the business" (*Journal News*, Westchester County, New York, July 28, 2003). Reinemund eliminated trans-fatty acids, which raise bad cholesterol and lower good cholesterol, from the company's snack chips.

Reinemund likened the new initiative to an exercise in corporate responsibility. Without trust—from consumers, employees, and investors—PepsiCo would never become a world-class company, he said. "Creating that trust comes from the doing the right thing for these consumers. Students coming out of high school today don't want to work for a company that doesn't have the right corporate values and ethics" (*Journal News*, July 28, 2003).

But nutritionists criticized Reinemund's initiatives as a thinly veiled marketing ploy simply to sell more food. Said Marion Nestle, author of the book, *Food Politics: How the Food Industry Influences Nutrition and Health* and chair of the New York University Department of Nutrition and Food Studies, "The argument that all foods can be part of a healthy diet is the favorite argument of the food industry. It's still junk food" (*Journal News*, July 28, 2003). Hoping to allay some of those criticisms and strengthen the notion that drinking Pepsi and staying healthy are not mutually exclusive activities, Reinemund began partnering with the nutritional community and building on a health strategy that transcended the products his company makes. Pepsi contributed money to causes that encouraged kids to become more active, sponsoring the Web-based journal *Get Active Stay Active*, which helped teens track their physical activity, and donating $16 million over 10 years to help poor teens enroll in YMCA programs. Analysts applauded Reinemund's strategy. Said Bryan Spillane of Banc of America Securities, "He has put PepsiCo in a position to take advantage of consumers eating healthier" (*Business Week*, October 20, 2003).

A STRONG SHOWING IN THE COLA WARS

As of early 2004 PepsiCo's Frito-Lay division was the number one maker of snack chips, and its Tropicana Products unit led the world in juice sales. But its namesake soft-drink business was the longtime runner-up to the Coca-Cola Company. Reinemund had made a strong showing of reversing that trend. In 2003, for the first time in 10 years, Pepsi's price-to-earnings ratio matched Coke's. And PepsiCo secured longtime Coke contracts from the NFL and United Airlines.

Adding to the legacy he inherited, Reinemund's efforts appeared to be paying off in early 2004. According to annual rankings released in early 2004 by *Beverage Digest*–Maxwell, PepsiCo increased its share of the $64 billion U.S. soft-drink market to its highest level since 1992. Coca-Cola's U.S. market share fell .3 percentage points to 44 percent while the market share for PepsiCo grew .4 percentage points to 31.8 percent. While Coke struggled to replicate its success in 2002 with the debut of Vanilla Coke, Pepsi achieved a longtime goal of creating a lemon-lime drink—Sierra Mist—that could challenge Coke's Sprite brand. Sierra Mist was so successful that it landed on the list of top 10 soft-drink brands. Said John Sicher, editor and publisher of *Beverage Digest*, "Most notably, Pepsi has finally cracked the lemon-lime code and has a big new brand with Sierra Mist" (*Wall Street Journal*, March 4, 2004).

Pepsi was also number one in the United States in the non-carbonated beverages market, which includes its All Sport sports drink and Aquafina bottled water products. Analysts estimated that the market for noncarbonated beverages was expanding at least 60 percent faster than that for soft drinks.

AN UNCERTAIN FUTURE FOR PEPSI

Reinemund's legacy will depend on whether he can sustain momentum in the cola wars. Another key test will be his ability to move from a massive company with separate, individually operated business units to a more integrated firm. While other companies of Pepsi's size have eliminated separate sales teams, marketing departments, and even supply chains associated with each unit, Pepsi has yet to follow suit. Said Tom Pirko, president of BevMark, "They've been talking forever about how they're going to streamline operations and integrate systems and they're still talking. The commitment just hasn't been there" (*eWeek.com*, May 1, 2003).

Reinemund admitted as much during an analysts meeting in 2003. "I have to tell you, we've talked about this for years. I can remember in 1986 having a meeting with the division presidents at the time, and we talked about synergistic things we could do together, and we had a nice discussion for a couple hours and went back and nothing happened" (*eWeek.com*, May 1, 2003). But he made it clear that he had no intention of doing away with his company's autonomous business-unit structure. He envisions a subtle collaboration between business units that would strengthen the company's overall performance. In fact, he credited division competition as a key component of each unit's strategy. As he put it (*USA Today*, December 5, 2000), "If we were all about central business

directives to get results, it would destroy the cultures. The success of Pepsi in the future is based on the ability to create business opportunities and divisions where people can take ownership."

Some experts see this inability to choose sides between central control and business unit control as a mistake. Only time will tell. Said one former executive, "They've got one foot on the gas and one on the brake" (*eWeek.com*, May 1, 2003).

See also entries on Frito-Lay Company and PepsiCo, Inc. in *International Directory of Company Histories*.

SOURCES FOR FURTHER INFORMATION

Brady, Diane, and Monica Roman, "Pepping Up Pepsi," *BusinessWeek*, October 3, 2003.

Byrnes, Nanette, "The Power of Two at Pepsi," *BusinessWeek*, January 29, 2001, p. 102.

Byrnes, Nanette, with Julie Forster, "A Touch of Indigestion," *BusinessWeek*, March 4, 2002, p. 66.

Howard, Theresa, "Deal Puts Reinemund on the Fast Track: Once Set to Be Chairman and CEO in 2002, He Will Take the Positions Next Year," *USA Today*, December 5, 2000.

Klingbeil, Abigail, "Corporate Profile; Chairman and Chief Executive Officer," *Journal News* (Westchester County, New York), July 28, 2003.

"PepsiCo: No Deposit, No Return; Food Service: The Choice of a New Generation Is Rife with Options. Will Pepsi Prove Itself to Be up to the Challenge?" *eWeek.com*, May 1, 2003.

Terhune, Chad, "PepsiCo Sees Rise in U.S. Market Share," *Wall Street Journal*, March 4, 2004.

—Tim Halpern

Eivind Reiten

1953–

President and chief executive officer, Norsk Hydro

Nationality: Norwegian.

Born: April 2, 1953, in Midsund, Møre og Romsdal, Norway.

Education: University of Oslo, 1978, Master of Science in economics.

Family: Married Frøydis Odden; children: two.

Career: Ministry of Fisheries, 1979–1982, junior executive officer; Centre Party Parliamentary Group, 1982–1983, secretary; Ministry of Fisheries, 1985–1986, minister of fisheries; Norsk Hydro, 1986–1988, manager and vice president, Hydro Agri; 1988–1990, president of Energy Division; Ministry of Petroleum and Energy, 1989–1990, minister of petroleum and energy; Norsk Hydro, 1991–1992, senior vice president, special projects; 1992–1996, president of Refining & Marketing Division; 1996–1998, president of Hydro Aluminium Metal Products; 1999–2001, executive vice president, light metals; 2001–, president and chief executive officer.

Awards: Named Leader of the Year by Økonomisk Rapport, 2003.

Address: Norsk Hydro ASA, Drammensveien 264, N-0240 Oslo, Norway; http://www.hydro.com/en.

■ On May 2, 2001, Eivind Kristofer Reiten became president and CEO of Norsk Hydro, an industrial conglomerate with two major segments: light metals (aluminium) and energy operations. At the time of Reiten's takeover, Norsk Hydro was Norway's largest publicly traded industrial company and was 43.8 percent owned by the Norwegian government. A third segment, Norsk Agri, was spun off in 2004.

EARLY CAREER

Reiten came from the rural north of Norway, where his family was long established in farming and fishing. He origi-

nally intended to be an economist and graduated from Oslo University in 1978 with an economics degree. However, he spent his earliest working years as a politician with the Centre Party. In fact, he served for over a year as Norway's minister of fisheries, perhaps a fitting post for the son of a fisherman. However, in 1989 he took a position in the semipublic company Norsk Hydro and (with the exception of a term as Norway's minister of petroleum and energy) remained with this company.

NORSK HYDRO

Starting in 1989 Reiten held positions of increasing responsibility with Norsk Hydro. In 1999 he was appointed executive vice president and a member of corporate management, serving under the CEO and president, Egil Myklebust. To the surprise of the board, Myklebust announced his intention to step down from his position, and a committee began the search for a successor. In December 2000 their choice was announced: Eivind Reiten, who had worked in all three segments of Norsk Hydro, who had twice been a government minister, and who had extensive experience from various directorships in other companies. The formal change of command was scheduled for May 2, 2001.

When Reiten took over, he had already been a part of the corporate management team that had developed the strategy for Norsk Hydro's future, and he planned no sudden change of direction. However, change did come. The oil and energy segment was revitalized with the acquisition of VAW (a German aluminum group); the combination created the world's largest integrated aluminum company. On the other hand, Norsk Hydro divested itself of its fertilizer division since it was not seen as part of the company's core business. Norsk Hydro's stock market listings were streamlined. The result of this fine-tuning was that the company boosted its reputation among investment companies and bankers. Norsk Hydro entered into merger talks with its rival Statoil; however, the talks were terminated, and Reiten's name was one of those mentioned as a possible successor to Olav Fjellof Statoil. Reiten chose to remain with Norsk Hydro.

His tenure was not without controversy. He separated himself from his colleagues in the Centre Party who were strongly anti–European Union (EU). An article in *Aftenposten* (December 29, 2003) quotes him as saying, "I hesitate to declare myself an active 'Yes to the EU' person [but] it's becoming more and more difficult" to stay out of the Union. A salary increase of NK 550,000 (plus a bonus of NK 630,000) angered Norwegians, who saw the increase as obscene and destructive. Moreover, his unapologetic association with the oil and gas industry earned him the scorn of many in the environmental community.

It was Reiten's stated policy to keep a low profile, and he was not frequently discussed in the national papers for non-business matters. He was convinced that globalization is inevitable, and he supported openness, dialogue, liberalization of trade, and sustainable development. Reiten was quoted in *FDI* magazine as saying, "We believe attractiveness is linked to predictability through an established legal framework, a fair tax system and a highly qualified labor force."

See also entry on Norsk Hydro ASA in *International Directory of Company Histories.*

SOURCES FOR FURTHER INFORMATION

Andreassen, Kolbjørn, "Årets leder: Eivind Reiten," *Økonomisk Rapport*, February 5, 2004.

Cresswell, Jeremy, "Downgrade for Norsk despite Excellent Year," *Scotsman* (Edinburgh, Scotland), July 17, 2001.

Fosse Skeie, Synnøve, "Generaldirectøren," *Fædrelandsvennen*, June 16, 2004.

Hohler, Alice, "Norsk Hydro Gets Its Act Together," *Financial News*, March 7, 2004.

"Hydro Agri Faces a New Future," *Fertilizer International*, September-October 2003, pp. 14–15.

"Hydro Boss Warms Up to EU," *Aftenposten*, December 29, 2003.

"An Interview with Eivind Reiten," *FDI*, April 2, 2003, http://www.fdimagazine.com/news/fullstory.php/aid/219/cautious_optimism.html, (then choose Norway).

"Reduced and Improved State Ownership" (a white paper presented to the Norwegian parliament on April 19, 2002), http://odin.dep.no/nhd/engelsk/akruelt/p.10001607/024131-070005/dok-bn.html.

—Barbara Gunvaldsen

Glenn M. Renwick

1955–

President, chairman, and chief executive officer, Progressive Casualty Insurance Company

Nationality: American.

Born: May 22, 1955, in New Zealand.

Education: University of Canterbury (New Zealand), BA; University of Florida, MS.

Career: Progressive Casualty Insurance Company, 1986–1988, auto product manager for Florida and then Georgia; 1988–1990, president of the Mid-Atlantic States; 1991–1993, president of the California division; 1993–1998, president of program operations, division of consumer marketing; 1998–2000, business technology process leader and chief information officer; 2000–2001, chief executive officer of insurance operations; 2001–, president, chairman, chief executive officer.

Address: Progressive Casualty Insurance Company, 6300 Wilson Mills Road, Mayfield Village, Ohio 44143; http://www.progressive.com.

■ Glenn M. Renwick served as president, chairman, and chief executive officer of Progressive Casualty Insurance Company. At Progressive he was able to create long-term profitability through his accurate predictive insurance models, which allowed the company to insure high-risk drivers. Renwick was known as a responsive and accessible leader who welcomed new innovations in technology and believed in truthfulness in business.

LEARNING ABOUT AND MARKETING TO THE CUSTOMER

Renwick joined Progressive Casualty Insurance Company in 1986 as an auto product manager for Florida. As he worked in the day-to-day local operations of the company, he learned much about Progressive's clients. Foremost among these lessons was that customers find it hard to shop for car insurance.

The easier a company makes it to buy a policy, the more likely a customer is to purchase the insurance. He also learned that good, accessible customer service can make the difference in a company's reputation, whether the customer is shopping for insurance or submitting a claim following an accident. These customer details became very important to Renwick when he entered Progressive's brand advertising and marketing department.

Remembering the lessons learned in Progressive's local operations, Renwick developed a strategy to help customers shop for insurance. His idea was to focus Progressive's marketing campaign on the specific services that assisted customers in their search for the best insurance carrier. These services included competitively priced auto insurance rates, excellent customer services, and a practice of giving customer's quotes from other competitive insurance companies as well as their own. Progressive's successful marketing campaign resulted in an increase of market share: from 1.5 percent in 1993 to 6 percent in 2003.

USING THE INTERNET

After his successes in the consumer marketing group, Renwick moved into a new role as chief information officer in 1998. The position of CIO at Progressive proved to be an intense and important role, since Progressive placed so much weight on technology and customer education. One of Progressive's most marketed features was their provision of insurance quotes and the selling of insurance over the Internet, beginning in 1997. Renwick extended Progressive's Internet services through creation of online interactive customer services, through which customers could look up their policy information, obtain a policy quote, check the status of a claim, make online payments, and update personal account information. Renwick considered the project, named Personal Progressive, one of his best customer-focused innovations, because it allowed customers to examine their insurance policies without going through an insurance agent or customer service representative.

As part of his plan to educate customers, Renwick added the Insurance Institute for Highway Safety's side-impact head-protection crash videos to the Progressive website. The stated purpose of the videos was to help Progressive's customers make informed vehicle- and insurance-purchase decisions. The posting of the videos on Progressive's website garnered considerable media attention, since it was the only authorized online outlet for viewing the crash-test videos at that time. In recognition of its usefulness and functionality, the company's Web site was named one of *InfoWeek* magazine's "top 10 Web sites that work in 2001" and also was named to *Smart Business* magazine's Smart Business 50.

Later in his term as chief information office, Renwick used his finance and engineering skills to create an accurate predictive formula to determine insurance rates. The formula models were set up as a detailed, oriented approach to calculating insurance rates based on how much, when, and where a particular person drives. The high level of predictive accuracy from the calculations allowed the company to profitably insure high-risk drivers. The main goal of the CIO during Renwick's tenure was to ensure that Progressive's technology remained ahead of the other industry leaders, and he met it with great success.

THE BIG PICTURE: SHORT-TERM LOSS FOR A LONG-TERM GOAL

In 2000, after two successful years as CIO, Renwick became Progressive's chief executive officer. As CEO, Renwick made the tough decision to raise insurance rates, because it was the only strategy that would keep rates accurately reflecting current costs. At the same time, Renwick changed the duration of the insurance policies from 12 months to six months. Although a survey of customers found that most people prefer a longer-duration policy, Renwick felt that a shorter policy would allow the company to enhance the accuracy of their insurance rates. Wall Street and other industry leaders immediately criticized Renwick for his rate hike, and in 2001 Progressive had only 2 percent net new business. However, the company soon gained more new business when larger companies, such as State Farm Insurance, had to start aggressively raising their insurance rates after their artificially low rates resulted in large financial losses. By 2002 Progressive's new net business was booming, and the company had a 30 percent increase in new-insurance premiums.

As Progressive's new CEO, Renwick felt that it was best to categorize and prioritize the different challenges confronting him. He narrowed his management goals to making operations more efficient, improving customer services, and keeping expenses low. To decrease expenses and improve corporate efficiency, Renwick reorganized and clarified Progressive's management structure and focused on new technologies to boost efficiency. As a way to keep his finger on the pulse of clients' needs, Renwick created a series of customer questionnaires. Outside his goals as CEO, Renwick's priority for the company was to ensure that the insurance company's rates and reserves remained adequate. Progressive's focus on the accuracy of rates

helped the company remain true to its slogan to make their business "all about the customer."

INNOVATION AND INFORMATION TECHNOLOGIES

When Renwick became CEO after the tenure of the eccentric, visionary Peter Lewis, Progressive was already known for its ability to implement new and innovative ideas successfully. Renwick continued the company's policy of innovation by concentrating on the weaknesses of the car-insurance business and trying to find creative solutions to solve the problems. For example, Renwick recognized that car-insurance companies have the least control over events when customers are most anxious, right after an accident. To address this issue, Renwick created a network of "one-stop shopping" centers that allow the customer "to bring in the damaged car and get a replacement car immediately, and also get a beeper so that the insurer can get in touch with the customer when the car is ready." (*BusinessWeek Online*, April 16, 2003) These one-stop-shopping centers helped lessen customer confusion following an accident and increased the speed with which claims were processed.

In keeping with his former role as CIO, Renwick created another model for Progressive to track information technology (IT) expenses. Given the large number of technological innovations implemented throughout the company, it was important to efficiently track the amount of profit directly related to the cost of specific IT developments. With an IT expense tracking model, Renwick was able to develop a simple budget that kept tabs on specific innovations, their cost, and their overall impact on business operations. If a project was costing more money and having a minimal positive effect compared with other innovations, Renwick and his managers would be aware of it and could further evaluate the merit of that particular IT innovation.

MANAGEMENT STYLE

Renwick was known as a responsive and communicative leader who welcomed new innovations in technology. When he became CEO of Progressive, he focused on the company's organizational structure so that every employee would understand his or her job objectives and responsibilities. By establishing accountability and clear objectives, Renwick encouraged employees to focus fully on their position's goals and thus improve company productivity, and he communicated openly and honestly with his employees and shareholders so that they understood the motivations behind the business decisions made in the company. In fact, to emphasize his position, Renwick placed a picture of a naked man and the title "Bare All" on the company's 2003 annual report. He believed that the atmosphere of candor and openness at Progressive was responsible for the success of the company. As he put it, "In insurance, the foundation of success is trust. To be trusted, you need integrity and you need to be open" (*Intelligent Enterprise*, March 20, 2004).

SOURCES FOR FURTHER INFORMATION

Gallagher, Julie, "Alone in the Spotlight?" *Insurance and Technology*, June 1, 2003, pp. 13–14.

Gogoi, Pallavi, "Progressive: Ahead of the Curve; Making It 'All about the Customer' Has Helped Drive the Car Insurer to the No. 3 Slot in Its Industry and No. 5 on the BW50," *BusinessWeek Online*, April 16, 2003, http://www.businessweek.com.

Tapscott, Don, "Fear No Truth," *Intelligent Enterprise*, March 20, 2004, pp. 10–11.

—Dawn Jacob Laney

◼◼◼
Linda Johnson Rice
1958–
President and chief executive officer, Johnson Publishing

Nationality: American.

Born: May 22, 1958, in Chicago, Illinois.

Education: University of Southern California, BA, 1980; Northwestern University, MBA, 1987.

Family: Daughter of John H. Johnson (publisher and chairman of Johnson Publishing) and Eunice W. Johnson (secretary-treasurer of Johnson Publishing and producer-director of Ebony Fashion Fair); married André Rice, 1984 (divorced 1994); children: one.

Career: Johnson Publishing, 1980–1985, fashion editor of *Ebony*; 1985–1987, vice president; 1987–2002, president and chief operating officer; 2002–, president and chief executive officer.

Awards: Phenomenal Woman Award, 2000; Alumni of the Year, Kellogg School of Management.

Address: Johnson Publishing, 820 S. Michigan Avenue, Chicago, Illinois 60605; http://www.ebony.com.

◼ Linda Johnson Rice was the first African American woman to be named chief executive officer of a company listed among the top five of the Black Enterprise 100s, the nation's largest black-owned companies. Johnson Publishing, founded by Rice's father, John H. Johnson, had more than $400 million in sales as of 2002 and was the number one black-owned, privately held publishing company in the world, worth $350 million and employing more than 2,500 people. The company opened the eyes of mainstream American businesses to the multibillion-dollar influence of the African American consumer market by convincing mainstream companies that they would be well served by advertising in magazines aimed at black readers. At the same time, the company played a key role in establishing the careers of many African American professionals in publishing and advertising.

EARLY LIFE

Born in Chicago, Rice developed interests as an equestrian and opera singer. However, she always had a keen interest in the family business. From the age of six, she often went straight from school to the Johnson Publishing headquarters south of Chicago's downtown loop. "It was a giant baby-sitter," Rice recalled (*USC Trojan Family Magazine*, Winter 2002). As she grew, the young Rice began to play a role in the family business. Her father would often include her in meetings with editors debating about which photos to feature as *Ebony* covers, and the precocious schoolgirl participated actively in the discussions. In addition, Rice would often travel with her mother to France and Italy to shop for haute couture for the Ebony Fashion Fair, a traveling fashion show that raised money for charity.

Rice attended the University of Southern California (USC), earning a BA in journalism in 1980. She collected her first full-time paycheck in 1980 when she became the fashion editor at Johnson Publishing. Over the next several years she held the titles of vice president, president, and chief operating officer. At the same time, she attended Northwestern University's J. L. Kellogg School of Management, earning an MBA in 1988. Rice's early years at Johnson Publishing were noted by William Berry, a University of Illinois journalism professor who was an editor at *Ebony* for seven years: "I've watched her career over the years, and she's retained the availability of an ordinary person who has extraordinary access to power and capital" (*USC Trojan Family Magazine*, Winter 2002).

BUSINESS ACHIEVEMENTS

After her promotion to CEO in 2002, Rice oversaw the production of *Ebony* and *Jet* magazines and was executive producer of a television show, *Ebony/Jet Showcase*. In addition, she developed an aggressive advertising campaign for Fashion Fair Cosmetics, which included special events, more gifts with purchases, and glitzier signage in stores. Without changing any of the products, she attempted to further brand them in various arenas, such as video and television.

Rice sat on several corporate boards of directors, including Continental Bank Corporation, Kimberly Clark, and Bausch & Lomb. She was also on the board of the Boys & Girls Clubs of Chicago, the board of directors of Magazine Publishers of

America, the Museum of Contemporary Art Board of Trustees, and the USC Board of Trustees. She was also a member of the National Association of Black Journalists.

MANAGEMENT AND LEADERSHIP STRATEGIES

Johnson Publishing's change in leadership from John H. Johnson to Linda Johnson Rice was managed sensitively and smoothly, said employees, because of Rice's vision and ability to inspire. In her first few months as CEO, she spent a large portion of each day meeting with groups of employees at all levels of the company. "My door is hardly ever closed," she said. "I'm not the type of CEO that runs a dictatorship, because I don't think that gets you anywhere" (*USC Trojan Family Magazine*, Winter 2002). Like her father, Rice took pride in knowing the details of the company, approving story lists for each issue and making the final decisions on *Ebony* covers. According to Rice, "Out of 12 covers a year, you want 12 hits. You want something out there that is appealing and eye-catching. I'd be crazy not to look at them" (*USC Trojan Family Magazine*, Winter 2002).

With the transition in leadership came a change in managerial style. Rice described her father as an entrepreneur with a fiery temper and the vision required for the birth and growth of a business, while she described herself as a more patient operations person dedicated to managing the size and growth of an established business. Even with more than 2,500 employees nationwide, Johnson Publishing maintained a family atmosphere that reflected the company's leadership, keeping an open-door policy, hand-signing paychecks, and retaining many employees 30 years or longer. Rice was also dedicated to maintaining a healthy mix of business and family time, making a habit of eating Sunday dinners at various local restaurants with her daughter and friends.

BUSINESS STRATEGIES AND PHILOSOPHY

Rice responded to critics that claimed *Ebony* and *Jet* were not serious reflections of African American issues by stating, "We are not an investigative magazine. . . . We are a feature magazine. We are not here to pick apart African Americans. We are here to celebrate, and uplift, and inspire" (*USC Trojan Family Magazine*, Winter 2002). Nonetheless, Rice planned to devote more space in both magazines to the issues of economic equality, education, and drug abuse.

Not a believer in complacency or stagnation, Rice said her drive was inspired both by seeing employees work hard to put out the magazines and hearing the positive responses of readers. "My father built an incredible business, and I don't want to let him down," she said (*USC Trojan Family Magazine*, Winter 2002). Despite several offers, Rice never considered selling the family business, maintaining the spirit of family pride in ownership and control that outweighed the spirit of capitalism.

Rice took the reins to guide the company through a turbulent time in publishing, with advertising revenues throughout the industry the lowest in years. Although *Ebony* and *Jet* overwhelmingly dominated the black publishing market in 2002, they faced mounting competition from emerging niche magazines, such as *Essence*, *Vibe*, and *Black Enterprise*. Despite the proliferation of magazine titles, however, *Jet* had a circulation of more than 950,000, and *Ebony* maintained a circulation of more than 10 million readers and 1 million subscribers.

At the same time, Fashion Fair Cosmetics competed with major makeup manufacturers such as Estée Lauder for consumers of various ethnic backgrounds. However, Fashion Fair Cosmetics, the largest black-owned cosmetics firm in the world, selling in 2,500 stores on three continents, was the world's number one line of makeup and skin care products for women of color. In addition, as of 2004 more than 300,000 patrons attended the Ebony Fashion Fair per year, and the show had raised a total of $49 million for charity, the majority of which was used for scholarships for 475 students.

See also entry on Johnson Publishing Company in *International Directory of Company Histories*.

SOURCES FOR FURTHER INFORMATION

Bengali, Shashank, "Jetsetter," *USC Trojan Family Magazine*, Winter 2002, http://www.usc.edu/dept/pubrel/ trojan_family/winter02/jetsetter.html.

Bennett, Lerone, *Succeeding against the Odds: The Inspiring Autobiography of One of America's Wealthiest Entrepreneurs*, New York: Warner Books, 1989.

Clarke, Caroline V., "At Ebony, a New Johnson Is CEO," *Black Enterprise* 32, no. 11 (June 2002), pp. 136–137.

Henderson, Eric, "Ebony and Jet Forever!" *Africana*, http:// www.africana.com/articles/daily/bk20030528ebonyjet.asp.

Lenoir, Lisa, "Revolutionary Fashion Fair Fights to Keep Its Edge," *Chicago Sun-Times*, November 13, 2003.

—Lee McQueen

■■■
Pierre Richard
1941–
Chairman of the management board and chief executive officer, Dexia Group

Nationality: French.

Born: March 9, 1941, in Dijon, France.

Education: Attended University of Dijon, BS; Ecole Polytechnque, master's in engineering; Ecole Nationale des Ponts et Chaussées, and University of Pennsylvania; attended Columbia University, 1966–1967.

Career: Institute for Urban Studies, Paris, 1967–1968, professor; Cergy-Pontoise, 1967–1972, deputy manager, Urban Planning Department; Ministry of Housing and Urban Development, 1972–1974, technical advisor; General Secretary of the President of the French Republic, Secrétariat general de la présidence de la République, 1974–1978, technical advisor; French Ministry of the Interior, 1978–1982, head, local authorities department; Caisse des dépôts et consignation, 1982–1985, deputy manager; Crédit local de France, 1985–1987, head of the board of trustees and vice president; 1987–1996, president and chief executive officer; Dexia Group, 1996–1999, cochairman; 1999–, chief executive officer.

Awards: Order of the Legion of Honor, Officer of the National Order of Merit and Commander of the Order of Léopold II.

Address: Square de Meeûs, 1 B-1000 Brussels, Belgium; http://www.dexia.com.award>

Pierre Richard. © *Reuters NewMedia Inc./Corbis.*

■ Pierre Richard was the chairman of the executive committee and group CEO of Dexia Group. He was cochairman with Francois Narmon until 1999, when he assumed the role of CEO. Before cofounding Dexia with Narmon, Richard had been chairman and CEO of Crédit Local de France, deputy general manager of the Caisse des Dépots et Consignations, and head of the Local Authorities Department at the French Ministry of the Interior. Richard, who was said to favor an American model of corporate governance, also served on several boards of directors, including those of the European Investment Bank, Compagnie Nationale Air France, *Le Monde,* Crédit du Nord, Generali France Holding, and Financial Security Assurance.

Dexia was created in 1996 by a merger between Crédit Local de France and the Crédit Communal de Belgique. The name Dexia was adopted in 1999 after a merger with Banque International Luxembourg. Dexia was one of the first transnational banks and specialized in local public financing. The group was established in anticipation of the European monetary union, which took place in January 2002. Dexia became one of the 15 most important banks in the European Union. The company offered retail banking services in more than one thousand branches in Belgium and Luxembourg, where its traditional banking activities were principally located. The group was also present in Italy, Sweden, Germany, Austria, and

Spain. With an aggressive acquisition policy, Dexia targeted markets in the United States, the Benelux countries, Switzerland, and the United Kingdom. Its worldwide presence was consolidated after Dexia opened offices in the Americas, Asia, and Australia. Other Dexia services included asset management, private banking, and financial insurance.

BUILDING A CITY AND A CAREER

Richard was trained as an engineer and spent much of his career as a civil servant and urban planner. He was one of the principal planners of the Paris suburb of Cergy-Pontoise, an optimistic attempt at rational demographics and urban planning that went horribly wrong. Cergy was a collection of *cités*, or housing projects, intended to provide assistance to low-income families, but by the 1990s it had become a synonym for social alienation, poverty, and crime.

Richard's background as an urban planner made him something of an outsider among France's banking elite, who initially regarded him with condescension. If he was an outsider, he was an outsider from the inside, having been educated at the elitist and exclusive Ecole Polytechnique and later at the Ecole des Ponts et Chaussées. His years as a civil servant and urban planner, nevertheless, provided Richard with a comprehensive understanding of the intricacies of public finance.

In 1972 the secretary of state Christian Bonnet recruited Richard as a technical advisor in his cabinet. After the general elections of 1974 President Valéry Giscard d'Estaing appointed Richard technical advisor to the General Secretary of the President of the French Republic. Richard's work as an urban planner was sufficiently impressive to allow him to take part in the creation of the Ministry of the Environment and Quality of Life. He was then appointed to head the local authorities department in the Ministry of the Interior. Richard entered the financial world in 1982, when Robert Lion picked him to be general manager of the Caisse des dépôts et consignations. In 1985 Richard was appointed head of the board of directors of the public financing bank Crédit local de France and worked his way up the corporate ladder to become vice president then president and CEO.

BEARDS AND BEASTS: DOING IT HIS WAY

Richard's rise to become head of the Dexia group, Europe's 15th largest bank and at the time the leading bank in public finance, was remarkable for the fact that he was not a tax inspector, practically a requirement in France for qualifying as CEO of a bank. Tenacity in the face of adversity explained his success. Richard flouted the mores of his community by sporting a beard, however neatly cropped. Richard had grown the beard as a sign of radical individuality during the student riots of 1968, a time when beards in France were considered controversial. When he was a candidate to be an adviser on housing to Giscard d'Estaing, Richard was informed that the French president did not like beards. Richard replied that he would discuss the issue only with the president himself. Richard kept the beard throughout his career.

Richard relished his reputation as a nonconformist, and Dexia under him had a unique corporate culture. "Investors say Dexia is a strange animal and I am not sure if this is a positive or a negative. We don't say we are better than other banks, only that we are different," Richard noted to Brian Caplen of the *Banker* (February 1, 2004). While transforming Dexia into a banking giant, Richard remained conscious of his role as an outsider among banking giants. He made a career out of pitting himself against larger beasts, and in his private life he practiced dressage once a week. "I like it as it is a lesson in humility, a way to surpass my fears since the horse has an independent personality. In our personal life we succeed when we surpass our fears," Richard told Karina Robinson of the *Banker* (August 1, 2001).

Richard's management style was influenced by his years in the United States. Alexis de Tocqueville, the author of *Democracy in America*, was a major role model for Richard and a principal source of inspiration. A portrait of the social philosopher hung on a wall in Richard's office. Richard pointed out that de Tocqueville was an advocate of decentralization and was in charge of the law to decentralize France in the 19th century. Accordingly, Richard had a democratic rather than autocratic approach to running his shop. "We have a collegial management, much more so than a French bank," he told Robinson. Nevertheless, in 1999 Dexia was reorganized, and Richard found himself indisputably in charge.

A TRUE EUROPEAN: RICHARD'S LEGACY

Richard was an energetic CEO who created and later led the first truly European bank. He transformed Dexia into a worldwide competitor and established a banking and management model that would be an example for the rest of Europe. Although Dexia was not a universal bank, Richard expanded operations into carefully chosen niche markets. Through an aggressive acquisition policy, Dexia became a lasting and influential enterprise. Most notably Richard resisted the strong tendency in France to promote a French national banking champion, which he considered to be a vain and misguided goal. "In this global economy if we want to compete with the U.S. economy, we must promote a European champion, not a French champion," Richard told Robinson (August 1, 2001).

See also entry on Dexia Group in *International Directory of Company Histories.*

Pierre Richard

SOURCES FOR FURTHER INFORMATION

Caplen, Brian, "Cross-Border Pioneer Fights On," *Banker*, February 1, 2004.

Robinson, Karina, "A Different Kind of European Union," *Banker*, August 1, 2001.

—John Herrick

Kai-Uwe Ricke

1961–

Chairman of the board of management, Deutsche Telekom

Nationality: German.

Born: August 1961, in Krefeld, Germany.

Education: Attended European Business School.

Family: Son of Helmut Ricke (former chairman of Deutsche Telekom).

Career: Talkline, 1990–1995, chief executive officer; 1995–1997, chairman; DeTeMobil Deutsche Telekom Mobilnet, 1998–2001, chairman of the board of management; Deutsche Telekom, 2001–2002, chief operating officer; 2002–, chairman of the board of management.

Address: Deutsche Telekom, Friedrich-Ebert-Allee 140, 53113 Bonn, Germany; http://www.telekom.de.

Kai-Uwe Ricke. *AP/Wide World Photos.*

■ German-born Kai-Uwe Ricke was appointed chairman of the board of management of Deutsche Telekom, a European telecommunications giant, when he was just 41 years of age. Although his father, Helmut Ricke, had once held the same position at the company, Ricke was not the board's first choice and was offered the job only after a number of more seasoned executives declined. Faced with a daunting challenge, Ricke, who had cut his teeth in the wireless sector, was able to turn around the struggling company in under two years, relying on a disciplined approach that valued the implementation of incremental steps over radical change. Despite his lack of top-level executive experience, Ricke proved to be unflappable. When making decisions he was known to be receptive to ideas from others but was quick and purposeful upon acting. Unlike his predecessor at Deutsche Telekom, Ron Sommer, who had harbored global aspirations, Ricke was content with the company's becoming the most profitable integrated telecommunications operation in Europe. According to the *New York Times*, Ricke "clearly [did] not care if he [was] known as a globetrotting mogul" (May 18, 2004).

Ricke was born in 1960 in Germany in the Rhine River port city of Krefeld. He gained his business education by studying at the European Business School in Schloss Reichartshausen, Germany, and by serving an apprenticeship at a bank. Ricke began his business career at the global media company Bertelsmann, serving as an assistant to the board. He would next become head of sales and marketing at Bertelsmann's Swedish subsidiary, Scandinavian Music Club. Ricke's first major appointment came in 1990, when he was named chief executive officer of Talkline, a new mobile phone service provider, at a time when the mobile phone boom was just beginning. In July 1995 he took over the additional post of chairman of Talkline. Ricke joined Deutsche Telekom in January 1998 as chairman of the board of management of DeTeMobil Deutsche Telekom Mobilnet—the mobile telephone business that would change its name to T-Mobile Deutschland with the formation of T-Mobile International. In February 2000 Ricke was named chairman of this new consolidated wireless unit. His final step before landing the top job at Deutsche Telekom was the May 2001 appointment to the position of chief operating officer of the parent company, responsible for both the wireless and the Internet businesses.

DEUTSCHE TELEKOM ROOTS IN STATE POSTAL SERVICE

Deutsche Telekom grew out of the state-owned postal service, Deutsche Bundespost. In 1990 telecommunications reform legislation led to the division of the Bundespost into three independent, state-owned entities: postal services, Post-Bank, and telecommunications, which was known as Deutsche Bundespost Telekom. Ricke's father, Helmut, headed the telecommunications company from 1990 to 1994 as it made the transition from state utility to commercial company. The elder Ricke was responsible for the first global initiatives: establishing an alliance with France Telecom and buying an interest in Sprint. Concerned by the makeup of his supervisory board, shaded by politics, he declined a contract extension. On January 1, 1995, the second phase of the national postal and telecommunications reform went into effect, transforming Deutsche Bundespost Telekom into Deutsche Telekom, which was initially a state-owned stock company. Helmut Ricke's recommended replacement, Ron Sommer, who had been Sony Corporation's head of German operations, was appointed to run the company. Not only was he able to sell the board on his vision of the future of telecoms, but he was also able to convince investors. In November 1996 Sommer guided Deutsche Telekom through its initial public offering, the largest in Europe to date, grossing some $20 million in stock. With a massive war chest at his command, Sommer set out to make Deutsche Telekom a global telecommunications conglomerate, completing a number of sizable acquisitions. Along the way, Ricke and his success at Talkline caught Sommer's eye, and in 1998 Sommer hired Ricke to run the company's mobile phone business. Sommer soon recognized that Ricke had the potential to succeed him and promoted him to the position of chief operating officer.

In a matter of 18 months, Sommer spent about $80 billion to expand Deutsche Telekom's global reach. One of those acquisitions, the $38 billion purchase of VoiceStream Wireless Corporation, which was based in the United States, was made with the firm support of Ricke. Because of the high cost of the acquisition, it was considered a make-or-break deal for Sommer. By the summer of 2002, with the drop in the telecom sector worldwide, the collapse in the price of Deutsche Telekom stock, and the huge debt that the company had taken on in its acquisition spree, Sommer's high-wire act was on the verge of being shut down by the German government, which still owned a 43 percent stake in the company. In the midst of an election season, Chancellor Gerhard Schroeder had been enduring severe criticism from Germany's conservative opposition. Becoming an election issue only exacerbated the prob-

lems hindering Deutsche Telekom, which had been trying to prove that it was indeed independent of government influence. A Schroeder aide reportedly approached several high-profile German executives about replacing Sommer, but given the political implications, no one was interested.

RICKE ASSUMES POST FEW WANTED

Although there was no successor in the wings, Sommer was ousted in July 2002, leaving Deutsche Telekom to be headed by an interim chairman until Ricke was appointed in November 2002. According to London's *Sunday Business,* "It was the job that no one wanted. Porsche chairman Wendelin Wiedeking is said to have turned it down; TUI chairman replied nein danke, as did a slew of other German business leaders and politicians" (November 17, 2002). The lack of interest was not surprising, given the problems Ricke now faced: huge debt, a slow-growth business, and a bureaucratic corporate culture.

Ricke also had to reassure disillusioned investors, many of whom had not forgiven him for his part in the VoiceStream acquisition (which became T-Mobile USA) and indeed considered him part of Deutsche Telekom's problems. They were hardly reassured when Ricke's initial strategy to trim the company's debt—the sale of assets and some restructuring—was essentially the plan Sommer had already begun instituting. Many shareholders wanted Ricke to sell off T-Mobile USA to cut debt, but he resisted giving up the business. Instead, he divested nonstrategic assets, such as real estate and cable television operations.

NOVEL APPROACH TO STAFF CUTS

Aside from lowering interest payments by cutting debt, Ricke needed to cut costs in other ways, in particular by trimming the workforce. But when it came to labor issues, he once again met political obstacles. Not only was the government fearful of the electoral ramifications of layoffs, but also the labor union held half of the 20 seats on the company's supervisory board. One area in which Ricke hoped to have a greater impact was in changing Deutsche Telekom's corporate culture. He declared that he wanted a new leadership style: "I want to encourage open and controversial discussion, but then I expect swift and speedy decisions" (*Newsweek International,* December 30, 2002).

Ricke was not at his post very long before he had the unpleasant task of announcing that Deutsche Telekom had lost $27.1 billion in 2002, the largest annual loss ever suffered by a European corporation. Mostly to blame were massive writedowns on investments that the company had made during the heady days of the late 1990s technology stock bubble. In a statement that accompanied the release of the year-end numbers, Ricke maintained, "We are well aware of the scale of the figure. We are in no way trying to gloss over this" (*New York Times*, March 11, 2003). Nevertheless, there were some bright signs for the company. Debt was coming down steadily; business was picking up for T-Mobile in the United States, where the subsidiary was the fastest-growing wireless operator; and business was also improving in the German market, due in large part to a drop in competition as lean times winnowed the field of competitors.

RICKE ACHIEVES QUICK TURNAROUND

A little more than a year after taking charge of Deutsche Telekom, Ricke had completed an impressive turnaround. Debt was under control, there was no further need to sell off assets, and the company had returned to profitability. Ricke's ambitions were modest, which was reassuring to investors during a period of lowered expectations. But he also revealed some creativity when he found a way to take advantage of a new law to address his labor problems. Approximately 12,000 employees were transferred to a subsidiary that acted as a personnel service agency and hired them out to other companies—as well as serving the temporary employee needs of Deutsche Telekom. The savings were in the tens of millions, and should the economy improve and the need for temporary employees grow, the company would stand to save even more. As a result of Ricke's achievements, many of his skeptics were appeased. In the words of one analyst quoted in *BusinessWeek* in December 2003, Ricke has "got a real sense of discipline, a willingness to just get things done."

Ricke's ongoing strategy was "vague," according to *BusinessWeek* (December 15, 2003): "a six-point plan that includes continuing to push broadband, cutting labor costs and selling more services to corporations such as maintenance of local area networks or security measures." Ricke was open to a return to selective acquisitions but clearly did not possess the grand ambitions of his predecessor. He appeared content to lower his sights to Europe, the German market in particular. As for T-Mobile, he saw the U.S. unit as a hedge against business in Germany, although he was not opposed to selling it, especially in light of the consolidation taking place in America's cellular market. Ever practical, Ricke explained, "I'm not in the U.S. to own a Rolls-Royce. I'm in the U.S. to get a reasonable rate of return" (*New York Times*, May 18, 2004).

See also entry on Deutsche Telekom AG in *International Directory of Company Histories.*

SOURCES FOR FURTHER INFORMATION

Boston, William, "Recovering From the Tech Bubble," *Newsweek International*, December 30, 2002, p. 52.

Culp, Eric, "Deutsche Telekom Names New Chief," *Sunday Business* (London), November 17, 2002.

Eakin, Hugh, "Deutsche Telekom Posts Biggest Loss in Europe's History," *New York Times*, March 11, 2003.

Ewing, Jack, "What's Ricke's Next Trick?" *BusinessWeek*, December 15, 2003, p. 30.

Landler, Mark, "Progress at Deutsche Telekom After Returning to Its Roots," *New York Times*, May 18, 2004.

Latour, Almar, and Matthew Karnitschnig, "Deutsche Telkom Announces New CEO and Posts Hefty Loss," *Wall Street Journal*, November 15, 2002.

—Ed Dinger

■■■

Stephen Riggio
1954–
Chief executive officer, Barnes & Noble

Nationality: American.

Born: 1954, in New York City, New York.

Education: Brooklyn College, AB, 1974.

Family: Son of Steve Riggio (semiprofessional boxer and cab driver); married (spouse's name unknown); children: three.

Career: Barnes & Noble Bookstores, 1974–1978, positions in buying and marketing departments; 1978–1981, general merchandising manager; 1981–1987, vice president and general manager of direct mail and publishing divisions; 1988–1995, executive vice president of merchandising; B. Dalton Bookseller, 1993–1995, president; Barnes & Noble, 1995–1997, chief operations officer; 1997–2002, vice chairman; Barnesandnoble.com, 1997–1999, chief executive officer; Barnes & Noble, 2002–, chief executive officer.

Address: Barnes & Noble, Inc., 122 Fifth Avenue, New York, New York 10011; http://www.barnesand nobleinc.com.

■ Stephen Riggio worked for his brother, Leonard, at Barnes & Noble for nearly 28 years in a variety of capacities before being appointed chief executive officer in 2002. Riggio was largely responsible for the launch of the company's online subsidiary, Barnesandnoble.com, in 1997. In contrast to his brother's outspokenness, Riggio was known to be more reserved and intellectual.

FOLLOWING IN HIS BROTHER'S FOOTSTEPS

Although Stephen Riggio experienced some of his success due to his own leadership skills, his assent to the position at the top of Barnes & Noble was thanks in no small part to the work of his brother, Leonard. The Riggios grew up in Brooklyn, New York, in a home filled with extended family members, such as grandparents, aunts, and uncles. The brothers' fa-

ther was Steve Riggio, a semiprofessional boxer from 1939 to 1948 who once defeated the eventual middleweight champion Rocky Graziano. The elder Steve Riggio, who died in 1982, later became a cab driver in New York City. Leonard, who was 14 years older than Stephen, opened a bookstore on the campus of New York University in 1965. He later convinced bankers to loan to him $1.2 million to buy Barnes & Noble, an old bookstore located on Fifth Avenue in New York City.

Riggio was still a teenager when his brother began running these bookstores. After graduating from high school, Riggio enrolled at Brooklyn College, earning a bachelor of arts degree in anthropology in 1974. He immediately went to work for his brother upon graduation. Riggio joined his brother's business during the same year in which Leonard initiated a plan to provide major discounts. For instance, books on the *New York Times* best-seller list were marked down 40 percent while best-selling paperbacks were marked down 20 percent. Leonard Riggio's plan was later credited with changing the economics of the bookselling industry.

Riggio worked at Barnes & Noble in New York in various capacities from 1974 through 1987. He began working in the company's buying and marketing departments before being promoted to general merchandising manager in 1978. Three years later he was promoted to vice president and general manager of the company's direct mail and publishing divisions. Leonard Riggio's quest for growth culminated in the purchase of one of his company's competitors, B. Dalton Bookseller, in 1986. The acquisition made Barnes & Noble the largest bookseller in the United States. In 1987 Stephen Riggio was appointed executive vice president in charge of marketing.

INSTRUMENTAL IN BUILDING BOOK SUPERSTORES

Leonard Riggio borrowed an idea from such retailers as Circuit City and Toys "R" Us to develop a chain of book superstores. The idea behind the construction of these stores was to offer a vast selection of books at discounted prices and to attract customers by offering such amenities as reading tables, comfortable chairs, and coffee shops. Stephen Riggio was instrumental in the development of these superstores, which began in earnest in 1991.

Riggio remained executive vice president of Barnes & Noble through 1995. In 1993 he added a second title when he was named president of B. Dalton Bookseller. He moved into the newly created position of chief operating officer of Barnes & Noble in 1995. Two years later, in 1997, he was named vice chairman of the company.

ATTEMPTING TO COMPETE WITH AMAZON

Leonard and Stephen Riggio were shocked during the mid-1990s with the rapid growth of Amazon.com, an online bookseller. In 1996 Stephen convinced Leonard that the company should create an online presence, although initially the brothers envisioned a Web site that would be used to market the company's physical bookstores. However, Amazon grew rapidly and began to cut into Barnes & Noble's profits. The Riggios decided to compete directly with Amazon, believing that they would destroy the start-up company on the strength of Barnes & Noble's name as a retail outlet and because of the company's deep pockets.

Riggio was named chief executive officer of the online subsidiary, Barnesandnoble.com. Although technicians did not believe that the company's online site was ready, Riggio ordered the site to go live in March 1997. Although Barnes & Noble's online subsidiary had an agreement with America Online to be the latter's exclusive bookseller, the site failed to compete effectively with Amazon. Riggio, who maintained dual duties as CEO of the online company and vice chairman of the parent company, did not devote his full attention to Barnesandnoble.com. In an interview with *Wired* (June 1999), one executive questioned, "If you are trying to significantly compete against your archenemy, do you think it's smart to have the chairman treating it as a part-time job?"

Riggio was phased out as CEO of Barnesandnoble.com in 1998, and in 1999 he resumed his full-time duties as vice chairman of Barnes & Noble. His experience with the online subsidiary did not end there, however, as he was partially responsible for focusing on the improvement of delivery times for online sales. Barnesandnoble.com did not have a CEO for nearly two years in the early 2000s, and Riggio served as the subsidiary's acting chief executive during that time until the appointment of a replacement in 2002.

INEVITABLE COMPARISONS BETWEEN BROTHERS

Riggio was never able to avoid comparisons with Leonard, though their styles stood largely in stark contrast to one another. Leonard Riggio developed a reputation for being confrontational as the leader of Barnes & Noble. He was reviled by many due to the success of Barnes & Noble, which caused the closure of countless independent bookstores throughout the United States.

Despite the criticism, Leonard remained outspoken and at times contemptuous towards his competitors. By comparison, Stephen was known to spend his spare time with his family at his New Jersey home. He was regarded as being more reserved and more likely to avoid confrontation than his older brother. "Len is the tough one and he's an incredible negotiator," said one family friend. "Steve is more intellectual and reads a lot of books" (*Wired*, June 1999). The brothers' opinions were known to clash.

PROMOTED TO CHIEF EXECUTIVE OFFICER

Riggio's years in the number two position at Barnes & Noble ended in 2002, when Leonard announced that he was stepping down as chief executive officer and that Stephen would be promoted to the position. Leonard Riggio remained as the company's chairman. Although Stephen Riggio had nearly 28 years of experience with the company, some analysts questioned the move, noting potential conflicts of interest because Leonard Riggio remained the company's largest shareholder. Some commentators also questioned whether Stephen's leadership style would be as successful as his older brother's. Barnes & Noble stayed the course after Riggio took over the company, opening more than 30 new stores in 2003. The company's overall growth remained steady. In 2003 the company announced that the online subsidiary Riggio had run would go private, with the company repurchasing all of the outstanding stock. Riggio was active on the boards of the National Book Foundation, the Association for the Help of Retarded Children, and the National Down Syndrome Society.

See also entries on Barnes & Noble, Inc. and B. Dalton Bookseller Inc. in *International Directory of Company Histories*.

SOURCES FOR FURTHER INFORMATION

Dugan, I. Jeanne, "The Baron of Books," *BusinessWeek*, June 18, 1998, http://www.businessweek.com/1998/26/b3584001.htm.

Kirkpatrick, David D., "A Shifting of Leadership at Bookseller," *New York Times*, February 14, 2002.

St. John, Warren, "Barnes & Noble's Epiphany," *Wired*, June 1999, http://www.wired.com/wired/archive/7.06/barnes_pr.html.

Wilner, Richard, "Ring-Around with Riggio's Resume," *New York Post*, November 11, 1998.

—Matthew C. Cordon

■■■
Jim Robbins
President and chief executive officer, Cox Communications

Nationality: American.

Education: University of Pennsylvania, BA; Harvard University, MBA.

Career: WBZ-TV, 1969–1972, assistant producer, then managing news editor; Continental Cablevision of Ohio and Montachusett Cable Television, 1972–1979, various management positions; Viacom Communications, 1979–1983, vice president and general manager for Viacom Cable of Long Island, then senior vice president of operations; Cox Communications, 1983–1984, vice president of New York City operations; 1984–1985, senior vice president of Atlanta and New Orleans operations; 1985–, president; 1995–, president and chief executive officer.

Awards: Named one of *Forbes* magazine's Most Powerful People, 2000 and 2001.

Address: Cox Communications, 1400 Lake Hearn Drive NE, Atlanta, Georgia 30319; http://www.cox.com.

■ In 1985 James (Jim) Robbins became president of Cox Communications, the third-largest cable-television provider in the United States. Ten years later the position of CEO was added to his duties. A veteran of the television industry, Robbins ran operations for several cable systems before joining Cox. While at its helm, he always stressed a commitment to customer service and an unwavering dedication to the cable industry.

AN EARLY INTEREST IN BROADCASTING

Robbins graduated from the University of Pennsylvania and then served two tours of duty in Vietnam. On his first tour he served with the U.S. Navy as a line officer on a destroyer. On his second tour, and by now interested in broadcasting, Robbins was assigned to the post of deputy public-affairs officer for the mobile riverine force, stationed on the Mekong River. "It taught me a lot about the news business," he told *Broadcasting* (February 15, 1988).

When he returned from Vietnam, Robbins had the choice of working as a reporter for a Tulsa, Oklahoma, television network affiliate, or pursuing an MBA at Harvard. He chose the latter, but remained interested in television. While still in school he took a job as an assistant producer for WBZ-TV in Boston. He stayed on at WBZ after receiving his degree, eventually becoming the managing news editor.

ENTERING THE CABLE INDUSTRY

Robbins enjoyed the production end of the television business, but he wanted to apply the business and management training he had gained at Harvard. He took a job running a small cable system for the Adams-Russell Company, where he increased the number of subscribers, raised rates, and improved programming. He also met H. I. Grousbeck, then chairman of Continental Cablevision, who hired him to build franchises near Dayton, Ohio. When he had finished that task, Robbins moved on to Viacom, where he had the job of fixing the company's troubled Suffolk County system on Long Island. He described the operation when he arrived as "a disaster." Robbins got the system under control and improved customer service. "My career in the cable business has taken me into very tough situations, turnaround situations," Robbins told *Broadcasting* (February 15, 1988).

JOINED COX COMMUNICATIONS

In 1983 Robbins was offered the position of running Cox's cable partnership in Staten Island, New York. He did that for a year, and then he moved to the company's Atlanta headquarters to oversee Cox's Louisiana and California operations. In 1985 he was named president of Cox Communications, which was then the country's fifth-largest multiple-service operator (MSO), a cable company that operated more than one cable system.

Robbins was a stickler for customer service. He boasted that under his leadership Cox's customer-service representatives answered calls within 25 seconds and its service technicians handled repairs within three days. He also developed the strategy of wooing customers with reasonable rates and then gradually increasing the rates over time. In 1991 Robbins took over as chairman of the National Cable Television Association.

In that role he fought against the entry of telephone companies into the cable-television business, a move he said would reduce competition and hurt consumers. He also pushed for the cable industry to improve customer service, keep rates under control, improve its negative image in the media, and become more involved in the community—especially in education. Robbins was a big proponent of the Cable in the Classroom program, which brought educational television shows into schools around the country.

LOOKING TO THE FUTURE AT COX COMMUNICATIONS

Meanwhile, Robbins kept busy modernizing his company. In the late 1990s Cox entered the digital age, offering digital cable and high-speed Internet access. And even though Robbins had fought the entry of telephone companies into the cable industry a decade earlier, under his leadership Cox began offering its customers telephone service. In 1999 Congress was considering regulating access to Internet service, which would have forced Cox to open its high-access lines to competing Internet service providers. Robbins urged the government to stay out of Internet regulation, claiming that it would reduce competition and slow new investment in technology.

Also in 1999 Robbins surprised analysts by acquiring TCA Cable TV, a Texas cable operator. Whereas most of Cox-owned systems were in major metropolitan areas, TCA served less-profitable rural areas. Robbins claimed the purchase added a strategic one million new customers, but after making the move he admitted that Cox would probably stay away from similar acquisitions in the future. In 2001, with the telephone business proving less popular than he had anticipated, Robbins scaled back the company's expansion of phone service. At the time, it had only 245,000 phone customers out of its 6.2 million home subscribers.

In 2003 lawmakers and the cable industry began battling over rising cable costs. Robbins and other cable-system owners blamed the increasing costs on programmers. In 2003 Robbins testified before Congress, calling for regulations on programming prices, especially on sports-network licensing fees. He was especially concerned about ESPN, which had raised its rates several times. Cox and other cable systems had to pass those additional costs on to their customers, he claimed. He suggested that cable operators offer sports programming to their customers on a separate tier for an additional charge. Disney's Michael Eisner, whose company owned 80 percent of ESPN, responded by calling Robbins "a whiner." Robbins fired back, accusing Eisner of using "Goofy math" (*Broadcasting & Cable*, June 9, 2003).

The following year the Senate aimed its concern over rising prices squarely at the cable industry. Senators threatened new cable regulations if operators did not rein in soaring prices and offer customers greater channel choice. But Robbins and other cable operators again asserted that rising costs were merely a reflection of increasing prices for programming, and he said that a move to à la carte pricing would only increase prices and result in fewer programming choices for consumers.

OTHER INTERESTS

Robbins served on C-SPAN's executive committee and the board of trustees of STI Classic Funds, a mutual-fund affiliate of Sun Trust Bank. He also served as chairman of the board of the National Cable Television Association from 1991 to 1992 and 1999 to 2000. A firm believer in community service, Robbins was actively involved in the local and national chapters of the National Diabetes Foundation (one of his children has diabetes). He served as chairman of the board of the Juvenile Diabetes Research Foundation, International.

See also entry on Viacom Inc. in *International Directory of Company Histories*.

SOURCES FOR FURTHER INFORMATION

Higgins, John M., "Cox, ESPN Brawl Gets Nasty: Eisner Calls Robbins a 'Whiner'; Robbins Accuses Disney of 'Goofy math,'" *Broadcasting & Cable*, June 9, 2003, p. 8.

"James Robbins: Putting the Community in CATV," *Broadcasting*, February 15, 1998, p. 159.

—Stephanie Watson

■■■

Brian L. Roberts

1959–

President, chief executive officer and chairman, Comcast

Nationality: American.

Born: June 28, 1959, in Philadelphia, Pennsylvania.

Education: Wharton School, University of Pennsylvania, BS, 1981.

Family: Son of Ralph Roberts (founder of Comcast); married Aileen Kennedy; children: three.

Career: Comcast, 1981–1989, comptroller, Trenton office; 1990–, president; 2002–, chief executive officer and president; 2004–, chairman of the board.

Address: Comcast, 1500 Market Street, Philadelphia, Pennsylvania 19102; www.comcast.com.

■ Brian L. Roberts took the helm of Comcast, the business his father had started in the late 1960s, and oversaw its growth into the largest U.S. cable-television operator. The company finished 2002 with at least $12.5 billion in sales. To build a collection of programming content, Roberts purchased stakes in several cable channels, including QVC, which supplies more than half of the company's revenues, E! Entertainment Television, and two Philadelphia sports teams. But Comcast's 2001 acquisition of AT&T Broadband, which boosted its subscriber count to 21.3 million, is the deal that placed Brian Roberts on the corporate map. Roberts believed that the future of the cable industry was in the broadband platform, and he aggressively pursued the implementation and delivery of high-profit services such as digital video, high-speed data, and voice. Roberts's leadership style, not to mention every major business decision he made, was inextricably linked to his hero and mentor—his father.

A FAMILY BUSINESS IS BORN

The Roberts family was shaped by the Depression. Ralph Roberts, the founder of Comcast, was born into affluence—the family even had a chauffeur for a while—but the wealth

Brian L. Roberts. *AP/Wide World Photos.*

quickly disappeared. Said Ralph Roberts: "My father died, and we lost all our money. People who never had a financial problem in their lives can never understand what terror there is in that" (*New York Times,* June 22, 1997). Driven by his family's past, Ralph Roberts acquired an entrepreneurial streak, starting a company that sold belts, suspenders, and other men's accessories. He traded in fashion for cable after hearing in a poker game about a company looking for investors. Along with two colleagues, he bought American Cable Systems, renamed Comcast, in 1969.

In its formative years, cable was a mom-and-pop business. As the industry grew, however, it quickly acquired a cutthroat streak, with smaller operators cashing out and handing over their subscribers to bigger businesses. Comcast was the exception. Since its modest beginnings in 1963 as a single system in Tupelo, Mississippi, Comcast went public in 1972 and grew eightfold from 1987 to 1992, but still managed to remain a tightly knit family business. Comcast's CFO, Julian Brodsky, once told Ralph Roberts that he would make millions if he took the company private, to which Roberts replied: "I don't want to be rich. I want to build a great company that I can turn over to Brian" (*Fortune*, October 29, 2001).

A TEENAGE *WALL STREET JOURNAL* READER

For Brian Roberts, the decision of what to do with his life was determined from childhood: He would proudly follow in his father's footsteps. As a child he helped assemble the coupon books that were mailed to Comcast's customers. As a teen he was fascinated by facts and figures. The road to a finance degree at the University of Pennsylvania's Wharton School began in high school, where Roberts read the *Wall Street Journal* between classes to check on his stock investments. He also had his own financial advisor, with whom he would meet frequently. Another high-school activity was accompanying his father to meetings with bankers to negotiate loans. Said Brodsky: "I think we have known that Brian would take over the company since he was about eight years old" (*Fortune*, October 29, 2001).

AN UNUSUAL FATHER-SON RELATIONSHIP

After college, Ralph Roberts encouraged his son to assert his independence by finding work outside the family business. But Brian Roberts doggedly pursued employment at Comcast, and his father relented on the condition that he would join the company at the bottom and work his way up on his own merit. His first jobs involved selling cable service door-to-door and climbing utility poles to string cable.

But while Ralph Roberts insisted on the merit system, after his son proved himself, Brian Roberts was given opportunities to shine. In 1986 Comcast joined an industry bailout of debt-ridden Turner Broadcasting System. Most assumed that Ralph would be the company representative to join the Turner board, but he sent his son instead. Said Terry McGuirk, a Turner executive and friend of Ralph Roberts: "It was an important experience for Brian. The people who sat around that table were the most powerful in the industry, and Brian was recognized as a peer" (*Fortune*, October 29, 2001).

A NEW GENERATION TAKES OVER

Not long after the Turner deal, Comcast aligned with TCI president John Malone to purchase half of Storer Communications, a move that made Comcast the nation's fifth-largest cable company, with more than two million subscribers. As the company grew, so did Brian's clout. In 1990 Ralph Roberts named himself Comcast's chairman and his 30-year-old son president.

Families that work together have been known to implode under the pressure, but Ralph and Brian Roberts appeared to have escaped that kind of tension and bruised egos. Leo Hindery, former president of AT&T Broadband, said, "Ralph and Brian have the most remarkable father-son relationship I've seen in any context. Rather than battling each other, as fathers and sons often do in a family business, they have this supportive, loving relationship" (*Fortune*, October 29, 2001).

The Roberts team set up adjoining offices and confided with one another about important business decisions. Said Brian Roberts: "We do months of work with advisers, bankers, financial analysts, corporate strategists, lawyers, and then you get to the moment of truth: Should we do it? That's when I walk into Ralph's office and say, 'OK, what's the call?'" (*San Francisco Chronicle*, February 15, 2004). This family relationship helped drive impressive financial results, as Comcast stock split 12 times between 1971 and 2004. Together, the Robertses decided against several merger offers that would have increased the company's shareholder value in the short term because they would have ultimately weakened the family's control of the company.

ASSERTING POWER OVER AN INDUSTRY MOGUL

In 1994 the revered Hollywood mogul Barry Diller attempted to sell QVC, the home-shopping network he ran, to CBS. Comcast already owned 15 percent of QVC and, unbeknownst to Diller, was anxious to secure the rest. Just hours before Diller was to sign off on the deal, the father and son surprised him with their intentions at a New Jersey airport, where he had arrived in his private jet. The CBS-QVC merger died and Comcast bought the network for $2.5 billion. The decision was prescient. In December 2001 the network set a record by securing $80 million in orders, including 30,000 Dell computers.

THE FUTURE OF CABLE

During the 1990s Roberts gradually assumed a leading role in his family's business during a time when the future of the industry was dubious. Congress had re-regulated the industry and opened the doors for the Baby Bells, the seven telecom companies formed after the breakup of AT&T in the mid-1980s, to compete. Meanwhile, satellite competitors like DirectTV aggressively pursued cable's customers. Recalled Brian: "We did some soul searching. Was the cable industry obsolete? Was it an opportune time to get out? Our conclusion was that if you rebuilt your system with this new fiber-optic coaxial hybrid—which we now call broadband—the glass was half full, not half empty. We could compete" (*San Francisco Chronicle*, February 15, 2004).

It would not be cheap. Comcast invested $5 billion to create a digital-cable company that offered all of the trappings of modern U.S. television service: two hundred channels, high-speed Internet access, and video on demand. An important vote of confidence came from Bill Gates in 1997. During a dinner in Seattle with several cable moguls, the Microsoft CEO asked what could be done to accelerate broadband's growth. Brian Roberts replied: "Why don't you buy 10 percent of the industry? Most of us are here tonight" (*Fortune*, October 29, 2001). Instead, Gates decided to buy 10 percent of Comcast in a deal that cemented Comcast's industry standing. Recalled Brian: "We had 650 analysts on the conference call to discuss the deal. Usually we have about 200" (*New York Times*, June 22, 1997).

EYEING A MEGADEAL

In 2000 AT&T announced that it would split into three separate entities, including its giant cable unit, AT&T Broadband, which claimed 13 million subscribers and dismal finances; AT&T Wireless, at one time the nation's largest wireless company; AT&T Business—the network, the labs, the AT&T brand—and $28.4 billion in revenues from wholesale and corporate customers; the AT&T Consumer unit that became a tracking stock for consumer long distance; and whatever the company could put together in D.S.L., as well as its Internet access business.

But AT&T Broadband continued to struggle in 2001, with profit margins hovering around 18 percent in some cities versus industry averages of about 35 percent or better. Roberts viewed an acquisition of AT&T Broadband as a great opportunity.

Brian Roberts wanted the deal badly, and few in the industry questioned his competitive streak. In college, he had joined Penn's squash team as a freshman and was one of the worst players on the team; by the time he graduated he was all-American player, known for his intense drive and sharp sense of strategy. He also claimed three silver medals from his contribution to the U.S. squash team at the Maccabiah Games (the Jewish Olympics) in Israel in 1981, 1985, and 1997.

In 2002, Comcast acquired AT&T Broadband for $29.2 billion in stock and the assumption of more than $24 billion in AT&T debt. The transaction made Comcast the nation's largest cable operator with 22 million subscribers, nearly twice as many as second-place AOL Time Warner Inc.

A MEDIA EXECUTIVE WHO AVOIDED HYPE

The Comcast-AT&T deal was the biggest in the industry since the AOL-Time Warner merger in 2001. With cable subscribers, broadband users, and a modest programming business, the new Comcast contained the key components of a media empire. Still, Roberts, an understated business executive who preferred mass transportation to limousines and for years held the company's annual meeting in the cafeteria, avoided grand pronouncements. When asked about the impact the deal would have, he replied: "We will go from a regional cable company to being a premiere provider of entertainment and communications services into people's homes." His father's own past played a role in this tempered enthusiasm. "My father watched his parents lose it all," he said. "You talk to anybody in the company and they'll say, 'Brian's a fatalist. He's constantly wary.' It could all go away in an instant" (*BusinessWeek*, November 18, 2002).

ROLLING THE DICE ON AN OPPORTUNITY OF A LIFETIME

The AT&T Broadband acquisition left Comcast in a financially vulnerable position at a time when the industry was suffering. Media and cable companies were going out of business and those that remained were affected by accounting improprieties at several cable companies that created a general distrust of the entire industry. Competition from satellite services threatened to cripple the industry even more. In 2001 cable shares lost 57 percent of their value and Comcast's shares fell nearly 34 percent to about $25. Said industry analyst Alan Bezoza of CIBS World Markets: "Investors want to see the proof in the pudding. Where's the cash? It's that simple" (*BusinessWeek*, November 18, 2002).

It was some time before Brian Roberts could answer that question. The acquisition meant that Comcast would have to take on enormous debt in a weak economy. In addition to reducing that debt he would also have to get revenues flowing again. This required that he spend about $2 billion to upgrade AT&T's rundown cable systems while working hand-in-hand with a vocal critic of the merger, former AT&T chief executive C. Michael Armstrong, who became nonexecutive chairman of the new company, replacing Ralph Roberts. Yet Roberts felt that the potential rewards of purchasing AT&T's cable business surpassed the risks. "You only get one chance to redefine your company, and this was ours" (*BusinessWeek*, November 18, 2002).

Much of Roberts's plans hinged on the growth of broadband services. Some analysts predicted that about 30 percent of Comcast's subscribers—about 6.7 million homes—would be buying high-speed data by the end of 2006. Others warned that such projections were too optimistic. Said Leo Hindery, a former president of AT&T Broadband who had become CEO of the Yankees Entertainment & Sports Network: "I'd be shocked if you get 20 percent of homes on high-speed data" (*BusinessWeek*, November 18, 2002).

TRYING TO CATCH A MOUSE

By the end of 2003 Comcast had boosted profit margins at AT&T Broadband's old cable networks, helping earn Roberts the distinction from *Institutional Investor* magazine as one of "America's best CEOs." Hungry for an even bigger deal, Comcast announced that it would sell its 17.9 percent stake in Time Warner Cable, the second-largest cable company in the United States, thus setting the stage for a surprise February 11, 2004, Comcast announcement of a $66 billion hostile takeover bid for the Walt Disney Company.

Under the deal, Comcast would pay $54 billion in stock for Disney. The deal would add Disney's $12 billion debt to Comcast's already debt-laden books. In return, Comcast would get what every cable-delivery company wanted: original programming content such as feature films and network television shows. Disney owned Miramax, ESPN, ABC, the Mighty Ducks of Anaheim hockey team, and some of the most recognizable films and animated movies in the world. The acquisition would make Comcast the world's largest media conglomerate, surpassing even Time Warner.

A TAKEOVER BATTLE ENDS QUICKLY

The board of Walt Disney, however, unanimously rejected the offer from Comcast as being too low. The board noted that the offer was worth $3.60 less per share than the market price of Disney's stock. The board also reaffirmed its confidence in embattled CEO Michael Eisner, saying that it expected Disney's current structure and strategy to enhance shareholder value. Eisner had been under siege from several factions, including disgruntled former board members, corporate partners, restless shareholders, and, now, Comcast.

In April 2004 Comcast dropped its offer. Roberts had misread his own shareholders, who drove the company's stock price down, making it easy for the Disney board to ignore the bid and difficult for Comcast to sweeten the pot. Foreseeing Wall Street's disapproval, Comcast timed the news with the announcement of its first-quarter earnings: revenue of its cable systems rose 9.8 percent from the first quarter of 2003 to $4.65 billion. The company earned a profit of $65 million compared with a loss of $297 million a year earlier. Still, the company's shares remained 11 percent lower than they had been before Comcast's offer for Disney. Said Craig Moffett, a cable analyst at Sanford C. Bernstein & Company: "Some damage has still been done. It's not that easy to put all this be-

hind you. The after effects of the bid are going to linger" (*Wall Street Journal*, April 29, 2004).

RECOVERING FROM A PUBLIC BLOW

The failed takeover threatened Roberts's reputation as a highly skilled dealmaker. A chance to restore some of his luster came in the form of a potential acquisition of Adelphia Communications, the country's fifth-largest cable company, which had been operating under bankruptcy protection. In April 2004 Adelphia's board voted to explore the possibility of selling the company, and Roberts said that Comcast would consider an offer.

Comcast also had strong prospects in its broadband business. In early 2004 it announced plans to begin offering telephone service using Internet technology, which could lead to the introduction of other services, such as videophones. As for the Disney debacle, Roberts refused to dwell. "Being disciplined means knowing when it's time to walk away. That time is now" (*Wall Street Journal*, April 29, 2004).

See also entry on Comcast Corporation in *International Directory of Company Histories*.

SOURCES FOR FURTHER INFORMATION

Fabrikant, Geraldine, "The Heir Clearly Apparent at Comcast," *New York Times*, June 22, 1997.

Grant, Peter, "Comcast Drops Offer to Buy Disney," *Wall Street Journal*, April 29, 2004.

Helyar, John, "The First Family of Cable," *Fortune*, October 29, 2001, p. 137.

Jones, Del, "Comcast CEO Keeps a Pretty Low Profile," *USA Today*, February 12, 2004.

Lieberman, David, "Father-Son Odd Couple Make Bid to Rule Cable," *USA Today*, July 23, 2001.

Lowry, Tom, "A New Cable Giant," *BusinessWeek*, November 18, 2002, p. 108.

Wallack, Todd, "A Father-Son Team that Usually Wins," *San Francisco Chronicle*, February 15, 2004.

—Tim Halpern

■■■
Harry J. M. Roels
1948–
President and chief executive officer, RWE

Nationality: Dutch.

Born: July 26, 1948, in Netherlands.

Education: University of Leiden, degree in physical chemistry, 1971.

Career: Shell, 1971–1996, petroleum engineer; various positions in exploration and production; senior petroleum engineer, Turkey and Norway; technical manager, Norske Shell; director, corporate development, Shell Internationale Petroleum Maatschappij, The Hague; manager, Offshore Business Division, Nederlandse Aardolie Maatschappij; area coordinator, numerous Latin American countries, Shell International Petroleum Company, London; 1996–1998, regional business director, Middle East and Africa, Shell International Exploration and Production, The Hague; 1998–1999, general manager, Nederlandse Aardolie Maatschappij; 1999–2002, member, board of management, Shell Nederland; group managing director, Royal Dutch/Shell Group; RWE, 2003–, president and chief executive officer.

Address: RWE, Opernplatz 1, Essen, 45128 Germany; http://www.rwe.com/en.

Harry J. M. Roels. *AP/Wide World Photos.*

THREE DECADES AT SHELL

Roels was born in the Netherlands and graduated with a degree in physical chemistry from the University of Leiden in 1971. He joined Shell, now known as Royal Dutch/Shell Group, that same year. He began his career as a petroleum engineer and went on to hold various positions in exploration and production before becoming a senior engineer for petroleum in Turkey and then in Norway. While working in Norway he was promoted to technical manager of Norske Shell. Following this appointment, he became director of corporate development for Shell Internationale Petroleum Maatschappij in The Hague.

Roels's next position was head of the Offshore Business Division of Nederlandse Aardolie Maatschappij, a joint venture between Shell and Exxon. Later he was promoted to area coordinator for several Latin American countries at Shell Interna-

■ When Harry J. M. Roels was named president and CEO of RWE in 2003, he took charge of Germany's second-largest utility company, which was underperforming and burdened with debt. His predecessor had gone through a wide-ranging acquisition spree to build a utility company that was involved in electricity, water, recycling and waste management, coal mining, petroleum, natural gas, and related products. Overall, the acquisitions cost approximately $30 billion. According to market analysts, Roels conducted a conservative revolution, cleaning up the utility with efficiency and surprising analysts and stockholders with better-than-expected debt reduction, cost cuts, and dividend growth.

tional Petroleum Company, London. He returned to The Hague in 1996 as regional business director for the Middle East and Africa, working for Shell International Exploration and Production. Roels then took on the responsibilities of serving as general manager of Nederlandse Aardolie Maatschappij and as managing director of Shell Nederland. In 1999 he became a managing director at Royal Dutch Petroleum Company and a member of the board of management of the Royal Dutch/Shell Group.

TAKES OVER AT RWE

In January 2002 Roels abruptly announced his retirement from Royal Dutch/Shell after 30 years with the company and just six years before his retirement. He said that he was quitting for personal reasons, and the company offered no further explanation. As reported in *Power Economics*, however, some industry insiders speculated that Roels quit because he had been passed over for the position of chairman.

With over 30 years of international experience and expertise in the energy field, Roels joined RWE, which was limping along after a mammoth spending spree that included purchasing Thames Water and Innogy of Great Britain and the $4.6 billion acquisition of American Water Works, the largest water company in the United States. Laboring under EUR 25 billion of debt and trying to work with an outdated structure of 13 almost totally independent divisions, the company turned to Roels for leadership and appointed him as president and CEO effective February 1, 2003.

As reported by the *Sunday Times* in London, some analysts believed that Roels's task as the new CEO of the vast utility business should have sent prospective candidates for the job running in the opposite direction. In April 2003 the company reported a 22 percent drop in full-year net profit, largely because of acquisitions and ongoing weak performances from its noncore divisions, including civil-engineering contractor Hochtief and Heidelberger Druck. But Roels said he relished the challenge, and he set out to overhaul the company. He told the *Sunday Times*, "I never thought that the job would be easy. RWE had 13 businesses, and the criticism was that we had many people responsible for one customer" (September 28, 2003).

One of Roels's first moves was to replace the company's multiple business units with seven divisions. For example, the company's energy-trading businesses had been spread throughout different parts of RWE, but Roels organized them into one distinct operation. He also emphasized that all divisions and companies had to take the RWE brand name; Thames Water, for example, was renamed RWE Thames. Roels said that the idea was to give RWE customers a single point of contact, while marketing could be carried out on a regional basis. Roels also noted that under his program the

global workforce of 138,777 could eventually be cut by as many as ten thousand employees.

Roels began to reorganize the company's investments and expectations as well. For example, he reduced RWE's investment in the American coal business Consol and let the company's environmental-services business, RWE Umwelt, know that he expected improved returns or the business would be changed radically and perhaps even cut loose. By January 2004 analysts were commending Roels for how he had, as the *Financial Times* noted, "quietly concentrated on cleaning up its existing businesses" (January 7, 2004).

Nevertheless, Roels and RWE continued to pay for past acquisition excesses, which often had hurt the company's overall value. Goodwill charges and interest payments on debt were expected to depress the company's earnings for many years. However, as noted in the *Financial Times*, "the more than 20 percent rise in operating profits from its core businesses suggests that Mr. Roels has made a decent start—although last year's excellent performance in German electricity might prove difficult to repeat" (January 7, 2004).

Within his first year at RWE, Roels had outperformed analysts' expectations in debt reduction, cost cutting, dividend growth, and integrating the company's electricity, gas, and water businesses into a single entity. Although some analysts still questioned RWE's multiutility approach, they commended Roels for focusing on the company's prime utility businesses by disposing of many of its noncore assets. From November 2003 through February 2004 the company's share price gained 40 percent. The *Financial Times* noted that Roels went from "value destroyer to crowd pleaser" (February 27, 2004).

MANAGEMENT STYLE: SETTING GOALS

According to a February 2004 article in the *Financial Times*, analysts called Roels a quiet revolutionary who cleaned up RWE with great efficiency. They also noted that his lack of political ties in Germany's industrial heartland helped him; owing no allegiance to any political group or constituency, he was better able to fight off initial resistance to his plans from municipal shareholders.

Roels also focused on changing the corporate culture at RWE. He showed that he had the leadership skills to integrate the company's different cultures and create diverse management teams in the process. Although Germans dominated RWE's top jobs, Roels instituted a new management committee that included non-Germans working alongside top German managers for the first time. He also implemented new programs designed to ferret out employees who showed talent for future leadership. Analysts noted that Roels's management changes were good moves. Bill Alexander, who headed RWE

Thames, said in the *Sunday Times*, "If you look around a room of RWE managers today, they are much younger and more international in their outlook than they used to be" (September 28, 2003).

Roels managed by setting objectives both for the businesses in general and for individuals and management teams. For example, he initiated a scorecard approach that was used throughout the company to rate how the staff was achieving its goals and potential. In terms of his business divisions, Roels noted in the *Sunday Times*, "Every division has established targets, and one goal we want to achieve is that every unit's returns are above its cost of capital" (September 28, 2003).

CONTINUED COST CUTTING

Roels reduced RWE's debt to EUR 17.8 billion by the end of 2003, and he was praised by analysts for being ahead of his schedule for cutting the debt, which he first predicted would inch below 20 billion by 2005. Roels continued to cut costs by offloading the company's units that could not be linked with its electricity and water activities. These moves included the sale of RWE Umwelt and approximately half of its stake in the German printing-machinery maker Heidelberger Druckmaschinen. By the end of the first quarter of 2004 RWE, which had become Europe's third-largest utility, reported a quarterly profit that had more than doubled, with net income rising to EUR 925 million, up from EUR 432 million. In addition, operating profit advanced 12 percent to EUR

1.97 billion, beating analysts' forecasts despite a substantial fall in profits at its two British subsidiaries, RWE Innogy and RWE Thames. During the first quarter, RWE shares had the largest percentage gain on the Dow Jones index of 50 European stocks. Market analyst Felix Schleicher was quoted as saying, "RWE has delivered what the market had hoped for" (*Bloomberg.com*, May 11, 2004).

See also entries on Royal Dutch/Shell Group and RWE Group in *International Directory of Company Histories*.

SOURCES FOR FURTHER INFORMATION

Betts, Paul, "A Very Conservative Revolution at RWE," *Financial Times*, February 26, 2004.

"Electronics Firms Rue End of Glory Days," *Sunday Times* (London), September 28, 2003.

"Royal Dutch/Shell Group (People on the Move)," *Power Economics*, February 2002, p. 3.

"RWE 1st-Quarter Profit Doubles on Asset Sales, Prices," *Bloomberg.com*, May 11, 2004, http://quote.bloomberg.com/apps/news?pid=10000085&sid=aQFRsRAHEL6M&refer=europe.

"RWE the Lex Column," *Financial Times*, January 7, 2004.

"RWE the Lex Column," *Financial Times*, February 27, 2004.

—David Petechuk

■■■
Steven R. Rogel
1942–
Chairman, president, and chief executive officer, Weyerhaeuser Company

Nationality: American.

Born: October 25, 1942, in Ritzville, Washington.

Education: University of Washington, BS, 1965.

Family: Married Connie Schuler, 1964; children: three.

Career: St. Regis Paper Company, 1965–1970; St. Anne–Nackawic Pulp and Paper, 1970–1972, assistant manager; Willamette Industries, 1972–1995, technical director; 1995–1997, president and chief executive officer; Weyerhaeuser Company, 1997–1999, president and chief executive officer; 1999–, chairman, president, and chief executive officer.

Awards: Global CEO of the Year, Paper/Forest Products Global Outlook Conference, 2002.

Address: Weyerhaeuser Company, 33663 Weyerhaeuser Way South, Federal Way, Washington 98003-9620; http://www.weyerhaeuser.com.

Steven R. Rogel. *AP/Wide World Photos.*

■ Steven R. Rogel, chairman, president, and chief executive officer of Weyerhaeuser Company, stirred up a hornet's nest when he led Weyerhaeuser's hostile takeover bid for Willamette Industries, where he had worked until jumping to the bigger company in 1997. The Willamette takeover pitted Rogel against the smaller company's chairman, who had been his mentor for much of the Rogel's 25 years with Willamette. Although Rogel and Weyerhaeuser ultimately prevailed, it took more than a year to hammer out a deal acceptable to Willamette. In the end, Weyerhaeuser had to raise its bid substantially from the initial offer and Rogel had to endure vitriolic attacks from Willamette's executives and workers.

Rogel's relationship with Willamette chairman William Swindells—that of protégé and mentor during Rogel's 25 years at the Oregon-based forest-products company—had gone sour the day Rogel announced his plans to leave and take a job with its bigger rival, Weyerhaeuser. According to Stanley Holmes of *Business Week*, Swindells insisted that Rogel leave the company immediately, and the two had not spoken since. Despite the bitterness he knew the takeover bid would generate among his onetime colleagues at Willamette, Rogel said he was comforted by his certainty that the acquisition would benefit both companies. "I slept well at night," he told Holmes (March 11, 2002). "I was doing the right thing not just for Weyerhaeuser but for good friends at Willamette."

One of America's largest forest-products companies, Weyerhaeuser has fared well under Rogel's leadership. In addition to its expansion through the acquisition of Willamette, the company significantly increased its revenue in the opening years of the new millennium. Total sales climbed from roughly $15.9 billion in 2000 to nearly $20 billion in 2003. The company harvests timber not only in North America but also from such far-flung woodlands as those of Australia, France, Ireland,

New Zealand, and Uruguay. Weyerhaeuser produces a wide range of forest products, including solid wood products, pulp and paper, containerboard, and packaging materials. The company's real estate division develops both residential building lots and single-family housing for sale. Asked by *PaperAge* editor-in-chief Jack O'Brien to summarize his business philosophy, Rogel said, "I believe that people who are successful must have first a good battle plan and then stick with it" (March 2003).

RAISED IN GRAIN COUNTRY OF EASTERN WASHINGTON

Rogel, born in Ritzville, Washington, on October 25, 1942, grew up in the grain-growing and livestock-raising country of eastern Washington. After finishing high school in Ritzville, he enrolled at the University of Washington in Seattle to study chemical engineering. His interest in the forest-products industry was awakened during a 1964 summer internship at the Tacoma kraft mill of St. Regis Paper Company. Rogel told *PaperAge* that the experience convinced him of the value of internships. "They bring you into the real world. Even though I was a chemical engineer and had opportunities to enter the chemical and oil industries, I chose forest products" (March 2003).

In 1964, a year before graduating from the University of Washington, Rogel married Connie Schuler, his high school sweetheart. Fresh out of college, Rogel took a job with St. Regis, where he remained until 1970. He next moved to the other side of the continent, taking a job as assistant manager at St. Anne–Nackawic Pulp and Paper in Nackawic, New Brunswick, Canada. Two years later he got an offer to work as a technical director in the Albany, Oregon, facility of Western Kraft, which was soon to become part of Willamette Industries. Thus began a career of about 25 years with Willamette.

Quickly singled out as a promising candidate for a top management position, Rogel moved rapidly up the ladder at Willamette. After holding several management positions at the company's Albany, Oregon, and Campti, Louisiana, mills, he was elected a vice president in 1979. Nine years later he was named executive vice president, and in 1991 he became Willamette's president and chief operating officer. Groomed as a successor to the company's longtime chairman and CEO, William Swindells, Rogel took over as Willamette's CEO on October 1, 1995. Swindells, however, remained as chairman.

WON PRAISE AS WILLAMETTE'S CEO

Over the next two years, Rogel's leadership of Willamette won plaudits from Wall Street analysts. Less than a year after taking over as CEO, Rogel engineered Willamette's acquisition of nearly 400,000 acres of prime forestland in Oregon's Pacific Coast and Cascade ranges, making the company the biggest private landowner in the state. In an interview with Hal Bernton of the *Oregonian* (June 25, 1997), Rogel said that his goal for Willamette was to be recognized as "one of the outstanding companies in the industry, not only for financial performance but also for safety, environmental policies, and contributions to local communities." In 1996, Willamette's first full year under Rogel as CEO, the company managed to post net earnings of $192 million on revenue of $3.4 billion despite the impact of soft markets on Willamette's paper and pulp mills.

Rogel maintained Willamette's well-established reputation for strong growth and high rates of return on investment. In the five years that ended December 31, 1996, the company generated an average annual rate of return of 21 percent. According to Morgan Stanley forest-products analyst Matt Berler, quoted in the *Oregonian*, "Willamette is the premier company in the pulp and paper industry" (June 25, 1997). Berler added that the company had generated "the highest, most consistent returns in the industry and . . . sustained the fastest growth rate."

Although Rogel said that he was happy at Willamette, which for its part seemed pleased with the job he was doing as CEO, in 1997 he received an offer he felt that he could not refuse. Rogel told O'Brien of *PaperAge* (March 2003) that he was first approached by Jack Creighton, who was then Weyerhaeuser's president and CEO, and later contacted by George Weyerhaeuser Sr., the company's chairman and great-grandson of its founder. Both told Rogel they wanted to bring changes to Weyerhaeuser and felt that he was the man to do the job. "This presented a challenge I couldn't resist—the professional challenge of my entire career!"

DEPARTURE ANGERED WILLAMETTE EXECUTIVES

Rogel's decision to leave Willamette for Weyerhaeuser was not at all well received by the former's executives, particularly Swindells, who saw their CEO's defection to a larger rival as a betrayal. Weyerhaeuser, for its part, was delighted that Rogel had been persuaded to join the company as its new president and CEO. Many observers found the hiring a bit surprising, given Weyerhaeuser's previous record of filling its top executive positions from within. However, in announcing the appointment, Creighton made clear that the company had chosen Rogel because "he is a proven leader at the CEO level," according to the *Seattle Post-Intelligencer* (November 18, 1997).

Rogel wasted no time in defining his vision of a new, more focused, nimble, and efficient Weyerhaeuser. Within months of coming on as CEO in December 1997, he took steps to rationalize Weyerhaeuser's corporate structure, began using the company's buying power as leverage in its dealings with major suppliers, and put greater emphasis on Weyerhaeuser's core businesses. He also moved quickly to grow the company's holdings, acquiring MacMillan Bloedel, a Canadian forest-products company; TJ International, MacMillan Bloedel's partner in Trus Joist MacMillan; and three Canadian mills owned by Bowater.

WILLAMETTE TAKEN OVER

The next step in Rogel's long-term strategy for Weyerhaeuser—the acquisition of Willamette—revived and intensified all the ill feelings that had first been generated by his decision to leave more than three years earlier. In what was to be a lengthy war of wills, Rogel fired the opening shot on November 6, 2000, when he offered Willamette's shareholders $48 per share for their stock. In addition, Weyerhaeuser's offer provided for the assumption of roughly $1.7 billion in Willamette debt, bringing the total value of the offer to about $7 billion. Willamette's board quickly rejected the hostile takeover bid, hoping to slam the door on Weyerhaeuser's unwelcome acquisition campaign.

Rogel had no intention of giving up that easily, however. As he told Holmes in *BusinessWeek*, "I knew [the takeover bid] would be upsetting to them [Willamette management] and come back on me personally" (March 11, 2002). Over the next 14 months or so, the battle got very personal indeed. Willamette executives taped a picture of Rogel to a voodoo doll and stuck pins into it, and thousands of Willamette's workers wore buttons that read "Just Say No Wey." Despite the personal attacks, Rogel continued to press the bid. Weyerhaeuser's offer was steadily sweetened, eventually reaching $55.50 per share, which with the assumption of debt, brought the total price for Willamette to about $7.9 billion. In January 2002 Willamette finally accepted the offer, and in March 2002 the company became a wholly owned subsidiary of Weyerhaeuser.

Although the standoff between Weyerhaeuser and Willamette had been unpleasant, in the end, Rogel told *PaperAge*, "Willamette people came with the attitude, 'we may not have wanted this, but let's get on with it and make the very best company we can'" (March 2003). To facilitate the integration of his latest acquisition into the Weyerhaeuser corporate structure, Rogel tapped a number of Willamette people from throughout the company for management positions at Weyerhaeuser.

CONCENTRATING ON WEYERHAEUSER

With the Willamette acquisition behind him, Rogel in early 2003 began to focus his energies on making Weyerhaeuser "lean, nimble, quick, opportunistic," according to *Official Board Markets* (April 19, 2003). He told shareholders that the company must reinvent itself to increase both its efficiency and its profitability. He suggested that short-term priorities might include expansion of Weyerhaeuser's international operations, a critical reassessment of its wood and paper operations, and redoubled effort to control expenses. He told *Official Board Markets* that company employees had been told: "You're going to find our workplace of the future fulfilling, exciting, and rewarding if you're the kind of person who is customer-focused and results-oriented" (April 19, 2003).

In addition to his responsibilities at Weyerhaeuser, Rogel sat on the boards of various forest-products industry organizations, including the World Forestry Center, Wood Promotion Network, and American Forest & Paper Association. He also served as a director of Kroger Company and Union Pacific Corporation and a trustee of Pacific University. Rogel was vice president of administration for the Western Region of the Boy Scouts of America. In 2001 Rogel was picked as Global CEO of the Year in a survey of forest-products analysts conducted by *Pulp & Paper* and *PPI* magazines, and in 2003 he was named Executive Papermaker of the Year by *PaperAge* magazine.

See also entry on Weyerhaeuser Company in *International Directory of Company Histories*.

SOURCES FOR FURTHER INFORMATION

Bernton, Hal, "Rate of Return at Willamette Industries Pleases Wall Street," *Oregonian*, June 25, 1997.

Erb, George, "Not Lumbering: Weyerhaeuser's Steven Rogel Quickly, Decisively," *Puget Sound Business Journal*, April 26, 2002.

Holmes, Stanley, "Pulp Friction at Weyerhaeuser," *BusinessWeek*, March 11, 2002.

"Is a New Weyerhaeuser Here?" *Official Board Markets*, April 19, 2003.

O'Brien, Jack, "Weyerhaeuser's Steve Rogel: Executive Papermaker of the Year," *PaperAge*, March 2003.

"Resume: Steven R. Rogel," *BusinessWeek*, March 11, 2002.

"Rogel Rewrites Weyco Roadmap," *Official Board Markets*, February 23, 2002.

"Steven Rogel," *Marquis Who's Who*. New Providence, N.J.: Marquis Who's Who, 2004.

Virgin, Bill, "Weyerhaeuser Goes Outside to Find a CEO; Less Traditional Choice Is the Head of a Smaller Rival," *Seattle Post-Intelligencer*, November 18, 1997.

—Don Amerman

■■■

James E. Rogers

1947–

Chairman, president, and chief executive officer, Cinergy Corporation

Nationality: American.

Born: September 20, 1947, in Birmingham, Alabama.

Education: University of Kentucky, BBA, 1970; JD, 1974.

Family: Son of James E. Rogers and Margaret (Whatley) Rogers; married Robyn McGill (divorced); married Mary Anne Boldrick; children: three (first marriage).

Career: Commonwealth of Kentucky, assistant attorney general; Federal Energy Regulation Commission, assistant to the chief trial counsel, then deputy general counsel for litigation and enforcement; Supreme Court of Kentucky, law clerk; Akin, Gump, Strauss, Hauer & Feld, 1985–1986, partner; Houston Natural Gas, executive vice president; PSI Energy, 1988–1994, chairman, president, and chief executive officer; Cinergy Corporation, 1994–, president; 1995–, chief executive officer; 2000–, chairman.

Awards: Received an honorary doctor of Law degree from Indiana State University, 1991; named to the University of Kentucky College of Business and Economics Hall of Fame, 1994; listed in "America's Most Powerful People" by Forbes, 2000.

Address: Cinergy Corporation, 139 East Fourth Street, Cincinnati, Ohio 45202; http://www.cinergy.com.

■ James E. Rogers catapulted from a successful career as a lawyer to become the chairman, chief executive officer, and president of Cinergy, one of the largest utility companies in the United States. After earning his law degree in 1974, Rogers served as assistant attorney general for the Commonwealth of Kentucky, as a law clerk for the presiding justice for the Supreme Court of Kentucky, and as a partner with the law firm of Akin, Gump, Strauss, Hauer & Feld in Washington, D.C. He moved on to become executive vice president for Houston Natural Gas, the predecessor to Enron. He was later named president of Public Services Indiana (PSI) and was highly responsible for the merger between PSI and Cincinnati Gas and Electric Company that formed Cinergy. Rogers was well known not only for his innovative business strategies at Cinergy but also for his environmental advocacy.

EARLY LESSONS IN FREE ENTERPRISE

Rogers was born in Birmingham, Alabama, in 1947 and grew up in Kentucky. His father, a laborer for the Southern Railroad, taught him his first lesson in entrepreneurship when Rogers was 12. Rogers's father had developed a solvent to seal leaks in car radiators, and he had Rogers put labels on the barrels of the solvent. Four years later, at age 16, Rogers found the opportunity to sell the solvent at local gas stations. Rogers told the New York Times in 1994 that the experience "taught him to be fast and persistent" (November 13, 1994).

CAREER IN LAW AND GOVERNMENT

After graduating from high school, Rogers attended Emory University in Atlanta, Georgia, for a time before returning to his home state to attend the University of Kentucky. In 1970 he earned a bachelor of business administration degree from the University of Kentucky, where he earned membership in Beta Gamma Sigma, a national honor society for business and management. After earning his undergraduate degree, he enrolled at the University of Kentucky College of Law. During his law school career, he was a member of the Kentucky Law Journal and published an article as a student in 1973. Despite his success as a law student, Rogers was desperate for work. He worked for a time at a funeral home and then asked an editor at the Lexington Herald Leader for a job as a rewrite man. Although he had no experience for the position, he got the job after he told the editor, "Look, you can train me the way you want" (New York Times, November 13, 1994).

Rogers earned a juris doctor degree in 1974 and became a member of the Kentucky bar. By this time he was married and already had three children. After earning his law degree, he accepted a position as assistant attorney general for the State of Kentucky. He gained early experience with utility companies by fighting utility rate increases, and he later moved on to join the Federal Energy Regulatory Commission (FERC), where he served as assistant chief trial attorney. He later became the deputy general counsel for enforcement and litigation, assisting the agency in enforcing environmental regulations.

Rogers continued his success as a lawyer, becoming a law clerk to the presiding justice of the Kentucky Supreme Court. He moved on to join the Washington, D.C., office of the law firm Akin, Gump, Strauss, Hauer & Feld, which represented several utility companies. Rogers was later named a partner in the firm.

MOVING FROM LAW TO MANAGEMENT

During the mid-1980s Rogers left a successful career in law for a career in business, joining Houston Natural Gas, where he served as executive vice president. At Houston Natural Gas, which later changed its name to Enron, Rogers was in charge of the company's interstate pipelines—a $2.6 billion business. Two years later, in 1988, Rogers had an opportunity to take over as chairman, president, and chief executive officer of a fledgling electrical utilities company, Public Services Indiana, later known as PSI Energy.

PSI gave Rogers a mandate to clean up the utility company. In one of his first actions as head of the company, he met with several groups who protested the company's plan to install a nuclear reactor. Prior to Rogers's taking over as president, PSI had invested a reported $2.6 billion in the construction of a nuclear reactor but had later abandoned the project. Rogers met with opponents of the plant to mend relations. The co-founder of one of the opposition groups, Michael A. Mullett, told the New York Times, "Rogers came in as the white knight. He reached out to people" (July 6, 2003).

A "CATALYST FOR CHANGE WITHIN THE INDUSTRY"

Rogers took unprecedented steps in making PSI a competitive utility. In an industry that had been strictly regulated, in which utility companies enjoyed regional monopolies, Rogers in 1990 allowed PSI customers to shop around to find cheaper utility alternatives. Considered "heretical" among energy companies, the risky plan paid dividends, however, as PSI was among the first companies to break free from regulatory control and to be able to negotiate long-term energy contracts. Vicki Bailey, a member of the FERC, told the New York Times, "He's a catalyst for change within the industry. He definitely does not seem to be afraid of the new competitive era that we're going into" (November 13, 1994).

In 1992 Congress enacted legislation that opened up the market for energy in an effort to increase competition. This legislation led Rogers to negotiate a merger, which was announced in 1992 and took place in 1993, with Cincinnati Gas and Electric Company. The new company was called Cinergy. Rogers was named as the company's vice chairman and president. Jackson H. Randolph, formerly the chairman, CEO, and president of Cincinnati Gas, was named chairman and chief executive.

The move to form Cinergy allowed the two companies to reduce their costs. PSI anticipated a $1.2 billion construction project that was necessary to ensure compliance with federal law. The move also improved the merged company's ability to compete in a more open marketplace. In 1992 Rogers noted, "From a strategic standpoint, we see change starting to sweep through our industry, eventually resulting in fundamental transformation" (New York Times, December 15, 1992).

Cinergy remained the only utility company in the United States that voluntarily allowed industrial customers to shop for their power. Rogers maintained that the reasoning behind this strategy was anticipation of future competition. In an interview with the New York Times in 1994, Rogers pondered, "How do you convince a customer that you are the best choice for their electric supplier if you fought until the last dog was dead to keep out competitors?" (November 13, 1994). The strategy earned Rogers respect among his colleagues. According to Stanley T. Skinner, the president and chief executive officer of Pacific Gas and Electric, "Rather than resist the approaching change, or try to stuff the genie back in the bottle, [Rogers] is using his energy to dramatically reshape the way his company will do business. The customer is going to be relentless in pushing open markets" (New York Times, November 13, 1994).

Rogers became chief executive officer in 1995 and later became chairman when Randolph retired in 2000. Cinergy's first 10 years, as Rogers announced in 2004, were quite successful. The company grew at an average annual rate of 4 to 6 percent during its first 10 years. Shareholders received 191 percent in returns, including about $1 billion in dividends, between 1994 and 2004. The company was able to reduce emissions of sulfur dioxide by 50 percent as well as to decrease nitrous dioxide emissions by 40 percent.

UNUSUAL ADVOCACY ROLES

Because Rogers spent several years enforcing environmental regulations, his role as head of a major utility company was sometimes unusual. He spoke at hearings before congressional committees more than a dozen times, often advocating for limits to be placed on emissions. He told the New York Times in 2003, "Having been on many sides of the issue gives me a unique perspective. My whole career has been predicated on making common cause with other groups" (July 6, 2003). Even those who were often critical of utility companies showed their admiration for Rogers. "He's one of a new breed of utility executives," David G. Hawkins of the National Resources Defense Council, a New York environmental group, said of Rogers (New York Times, July 6, 2003).

Although the company pledged to reduce carbon dioxide emissions, it was still targeted as one of the nation's largest pollutants. Cinergy's plants burned an estimated 30 million tons of coal annually, prompting some of its shareholders to include the company within the so-called "Filthy Five," referring to top utility companies that produced high levels of carbon dioxide emissions. Rogers personally supported limitations on carbon dioxide emissions in testimony before a congressional committee in 2001 but later reversed his stance. He continued, however, to support legislation that would reduce emissions of sulfur dioxide, nitrogen oxide, and mercury—a position that was consistent with proposals introduced by the administration of President George W. Bush.

ACTIVE IN INDUSTRY, EDUCATIONAL, AND CIVIC ORGANIZATIONS

Rogers was highly active in industry, educational, and civic organizations. In addition to his responsibilities at Cinergy, Rogers served as director of First Bancorp and Fifth Third Bank as well as Duke Realty Corporation. He also served on the board of directors for Edison Electric Institute, the Indiana chapter of the Nature Conservancy, and the Cincinnati Museum Association. He was a founding member of the University of Kentucky Business Partnership Foundation and served as a trustee of the National Symphony Orchestra.

In 1991 Rogers received an honorary doctor of law degree from Indiana State University. He was later inducted into the University of Kentucky College of Business and Economics Hall of Fame in 1994. He was also listed among "America's Most Powerful People" by *Forbes* magazine.

SOURCES FOR FURTHER INFORMATION

Boyer, Mike, "Cinergy Plans to Think 'BIG,'" *Cincinnati Enquirer*, May 5, 2004.

"Cinergy Energy Chief James Rogers Speaks His Mind," *Industrialinfo.com*, April 8, 2004, http://www.industrialinfo.com/.

"Cinergy's Rogers Laments Midwest RTO Scene, But PJM Chief Says It Has Imposed 'Discipline,'" *Electric Utility Week*, April 5, 2004, p. 5.

Cortese, Amy, "From Green Knight to Utility King," *New York Times*, July 6, 2003.

Golden, Mark, "Cinergy CEO: Regulatory Uncertainty Good for Earnings," Dow Jones International News, February 13, 2004.

Newberry, Jon, "Cinergy Boss Cites Gains, Challenges," *Cincinnati Post*, May 5, 2004.

Salpukas, Agis, "Utility Competition Is Coming! (He's Ready, of Course)," *New York Times*, November 13, 1994.

Wald, Matthew L., "Cincinnati Utility to Merge with Indiana Counterpart," *New York Times*, December 15, 1992.

—Matthew C. Cordon

■■■
Bruce C. Rohde
1948–
Chairman and chief executive officer, ConAgra

Nationality: American.

Born: December 17, 1948, in Sidney, Nebraska.

Education: Creighton University, BS, 1971; BA, 1971; JD, 1973.

Family: Married (wife's name unknown; divorced); married Sandra (maiden name unknown); children: five (from second marriage).

Career: McGrath, North, Mullin & Kratz, 1973–1996, attorney; ConAgra, 1996–1997, vice chairman and president; 1997–, chief executive officer; 1998–, chairman.

Awards: Business Information Professional of the Year Award, 2000; named Frost & Sullivan's Food & Beverage CEO of the Year, 2004.

Address: ConAgra Inc., 1 ConAgra Drive, Suite 302, Omaha, Nebraska 68102-5001; http://www.conagra.com.

Bruce C. Rohde. *AP/Wide World Photos.*

■ Bruce C. Rohde was chairman and CEO of ConAgra, the leading North American food-service supplier and the number two supplier to grocery stores. First serving the company as its general legal counsel, Rohde worked in transforming the company from a largely agricultural supplier to a diversified name-brand foods company. To that end Rohde worked on a number of important acquisitions that eventually led the company in a more focused direction while restructuring ConAgra better to meet the challenges of the 21st century. Rohde's strong leadership and vision enabled him to take ConAgra to a healthier financial future as one of the leading and most competitive food companies in the country. Rohde was also part of a new class of emerging CEOs consisting of attorneys appointed to leadership positions within many major companies.

EARLY LIFE AND CAREER

Rohde was born in Sidney, Nebraska, on December 17, 1948. His family later moved to Omaha, where Rohde father's was president of Electric Fixture & Supply Company, the largest electric supply wholesaler in the state. After finishing high school, where Rohde lettered in track and field, he entered Creighton University in Omaha, graduating in 1971 with a degree in business administration and a major in accounting. He then entered Creighton's law school, graduating cum laude in 1973. He was admitted to the state bar the following year.

Rohde went to work for the law firm of McGrath, North, Mullin and Kratz—the second-largest law firm in Nebraska, noted for its expertise in business and corporate law. Rohde's introduction to ConAgra came in 1974, when he was made the company's principal attorney. By 1984 Rohde had become general legal counsel to the company.

Founded in 1919 by Alva Kinney, ConAgra began business as Nebraska Consolidated Mills (NCM), which consisted of four grain mills. It was NCM that created Duncan Hines cake mix in the 1950s in an attempt to drum up sales for its flour. But the product did not do as well as the company had hoped, and NCM later sold the brand in order to expand its flour and feed production. However, in the process the company ignored the trend toward prepared foods. By the 1960s NCM had expanded into animal feed and poultry production. The primary focus was on the idea of "dirt to dinner," or on the ingredients that made prepared foods such as meat and grains.

When Rohde joined the company as legal counsel in 1974, its name had changed from NCM to ConAgra, derived from the Latin for "with the land." ConAgra also wanted to change its image as an agricultural-based company and for the next several decades concentrated on acquiring brand-name foods, particularly nationally recognized, processed and prepared food items. Among the companies and brands that eventually came under the ConAgra umbrella were Banquet Frozen Foods, Armour, Del Monte (including Morton, Patio, and Chun King), and the Swift Independent Packing Company. By 1991 ConAgra had gone from being a $500 million company to being a $20 billion company. During this period of expansion and acquisition, which lasted from 1975 until 1991, Rohde was responsible for putting together the deals for 241 of the company's new acquisitions.

RISING TO THE TOP

By 1984 Rohde was participating in management meetings for the company and consulting with other company executives to devise strategies for ConAgra's expansion. His abilities caught the eye of senior company officials, and in 1996 Rohde was promoted to president and vice chairman of the company. A year later Rohde was promoted again, this time to CEO; in 1998 he was named chairman of the board of directors.

Rohde's appointment as CEO and chairman caught company outsiders off guard. Even though the company had undergone a lengthy and extensive search, which included interviewing more than one hundred candidates to fill the position, many believed that the person they were looking for was right under their noses. Although Rohde's background as an attorney hardly seemed to make him CEO material, those in the company believed that ConAgra could not have done better. One ConAgra executive noted that Rohde, in his time with ConAgra, came to understand the company better than many with a background in business. In addition, Rohde valued the entrepreneurial spirit of ConAgra.

RESTRUCTURING THE COMPANY

In taking over the reins of ConAgra, Rohde had his work cut out for him. During the early 1990s ConAgra continued to swallow up smaller competitors while at the same time paring down its own operations. In 1995 the company began its

first major reorganization by closing 29 mills and meat-processing plants and selling its chain of Country General convenience stores. Rohde continued the reorganization, and in June 1998 ConAgra grouped its grain and commodity operations under ConAgra Trade. A year later Rohde instituted "Operation Overdrive," closing several production plants and storage facilities and cutting the workforce by seven thousand employees. The estimated savings from "Operation Overdrive" was calculated at close to $600 million a year.

Rohde also faced other problems in the first few months of his tenure as CEO. In 1998 a glut of meat products, grains, and poultry had overburdened commodities markets when Asia closed its doors to exports. As a result, prices and profits for the company declined precipitously. The 80 companies now falling under the ConAgra banner were used to running themselves, often not even bothering to check in with other divisions—a situation that was also hurting the parent company. Rohde soon found out that the company's food-processing divisions and meatpacking plants were buying their goods from competitors instead of from other ConAgra companies. Representatives from several ConAgra divisions, all selling similar products, visited the same restaurants and groceries. Clients quickly became frustrated with this lack of coordination and communication and let Rohde know that something needed to be done. Rohde listened and began utilizing a teamwork approach that avoided overlapping of resources.

Rohde continued retooling the company and by 2000 had collected 10 product groups under three divisions: food service, which focused on restaurants; retail and grocery stores; and agricultural products. By 2003, though, rumors were circulating that the company would eventually be dropping those products. Rohde stepped up marketing as well, working with grocery stores to create displays of ConAgra products.

In the meantime, expansion continued as ConAgra bought such products and companies as Nabisco's Egg Beaters and table spread, Choice One Foods, a California supplier of meat to restaurant chains, and Home International Foods in a $2.9 billion deal that gave the company the Chef Boyardee, Bumblebee Seafoods, and Gulden's mustard brands. By 2004 ConAgra owned more than 70 name brands, including Healthy Choice, Orville Redenbacher products, and Peter Pan. Although getting out of the meatpacking business in 2002, ConAgra became one of the nation's top meat and poultry sellers, counting such brands as Butterball and Armour among the company's holdings. Under Rohde's leadership, ConAgra began generating 75 percent of its food profits from sales of name-brand products. Rohde's changes also helped the company financially, as ConAgra earned approximately $12 billion in retail sales annually, with another $10 billion per year coming from the purchase of food products by restaurants and institutions.

MANAGEMENT STYLE

In the beginning Rohde's management style caught many off guard. As CEO, Rohde looked for ways in which ConAgra could solve its problems creatively and still keep an eye on the bottom line. He encouraged the independence of ConAgra's operating companies. His philosophy was if people have the power to make decisions rather than having to wait for all decisions to come from a centralized source, they will get more done. Still, he sought to facilitate better communication within ConAgra. This strategy worked especially well in the area of acquisitions in that after acquiring a company, ConAngra already had a supplier somewhere within its ranks. This setup allowed for almost all of the functions, from materials to processing and preparation, to stay within the company. Rohde also believed in keeping in touch with his employees—over 80,000 of them as of 2004—by regularly providing employees with news and listening to their concerns. Rohde encouraged replies, and while the response was not overwhelming, he ordinarily received between one hundred and two hundred responses to one of his e-mails.

Rohde continued to forge ahead despite discouraging economic news. As grocery store chains pushed their own brand names, which tend to be cheaper than other national brands, ConAgra needed to come up with ways to stay competitive. A growing headache was dealing with changing tastes. Increasingly Americans ate out, which meant that ConAgra products were not selling as briskly as Rohde would have liked. Rohde hoped to counteract this trend by stepping up sales of food ingredients needed by restaurants, such as processed potatoes used for french fries by fast-food chains like McDonald's or chicken for chains like Wendy's and Arby's. Some analysts suggested that Rohde was too cautious and that if the company were to remain profitable, he would need to take bigger chances in the acquisitions game.

See also entry on ConAgra, Inc. in *International Directory of Company Histories.*

SOURCES FOR FURTHER INFORMATION

"Bruce Rohde of ConAgra Foods Named Frost & Sullivan's Food & Beverage CEO of the Year Award," Frost & Sullivan Press Release, May 20, 2004, http://biz.yahoo.com/bw/040520/205114_1.html.

Copple, Brandon, "Synergy in Ketchup?" *Forbes*, February 7, 2000, p.68.

Kawar, Mark, "CEO: ConAgra Had to Centralize: Bringing It All Together," *Omaha World Herald*, September 25, 2003.

Neff, Jack, "The Biggest Nobody Really Knows," *Food Processing*, February 2001, p.19+.

Pollock, Ellen Joan, "Order in the Boardroom: Lawyers Rise to CEO," *Wall Street Journal*, September 11, 1996.

Ruff, Joe, "ConAgra Getting Out of Meatpacking," *Omaha World Herald*, September 24, 2002.

———, "New CEO Puts ConAgra into 'Overdrive,'" *Dayton Daily News*, May 5, 2000.

Taylor, John, "ConAgra Attorney Rohde to Fill Long-Vacant President's Office," *Omaha World Herald*, August 27, 1996, p. 16.

———, "Lawyer Joins Ranks of ConAgra 'Hunters,'" *Omaha World Herald*, November 17, 1996.

—Meg Greene

■■■
James E. Rohr

1948–

Chairman and chief executive officer, PNC Financial Services Group

Nationality: American.

Born: October 18, 1948, in Cleveland, Ohio.

Education: University of Notre Dame, BA, 1970; Ohio State University, MBA, 1972.

Family: Son of Charles E. Rohr and Loretta Kramer; married Sharon Lynn Chambers, 1970; children: three.

Career: PNC Financial Services Group, 1972–1989, joined company's management development program and subsequently moved through series of marketing and management positions in corporate banking sector; 1989–1990, vice chairman; 1990–1992, vice chairman and director; 1992–1998, president; 1998–2000, president and chief operating officer; 2000–2001, president and chief executive officer; 2001–2002, chairman, president, and chief executive officer; 2002—, chairman and chief executive officer.

Address: PNC Financial Services Group, 1 PNC Plaza, 249 5th Avenue, Pittsburgh, Pennsylvania 15222–2707; http://www.pnc.com.

■ James E. Rohr, who had spent his entire career with PNC Financial Services Group and its predecessor companies, became the banking corporation's chairman and chief executive officer (CEO) on May 1, 2001. Within months he found himself in the midst of a major accounting scandal that threatened to sweep him and most of the company's top executives from office. While others did pay the price for the accounting irregularities, Rohr survived and struggled valiantly to rebuild PNC's tarnished reputation and to maintain its independence.

As some measure of Rohr's success in reassuring investors, PNC's stock had climbed back into the upper $50s per share by early 2004, a sharp improvement from the high $30s to which it had plummeted in the wake of PNC's accounting irregularities. The company's stock, which was trading at about 10 times its earnings per share in August 2002, entered 2004 valued at roughly 15.5 times its earnings per share, not far

below the industry average of 17.2. Rohr also underscored his determination to protect the financial-services company from takeover by announcing the bank's acquisition of the New Jersey-based United National Bancorp in August 2003. The acquisition of the holding company for UnitedTrust Bank, which operated 52 branches in New Jersey and Pennsylvania, was expected to increase PNC's customer base by more than 100,000 households and businesses.

PNC'S GROWTH AS FINANCIAL-SERVICE PROVIDER

As one of the top managers at PNC since 1992, Rohr was instrumental in shepherding the group from a local Pittsburgh-area banking institution into an influential regional provider of diversified financial services. Under his watch, PNC steadily moved away from such low-margin banking staples as mortgage services into higher-margin financial services, such as brokerage and treasury management, thus paving the way for accelerated growth. Rohr was also an early champion of the integration of technology into all of PNC's core businesses.

EARLY PROFESSIONAL LIFE

James Rohr was born in Cleveland, Ohio, on October 18, 1948. He attended schools in the Cleveland area and after graduating from high school enrolled at the University of Notre Dame in nearby Indiana. Rohr received his bachelor's degree in 1970 and returned to Ohio to pursue his master's degree at Ohio State University in Columbus. On December 29, 1970, he married Sharon Lynn Chambers. After earning his MBA at OSU in 1972, Rohr interviewed with a number of companies but was particularly impressed with PNC, which was then a small regional bank, headquartered in Pittsburgh, with less than $2 billion in assets. In a 2003 interview with *Leaders* magazine, Rohr recalled, "When I interviewed at PNC, I liked the people I met, which really differentiated the company for me."

After completing PNC's management-development program, Rohr moved through a series of marketing and management positions in the bank's corporate-banking department. Within PNC, Rohr's organizational and management skills caught the attention of high-level executives, who in 1989 named him vice chairman of the company. A year later he was given the added responsibilities of director. In 1992, Rohr was elected president, and he assumed the additional post of chief operating officer (COO) in 1998. During his years at the upper end of management, Rohr helped steer PNC away from its heavy reliance on interest income to increasing dependence on fee-based income.

OVERSAW PNC'S ACQUISITION OF BLACKROCK

Rohr played a major role in PNC's 1995 acquisition of BlackRock Financial Management, a fixed-income investment management firm based in New York. At the time of its acquisition, BlackRock had roughly $25 billion in assets under management. As of the end of 2003, that figure had skyrocketed to more than $309 billion. Four years after acquiring Black-Rock for $240 million, in 1999 PNC sold 15 percent of the investment-management company to its employees and another 15 percent to the public. PNC retained a majority interest in BlackRock. To ensure that BlackRock continued to operate efficiently after its acquisition, PNC did something unusual for banks taking over an asset manager: It retained the partners of BlackRock—CEO Larry Fink and President Ralph Schlosstein. In discussing with *U.S. Banker* the working arrangement between PNC and its majority-owned subsidiary, Rohr said, "We work together on a lot of things; we have a lot of joint customers. Larry is in my staff meeting every Monday morning."

According to *U.S. Banker*, the acquisition of BlackRock and other moves directed by Rohr resulted in a sharp rise in the percentage of PNC's total revenue generated from non-interest income. In 1996 PNC posted $2.4 billion in net interest income and $1.4 billion in non-interest income. By 2000 net interest income had dropped to $2.2 billion, while non-interest income had climbed to $3.2 billion. According to PNC's preliminary earnings report for 2003, net interest income was roughly $2 billion, while non-interest income was close to $3.3 billion. Over the space of eight years, non-interest income had grown from about 36 percent of total revenue to approximately 62 percent.

Appointed president and CEO in 2000, Rohr moved quickly to accelerate PNC's transformation from a regional bank into a provider of diversified financial services. Under his direction, PNC saw its stock price climb from a low of less than $40 a share in early 2000 to more than $70 a share by the end of the year. After a brief and slight drop at the beginning of 2001, the stock climbed above its 2000 level, but the good times for PNC stock were not to last.

On May 1, 2001, Rohr succeeded Thomas H. O'Brien as chairman, while retaining his positions as president and CEO. Early in 2002 Rohr faced an accounting scandal that threatened for a while to topple him from his leadership of PNC.

Government banking regulators announced that approximately $760 million in troubled loans and venture-capital investments had been moved off the company's balance sheets for 2001, artificially inflating PNC's profit. In addition to ordering the bank twice to restate its earnings, regulators in July 2002 put PNC under a six-month watch. The Securities and Exchange Commission issued a cease-and-desist order, maintaining that PNC made "materially false" disclosures. As part of the regulators' settlement agreement with PNC, the company was required to hire an outside consultant to assess the performance of top management and "take all steps necessary to ensure that the bank is deemed to be well managed," according to the *Pittsburgh Post-Gazette* (July 19, 2002).

ROHR SURVIVES THE SCANDAL

Although two of his top lieutenants, vice chairman Walter Gregg Jr. and COO Robert Haunschild, were forced to step down in the aftermath of the accounting scandal, Rohr emerged from the storm somewhat battered but still firmly in charge. In August 2002 Rohr surrendered the president's job to a 30-year PNC veteran, Joseph Guyaux, but remained as chairman and CEO. At the same time, PNC's board of directors "unanimously reaffirmed" its support of Rohr's leadership, according to the *Pittsburgh Business Times* (August 28, 2002). In view of the widespread calls for his replacement, including an editorial in *BusinessWeek* headlined "Show Rohr the Door," Rohr's survival surprised many.

By the summer of 2002 Rohr was telling anyone who would listen that the bank's accounting problems were behind it, both "from a customer and an employee point of view," according to the *Philadelphia Inquirer*. To help mend its relationship with federal banking regulators, Rohr brought in Jack Wixted from the Federal Reserve Bank of Chicago to fill PNC's newly created position of chief regulatory officer. Wixted, a senior vice president responsible for the supervision and regulation of more than one thousand financial institutions in the Seventh Federal Reserve District, was assigned to manage all of PNC's issues related to regulatory affairs and compliance. In announcing Wixted's appointment, Rohr said in a company press release, "He brings a breadth of knowledge and depth of experience, and he shares our belief in the importance of a constructive relationship between banking companies and their regulatory agencies" (July 18, 2002).

MAXIMIZES BENEFITS OF TECHNOLOGY

Rohr was widely credited with positioning PNC early on to make the most of new technology in its servicing of bank customers. In an interview with *Leaders* magazine in late 2003, he described how the bank's data warehouse enabled PNC to manage information in the most efficient manner possible.

Rohr also touted the bank's call center and the extension of the company's Internet operation to all its branches. "In fact, I believe our online banking program has the second-highest penetration rate in the industry. As a result, we can provide a common customer experience" whether transactions are conducted online, through the call center, or at PNC's network of ATMs. Asked by *Leaders* to define his role as CEO, Rohr said he saw his primary responsibilities as mapping out, in concert with the board of directors, the strategic direction in which the bank should be moving and then communicating that message to employees at all levels within PNC. "So I have to create an atmosphere in which people understand, embrace, and commit to our direction. In addition, I have to select the right leaders and empower them to make a difference."

Rohr and his wife, the former Sharon Chambers, had three children. Both Rohr and his wife were active in Pittsburgh-area civic affairs. They cochaired the September 2003 Showplace Cabaret gala of the Pittsburgh Cultural Trust, which Rohr served as chairman. He also chaired the board of Pittsburgh's Civic Light Opera and sat on the boards of United Way of Allegheny County and the Greater Pittsburgh Council of the Boy Scouts of America. Rohr's business responsibilities outside PNC included seats on the boards of Allegheny Technologies and of Equitable Resources. He was a member of the American Bankers Association, International Monetary Conference, and the Financial Services Roundtable. In July 2002 he was elected to the board of trustees of RAND, a nonprofit research organization that seeks solutions for challenges facing both the private and public sectors around the world.

See also entry on PNC Financial Services Group Inc. in *International Directory of Company Histories*.

SOURCES FOR FURTHER INFORMATION

Bennett, Robert A., "Pulling Ahead of the Pack," *U.S. Banker*, December 2000.

Boselovic, Len, "PNC's Rohr Keeps Job, Gets Bonus," *Pittsburgh Post-Gazette*, March 15, 2003.

DiStefano, Joseph N., "Chairman Struggles to Regain PNC Financial's Credibility," *Philadelphia Inquirer*, August 11, 2002.

"Helping a Little BITS at a Time," *Bank Systems & Technology*, August 1, 2002.

Hoover's Online, "The PNC Financial Services Group, Inc.," http://www.hoovers.com/pnc-financial/—ID__11138—/ free-co-factsheet.xhtml.

"It's All about People and Execution," *Leaders*, October–December 2003.

"James Edward Rohr," *Marquis Who's Who*, New Providence, N.J.: Marquis Who's Who, 2004.

"John J. Wixted Jr. to Join PNC as Chief Regulatory Officer," company press release, http://www.prnewswire.com/cgi-bin/ micro_stories.pl?ACCT=701257&TICK=PNC&STORY=/ www/story/07-18-2002/0001766429&EDATE= Jul+18,+2002.

Panepento, Peter, "Executive Discusses His First Year at Helm of Pittsburgh-Based Banking Company," *Erie Times-News*, May 13, 2001.

Reuters.com, "Financial Snapshot for PNC Financial Services Group," http://www.investor.reuters.com.

Sabatini, Patricia, "Regulators Put PNC Financial under Six-Month Watch," *Pittsburgh Post-Gazette*, July 19, 2002.

"Seeking to Rebuild Confidence, PNC Adopts New Standards," *Pittsburgh Business Times*, August 28, 2002.

Tascarella, Patty, "The Mouse That Rohred: PNC Chief Takes the Stage," *Pittsburgh Business Times*, July 20, 2001.

Weber, Joseph, "Finance: Commentary: Memo to PNC: Show Rohr the Door," *BusinessWeek*, September 9, 2002.

—Don Amerman

■■■

Matthew K. Rose

1960–

Chairman, president, and chief executive officer, Burlington Northern Santa Fe Corporation

Nationality: American.

Born: 1960, in Salina, Kansas.

Education: University of Missouri, BS, 1981.

Family: Married (wife's name unknown); children: three.

Career: Burlington Northern Railroad, 1994–1995, vice president, vehicles and machinery; Burlington Northern Santa Fe Corporation, 1995–1996, vice president, chemicals; 1996–1997, senior vice president, merchandise business unit; 1997–1999, chief operations officer; 1999–2000, president and chief operating officer; 2000–2002, president and chief executive officer; 2002–, chairman, president, and chief executive officer.

Address: Burlington Northern Santa Fe Corporation, 2650 Lou Menk Drive, 2nd Floor, Fort Worth, Texas 76161-0057; http://www.bnsf.com.

■ Matthew K. Rose became the first member of the baby-boom generation to head a major North American railroad when he was named the CEO of Burlington Northern Santa Fe Corporation (BNSF) in 2000. He brought a new attitude to the staid industry, which had been notorious for its lack of younger members in top management. Having spent part of his career in marketing, Rose also came to his job with a focus on customer service, an outlook that for some time had been sorely lacking in an industry with a reputation for unreliability. Rose's experience in the trucking industry also helped him to transform BNSF. As a leader, he was optimistic, open, and supportive, but also decisive and tough-minded.

Rose was born in 1960 in Salina, Kansas. He went to college at the University of Missouri, and during the summer he worked as a brakeman and switchman for the Missouri Pacific Railroad. He graduated in 1981 with a BS degree in marketing and a minor in logistics and went to work as a management trainee with Missouri Pacific. After reaching the position of assistant trainmaster, he left the railroad industry to work for the trucking conglomerate International Utilities and the largest truckload carrier in the United States, Schneider National. His next stop was Triple Crown Services, a truck and rail intermodal service, where he became vice president of transportation. In 1993 he joined Burlington Northern Railroad and in June 1994 was appointed vice president of vehicles and machinery.

Burlington Northern and Santa Fe Railway merged in September 1995, forming Burlington Northern Santa Fe Corporation. After the merger Rose became vice president of chemicals, a position he held until May 1996, when he was promoted to senior vice president of the merchandise business unit. His quick rise through the management ranks of BNSF continued in August of the following year with his promotion to senior vice president and chief operations officer. He was now in charge of coordinating transportation, maintenance, quality, purchasing, labor relations, and information services. In June 1999 Rose was named president and chief operating officer, with the clear understanding that he was now being groomed to succeed BNSF's chief executive officer, Robert D. Krebs.

Krebs was the longest-serving railroad chief executive at the time, having started out in 1981 as the president of Southern Pacific Transportation Company and then moving to Santa Fe Southern Pacific Corporation, which became part of the 1995 Burlington-Santa Fe merger. Krebs maintained that finding a successor who could command the confidence of both management and the board was one of the most important responsibilities in his career. He settled on Rose because of his varied experience in marketing and operations, in both the rail and trucking industries. While preparing for the top spot, Rose also demonstrated the further advantage of having grown up as part of the computer generation. He played the lead role in the establishment of FreightWise, an online transportation exchange in which BNSF owned a majority interest.

Rose became the CEO at BNSF in December 2000, with Krebs retaining the chairmanship. Krebs had nothing but high praise for his 41-year-old protégé. He told the *Journal of Commerce*, "He is tough-minded, but he is an optimist. He is decisive, yet thorough. He is open and supportive.... People want to work for Matt" (December 8, 2000). Although people in the railroad industry acknowledged that losing Krebs was upsetting, Rose's appointment was received positively. The need for younger leadership in railroads was obvious, and Rose was expected to become the most progressive chief executive in the industry. For many, he represented a symbol of change.

Rose took over a railroad that operated on 35,500 route miles of track in 28 western states and two Canadian provinces and generated more than $9 billion in annual revenues, second in size only to Union Pacific. The hard-driving Krebs had done a good job in cutting costs, which allowed BNSF to survive and start to invest in capital improvements, leaving Rose with different priorities, which included growing revenues to meet rail's ferocious appetite for capital, investing in new facilities, and acquiring more efficient locomotives and freight cars. To accomplish these goals, he had to win back market share from truckers as well as forge partnerships between trucking and rail. One tool he hoped to utilize more was the Internet, putting to use some of the techniques used by airlines to better match supply and demand for rail service as a way to maximize revenue.

Rose also began working with major retailers to encourage them to make increased use of railroads to transport goods. But perhaps the most important and challenging task he faced was changing the mindset of the workforce, keeping it aware of financial matters but also looking to better serve customers. After years of hearing promises about customer service, most shippers—with the exception of giant accounts—had grown disenchanted with the railroads, which had been notoriously unreliable for so many years that it was a tall order to restore confidence. Without this trust, BNSF and the rest of the industry would be unable to grow revenues.

Making his job more difficult, Rose took over during difficult economic conditions and reduced rail traffic. To stimulate business BNSF resorted to money-back guarantees on 10 service corridors and offered some discounts on intermodal services. Despite these challenges, Rose remained characteristically optimistic, expressing his belief that without railroads the United States would experience a strain on the nation's highway infrastructure and an untenable level of congestion in metropolitan areas. "That's why," he told the *Dallas Morning News*, "I believe we have a bright future" (December 8, 2000). The transition of power at BNSF was completed in April 2002, when Krebs retired and Rose was named chairman in addition to his roles as president and CEO.

See also entry on Burlington Northern Santa Fe Corporation in *International Directory of Company Histories*.

SOURCES FOR FURTHER INFORMATION

Hooper, Michael, "Railroad on Right Track," *Topeka Capital-Journal*, April 14, 2004.

Kaufman, Lawrence H., "Rose Succeeds Krebs as BNSF's Chief Executive," *Journal of Commerce*, December 8, 2000.

Machalaba, Daniel, "Burlington Northern Names Rose CEO," *Wall Street Journal*, December 8, 2000.

Shah, Angela, "New Chief Takes Over at Burlington Northern Santa Fe," *Dallas Morning News*, December 8, 2000.

Siekman, Philip, "New Hope for Trucks and Trains," *Fortune*, December 11, 2001.

—Ed Dinger

Bob Rossiter

1946–

Chairman and chief executive officer, Lear Corporation

Nationality: American.

Born: February 15, 1946, in Detroit, Michigan.

Education: Northwood University, BA, 1992.

Family: Married Pamela Kittleson; children: two.

Career: Lear Siegler, 1971–1998, sales; Lear Corporation, 1988–2000, president and chief operating officer; 2000–2003, president and chief executive officer; 2003–, chairman and chief executive officer.

Address: Lear Corporation, 21557 Telegraph Road, Southfield, Michigan 48086; http://www.lear.com.

■ Robert E. "Bob" Rossiter, who preferred employees and colleagues to call him Bob, crowned more than three decades at Lear Corporation by becoming its chairman and chief executive officer in 2003. Lear was the world's largest supplier of automotive interior systems in 2003, with $15.7 billion in revenues. The company's rapid growth resulted from an aggressive acquisition and globalization strategy that started in the 1990s. Rossiter was part of this strategy as a member of the board of directors starting in 1988. He assumed the role of board chairman as well as the company's CEO in 2003, taking responsibility for the strategic direction and operational leadership of the corporation. His stated goal as head of Lear was to ensure that the company eliminated all forms of waste, to continually raise the bar on customer satisfaction levels, and to grow the company's market-leading position.

LIVING INSIDE THE AUTOMOTIVE WORLD

Rossiter was born into a working-class family in post–World War II Detroit, one of eight children. Raised in a blue-collar culture in which employees stayed with one company for decades and hard work was valued over education, Rossiter joined what was then called Lear Siegler as a sales rep-

resentative in 1971 and served in various sales positions until 1988. That year he became president and chief operating officer of the company after a management buyout that gave control to a core of executives who had risen through the ranks of the organization. The managers behind the buyout still ran Lear at the beginning of the 21st century. To help finance the 1988 buyout, Rossiter took out a second mortgage on his house.

Through the 1990s, Rossiter was known as "Mr. Outside" to CEO Ken Way's "Mr. Inside." Way directed Lear's growth, overseeing its transformation from a relatively small supplier of seats to the Big Three automakers to a far-reaching producer of automotive interiors and electronics. Meanwhile, Rossiter cultivated relations with companies in the United States and worldwide, using his knowledge of the industry to help shape company growth.

Rossiter and the Lear management team experienced seismic shifts in the automotive world that shaped their careers from the 1970s into the 2000s. During that era Detroit lost its dominance as the world's automotive hub, ceding its manufacturing dominance to Japan and learning to adapt to a world of global outsourcing of components, supplies, and services. Rossiter and Lear's other managers proved skillful in adapting to the changing environment.

A GLOBAL APPROACH THAT EMPHASIZED QUALITY

As chairman, Rossiter made his awareness of customer concerns a central part of his management approach, and he set the company on track toward a sales goal of $25 billion in 2005, up from nearly $16 billion in 2003. Rossiter worked to eliminate all forms of waste in the company's structure and accounting, fostering continual improvement in customer satisfaction and stimulating company growth into a world-leading supplier of complete automotive interior systems. According to Rossiter, Lear's growth strategy was based on the following components: find your customers, get their businesses, take care of your customers, throw out your ego, never pat yourself on the back for a job well done, what you get is what you give, work hard, make decisions, do not be afraid to fail, and learn from your mistakes.

Part of that growth came from the expansion of Lear's international operations based in Sulzbach, Germany. Sulzbach was the touchstone of Lear's aggressive acquisition of suppliers in the 1990s to bolster its Detroit operations. Such an approach was necessary, Lear managers maintained, as the automotive industry itself became more global. At the turn of the century, more than 70 percent of Lear's business remained with the Big Three Detroit auto companies, but the company set a goal of boosting its Japanese business from less than one-tenth to almost one-fifth of its revenues.

The company also had the good fortune of being a leader in interiors for trucks and sport utility vehicles, which exploded on the North American market in the 1990s. Lear also expanded its offerings as an automotive supplier, implementing an electronics growth strategy with the purchase of the Dearborn, Michigan, company Supplier United Technologies Automotive for $2.3 billion in 1998. A slowdown in the North American auto industry in the middle of the 21st century's first decade posed challenges for the company that were softened somewhat by its global diversification of assets, the result of earlier positioning by the company. At the end of 2003, Lear had 289 facilities located in 34 countries, with more than 110,000 employees worldwide.

Rossiter also made sure that Lear never became too hierarchical, using his own experience in the company's trenches to relate to and communicate with workers who in many businesses would not have had an opportunity to interact with the boss. Given its origins in the management buyout, Lear was an entrepreneurial company in which division heads controlled much of the decision-making process, and attracting young management talent was a priority. Rossiter approached his job as a politician-salesman, gleaning information from various sources before deciding on a course of action. A former executive told *Automotive News International* that Rossiter "will come up to a guy he met five years ago and say, 'Hey, Bill, how are you doing?' . . . He is the consummate salesman. He knows what you want and how to get it. He has the gift of gab" (December 1, 2000). Rossiter also had the gift of stamina and tried to set an example of hard work from the top. On Saturdays he was usually at his desk by 9 a.m. He did play golf but said he never took the time to be good at it.

With its entrepreneurial, diffused-power approach, Lear became an industry model. As it rocketed up the Fortune 500 list along with its sales, Lear gained recognition both inside and outside the automotive industry for its innovation and quality. In 2004 *Fortune* magazine recognized Lear as America's Most Admired Company in the motor vehicle parts sector, with a number one ranking for each attribute of reputation in the magazine's annual survey. Lear also received four Ford Motor Company World Excellence awards for its superior performance in 2003. "Improved quality is the bedrock of our strategy to move our company forward," said Rossiter on receiving the recognition. "Achieving quality improvement is not easy" (May 3, 2004).

CONTINUED CHALLENGES

In 2004 Lear faced the corporate challenge of international competition along with the more serious threat to its internal culture that focused on the tight core of executives who originally bought the company. At the beginning of that year the Securities and Exchange Commission (SEC) launched an informal probe into possible padding of the Lear payroll with family members of the executives who ran the company. Attracting the SEC's interest were $7.2 million in payments made in 2001 to Analysts International for software services and computer equipment. Analysts International's Sequoia Services Group employed Terrence Kittleson, Rossiter's brother-in-law, as a sales representative, along with other employees connected to Lear managers. Lear maintained it had nothing to hide and was cooperative with the SEC probe.

Meanwhile, the company continued to work to reduce its debt and unload its poorer-performing assets while maintaining its sales targets. The debt load was the by-product of the company's growth strategy in the 1990s, when the already highly leveraged company took on even more debt to fuel its expansion in automotive interiors. Hit by the automotive recession in 2002, Lear laid off more than 6,500 American workers as part of a cost-cutting strategy to maintain global competitiveness. At the same time, Rossiter became convinced that Lear management needed to expand globally. In a meeting with representatives of DaimlerChrysler, the company formed by a German takeover of the Chrysler corporation, the DaimlerChrysler executives started speaking in German and Rossiter needed a translator. Rossiter, who seldom ventured beyond vacations in northern Michigan when traveling for any reason other than business, said the experience further reinforced his belief that the company needed foreign executives. "Americans don't travel as well as some other people," he said (*Automotive News International*, December 1, 2000).

As 2005 approached, Lear had apparently stemmed layoffs and brought its heavy debt load under control. Rossiter expected no new major acquisitions, meaning the company's aggressive revenue growth targets would have to be met the hard way, through internal sales growth and by winning new contracts worldwide. The company set up operations in Brazil and Thailand to continue to penetrate global markets and added some of the foreign executives Rossiter desired. The company also heavily bet on growth in its European markets, where Rossiter felt the company's foreign operations and leaner cost structure would make it competitive in markets where European suppliers had traditionally reigned supreme. "Despite challenging industry and economic conditions, we continued to meet aggressive customer requirements and post solid financial results," Rossiter said in April 2004. "We intend to maintain our positive momentum by staying focused on what we can control—quality, customer service, cost and delivery" (*PR Newswire*, April 26, 2004).

See also entry on Lear Siegler Inc. in *International Directory of Company Histories*.

SOURCES FOR FURTHER INFORMATION

"Bob Rossiter Profile," *Northwood Idea: The Journal of Northwood University*, September 2003, pp. 3-4.

Carter, Sharon Silke, "Auto-Parts Supplier Under Scrutiny Over Filing," *Dow Jones News Service*, January 21, 2004.

"Lear Honored with Ford's 2003 World Excellence Awards, PR Newswire, May 3, 2004.

"Lear Posts Record First Quarter Net Sales of $4.5 Billion," PR Newswire, April 26, 2004.

Sedgwick, David, "The Buying Binge Is Over," *Automotive News International*, December 2000, pp. 16-21.

Truby, Mark, "Lear Thrives, Building More Into Each Vehicle," *Detroit News*, July 29, 2003.

—Alan Bjerga

■■■

Renzo Rosso

1955–

Owner, chief executive officer, and designer, Diesel

Nationality: Italian.

Born: 1955, in Brugine, Italy.

Education: Graduated from an Italian textiles school, 1975.

Career: Moltex, 1975–1978, production manager; Genius Group, 1978–1985, designer; Diesel, 1978–1985, designer and partner; 1985–, owner, chief executive officer, and designer; La Maison Martin Margiela, 2002–, majority owner and investor.

Awards: Best Italian Company of the Year, Premio Risultati award of the Bocconi Institute, Milan, 1996; nominated by Ernst & Young as Entrepreneur of the Year, 1997; chosen one of the 100 Most Important People in the World, *Select* magazine, 1997; honorary MBA, CUOA Foundation of Italy, 2000.

Address: Diesel, Via dell'Industria 7, 36060 Molvena, Vicenza, Italy; http://www.diesel.com.

Renzo Rosso. *AP/Wide World Photos/Fashion Wire Daily.*

■ Renzo Rosso never looked or acted like a chief executive. He attended corporate meetings and interviews in what could only be described as eccentric fashion—faded jeans, cowboy boots, and whatever else might have sparked his imagination on any particular day. Rosso never apologized for his attire nor his singular vision for Diesel, the company he founded and made into a multimillion-dollar fashion empire. Rosso was an original, and his vision turned a small wholesale clothier into an international sensation.

BEGINNINGS

Rosso was born in 1955 in the town of Brugine, located in northeastern Italy. He was raised in a small farming village and attended a local industrial textiles school. After graduating in 1975, Rosso went to work at jeans maker Moltex as a production manager. While at Moltex, Rosso partied at night and cared little about his job. When he learned Moltex's owner,

Adriano Goldschmied, was going to fire him, Rosso saved his job by creating a business plan to increase production and decrease costs. Goldschmied was impressed, kept Rosso on, and eventually offered him a stake in the company. The two launched the Genius Group in 1978, which became the home of several up-and-coming designers, including Katherine Hamnett.

Designing under the name "Diesel," reportedly because it was pronounced the same in all languages, Rosso began to make his mark in the fashion world in the early 1980s with jeans and casual wear. An outlet store was opened in 1982, and three years later Rosso, seeking his independence, was ready to take sole control of Diesel. He bought out Goldschmied and several other Moltex business units and assumed full responsibility for Diesel's future. As Rosso declared many times,

"Diesel is not my company, it is my life," and his complete devotion to the company proved this sentiment repeatedly.

FASHION OUTLAW

Rosso differed from most fashion houses in that he pushed creativity over the bottom line. Once designers proved themselves, they were given much freedom to design as they saw fit. Rosso wanted to create an international market for Diesel, and he slowly tested the waters. Within five years of taking control of Diesel, the firm had reached sales of more than $130 million and was available through retailers in more than three dozen countries.

As Diesel's jeans and casual clothes gained notice, so did Rosso. He was outspoken and irreverent and often flamboyant. He bought an art deco hotel in Miami's South Beach in 1991, giving it a stylish, if not somewhat outrageous, makeover. Ross also learned how to use the media to his full advantage, launching controversial advertising campaigns that gave Diesel prominent coverage in newspapers and magazines. No subject was too touchy for Rosso; he reveled in the attention, along with increased brand recognition and sales. By 1994 revenues approached $330 million.

An early foray into licensing in 1994 produced popular Diesel Shades (sunglasses) with in-your-face style names. The following year Diesel introduced its first fragrance, eponymously named and for both sexes. As the extreme sports phenomenon raged, Diesel launched a collection of extreme sportswear called 55DSL. Diesel's outrageous ad campaigns continued during the 1990s and picked up Clio and Cannes Film Festival awards in the process. By the time Rosso launched a Diesel Web site in 1995, the company had a huge cult status and received thousands of hits per day on a site that was more psychedelic than retail, since it was designed to sell image, not product.

CONQUERING THE UNITED STATES AND THE WORLD

The first Diesel store opened in New York City in 1996, and it was followed by a store in London. Within two years there were 24 more stores in the top retail areas of the United States. In 1999 Diesel signed with Fossil to produce watches. In 2000 Rosso bought the Italian luxury clothier Staff International, which licensed Vivienne Westwood apparel, and brought in annual sales of $380 million, which it bested in 2001 with $495 million in sales.

In September 2002 Rosso created a stir by buying a majority stake in Martin Margiela's Paris-based fashion operations. Most of the industry found this an odd pairing; the quiet, avant-garde Belgian and the flashy outspoken Rosso seemed akin to oil and water. Rosso stressed that the investment was not an acquisition and that he had no plans to change anything about Margiela's designs or business. Since he had long criticized fashion conglomerates like LVMH (Moët Hennessey Louis Vuitton) for their pursuit of profits at any cost, Rosso was quick to clarify his actions. "I'm not buying a fashion company like other groups have done," he told Robert Murphy of *Women's Wear Daily*, "I'm investing in Margiela so two friends can work together to grow a very special brand" (September 5, 2002).

By the end of year, Rosso's empire had annual sales of more than $600 million. In his many years in fashion, Rosso had been called radical, eccentric, and a host of other colorful terms as the maestro behind Diesel's success. He continued to push the limits of the industry with ironic, outrageous advertising in the early 2000s and was rewarded for his efforts with several Italian awards and an honorary MBA from Italy's CUOA Foundation.

Rosso explained his take on the fashion industry to Courtney Colavita of the *Daily News Record*: "Fashion companies—the ones that really drive the market—shouldn't work to produce numbers but rather should work to sell dreams, to create products that make you feel good and are right for the moment in which you live. Sure, a company has to be healthy financially, but the more we move forward the more people really want something that makes them an individual. Fashion companies have to focus on not being big but instead focus on being more of a niche product" (September 15, 2003). While number crunchers disagreed with Rosso's unique vision, they could not dispute his success. Diesel brought in sales of over $750 million in 2002, which qualified the brand as serving considerably more than a niche market.

In September 2003 Rosso celebrated Diesel's 25th anniversary with characteristic zeal, hosting an enormous party for 25,000 friends in Molvena, Italy. By 2004 Diesel products were sold in more than 75 countries through retailers, luxury department stores, catalogs, and about two hundred Diesel stores worldwide. The Diesel name appeared on children's clothing, undergarments, jewelry, leather goods, eyewear, fragrances, and footwear. Diesel jeans, however, remained the firm's primary claim to fame, with trendsetters willing to pay $100 to $200 for a pair.

See also entry on Diesel SpA in *International Directory of Company Histories*.

SOURCES FOR FURTHER INFORMATION

Colavita, Courtney, "Diesel's Engine," *Daily News Record*, September 15, 2003.

Dillabough, Chris, "Diesel Runs Rich-Media Ads on High-End Fashion Sites," *New Media Age*, March 20, 2003, p. 11.

Manuelli, Sara, "Fuel for Thought," *Design Week*, July 10, 2003, p. 15.

Murphy, Robert, "Opposites Attract: Diesel Buys Martin Margiela," *Women's Wear Daily*, September 5, 2002, p. 1(2).

Preston, Pieter, "Choosing A Unique Look," *New Media Age*, May 20, 2004, p. 20.

"Renzo Rosso," *Biography Resource Center Online*, Gale Group, 2003.

Sansoni, Silvia, "Full Steam Ahead for Diesel," *BusinessWeek*, April 29, 1996, p. 58.

Webdale, Jonathan, "Diesel Considers Loyalty Card on Eve of Online Campaign," *New Media Age*, January 24, 2002, p. 7.

White, Constance C. R., "New Line, New Images," *New York Times*, December 10, 1996.

—Nelson Rhodes

■ ■ ■
John W. Rowe
1944–
Chairman and chief executive officer, Aetna

Nationality: American.

Born: June 20, 1944.

Education: Canisius College, BS, 1966; University of Rochester School of Medicine, MD, 1970.

Family: Married Valerie A. DelTufo; children: three.

Career: National Institute for Children's Health and Human Development, 1972–1974, clinical associate; Harvard Medical School at Massachusetts General Hospital, 1974–1975, researcher and clinical fellow; Harvard Medical School, 1976–1988, professor of medicine, founding director of the Division on Aging; Beth Israel Hospital, 1980–1988, chief of gerontology; Mount Sinai School of Medicine and Mount Sinai Hospital, 1988–1999, professor of geriatrics and medicine, president; Mount Sinai NYU Health, 1998–2000, chief executive officer; Aetna, 2000–2001, chief executive officer; 2001–, chairman and chief executive officer.

Address: Aetna, 151 Farmington Avenue, Hartford, Connecticut 06156; http://www.aetna.com.

■ In 2000 Dr. John W. Rowe became the CEO of Aetna, making him the first trained physician to lead a health-maintenance organization (HMO). Aetna was ailing, and Rowe engineered a turnaround strategy that included jettisoning unprofitable customers, downsizing a mammoth organization, and focusing on earnings-boosting business, such as administering self-insured health-care plans for companies. As Rowe put it, his company was out of the ICU, but a complete recovery would take more time.

With 2003 sales of almost $17.9 billion, Aetna was a managed-care company on the rebound. After radically restructuring its operations by selling the financial-services division and its international businesses to the Dutch insurer ING Group, Aetna stuck to the health and benefits business. Aetna's shift in focus was largely due to government reimbursement cutbacks and a growing managed-care backlash. The company

covers more than 13 million individuals under its health plans, plus more than 11 million dental-plan members and some 11 million group-insurance members.

AN ADVOCATE OF THE AGING

After medical school Dr. Rowe became a well-regarded gerontologist with a passion for education. He said "You can't just walk into a classroom and say, 'We're going to teach you to be geriatricians.' If we do that, geriatrics will just be a passing fad. I feel that we have to develop a standing among academicians, first, in order for the field to get a grounding and, second, because we really don't know that much about old people" (*New York Times*, December 12, 1985). A former professor of medicine and the founding director of the Division on Aging at Harvard Medical School, he also served as chief of gerontology at Boston's Beth Israel Hospital. He was a director of the MacArthur Foundation Research Network on Successful Aging, served on the board of governors of the American Board of Internal Medicine, and was president of the Gerontological Society of America. Rowe authored over two hundred scientific publications, primarily on the physiology of the aging process. The coauthor of *Successful Aging*, Rowe's research placed particular emphasis on examining why some elderly people remain healthy and effective.

TRANSITIONING FROM ACADEMICS TO ADMINISTRATION

Following his tenure at Harvard, Rowe became president of the School of Medicine at Mount Sinai in New York. Rowe claimed that under his leadership Mount Sinai Medical Center, including the medical school and the hospital, sustained superior financial performance through a period of significant fiscal pressures on academic medical centers. He is credited with establishing the Mount Sinai Health System, which grew to be the largest integrated health-care system in the region, and with improving Mount Sinai's clinical services and effectiveness, with significant increases in patient volume and in the complexity of services rendered. During his tenure as president of the School of Medicine, Mount Sinai's basic- and clinical-research efforts grew dramatically, as reflected in the construction of major new research facilities, a near tripling of federal research grant support, increases in the national ranking of the medical school, and a substantial increase in the academic credentials of the student body.

HOSPITALS NOT IMMUNE TO BUSINESS TRENDS

The forces of consolidation—rising health-care costs, changing government reimbursement rates, and increased pressure from insurance companies—all created a tenuous health-care climate during the 1990s. Many medical centers merged or ceased to operate. Rowe conceived of and executed the 1998 merger of the Mount Sinai and NYU medical centers, one of the largest hospital-system mergers in history.

In 2001 Mount Sinai NYU Health had $1.8 billion in revenue and 31,000 employees. Rowe was responsible for the integration of the two organizations. By 2002, however, both medical centers publicly acknowledged that their merger was a failure and that they planned on reallocating all shared administrative services. In September 2002 Moody's downgraded Mount Sinai NYU Health's bonds, primarily due to Mount Sinai's considerable operating losses. Despite the dubious outcome of the merger, Rowe's contributions to the hospitals were significant.

A COMPANY IN NEED OF A DOCTOR

Leading two of the nation's top medical centers prepared Rowe for the next phase in his career, serving as a top health-care CEO. In 2000 flagging earnings at Aetna prompted transitions and replacements of senior executive. Rowe was named CEO in September 2000 and assumed the chairmanship of Aetna in April 2001.

Rowe had acquired a company that seemed headed for disaster. Doctors disdained Aetna, mostly for the tight controls on medical services imposed by its managed-care plans. Lawyers were targeting it with an onslaught of litigation, employee morale was very low, and the company had yet to fully recover from several acquisitions, including that of U.S. Healthcare. Yet the company was reporting a small operating profit and seemed to be holding its beleaguered business together. Said Rowe: "Most people expect that I came here and there was blood in the hall and things were in disarray. In fact, that wasn't the case. There was an appearance of stability" (*Hartford Courant*, November 27, 2003).

But the cracks in the company's seemingly secure foundation quickly revealed themselves. In January 2001 Aetna's chief financial officer indicated that profits were disappearing; even with price hikes, income was not keeping pace with spiraling claim costs. Management took false solace in the hope that financials would improve. By the end of 2001 the company lost a total of $266 million. Said Rowe: "I don't think anyone in management saw it coming. It's not like they sold me a bill of goods or something like that. I think everybody was flabbergasted at the severity of the problem" (*Hartford Courant*, November 27, 2003).

SEEKING TO CHANGE HEALTH CARE

Although Rowe was energized by the challenge of turning around an embattled company, he was also attracted to a grander cause: changing the very nature of the health-care system. He hoped to create a system in which insurance companies partnered with physicians and hospitals to deliver superior care. It was an idealistic notion, but Rowe claimed he was up to the challenge: "This can be done. It may not happen immediately. Not only can it be done, but this is important. If we get this right, this is going to make a difference," he said (*Modern Physician*, October 1, 2000). Still, the pressure was enormous. Thanks to regulatory pressures and an adversarial relationship with the medical community, in 2002 one in seven insurance-industry CEOs left office; many of them were fired, according to a study by the consulting firm Booz Allen Hamilton.

DAMAGING LITIGATION

Much of Rowe's early responsibilities entailed boosting Aetna's public image. In 2002 a lawsuit was filed in U.S. District Court in Brooklyn against Aetna, the FleetBoston Financial Corporation, and the CSX Corporation claiming that they profited from the slave trade. In 2000 Aetna had apologized for its involvement in slavery.

In May 2003 Aetna agreed to a $470 million settlement with about 700,000 physicians who claimed the insurer systematically reduced their payments and interfered with their treatment of patients. Aetna was the first major HMO to settle a longstanding class-action suit filed by the nation's physicians, who contended that the business practices of major managed-care companies were robbing them of reimbursements, jeopardizing patient care, and tying their hands with needless bureaucracy. In its landmark settlement, Aetna agreed to revamp its payment system, reduce administrative hassles for doctors, create a foundation to focus on patient safety, and establish a National Advisory Committee of Practicing Physicians to provide guidance to Aetna on key issues involving doctors. The fact that these pioneering changes were instituted under Rowe's watch was both ironic and critical to his notion of building a more democratized system of health-care.

LEADING A TURNAROUND

A primary component of Rowe's turnaround strategy was shifting the company's focus from size to profits. After years of spending billions on acquisitions to increase enrollment,

Aetna began scaling back, dropping customers who were not profitable and terminating health plans in many states. In just a few years the company downsized from 21 million to 13 million members. Additional cost savings came from the elimination of about 15,000 jobs. Said Rowe: "The easiest way to start making money is to stop losing it. We're being much more disciplined as a company about how we and where we compete" (*Rochester Business Journal*, April 5, 2002).

Meanwhile, the company made an aggressive move into the self-insured market. In such arrangements, employers assume the financial responsibility for the health-care costs of their employees and use a third party, such as Aetna, to administer the plans. Since the employer assumes the risk of claims, Aetna avoids unpredictable medical costs. One of the most important breakthroughs in that market came with Aetna's 2002 deal with the University of Rochester, Rowe's alma mater.

The University of Rochester's move to hire Aetna gave the company a strong entry into a market that for nearly half a century was almost exclusively served by nonprofits. Rowe said: "Self-insurance is part of a nationwide trend among employers seeking protection from double-digit health cost inflation. To provide health coverage for employees while remaining competitive, employers want health programs that reduce costs while enhancing employee productivity and satisfaction" (*Rochester Democrat and Chronicle*, April 5, 2002).

VITAL SIGNS IMPROVING

The first signs of an Aetna turnaround came in early 2002, when financial results indicated that Aetna was retaining valuable customers, despite steep price increases. In April 2002 the company reported its first quarterly operating profit in more than a year. Unlike the 3¢ analysts expected, Aetna posted a respectable 44¢ a share. Rowe commented: "That was the day we got off the runway. It was then that it became clear to everyone inside the company and outside the company that in fact we were going to save the company. It wasn't going to get taken over. It wasn't going to get broken up further and the patient was going to make it. The patient was out of the ICU" (*Hartford Courant*, November 27, 2003). In addition to mak-

ing money again, the company was cultivating once-alienated employers and benefits brokers, as well as doctors, who began viewing the company with newfound trust. In 2003 the stock price rose 56 percent.

FAR FROM A CURE

Yet the company still faced a host of challenges. Aetna lagged behind its peers in profits yet trumped them in overhead expenses. Further, the spate of jobs cuts and benefit reductions left remaining employees with dwindling levels of job satisfaction. A 2003 company survey indicated improvement, but Rowe conceded that employee satisfaction still trailed industry averages. In interviews with the *Hartford Courant*, some employees described morale as "awful" and "kind of in the crapper." Said Rowe: "We're making great progress, but the fat lady has not yet sung here. And we have a long way to go" (*Hartford Courant*, November 27, 2003).

See also entry on Aetna, Inc. in *International Directory of Company Histories*.

SOURCES FOR FURTHER INFORMATION

"Aetna Inc. Sees UR as Toehold for Efforts Here," *Rochester Business Journal*, April 5, 2002, p. 1.

Hallowell, Christopher, "New Focus on the Old," *New York Times*, December 12, 1985.

Lentz, Rebecca, "Tough Rowe to Hoe; New Physician CEO Aims to Repair Aetna's Troubles," *Modern Physician*, October 1, 2000, p. 18.

Levick, Diane, "Prognosis Good for Aetna's Continued Recovery," *Hartford Courant*, November 27, 2003.

Rowe, John W., "Insurance Competition is Healthy for Community," *Rochester Democrat and Chronicle*, April 5, 2002.

—Tim Halpern

Allen R. Rowland

1944–

Former president, chief executive officer, and director, Winn-Dixie Stores

Nationality: American.

Born: June 24, 1944.

Career: Miller's Supermarket, 1963–1970, store manager; Albertsons, 1971–1996, held various positions, eventually becoming senior vice president; Smith's Food and Drug Centers, 1996–1997, president and chief executive officer; Winn-Dixie Stores, 1999–2003, president, chief executive officer, and director.

■ Allen R. Rowland spent his entire career in the grocery business, beginning as a grocery-store clerk at the age of 19. Within three years he moved into the position of store manager of Miller's Supermarket in Colorado Springs, Colorado. He established his reputation through 25 years at Albertsons, a large retail food chain located in Boise, Idaho. He left Albertsons in 1996 after reaching the rank of senior vice president and running retail operations in the southeastern United States. He then became the president and chief executive officer (CEO) of Smith's Food and Drug Centers, where he led the company through its acquisition by Fred Meyer in 1997. In 1999 he became the president, CEO, and director of Winn-Dixie, one of the largest food retailers in the United States, with nearly 1,200 stores in 14 states and the Bahamas.

Rowland became a highly respected business leader with a reputation for taking decisive and swift action. His strength lay in his ability to instill organization while increasing profits and efficiency. He retired in June 2003 after setting Winn-Dixie on a course for higher revenues following four years of major reorganization and expansion.

EFFICIENCY AND PROFITABILITY: HALLMARKS OF A CAREER

When Winn-Dixie announced the choice of Allen R. Rowland as its CEO in November 1999, it focused on Rowland's previous achievements. He steered Smith's Food and Drug

Centers through a major period of reorganizing its operations, keeping the company focused simultaneously on improving its efficiency and profits. He developed a reputation among industry insiders as a leader who could create order in the most disorderly of situations. When Rowland joined Smith's, this small family-based business wanted to put itself on the market for purchase, but it needed a major overhaul to be competitive. In just over a year at the helm, Rowland negotiated Smith's sale to Fred Meyer, better known as Kroger, for $2 billion. At Albertsons, Rowland earned a reputation in the retail food industry as a cost cutter and streamliner. His past record reflected his ability to make quick, decisive, and successful decisions.

The chairman of Winn-Dixie, A. Dano Davis, noted Rowland's experience in large-store operations with an emphasis on customer service as one reason for his appointment as CEO. Industry insiders also noted that Rowland's experience with a family-owned operation in need of organization was a major benefit for Winn-Dixie, which many felt in 1999 needed to be reorganized and turned around. By the time of Rowland's retirement in 2003, Davis said that Rowland had not disappointed them and that store operations had improved along with Winn-Dixie's financial position.

Rowland introduced customer-reward cards as a way to boost sales. He improved store operations and customer service while eliminating under-performing products. Rowland called these changes "rightsizing." One example of rightsizing was the replacement of salad bars with bagged salads. Ice-packed melon bars also disappeared in Winn-Dixie stores under Rowland's leadership. Instead, cut pieces of melon were placed in plastic containers in refrigerated cases, which ensured less waste and higher quality for customers.

Rowland introduced popular programs such as Upromise Grocery Service, which allowed families to have a percentage of their Winn-Dixie purchases deposited in a college-savings account. He is credited with developing a strong senior-leadership team. He consolidated stores, aggressively restructured management, and instituted performance-based incentives for employees, while centralizing departments such as real estate, accounting, purchasing, and marketing.

AGENT OF CHANGE

A. Dano Davis called Rowland an "agent of change." Merrill Lynch noted in 2001 that, after two years in his leadership role, Rowland had made impressive changes necessitated by the "mess" he had inherited when he took over the reigns of Winn-Dixie, Florida's third-largest public company. *Florida Trend* magazine said in 2001 that Rowland had taken action quickly and decisively, "shaking up the grocery chain." He cut costs, removed unprofitable business lines, and reorganized the company's decentralized management structure. The magazine noted that one of his first decisions had been to change advertising agencies after 35 years of using the same company.

In his first year at Winn-Dixie, Rowland cut jobs and closed stores, which resulted in a $400 million annual reduction in costs. The *Florida Times-Union* reported that Winn-Dixie closed 112 unprofitable stores, four manufacturing plants, three distribution centers, and laid off 11,000 employees. In the middle of the restructuring, Winn-Dixie bought 106 stores from Jitney-Jungle of America, in Jackson, Mississippi, for $85 million. Rowland wrote in a press release on October 31, 2000, as quoted by the *Florida Times-Union,* "This acquisition is a very good strategic fit for Winn-Dixie" (October 31, 2000). He predicted that the purchase would improve Winn-Dixie's buying power. Industry insiders said the move could be good for the company, but only if Rowland's restructuring plans continued.

The restructuring did continue and was completed within a year of its initial announcement. Gross profits reached the projected level. Rowland continued the expense-reduction programs and focused on training and working with employees to improve customer service. Not all customers were pleased, however, as was made clear when the *Florida Times-Union* interviewed shoppers in 2001. One woman said that even though she enjoyed the service she received at the store, she had difficulty finding items because they kept moving them on the shelves. Winn-Dixie responded by saying they were trying to determine what products each of their stores needed on the shelves, to better satisfy customers in individual neighborhoods.

Rowland's restructuring of Winn-Dixie's management team earned high praise from food-retail watchers. Burt Flickinger III, a food-retailer professor at Cornell University, told the *Florida Times-Union* in 2000 that this initiative was "a brilliant master stroke," and he saw Rowland's decisions as allowing a more democratic structure into the business. Rowland brought all levels of management into the decision-making process, regardless of seniority. Industry analysts such as Flickinger saw this strategy as necessary to revive the stale corporate culture that had permeated Winn-Dixie in the late 1990s.

Rowland noted that he embraced working with a healthy mix of people with different experiences. His strategy emphasized developing a new corporate culture while stressing the need to give customers what they want. Representatives from Standard & Poor's noted the ambitious restructuring plan and watched the retail food chain carefully before they raised Winn-Dixie's credit ranking.

Rowland was not known for his interviews with media. When the *Florida Times-Union* attempted to interview him in 2000, he refused, but he did respond to written questions. *Florida Trend,* a magazine devoted to business in Florida, noted in its May 1, 2000, issue that "Winn-Dixie's executives are notorious for shunning interview requests, and the tradition continues with the company's newest CEO." The magazine was told that Rowland did not have an interest in interviews. Most of the information used in articles on Rowland's career came from press releases from the companies where he worked.

STREAMLINING AND ORGANIZING

Upon his appointment as Winn-Dixie's CEO, Rowland began applying what he had learned at other companies. At the time, ten separate buyers within its ten regional divisions negotiated and purchased retail items. Within a month of his appointment, he announced that the company would unify the buyers into a single department, which increased Winn-Dixie's buying and bargaining power. Rowland announced this change in a press release on January 18, 2000. He stated that the move would improve efficiency by assigning "our most talented procurement, marketing and merchandising associates" to corporate teams. Rowland said the changes would "improve sales, reduce costs and enhance our bottom line." Within a year those goals had been achieved.

Winn-Dixie had worked with the same ad agency for 35 years. In 2001, however, Rowland switched to Cramer-Krasselt, the fourth-largest independent marketing agency in the country. He said that effective communication with current and prospective customers had become essential to Winn-Dixie's goal of increasing business.

Rowland's announcement of his major restructuring plan for Winn-Dixie came on the heels of a dismal financial report in fiscal year 2000, with decreased profits of $20.9 million from the previous year. Rowland refused to be interviewed by *Florida Trend* regarding the dismal results, but in a press release issued by the company on April 20, 2000, he called the results "disappointing and totally unacceptable." The day of the announcement, the board of directors approved his restructuring plan.

The plan included the closing of three division offices, in Tampa, Atlanta, and Louisville, as well as shutting down two manufacturing facilities in Jacksonville. It also involved the renovation of six hundred stores and the closing of nearly 30 stores, mostly in the Atlanta, Tampa, and Louisville areas where Winn-Dixie had been struggling to retain its market share against other companies. Burt Flickinger III noted that Rowland was doing with Winn-Dixie what he had done at Smith's by providing shock therapy for a business that had been stagnating in an age in which megacorporations were taking over smaller family-run chains. As quoted by Matthew I. Pinzur in the *Florida Times-Union*, Flickinger said Rowland was turning Winn-Dixie into "an operational powerhouse" (April 21, 2000).

Rowland aimed to provide the best possible atmosphere for customers in Winn-Dixie's grocery stores. He wanted to exceed customers' expectations for good-quality products and clean, sanitary stores. This goal coalesced with his strategies in streamlining management and involving employees at all levels in the process. As quoted by Paul C. Peralte in the *Florida Times-Union*, Rowland said he intended to staff stores with "the friendliest, most helpful people in the community" (February 14, 2000).

SETS STANDARDS

Winn-Dixie, a family business and one of the South's leading grocery chains, chose Rowland because of his ability, demonstrated at Smith's, to take a family business through a transitional period. By 1999 experts and analysts in the supermarket industry wondered if Winn-Dixie had appointed Rowland to ready the company for acquisition. Winn-Dixie maintained that it wanted to remain an independent chain, while still being competitive. The industry watched as Rowland immediately began making successful changes.

Industry insiders said that Winn-Dixie had been slow to change and not aggressive enough to maintain its market share. One food-retail analyst said in 2000 that Winn-Dixie had been known as a chain going nowhere, and Wall Street viewed the company as one without a clear focus. With their eyes on Rowland's appointment as CEO, the experts viewed it as Winn-Dixie's move to become a major player in the retail food business.

Prior to his appointment as CEO at Winn-Dixie, Rowland was known as a genius and a coveted executive. One analyst noted that Rowland was considered a "superb strategist" in the supermarket industry because he knew how to cut out the dis-

eased parts of a corporation. Once Rowland had brought Winn-Dixie to the level of excellence he envisioned, he decided to retire at the age of 59. Before announcing his intentions, he brought in his successor, Frank Lazaran, to continue his strategies. A. Dano Davis said that Rowland, who was hired by Winn-Dixie to be an "agent of change," had been successful: as of 2003 Winn-Dixie ranked 149th on the Fortune 500 list.

See also entries on Albertson's Inc., Smith's Food and Drug Centers, Inc., and Winn-Dixie Store, Inc. in *International Directory of Company Histories*.

SOURCES FOR FURTHER INFORMATION

Daniels, Earl, "Winn-Dixie Buys Stores from Chain in Bankruptcy," *Florida Times-Union*, October 31, 2000.

Hallman, Cinda, "5 CEOs To Watch," *Florida Trend*, July 2001, p. 98.

Peralte, Paul C., "Winn-Dixie Plans To Cut 11,000 Jobs," *Florida Times-Union*, February 14, 2000.

Pinzur, Matthew I., "President and CEO Known For Resuscitating Companies," *Florida Times-Union*, April 21, 2000.

"Questions for new Winn-Dixie CEO," *Florida Trend*, May 1, 2001, p. 25.

"Winn-Dixie Announces Restructuring of Staff Organizations to Reduce Expense and Improve Efficiency," company press release, January 18, 2000, http://www.winn-dixie.com/company/news/2000/releases/01182000-1.asp.

"Winn-Dixie Reports Third Quarter Results," company press release, April 20, 2000, http://www.winn-dixie.com/company/news/2000/releases/04202000.asp.

—Patricia C. Behnke

Patricia F. Russo

1953–

Chairwoman, president, and chief executive officer, Lucent Technologies

Nationality: American.

Born: 1953, in Trenton, New Jersey.

Education: Georgetown University, BS; Harvard Business School, Advanced Management Program, 1989.

Family: Daughter of a physician and homemaker; married; stepchildren: two.

Career: IBM Corporation, 1973–1981, sales and marketing management; AT&T, 1981–1992, management and executive positions in strategic planning, marketing, human resources, and operations; 1992–1996, president of AT&T's Business Communications Systems unit; Lucent Technologies, 1997–1999, executive vice president of corporate operations; 1999–2000, executive vice president and CEO of Service Provider Networks Group; Eastman Kodak, 2001, president and COO; Lucent Technologies, 2002–, chairwoman and CEO.

Awards: 50 Most Powerful Women in American Business, *Fortune*, 1998, 1999, 2001.

Address: Lucent Technologies, 600 Mountain Avenue, Murray Hill, New Jersey 07974; http://www.lucent.com.

Patricia F. Russo. *AP/Wide World Photos.*

■ Patricia Russo rose through the ranks of the telecommunications giant AT&T and helped launch its spin-off company, Lucent Technologies. Lucent developed into a leading supplier of communications hardware, software, and services, riding the telecommunications boom of the late 1990s. When the telecom bubble burst, Russo left Lucent to take the number two spot at Eastman Kodak. Her reign there was short; in less than a year she returned to tend to the beleaguered Lucent. After taking over as president and CEO, she resolutely cut costs and trimmed staff in order to improve the company's financial outlook and restore consumer confidence.

Reporters and colleagues alternately described Russo as conservative and dynamic. In the *Calgary Herald* she said of herself, "I'm deliberate, and I believe in letting people who

have a stake in things weigh in. But I wouldn't call that cautious; I'll make the decisions we need to make" (June 16, 2003).

THE EARLY YEARS

Russo grew up in a large middle-class family in a New Jersey suburb. A natural athlete, she was cocaptain of her high school basketball team and captain of the cheerleading squad. After graduating from Georgetown University with a degree in political science and history, she joined the sales and marketing department at International Business Machines (IBM). She was there for eight years and eventually rose to the position of marketing manager.

Even when she was just starting out in the business world, Russo dared to tread on territory where few women had ventured. When she joined IBM, she was one of the only women selling mainframes. "Early in my career there were some people who didn't believe a woman belonged in sales," she told *Business Week*; "but I worked hard on the accounts I was given and made sure I met the customers' needs and focused on producing results for the company. What I found is that results matter—it's hard to argue with them. People who produce results rise to the top" (May 29, 2003).

MOVING UP THROUGH THE RANKS OF AT&T AND LUCENT

Russo was hired by AT&T in 1981 and quickly began moving up within the ranks of the sales and marketing departments. In 1992 she was called upon to overhaul the company's struggling Global Business Communications Systems. She focused the division's efforts on voice systems, improved its core products, cut costs, and spurred overseas expansion. Through these efforts she was able to stem huge financial losses and boost revenues by 43 percent, to $5.7 billion, transforming the unit from a money bleeder into a clear profit maker.

Russo was still with AT&T when the telecommunications giant decided to spin-off its equipment division in 1996; Lucent Technologies was born. In 1999 she became executive vice president and chairwoman of Lucent's $24 billion Service Provider Networks Group, a position that placed Russo in charge of 80,000 employees.

Although Russo's career was going strong, her company would soon face rough roads. In 2000 Lucent began a sharp downturn; telecommunications spending had dropped, and the company's sales and stock prices suffered as a result. Most of the blame for the company's troubles was placed on the CEO Richard McGinn. To stop the bleeding, he began to spin off Lucent divisions; in the end virtually all that was left was Russo's Service Provider Networks, which McGinn brought under the corporate umbrella, essentially squeezing Russo out. Experts say her reduced role, the constant infighting between McGinn and his staff, and McGinn's questionable accounting practices (he allegedly reported revenue on sales that were not final) ultimately drove Russo out the door in August 2000.

A CAREER SHIFT

Russo enjoyed a brief period of time off, painting and catching up on sleep. In April 2001 she found herself back on the corporate fast track when Eastman Kodak wooed her to its Rochester, New York, headquarters with the offer of its number two slot. She became president and chief operating officer, the highest position ever attained by a woman at that company. Management hired her because of her track record and because it was hoped her technological expertise would help Kodak modernize from film to digital imaging. The chair-

man Daniel Carp said in *Business Week* that she brought skills to exactly where the company needed them—"right in the sweet spot" (April 23, 2001). She was charged with helping the film and photo company integrate its imaging products with the latest technologies, overseeing the day-to-day functions of the operating divisions, and seeking out new business opportunities.

While Russo tended to Kodak, her former employer was ailing. Excess network capacity left over from the Internet boom combined with lagging consumer demand were taking their toll on the telecom industry as a whole. Lucent's customers—telephone and wireless companies—were themselves suffering from slow sales and as a result cut back on their equipment purchases. In 2001 Lucent reported a $16.2 billion net loss; the value of its stock had fallen nearly 50 percent within a single year. Lucent management was in a state of upheaval. McGinn had been let go in October 2000, with Henry Schacht serving as interim CEO and trying to find a replacement. He eventually turned his attention to Russo.

A QUICK RETURN

Less than one year after she had left, Russo returned to Lucent, taking over as CEO on January 7, 2002; she asked Schacht to stay on as her senior advisor. She was reportedly lured back with an attractive compensation package: a $1.2 million salary plus a $1.8 million bonus package and 4.7 million stock options. When she returned, she told the Associated Press, "It's like coming home" (January 8, 2002). At the time Russo was one of only six female CEOs running Fortune 500 companies. And, just like Carly Fiorina of Hewlett-Packard and Anne Mulcahy of Xerox, Russo was put in charge of a company in crisis.

The company had spun off its Agere Systems Unit, which produced integrated circuits and optical-electronics systems, and Avaya (formerly Business Communications, which she had run), supplier of office-telephone and voice-messaging systems. In 2002 capital spending by phone companies in the United States fell 38 percent. As a result Lucent was struggling in a sea of debt. Thus, being named Lucent CEO "wasn't like inheriting a world championship team," Steve Kamman, an executive director at CIBC World Markets, told *Business Week* (May 29, 2003).

The response to Russo's return was mixed. Some industry insiders predicted that she would boost sagging company morale. Company leaders felt that her insider status and familiarity with Lucent's products would facilitate her helping the company return to profitability. In a statement in *Network World*, Schacht said, "Pat brings deep knowledge of our industry and our customers, coupled with the ability to lead a large organization through change. She understands and embraces our strategic and restructuring plans, and she can step in as CEO without missing a beat" (January 7, 2002).

But some analysts were concerned that her return simply signaled a reemergence of Lucent's old bureaucratic ways, an unfavorable reminder of the AT&T days. "I'm concerned that the management team at Lucent is heavily concentrated with people who have been there for 10 to 15 years," the Lehman Brothers analyst Steve Levy told *Telephony* (January 14, 2002).

Even as pressure mounted, Russo maintained her composure. Stephanie Mehta of *Fortune* commented on her "flawless posture and the way she chooses her words. She comes across as well prepared and in command" (April 15, 2002). Although she was known and respected for her firm leadership, she also had a softer side that she was quick to exhibit in the company of friends and employees. She reportedly carried chocolate, a favorite food, wherever she went in order to prove that she was a real person.

Russo was determined to turn Lucent around and show a profit by September 2003 (she later had to revise her estimate to 2004). Her first order of business was to execute the turnaround plan that Schacht had drafted, which focused on the sales of Lucent products to wireless-telecommunication companies (such as AT&T and Verizon Wireless) and Internet service providers. Lucent faced a lot of competition in that arena, however, from companies such as Cisco Systems and Ciena Corporation.

Russo set to work reducing operating expenses, vendor-financing commitments, and working capital. The reduction of expenses necessitated spinning or selling off businesses that no longer fit within the company's sharpened focus. Another more difficult part of reducing expenses was the cutting of staff. By the time Russo took charge, the company had already trimmed the number of employees by nearly half (removing about 44,000 jobs). Russo would oversee thousands more layoffs.

In an effort to return to profitability, Lucent began to reshift its focus from simply providing equipment to the telecommunications industry to providing customer-centric services. Rather than just promote the company's existing products, Lucent asked customers what they wanted and designed offerings accordingly. The new Lucent offered a wide range of services, from installation to network optimization and outsourcing. The company began looking at establishing new partnerships—some even with rivals. In May 2003 Lucent signed a deal to resell products produced by its competitor Juniper Networks.

Russo also focused on the company's strongest money-making potential: its sales force. "In many ways I am Lucent's chief salesperson. Now more than ever, an experienced, creative, and committed sales team is absolutely critical to our turnaround and success going forward," she told *Sales and Marketing Management* (November 1, 2002).

It was not surprising that Russo so aggressively pursued sales, as she was well known for her competitiveness. Colleagues had reportedly asked her not to participate in golf and tennis matches on corporate retreats because she tended to win every game. In 2002 *Golf Digest* ranked her among the top 100 CEO golfers in the country.

Despite Russo's efforts, in October 2002 Lucent's market position had not improved. The company posted its 10th straight quarterly loss, to the tune of $2.88 billion. Its stock, which had soared to more than $80 a share in 1999, had subsequently plunged more than 90 percent to less than a dollar. Standard & Poor's dropped Lucent's credit rating, which was already considered junk. Some investors talked about the possibility of bankruptcy, a suggestion Russo and other company executives quickly dismissed. She told the *Boston Globe*, "When this storm is over, we expect to be a leader" (October 12, 2002).

WEATHERING THE STORM

In February 2003 Russo was named chairwoman of Lucent; after a tough couple of years, things were starting to look up for the beleaguered company. Eight months later in October Lucent reported a profit for the first time in three years. Although she admitted the company would probably still have its financial ups and downs, Russo announced that Lucent was finished downsizing (having reduced the number of employees from the 150,000 of three years before to about 35,000) and would not lay off any additional staff. "We have weathered the storm," she told the Associated Press (October 22, 2003).

Russo sat on the boards of Schering-Plough Corporation, Xerox Corporation, New Jersey Manufacturers Insurance Company, and her alma mater, Georgetown University. In addition to her degrees from Georgetown and Harvard, Russo received an honorary doctorate in entrepreneurial studies from Columbia College in South Carolina.

See also entry on Lucent Technologies Inc. in *International Directory of Company Histories.*

SOURCES FOR FURTHER INFORMATION

Duffy, Jim, "Lucent Taps Russo as CEO," *Network World*, January 7, 2002.

Gilbert, Jennifer, "Tough Sell," *Sales and Marketing Management*, November 1, 2002, p. 30.

Howe, Peter J., "Lucent Plans to Chop Another 10,000 Jobs," *Boston Globe*, October 12, 2002.

Johnson, Linda A., "Patricia Russo Returning to Lucent as Chief Executive," *Allentown Morning Call*, January 8, 2002.

Kharif, Olga, "Patricia Russo: Lucent's Best Hope?" *BusinessWeek Online*, May 29, 2003, http://www.businessweek.com/technology/content/may2003/tc20030529_9745_tc111.htm.

Patricia F. Russo

"Lucent Attempts a Russo Resuscitation," *Telephony*, January 14, 2002, p. 8.

McKay, Martha, "Why Patricia Russo is Lucent's Guiding Light," *Calgary Herald*, June 16, 2003.

Mehta, Stephanie N., "Pat Russo's Lucent Vision" *Fortune*, April 15, 2002, p. 126.

Mulvihill, Geoff, "Lucent Posts First Profit Since 2000," Associated Press, October 22, 2003.

Smith, Geoffrey, "Will She Click at Kodak?" *BusinessWeek*, April 23, 2001, p. 50.

—Stephanie Watson

■ ■ ■

Edward B. Rust Jr.

1950–

Chief executive officer and chairman, State Farm Insurance Companies

Nationality: American.

Born: August 3, 1950, in Chicago, Illinois.

Education: Illinois Wesleyan University, bachelor's degree, 1972; Southern Methodist University, MBA, 1975, and JD.

Family: Son of Edward Barry Rust Sr. (former chief executive officer and chairman of State Farm Insurance Companies) and Harriett (Fuller) Rust; married Sally Buckler; children: one.

Career: State Farm Insurance Companies, 1975–1981, corporate attorney; 1981–1983, vice president; 1983–1985, executive vice president and chief operating officer; 1985–, chief executive officer; 1987–, chairman.

Address: State Farm Insurance Companies, State Farm Plaza, Bloomington, Illinois 61710-0001; http://www.statefarm.com.

■ Like his grandfather and father before him, Edward B. Rust Jr. became the chairman and chief executive officer of State Farm Insurance Companies. Having been associated with the company his entire life, Rust was well steeped in the mutual insurer's corporate culture, which placed a great deal of emphasis on serving policyholders, who were the legal owners of the company, and avoiding spending money unnecessarily. However, despite a lifelong association with State Farm, Rust maintained that growing up in the Midwest and learning rural values provided a moral foundation that would become more important to his achieving success as a chief executive. One of those values was respect for education. Rust, who held advanced degrees in business administration and law, became devoted to the advancement of education in America and instrumental in State Farm's contributions in this area, in terms of both money and the time of its employees. Rust served as a trustee of his alma mater, Illinois Wesleyan University, and was a member of the Business Advisory Council of the University of Illinois College of Commerce and Business Administration as well as a member of the advisory council of the Stanford University Graduate School of Business. In addition, he was the cochairman of the Business Coalition for Excellence in Education and was a member of President George W. Bush's transition advisory team on education.

DEEP FAMILY TIES TO STATE FARM

When Rust was born in 1950 in Chicago, his family was already deeply involved in the affairs of State Farm. The company was founded in 1922 by George J. Mecherle of Bloomington, Illinois. His idea was to form a mutual insurance company for rural and small-town drivers, who paid higher premiums than urban drivers despite having fewer accidents. By linking insurance rates to risk levels, Mecherle was able to offer much lower premiums than his competitors. He also signed agreements with the state farm bureaus, which received a fee for each of their members who purchased policies—hence the State Farm name. State Farm soon covered city drivers as well and in 1929 added life insurance. By 1942 State Farm was the largest auto insurer in the country. Rust's grandfather, Adlai H. Rust, was a young lawyer when he helped Mecherle found State Farm and became his right-hand man. Mecherle's son, Raymond, took over the presidency of the company in 1937, and when Raymond died in 1954, Adlai Rust took over as chief executive officer. His son, Edward B. Rust Sr., joined State Farm in 1941, succeeded him as CEO in 1967, and was named chairman in 1983.

According to Edward Rust Jr., his goal while growing up was not one day to work for State Farm. Rather he focused on his education, which was a point of emphasis in his family. His father graduated cum laude from Stanford University, majoring in economics, and was elected to Phi Beta Kappa. His mother, Harriett Fuller Rust, graduated with honors from the University of Southern California. Rust received his undergraduate degree in 1972 from Illinois Wesleyan University in Bloomington, where he was a two-year starting guard in football and became an accomplished wrestler. He then went on to Southern Methodist University in Dallas, Texas, earning a master of business administration and a law degree. Rust told *Best's Review* in a December 1996 article that going to work at State Farm was not on his mind while completing his education: "It was not until I got out of law school, and, frankly, had a couple good offers from law firms, that I decided to give State Farm a try."

Rust stayed in Dallas and in 1975 became a State Farm management trainee at the local office. After gaining an overview of how regional operations were handled, he returned home to Bloomington to become an attorney in the State Farm corporate law department. He next became involved in marketing and sales before finally moving into general management. In 1981 he made vice president and in 1983 was appointed executive vice president and chief operating officer and named a director. Rust maintained that "being the boss's son was no guaranteed ticket to success" (*Best's Review*, December 1996). In fact, being the subject of expectations from older generations was often a difficult burden to bear. He was also quick to note that he owed a debt to a number of mentors beyond his father and grandfather.

RUST SR. DIES IN OFFICE

In August 1985 Rust's father died at the age of 66 and his namesake, only 35 years old, was promptly appointed the new chief executive officer. According to a *Fortune* profile of State Farm, insiders at the company almost took the younger Rust's promotion for granted. However, outside directors, mostly academics and economists, gave some thought to conducting a national search to bring in someone with a prestigious background: "These directors knew Ed Sr. as very private, disciplined, and brilliant. They knew the son as more outgoing but unproved as a businessman" (April 8, 1991). The idea of looking elsewhere was quickly dismissed, however, and Rust was named to the post. He soon proved that despite his age, he was up to the job and two years later, in 1987, was named chairman of the board.

After nearly a decade heading State Farm, Rust outlined to *Fortune* what made a top executive, observations that were a reflection of his own management style and core values. He said, "You have to live and breathe the business, always exploring new horizons and learning to understand the ever changing world around us" (April 8, 1991). At the same time, Rust emphasized the need to surround oneself with capable people and to have the confidence to delegate authority to them. He also expressed the importance of striking a balance between a personal and work life. As for his role at State Farm, Rust narrowed it down to two areas: "The first is the development of people, and the second is an untiring effort to better understand the marketplace, how customer demands are changing" (*Best's Review*, December 1996).

With Rust's family fortunes so intertwined with State Farm's history, it was difficult clearly to distinguish the corporate culture from the CEO's personal worldview. The insurer remained conservative in its approach to business, essentially content to continue selling reasonably priced auto and home insurance. In the words of one industry analyst quoted in a 1999 *BusinessWeek* article, "They don't throw the long bomb; they just move the ball ahead slowly and steadily" ("Father Knew Best—and So Did Grandfather," November 8, 1999). The company was so committed to controlling costs in the name of its policyholders that its corporate culture appeared to take on the zeal of religion, and to many it went too far. In 1989 State Farm was accused in a policyholder lawsuit of being too conservative in maintaining reserves, with the effect of trimming dividend payments to policyholders.

LEGAL PROBLEMS TROUBLE STATE FARM

During the 1990s Rust would face a number of legal problems that critics said were an outgrowth of State Farm's inbred culture and obsession with cost controls. A 1994 earthquake in the Los Angeles area led to lawsuits by homeowners, who charged that the company had secretly reduced their earthquake coverage. The matter was settled in 1997, when State Farm agreed to make $100 million in payments. In 1998 State Farm was "rocked by a string of blistering punitive damage decisions," as reported by *BusinessWeek* ("State Farm: What's Happening to the Good Neighbor?" November 8, 1999). As the article noted, in Utah the company was fined $25 million in punitive damages, in part for the "systematic destruction of documents" and "systematic manipulation of individual claim files to conceal claim mishandling." An Idaho appeals court then fined the company $9.5 million in punitive damages for making use of "a completely bogus" outside bill-review company that helped lower the cost of medical claims. In October 1999 an Illinois jury rendered a $456 million judgment against State Farm. That amount was then stiffened by an additional $730 million in punitive and other damages awarded by the judge for the insurer's breach of contract with auto policyholders by relying on generic replacement parts. Although the case revealed a number of damning internal documents, Rust was adamant in his insistence that State Farm had not committed fraud. A trained lawyer, Rust made his opinion of the current state of the court system a matter of public record. In 1995 he spoke before the Appellate Lawyers Association, outlining his belief that the civil justice system had undergone a fundamental shift in the years following World War II: "It has gone from a fault-based to a pseudo-compensation-based system" (*Vital Speeches of the Day*, September 15, 2003). In his opinion, this change was in many ways a reflection of people's decreased willingness to accept responsibility for their actions. Moreover, lawsuits were becoming viewed "a bit like a lottery," with a large number of people looking to turn misfortune into a jackpot. At a lower level, people were more willing than ever to pad insurance claims, but even this activity, he said, was fraud. It was not the insurance company that would foot the bill, of course; the policyholder would pay because in the end, it was the policyholder's money that was at stake. In the corporate culture of State Farm with which Rust so identified, protecting the interests of the policyholder was sacrosanct.

A COMMITMENT TO EDUCATION

While conservative business practices and a devotion to keeping a tight rein on policyholders' money were core values that Rust had essentially inherited from his forebears at State Farm, his devotion to advancing education was very much his contribution to the company's culture. Starting in 1995 State Farm offered its more than 75,000 employees one paid day off each year to offer help at a school, whether that help involve accompanying a class on a field trip or providing expert advice to school administrators. In 1997 State Farm became involved with the National Board for Professional Teaching Standards, a teacher-founded organization that sought to improve the quality of teaching and to provide certification. Moreover, State Farm provided funds for new buildings, fellowships, and other programs at colleges and universities across the country as well as support for the Beyond the Books Educational Foundation, which provided grants to elementary and secondary teachers for special projects that could not be funded at the local level. Rust's personal commitment to education was also evident in his willingness to serve as a trustee and adviser to Illinois Wesleyan University, the University of Illinois, and Stanford University as well as serving as the cochairman of the Business Coalition for Excellence in Education and on President Bush's transition team covering educational issues.

With the start of the 21st century, Rust faced a number of challenges in leading State Farm into the future. The insurance industry was adversely impacted by a string of events: asbestos claims, the sudden drop in the stock market, Enron and other corporate scandals, and the uncertainty that resulted from the terrorist attacks of September 11, 2001. While some were short-term problems, others carried long-term implications for the insurance industry. How Rust would be able to guide State Farm through this period of great uncertainty remained to be seen.

SOURCES FOR FURTHER INFORMATION

France, Mike, "Father Knew Best—and So Did Grandfather," *Business Week,* November 8, 1999, p. 142.

France, Mike, and Andrew Osterland, "State Farm: What's Happening to the Good Neighbor?" *Business Week,* November 8, 1999, p. 138.

Loomis, Carol J., "State Farm is Off the Charts," *Fortune,* April 8, 1991, p. 76.

Major, Michael J., "Reaching the Top," *Best's Review,* December 1996, p. 57.

McKinney, Kathy, "State Farm Chief Charts Major Shifts in Legal System," *Pantagraph* (Bloomington, Ill.), April 28, 1995.

Rust, Edward B., Jr., "Our Nation's Schools," *Vital Speeches of the Day,* September 15, 2003, p. 731.

—Ed Dinger

■■■
Arthur F. Ryan
1942–
Chief executive officer and chairman, Prudential Financial

Nationality: American.

Born: 1942, in Brooklyn, New York.

Education: Providence College, BA, 1963.

Family: Married Patricia (maiden name unknown; community activist); children: four.

Career: Control Data Corporation, 1965–1972, various positions; Chase Manhattan Bank, 1972–1975, project manager, data processing; 1975–1976, securities processing; 1976–1978, head of securities processing; 1978–1982, oversaw domestic wholesale operations; 1982–1984, head of bank's systems worldwide; 1984–1985, executive vice president, worldwide retail-banking operations; 1985–1990, vice chairman, retail banking; 1990–1994, president and chief operating officer; Prudential Insurance Company of America, 1994–2001, chief executive officer and chairman; Prudential Financial, 2001–, chief executive officer and chairman.

Awards: National Alumni Personal Achievement Award, 75th Anniversary Alumni Services Award, and the Diamond Anniversary Award, Providence College.

Address: Prudential Financial, 751 Broad Street, Newark, New Jersey 07102-3777; http://www.prudential.com.

■ As the first outsider to be named chief executive officer (CEO) and chairman of Prudential Insurance Company of America, Arthur F. Ryan took charge at a time of turmoil. He oversaw the conversion of the company from a mutual form of ownership, in which policyholders owned the insurer, to stock ownership, resulting in the publicly traded Prudential Financial, which gained a listing on the New York Stock Exchange in 2001. Although regarded as unpretentious and possessing a warm and friendly manner, Ryan was also known for his tough management style. While serving as president of Chase Manhattan Bank he earned the nickname "the gorilla." His technology background (he began in Chase's data-

Arthur F. Ryan. *Getty Images.*

processing department) was also seemingly at odds with his people-oriented approach to business. Ryan devoted a good deal of time to charitable works while at Prudential, as the company donated millions of dollars to support the arts and educational activities in its home state of New Jersey. Ryan regarded many of these public works as simply good business, thereby demonstrating his ability to balance the hard-nosed and amiable sides of his personality. If he had not become a chief executive at a major corporation, Ryan claimed he would have become a teacher.

BROOKLYN BORN, LONG ISLAND RAISED

Ryan was born in 1942 in Brooklyn, New York, and raised on Long Island. He graduated from Providence College in 1963, earning a BA in mathematics. It was during his college days that he gained his only sales experience: selling magazines during one summer. He then served a two-year stint as a lieutenant in the U.S. Army, serving in Washington, D.C., with the Army Security Agency. During his time in Washington he furthered his education by taking classes at American University. Following his discharge in 1965, Ryan went to work as a computer-systems designer for Control Data Corporation and later gained managerial experience when he was appointed area manager. He would put this combination of experience to use at Chase when he joined the bank in 1972.

THOMAS LABRECQUE: A CAREER CATALYST

Ryan began his career at Chase as a project manager in the data-processing division and soon began ascending the ranks of the institution. In 1975 he was put in charge of securities processing, and a year later became head of the entire securities processing business. Ryan received a major career break in 1978 when a treasury department executive, Thomas G. Labrecque, recognized his potential and promoted the relatively obscure Ryan to oversee all of the bank's domestic wholesale operations, including check processing, wire transfers, and trust and securities services. More importantly, Ryan formed a close bond with Labrecque, who in 1980 became a surprise choice for president at Chase. Ryan reported directly to Labrecque for the rest of his tenure at the bank. The two men formed a good team, possessing complimentary abilities. Labrecque was described as aloof and "pedigreed," a far cry from the rolled-up-sleeves, straight-talking approach of Ryan.

In 1979 Ryan was appointed to the bank's policy and planning committee, which was composed of 17 top executives who met on a quarterly basis to determine bank policy. In 1982 Labrecque expanded Ryan's job, giving him overview responsibilities for all of the bank's systems worldwide, including those employed by retail operations. The experience he gained on the retail side would be put to good use two years later. In 1984 Chase's consumer-banking business was reorganized, and Ryan was installed as its head with the title of executive vice president, responsible for retail-banking operations around the world. A year later he became a vice chairman. For the personable and down-to-earth Ryan, the move into the consumer area was a welcome change, allowing him to put his own experience as a consumer to good use in determining new product lines. "It's always nice to be in a business where you're one of them," he told *American Banker* in a 1990 profile. The consumer bank performed well under his leadership, enjoying a compound growth rate of 24 percent over the next four years. Ryan gave much of the credit for the operation's success to the decision of Labrecque and chairman Willard C. Butcher in the late 1970s to aggressively pursue the retail business, at a time "when it wasn't a very popular choice to make." Ryan went on to tell *American Banker*, "I had the opportunity to demonstrate that if we had the resources and spent them wisely, we could really do something."

"THE GORILLA"

Labrecque succeeded Butcher as chairman in 1990 and named Ryan as his replacement as president and to serve as his second in command. The two faced some major challenges. Along with Butcher they had been instrumental in taking Chase public in October 1989, offering such a promising picture of earnings that Chase was able to raise $625 million rather than the $500 million envisioned. Investors were not pleased, however, when the bank soon developed problems with some real-estate loans and the corporate-financing market went soft, resulting in Chase falling short of its projections. Labrecque and Ryan responded by ruthlessly slashing costs, streamlining the operation by eliminating layers of management, and focusing the bank's resources on its strongest businesses. As a result, they restored Chase to profitability, and Ryan earned his reputation as "the gorilla." He may have been informal and warm, but according to one colleague, "At the end of the day, you deliver or you are history" (*BusinessWeek*, August 5, 1996).

Ryan, at 52 years of age, had reached a plateau in his career at Chase. With Labrecque only four years older, there appeared little chance that he would ever take the next step and become chairman of the bank. Thus, when presented with the opportunity to become CEO and chairman at Prudential Insurance, Ryan accepted. His appointment marked the first time in the insurer's 120-year history that it had turned to an outsider, and someone without experience in the industry. But given the difficult straits in which Prudential found itself, there was good reason to look outside the company, even if the move risked demoralizing the executive ranks.

CHALLENGES AT PRUDENTIAL

For decades Prudential had traded on a solid reputation, portraying itself as "The Rock." But the mutual company, which came into existence to provide industrial insurance to the working class, paying for funeral and burial costs, expanded in the 1980s into financial products and landed in trouble. By the early 1990s the company was beset by a number of scandals as well as other endemic problems. The insurer had to admit that its securities unit had sold partnerships fraudulently, a mistake that would cost $1.5 billion to correct. Prudential also faced scrutiny on its life-insurance-sales practices, leading to a multistate regulatory investigation. In addition, the company posted a string of disappointing earnings and endured high restructuring costs that—along with $1.6 billion in losses from Hurricane Andrew in 1992 and a drop in the value of its real-estate and bond holdings—hurt profitability. Ryan also faced the difficult challenge of fundamentally changing a staid corporate culture that could in its own way warrant being called "The Rock." *BusinessWeek* offered one insider's take of the situation in a 1996 article: "This has been a company where the CEO could make a decision and some guy four layers down could derail it" (August 5, 1996).

REBUILDING "THE ROCK"

To address the problems at Prudential, Ryan had to use both the personable and the tough sides of his character, as well as rely on his technical background. To resolve the company's life-insurance-sales problem, Ryan encouraged New Jersey's insurance commissioner to launch an investigation, even though Prudential's home state was not one of the six looking into allegations that Prudential agents had deceived customers into buying new, expensive life-insurance policies as a way to pocket commissions without regard for the needs of the policyholders. Thus, New Jersey examiners led the multistate probe that resulted in Prudential being fined $35 million, the largest fine ever levied against an insurer, and agreeing to a settlement package that would pay $410 million to $1 billion to victimized policyholders. Although on the surface the punishment appeared stiff, critics claimed that Ryan had in fact engineered a sweetheart deal. Given that Prudential held assets worth $219 billion, the $35 million fine was not especially significant, and the terms of the settlement placed the burden of proof on policyholders to show they had been wronged. The day after the settlement was announced, Ryan began the process of repairing Prudential's tarnished image, taking out full-page newspaper ads to apologize for the company's "intolerable" sales practices (*BusinessWeek*, August 5, 1996). He fired hundreds of agents and managers, restructured the sales system, and established strong internal controls.

Ryan took other steps to improve the financials, both for the short- and long-term. He launched an $800 million annual cost-savings program and sold off more than $1.4 billion in businesses that were not considered core to the company's future. As he had done at Chase, Ryan also streamlined Prudential's management. Although he placed a great deal of emphasis on saving money, Ryan was not averse to making investments that would benefit Prudential over the long haul. He may have been an out-of-date technologist, but he still recognized the need to improve the company's information technology (IT). He spent large sums to upgrade Prudential's IT infrastructure, and under his leadership the company was in the vanguard of providing laptops, and later wireless handheld computers, to sales agents. In 1995 Ryan first began discussing the programming problems associated with the change to the year 2000. According to his chief information officer, Bill Friel, "He recognized all the metrics, the code, the function points and understood the issues associated with that, and how to plan and manage the program" (*Insurance and Technology*, September 1998). As a result, Prudential was able to get started on the conversion well before its rivals. Ryan's understanding of the role technology could play in business was also evident in the way he incorporated IT functions throughout the com-

pany to employ technology for even greater effect. He also looked to technology to help Prudential deal with compliance issues, especially important in light of the sales scandals the company had endured in recent years.

A HANDS-ON APPROACH

Just as Ryan was making progress on some fronts, his momentum in turning around Prudential would be stunted by fresh problems. The company's health-insurance business, for instance, was losing hundreds of millions of dollars. Prudential had been one of the pioneers in health care, establishing a health-maintenance organization in the early 1970s, but with increased competition in the managed-care sector in the 1990s Prudential was unable to keep expenses in line with revenues. As a result the company underperformed the market, leading to the resignations of the division's top two executives. Always the hands-on leader, Ryan stepped in to run the division himself until replacements could be hired. He ultimately decided Prudential needed to leave the health-care industry, aside from providing long-term coverage. Ryan and Prudential also faced continued problems with state regulators, dissatisfied with the life-insurance settlement. The Florida insurance commissioner, in particular, threatened to suspend the company's license to do business in Florida.

CHARITY A PRIORITY

From the start of his tenure at Prudential, Ryan attempted to treat the insurer as a public company in preparation of one day demutualizing it (converting the company from a mutual form of ownership, in which policyholders owned the insurer, to stock ownership). Part of that effort involved good corporate citizenship and involving Prudential in charitable works. For Ryan, whose wife Patricia was a community activist, public work was a personal value as well. Much of Prudential's financial support was devoted to Newark, New Jersey, where the company was headquartered. It spent $6.5 million to have the main concert hall of the New Jersey Performing Arts Center named after it, and coendowed a foundation that would buy and provide master plans for properties surrounding the arts center. Ryan and his wife supplemented the donation to the arts center with personal contributions. Prudential also established a $1 million challenge grant for the city's public schools and donated $200,000 of the $500,000 needed to subsidize the fee-based buses that circled downtown Newark in a further effort to revitalize the city. In addition, Ryan made a personal commitment to educational activities. He served as a trustee to Providence College, where he also established the Arthur Ryan Family Scholarship. In New Jersey, Ryan agreed to help lead New Jersey United, an organization established to improve public education by supporting a standards-based educational approach to public schools. Ryan also procured funding from Prudential for New Jersey United and donated staff time of two Prudential employees.

LEADS PRUDENTIAL'S CONVERSION TO STOCK OWNERSHIP

In the late 1990s Ryan began the formal process of converting Prudential from a mutual to a stock company, following on the heels of other mutual insurers who had taken the step earlier in the decade. An initial bill authorizing the change was passed by the New Jersey legislature in 1998, but it was not until 2001 that the process was completed. A new company, Prudential Financial, was incorporated and taken public to acquire the assets of Prudential Insurance. Ryan retained the CEO post and chairmanship of the new stock company, which on December 13, 2001 began trading on the New York Stock Exchange. With stock at his disposal Ryan was better positioned to move the company forward in a highly competitive environment where insurance and financial products were sold by insurers and bankers alike. Prudential could now supplement pay packages with stock options, an increasingly key element in attracting top-notch executive talent. Moreover, Prudential had the capacity to use stock to fuel growth. After the conversion, Ryan engineered a number of acquisitions, including the purchase of American Skandia, which was the largest distributor of variable annuities through independent financial planners in the United States. Prudential was able to create a retail-brokerage business with Wachovia Corporation. The resulting Wachovia Securities, was one of the largest retail financial-advisory organizations in the United States. In 2004 Prudential paid $2.1 billion for the retirement business of Cigna Corporation, making it the largest manager of stable-value and funding-agreement assets, serving more than 3.3 million active workers and retirees. Prudential also looked overseas, acquiring two South Korean asset-management companies. Ryan, who had come to Prudential Insurance with no experience in insurance, was now taking Prudential Financial into many of the retail-banking areas he had nurtured during his tenure at Chase. At the same time, he continued to repair Prudential's tarnished image.

See also entry on Prudential Insurance Company of America in *International Directory of Company Histories.*

SOURCES FOR FURTHER INFORMATION

Applebaum, Alec, "Prudential's Art Ryan Moved Quickly to the Top," *Business News New Jersey,* September 7, 1998, p. 6.

Bryant-Friedland, Bruce, "Prudential Insurance Rocked by Controversy, CEO's Efforts Overshadowed by Litany of Problems," *Florida Times-Union,* January 6, 1997.

Kantrow, Yvette D., "Promotions Come Naturally to Chase's Arthur F. Ryan," *American Banker,* June 25, 1990, p. 2.

"Money-Maker Ryan Heads for No. 2 Spot at Chase," *United States Banker,* April 1990, p. 46.

Rea, Alison, "Can Art Ryan Move 'the Rock'?" *BusinessWeek,* August 5, 1996, p. 70.

Scism, Leslie, "Ryan Carves a Fresh Profile for Prudential," *Wall Street Journal Europe,* January 18, 1996, p. 19.

Scism, Leslie, and Steve Lipin, "Prudential Hires Chase's Ryan as Chairman, Chief Executive Officer," *Wall Street Journal,* October 21, 1994.

Tauhert, Christy, "The CEO Who's in the Know," *Insurance and Technology,* September 1998, p. 34.

—Ed Dinger

■■■
Patrick G. Ryan

1937–

Chairman and chief executive officer, Aon Corporation

Nationality: American.

Born: 1937.

Education: Northwestern University, BS, 1959.

Family: Married Shirley (maiden name unknown); children: three.

Career: Penn Mutual, dates unknown, life insurance agent; worked at father's Ford dealership; Ryan Corporation (became Ryan Group), dates unknown, owner; Aon (merged company), 1982–, chief executive officer; 1990–, chairman of the board.

Awards: International Executive of the Year, Brigham Young University, 2002; Golden Plate Award, Academy of Achievement in Ireland, 2002; Horatio Alger Association of Distinguished Americans Award; Crain's Chicago Business Executive of the Year Award, 1997.

Address: Aon Corporation, Aon Center, 200 East Randolph, Chicago, Illinois 60601; http://www.aon.com.

Patrick G. Ryan. *Jean-Marc Giboux/Getty Images.*

■ Patrick G. Ryan started out selling insurance policies at his father's car dealership in 1964 and eventually created his own company. He first sold warranties and then moved to other products, taking his business to Chicago. He hoped to "go national and create specialty insurance agents for every industry" (*Forbes*, August 23, 1999). Ryan Corporation went public in 1971 with $27 million in sales.

Ryan merged his own company, Ryan Group, with Combined International Corporation in 1982 into what came to be called Aon Corporation in 1987. "Aon" is Gaelic for unity or oneness. Combined International at that time was in financial trouble and approached Ryan to run the company. Ryan consented, but only if he could run the two companies, even though Combined was eight times the size of Ryan Group. Combined agreed, and Ryan became chief executive in 1982. Aon went on to become the world's second-largest insurance brokerage and consulting company, after March & McLennan.

STEADY GROWTH

The new company became a provider in risk management services, insurance and reinsurance brokerage, human capital and management consulting, and specialty insurance underwriting. The firm operated in three major segments: commercial brokerage, consulting services, and consumer service underwriting. The company's brokerage services included retail and wholesale insurance for groups and businesses.

Aon's smaller component, inherited from Combined International, offered insurance underwriting, such as supplementary health, accident, and life insurance as well as extended warranties for consumer goods. Aon employed 53,000 people in 2004, with six hundred offices in more than 120 countries. In 2003 Aon was the country's second-largest insurance broker, built mainly through Ryan's acquisitions. He liked to quote Horatio Alger: "I deal in calamity and misfortune" (*Forbes*, August 23, 1999).

Ryan expanded his company globally to the United Kingdom, Spain, France, and Germany. He acquired the Italian brokerage firm Nichols Group, along with Hudig-Langeveldt in 1991, Frank B. Hall in 1992, and Alexander & Alexander in 1997. In Europe, Ryan bought out more companies: Bain Hogg in the United Kingdom, Gil y Carvajal in Spain, and Groupe LeBlace de Nicolay in France. Starting in 1982 Ryan acquired 115 companies for $4 billion.

In 1999 more than half of Aon's earnings came from brokering. Ryan offered certain types of insurance online to customers as well. His vision for the company was to achieve steady growth by creating brand recognition and to offer current and potential clients more types of insurance under the umbrella of one company. For example, a corporation could take advantage of Aon's property insurance as well as policies covering employees. In 1999 Ryan told *Forbes* that his company would be helped by more name recognition and better advertising.

After the 2001 terrorist attacks, Ryan hired the consulting firm of Rudolph Giuliani, the former mayor of New York, to help revamp the Aon's image after the tragedy. Aon had 1,151 employees in 2 World Trade Center and lost 176. It reopened an office in Lower Manhattan in June 2003.

A 2004 inquiry subpoenaed Aon and other insurance companies, bringing them to task for paying their commercial insurance brokers to promote their coverage. This action may have portended a decrease in profits to insurance companies if it had the effect of increasing pressure on brokers and scrutinizing the information they shared with customers. Aon defended the practice, however, and told the *New York Times* that such payments were "a longstanding and common practice within the insurance industry" (April 28, 2004).

Ryan took an enthusiastic interest in causes outside the insurance business. As a part-owner of the Chicago Bears, Ryan convinced Mayor Daley to use public funds to refurbish the team's Soldier Field. For their philanthropic efforts, Ryan and his wife, Shirley, received the 1998 Distinguished Philanthropist Award for their work with the Pathways Center for Children and the Pathways Awareness Foundation.

See also entry on Aon Corporation in *International Directory of Company Histories*.

SOURCES FOR FURTHER INFORMATION

Machan, Dyan, "Devouring Risk," *Forbes*, August 23, 1999.

"The Richest People in America," *Forbes*, October 6, 2003, http://www.forbes.com/global/2003/1006/074_3.html.

"Term Lifers," *Forbes*, October 11, 1999.

Treaster, Joseph B., "An Inquiry into Insurance Payments and Conflicts," *New York Times*, April 28, 2004.

—Alison Lake

■■■
Thomas M. Ryan
1953–
Chairman, president, and chief executive officer, CVS Corporation

Nationality: American.

Born: 1953.

Education: University of Rhode Island, BS, 1975.

Family: Married Cathy.

Career: CVS Corporation, 1975, pharmacist; 1975–1988, various positions; 1988–1990, senior vice president of pharmacy; 1990–1998, executive vice president of stores; 1998–, president and chief executive officer; 1999–, chairman.

Awards: Honorary doctor of business administration, Johnson & Wales University, 1999; honorary doctorate of humane letters, University of Rhode Island, 1999; Gold Heart Award, American Heart Association, 2002; honorary doctorate of science in pharmacy, University of Rhode Island, 2003; Mass Market Retailer of the Year, *Mass Market Retailer*, 2003.

Address: CVS Corporation, One CVS Drive, Woonsocket, Rhode Island 02895; http://www.cvs.com.

■ Thomas M. Ryan joined CVS Corporation in 1975 as a pharmacist. He was promoted through progressively more responsible positions and was named vice president of pharmacy operations in 1985. Ryan became senior vice president of pharmacies in 1988 and executive vice president of stores in 1990. He was named president and chief executive officer in 1998 and was elected chairman in 1999. Ryan relinquished his position as president for a short time in 1999 and later resumed the role. He also served as president and chief executive officer of CVS Pharmacy.

CVS, which stands for "consumer value stores," was formerly known as Melville Corporation, and was part of the Melville retail group that also included Linens 'n Things, KB Toys, and Marshall's. CVS was the exclusive online pharmacy for Healtheon/WebMD, an Internet-based company that linked physicians, consumers, and corporations in the healthcare industry.

MANAGING CHANGE AND GROWTH

Ryan's main role in leading one of the largest retail pharmacy chains in the United States focused on controlling and managing growth. CVS had grown through acquiring other retail pharmacy chains, including Revco, People's Drug, Arbor, and Big B. The Revco acquisition alone doubled CVS's store count. Meanwhile, the company continued to build new stores. This rapid, exponential growth caused concerns about daily operations at the stores and the need for a unified approach to doing business.

In a relatively short time, CVS became independent from the Melville group, issued public stock, and tripled the number of stores in the chain. In an effort to bring the new stores and larger workforce together under the CVS umbrella, Ryan initiated a store relocation and redesign program. Inline stores were moved to freestanding sites, which helped to provide easier access and often included drive-through pharmacy service. At about the same time, CVS introduced its revolutionary customer loyalty program and created its leading-edge Pharma-Care subsidiary. PharmaCare became one of the top 10 pharmacy benefit managers in the United States, at one time handling pharmacy benefits for an estimated 14 million patients. A former pharmacist, Ryan ensured that CVS stores were equipped with the most technologically advanced systems, including automated workflow tools for pharmacists and an automated prescription refill service for customers.

CREATING CUSTOMER-CENTRIC VALUES

Integration was a key theme of Ryan's tenure at CVS. He promoted six values of success throughout the company: respect for the individual, integrity, teamwork, sense of urgency, openness, and a willingness to embrace change. Ryan guided CVS by the benchmarks of convenience, value, and service—another interpretation of the CVS name. By adhering to these standards, Ryan believed that each employee could contribute to making CVS the store of choice for busy consumers.

Ryan focused CVS on becoming the easiest retail pharmacy for shoppers to use. He was involved in every detail, from store layout through merchandising to customer service. Ryan's goal was to provide a shopping experience that supplied necessary items such as prescription and over-the-counter drugs as well as optional items such as magazines, candy, and household goods. Ryan wanted CVS to offer complete pharmacy coverage so that customers could get retail, mail-order, and prescription benefit manager services from a single source.

Ryan created a unified culture throughout CVS by supporting employee development within a learning organization. He promoted open communication to implement his vision and the programs that supported it. The theme of customer service was carried out externally as well as internally. Ryan held regular town hall meetings with employees. Under Ryan's leadership, every employee was empowered to make a difference, and all employees were held responsible for their duties.

POLITICAL ACTION FOR DRUG IMPORTS

Ryan caught national attention when he began to speak out in support of reforms of U.S. drug importation policies. Disagreeing with prevailing attitudes in the retail pharmacy industry, Ryan called for federal policy changes to reduce costs for prescription drug consumers. "We cannot allow millions of our fellow citizens to go without life-sustaining medications due to arbitrary international trade practices. We don't do it for sugar, rice, or corn, we shouldn't do it for life-saving medications," Ryan told *Chain Drug Review.*

Testifying before the U.S. Department of Health and Human Services Drug Importation Task Force, Ryan brought media attention to the growing use of reimportation by consumers using the Internet and international pharmacies. Ryan told Tony Lisanti of *Drug Store News,* "It is not acceptable to allow this trade to continue in the shadows." Advocating that the most logical solution would be to authorize retail pharmacy distribution of imported drugs, Ryan captured media attention with his blunt comments and simple proposals. He emerged as the leader and spokesman for the retail pharmacy industry.

MANAGEMENT STYLE AND PHILOSOPHY

Ryan's management style was upbeat, enthusiastic, optimistic, and outspoken. He saw a tremendous amount of potential for continued growth of the retail pharmacy industry. Ryan's goal was to make CVS into the preeminent global health-care retailer. Ryan worked to create an environment that emphasized the importance of individual people, praise and rewards for employees, and support for individual initiatives. He achieved an entrepreneurial environment that helped CVS grow from a regional chain into a national presence in the world of retail pharmacies. Of his overall strategy for leading CVS into the future, Ryan told David Pinto of *Mass Market Retailer,* "Any road will take you somewhere. I had to learn which was the right road for us. Even then, it's one thing to know, another to make it happen. Strategy tells you where you're going, execution gets results."

CHARITABLE AND CIVIC INVOLVEMENT

Over the course of his career, Ryan was associated with a number of professional and civic organizations. He was vice chairman of the National Association of Chain Drug Stores and a member of the boards of directors of Melville Corporation, Bank of America, Citizens Bank of Rhode Island, Fleet-Boston Financial Corporation, Reebok International, Yum! Brands, Ryanair Holdings, TriCon Global Restaurants, the Rhode Island Philharmonic, and the Trinity Repertory Company. He was a member of the Rhode Island Public Expenditures Council and a trustee of the University of Rhode Island and the Brown University School of Medicine.

Ryan created the CVS Charity Golf Classic, which contributed millions of dollars to charities. He made substantial personal donations to educational institutions, particularly the University of Rhode Island. He maintained a vital interest in leading-edge technology in the field of pharmaceuticals. "I believe community pharmacy can play an expanded role in improving the quality and delivery of health care in this country," Ryan said when he provided financial support for the creation of an endowed professorship in community pharmacy. In addition to personal gifts, Ryan funded scholarships and grants for University of Rhode Island students and faculty through the CVS corporate giving program.

See also entry on CVS Corporation in *International Directory of Company Histories.*

SOURCES FOR FURTHER INFORMATION

"Gift from CVS Chief Enables URI to Establish Second Endowed Chair in Pharmacy," October 27, 1998, http://www.uri.edu/news/releases/html/98-1027-01.htm.

Lisanti, Tony, "CVS' Ryan Offers Viable Solutions to Importation," *Drug Store News,* May 17, 2004, p. 16.

Pinto, David, "CVS' Ryan is MMR Retailer of the Year," *Mass Market Retailer,* January 12, 2004, p. 1–2.

"Ryan Discusses 'Pharmacy in the New Millennium,'" *Chain Drug Review,* April 27, 1998, p. 272.

"Ryan Looks Ahead, Finds Good Reason for Optimism," *Mass Market Retailer,* January 12, 2004, p. 16.

"Ryan to Lead CVS to Greater Heights," *Mass Market Retailer,* June 26, 2000, p. 165.

Walden, Geoff, "Ryan Throws Down Gauntlet on Drug Importation," *Chain Drug Review,* May 24, 2004, p. 3–4.

—Peggy K. Daniels